Identity, Character, and

Identity, Character, and Morality
Essays in Moral Psychology

edited by Owen Flanagan and
Amélie Oksenberg Rorty

A Bradford Book
The MIT Press
Cambridge, Massachusetts
London, England

First MIT Press paperback edition, 1993
© 1990 Massachusetts Institute of Technology

All rights reserved. No part of this book may be reproduced in any form by any electronic or mechanical means (including photocopying, recording, or information storage and retrieval without permission in writing from the publisher.

This book was set in Palatino by DEKR Corporation and printed and bound in the United States of America.

Library of Congress Cataloging-in-Publication Data

Identity, character, and morality: essays in moral psychology/
  edited by Owen Flanagan and Amélie Oksenberg Rorty.
    p.   cm.
"A Bradford book."
Includes bibliographical references.
ISBN 0-262-06115-5 (HB), 0-262-56074-7 (PB)
  1. Ethics—Psychological aspects. I. Flanagan, Owen J.
II. Rorty, Amélie. III. Title: Moral psychology.
BJ45.I34   1990
170—dc20   90-34927
                                                                    CIP

Contents

Acknowledgments   vii

Introduction   1
Owen Flanagan and Amélie Oksenberg Rorty

PART I
Identity, Commitment, and Agency

Chapter 1
Aspects of Identity and Agency   19
Amélie Oksenberg Rorty and David Wong

Chapter 2
Identity and Strong and Weak Evaluation   37
Owen Flanagan

Chapter 3
The Moral Life of a Pragmatist   67
Ruth Anna Putnam

PART II
Character, Temperament, and Emotion

Chapter 4
Natural Affection and Responsibility for Character: A Critique of
Kantian Views of the Virtues   93
Gregory Trianosky

Chapter 5
On the Old Saw That Character Is Destiny   111
Michele Moody-Adams

Chapter 6
Hume and Moral Emotions   133
Marcia Lind

Chapter 7
The Place of Emotions in Kantian Morality   149
Nancy Sherman

PART III
Moral Psychology and the Social Virtues

Chapter 8
Vocation, Friendship, and Community: Limitations of the Personal-Impersonal Framework   173
Lawrence A. Blum

Chapter 9
Gender and Moral Luck   199
Claudia Card

Chapter 10
Friendship and Duty: Some Difficult Relations   219
Michael Stocker

Chapter 11
Trust, Affirmation, and Moral Character: A Critique of Kantian Morality   235
Laurence Thomas

Chapter 12
Why Honesty Is a Hard Virtue   259
Annette C. Baier

PART IV
Rationality, Responsibility, and Morality

Chapter 13
Higher-Order Discrimination   285
Adrian M. S. Piper

Chapter 14
Obligation and Performance: A Kantian Account of Moral Conflict   311
Barbara Herman

Chapter 15
Rational Egoism, Self, and Others   339
David O. Brink

Chapter 16
Is Akratic Action Always Irrational?   379
Alison McIntyre

Chapter 17
Rationality, Responsibility, and Pathological Indifference   401
Stephen L. White

PART V
Virtue Theory

Chapter 18
Some Advantages of Virtue Ethics   429
Michael Slote

Chapter 19
On the Primacy of Character   449
Gary Watson

Bibliography   471

Contributors   485

Acknowledgments

Several of these papers were first presented at the conference Character and Morality held at Radcliffe College in April 1988. We are grateful to the participants of that conference and to Wellesley College and Radcliffe College for sponsoring it. Wellesley College also provided a generous grant to support the preparation of this book. Maureen Kelley deserves special thanks for her editorial assistance and her conscientious compilation of the comprehensive bibliography.

Identity, Character, and Morality

Introduction

Owen Flanagan and Amélie Oksenberg Rorty

Moral psychology straddles two fields. On one side, there is normative ethics. On the other, there is empirical psychology, analyses of the nature and function of cognition and reasoning, the emotions, temperament, conceptual and personality development, and socially constructed attributes. From a purely logical point of view, normative moral theory is independent of empirical psychology. On such a view, normative ethics sets standards of feeling, thinking, and conduct. Whether persons can measure up to these standards is fundamentally irrelevant to the project of setting them.

The papers in this volume start from a radically different premise. Normative ethics, as the authors of these essays see it, is appropriately constrained by psychology. This does not mean that the distinction between the actual and the ideal collapses. It simply means that articulating moral ideals and principles is appropriately constrained by knowledge of the basic architecture of the mind, core emotions, patterns of development, social psychology, and the limits on our capacities for rational deliberation.

There are several ways to support the fundamental idea of constraining normative reflection by psychological knowledge. First, every traditional moral theory presupposes a theory of the structure of character and agency. Second, proponents of each theory attempt to provide justifications for conceiving of morality in a way that can motivate agents and guide practical deliberation. They want to promote a specific way of life, certain sensitivities of thought and feeling, as well as appropriate actions and practices. In order to do this, it is necessary to know what sensibilities we should develop, which capacities we should energize, and which to suppress, moderate, modify, or redirect. It is also essential to understand characteristic patterns of psychological and social development. Perhaps it is possible to live a moral life guided by the categorical imperative, by the principle of utility, or by commitment to a moral contract. But the capacities required for Kantian, utilitarian, and contractarian deliberation do not simply emerge as a person matures. Individuals need to learn to reason in the required way. Even moral systems that aim at impersonal and unemotional deliberation may have to endorse certain emotional dispositions like trust, upon which the development of such deliberative ability depends. Certain ladders must be climbed before we can even consider throwing them away.

Similar considerations apply to virtue theories. Because virtue theories make character and its components the central concern of ethical theory, they recognize the relevance of psychology to morality. But virtue theorists must address a host of further moral-psychological questions: How are the virtues acquired, developed, and individuated? To what degree are the virtues functionally interdependent? How do the virtues function within the whole of a person's character; that is, how do they affect motives, perception, emotions, ideals and self-conception?

Another reason for linking normative and psychological reflection is that traditional moral theories have recently been criticized for being indefensibly utopian, enjoining an impossible reconstruction of our psychologies. Before we can judge whether a moral theory is too demanding, we need a better understanding of the psychological structures it presupposes. This is obviously no easy task. However difficult it may be, the project of describing the distinctive psychologies that are required to realize different moral systems and ideals is important to evaluating them. Envisaging the sorts of persons an ethical conception requires for its realization, and imagining a world populated by such persons, is one way of evaluating the underlying ethical conception.

The questions raised by contemporary moral psychology are daunting yet exciting. In the last two decades, the fertility of philosophy of mind, psychology, and the social sciences has promoted greater sophistication and precision in moral psychology. The papers in this volume reflect the happy confluence of recent thinking in ethics, philosophical psychology, and psychology itself. The following discussion of the five parts of *Identity, Character, and Morality*, traces the sequence of issues addressed by the papers in the volume.

Part I: Identity, Commitment, and Agency

Most philosophical discussions of personal identity revolve around two related questions. First, there is the metaphysical question of what makes some individual the same or virtually the same over time. Second, there is the epistemological question of what criteria are used to identify and reidentify an individual over time.

Ethical reflection requires a more robust conception of identity than is provided by the standard solutions to the metaphysical and epistemological problems concerning personal identity. Knowing that an individual is the same person over time because her psychological states satisfy some plausible condition of psychological connectedness, or because she physically endures, does not tell us what sort of person she is. But it is this more robust sense of identity that we seek to capture when we aim at self-understanding, when we attempt to engage and comprehend others, and when we make judgments about character, worth, and responsibility.

There are a number of difficult issues surrounding this more robust, substantive kind of identity. First, there are problems in characterizing exactly what identity in this sense consists in. From the objective point of view, identity is defined by a set of central functioning traits. The trouble is that the objective point of view may assume an unwarranted metaphysical realism. There may be no way of identifying a person independently of social and subjective ascriptions. But because both self-ascriptions and social ascriptions of identity can be mistaken, it is also unsatisfactory to identify a person solely by reference to them. One of the main problems, then, is that of characterizing a person's identity, her central character traits, without assuming an objectionable form of either realism or relativism.

One promising strategy involves conceptualizing the varieties of identity-constituting traits along different dimensions of centrality (Rorty and Wong). Traits can be objectively functional, subjectively appropriated, or socially ascribed. Standardly, the centrality of a trait can vary along these different dimensions.

A person's identity reflects the whole structure of her character, the traits that are central to her capacities for agency. Somatic, proprioceptive, and kinesthetic dispositions affect a person's moral capacities because they affect not only the way she is perceived and treated but also her self-conception. Besides a person's aspirations and ideals, other morally significant aspects of identity are central temperamental and psychological dispositions such as friendliness and shyness, social-role identity (daughter, professor, citizen), and socially defined group identity (age, ethnicity, gender). Ethical reflection informed by psychology and anthropology would analyze the ways that social structures and social norms affect action by affecting these complex aspects of identity.

Exploring ideal identity presents a cluster of specific problems (Rorty and Wong, Flanagan, Putnam). Recent philosophical discussions have suggested that a person's life is made meaningful by her attempt to live up to her ideals. These ideals may be characterized by a life plan or a ground project, by an unfolding array of projects that change over the course of a life, and by a range of personal commitments. A life lived according to its ideals might be meaningful because it is a self-chosen life or because there is a certain consonance and consistency between a person's ideals and her character and mode of life. Presumably, self-esteem and self-respect require this sort of consonance and consistency.

Characterizing a person's identity by her central projects and commitments seems plausible from the point of view of philosophical psychology, especially in our culture. But this picture of identity raises a problem for the philosopher who believes in the sovereignty or dominance of moral considerations over all others. The meaning-grounding commitments that constitute identity need not be moral, even if that term is taken very broadly. A person might, after all, live a life grounded in an aesthetic or an athletic project, or even in what seems like a totally frivolous project. But this means that there may be ineliminable tensions between moral ideals and personal ones. Those who hold that moral requirements outweigh all others must acknowledge that there may be circumstances in which the demands of morality and personal fulfillment cannot both be met.

Another set of issues involves the relation of identity, reflectiveness, and agency (Flanagan). Does moral agency require reflectiveness to any high degree? Can a person be moral who does not have an articulated moral conception, who cannot articulate her ideals? Is the identity of modern persons invariably tied up with some conception of moral goodness, even if such a conception does not dominate? To what degree is identity socially constituted? How important is it that an agent understand the social grounds of her identity? What connections does comprehension of the self in social terms have with a sense of communal respect and obligation? To what extent, and under what social circumstances, does reflection lead to the destabilization of the grounds of one's identity and of one's moral ideals?

Reflection on ideal identity illuminates the ways that solid, effective, and self-respecting identities are built and maintained. A better understanding of the social bases of identity can help locate the places where social practices can best be restructured to enable persons to possess and maintain firm, self-respecting, morality-sensitive identities.

Part II: Character, Temperament, and Emotion

Two issues haunt reflection on character and temperament. First, recent psychological work has called attention to the possibility that certain of our temperamental traits, shyness for example, are deeply rooted in our biological natures. Suppose this is true of many or even most of our temperamental traits. Temperamental traits ramify. A shy person is not shy only at parties and in other novel social settings. Her shyness can be partly constitutive of her identity, and her being shy can affect a wide range of feelings, thoughts, and actions. A complete picture of moral psychology will require mapping the different ways such temperamental traits ramify.

The biological bases and ramification of temperamental traits raises the question of the extent to which character can be chosen or self-constructed (Trianosky, Moody-Adams). Even if temperamental traits are not chosen, they are only partly constitutive of character. Furthermore, we exercise some control over them—minimally, we possess the ability to modify and modulate our temperamental traits. Even if our temperamental traits turn out to be relatively unmalleable, many identity-defining traits may still be partly self-chosen and self-constructed.

But another haunting problem—the problem of luck—emerges to deepen our worries. If having certain temperamental traits is a matter of luck, then the morality and meaning of an individual's life is also a matter of luck. It will depend on luck in an individual's upbringing, the values she is taught, the self-controlling and self-constructing capacities her social environment enables and encourages her to develop, the moral challenges she faces or avoids. If all of character, not just temperamental traits and dispositions but also the reflexive capacities for self-control and self-construction, are matters of luck, then the very ideas of character and agency are in danger of evaporation. What becomes of the idea that persons are responsible for their character and actions?

The problem can be framed less dramatically, but no less forcefully, if we drop the specter of luck and simply think in terms of its more mundane equivalent—causal necessity. If persons are simply complex creatures subject to natural laws, then some adjustment or reconceptualization of our ideas of character, agency, and responsibility are in order. Whether some or most of the original force of these concepts can be maintained within a more naturalistic psychological framework is a pressing concern requiring close philosophical analysis.

A closely related set of issues arises around the topic of the emotions. Some recent work on the emotions indicates, as Darwin anticipated, that certain basic emotions can be distinguished by specific characteristic movements of the facial musculature as well as by typical physiological responses. The claim is that such basic emotions as anger, fear, disgust, happiness, sadness, and surprise are the product of natural selection, cross-culturally recognizable, and easily activated.

If the emotions are ubiquitous features of human life and cannot be totally suppressed, their expression and direction are morally relevant (Lind, Sherman). Like temperament, emotions ramify. The project of morality must extend beyond a concern for autonomy and righteousness to a concern for the adequate expression and direction of a wide array of attitudes, including the emotions. But how are the emotions distinguished from mere feelings? How do the core emotions acquire their intentional objects? Some types of situations or stimuli, loud noises for example, may automatically activate certain core emotions. But by and large our emotions take as their objects social facts or artifacts, the responses to which are not constitutionally determined. Some psychologists believe that moral norms and values are acquired by connecting the core emotions and socially specific norms and values. This would help explain the powerful emotive elements associated with moral conviction, while at the same time preserving the intuition that the emotional force of a norm or value does not necessarily establish its worth or value.

Further important questions concerning the emotions include the following: Does the fact that certain basic emotional dispositions tend to promote specific values or goods establish the moral worth of those dispositions? Is the role of the emotions in morality an instrumental one such that certain emotions enable us to do what is right? Or are some emotions partly constitutive of morality, so that a type of action does not qualify as moral unless it is performed with the appropriate emotion? To what extent are such emotions as anger, which are normally considered disruptive, important for moral life? How, and under what circumstances, should emotional responses be moderated and modified? What roles do the social environment, rationality, and other aspects of character play in the modulation of emotional response?

Part III: Moral Psychology and the Social Virtues

Aristotle tells us that no one would choose to live a solitary life. Social relations are among life's greatest goods. Some—love and deep friendship, for example—are good in themselves. Others are more instrumental. Many are mixed, good in themselves and useful. Different types of social relations are supported by distinctive virtues, traits, and obligations. We need a sensitive taxonomy of the varieties of social relations and the psychodynamics that promote the most valuable types of relations.

One approach to the taxonomic project begins by challenging the contrast between personal relations that need no principled support because good action springs directly from affection or love, and impersonal relations that require the support of impartial principles because no fellow-feeling binds the parties (Blum). This contrast seems too simple. Many persons appear to act with care and compassion outside of intimate relations. Indeed, recent studies of Christian rescuers of Jews during the holocaust indicate that much rescue originated in a compassionate response to unanticipated encounters with needy strangers. On the other hand, much organized rescue involved articulating principles to guide communal rescue efforts. For many individuals, the appropriate principled conviction seemed sufficient to motivate appropriate action in the absence of any deep feeling for those in need of protecting.

Other sorts of actions cast doubt on a simple personal-impersonal dichotomy. Some of these are actions that express identity-defining and meaning-conferring social roles and vocations, for example, a teacher taking extra time to help a student for whom she has no special personal regard. Actions that stem from one's attachment to a wider community and the goal of helping that community to flourish also defy the personal-impersonal dichotomy.

"Care" and "compassion" appear to be complex cluster concepts, which do not denominate individual traits or dispositional kinds. They refer to complexly related sets of dispositions and response types that range across relations conventionally defined as either personal or impersonal.

Reflection on the complex features of the social virtue of care, understood as a cluster concept, can help elucidate lively contemporary debate about virtue and gender (Card). Some recent work in moral psychology suggests that there is a gender division of moral labor. Women tend to respond to moral issues primarily out of care, concern, and a sense of responsibility for the maintenance of relationships. For men, issues of right, justice, and fairness are central to moral response. The precise nature and degree of gender differences in moral psychology are in need of clarification. Furthermore, because "care" and "compassion" are complex cluster concepts, an ethic of care must proceed cautiously, particularly as care can be expressed impersonally by moral principles, vocational identification, and a deep commitment to the good of a particular community.

Reflection on the moral relevance of gender raises further difficult questions. What, if anything, is the basis of stereotypic gender differences? Should these differences be sustained? Some have argued that the allegedly distinctive moral orientations of men and women ought to be integrated so as to make us all more complete ethical beings. Others have argued that the distinctive ethical orientations cannot be integrated, because they require incompatible dispositions of perception and thought. Still others have recommended acknowledging and valorizing the neglected moral strengths of women in the way we have traditionally valorized the moral qualities associated with males. The trouble with the valorizing strategy is that the alleged gender-specific virtues developed in historical contexts of oppression. Care, compassion, and attention to the maintenance of close relations arose in situations of gender inequality. Promoting these traits as virtues may help sustain morally exploitive relationships. Similar questions must be raised for the stereotypic masculine virtues: virtues of autonomy and respect for justice and duty, impersonally construed. Moreover, the gender stereotypic virtues are each associated with a set of deficiencies. Care is associated with capacities for cunning, deceit, and manipulation. A concern for rights and liberty is associated with detachment and deficiencies of intimacy and compassion. We need to examine the relations between the constructive and harmful exercises of the traits that constitute the virtues, especially if certain virtues are typically associated with specific vices or deficiencies.

The issues surrounding the ethics of care raise further difficult questions. According to many deontological, contractarian, and consequentialist theories, we have obligations to promote the good or welfare of all persons independently of any special relations we might have to them. This seems to imply that it is morally problematic to give special treatment to our personal projects, commitments, and close relations. Some moral theorists have raised the disturbing question of whether morality might be an enemy of friendship and love (Stocker). Can morality allow special partisanship for these relations? When the demands of love or friendship conflict with the demands of duty, which takes priority? To what extent do love and friendship themselves involve duties? More generally, to what extent do love and friendship require respect for persons as ends and a concern for obligation?

The concept of trust presents another approach to these issues (Thomas, Baier). Trust is an integral part of social and moral life. Besides the affectional trust that obtains between friends, there is another kind of trust that obtains among the members of a healthy moral community. We depend on the decency of our fellows, on their refraining from wanton harm, and on their supporting schools, libraries, public works, and welfare programs, because they share our values, rather than merely out of narrow self-interest or a failure of imagination. When shared values are accepted mindlessly or from strategic egoism, we can trust others to maintain a minimal civic, civil moral life. But such trust is more akin to being predictable than it is to being trustworthy. Good personal and communal relations are vulnerable; they merely subsist when trust depends solely on predictable egoism or thoughtless conformism. Genuine flourishing requires trustworthiness as well as predictability.

Trust is intimately related to honesty. But honesty is a hard virtue, hard to characterize, hard to practice, and hard to design (Baier). We are taught a certain amount of reserve and reticence. These protect us from the mockery and censure that might come from revealing our most intimate thoughts and desires. We also withhold certain bitter truths from the young. But if reticence, reserve, and paternalism with respect to the truth are rational, then complete honesty is not. It seems implausible, however, to characterize honesty as the virtue of speaking the truth only when one is under pressure and when there is no risk of mockery or censure. It seems that certain goods—expansive openness, on the one hand, and the desire for privacy and self-protection, on the other—are in tension with each other. The good life is not analogous to a jigsaw puzzle with a space for every piece and with a single optimal solution. Because the virtue of honesty varies culturally and contextually, learning the difference between honesty and deception requires learning complex social rules, with *ceteris paribus* clauses and sensitivity to subtle contextual clues. Of course, following the conventions governing honesty is not enough to guarantee ethical honesty. Most societies have an interest in secrecy and silence, particularly about their own morally problematic features. Honesty may sometimes require breaking the local conventions of decorum concerning silence.

Part IV: Rationality, Responsibility, and Morality

Reflection on the social virtues, especially those displayed in intimate relations and those that serve one's community, suggests that morality must endorse worthy partisan commitments. The danger, however, is that this way of thinking may lead to chauvinism (Piper). Arguments for the rationality and morality of special relations and commitments could conceivably be used to justify vicious discriminatory attitudes and practices. A person who discriminates against a group typically constructs grounds to justify differential treatment, for example, characterizing black culture as primitive or regressive or homosexuality as a form of pathology. More sophisticated discriminators see that such grounds are spurious. They avoid cognitive dissonance by self-deception and denial. Typically, such discrimination uses a deflecting strategy. The discriminator denies contempt for Jews or blacks or homosexuals. Instead, she disvalues intellectual Jews or athletic blacks or sensitive homosexuals. Traits that are valued in others are disvalued when they are possessed by members of the group she holds in contempt.

It is possible that the special treatment allowed to personal relations and to the members of one's community can be justified on grounds that appeal to morally significant features of those relations. But work on the rationalization of sophisticated kinds of discrimination indicates that we are ingenuous at justifying just the special treatment that we initially want to justify. We are highly prone to pseudorationality of just the morally objectionable kind. This line of thought suggests that it may be necessary to retain some form of universalistic moral theory despite the difficulty of reconciling it with a morality that allows space for special relations and commitments.

One possible way out of this impasse involves reconciling the moral requirements of partiality with those of impartial deliberative rationality (Herman). Doing this requires dealing with the problem of moral conflict, since one of the main sources of moral conflict is alleged to lie at the point where performance obligations to do what is right from an impartial point of view meet obligations that arise from personal projects, relations, and commitments. There is a significant divide between philosophers who insist on the reality of moral conflicts that admit of no rational resolution, and those who believe that the conceptual connection between rationality and morality rules out the existence of moral conflict. Many philosophers want to avoid jeopardizing the role of rational deliberation in morality while acknowledging the experience of conflict and the associated attitudes of regret, remorse, and guilt. One proposal is to claim that there is fundamentally only one moral requirement, that of adopting the standpoint of practical rationality. A person's identity as a rational agent is constituted by her taking this standpoint, rather than by committing herself to a set of performance requirements that, once suitably ordered, provide clearcut solutions to all apparent moral conflicts. The standpoint of practical rationality defines a unitary field of deliberation. Everything that legitimately demands deliberative attention lies within the field. Seeing things this way has two important consequences. First, morality need not be seen as inimical to friendship and care-based relations. To be sure, we need to beware of chauvinism and pseudorationality, but friendship has a moral dimension and it occupies an important but not always dominant place in the deliberative field. First, there is nothing in the view of morality as a commitment to rational deliberation that makes friendship always subordinate to impartial obligations. Secondly, there are conflicts and tensions among different facets of the deliberative field. But since morality simply demands that we deliberate rationally, it does not demand that we always act impersonally.

On this view, rational deliberators bring the demands of personal and impersonal morality together onto a unified field of play. What of the person who has trouble doing this, who conceives of himself as a rational deliberator but has trouble seeing the rational force of traditional moral considerations for himself (Brink)? Rational egoism incorporates an agent-relative theory of rationality that assumes that sacrifice requires compensation. Since many other-regarding demands seem to go uncompensated, the egoist has grounds for doubting the rational authority of traditional moral obligations. There are a variety of possible responses to the rational egoist. One is to develop an agent-neutral theory of value according to which the reasons for an action are a function of its value, impersonally construed. But the egoist denies agent neutrality. He denies that value impersonally construed is the sort of value that matters to him. Two other strategies seem more promising because they allow the egoist his motivational structure. The first approach is strategic. The argument is that abiding by traditional morality is typically to the egoist's advantage. The second, neo-Aristotelian strategy involves trying to convince the egoist that his own happiness cannot be specified independently of the happiness of at least some others. There is a noncontingent relation between his own good and the good of some others.

Both strategies are defensible. But both have their limitations. Free riders and sensible knaves haunt the first approach. Furthermore, it seems at most to justify only a prudential morality. It justifies moral conduct perhaps, but not moral concern. Worries about the second, neo-Aristotelian approach arise from the implausibility of the claim that every individual's good is noncontingently connected with the good of every other individual. If identity is grounded in psychological continuity, then some few specific other persons might be thought of as other selves or as part of the self. Perhaps the egoist can come to understand certain personal relations as constitutive of his identity. But extending the egoist's field of reasons to include such relations still leaves a relatively narrow field. Even if these strategies can succeed in making morality more appealing to the egoist, thereby giving it a foothold in his psychology, questions still remain as to the scope and weight of a morality justified in either of these ways. The egoist need not see any reason to commit himself to a morality that extends beyond his primary identity-defining relations, nor need he accord moral considerations any overriding weight. Even if abiding by traditional morality is typically rational from an agent's point of view, its commands may sometimes have no hold on an enlightened egoist, even one who sees his own good as noncontingently connected with the good of some few others.

The phenomena of *akrasia*—an agent voluntarily not following the course she judges best—presents problems for many theories of rationality and morality (McIntyre). Philosophers who judge *akrasia* as irrational must explain how and why an agent would choose to act against her best judgment. On the naive assumption that the mind is transparent to reflection and that an agent can always reflect on the (internal) reasons that relevantly affect her action, all *akrasia* would be irrational. But if we don't accept these assumptions, some *akrasia* might be rational.

Consider the case of Huck Finn. Huck decides that he was wrong to help Jim to escape from his owner. He determines to turn Jim in at the earliest opportunity. But when he is faced with bounty hunters, Huck balks. According to one view, what Huck does is mysteriously irrational. But rejecting the assumptions of the mind's transparency and its optimal deliberative capacity enables us to read the story in another way. Huck is only aware of some of the reasons that move him. Other reasons that significantly figure in his motivational economy are more elusive to his reflection than is his thinking that he should obey the law. But his nontransparent internal reasons can nevertheless successfully motivate his actions. In not turning Jim in, Huck acts out of his own reasons, reasons that make this the best course of action, all things considered. On the analysis that recognizes the motivational and deliberate importance of internal but nontransparent reasons, what Huck does might be both rational and good.

The contast between internal and external criteria of rationality is useful in other areas of moral psychology (White). Like the akratic person, the sociopath, the psychopath, and others who seem undecipherable are often classified as irrational. But on an internalist view of rationality, ascriptions of irrationality are unwarranted when apparently suspect beliefs and desires are in reflective equilibrium with the rest of an individual's beliefs and desires. Similar considerations apply to ascriptions of responsibility. If an agent did what she really wanted, all things considered, she has no internal reason to feel regret, remorse, or guilt, even if her action is irresponsible or even heinous by our lights. The absence of regret in such cases may indicate moral blindness without indicating irrationality. Internalist ascriptions of irrationality and irresponsibility must find a foothold in the individual's own psychological economy.

One way of gaining such a foothold involves making use of the idea that an agent's reasons and their consequences are often not transparent to reflection. Someone who sees no wrong in having needlessly harmed someone might seem to be in internal rational and motivational equilibrium. But if she is committed to autonomy and rational consistency and also desires herself not to be harmed, she has desires and beliefs that provide her with internal reasons to hold herself responsible and blameworthy for causing needless harm. She may not acknowledge her reasons or what they imply, but they nevertheless provide a foothold for ascriptions of blame and responsibility within her own psychology. Normally, the desire not to be harmed and commitments to consistency, autonomy, and authorship provide internalist grounds for ascriptions of blame and responsibility. This leaves room for the possibility that the reigning concepts of rationality and responsibility might not apply to a psychopath who has none of these internal reasons.

Part V: Virtue Theory

The desire for a more psychologically sensitive ethics has resulted in the recent revival of virtue ethics. Virtue theory has been seen by many as the solution to certain shortcomings of contractarian, consequentialist, and deontological theories. These theories seem too rationalistic or cognitivist. They depend on a picture of the ideal moral agent as a deliberator who operates with a general-purpose moral principle, procedure, or ideal. It is also charged that these theories are not sufficiently sensitive to the heterogeneity of goods and the tensions among values. The claim that there is one general morality-conferring principle that also serves as a decision procedure appears to assume that there is a single metric or rule for evaluating and ordering all moral values and obligations.

Virtue theory appears to address both problems. It avoids the charge of excessive cognitivism by stressing moral functions of non-cognitive habits and dispositions. It avoids the assumption of the homogeneity of values by analyzing different virtues as suited for responding to different types of problems, each promoting different kinds of values.

One controversial way of trying to establish the special merits of virtue theory is to argue that it preserves, as many other theories apparently do not, the proper moral worth of agent-centered interests and well-being (Slote). The claim is that both commonsense morality and Kantianism join egoism in justifying an asymmetry between self-regard and regard for others. Egoism allows agents to favor themselves unrestrictedly. Kantian and commonsense morality both concede the importance of the well-being and happiness of agents, but both set moral limits on the pursuit of such well-being and happiness. According to this argument, although commonsense morality and Kantian morality give consideration to the well-being and happiness of individuals, they do so only as a concession. Taking care of oneself, developing one's intrapersonal virtues for their own sake, and promoting one's own projects and commitments have no intrinsic moral value on either view. An agent-centered prerogative is allowed by commonsense and Kantian morality, but it has no intrinsic or direct moral worth. The argument concludes that by giving the self and its projects only secondary, nonmoral value, both commonsense and Kantian morality (like consequentialism) devalue the self and alienate it from its projects. Since virtue theory allegedly treats both self-regarding and other-regarding virtues as equally valuable, it is not open to the charge that the self-regarding virtues are of only instrumental value. It does not require that others be favored or that the self be given moral weight only as a concession. According to this view, virtue theory seems to have the advantage that it does not require agents to alienate themselves from their own selves and projects.

This defense of virtue theory does not claim to establish that virtue ethics is complete or that it provides action-guiding principles. It also leaves open the possibility that the insights of virtue theory can be incorporated into other systems of morality. This raises the question of whether virtue theory is a genuinely different kind of theory from a consequentialist ethic or a deontological or contractarian ethic of requirement and obligation, or whether it supplements them (Watson). One way of showing that virtue theory is both independent and primary would involve establishing, first, that we can provide a theory of good character independently of a theory of what is right or what is consequently good, and second, that we can derive our criteria of action appraisal from a theory of good character. But there is reason to be skeptical that either of these can be done. If virtue theory needs to be complemented by deontological and consequentialist theories, they too for their part seem to require a theory of the traits that constitute a good character. Virtue theory must have a place within any moral theory that aspires to comprehensiveness.

The recognition that our theories of good character, good consequences, and the right are inextricably intertwined need not engender fears of vicious circularity or moral skepticism. To be sure, knowledge from psychology and the other human sciences radically underdetermines our normative theories. But it is a core assumption of the essays in this volume that reflection on psychology and character is essential to normative ethics. Normative ethics interwoven with empirical psychology, history, and anthropology is richer and more defensible than one that remains detached from the human sciences. But the directions and guidelines of such an ethic are provisional and corrigible.

Part I
Identity, Commitment, and Agency

Chapter 1

Aspects of Identity and Agency

Amélie Oksenberg Rorty and David Wong

Recent discussions of personal identity have focused on problems of reference and reidentification (Shoemaker 1963, Parfit 1984) or on the social and cultural dimensions of identity (Sandel 1982, MacIntyre 1981, 1984) or on the processes of self-definition (Frankfurt 1971, Taylor 1976). In sections 1 and 2 we shall explore aspects of identity neglected by those who are primarily interested in metaphysical issues; we propose to develop and expand the work done by those who have been focused on the social and psychological aspects of identity and agency. We will examine the practical import of personal identity, the various ways that the structure of identity traits affect habits and actions.[1] In section 3 we argue that the social aspects of identity are both more complex and more conflicted than many anthropologists have claimed. In section 4 we discuss several philosophical attempts to accord centrality to the social and ideal aspects of identity. Such attempts are best read as expressing normative recommendations that these aspects be accorded centrality. In section 5 we examine the pragmatic import of identity attributions. A decision to emphasize certain aspects of identity expresses a normative commitment and an attempt to direct attitudes and actions.

1 Identity and the Centrality of Traits

A person's identity is constituted by a configuration of central traits. In characterizing identity by the structure of central traits, we do not mean to imply that these traits remain constant throughout an individual's lifetime or that they individuate a person or that they serve as referential reidentifiers. We are focusing on traits that typically make a systematic difference to the course of a person's life, to the habit-forming and action-guiding social categories in which she is placed, to the way that she acts, reacts, and interacts. Of course, in principle any trait, however trivial, can affect the unfolding of a person's life, but we are interested in those sorts of traits that typically make systematic lawlike differences. The kinds of traits that form identity vary culturally, across class and gender lines, and indeed, individually. A trait can be central along numerous dimensions, and it can be central for one dimension without being central for others. The question of whether a trait is part of a person's identity generally has no simple and univocal answer; it is contextually subscripted to one or more dimensions of centrality.

We can distinguish a variety of ways by which a trait can be central to a person's identity:

- The degree of its objective ramification, the extent to which other traits (that is, dispositions to beliefs, desires, habits, attitudes, and actions) are dependent on it
- The degree of its contextual or regional ramification, that is, the extent to which a trait is exemplified across distinctive spheres (e.g., public and private domains, work and leisure) and across different types of relationships (as they are differentiated by gender, status, class, age, etc.)
- The degree to which it is difficult for a person to change the trait (which is often a function of its temporal persistence)
- The degree of its social ramification, the extent to which the trait affects the way the person is categorized and treated by others
- The extent to which it is dominant in situations that require coping with stress or conflict
- The extent to which it is dominant when it conflicts with other traits (e.g., when generosity conflicts with vengefulness)
- The degree to which it is appropriated as important in that the person regards herself as radically changed if the trait is lost or strongly modified. Such appropriations may, but need not be, explicitly articulated; they can be sporadic or contextualized; a person can appropriate a trait without succeeding in acting from it habitually. Sometimes what matters to a person's identity is that she centrally strives to strengthen and exercise a trait. Important traits are often also the focus of self-evaluation and self-esteem.

While many of these dimensions of the centrality of a trait can be correlated with one another, there is no necessary connection among them. For instance, a trait can be highly ramified without being considered important; it can be dominant as a coping strategy without being central to a person's self-evaluation. A person need not be aware of its role in forming her actions; she can be mistaken about the extent to which a trait is central to her identity. Without always succeeding, she can attempt to change the centrality of a trait, diminishing or enlarging the degree of its ramification in the configuration of her character.

A trait can be accorded a high degree of centrality by an individual's culture without its having a correspondingly high degree of either subjective or objective centrality in the configuration of her character. It can, for instance, figure significantly in a culture's practices of praise and blame without actually being strongly ramified. We can furthermore attribute dimensions of centrality to societies or cultures as well as to individual configurations of identity-defining traits. A culture's self-ascriptions—as expressed in political pronouncements and in cultural life—can differ from observer's analyses of the configuration of that culture's central traits.

2 Aspects of Personal Identity

How do the varieties of central traits enter into the formation of actions and into their individuation? How do such traits affect a person's values, beliefs, and motivations—the patterns of practical deliberation? Answering these questions requires differentiating distinctive aspects of identity and of action.

Somatic, Proprioceptive, and Kinaesthetic Dispositions

Initially such central traits (as deft or awkward, excitable or calm, muscularly strong or weak, active or passive, quick or sluggish, slender or heavy, flexible or stiff) are prelinguistic. Virtually any aspect of a person's somatic dispositions can come into focus as significant for identity.[2] Because a child's earliest self-awareness is noncomparative, it is usually preconscious. Even when somatic identity becomes conceptualized in a self-image or self-conception, it need not be articulated or appropriated, and a person can even be unaware of its practical import in forming her actions. Because there are social norms for many somatic qualities (e.g., slender, muscularly strong, or agile), those who stress the somatic aspect of identity attempt to conform to social ideals of body types. Central somatic dispositions affect the formation of action in several ways. Because they affect a person's posture, gestures, movements, they often individuate the modality of an action as graceful, sluggish, or abrupt, for instance. Somatic dispositions can also affect a person's beliefs, motives, and plans. Someone with a low sense of somatic self-confidence can feel alienated or unimpowered, act in a tentative and anxious way, limit her desires, avoid confrontational situations, expect failure, and so on (Bruch 1988).

Central Temperamental or Psychological Traits
Such traits as aggression or friendliness, shyness or gregariousness, generosity or withholdingness, trust or distrust affect the individua-· tion of actions by modifying the manner in which they are performed and described, e.g., by such adverbial modifiers as "He closed the door sullenly (apprehensively, expectantly)," "She voted enthusias- tically (cynically, carelessly)."[3] Central temperamental traits also dis- pose a person to develop certain sorts of motives and habits, but they can also affect actions directly, contrary to a person's desires.[4] While a shy person might, for instance, prefer to avoid social occa- sions, he could also sincerely desire companionship but find himself unable to move toward it.

Sometimes the way that temperament affects action is indirect: cultural narratives, popular songs, and stories provide a standard repertoire of ready-made action routines for typical temperaments.[5] (Theophrastus and Samuel Butler sketched the habits and tastes of various psychological types: the melancholic person, the pugnacious man, the licentious man, the envious man. These sketches are re- markably detailed and include the descriptions of the kinds of situ- ations, occupations, and actions toward which the various temperaments are typically drawn.) Because they standardly and widely elicit specific patterns of social responses, temperamental traits often tend to ramify to form clusters of mutually reinforcing dispositions. For instance, an aggressive person is likely to generate very different sorts of interactive action scenarios than would stan- dardly be generated by a friendly or gentle person. But temperamen- tal traits can also generate conflicting or erratic patterns of behavior: an aggressive person can also be shy.

Social Role Identity
Central traits can be acquired and entrenched by a person's being placed (or placing herself) in socially defined institutional roles or being cast to play a certain kind of role in the unfolding of social dramas. Social-role channeling tends to occur early within the fam- ily's cast of characters (Bowen 1978). Some of these roles are defined by established institutions and practices (family and occupational roles); others arise from the impetus of an unfolding narrative (e.g., the ingenue, the villain, the elder sister with advice, the tomboy, the victim, the liberator, the daredevil, the complainer, the outsider).[6] Somatic factors often influence role casting: a tall person with deep voice is often seen as reassuring, whether or not he initially has the desires or the skills for that kind of leadership. When a person is constantly channeled by the interactive minutiae of cooperation and

interaction, he tends to develop habits of perceptual salience, emotion, and motivation that are appropriate to the role in which he has been cast. When they are strongly socialized, reinforced, or rewarded, such habits can become central traits.[7] But there can also be a dramatic mismatch between social role casting and a person's somatic or temperamental traits. While mismatches of this kind can produce pathologies of cognitive dissonance or conflicted identities, they can also lead to a critical evaluation of existing social practices or to the development of new coping traits (Festinger 1965).

Social role casting can also provide norms for deliberation. For instance, parents are pressed into socially defined forms of practical reasoning, beliefs, and desires by virtue of being held responsible for the welfare of their children. These norms can often be difficult to integrate with the rest of their central traits.

Socially Defined Group Identity
Race, class, age, gender, ethnicity, or occupation tend to be associated with stereotypic traits that often set directions for role casting. Like role casting, group identity can be socially attributed without being subjectively appropriated or being objectively central.

A person's group identity can affect his actions in a number of ways. Ethnic groups often have distinctive child-rearing practices, many of which also direct the formation of gender- and class-specific traits and habits. Members of groups are often socially channeled into specific sorts of habit-forming institutional roles. Women were, for example, channeled into certain sorts of action-guiding institutional positions (nurses, secretaries), and immigrants often are streamed into certain sorts of ethnically stereotypic occupations. A person's group identity further tends to generate specific sorts of social interactions. The elderly or disabled are, for instance, stereotypically constrained and channeled in ways that can become strongly habitual, even to the extent of affecting beliefs and desires. Not surprisingly, group identity traits·often conflict with other aspects of a person's identity. (For instance, a strongly inventive and improvisatory person who is treated as dependent and passive in her old age is often catapulted into a limited set of action-forming attitudes of resentment or of forced cheer.)

Ideal Identity
A person's ideal identity sets directions for the development of central traits. Sometimes this involves imitating an idealized figure—an Eleanor Roosevelt or a Mahatma Gandhi. Sometimes it is envisioned from the acceptance of moral principles or ideology. Besides individ-

ually appropriated idealized figures, there are also culturally specific ideals—a Buddha or a set of saints whose lives set a pattern for the formation of central traits. The hagiographic traditions surrounding these figures are presented in narratives describing their values, deliberations, and choices. But ideal identifications need not always be so elevated: they can be set by popular culture, by rock stars or movie stars who provide models for the imitation of even the smallest gestures. Of course, a person can appropriate many different, sometimes conflicting ideals, she need not always be aware of her operative ideal identifications, and she need not always approve of those that are actually functioning. An adolescent who takes Gandhi as one of her idealized identity figures might nevertheless also unwittingly model herself on Lauren Bacall.

When they are capable of reflecting on the range of roles and group factors in identity, children can also appropriate ideal identities. Indeed, children often acquire other central identity traits by first being moved by the image of an ideal, which is often initially socially imposed before it is subjectively appropriated. But it seems at least possible that a tendency to idealize may precede socialization.[8] A child who is consistently cast as 'nurse' in playground games can come to accept that identity as an ideal, making it formative in her general behavior, first playing and then becoming solicitous. But despite always being lured into playing the nurse's role, a child might subjectively appropriate the ideal of a swashbuckling adventurer and attempt to graft bold, daring traits on the manner of her playing nurse. While such improvisatory grafts are often fruitful, they can also generate erratic or conflicted behavior.

Like other aspects of identity, a person's conception of her ideal self can enter into the individuation and the formation of actions in a number of different ways.[9] When it involves models, it can affect both the types of actions a person performs and her manner of performing them. Because the ideal self defines a set of general ends and values, it affects the details of practical deliberation and the directions of choice, often by determining what is salient. But it is frequently difficult to integrate the habits required to actualize an ideal identity with the rest of a person's central traits, particularly when the ideal involves a commitment to a relatively undefined long-range projects, like becoming a parent or a physician.

The psychological force of an ideal is distinguishable from the normative or moral authority accorded to it. For instance, a person might be unselfconsciously guided by a John Wayne ideal of masculine identity but not accept the moral values that support such an ideal. The extent of a person's success in appropriating an ideal as part of his action-forming identity is generally a function of the sources of this commitment to that ideal, its attraction for him, and the extent to which the habits required to realize the ideal can be integrated with the rest of his character. Sometimes when an ideal cannot be fully or successfully realized, the focus of a person's identity can lie in his continuous striving toward it. The ideal of rationality might, for instance, be expressed by a person's continuously attempting to entrench intellectual habits of disambiguation. Similarly, an ideal of empathy might be expressed by attempting to enrich habits of imagination.

Let us return to the questions with which we began this taxonomy. How are these aspects of identity related to one another? And what is their practical import in forming actions?

While these aspects of identity are independent, they are often mutually reinforcing, constraining, or conflicting. For convenience we've presented them in a roughly psychogenetic developmental order, beginning with an infant's earliest somatic dispositions and ending with intellectualized ideals. But we are not committed to any theory about the foundational importance of the chronologically earlier aspects of identity. A person's somatic and temperamental traits tend to affect the range of social roles in which she is cast. (For instance, an aggressive person is likely to be cast in the role of an explorer rather than that of a peacemaker.) On the other hand, the social roles into which an individual is cast can cause her to develop temperamental traits that might otherwise have remained relatively recessive. (For instance, a man who was not particularly nurturing can become so when he is centrally role-cast as a father.)

Similarly, a person can be unaware of, and even sometimes mistaken about, the connections among her central traits. For instance, the young woman who appropriates John Wayne as an identity ideal may be unaware or mistaken about the ways that her own somatic dispositions and those she acquired as a result of social role casting will resist her attempts to become a female version of John Wayne. In principle, the range of ideals that a person can appropriate is quite open. But idealized identity can be influenced by social role casting, even when its channeling practices are not publicly formulated or announced. Social values can also affect the selection of somatic traits that become central to identity: military societies focus attention on strength, while aesthetic societies emphasize refined thresholds of sensory discrimination. Individuals are normally presented with a relatively limited repertoire of appropriate ideals, as defined by their social roles and groups. For instance, while a young woman might take John Wayne as representing her ideal identity, she will find it difficult to realize the habits and actions associated with that ideal. Both the ramification of her own early traits and the dynamic force of her social interactions channel her in other directions. If she has a persistent and independent temperament, she may indeed move John Wayneward. But attempting to free oneself from social norms— or attempting to change those norms—often exacts social and sometimes psychological costs.

There are, as we saw, a number of different ways in which central identity traits affect actions.

- They affect what is (perceptually, imaginatively, emotionally, and cognitively) salient to an agent. In directing interpretations of situations and affecting the associations that such interpretations generate, central identity traits form (what might be called) the problematics of an agent's experience. They propel an agent into certain sorts of situations and problems, and they provide a relevance selector among the relatively indefinite number of action routines that might be elicited in any given situation.
- They affect the dynamics of social interaction, eliciting responses—sometimes supportive and cooperative, sometimes antagonistic—that set constraints and directions on the agent's actions.
- By affecting patterns of child rearing and socialization, they direct the formation of habits.
- They can affect systems of beliefs and desires. Ideals are often the best explanation of a person's having acquired or developed a pattern of desires, even when those ideals were initially socially inculcated. Similarly, a person's group or role identity can often provide the best explanation of her holding certain beliefs.
- They can set ends and values that direct practical deliberation.
- Central traits sometimes affect actions straightaway and directly. Though of course they do not justify actions, they can sometimes be question stoppers in the search for explanations.[10]

There is a distinction between the psychological force of a central trait and a person's (or a society's) normative evaluation of that trait. A person can recognize that a trait—an ideal or a group identity—is objectively central, widely ramified, and even dominant in the resolution of conflicts and yet value neither that trait nor its centrality.

3 Relative Centrality of Aspects

Just as traits vary in degrees of centrality, so too there are considerable individual and cultural variations in the degree to which different aspects of identity are central. One person might stress her role identity as a teacher, importing her pedagogic traits into a wide variety of contexts and according them priority in cases of conflict. Another might stress temperamental traits, leaving role relatively recessive. Similarly, one culture might stress the ramification of such temperamental traits as austerity and asceticism, while another might focus on channeling social roles.

Anthropologists have claimed that there are systematic differences in the ways that societies tend to weight the centrality of aspects of identity. Some have claimed that in certain societies the social-role aspect has a centrality it does not normally have in our culture. K. E. Read (1955, 278, 276) reported that "social role is an intrinsic constituent of each man's identity" among the Gabuku-Gama of New Guinea. Members of that congeries of tribes do move in and out of social roles and "thereby in a somewhat paradoxical sense, they lose or forfeit [what we would call] their identity." They note each other's idiosyncrasies and conceive of one another as distinct personalities, but these differences "are like a shimmer which overlies their social identity." They chiefly regard each other and themselves as "figures in a social pattern."

Read notes that moral reasoning among the Gahuku-Gama is "primarily contextual, dependent, that is, on the nature of specific social ties." The condemnation of homicide, for example, varies with the social status of the agent and victim. It is seriously wrong to kill a member of one's own subclan but commendable to kill a member of opposed tribes, even in peacetime (pp. 262–264). He contrasts the views of the Gahuku-Gama with the Western doctrine that human beings are owed respect because they possess intrinsic value independently of their social status or role (pp. 263, 260, 259–261). Read seems to have found a systematic cultural difference in the relative centrality accorded to the social ramification of role identity.

A similar point is made by Clifford Geertz, who contrasts Western with Balinese identity. The Balinese control interpersonal relations by a highly developed system of conventions and proprieties and define the "substance of the self" by a person's roles (Geertz 1984, 129). In commenting on the connection between identity and social role in Balinese public life, Geertz says that political and religious leaders become absorbed into their roles: "We, focusing upon psychological traits as the heart of personal identity, would say they have sacrificed their true selves to their roles; they, focusing on social position, say that their role is of the essence of their true selves" (1973, 386).

George de Vos holds that traditional societies like Japan accord a high degree of subjective and objective dominance to role identity, particularly in cases of stress and conflict. He believes that the varieties of identity tend to be absorbed into role identity in societies where roles are socially channeled and widely ramified (de Vos 1973). Richard Shweder and Edmund Bourne hold that the traditional "sociocentric" conception of the person does not differentiate the individual from his group and role, while the modern Western "egocentric" conception accords value and assigns duties to individuals independently of their social roles (Shweder and Bourne 1984, 166–168).

The distinctions that we have drawn between dimensions and aspects of identity suggest that the wholesale contrasts that many anthropologists have drawn between traditional sociocentric and modern egocentric conceptions of identity are too stark.[11] The sharp contrasts that Shweder and Bourne, along with some other anthropologists, have emphasized might be better understood as distinctions of degree. Traditional cultures have some identity-defining ideals and duties that are universally prescribed, independently of social roles. Hindu cultures, for example, prescribe certain ideal identities across socially defined caste and class divisions.[12] On the other hand, while social mobility in modern Western society is greater than it is in traditional societies, twentieth-century North Americans also have social identities; they too are group-cast along race, class, and gender lines. While Western societies tend to give more subjective centrality to role-independent temperamental and ideal traits than they do to role and group identity, the latter aspects normally have much greater objective centrality than is usually subjectively acknowledged.

Even when ideal traits are specifiable independently of any particular social roles, social contexts place significant objective and subjective constraints on their development and exercise. An individual's attempt to discount the centrality of group identity can often fail. The attempt to diminish the significance of race, ethnicity, or gender is often treated as itself a focal expression of the very identity whose centrality is denied. For example, blacks or African-Americans are now often called upon to give race relative dominance over other aspects of their identity.[13] Even if an individual African-American subjectively attempts to discount race and to stress his ideal identity, his refusal to privilege race identity is often socially interpreted as a form of racism. He may be charged with identifying with the oppressor, and he is likely to be continuously role-cast in ways that can override the centrality that he attempted to accord to his ideal identity.

There can be deep conflicts between the various aspects of identity. As we saw in section 2, aspects affect action in several direct and indirect ways. Different aspects can direct an agent toward incompatible courses of action: a person's ideals can direct a course of action that is countermanded by her temperament or her social roles; similarly, traits that have become widely ramified as the result of social channeling can be more dominant than traits of the ideal self. Conflicts of this kind can be diagnosed by an observer or theoretician who can trace the distinctive patterns of centrality accorded to various aspects. But they can also be experienced by an agent, who finds herself in conflict between different plans of action as they might be generated by distinctive configurations of her identity traits.

4 Identity and Practical Deliberation

Philosophers have drawn normative lessons from their conceptions of personal identity. Their work, however, does not adequately address the possibility of conflict among the several aspects. They may be criticized as having a simplistic conception of identity, focusing on one aspect to the exclusion of others. Or they may be understood as responding to certain moral and social problems of the time by urging us to strengthen one aspect of identity relative to the others.

Michael Sandel criticizes deontological ethics for picturing us as independent selves "in the sense that our identity is never tied to our aims and attachments" to various communities. But, he objects, "we cannot regard ourselves as independent in this way without great cost to those loyalties and convictions whose moral force consists partly in the fact that living by them is inseparable from understanding ourselves as the particular persons we are—as members of this family or community or nation or people" (Sandel 1982, 179). Acknowledging the extent to which others participate in the constitution of our identities might lead us to regard ourselves "more as participants in a common identity" (p. 143) and enable us to use our individual talents and skills in the common endeavors of community.

Sandel thinks that reflecting on the social formation and definition of motives has implications for our understanding of practical deliberation. It reveals the extent to which such deliberation goes beyond the evaluation of the relative strength of our desires in being guided by the commitments of our encumbered intersubjective selves. Sandel's work raises the questions of whether greater awareness of the central aspects of identity always leads to an affirmation of those aspects and whether such affirmation is always motivationally efficacious.

Sandel's analysis of the contribution of social identity is most applicable to those who affirm their social identities as relatively central. It is too simplistic for those for whom role and group are either much less central or represent attachments and habits to be rejected. Questions of identity tend to arise when there are problems of action and policy, when an "identity crisis" triggers an attempt to articulate an individual or collective identity, particularly when there is disagreement about their characterization and importance. To begin with, the relations we bear to the social structures that influence our identities are often ambiguous and indeterminate. More seriously, many of us have deep moral reservations about the very structures that have traditionally defined identity. We have reservations both about ways traits have been characterized and about the centrality accorded to the various aspects of identity. For instance, someone who has moral reasons for accepting the centrality of the family to his identity might nevertheless criticize the implicit hierarchical structure of the traditional family. Or someone who accepts the traditional definition of the role traits of the teacher might have moral reasons for rejecting the centrality accorded to role aspects of identity.

Perhaps Sandel's emphasis on the social aspects of identity is best read as a claim about the force and ramification of the social aspects of "the encumbered self." A sympathetic reading of Sandel would interpret him as attempting to persuade us to affirm and appropriate what we judge valuable in the social aspects of our identity, rather than as claiming that all social identities are morally legitimate. More reflection of this kind involves articulating tensions between our ideals and other aspects of identity; it involves evaluating the aims and attachments that are embedded in the social aspects of identity. Having argued that practical deliberation should include a critical evaluation of desires, Sandel should also acknowledge the possibility of a critical evaluation of social identity.

Charles Taylor has presented an account of the practical role of ideal identity that could provide grounds for a critique of social identity. He holds that "identity is defined by our fundamental evaluations," which form "the indispensable horizon or foundation out of which we reflect and evaluate as persons" (1977a, 124–125). Having an identity goes beyond weighing desires according to their relative strengths. It involves a "strong evaluation" of motives and existing social roles as base or noble, honorable or dishonorable, fragmented or integrated.

Taylor seems to accord the ideal aspect of identity absolute centrality. But as we saw, the contrast between an agent's ideal identity and her fortuitous system of desires is too simple to account for the variety of ways that different aspects of identity affect practical reasoning. A person's conception of the somatic or temperamental aspects of her identity can play a crucial role in her evaluation of the feasibility of her ideals. Someone who realizes that she is somatically fastidious and temperamentally methodical can recognize the impracticality of adopting the ideal identity of being a member of the Grateful Dead. A person's strong moral evaluations can conflict with her social and group identity in ways that severely constrain the viability and applicability of those ideals. Identity, as we saw in section 1, consists not only of what is subjectively appropriated but also of traits that can be objectively, contextually, and socially ramified independently of their acceptance or even acknowledgment by the agent.

In any case, as Taylor himself sometimes acknowledges, admirable persons need not be deeply reflective, and their actions can sometimes be determined by role, group, somatic, or temperamental traits rather than by their ideal identities.[14] A kind person's sensitivity to the needs of others can be perceptually "hard-wired" as salient without her being a "strong evaluator." She might navigate the world in a relatively unselfconscious fashion, without reflecting on what is worthy or unworthy, noble or base.

Taylor appears to overestimate the power of choice and reflection to effect an equilibrium in the relative importance that should be accorded to different identity aspects. While ideal identifications can sometimes provide a basis for critical evaluations of other aspects of identity, they are not necessary conditions for an individual to be a person with an identity, nor can a person have an identity only to the extent that he is actively engaged in strong evaluation. In any case, the viability of an ideal depends on the extent to which it can be integrated with a person's habits and existing social practices. The social contexts in which an individual pursues his ends and ideals set severe constraints on their realization and sometimes even on their formulation. Attempts to change existing patterns of social channeling can create paralyzing internal conflicts. If practical deliberation attempts to change the actual in favor of the ideal, it must pay attention to the ways in which the ideal is constrained by the intractable. The 'correct' balance of aspects of identity cannot simply be reached by an intellectual or visionary top-down evaluation by

the ideal aspects, nor are we forced in the absence of such an evaluation to a groundless radical choice. Instead, practical reasoning can
involve an attempt to reach a "reflective equilibrium" among the
various aspects of the self. We use the phrase from John Rawls (1971)
to refer to a mutual adjustment among the aspects.[15] No one aspect
is assumed to be absolutely privileged and exempt from adjustment.
Nor can general guidelines be given for determining what constitutes
a satisfactory adjustment.

A more sympathetic reading of Taylor would interpret him to be
making a rhetorical appeal, urging us to exercise the force of our
ideals to change what we judge wrong with existing habits and social
practices. Like Sandel, Taylor may be calling attention to an aspect
he believes should be strengthened. In focusing on one or another
aspect of identity, a philosopher is not only presenting a descriptive
analysis; he is also expressing a normative diagnosis, his own ideals.

5 The Pragmatic Implications of Identity Attribution

The configuration of identity—the relative centrality allocated to different aspects of identity—often varies contextually with the practical
significance of the allocation. For instance, the leaders of a political
party might stress the group and role aspects of identity in their
deliberations concerning the merits of various possible nominees for
office. Having selected their candidate, however, they are likely to
highlight the temperamental and ideal aspects of his identity to the
electorate in the interest of getting him elected. Sometimes such shifts
in emphasis involve falsification. Yet the difference in emphasis may
correctly reflect the aspect of identity that is importantly relevant to
the electorate.

But differentiating contexts does not always resolve apparent conflicts in descriptions of the configuration or structure of identity.
When there is strong disagreement about the direction of policy,
attributions of identity can be a mode of social channeling, and
sometimes of social control. Practical judgments that appeal to "tradition" are selective and normative; those that stress the primacy of
the agent's ideal identity also often implicitly introduce substantive
normative commitments. Consider Sartre's young man in occupied
France who faces a choice between remaining to sustain his mother
or joining the Free French in England. Different advisors with different normative commitments will stress different aspects of his
identity. The advisor who recommends staying in France privileges
the role aspect of identity, while the advisor who urges joining the
Free French takes political ideals to be primary.[16]

Attributions of identity are standardly declarative speech acts. But even when such attributions are true, they perform numerous functions besides reporting what is true. Indeed, the point of making an identity attribution goes beyond just telling the truth. There are, after all, an indefinite number of true and even interesting things a person can say in any given situation. When do questions about the relative centrality of traits arise? Why do we select those aspects we emphasize as relevant or central? Even within the boundaries of truth and relevance, attributions of identity have pragmatic and normative force. Identity attributions occur in practical contexts, usually when there is a choice about the direction of policy.[17] Even autobiographies and obituaries are triadic: a speaker describes a subject to a specific but sometimes unidentified audience, usually with a view to affecting its attitudes and so eventually its actions. Obituaries, for instance, are often directed to the children of the deceased; autobiographies are often written in self-justification or as warnings or apologias. Of course, sometimes audience and subject coincide; indeed, all three coincide.

If Sandel and Taylor are interpreted as presenting straightforward reports about the unqualified centrality of the social and ideal aspects of identity, their claims are surely radically oversimplified. More charitable interpretations of their positions suggest that their analyses are not only pragmatic but also normative: they are not merely reporting their philosophic conclusions but attempting to influence our identities. They present diagnoses of the cultural and political malaise of their audience; their reflections on its traditional and ideal identities are intended as therapeutic recommendations. Sandel's emphasis on the socially encumbered aspects of identity reveals his confidence in the compatibility of our social identities with the self-critical aspects of the liberal tradition. Presumably Taylor stresses the ideal aspects of identity because he is less sanguine about the self-corrective aspects of our social identities.

Like most philosophers, they are strongly committed to formulating their arguments in universal terms, attempting to detach their analyses from the specific historical or cultural problems that generated their investigations. They try to derive their conclusions neutrally without presupposing that their audience shares their prephilosophic intuitions. But they want to persuade us, historically and philosophically situated as we are, to appropriate a certain kind of identity. Sandel and Taylor attempt to combine the universalistic tradition of philosophical analysis with an older philosophical tradition that also tries to be rhetorically and normatively persuasive. It is ironically often the very strategy of casting their contextualized and normative views about personal identity in apparently neutral terms that makes their work rhetorically persuasive. It is sometimes difficult to decide whether to chide the disingenuousness of philosophers detaching analyses of identity from the highly specific contexts in which they arise or to admire the rhetorical ingenuity of their masks of neutrality. There is another view of philosophy, one developed in the spirit of Hume, that might make it possible to combine the two traditions, to unmask illusion in the name of analytic clarity and impartiality while also acknowledging the propriety and perhaps the inevitability of a philosophical rhetoric that attempts to persuade as well as to clarify.[18]

Notes

1. We shall use the terminology of traits to refer to dispositions of perception, imagination, and cognition as well as of behavior. Many of these dispositions are active: they do not depend solely on the chance of circumstance but rather generate the conditions that promote their exercise. Some but not all traits are habits of action; some but not all are habits of thought, of categorical, perceptual, and emotional salience. Our discussion of the practical role of such traits is neutral for different analyses of dispositional terms. It is intended to acknowledge the influence of culture on the identification and attribution of traits.

2. See Rousseau's *sentiment* (sense) of one's own existence (J.-J. Rousseau 1961), Merleau-Ponty's embodiment (M. Merleau-Ponty 1963, pp. 185–224, 226–249), Sartre's prereflective consciousness of the body's qualities (J.-P. Sartre 1943).

3. Contemporary psychological theories of personality are descended from the classical and medieval psychophysical theories that projected the range of humors or temperaments from combinations of the four elements and the "pure" psychological types associated with them. The psychological or temperamental traits of individuals were thought to be functions of the proportions of the elements that constitute their bodies. Both physical and psychological disorders were identified with disproportions in the balance of elements. Robert Burton's *The Anatomy of Melancholy* is a classical medical formulation of the theory of temperaments. Among the most elegant literary expression of this view is Chaucer's Prologue to the *Canterbury Tales*. Chaucer presents a rich array of social types by describing connections between somatic, temperamental, group, and role traits. In speaking of a person's temperamental identity, we are not, of course, committing ourselves to psychophysicalism or to the classical theory of the temperaments.

4. As a philosophical term, 'desires' has a broad and a narrow sense. In its broad or technical sense, it refers to any and all motivating states and dispositions. The narrower and more common sense of 'desire' refers to a specific subclass of motives: wants and wishes that are directed to particular satisfactions. Acting out of unreflective habit counts as acting out of desire in the broad but not the narrow sense. In claiming that habits and identity traits can form actions independently of beliefs and desires, we are referring to the narrower sense of 'desire'. We take no position on whether there are satisfactory analyses of the technical sense of 'desire' that capture the primary features of ordinary use except to note that the more that a technical sense diverges from the ordinary sense of desire, the less it

can be used to explain the ordinary sense of action. Once technical reconstruction is introduced, it must be followed through on all levels.

5. See S. Butler 1970, J. Earle 1811, Theophrastus 1967, R. Burton 1977, Chaucer 1985, La Bruyere 1965.

6. Molière 1869.

7. S. Ruddick 1989, N. Chodorow 1978.

8. Jerome Kagan (1984) discusses some interesting observations of children's distress at damaged or imperfect objects, which suggests that children may be guided by a desire for ideal objects. He links such phenomena with moral development and identity formation.

9. See Frankfurt 1971, C. Taylor 1976.

10. "Why did you go to cheer the Pope on his arrival in Bogata?" "Because I am a Pole." "Do you weight national solidarity as a central dimension of your identity?" "No, I don't like Poles, hate crowds, and had better things to do." "Were you then *akratic* in welcoming him? Do you regret what you did or think it was irrational?" "No, of course not. Like it or not, I am a Pole."

11. Alasdair MacIntyre, in chapter 3 of *After Virtue*, seems to make the same stark contrast. His most recent book, *Whose Justice? Which Rationality?* especially chapter 20, moderates the contrast.

12. For example, the ideals of noninjury, truth, purity, not stealing, charity, forbearance, self-restraint, tranquility, generosity, and asceticism, as stated in the *Arthasastra*. See O'Flaherty 1978 for an interesting discussion on attempts to resolve conflicts between role-specific duties and common duties.

13. Terminology often becomes centrally important to group identity. Whether a person is prepared to accord centrality to his racial identity will, of course, depend how the race is characterized and how it is related to his other group identities (e.g., to class or subculture). The differences between 'black', 'Afro-American', and 'African-American' are significant; they affect an individual's decision about whether to appropriate or to discount race as central to his identity.

14. Taylor (1989) has enlarged his conception of strong evaluations. There appear to be several strands in this conception. (1) The identity of persons is linked to reflexive self-awareness. This strand in Taylor's account derives from a Hegelian-Romantic commitment to self-realization through self-consciousness. In the most general formulation of this condition, reflexivity need not be intellectually articulated or defended (see, e.g., chapter 1, pp. 20–21). (2) Taylor sometimes links the reflexivity condition with a linguistic condition. The identity of persons is marked by their capacity for reflexive intentionality, construed as a capacity for the self constituting its identity through a linguistic self-description. Like the first reflexive condition, this condition need not be intellectualistic in the usual sense of that term. The linguistic condition can be satisfied with poetry (e.g., chapter 23, pp. 408–441). (3) The linguistic strand is linked to a communitarian theme, under which one's identity includes a "defining community" (chapter 2, p. 36). Even if an individual develops original understandings of herself and human life, she starts from a base in a common and public language, and she is a self "only in relation to certain interlocutors." The narrow, intellectualistic interpretation of this theme requires that a person with an identity be able to give reasons for her conception of the good (see chapter 4, pp. 91–107). Whether Taylor's conception of identity and of strong evaluation is intellectualistic or not depends on whether these themes are given broad or narrow interpretations. For a criticism of Taylor's intellectualist tendencies, see Owen Flanagan's chapter in this volume. Whether

or not Taylor is an intellectualist, he is committed to a top-down view according to which identity is constituted by a commitment to a set of ideals.

15. Our use of the term is an extension of the way Rawls uses it to refer to the mutual adjustment between considered convictions of justice and the most abstract and general theoretical principles of justice.

16. Sartre 1964. "Qui doit-on aîmer comme un frère, le combatant ou la mère?"

17. American historians are now increasingly sensitive to the ways that their research and analyses reflect their normative commitments about the central features of national identity. For instance, it is now generally recognized that the Beards' influential *A History of the United States* stressed those aspects of the tradition which they believed consistent with adopting a socialist program.

18. We are grateful to Laura Weisberg for her good counsel and for bibliographic suggestions and to Owen Flanagan for helpful comments. We also benefitted from comments and discussions with Larry Blum, Sissela Bok, and Eli Hirsch.

Chapter 2
Identity and Strong and Weak Evaluation
Owen Flanagan

1

What is the connection between identity and reflection, between possession of an integrated, motivationally effective self and articulate self-comprehension? To what extent is ethical self-evaluation necessary for personhood and for ethical goodness itself? I want to discuss these fundamental questions of philosophical psychology by exploring a provocative and influential recent attempt to answer them. This influential answer goes wrong in certain subtle but consistent ways. It overstates the degree to which rich and effective identity, as well as moral decency, are tied to articulate self-comprehension and evaluation. And it overstates the centrality of ethical identifications in human life.

Reflection is a good. But it is a relative, contingent good. Identity and goodness do not require reflectiveness to any significant degree, nor is distinctively ethical identification the indispensable font of all modern identity.

2

In several important papers (1977a, 1977b, 1981) and in his recent book *Sources of the Self: The Making of Modern Identity* (1989), Charles Taylor argues that the capacity for what he calls strong evaluation is a necessary feature of persons. He writes that "the capacity for strong evaluation in particular is essential to our notion of the human subject. . . . Without it an agent would lack a kind of depth we consider essential to humanity" (1977a, 28). "The capacity for . . . strong evaluation is an essential feature of a person" (p. 43). More recently, Taylor insists that strong evaluation is an inescapable feature of "undamaged" personhood. Strong evaluation involves "discrimination of right or wrong, better or worse, higher or lower, which are not rendered valid by our own desires, inclinations, or choices, but rather stand independent of these and offer standards by which they can be judged" (1989, 4). It is clear that Taylor conceives of the relevant capacity as one that is realized. It is an actualized potentiality, not a bare potentiality. An individual is a person if and only if she is a strong evaluator.

There are a number of significant modifications in the original picture of strong evaluation as it is used and described in *Sources of the Self*. Taylor does not remark on any of these changes. But since these modifications involve both improvements in the view, some of which blunt the force of certain criticisms I make, and certain new problematic twists in the characterization of strong evaluation, I will be careful to call attention to them as the discussion proceeds.

Taylor employs Harry Frankfurt's well-known (1971) distinction between first and second order desires as a basis for drawing the distinction between strong and weak evaluation. Here are several passes at an interpretation, each more refined than its predecessor, of the distinction Taylor wants to make.

> 1. In weak evaluation we are concerned ultimately only with how, given our circumstances, we can most effectively satisfy our first-order desires. Our second-order desires, in so far as we have any, are concerned with scheduling and ordering consummations, possibly within an overall hedonistic plan. In strong evaluation, on the other hand, we are concerned with the "qualitative *worth*" of different desires, values, and action tendencies (1977a, 16; 1977b, 65). The strong evaluator, unlike the weak evaluator, may "be called deep because what weighs with him are not only the consummations desired but also what kind of life, what quality of agent, they are to be" (1977a, 34).
>
> 2. This way of contrasting weak and strong evaluators turns out not to work exactly, since the weak evaluator need not weigh things in simple quantitative terms, in terms of what is more pleasure-producing along some single dimension. The weak evaluator might think a Southern vacation better than a Northern one along an axis, or along various axes, of qualitative distinctions—it is more beautiful in the South than in the North, the environment is more serene in the South than in the North, the diet more spare and elegant in the South, and so on.
>
> 3. The weak and the strong evaluator cannot be distinguished, then, simply in terms that the latter judges things qualitatively whereas the former does not, or that the latter is reflective while the latter is not (1977a, 23). The difference lies more precisely in the fact that the strong evaluator characterizes his "desires and inclinations as worthier, or nobler, or more integrated" (1977a,

25). The weak evaluator's qualitative assessments either do not involve her own motives, desires, and inclinations, or if they do, they involve only nonethical assessment of these motives, desires, and inclinations. The desire for the spare Southern diet fits better than the Northern diet with the plan of keeping her weight down, or the choice of a Southern diet will be perceived as classier by those whose impression of her she fancies most.

4. It might seem that what distinguishes the weak from the strong evaluator is that the strong evaluator has the ability to condemn and override some of her own desires as unworthy despite her powerful motivation to act in accordance with them. But the weak evaluator can do this too. She can decide that a Northern vacation is unworthy of a person as refined as herself, even though she would actually prefer to be in the North. If she is trying to live her life oriented around a ground project in which refinement, sophistication, and *savoir faire* are the central goals, she may well choose against what she prefers in this way. This shows that it is not the case that the weak evaluator's second-order evaluations are all instrumental, concerned only with how well her second-order plans and motives are suited to realizing her first-order desires. She may care about the quality of her sophisticated life in its own right. Furthermore, the standards of sophistication she abides may exist independently of her own inclinations and desires. Strong evaluators cannot be distinguished, therefore, from weak evaluators in terms of the independence or objectivity of the standards they abide (contra Taylor 1989, 20).[1]

5. Insofar as the contrast between strong and weak evaluators has to do with capacities to overrule one's own motives, it has to do not with the capacity itself but with the reasons behind such overriding. When the strong evaluator overrules her own desires, she does so on the basis of some sort of ethical assessment. The weak evaluator, if she evaluates and overrides at all, does so on the bases of other kinds of assessment—kinds that need not be purely instrumental, however.

Sometimes Taylor paints the weak evaluator as a simple wanton who blows whichever way the winds of his own motivational economy blow. But the overall picture is best understood as one in which weak evaluators range from the simple wanton who makes no motivational assessments at all to persons who do make motivational assessments along a wide variety of dimensions, so long as these dimensions are not ethical. Groucho Marx, Truman Capote, Gore Vidal, Paul Gauguin, Lucille Ball, and Mick Jagger might fit the bill of persons, even decent persons, whose lives are not, or were not, guided in any central way by ethical commitments or distinctively ethical evaluation. It seems best to think of weak evaluators as comprising an extraordinary variety of types. We might think of these types as sorted along a continuum that plots degree of reflectiveness. Or we might think of them as sorted along various continua individuated by motivational content, with each continuum plotting degree of reflectiveness within a content type. The aimless youths who "wild" in Central Park and the savvy, single-minded head of a drug cartel might both be seen as weak evaluators of a single-content type. Aesthetic types—think, for example, of Kierkegaard's character A. in *Either/Or* or of a Gauguin who does not see or otherwise experience the moral relevance of his prior commitments to Madame Gauguin and his children as he plans to pursue his artistic project in Tahiti—would form a different type. Within each type, self-comprehension might range from the virtually vacant to continuous, highly refined, and well-focused assessment of how well one is doing what one is trying to do or being what one is trying to be.

6. There is an ambiguity, however, in the concept of the ethical. This ambiguity is due in the first instance to the fact that the concept can be understood broadly or narrowly. In 1989 Taylor is explicit that he intends the broad conception of the ethical as including not simply obligations, respect for rights, and conflict avoidance but also a wide range of intrapersonal concerns as well—concerns with how one should live, what one should care about, and so on. Whereas Williams (1985) draws the distinction between the narrow and wide conceptions in terms of the "moral" on the one hand and the "ethical" on the other, Taylor draws it as one between the "moral" and the "spiritual" (1989, 3–4, 53). A life can be spiritually unworthy even if it is not, strictly speaking, immoral. Strong evaluators judge their lives in such broad ethical terms in a way that is "a bit broader than what is normally described as the moral" (1989, 4).

The conclusion we are drawn to is this. Strong evaluation is distinguished from weak evaluation not because only it involves second-order desires, nor because only it involves qualitative assessment from the second level, nor because only it involves assessment from the perspective of a long-standing life plan or in terms of objective social standards, nor even because only it involves depth—although it is sometimes marked from weak evaluation in these ways—but because of the kind of evaluation involved. The strong evaluator assesses his or her motives and life in specifically ethical terms, "ethical" now broadly understood.

> Implicit in this strong evaluation is thus placing our different motivation relative to each other, the drawing, as it were, of *a moral map of ourselves;* we contrast a higher, more clairvoyant, more serene motivation, with a baser, more self-enclosed and troubled one, which we can see ourselves as potentially growing beyond, if and when we come to experience things from the higher standpoint. (Taylor 1977b, 67, my emphasis)

3

Taylor wants there to be a distinction between weak and strong evaluators. From what I have said so far, one might reasonably suspect that the distinction between weak and strong evaluators will be hard to draw in any unequivocal terms. This is a reasonable suspicion. Five reasons weigh in its favor. First, the ethical is not neatly cordoned off from other domains of life, especially once one opts, as Taylor now does, for a broad conception of the ethical. Second, the domain of the ethical and thus what counts as ethical assessment is notoriously observer-relative. What looks like nonethical assessment from an outsider's perspective may be ethical from an insider's perspective (Taylor himself makes this sort of point in his 1982 essay). Third, evaluation can be nonethical without being counterethical. Imagine a person who lives a life built around love of baseball or the person Rawls imagines who lives a life absorbed in the fate of blades of grass. Presumably even if we construe the ethical in broad terms, it will not include everything. Strong "spiritual" evaluation will still need to involve "discriminations of right or wrong, better or worse, higher or lower, which are not rendered valid by our own desires, inclinations, or choices" (1989, 4). The trouble is that we can imagine complex disagreements about whether the lives I have imagined fit the bill. And we can easily imagine that the persons who live lives built around baseball or the fate of grass or sophistication might fully abide what morality, commonsensically construed, demands.

Fourth, there simply is no such thing as a pure strong evaluator (whether there can be a pure weak evaluator is a separate question). Normal persons sometimes behave wantonly; for example, we scratch where it itches. And even when we assess and evaluate our motives, we often do so in nonethical terms. Persons who go in for strong ethical evaluation often make vacation plans on the same bases as savvy weak evaluators. It would be unrealistic as well as excessively moralistic to think that they should do otherwise. Fifth and relatedly, in so far as there are strong evaluators, they, like weak evaluators, reflect to various degrees of depth and breadth, and they deploy vocabularies whose primary saliencies are not only Taylor's Nietzschean parade of nobility, worth, and their suite but also concepts of justice, love, humility, and many others besides (this point is quietly conceded in 1989 in a way it was not in 1977a, 1977b, and 1981).

My proposal that we think of weak evaluation as involving any kind of nonethical assessment, with the caveat that what counts as ethical assessment is a matter of social construction and thus a matter of interpretation and relativity, fits with most of what Taylor says, but not with everything. Usually he grounds strong evaluation in ethical evaluation, but sometimes he grounds it in any evaluation that is Nietzschean in the sense that it deploys a vocabulary of nobility and worth, but not necessarily a vocabulary of ethical nobility and worth, even broadly construed. Taylor rightly points out that such evaluative categories are sometimes used to make assessments of one's own and other's bearing, style, and demeanor (1977b, 68). This is because "the languages of qualitative contrast embrace more than the ethical" (1982, 239). Furthermore, in such cases, both insiders and outsiders would agree that such assessments are not intended as ethical ones.

The contrast between strong and weak evaluation will be much less useful (see Slote 1988 for an argument to the effect that it already is useless), as well as internally inconsistent with the dominant line of analysis in Taylor's writings, if we make formal linguistic properties—the mere use of certain evaluative terminology—criterial for it. If we understand the ethical so broadly that anyone who evaluates her desires in terms of "better" and "worse" is a strong evaluator, then the person convinced of the superiority of her style, fashion, or social class will turn out to be a strong evaluator. I conclude that the best way to understand the contrast between strong and weak evaluation is as one involving ethical assessment, on the one hand, and any kind of nonethical assessment, on the other hand. Counting the sophisticate as a strong evaluator cuts too much against Taylor's dominant line that it is definitive of modern identity that we are strong evaluators who are concerned with the quality of our lives in broad ethical terms. The downside for Taylor of thinking of the contrast in the way I recommend, and thus not counting all qualitative assessment as ethical, is that it means that not everyone is a strong evaluator.

4

We now have a firm interpretation of how the contrast between weak and strong evaluation is supposed to work. The next step is to examine two different sorts of claims Taylor makes about strong evaluation. One set of claims is descriptive or empirical; the other set is normative. There are two main descriptive claims. First, "the human beings we are and live with are all strong evaluators." Second, "our identity is defined by our fundamental [strong] evaluations" (1977a, 34). Taylor elaborates on the second claim in this way:

> The notion of identity refers to certain [strong] evaluations which are essential because they are the indispensable horizon or foundation out of which we reflect and evaluate as persons. To lose this horizon, or not to have found it, is indeed a terrifying experience of disaggregation and loss. This is why we speak of an "identity crisis" when we have lost our grip on who we are. A self decides and acts out of certain fundamental [strong] evaluations. (1977a, 35)

Because the two claims are broadly empirical—that all contemporary persons *are* strong evaluators and that only strong evaluations, but not weak evaluations, can constitute identity—they can be assessed as such.

These empirical claims are distinct, however, from the normative claims that strong evaluation is necessary for ethical goodness, for ethical excellence, or for gaining, in the deepest possible ways, nonatomic self-understanding, autonomy, a sense of communal obligation, and so on. Fortunately for the defender of strong evaluation, the falsity of the empirical claims is compatible with the truth of the normative claims.

Is Taylor right that a realized capacity for strong evaluation is criterial for personhood in these two senses—the first empirical, the other normative? I think not. In order to make out this case, it will be useful to set out three theses about persons that I claim should be accepted by any credible philosophical psychology. These three claims are prior to and less controversial than the claims in question. They will help us understand better where and how the strong evaluative picture goes wrong.

First, there is the claim for the *intersubjective conception of the self*, the claim that identity is invariably created in the context of some social relations or other and is formed or constituted from the cloth of prior social forms and the possibilities available therein. Prior social forms enter into our formation as persons through the activity of previously socialized caretakers, and we are sustained and tained as persons with certain kinds of structured identities in social relations that we help change and modify but do not in the first instance create. We are neither creators nor sole guardians of our identities. The intersubjective conception of the self is something every moral or political conception should accept. It is a fundamental truth of philosophical psychology that we are intersubjective selves.

The second fundamental truth is that we are *self-comprehending creatures*. Some minimal form of self-awareness is criterial for being a person. According to child psychologists, a sense of self is pretty firm by age 2 (Kagan 1984, Stern 1985). However, one needs to be careful not to pack too much into this fact. Compatible with the bare-bone truth that all normal *Homo sapiens* develop self-awareness and are self-comprehending in some minimal sense is the fact that normal persons often lack a deep reflective appreciation of who they are. The sort of self-awareness required for personhood can be extremely dim and inchoate. Furthermore, it can fail to track the truth.

It is important to keep these two things separate: dim and inchoate self-comprehension, on the one hand, and epistemically misguided self-comprehension, on the other hand. A person would be making a mistake if she were actually to deny the truth of the intersubjective conception—if she saw herself as a pure self-creation, if she denied her dependence on prior social structures and relations, and if she saw her identity as in no way sustained by certain ongoing social relations. It would be good, because true, to comprehend one's life in intersubjective terms.

However, it does not follow from this that every individual person must comprehend herself in terms expressed by the intersubjective conception of the self. That is, although it would be a mistake for any individual to deny the truth of the intersubjective conception and its applicability to herself, it is not so obviously an error not to have articulated this truth and incorporated it into one's reflectively held self-conception. One might simply not have a very reflectively held self-conception. One might even lack the ability to understand and thus to assent to (or dissent from) the appropriately formulated sentences when they are expressed in abstract philosophical terms. Both possibilities are compatible with being a self-comprehending and self-interpreting creature. The characters of many of Tolstoy's stories are unreflective and inarticulate in something like the relevant senses. I am thinking, for example, of Simon, the cobbler, and his wife, Matrena, in "What Men Live By," Efim and Elisha in "Two Old Men," and Nikita, the servant to Vasali Andreevich Brekunov, in "Master and Men." Most of Tolstoy's characters comprehend themselves to some degree and care that their lives express certain values: compassion and love, on the one hand, and a certain calm resignation to God's will, on the other hand. The intersubjective conception is true of the lives of the characters in Tolstoy's stories because it is true of every life. Furthermore, his noble peasants typically express a humble comprehension of their role in carrying out certain communal projects whose origins are antecedent to their own births and that will continue long after they die. But it is not clear that their intersubjectivity is very reflectively held or that it is subject to articulate containment by them in the form of some abstract philosophical truth.

Tolstoy's peasants serve as reminders that we must distinguish between the truths of philosophical psychology or anthropology that any acceptable moral or political theory must give articulate expression to, and the requirements we place on individual persons to know and articulate these same truths (see Taylor 1989, chap. 4, for a general defense of the worth of articulating the good in some sort of "philosophical prose").

Tolstoy's peasants (occasionally they are noble merchants, for example, Ivan Dmitrich Aksenov in "God Sees the Truth, but Waits") allow a second distinction. There is in the first place the ubiquitous truth of philosophical psychology or anthropology expressed by the intersubjective conception. There is in the second place what I will call *normative intersubjectivity*. Normative intersubjectivity comes in multifarious forms. Roughly, a life (or an ethical conception) expresses normative intersubjectivity if it treats it as good or worthy to partake of social union and if it treats the worth of social union as more than merely instrumental. I say "treats" rather than "sees" or "understands" because I want to allow for comprehension of the good of social union of the dim and inchoate sort that I have been emphasizing and I want to allow for a life that expresses the truth of normative intersubjectivity in the activities of living rather than, in the first instance, in how one linguistically conceives of things.

I cannot argue for normative intersubjectivity here. But it seems fair to say that especially in the bare-bone terms just expressed, it constitutes a third truth that, like the intersubjective conception itself and the idea that we are self-aware, self-comprehending creatures, is part of any credible philosophical psychology.

The analysis so far suggests this much: the three core truths of philosophical psychology express certain necessary conditions of distinctively human lives. But satisfying these conditions is compatible with not being a strong evaluator. Persons can satisfy these three truths and live morally good lives without satisfying the further conditions of strong evaluation.

Tolstoy's peasants are a case in point. Taylor stresses that the strong evaluator evaluates within some sort of contrastive space, and—at least in his original formulations—he seems to think that such contrasts can only be drawn within linguistic space. "The strong evaluator can articulate superiority just because he has a language of contrastive characterization" (1977a, 24). Most of Tolstoy's noble peasants are inarticulate. Indeed, Tolstoy often uses articulateness as a dimension along which peasants are contrasted with persons of means, education, and refinement. In stories like "Master and Man" and the earlier "Three Deaths," the person of means, education, and refinement uses language to express querulousness, elitism, acquisitiveness, self-absorption, self-righteousness, and a rageful inability to accept the contingencies and vagaries of human experience, especially human finitude. This is contrasted with the goodness and calm resignation of the uneducated and inarticulate peasant.

Tolstoy's characters typically comprehend the contrast between a Christian life of love and compassion and its alternatives. If an agent can contrast her life or the values it expresses with alternatives, even if the alternative is only that of not living the life she knows in her sinews and bones to be good, then perhaps she can be said to possess a minimal language, or better, a minimal sense, of contrastive characterization. But Tolstoy's peasants cannot be very articulate about this contrast.

If comprehension of some contrastive space and motivation and evaluation that originate from some morally informed location within that contrastive space are sufficient for strong evaluation, then Tolstoy's peasants are strong evaluators. But if articulateness is taken as necessary as well (as it is by Taylor, but see the change in 1989 discussed below), then they will not fit the bill. In either case, the alleged link between strong evaluation and moral personhood is weakened. This means that there is no easy route to the claim for the normative necessity of strong evaluation by way of an argument for its necessity for moral agency. Tolstoy's peasants are good, and they are good because their lives exemplify what they value and because what they value is good. That much seems firm.

We might question even the idea that comprehension of contrastive ethical space is necessary for being counted among the strong evaluators, or if it is necessary for being counted among them (because Taylor stipulates that it is), we might question whether contrastive comprehension is partly constitutive of being a good person with a rich identity, ethical motivation, and agency. There seems to be no impossibility in the idea that a particular individual, perhaps a whole social group, might see no other way to be. Not living as they do is not seen or otherwise experienced as a genuine possibility. Occasional temptations not to muster the effort to live their life as it should be lived provide at most a "notional" sense of contrast, not a "real" sense of contrast. Such persons could easily be imagined to gather motivational strength from their life form, and their integrity and self-worth might be totally tied up with living the life they live. If such persons are possible, then it is not a truth of any acceptable philosophical psychology that evaluating one's life contrastively in any very robust sense is necessary for being a person.[2] If firm, self-respecting identity is possible for persons who are both inarticulate and (let us suppose) unaware of contrastive possibilities, and if both these things are necessary for strong evaluation, then it follows that strong evaluation is not a necessary foundation and indispensable font of identity and motivation. And if some such persons are appropriately judged as good, strong evaluation is not necessary for moral goodness.[3]

Tolstoy's peasants have identities, as do the persons I have just been imagining, yet they do not fit the original characterization of strong evaluation. But surely Tolstoy's peasants are not properly characterized as weak evaluators. They are not simple weighers of desires. They have rich identities that they express in action. Their identities are morally informed and express good, possibly excellent, values. This suggests that Taylor's distinction does not usefully capture many types of persons. For one thing, it is too intellectualist.

The analysis also implausibly projects a realized capacity for ethical self-appraisal onto the minds or consciousnesses of all our contemporaries. The idea that all contemporary persons are strong evaluators who cast their lives in terms of nobility, integration, and worth seems patently false. It conceals not only the good and unreflective types depicted by Tolstoy, but the hedonist, the amoralist, and the immoralist as well. One response is that the immoralist is a strong evaluator with bad standards. But this is utterly implausible as a generalization in its own right. Furthermore, it does nothing whatsoever to account for the hedonist, the rich, conspicuously consuming modern character who is committed to being a savvy weak evaluator, or for the amoralist, the aesthete of Kierkegaard's *Either/Or*, who does not care about or go in for ethical evaluation. Further evidence that there is something wrong with Taylor's picture comes from the psychological sources on which he claims to depend.

There is nothing in the canonical descriptions of persons who are suffering identity crises, and who are thereby immobilized and alienated from their own lives, that requires that we think of them as former virtuosos at strong evaluation or alternatively as persons who have never discovered the good of strong evaluation and have thereby come undone (see Taylor 1977a, 35). Even among those who suffer identity crises and were formerly strong evaluators, there is no necessity in thinking of their loss of identity as rooted primarily or exclusively in the loss of their capacities for strong evaluation. It seems plausible to think that in such cases the loss of strong evaluative identity is sometimes—perhaps often or usually—the effect of some awful process that makes all aspects of identity come undone, rather than its cause. Erik Erikson writes,

> The term "identity crisis" was first used, if I remember correctly, for a specific clinical purpose in the Mt. Zion Veterans' Rehabilitation Clinic during the Second World War. . . . Most of our patients, so we concluded at that time, had neither been "shellshocked" nor become malingerers, but had through the exigencies of war lost a sense of personal sameness and historical continuity. They were impaired in that central control over themselves for which, in the psychoanalytic scheme, only the "inner agency" of the ego could be held responsible. Therefore I spoke of loss of "ego identity." (1968, 16–17)

Individuals in identity crisis, of the sort Erikson describes, possess a sense of "mere" identity. That is, they normally experience themselves as the locus of a set of subjectively linked events, as a sort of conduit in which a certain bland and low-level sameness and continuity subsists. What they lack, and what horrifies us and immobilizes them, is any sense of coherent and authoritative "me-ness," of personal sameness—any sense that these subjectively linked events occurring to and in them constitute a person, a self, a life. Erikson asks what "identity feels like when you become aware of the fact that you undoubtedly *have* one," and he answers that it consists of "a *subjective sense* of an *invigorating sameness* and *continuity*" (1968, 19). Without the invigorating sense of self there is no person and thus no coherent cognitive and motivational core from which the individual can generate purposes or in which he could find the energy required to sustain them were he able to find any in the first place.

Taylor claims to depend on standard notions of identity and identity crises in framing the notion of strong evaluation. But there is nothing in the passage quoted from Erikson, nor in the text around it, that indicates that persons in identity crises are all former strong evaluators. Identifying powerfully with one's desires, whatever they are, or with a superficial scheme of evaluation, such as persons who are centrally absorbed with style or fashion do, is enough to stave off an identity crisis in Erikson's sense. The best analysis of what persons in identity crises have lost is what Wong (1988) calls "effective identity." Persons in identity crises have a dim and inchoate self-awareness. But the self of which they are aware is ghostly. It lacks robustness and vivacity, and it fails to energize. Persons in identity crises are in some significant sense care-less. It is because they have lost the capacity to care or are numb to caring that they are unmoved, that their agency is immobilized.

It is unclear whether the loss of the capacity to find one's self and gain one's motivational bearings through the self is best conceptualized as a loss of some reflexive capacity, so that a self cannot be found although there is still, so to speak, a self there, or whether the problem should be seen as rooted in the dissolution of the self, so that although one still has capacities for self-comprehension, self-control, and so on, there is no longer any robust self—no set of cares and identifications—to provide motivation, to be comprehended, controlled, and so on. The first problem would involve an access problem; the second a wipeout. But in neither case need the "lost self" be thought of as one (formerly) essentially constituted by ethical aims and purposes, and even less plausibly as a self whose whole horizon of being and motivational power was grounded in ethical aims and purposes.

Weak evaluators possess actual identities, which engender some subjective sense of who they are, and which they can lose touch with or which can become extremely disintegrated or dissolute. Recall that weak evaluators (if there are any) range from those types of persons who have only a dim and inchoate sense of who they are to persons who possess a perfectly clear and firm awareness of themselves as systems constituted by aims of a certain kind. The weak evaluator's life is built around nonethical aims but is not, I emphasize again, necessarily counterethical. It is easy enough, I think, to imagine Groucho Marx in an identity crisis. Indeed, the picture I am drawn to is one in which most weak evaluators will possess ethical standards and have the capacity to see their lives in ethical terms—it is just that doing so will not be central for them. A weak evaluator's loss of his sense of himself—of his sense of where his "center of narrative gravity" lies and in what it consists (Dennett 1988)—can be sufficient to cause an identity crisis in Erikson's sense, and it can lead to the immobilization of agency. Many professional athletes, whom we would not think of as particularly reflective or as centrally motivated by ethical concerns, fall prey to identity crises when they lose their central project, when the framework of their lives changes at the end of their playing career. Mental hospitals and therapists' offices are not disproportionately filled with formerly strongly reflective types.

As a consequence, it is not a simple truth of psychology that a "self decides and acts out of certain fundamental [strong] evaluations." Persons who don't go in for strong evaluation do not do so. Some such persons are familiar to most everyone, and some of them are pretty good (accidentally perhaps) and happy to boot. Being a weak evaluator is a necessary condition for being any person whatsoever. Nonetheless, being a strong evaluator, one who has well-developed capacities for specifically ethical evaluation and even, more implausibly, for whom such evaluation is the pivot on which her being turns, the basis on which all other motives are assessed, is neither a standard feature of all persons nor is it unambiguous and unproblematic as a moral ideal. Since the empirical claim is false, the unabashedly essentialist claim Taylor makes in *Sources of the Self* (1989) is false as well. He puts the essentialist claim this way: "I want to defend the strong thesis that . . . the horizons within which we live our lives and which make sense of them have to include these strong qualitative discriminations. Moreover this is not meant just as a contingently true psychological fact about human beings" (1989, 27). Indeed, it is extremely puzzling that such a historicist as Taylor is tempted to make such essentialist claims at all. I suspect that the cause lies in the theism that lurks ever more prominently in his writing.

Furthermore, the fact that every conceptual scheme leaves certain things unseen and characterizes some things it sees in self-serving, ethically, or epistemically dubious ways means that nothing guarantees that a person who engages in strong evaluation sees herself clearly, makes the right qualitative assessments, has the power to make the needed character adjustments in light of these assessments, or actually decides and acts on the basis of the considerations she thinks she decides and acts on. Taylor stresses that strong evaluation is essentially linked to articulateness. This is true. Articulateness is necessary for strong evaluation as he describes it (1977a, 1977b, and 1981). But it is not sufficient for it.[4] Weak evaluators can be articulate. Furthermore, articulateness can be the able servant of self-deception and manipulative and mendacious self-presentation, as well as of accurate self-interpretation and honest and sincere self-presentation. One can have strong-evaluative identity in Taylor's sense and have everything wrong.

Of course, Taylor never claims that articulateness or strong evaluation is sufficient for moral goodness, only that articulateness is
necessary for strong evaluation, which is in turn necessary for personhood in general, and moral personhood in particular. I have called
these last two necessary-condition claims into question. Once these
claims are called into question and the compatibility of strong evaluation with severe self-deception, immorality, and neurosis are high-
lighted, one might wonder whether it is even true that strong
evaluation is a friend to the ethical life by way of certain characteristic
relations it allegedly has to it. I will come back to this issue shortly.
But first I want to diagnose why the strong evaluative picture goes
wrong in the ways I have isolated so far.

5

The mistake in Taylor's original picture of personhood has, I think,
two main sources. First, he ties the sort of self-comprehension that
is necessary for personhood too closely to linguistic competence.
Second, he ties motivation too closely to judgment, or better, to
judgment of a heavily cognitive sort. These two problems are closely
related, but let me develop each in turn.

Taylor rightly points out that we are language-using creatures and
that the sort of self-interpretation that is constitutive of being a person
is typically linguistically informed. The strong evaluator differs from
the weak evaluator because he possesses a vocabulary of ethical
evaluation and because he frames his self-interpretation in terms of
this vocabulary. The strong evaluator possesses a "vocabulary of
worth" (1977a, 24). "The strong evaluator envisages his alternatives
through a richer language" (1977a, 23). "The strong evaluator can
articulate superiority just because he has a language of contrastive
characterization" (1977a, 24). The strong evaluator has "articulacy
about depth" (1977a, 26).[5]

Although it is true that we are essentially language-using animals
and that identity and self-comprehension are in large part linguistically created, sustained, and informed, it is a mistake to think that
all self-comprehension, all self-interpretation, is linguistic. Piaget's
psychology provides the relevant theoretical alternative (see Taylor
1971 for a valuable assessment of Piaget that nonetheless fails to see
clearly enough the implications of this aspect of his psychology).
Piaget's genetic epistemology is a well-respected theory in which the
picture is one in which the child develops various competencies,
with conservation, space, number, even morality (1932), and engages
in reflexive comprehension and deployment of these competencies

prior to the emergence of the capacity to linguistically formulate what he or she is doing. Children understand conservation and solve conservation problems long before they can linguistically formulate their comprehension or solution strategies (see Van Gulick 1988 for another interesting analysis of self-comprehension, which wisely shies away from tying it too closely to linguistic competence).

To be sure, our emotions, the imports they have for us, and the standards associated with them are gathered together for us, and accrue the meanings they have, by being given various culturally specific significances. And these significances are typically attached partly by linguistic means—minimally by way of some linguistically mediated reinforcement provided by primary socializers. Selves are constituted within "webs of interlocution" (Taylor 1989, 36). Furthermore, a linguistic map of the network of signification can invariably be drawn. But, and this is one point I want to stress, the map of signification cannot always be drawn by the agent for whom the significances obtain. To be sure, Taylor is right that even our "prearticulate sense of our feelings is *not* language independent. For they are the feelings of a language being, who therefore can and does say something about them, for example, that he feels something disturbing and perplexing, which baffles him, and to which he cannot give a name. *We* experience our pre-articulate emotions as perplexing, as raising a question. And *this* is an experience that no non-language animal can have" (1977b, 74). And he is right to emphasize that "our sense of dignity, and shame, and moral remorse, and so on" are very different from the experience of a baboon (assuming he can experience relatives of these emotions), since our sense of these things "are all shaped by language" (1977b, 69). But to accept that nothing in our experience is *language-independent* does not remotely entail that all self-comprehension requires that the self so comprehended be linguistically corralled. Taylor often speaks as if it does (1977a, passim; 1977b, passim; 1983, 103). But there is no incoherence whatsoever in thinking that identity and self-comprehension can accrue in environments that are relatively impoverished linguistically and by means of all manner of intrapersonal and extrapersonal feedback mechanisms: by way of feelings of coordination, integration, and integrity, of fit with the social world mediated by the body language of others, and so on. Such self-comprehension might involve an evolving sense of who one is, of what is important to oneself, and of how one wants to live one's life. But the evolution of this sense might proceed relatively unreflectively, possibly for the most part unconsciously. It might be conceived of along the lines of the acquisition of athletic know-how and savvy by way of continuous practice.

Great athletes often cannot coach, because they cannot say how they do what they do. It is not that they linguistically know how they do what they do but simply cannot get at the module that contains the relevant linguistic description. Often, if they were not themselves coached in certain ways, there was never cause to linguistically formulate the relevant skills. But surely what such athletes are able to do involves highly developed know-how, reflexive comprehension, and self-control.

Taylor (1989, 77–78, 91–92) now concedes this point that moral comprehension can be "prearticulate." In discussing the ancient warrior ethic, he writes that "the framework within which we act and judge doesn't need to be articulated theoretically. It isn't usually by those who live the warrior ethic" (p. 20). But this reasonable retraction of the articulacy requirement is, I want to insist, a genuine change in his view, and it is in tension with the emphasis Taylor continues to place on the powerful connection between identity, meaning, and articulation. For example, Taylor writes that we "find the sense of life through articulating it" (1989, 18). But if my argument is right and if Taylor's recent retraction of the articulation requirement is motivated by considerations of the sort I have raised, then finding "the sense of life" cannot be so closely linked to articulating what that sense consists in.

The implausible idea that all self-comprehension is linguistic is related to a second implausibility. This is the mistake of thinking that "our identity is defined by our fundamental [strong] evaluations" (1977a, 34) and that "a self decides and acts out of certain fundamental [strong] evaluations" (1977a, 35). Taylor gets things right, I think, when he says that "what is crucial about agents is that things matter to them" (1983, 98). And he is right when he says that to "be a moral agent is to be sensitive to certain standards." He is right still when he adds, "But 'sensitive' here must have a strong sense: not just that one's behavior follow a certain standard, but also that one in some sense recognize or acknowledge the standard" (1983, 102). But the point that needs to be stressed, and that is in tension with Taylor's heavily linguistic picture, is that one can be sensitive to a standard and "in some sense recognize or acknowledge" it without ever having linguistically formulated that standard and without even possessing the ability to do so when pressed.[6]

The idea that identity is defined by our strong evaluations is Taylor's way of trying to express the idea that identity is constituted by what is important to us, by what we care (most) about. Frankfurt puts the relevant idea this way: "A person who cares about something, is, as it were, invested in it. He *identifies* himself with what he cares about in the sense that he makes himself vulnerable to losses and susceptible to benefits depending upon whether what he cares about is diminished or enhanced" (1982, 83).

It seems to me that this way of thinking about identity, like the picture of identity as constituted by the plans, projects, and commitments in accordance with which a particular individual lives, are better ways than Taylor's of getting at what is essential about identity. The advantages of the latter sorts of characterizations over Taylor's heavily intellectualist picture are twofold: First, they allow for identity in people whose lives are guided by cares, concerns, imports, and commitments, but who are, for whatever reason and to whatever degree, inarticulate about them. Second, these ways of characterizing identity are nonmoralistic in a way the strong evaluative picture is not. For better or worse, what a particular human individual cares about can involve all manner of nonethical concerns (not all of which are thereby loony and low-minded, although they might be) and involve almost nothing in the way of ethical valuation.

There is an idea recently floated in the literature that might seem to help Taylor here but that actually works against him. This is Dennett's (1988) idea that the self is the "center of narrative gravity." Dennett's fruitful metaphor is an attempt to point to the fact that what we call the "self" is a construction that involves locating what in one's motivational economy one perceives as most important, what one cares most about. But Dennett's picture of the self is wisely neutral on the question of whose narrative web the self is captured in. A particular self might be self-comprehended without being subject to elegant narrative construction by the self who so comprehends it. A third party might be better at spinning out the relevant narrative. The only constraint, except in cases of self-deception, is that the narrative told from the third-person, heterophenomenological point of view resonates with autophenomenological, first-person comprehension, insofar as there is any, and with the cares, concerns, and projects as revealed in how the person lives.

6

In 1989 Taylor introduces an interesting equivocation in the way he describes strong evaluation, an equivocation that ironically moves the idea in a more plausible direction. Taylor writes (pp. 29–30) that for us, strong evaluative identity involves some "strongly valued good." It involves finding a framework that renders life meaningful. This way of putting things is more consonant with the Frankfurt-Williams-Dennett formulation and with the conception of identity I argued for in section 4. It does not require that identity be grounded in an articulate sense that one lives an ethically noble life. Identity in the first instance requires that there be something or someone—baseball, sophistication, concern for the fate of grass or one's teammates—with which one strongly identifies. The original and less plausible formulation focuses on the link between identity and reflection and evaluation of a certain distinctively ethical kind. The new, equivocal, and more plausible formulation links identity to the strength of one's identifications—to absorption in some end or ends, whatever that end or those ends might be.

There is another important change marked in *Sources of the Self* (1989). Originally, the idea of strong evaluation was linked, as I have argued, to locating and orienting one's life from the perspective of some ethical, meaning-grounding framework. This framework was to provide the grounds for both identity and agency. But one of the main themes of this book is "that frameworks today are problematic" (p. 17). We moderns find no framework immune to skeptical doubts. We find no rational grounds sufficient to warrant our adherence to the ethical values we avow. We have high ethical standards—powerful commitments, for example, to justice and benevolence—but we cannot, upon reflection, find sources strong enough to support these values.

The point about the fragility of frameworks seems right, as does the point that to the degree that one lacks confidence in one's framework and cares that one possesses such confidence, problems of meaning can arise and identity crises may ensue. But this point leads to an interesting problem for Taylor. According to the original view, all contemporary persons are strong evaluators. Most strong evaluators are reflective and posses identities constituted by frameworks that have passed scrutiny. Normally, the scrutinizing of the framework engenders confidence in the framework. Strong evaluation legitimizes a framework. It is only when reflective evaluation fails to engender such confidence then the agent is prone to an identity crisis. But now we discover that *all* frameworks are problematic—none of the available ones can pass muster in the face of stringent reflective scrutiny. This would seem to imply that all strong evaluators, that is, all contemporary persons on Taylor's view, are either in identity crises or highly vulnerable to them. Indeed, the stronger and deeper the evaluation, the more likely will it be that the framework being scrutinized will be seen as unstable, and thus the more likely will it be that the person will succumb to a crisis of identity.[7]

But this doesn't quite seem to be an accurate picture of us—teetering so precariously on the edge of our own identities. Furthermore, if it is, then strong evaluation reveals a particularly disturbing downside—it makes identity and agency prone to coming undone by demanding that our frameworks pass tests they cannot pass. It is puzzling why we would want to recommend a way of being that is destined, at least in our time, to make demands that cannot be met. Third, and relatedly, a new implausibility begins to lurk—this is the implausible idea that frameworks need to be seen as extremely secure if they are to ground identity and agency. Taylor (1989, 520–521) thinks that unless we can find some transcendent ground for our projects, commitments, and ethical frameworks, we will suffer losses in identity and agency (indeed, it is a consequence of his view that we already have).[8] But here, I think, he misses an important feature of the psychology of many contemporary persons. There are many people who have come to grips with the contingency of their selves, with their fallibility, and with their naturalness, in ways that do not throw them into existential turmoil when they experience their frameworks as lacking transcendent grounding. There is no incoherence in the idea of persons, be they strong or weak evaluators, operating effectively and happily within frameworks that they simply do not see or experience as final or foundational (see R. Rorty 1989).[9]

7

So far I have called into question the idea that there are any essential empirical or normative connections between strong evaluation, possession of a rich and effective identity, personhood, and moral goodness. Rejection of these claims is compatible with thinking that it is a worthy ideal to possess an identity that involves an accurate evaluative conception of where one stands, that has withstood deep critical reflection, and in accordance with which one assesses one's motives and guides one's activities.

In this final section I want to explore briefly some of the ways the idea of strong evaluation gets tied up with certain ideas in political philosophy, in particular with communitarianism. Taylor (1979) suggests an interesting connection between a certain kind of reflective evaluation (which need not, I think, be identified with distinctively strong evaluation) and recognition of communal duties. Sandel (1982, 143–144, 154–161) links strong evaluation to what he calls "expansive self-understanding," which he in turn links to fraternal motivation, to a desire to nourish and sustain one's community partly out of a sense that by so doing one is nourishing and sustaining one's own identity.

I admit to having been initially puzzled in seeing the use both Taylor and Sandel make of the idea of strong evaluation in their defenses of communitarianism.[10] Strong evaluation involves a depth of criticism, reflection, and evaluation that seems, at least at first, in tension (for reasons just mentioned in the previous section) with the emphases on shared values, strong group identification, likemindedness, homogeneity, and the stability of character and identity strongly associated with communitarian thinking. Most communitarians abhor the idea that, in theory, all one's ends might become an object of critical scrutiny, and they disdain communities in which the contrastive possibilities are so multifarious that every single thing—individual selves, interpersonal relations, social practices, and political structures—can be made to look deficient against some other socially available option or ideal.

This ambivalence about critical reflection is rooted partly in the correct perception that reflection has the capacity to reduce confidence in and admiration of the object reflected upon—be that object a set of social arrangements, particular others, or even the self. In cases where alternatives are available to improve upon or to replace those that lose some status to reflective scrutiny, the grounds are ripe for a certain amount of social or personal upheaval. For reasons such as these, many of the more Aristotelian communitarians, especially those who stress the good of unreflective lives rooted in habitual responses that are learned and sustained within good communities, would not, I think, find much attractive in the suggestion that strong evaluation is necessary for certain traits dear to their hearts: nonatomistic self-comprehension, a firm sense of identity suited to the narrative ideal of life, comprehension of communal obligations, and moral goodness.

If sound, the argument linking ethical reflection to communitarian ideals is important, however. Indeed, if Taylor is right about these links, then some of the distance between communitarian and liberal conceptions is closed. Reflectiveness of something like the strong evaluative variety will be a virtue on both views, although, for reasons already suggested, not necessarily a mandatory virtue.

One possible route to the desired conclusion might deploy the bare-bone truths of philosophical psychology discussed earlier. A person can comprehend herself only in social terms, as one whose abilities, plans, projects, and self-respect are rooted in past and present social relations and in preexisting social and institutional structures (the intersubjective conception of the self). And one can grasp the good of social union (normative intersubjectivity) only if one is a strong evaluator.

But this argument is unsound. I showed earlier that unless we require self-comprehension to have a highly articulated structure and in this way beg the interesting question, certain relatively unreflective persons can be said to comprehend both these truths.

The argument fails on another basis as well. Even if we demand reflective articulation, there is no incoherence in the idea that a reflective and articulate social psychologist, for example, might know that both truths obtain. Furthermore, he might consciously infer that both apply to his own case. This would involve, at a minimum, a recognition of the fact that he finds noninstrumental good in certain human relations and that his identity, interests, abilities, self-esteem, and so on, have sources in the activities of past and present others. This might even lead him to appreciate more than he did before the contributions that others made and continue to make to his flourishing. But such a person might not be a strong evaluator. There is nothing in the picture I have drawn so far that would require deployment of a vocabulary of ethical assessment, and in particular one in which the central concepts are those of nobility, worth, and so on. Being the sort of social psychologist I have imagined, who knows that the intersubjective conception is true, who finds good in social union, and who consciously appreciates such union, is compatible with being largely (but probably not completely) ethically indifferent.

However, a different and better case for the normative superiority of a high degree of reflectiveness involving the deployment of an array of ethically sensitive standards can be made, although, for reasons that have emerged, I do not think such reflectiveness needs to be identified with strong evaluation in Taylor's sense. Here is the argument: Although a weak evaluator may in some sense know her center and fully identify with her constitutive ends and be moved by them, she is not in a position, since she hasn't engaged in the requisite reflection, to try to recognize, change, or modify possibly problematic features of her moral personality. The problematic features may be problematic only in unlikely counterfactual situations. But as the case of the Holocaust shows, such features can cause untold moral harm if the unlikely and unanticipated possibilities do arise, and thus there is much to be said for modifying problematic dispositions in anticipation of the counterfactuals. Call this "the counterfactual advantage." The argument linking reflectiveness to the counterfactual advantage can be bolstered by noting that there is almost always room for ethical improvement. So unreflective persons can be good, as can reflective persons who do not normally conceive of their lives in ethical terms. But all things equal, an ethically reflective person has more resources at her disposal for ethical improvement, for satisfactorily meeting unusual and unanticipated ethical situations, and so on.

Securing this argument is more difficult than it might at first seem, for among other reasons, reflectiveness can have, as we have seen, a confidence-undermining downside. Furthermore, many morally vicious persons, many Nazis for example, were articulate, reflective, and self-scrutinizing. The problem was that they scrutinized and reflected with vicious values. We must keep constantly in mind that reflectiveness is a virtue of form (Rawls 1971), not of substance. Reflectiveness is good if and only if it is carried out with decent ethical standards.

But let us assume, what seems generally true, that the capacity for reflectiveness is a necessary condition for *efficiently* criticizing one's ends, and that criticizing one's ends is in many cases essential to recognizing one's deficiencies, to ethical improvement, and so on. I don't want to say that it is absolutely necessary for the refinement and adjustment of ends, for seeing one's deficiencies and seeing how one can improve, because I think these sorts of things are done all the time by relatively unreflective and inarticulate persons. The connection is between reflection and articulateness, on the one hand, and *efficient* criticism, not between reflection, articulateness, and criticism as such.

There is a third argument that might be mustered to bolster the reasons for succumbing to the belief in the great worth of reflective criticism of wide scope and depth. This third argument is similar in certain respects to the first argument considered above, which I claimed failed. This one, however, works. How can this be? The argument works, so to speak, for pragmatic reasons rather than for purely logical reasons. It provides a rationale for reflectiveness of a certain sort for those with a prior commitment to reflectiveness but who reflect with too narrow a conception of personhood and who, because of this narrow picture, are unable to see any firm ground for communal obligations and responsibilities. The argument works to move persons who are already reflective but who have what Taylor calls "ultra-liberal" sensibilities and who conceive of persons "atomically" in strongly possessive, individualist terms. The argument works in effect because it is well designed for a certain audience. It is designed both to persuade this audience of the truth of the intersubjective conception of the self and of normative intersubjectivity, to enable them to see more clearly what these truths mean and to move them to see the links between these truths about our social natures and our possession of certain communal obligations (see Wong 1988).

The conclusion the communitarian wants the ultraliberal—the atomistic philosophical psychologist—to draw is that in virtue of being socially formed and in virtue of being constituted, encumbered, and implicated in a certain way of being, we incur certain responsibilities and obligations to particular others, as well as to the form of life itself, within which we are formed.

On one standard analysis of responsibility and obligation, call it the "explicit contract analysis," the very idea of responsibilities and obligations one simply has or acquires by virtue of having a certain history, by being a certain kind of person, or by way of one's nonverbal behavior will seem incoherent. On such an analysis, P has an obligation to do q for S if P has reached a voluntary agreement with S to do q.

This notion of responsibility is in the end too narrow. It fails to make room for "tacit" agreements of the sort a citizen has with her state or for the responsibilities we rightly think parents bear toward their children. Furthermore, even for persons who find such a strong analysis appealing, the voluntary-agreement condition must be interpreted as only providing grounds of prima facie obligation. The reason is simple: if one agrees to perform some morally heinous action, one is *not*—on any credible account of obligation—obligated to do that act.

It is important to see that this sort of objection is an objection not only to an unconditional, explicit contract analysis. It is a legitimate objection to *any* view that grounds obligations on purely formal grounds and pays insufficient attention to their ethical content. As such it is an objection that can be brought against certain kinds of role moralities, as well as against all notions of responsibility and obligation that turn too unconditionally on one's encumbrances or on the conditions for maintaining an integrated unalienated identity (Flanagan 1991). It is a plausible constraint on any acceptable theory of obligation that prima facie obligations become bona fide ones only after there has been (or could be) a passable qualitative assessment of the promises, activities, traditions, or kinds of persons one is helping to sustain by being or behaving in the prescribed way.

This means that on all accounts, we do best if we reflectively examine the encumbrances we have and judge what kinds of goods, if they are goods at all, these encumbrances are (or at least if we are disposed to do so and capable of so doing when the need arises). The operative notion of obligation is one in which the existence of an obligation is linked to passing such inspection, or to the ability to do so if scrutinized. One plausible and suitably weak analysis of the underlying idea is that respect and gratitude and a certain amount of reciprocity are appropriate when one is given something of worth (libertarians might object that nothing is owed even in such cases if the benefits were not specifically requested).

Taylor eloquently expresses the relevant set of ideas in the specific context of the modern ideal of the autonomous agent. He writes,

> The free individual or autonomous moral agent can only achieve and maintain his identity in a certain type of culture . . . [the relevant facets of which] do not come into existence spontaneously each successive instant. They are carried on in institutions and associations which require stability and continuity and frequently also support from society as a whole. . . . [I] am arguing that the free individual of the West is only what he is by virtue of the whole society and civilization which brought him to be and which nourishes him; that our families can only form us up to this capacity and these aspirations because they are set in this civilization. . . . And I want to claim finally that all this creates a significant obligation to belong for whoever would affirm the value of this freedom. (1979, 205–206)

Although Taylor is skeptical of the objection that claims that past gifts do not necessitate ongoing gratitude or obligation, he suggests a reply that might persuade even someone who is tempted by such an objection.

> Future generations will need this civilization to reach these aspirations; and if we affirm their worth, we have an obligation to make them available to others. This obligation is only increased if we ourselves have benefited from this civilization and have been enabled to become free agents ourselves. (1979, 206)

In these passages, obligation to one's society is tied in the first instance to both gratitude and a kind of self-consistency. If "we ourselves have benefited from this civilization" and if "we affirm the value" of its institutions in forming us the way they have, then there are credible grounds on the basis of which we can be said to have obligations toward those institutions. The postulation of motivational concern for the good of future generations provides further reason for sustaining a life form one thinks is good.

The question remains, of course, as to whether one has been given something of worth, or more probably, what aspects of the traditions and persons to whom one rightly owes one's identity formation are most worth sustaining, respecting, and shoring up. In order to answer such questions, it follows than an acceptable communitarian account of obligation to one's tradition(s) will need to be content-

sensitive. But such content-sensitivity requires possession of a sophisticated set of reflective tools (whether it requires these to be
applied consciously and with analytic acuity is something I am more
skeptical of). The communitarian proposal, then, is best read as
involving the following plausible claim: if one's life form passes
reflective scrutiny and is judged as good, or at least above a certain
acceptable threshold of decency, then claiming and perpetuating this
life form is in part a way of staking and discovering the good of one's
own identity and it is ethically acceptable as well. The overall conclusion, then, is this: reflection is good in two respects: First, it can
help ultraliberals to understand themselves in less atomic terms and
thereby to see the grounds on the basis of which they incur communal obligations. Second, reflectiveness is good because it provides
one with the critical tools needed to assess the content of one's life
form so that one can judge the *ethical* bases for such communal
obligations.

I close by pointing to a paradoxical feature of this last argument. I
have claimed that the argument is effective against a certain liberal,
individualist way of thinking about things. The argument shows that
for persons socialized within a certain liberal life form that
(over)emphasizes personal autonomy, individual projects, self-ac-
tualization, and so on, it has become hard to see why we should care
about others. The argument I have just rehearsed provides an argument for those who need it. It is a good argument relative to a
certain audience. The facts that certain contemporary ultraliberals
need to hear this argument, that they can understand it only if they
are reflective, sensitive to reason and argument, and so on, does not
show that having these last attributes is a necessary condition for
possessing the desired communitarian sensibilities. These highly reflective attributes are necessary for those who do not possess the
relevant communal sensibilities and have beliefs and desires that
militate against developing them. But one can imagine that persons
socialized within a different life form that imbued neophytes with
less individualist sensibilities might already express in their personal
lives and political structures the relevant sensibilities and thus might
have no overwhelming need for the sort of deep reflection on their
social natures designed to make them open to communitarian sentiments.

However, the fact would remain that human life is subject to great
contingency, including the possibility of being formed within ethically problematic social systems. Having communitarian sentiments
is good if one's community is good, but it is obviously not good if
one's community has bad values, values that one is motivated to

sustain and maintain because of these sentiments. This is where the second, content-sensitive aspect of reflectiveness becomes important. The realistic possibility that one will live in a community with some or many ethically problematic features means that it is probably never bad in and of itself to have realized reflective capacities and to be open to rational argument. But, and this is the conclusion I am drawn to at every turn, such reflectiveness is not necessary for identity, personhood, or moral goodness. It is an intellectualist projection to think otherwise. Deep critical reflection is a good, and it rightly has a valued place in our conception of the good life. But it is not a truth of philosophical psychology that all persons, even all ethical persons, are reflective.[11]

Notes

1. Actually, in Taylor 1989 there is no characterization of weak evaluation, while strong evaluation continues to figure prominently as a defining feature of modern identity. This may be because Taylor is convinced that there are no persons who fit the description and thus no such persons to draw our attention to. This fits with Taylor's claim (p. 27) that the characterization of personhood in terms of strong evaluation captures an essential truth, not a contingent psychological truth.
2. In 1979, p. 204, Taylor acknowledges the possibility of persons who can conceive of no other way to be. But he rightly denies that persons who live such lives have the kind of freedom made available within modern liberal democracies in which many of the possibilities revealed in our contrastive spaces present live social options.
3. There is a widespread belief in the idea that evaluative concepts can only be comprehended contrastively. I admit to being unable to see why this view seems so obvious. First, we do not think that comprehension of most concepts in our language require contrast. "Table," "chair," "red," "electron," are all comprehensible in their own right without being contrasted with anything else. To be sure, in an actual world in which there is a perceived contrast between what is good and evil, what tastes good and bad, and what is beautiful and hideous, the contrastive space affects comprehension at both ends of the spectrum. But I have trouble seeing how it follows that comprehending what is morally good, what tastes good, or what is beautiful requires contrast, especially contrast with its opposite. One could understand how something that satisfied the description "moral," or "beautiful" could fail to satisfy that description, namely by failing to possess the relevant properties, without understanding the description in some sort of yin-yang space. Negation alone might be thought to be sufficient to establish the relevant contrast. But this cannot be right. First, if there are no things around deserving negation, it seems implausible to think that we will necessarily formulate the relevant negated thought. Second, even if we do formulate the negated thought, it is not clear that it will have determinate content in situations where it lacks clear referents, nor again is it clear why having the negated thought would be remotely necessary for clear comprehension of the affirmative referring term.
4. In 1977a, p. 28, Taylor wonders perhaps whether Camus's Meursault in *L'Etranger* isn't perhaps the exception who proves the rule that all contemporary persons are

strong evaluators. One interesting thing about Meursault is that he is very articulate; he simply does not use ethical categories to judge lives or motives as more
or less worthy. One life, Meursault says, is "as good as another." And after he
murders his Arab attacker, firing four gratuitous shots into his dead body, he
acknowledges that regret is not an emotion that he is capable of experiencing. But
if Meursault is an example of a weak evaluator, it is not because he is inarticulate
or because he is unreflective, it is because he does not evaluate in ethical terms.
Actually, he may be a good example of a person in an identity crisis, for on one
reading, he fails to see worth along any dimensions whatsoever. He is articulate
and reflective, but he evaluates neither weakly nor strongly, neither in moral terms
nor in nonmoral ones. But he is not a wanton either.

5. It is this side of Taylor's view that has led Annette Baier to write that Taylor "takes
men with their rational wills to be special, if not a Father God's favorites at least
his speaking likenesses. This remarkable tradition, for which Taylor is an eloquent
spokesman, is a cultural artifact of enormous expressive power. It fascinates, and
will continue to fascinate more naturalist anthropologists, as they are fascinated
by the mitres, head dresses, breastplates, mirrors and fetishes of less intellectual
tribes" (1988, 594).

6. As I indicated above, Taylor (1989) now thinks that there is a "sense" of qualitative
distinction that can be revealed in the lives of the inarticulate. Indeed, it may be
entirely up to third parties to articulate what the guiding frameworks of such lives
are.

7. The structure of modern identity actually consists of three levels: there are first-
order desires, there are the second-order desires and valuations deployed in strong
evaluation of the first-order desires, and there are (often) what Taylor calls "hypergoods." Hypergoods "provide the standpoint from which [strongly valued
goods] must be weighed, judged, decided about" (1989, 63). The three-level picture
is credible. But Ken Winkler has pointed out to me that it has the following
consequence: assuming that a hypergood is part of one's framework, it follows
that frameworks can be self-undermining, since, as Taylor points out, a hypergood
can lead to the rejection of goods that are valued at the second level (1989, 65).

8. Taylor admits that he has no argument (yet) for this view.

9. Taylor acknowledges that some persons identify with their framework in a "tentative, semi-provisional way" (1989, 17). But he seems to think that such persons
need to be seen as on a "quest," as seeking some firmer ground. The possibility I
am suggesting is that one can identify fully with one's framework while at the
same time seeing it as imperfect, subject to revision, and as hardly the only or
best framework. Or to put it another way, one can see one's framework as nonfinal
in Richard Rorty's sense without one's absorption in one's framework being half-
hearted or tentative.

10. It is a significant feature of Taylor (1989) that communitarianism (with his liberal
coloration) no longer appears to be able to function for him as the sort of framework
that can unproblematically ground a meaningful life. The book ends with poignant
hopes that we can once again find some sort of transcendent ground for meaning—
larger and more significant than even deep and fulfilling social relations. One can
only infer that reflection undermined Taylor's conviction that communitarian social
ideals could play the role of a grounding framework for him. Atomism is still
criticized for being too individualistic and for dividing us from each other (pp.
500–501). But Taylor is strangely silent—"inexplicit" is a better word—as to what
aspects of communitarianism he has come to find wanting. The insufficiency has
something to do with the failure of philosophical arguments for communitarian

social arrangements to agree on what such arrangements would be like, and even where there is agreement on the right kind of arrangements, these arguments are insufficient to win the case for specifically communitarian ideals against rivals. It is Taylor's sense of the ubiquity of such underdetermination relative to all contending ethical ideals that seems to have headed him more firmly in a theistic direction.

11. I am grateful to David Wong for extremely helpful comments and criticisms and especially to Ken Winkler for his acute reading of both my paper and Taylor's *Sources of the Self* (1989).

Chapter 3
The Moral Life of a Pragmatist
Ruth Anna Putnam

The title of William James's only systematic essay in moral philosophy—"The Moral Philosopher and the Moral Life"—suggests that
serious systematic thought about morality needs to focus on a whole
life. Bernard Williams (1981a, 38) has suggested that a life consisting
of a string of dutiful actions chosen one by one simply because they
are dutiful does not deserve to be called a life, for an agent leading
such a life would be unable to pursue any projects of her own. James
has taken this thought at least one step further. For him, choosing
what to do, when the choice is a difficult moral one, is choosing who
one is going to be. Who one is, or is going to be, and what projects
one will pursue turn out to be two ways of looking at the same
problem. But one's character and one's ends play crucial roles in
one's moral life not only at moments of difficult choice but also during
tranquil periods. Here I want to expound some of James's writings
in order to examine the place of character and of ends in our moral
lives. Specifically, section 1 provides a brief survey of the moral life,
section 2 examines the interdependence of character and ends, section 3 raises some further questions about character, and section 4
examines James's standard of an "inclusive ideal."

1

In an early talk James asked "What makes a Life Significant?" and
concluded,

> Culture and refinement alone are not enough to do so. Ideal
> aspirations are not enough when uncombined with pluck and
> will. But neither are pluck and will, dogged endurance and
> insensibility to danger enough, when taken all alone. There must
> be some sort of fusion, some chemical combination among these
> principles, for a life objectively and thoroughly significant to
> result. (1983, 165)

James mentioned that "culture and refinement" do not suffice for a significant life. Here I want to emphasize that they are also not necessary. That the lives of people living precariously and simply may be rich in significance was brought home to James when he encountered poor farmers creating clearings for themselves in the mountains of North Carolina. These farmers and their families, though they worked hard from sunup to sundown and lacked anything that might be called "culture and refinement," told James that "we ain't happy here unless we are getting one of these coves under cultivation" (James 1983, 134). What they had in additon to what James would call an "ideal," namely the goal to get a cove under cultivation, and in addition to "pluck and will" was just enough to eat to keep them healthy enough to pursue their ideal with "dogged endurance." Thus, culture and refinement are not required for a significant life, but human beings so derprived of the necessities of life that they are unable to formulate, however inarticulately, some goal or aim or purpose that makes sense of the daily routine beyond that routine itself, or so deprived that they are unable to pursue their goals with some chance of success, cannot be said to lead significant lives. Here one should also mention the need for positive relationships with other human beings. Social isolation can be, and for most persons is, as debilitating as lack of the material necessities of life.

James emphasizes not only that the moral life requires "pluck and will, dogged endurance and insensibility to danger," but also that this "strenuous mood" can be sustained only if one believes "that acts are really good or bad," and that involves, for him, both a belief in indeterminism (James 1979b, 135) and in the objectivity of moral values. Morality, objective values, and with them obligations exist whenever there are persons who care for one another. "One rock with two loving souls upon it . . . would have as thoroughly moral a constitution as any possible world. . . . There would be real good things and real bad things; . . . obligations, claims and expectations; obediences, refusals, and disappointments; . . . a moral life, whose active energy would have no limit but the intensity of interest in each other" (James 1979c, 150). Objectivity in ethics depends, then, on the possibility of resolving conflicts, of arriving at shared values, of jointly espousing more inclusive ideals. That possibility rests on the fact that we have sympathetic as well as egoistic instincts, which "arise, so far as we can tell, on the same psychological level" (James 1950, vol. 1, p. 325). However, for James, objectivity is more than mere intersubjectivity. His insistence on the imperfections of the world and on the possibility of moral progress suggests that there is a standard outside not only this or that thinker but outside any particular collection of them, just as scientific truth is not determined by the opinions of any particular collection of scientists. "There can be no final truth in ethics any more than in physics until the last man has had his experience and said his say" (James 1979c, 141). In ethics, though not in physics, this notion of a final truth seems to be not clearly distinguishable from belief in a divine thinker. For, though James says that "ethics have as genuine and real a foothold in a universe where the highest consciousness is human, as in a universe where there is a God as well" (James 1979c, 150), he also asserts that "in a merely human world without a God, the appeal to our moral energy falls short of its maximal stimulating power. Life, to be sure, is even in such a world a genuinely ethical symphony; but it is played in the compass of a couple of poor octaves, and the infinite scale of values fails to open up" (James 1979c, 160). I want to put this aside.[1] The important point to retain is the idea that we do not have the final truth, that we can and must continue to learn in ways that will alter not only our beliefs but also our behavior. For this caring and other altruistic virtues are as indispensable as courage, determination, and endurance. We may take it, therefore, that a fuller account of the virtues would for James include the altruistic virtues as well as the executive virtues mentioned in the passage concerning life's significance.

Finally, what about "ideal aspirations"? In order to lead significant lives, human beings need enough of the necessities of life to be able to formulate some goal or have some purpose that will make sense of the routine of their lives. Routine alone does not give meaning to one's life, although it may carry one across some meaningless stretches, keep one going while one sorts things out or simply waits for things to sort themselves out. Habits work in the same way. Indeed, a well-established routine becomes a habit, and a firm habit will, in novel circumstances, establish a new routine. What routines and habits do for us is this: they obviate the necessity to decide at every moment what to do next; they provide an easy explanation of a host of actions. Without thinking, one gets up at a certain hour because one always gets up at that hour. The luxury and the difficulty of vacations consists in part in being able to stay in bed, hence in having to decide to get up. One gets up at the right hour because one has to go to work. Retirement removes that reason. Hence the danger of not getting up, of feeling that life has lost its purpose because it has lost its rhythm. Children who have looked forward to school vacation with great eagerness become bored and cranky after a few days of vacation. Because their activities are not structured, they say, "There is nothing to do," although much could be done.

However, structure is not enough. There can be too much structure, as in a slave-labor camp, or a structure of despair, as in a famine-relief camp, where the days consist in waiting for the next doling out of food and there is no energy to fill the periods of waiting with anything other than waiting. These people do not flourish, not merely because they are hungry, exhausted, ill, and in the former case, mistreated, but because life doesn't derive its purpose from a routine. Rather, most people have purposes that impose a routine on their lives. Even if one's purpose does not impose a routine, or if the routine varies frequently or leaves much to be decided from day to day, one's purpose gives one's life a shape, guides one's choices, and explains one's activities. Or again one's purpose may be only indirectly related to one's routine; one may spend one's days doing a job that is just a job, any other would do as well, in order to support one's family. Or one may work at a routine job for the sake of having the free time and free mind to do what one really wants to do after hours. Think of a musician who makes her living as a waitress and composes in her "free" time. We must then look at purposes, projects, ideals, or plans.

Purposes, projects, ideals give shape or coherence to a life or at any rate longer or shorter periods thereof. They loom large in forming what John Rawls calls, perhaps too grandly, a rational life plan (most people's plans are neither as long-range nor as passionless as that term suggests). But our students do decide that they want to be philosophers or lawyers or whatever and so they put their energy, their time, and a good deal of their emotions into learning to be a philosopher or a lawyer or whatever. Many of their daily and even longer-range priorities are ordered by these aims. A few may also plan when to fall in love, when to get married, when to have children, etc., though we "adults" suspect that these are the kinds of plans that go often awry. In other walks of life, in other times or places, these matters seem to be determined to a large extent by the society and/or the circumstances of one's birth. Generations of coal miners grew up expecting to work in the mines and did so; generations of civil servants raised their children to be civil servants; etc. In those circumstances it takes courage and imagination to pursue another path. Some projects, e.g., becoming a world-class concert pianist, require more planning—more years as well as more hours of each day are covered by the plan—than others, e.g., reading all of George Eliot's novels. I am interested here in projects and ideals and their bearing on the moral life; I am not interested in plans as such.

Projects explain, and within limits justify, what one does by show-ing how that action fits into the life dominated by that project. Gauguin's leaving his family in order to paint fits into his life in this justifying way. Character plays a similar role; it too shapes a life and determines what is fittingly done in that life. When at the end of *Portrait of a Lady* Isabel Archer refuses the love of Caspar Goodwin and returns to her unlovely husband, she does what fits into her life, what befits the person she has chosen to be.

I do not mean to suggest that every action needs moral justification. Dewey, who agrees with James in emphasizing the centrality of the moral life, points out that it would be morbid to subject each act to moral scrutiny; a well-formed moral character knows when to raise moral issues (Dewey 1960, 12). But choices that affect one's own life over a considerable period of time and choices that affect the lives of others (the choices just mentioned fall into both categories) do raise moral issues, issues that cannot be settled adequately unless one inquires how the contemplated alternatives would fit into the agent's life as well as how they would affect the lives of others. It is the great merit of James, as of Dewey, to have suggested that the moral life should be the center of attention in our moral philosophizing. How, then, do projects and characters shape a moral life?

2

In "The Moral Philosopher and the Moral Life" (1979c) James distin-guishes three questions "which must be kept apart":

> The psychological question asks after the historical origin of our moral ideas and judgments; the metaphysical question asks what the very meaning of the words "good," "ill," and "obligation" are; the casuistic question asks what is the measure of the various goods and ills which men recognize, so that the philosopher may settle the true order of human obligations. (James 1979c, 142)

From the perspective of living a moral life, the casuistic question is central. In our private lives, though not for the philosopher *qua* philosopher, that question comes itself in two forms—it may focus on choosing goals and the means thereto, or it may focus on choosing who one is to be—as James makes clear in the following crucial paragraph from the *Principles:*

> We reach the plane of Ethics, where choice reigns notoriously supreme. An act has no ethical quality whatsoever unless it be

chosen out of several all equally possible. To sustain the arguments for the good course and keep them ever before us, to
stifle our longing for more flowery ways, to keep the foot un-
flinchingly on the arduous path, these are characteristic ethical
energies. But more than these; for these but deal with the means
of compassing interests already felt by the man to be supreme.
The ethical energy par excellence has to go farther and choose
which interest out of severally, equally coercive, shall become
supreme. . . . When he debates, Shall I commit this crime?
choose that profession? accept that office or marry this fortune?
his choice really lies between one of several equally possible
future Characters. What he shall become is fixed by the conduct
of this moment. Schopenhauer, who enforces his determinism
by the argument that with a given fixed character only one
reaction is possible under given circumstances, forgets that, in
these critical ethical moments, what consciously seems to be in
question is the complexion of the character itself. The problem
with the man is less what act he shall now choose to do, than
what being he shall now resolve to become. (James 1950, vol. 1,
pp. 287–288)

James contrasts in this paragraph what I shall call "normal moral
life" with "critical ethical moments." That is not, nor do I mean to
suggest that he thought it was, a hard and fast distinction, but
making it enables us to begin to chart the moral life. The choices of
normal moral life are made against a background of (relatively) stable
values by a (relatively) stable character in more or less stable conditions and not very surprising situations. Even in normal moral life
there are two types of choice situation, which seem to be related to
ends and character respectively: sometimes one decides what to do;
sometimes one needs to resist the temptation not to do what one
has chosen. In normal moral life an agent has goals, principles,
values, not all of which can be realized. Thus she must choose among
alternative course of action. Presumably, she wants to maximize what
she values, which may include others' welfare as well as her own,
doing her duty as well as succumbing to temptation. The course of
action she chooses and pursues may, of course, prove to be less
felicitous than she had hoped. That will be a reason for reexamina-
tion, reevaluation, a change of course. Be that as it may, after she
has chosen "the good course," an agent needs to be ever vigilant lest
she succumb to temptation. Resisting temptation is rather different
from choosing how best to accomplish one's aims. It is, for example,
one thing to decide to follow a strict diet rather than to use medication

to control one's cholesterol level; it is another thing to resist the temptation to violate the diet. Nevertheless, to stick with the diet is after all to decide yet again that one prefers diet to medication, on the assumption all along that one prefers a lower cholesterol level. That is why James speaks of "sustaining the argument." Being resolute and having a certain goal in any serious sense turn out to be intimately connected. For pragmatists it makes no sense to say that someone has a certain purpose but does nothing to further it. With common sense they will say, "If she doesn't diet, then she doesn't really want to lower her cholesterol level." James goes beyond making this point and finds such a person contemptible. "The more ideals a man has, the more contemptible" we deem him if he lacks the virtues required "to get them realized" (James 1983, 164).[2]

A *critical moment* is a situation in which, according to James, one chooses which of several equally coercive interests shall become supreme, which of several equally possible characters one shall become. Here too it may be well to begin by distinguishing between choosing a supreme, life-shaping interest and choosing what kind of person one is to be, though it will become apparent that these are, as James's words suggest, two aspects of one problem. Consider this rather simple case—one is almost tempted to say that it belongs to normal moral life. A young woman who is about to graduate from college finds that she has interest and considerable ability in two fields, she could become, let us say, a philosopher or a biologist. Here we want to say that she chooses between two interests, she cannot pursue both, and whichever one she chooses will be supreme in her life from then on. At first blush this does not seem to be much of a choice of character. In either case, she chooses to develop the virtues of a scholar; in either case, she may or may not become viciously competitive, she may or may not subordinate friendships and family life to her career, etc. These latter choices, on the other hand, do appear to be choices of character. Someone might choose not to become an academic of any kind because she does not want to be tempted (or, as it might appear to her, forced) to subordinate her personal relationships to her professional life. But what then determines our young woman's choice? Presumably, if her interests and abilities are indeed equally balanced, it is that one of the alternatives promises a life in which she can satisfy more of her other longings. Perhaps she believes that she can be more useful as a biologist, so that becoming a philosopher appears to her as becoming a self-indulgent person, and that is not what she wishes to become. Perhaps she believes that a biologist's long hours in the laboratory are less compatible with raising children than a philosopher's work in her study at home. She does not see herself as choosing the person she wants to be, yet her choice expresses her personality. The young woman is choosing a life, or at any rate a probable life, and in so choosing she chooses to become the sort of person who, with luck, will lead that sort of life both successfully and contentedly. That choice requires self-knowledge, for surely even if one sides with James as against Schopenhauer, one cannot become just anyone one chooses to be. One person who commits a crime will be destroyed by remorse even if she is not caught, while another will take pride in her accomplishment if she is not caught and merely bewail her "bad luck" if she is.[3]

It is important to emphasize here that choosing what "being [one] shall now resolve to become" does not refer to any ego-centric preoccupation with self, nor to a hyperfastidious concern to keep one's hand clean. Nor is it a simple reminder that whatever one may deliberate about, one's action will affect oneself as well as others. Nor, finally, is it an invitation to ignore others and the effects of our choices on them. Rather, the central point made here is that some of our moral choices will change us radically, while others will do so, if at all, only slowly and in minor ways. Alternatively, some of our moral choices deliberately and dramatically reaffirm our character, while others simply reflect the being we are. Thus, when Isabel Archer returns to Osmond, she reaffirms the character she has become, has made herself through her decisions to marry Osmond and to remain with him in spite of his utter selfishness. When Gauguin chooses to go to Tahiti and be a painter rather than to stay with his family and continue to work in his office, he chooses both which interest is to be supreme in his life and the kind of person he is to be, namely the sort of person who can live with the thought that he has left his family and who can devote himself single-mindedly to painting, or do so at least sufficiently to justify his choice.

Bernard Williams (1981a) discussed Gauguin (a slightly fictionalized Gauguin) in order to draw attention to the role of moral luck in our moral lives in order to make the distinction between normal moral life and what might be called "existential" choices (James's critical moments), choices that cannot be justified at the time of choosing by their reasonably anticipated consequences because success, in these cases, cannot be foreseen. With some modification and elaboration, the same case may be used to explore the interdependence of character and ends. The Gauguin here envisaged is a family man who is keenly aware of his family responsibilities; he is also a man who (unlike Williams, at least in his discussion of the case) recognizes and deeply feels a moral obligation to realize his talents as a painter. After agonized reflection he decides that he must abandon his family in order to realize his talents as a painter. One might say, then, that he knows that he will shirk some duty whatever he does, but he can be sure of doing something right only if he stays with his family. But can he? If he chose to stay, he might come to see his family as nothing but a burden, a source of perpetual irritation. We may imagine that as the years go by, he becomes more and more morose, perhaps even abusive; perhaps in the end he takes to drink. That, of course, represents a failure of character, and one might say at that point that he should have known himself well enough to know that he would not be able to bring it off. Just so, if he goes to Tahiti but succumbs to the temptations of Polynesian life and fails to paint at all, or paints only rarely and fitfully, one would say that he should have known himself better. There is, then, a connection between the person one is and the kind of interest one can justifiably make supreme. Just as a person who needs to be physically active should not choose a desk job, or someone excessively shy should not choose to be a receptionist, so too one's moral strengths and weaknesses are relevant to one's critical moral choices. Just as Gauguin, according to Williams, was unable to know whether he had a genuine talent, so one is unable to know one's character, how one will react and behave in unfamiliar situations. Still, both will respect to one's talents and with respect to one's character and personality, one is not entirely in the dark, one can often know of weaknesses that should preclude certain alternatives.

However, Gauguin might have turned out to be a merely mediocre painter, someone who painted steadily and conscientiously but never produced a work of museum quality. Would Williams regard that as a justifying success? I assume not, since one would hardly say of such a man that he "is a genuinely gifted painter who can succeed in doing genuinely valuable work" (Williams 1981a, 26). Nevertheless, I would say of such a man that his decision and subsequent actions fit into his life and were justified, if one is ever justified to abandon one's family in pursuit of the realization of one's talents. Consider a parallel case. One could say of Martin Luther King, Jr., that he abandoned his family when he devoted himself to a cause that would almost certainly lead to periods of imprisonment and perhaps to an early, violent death. What justified King's choice was his profound commitment to social justice and his conviction that he could best further that cause by becoming a highly visible, highly exposed leader in that struggle. What King could not know, as Gauguin could not know the extent of his talents, was how competent and inspiring a leader he would prove to be, how visible he would become, how much he would contribute to the success of the Civil Rights Movement. Others whose talents were more limited or merely different, who played lesser roles and contributed in more limited or less visible ways, made the same choice out of the same deep commitment. We do not doubt that they were as justified as was King himself. I am suggesting that if one is justified in putting one ideal above another, in slighting one obligation for the sake of another, then one's success in realizing that ideal is not nearly as morally important as Williams suggests. Only failure due to one's moral failings, which may include self-deception, is morally relevant.

Needless to say, not any project justifies any action undertaken in its behalf. Perhaps painting in general, or the project of producing Gauguin's paintings in particular, does not justify abandoning one's family, but if it does not, then it also does not become justified by the project's success. Here we confront the philosopher's casuistic question, the question of "the true order of human obligations." Both for the philosopher and for us as agents, that question is directly related to the question of choosing "which interest . . . shall become supreme." First, however, more needs to be said about choosing who one is to become.

3

Gauguin's case enables us to see that one's character may be particularly suitable or unsuitable to one's projects, so that one should attempt to know oneself and take that self-knowledge into acount in choosing one's projects. Osmond's case provides an example of a man whose project seems almost determined by his character. Osmond's aesthetic sensibility leads him to collect fine things. His selfishness allows him to pursue that project at the expense of other people's happiness. Given his poverty, he could not have pursued it otherwise. So it is his total character that enables him to make the interest in fine things supreme.

Recently Paul Seabright (1988) has suggested yet another way in which character and projects may be related. According to Seabright's reading of *Portrait of a Lady,* Isabel Archer is a woman who makes it her project to have a certain character. Seabright raises questions concerning the possibility of success for such a project. In particular, he argues that "character may be subverted by the desire to have or to form character" (p. 214) because one would concentrate one's attention inward, on one's being generous, rather than outward to discern situations that call for generosity and then to act accordingly. In her comment on that paper Martha Nussbaum (1988) points out that if Seabright's concerns were to remain unanswered, they would undermine a character-based ethics. She then argues that in the Aristotelean sense of the word, the aim to have a good character is not self-subverting in the manner suggested by Seabright. "So the motivation to be a just person is supposed to be a motive that is what we might call morally transparent: it is focused not upon the agent as the author of the act, but directly upon the act itself, and its valuable characteristics" (Nussbaum 1988, 333–334). That seems to be right. Nussbaum is also right in pointing out that Henry James understands how one might become a just person through a process of education that would focus the attention of the learner away from her own future role and to the problems that are to be solved. Lord Warburton is the result of just such an education. But that reflection gives rise to a related problem.

Every action is an interaction; it changes both the world and the agent. This appears to lead to paradox. It is easy enough to understand that character limits the choices that are actually open to the agent, that are what James calls "live options," but then it appears that the adult agent willy-nilly reinforces her virtues as well as her vices. The child, on the other hand, has her virtues reenforced and her vices discouraged by others. That does not quite say that one could never have chosen other than as one did choose, but it does seem to say that our choices only reenforce our character—pharaoh's heart can only become ever more hardened, criminals are beyond redemption, but the good may be trusted implicitly. What then would be the point of a moral philosophy that emphasizes the critical role of character; how could we ever be said to choose who we want to be?

The problem just raised seems to be the hoary problem of free will. James, as is well known, believed in free will, but an ethics that emphasizes character development can be shown to be empirically grounded and thus practically relevant without an appeal to free will. James points out that new habits can be and are formed as the result of new experiences. "Now life abounds in these, and sometimes they are such critical and revolutionary experiences that they change a man's whole scale of values and system of ideas. In such cases, the old order of his habits will be ruptured: and if the new motives are lasting, new habits will be formed, and build up in him a new or regenerate 'nature'" (James 1983, p. 53). There are examples of sudden conversions, but for the most part, the dynamics of character formation or character change in the adult must be understood as a slow process. All of us know regretfully of virtues lost through neglect, and perhaps some of us know of virtues gained through determined vigilance. As one's children grow up, one is apt to lose that special vigilance without which they would not have survived their early years; in its place one learns to develop a certain toughness, an ability to let them get into trouble and to let them extricate themselves by themselves. Luck, good or ill, may prompt other changes. A man who has always been demanding and impatient may learn to be helpful and patient when his wife becomes seriously ill. It is not the case, then, that as adults we are reduced to reinforcing our already settled characters. Life presents us again and again with the opportunity to change, to grow. We must grasp these opportunities lest we diminish. This point is made most emphatically by John Dewey. "Everywhere," he says, "there is an opportunity and a need to go beyond what one has been, beyond . . . the body of desires, affections, and habits which has been potent in the past. . . . The good person is precisely the one who is . . . the most concerned to find openings for the newly forming or growing self" (Dewey 1960, 173–174).

Because James believes that we can form our own character, he offers advice on how to form habits. This advice is directed not merely at teachers attempting to aid their students in developing good habits but at anyone committed to leading a moral life. He tells, for example, a cautionary tale concerning Darwin, who is said to have lost the ability to enjoy poetry because he failed to read it regularly. He states in at least two separate publications: "Keep the faculty of effort alive in you by a little gratuitous exercise every day" (James 1983, 52; 1950, 126). For, according to James, "the deepest difference, practically, in the moral life . . . is the difference between the easy-going and the strenuous mood" (James 1979c, 159), and it is the latter that James advocates again and again.

If James is right, we have some control over who we shall continue to be or how we slowly change during normal moral life, and in critical moments we sometimes have the opportunity to change quite dramatically. The man whose wife has become seriously and permanently disabled is caused by that event to ask himself what kind of a man, what kind of a husband, he is and wants to be. He could have left her care to strangers; he could have provided only minimally for her needs. Instead, so I imagine, he realizes for the first time how self-centered and neglectful he has been, and he decides to change, to learn to be sensitive to her needs, to do within his means what is best for her.

Who is this man who realizes what kind of man he was, whose remorse does not concern a particular "uncharacteristic" action but his conduct over many years, who wants to become a "new man"?

Who is the self that can say, "I don't like myself," that can decide to change? James distinguishes a number of different selves, but the self here at issue is what he calls the "social self" (James 1950, 293). The voice of conscience is for James the voice of real or imagined others. We learn our values, our principles, our image of a worthy person from parents, teachers, friends, the society in which we grow up and live. Nevertheless, for James, though we learn our morality from the human beings that surround us, morality is not ultimately relative to culture or tradition. Moral progress—the search for and realization of ever more inclusive ideals—requires that one reach beyond one's actual social self toward a potential or ideal social self, a social self approved of by an ideal judge (James 1950, 315 ff). For James, that ideal judge is God, but it suffices for the purposes of this paper that reflection prompted by "new experiences" may cause one not only to seek new ways to realize old ideals but to change one's ideals, not only to regret this or that action but to resolve to change one's habits and to become a different person. Both the self one is and the self one seeks to become are what one's intelligence and temperament make of one's experiences and of the fortunately somewhat incoherent influences of one's society.

A life is not a string of actions chosen one by one. A life has a shape, a coherence due to the character and the aims of the person whose life it is. So far this paper has paid more attention to character than to ideals, although these were seen to be closely connected, especially in critical moments. Still, knowing a person's character does not suffice to tell one her ideals. Moreover, when James concentrates on the casuistic question as it confronts the philosopher *qua* philosopher, he speaks of ideals. The moral philosopher is to bring the ideals she finds into a coherent system. We therefore must turn now to ideals.

4

What, then, is an ideal? In "What Makes a Life Significant" (1983) James tells us that an ideal must be something "intellectually conceived" and that it must contain "novelty," but again he does not quite mean what he says. He is, in that essay, weighing a Tolstoyan admiration for the virtues of simple peasants against the sense that, after all, the virtues, any virtues, are of greater worth "to the universe" if "the possessor of these virtues is in an educated situation, working out far-reaching tasks." He admits that to keep out of the gutter may be for many a "legitimate and engrossing ideal," having just said that we do not raise monuments to the laborers in the subway because they endure their long hours and hard toil only "to gain a quid of tobacco, a glass of beer, a cup of coffee, a meal, and a bed, and to begin again the next day and shirk as much as one can" (James 1983, 159–163). Finally, James recognizes that for many the ideal will always be to cling to the familiar goods. For James, we may conclude, an ideal is not any object of desire; rather, it is the sort of conception, aim, or project that shapes a significant part of a life, either the life of an individual or that of a community. Thus James speaks of the philosopher's ideal of "a genuine universe from the ethical point of view," which sets her a lifelong task, and of the "punitive ideal," i.e., the notion of retributive justice, which has thus far shaped criminal law (James 1979c, 141, 144).

Why, then, are ideals a necessary ingredient in a significant life? We have learned from the Greeks that the moral life is an examined life; it requires the opportunity to reflect. What one reflects upon may be the sort of person one is or wishes to be; or it may be the ends, the projects, and ideals that make one's life a life. One examines and reaffirms actions, habits, and customs that lead to or maintain desired ends; one criticizes and changes actions, habits, and customs that fail to accomplish one's projects or to realize one's ideals. Ends, in turn, may be reconsidered, reshaped, even replaced by other ends because (changed) circumstances make their attainment impossible or because we find that they can be realized only at a cost we are unwilling to pay. Thus, "separate but equal" was rejected by our society because separate was found to be inherently unequal, but we still seek that elusive balance of freedom and equality called justice. Or painting in Tahiti enables (the real) Gauguin to provide for his family and to give full play to his creativity and talent.

The claim, central to pragmatist ethics, that there can be no moral life without reflection and no reflection without ideals, projects, aims, ends in view needs defending. One objection against it is that reflection is a rather cerebral activity, so that demanding reflection seems to relegate a lot of simple people, people who are kind, who "see" what is amiss and how it is to be helped, who do the right thing habitually, etc., to a lower moral rank than they deserve. Insistence on reflection appears to be intellectual snobbery. The answer to that is, I think, twofold. First, it is the objector rather than the Pragmatist who thinks that "simple people" (Tolstoyan peasants?) are incapable of moral growth through reflection. We know that some of those who courageously saved Jews from the Nazis—men and women who rejected both the conventional wisdom of timidity and the dominant anti-Semitism—were simple people with only an elementary education. To be sure, the first move toward saving a Jew was often done "without thinking," as something one just had to do, but in the days, the weeks, and sometimes the months to come, reflection was inevitable, not only reflection on how best to achieve the aim of saving this Jew but on whether to continue with the dangerous endeavor. Second, in fortunate circumstances the results of reflection may not be any startling deviation from the norm, it may show itself only in doing better what everyone says ought to be done. Seeing better, in the sense emphasized by Murdoch (1971), is itself a result of reflection. Finally, a sense of doing the right thing, or having done the right thing, without thinking, and hence without choosing, is a common constituent of normal moral life and may well occur without any subsequent reflection. That is quite compatible with Dewey's claim that moral *growth*, whether in the individual or in the society, requires reflection.[4]

Let us now turn to reflection on ideals. This is one form of the casuistic question (the other being reflection on one's own present and future character). Here James distinguishes between the philosopher *qua* philosopher and the individual moral agent. The philosopher's task is to weave the ideals she "finds existing in the world" into "the unity of a stable system," while the task of the individual moral agent is to "seek incessantly, with fear and trembling, so to vote and to act as to bring about the very largest total universe of good which we can see" (James 1979c, 141–142, 158). The crucial differences here is that the moral philosopher is to be impartial—she finds ideals existing in the world—while the moral agent will and should favor her own ideals while being, as far as possible, respectful of those of others. Moral agents, not moral philosophers, are the engines of moral progress." Although a man always risks much when he breaks away from established rules and strives to realize a larger ideal whole than they permit, yet the philosopher must allow that it is at all times open to anyone to make the experiment, provided he fear not to stake his life and character upon the throw" (James 1979c, 156). One again, ideals and character are found to be inextricably intertwined.

It is apparent from the above that James is a consequentialist. However, although he wrote that pragmatism agrees "with utilitarianism in emphasizing practical aspects" (1978, 32) and dedicated *Pragmatism* to the memory of John Stuart Mill, he is not a utilitarian in the Benthamite sense, because he is not a hedonist.[5] A distinction made repeatedly by John Dewey, the distinction between valuing and evaluation, prizings and appraising (see, e.g., Dewey 1960, 122–123), is useful here. What James calls the psychological question is an inquiry into the origins of our valuings, while the casuistic question deals with evaluation. Although James grants that many of our valuings have arisen in direct association with bodily pleasures and reliefs from bodily pains and that others result from the influence of public opinion, he insists both in "The Moral Philosopher and the Moral Life" (1979c) and more emphatically in the last chapter of the *Principles* (1950) that we have what he calls there a "higher moral sensibility." This makes us feel immediately how hideous it would be to achieve the felicity of millions at the expense of the unending torture of one lost soul, it explains the feelings that cause many to eschew the eating of meat, etc. James's consequentialism thus includes already among the consequences to be counted any moral goods that one might fear would be endangered by consequentialism. Whether James can defend himself against the following objection by Philippa Foot is less clear. Concerning utilitarianism Foot says, "There will in fact be nothing that it will not be right to do to a perfectly innocent individual if that is the only way of preventing another agent from doing more things of the same kind" (Foot 1985, 198). Presumably, compassion would prevent many from committing such actions, and James regards compassion as one of the basic emotions without which morality cannot gain a foothold. (In his notes for lectures on ethics he asks himself repeatedly whether one could persuade a person who lacks the altruistic impulse to act morally (James 1988, 303 ff).) However, even if justice is, as James maintains, a value of which we are immediately sensible, it is not clear that the Jamesian agent must refuse to do an injustice to one even when that means letting others do an injustice to many. Saying that one would feel immediately how hideous it would be deliberately to purchase the happiness of millions at the cost of one soul's eternal suffering does not commit James to rejecting that bargain after reflection or, needless to say, to accepting it. There are perhaps more moral dilemmas in James's moral world than in Foot's, and that may be all to the good. A theory that claims to resolve all moral dilemmas may well fail to do justice to the complexity of our moral lives. However, opening the doors so widely to our moral intuitions will complicate the casuistic question, the question of evaluation, of establishing "the *measure* of the various goods and ills which men recognize" (James 1979c, 142).

The moral philosopher is to weave the ideals she finds in the world into the unity of a stable system without giving any special weight to any ideals of her own except for this ideal of coherence. This turns out to be an impossible task. Since the "elementary forces in ethics are probably as plural as those of physics are," which rules out any form of reductionism, and since all ideals cannot be satisfied simultaneously, the moral philosopher must ultimately appeal to her own moral sensibilities. That idea fills James with horror. "Better chaos forever than an order based on any closet-philosopher's rule, even though he were the most enlightened member of the tribe." But James is not prepared to fall back upon moral skepticism. Rather, what this attempt at a priori ethics has taught him is that "so far as the casuistic question goes, ethical science is just like physical science, and instead of being deducible all at once from abstract principles, must simply bide its time, and be ready to revise its conclusions from day to day" (James 1979c, 153, 155, 157). What James is prepared to offer his readers is not a system but rather a criterion.

> Since everything which is demanded is by that fact a good, must not the guiding principle for ethical philosophy (since all demands conjointly cannot be satisfied in this poor world) be simply to satisfy at all times *as many demands as we can?* that act must be the best, accordingly, which makes for the *best whole,* in the sense of awakening the least sum of dissatisfactions. In the casuistic scale, therefore, those ideals must be written highest which *prevail at the least cost* or by whose realization the least possible number of other ideals are destroyed." (James 1979c, 155; italics in the original)

Unfortunately, this passage raises the suspicion that James is simply inconsistent. I shall argue that he is not. The suspicion arises as follows. If the *guiding principle* for ethical philosophy is

(1) That act is best that awakens the least sum of dissatisfactions,

then James appears after all to be an act-utilitarian, though not a hedonistic one, since, as mentioned above, he denies that all demands are reducible to desires for physical pleasure and aversion to physical pain. But this "guiding principle" is glossed as follows:

(2) Those ideals must be written highest by whose realization the least number of other ideals are destroyed.

Though (2) is vague—how would one count ideals?—it coheres far better than (1) with the account I have given of James's views. We should, therefore, let (2) guide us in our interpretation of (1). This results in the following reading of our troubling passage.

James does not intend us to take all existing desires as they happen to be and to seek what will satisfy the greatest number of them. Rather, we are to pursue those ideals that can be realized at the least cost to other ideals. If not every object of desire is an ideal but only those that shape lives, or at any rate significant parts thereof, then large numbers of more or less temporary desires may well be sacrificed for the realization of an ideal. That, it seems to me, is an accurate description of how we actually manage to lead reasonably contented, reasonably coherent lives. Again and again we sacrifice small desires to long-range projects. Why should we not apply to the public domain what stands us in good stead in our private lives? If this is right, "the best act" is the act that fits into the most inclusive ideal and that, of all acts that so fit, awakens the least sum of dissatisfactions.

However, we are not yet home free. What is inclusiveness when it comes to ideals? There are several possibilities. An ideal may be more inclusive than another because it is espoused by a greater number of persons, because it benefits more people, or because it encompasses a greater number or lesser ideals, perhaps as the result of a process of compromise and accommodation. Thus we might say that the ideal of freedom of conscience is more inclusive than the ideal of toleration for Christian sects only, since it benefits more people; we might also say that the ideal of respect is more inclusive than the ideal of mere tolerance, since it includes the latter. However, though realization of the ideal of freedom of conscience would have benefitted the greater number of persons at all times, this ideal was espoused for most of human history only by a small number. Moreover, the question of benefit depends, at least sometimes, on what people demand. Religious fundamentalists believe that freedom of conscience threatens the very values that it leaves them free to pursue in our pluralist society. Were they the majority, they would attempt to impose their faith on everyone and consider themselves and us the beneficiaries. Nevertheless, religious freedom is the more inclusive ideal, since it permits, the realization of the greater part of the fundamentalists' ideals as well as the realization of the greater part of the ideals of those of other persuasions.

We seem to have reached an impasse. What is seen as the more inclusive ideal in the eyes of someone committed to what James refers to approvingly as "our ancient national doctrine of live and let live" (James 1983, 5) would be rejected by some, perhaps many, of its beneficiaries. That would be an impasse if they too were committed to finding and promoting the most inclusive ideal, but they are not. What this difficulty shows is, rather, that in advocating the most inclusive ideal, James, the philosopher, has in fact imported an ideal of his own. It seems to be indeed impossible to proceed with moral philosophy unless one brings to the task ideals of one's own. It is not only the case, as James acknowledges, that the moral philosopher is "no better able to determine the best universe in the concrete emergency than other men," that she is "just like the rest of us non-philosophers, so far as we are just and sympathetic instinctively, and so far as we are open to the voice of complaint." If her function is, as he says, "indistinguishable from the best kind of statesman," she cannot be an impartial judicial investigator but must be an advocate (James 1979c, 158–159). There are those who find it a tragedy that there is no transcendental perspective from which one can demonstrate the superiority of the values of the Enlightenment. I do not agree with that judgment. The values of the Enlightenment are indeed worth preserving and propagating, and a pragmatist ethics seems to me to be both an expression of those values and a brilliant example of how these values may be incorporated into a comprehensive moral philosophy.

There is another interpretation of "more inclusive." An ideal may be said to be more inclusive than another if the included ideal was taken into account in the argument or conversation that terminated in the adoption of the more inclusive ideal.[6] The argument or conversation would, of course, have to be fair in some sense to be specified. One might think, for example, of the conversation in a Rawlsian original position. Indeed, the Rawlsian principles of justice, in particular the difference principle, may then be seen as including the ideal of absolute socioeconomic equality, since that ideal was taken as the starting point for the conversation (Rawls 1971). On this reading, an ideal adopting after free and equal parties reached consensus in a nonthreatening, noncoercive setting would include those ideals that were modified or even abandoned during the discussion. That such consensus can be reached on issues of vital importance—avoiding nuclear war, preserving the biosphere, raising the standard of living in the have-not nations—is indeed our last, best hope, but the rules governing this type of discussion reflect once again respect for the dignity of the participants.

Respect for the dignity of the individual and the freedoms and equalities that such respect implies cannot be grounded in a deeper foundation. We can only exhibit their glory. That is why James is right to tell us that "books upon ethics, therefore, so far as they truly touch the moral life, must more and more ally themselves with a literature that is confessedly tentative and suggestive rather than dogmatic—I mean with novels and dramas of the deeper sort, with sermons, with books on statecraft and social and economic reform" (James 1979c, 159). To be sure, James was moved to this declaration not by apprehending that the ideal of an inclusive ideal is itself not morally neutral but rather by a lively appreciation of the fallibility of all philosophers. "Like the rest of us non-philosophers," the philosopher "cannot know for certain in advance" which is the most inclusive ideal.

For James, moral progress occurs when more and more human beings in their demands and in their actions realize ideals that encompass greater and greater numbers of lesser ideals. That presupposes that one knows what those ideals are. That is why one must begin with the ideals one finds existing in one's society, but it is also why that can be only a starting point. One's problem is set precisely because one is confronted by a clash of values, a conflict of demands, incompatible standards. The task of finding more inclusive ideals is, therefore, truly formidable. One is tempted to fall back on the wisdom of mankind, which in practice means endorsing the scale of values of the narrower society to which one happens to belong. This temptation is further encouraged by the fact that James believed, as we perhaps do not, that mankind has made, was making, and would continue to make moral progress. He was "confident that the line of least resistance will always be towards the richer and the more inclusive arrangement, and that by one tack after another some approach to the kingdom of heaven is incessantly made" (James 1979c, 157). To the extent that present ideals clash with earlier ones, it would then appear that the earlier ones gave way to the later ones because they could not be accommodated in a coherent comprehensive scheme. Nevertheless, may there not be ideals espoused by our predecessors that might offer solutions to some of our pressing contemporary ills? Should we not, in the interest of both objectivity and further moral progress, reconsider all past ideals? That would appear to be a waste of effort. Surely, the result of humanity's experiments with slavery are sufficiently clear that we need no longer ask what is wrong with it. Nevertheless, as philosophers we must resist the temptation to be blind partisans of the present. On the other hand, any past ideal that has contemporary champions, e.g., the communitarian ideal, must be reconsidered, even if the reconsideration serves only to remind us why we rejected it before. On the other hand, though the presumption both in science and in morality is in favor of the accepted opinion, progress in both is due to those courageous individuals who "may replace old 'laws of nature' by better ones [or,] by breaking old moral rules in a certain place, bring in a total condition of things more ideal than would have followed had the rules been kept" (James 1979c, 157–158). James mentiones Tolstoy's ideal of nonviolent resistance, we may think of Martin Luther King, Jr., as an American who broke the old rules to bring about more ideal conditions. Here it is worth recalling that the revolutionary must choose "with fear and trembling" and be prepared "to stake his life and character upon the throw." James does not encourage armchair utopianism. Indeed, he regards it as contemptible.

5

We have come full circle. Moral life consists of normal stretches punctuated by critical moments. During the normal stretches our conduct is shaped by our virtues and vices and directed by our ideals. Our problems consist on the one hand in resisting temptation and on the other in finding the best means to our ends. During the critical moments we choose new ideals or reaffirm or modify old ones guided by nothing but ourselves. Our character limits our choices and will be modified by the choice we make. The right act is the act that fits into a certain life, fits the character one is and wants to become. The right act is also the act that fits into the most inclusive ideal. These are not incompatible characterizations, for the character and the ideal are not independent. Together they constitute the agent, the person, who she is. To be sure, another person may judge that a certain action, though it fits into the agent's most inclusive ideal, fails to fit into the most inclusive ideal of the relevant community. A theory of the moral life that denied the possibility of conflict between an individual and her society would not be true to the facts. It would also fail to do justice to James, who was fully aware of the need for social criticism and reform. But with this acknowlegment I must drop this matter here.

These criteria of fitting (into a life, with a character, into an ideal) sound less consequentialist than James's concern with the most inclusive ideal would suggest. In practice, however, they are, often the only criteria available at a moment of critical choice, for often the consequences cannot be known. That makes the choice one to be undertaken with fear and trembling. However, having chosen, having acted, we must listen for the cries of the wounded, who would inform us if we had made a bad mistake and would motivate us to begin anew.

Having dealt at length with the casuistic question as well as, though more briefly, with the psychological one, I want to return in conclusion to the issue of objectivity, James's metaphysical question. For James, values exist only insofar as they are realized (felt) in some mind, but they exist as soon as they are so experienced. That, however, does not yet provide for objectivity. For "truth," he writes, "supposes a standard outside the thinker to which he must conform" (James 1979c, 146). That standard is provided by a community of thinkers who make demands upon one another and acknowledge these demands. In practice we learn that our moral judgments have been mistaken when those we have wounded respond to our actions with cries of pain and indignation. Our capacity to care for one another thus lies at the very foundation of the objectivity of moral judgments. But it is entirely compatible with this approach that different cultures, different traditions, should forever believe in and attempt to realize different ideals. James's account is, to say the least, too sketchy to offer a clear response to the charge of cultural relativism. Such a response would begin by saying that James's falliblism with respect to ideals means simply that we shall continue to learn from experience, and his pluralism means that the final inclusive ideal will leave room for many ways of life that will share that commitment to pluralism. James's moral philosophy calls for a sympathetic reader to interpret, interpolate, and smooth over what appear to be contradictions. I have only begun to do that here. Nevertheless, I hope to have shown that a pragmatic ethics has more to offer than has been acknowledged by most contemporary moral philosophers.[7]

Notes

1. James clearly believed in a God who cared about his creation. James believed both that God needed our help in making the world a better place for his creatures and that he, in a sense, guaranteed our success in that endeavor. James believed not only, as we all do, that our efforts can make a difference to how the world will be—that there are causal lines that run through our persons—but also that we have free will—that we can and do initiate causal chains. While these beliefs may well serve as motivating factors, they cannot in any sense help us to know what ideals to embrace, what persons to be, for we cannot read God's mind. I shall therefore set this question aside for another occasion.
2. I have discussed choices in normal moral life. It is worth pointing out, however, that the choices of normal moral life tend to be relatively rare, or at least are hardly noticed. Our priorities are set and almost dictate our course of action. Our habits, virtuous or otherwise, enable us to act in familiar situations almost without thinking.
3. For a different account of moral choice in critical moments, see Owen Flanagan's chapter in this volume.
4. For a more sustained discussion of the role of reflection in our moral lives, and in particular of Tolstoyan peasants, see Owen Flanagan's chapter in this volume.
5. My colleague Ken Winkler correctly pointed out that John Stuart Mill was also not a hedonist. It would lead too far afield to examine the differences between James and Mill, or the question whether Mill was strictly speaking a utilitarian. Here it suffices to defend the claim that James was not a utilitarian.
6. This suggestion is due to Ken Winkler.
7. An earlier draft of this paper was presented to the Philosophy Club at the University of Virginia. I benefitted from the discussion that followed, especially from remarks

by Cora Diamond and by a student whose name I do not know. I was also helped by conversations with Owen Flanagan and Amélie Rorty. The pen-ultimate draft of this paper was read with great care by Ken Winkler, whose comments prevented me from making at least one serious blunder and enabled me to be clearer than I otherwise would have been. To all these people I am most grateful.

Part II
Character, Temperament, and Emotion

Chapter 4

Natural Affection and Responsibility for Character: A Critique of Kantian Views of the Virtues

Gregory Trianosky

Kantians characteristically claim that natural benevolent and kind motives cannot be virtuous unless they are supplemented by some awareness of the rightness or goodness of promoting well-being.[1] Different forms of supplementation may be held to be required, but in any case, we may call this sort of view a view of no moral worth without formal motivation. Thus suppose we think of a Noble Innocent as one who, like Adam and Eve in the Garden of Eden, has not "eaten of the tree of the knowledge of good and evil." His conduct is unreflective, involving no articulated awareness of the morality of what he does. One familiar eighteenth-century view has it that the conduct of such an Innocent would nonetheless be guided by a powerful and steady flow of kindness and fellow feeling. But the view in question maintains that however reliable and influential such feelings might be in the life of the Noble Innocent, his very innocence entails that he cannot possibly be virtuous. In this chapter, I wish to begin a defense of the virtue of the Noble Innocent.

1

Opposition to this Kantian claim has persisted from his Romantic critics to present-day "personalists" like Blum and Williams. As recent defenses of no moral worth without formal motivation suggest, it is not always clear that these critics are addressing a version of the view that Kant or any of his followers in fact hold. Moreover, although I have called these views "Kantian," in point of fact they have been widely propounded by a great variety of thinkers before and since Kant. Leaving aside these pointed questions of parentage and identity, however, there remains a central argument in favor of the "Kantian" views that has not yet received much discussion from either side. Ironically, it is Kant himself who puts the argument in a very familiar passage. His remarks about the moral worth of actions done from wholly unreflective altruistic motives, or "natural affections," as they were called in the eighteenth century, are worth quoting in full:

To be beneficent when one can is a duty; and besides this, there are many minds so sympathetically constituted that, without any other motive of vanity or self-interest, they find a pleasure in spreading joy around them, and can take delight in the satisfaction of others so far as it is their own work. But I maintain that in such a case an action of this kind, however proper, however amiable it may be, has nonetheless no true moral worth, but is on a level with other inclinations, for example, the inclination to honor, which, if it is happily directed to that which is in fact honorable, *deserves praise and encouragement, but not esteem.* For the maxim lacks the moral import, namely, that such actions be done *from duty,* not from inclination. (Kant 1964a, 398; first italics mine)

The little-noticed thread in these remarks of Kant's has nothing to do with the reliability or capriciousness of the natural affections. Instead, roughly sketched, it is this. There are all sorts of qualities that people may have or develop and that we are glad they have. We may call such qualities *praiseworthy,* or worth encouraging. However not all such praiseworthy qualities are ones for which the person himself deserves credit or *esteem.* Consider, for example, a young adult, say a daughter, who has easily and unthinkingly maintained the values imparted by a very strict upbringing. Such a person may be a credit to her parents. But even if her values are noble ones, perhaps *she* deserves no credit for having them. After all, praiseworthy though her actual commitments may be, this young adult might have just as meekly and uncritically adopted any old parental values, noble or base.

Armed with this rough and intuitive distinction between praise and credit, Kant seems to assume that the moral virtues must be not only praiseworthy but also to the credit of the agent who has them. Moreover, because the natural affections involve no articulated conception of rightness or goodness, they do not have a properly formal intentional structure. Hence, Kant argues, they do not and cannot reflect credit on their possessor. Hence, they cannot be moral virtues.

Both of the crucial premises in this argument seem to me mistaken. It is not necessarily true that moral virtues must be to the credit of their possessor, and it is not necessarily true that the natural affections must fail to reflect credit on their possessor. To appreciate both these points of disagreement requires a more careful account of the distinction between praise and credit.

2

Praising something essentially involves thinking it valuable and expressing that thought in an approving or commending way. Typically, whether we praise a certain trait of character and whether we think it valuable to have are to a large extent independent of its genesis. In this, praise and admiration are akin. Thus one can admire Kant's own well-known "sentiment of humanity" or his self-control, for example, and think these traits worth having in his case, even if they turn out to be nothing more than the lingering imprint left on the young Kant's superego by a rigorous Pietistic upbringing.

It is easy to miss this point because there are certain ways of developing a trait that do seem incompatible with its being a virtue. One who is liberal with his money does not display the virtue of generosity, for example, if his disposition to liberality is simply the product of a continuing, childlike desire to win the approval of now-absent parents. But this is because to be generous, truthful, kind, or just is to pursue certain things for their own sake, or perhaps for the sake of what is right and good in them. The parent-pleasing money giver is someone whose concern lacks the proper intentional focus: he gives not for the sake of the recipients but for the sake of parental approval.

In such cases, however, facts about how the agent came to be liberal with his money are relevant only because they illuminate the structure of the motives he currently has. What obscures this point in the case of standing motives like the ones just mentioned is the closeness of the psychologically explanatory connection between the particular genesis of a motive and its precise content. The point is quite clear if we think of virtues that are not species of motivation at all but skills or abilities like self-control or what Hume calls "dexterity in business." Here, as with skills or abilities in general, the very close explanatory tie with genesis is often missing. It is plain that whether someone has an admirable ability to keep his temper or to prevent his feelings from inappropriately influencing his judgment is a question that is not typically illuminated by an investigation of how he came to develop his traits.

How one comes to have a trait and who is the cause of one's having it, however, are precisely the questions that must be answered before one can rightly be given credit or esteem for one's character. A person deserves credit for his moral character if and only if that character is virtuous, and *he* is the one primarily responsible for its being so. (In this respect, though perhaps not in others, attributions of credit for moral character are very much like attributions of responsibility for action.) Thus, intuitively, the uncritically accepting but nobly motivated young adult may really care deeply about the poor and take the relief of their suffering to be a duty. He does not act just to please his parents or even with any thought of them at all. He has thoroughly internalized the values they taught. His concern for the poor is consequently a genuine, intrinsic concern. Yet he has it only because he was a docile and malleable child who is now set in the ways of his childhood and because he was fortunate enough to have good parents. If he had had bad parents, he would now be just as profoundly committed to bad values.[2]

Hence intuitively it seems that it is no credit to *him* that he is a charitable person. At most, if his parents were genuinely good people who tried to raise their malleable and uncritical child to be the same, it is they who deserve the credit for his virtues, for it is they who are responsible for the content of his moral character.

This case suggests a more precise account of the conditions for a trait's being to an agent's credit:

(1) The trait must be a praiseworthy one.

(2) The trait must have the content it does primarily because of the agent's active discrimination rather than the discriminations made by others.

(3) Reference to the value-making features of the trait (or of what it aims at) must figure essentially and fairly directly in the explanation of why the trait is developed and maintained.

Condition (1) is straightforward enough. Conditions (2) and (3) flesh out the idea of responsibility for character.

3

It is one question whether a character is a good one. It is another to what extent it is *one's own*. Of course, there is an obvious sense in which one's character is always just as much one's own, regardless of its genesis. Moreover, one's character is not a possession like fine clothes or a house or even a Ph.D. Nonetheless, it may still be more or less one's own in a familiar sense, just as one's opinions and creed may be more or less one's own. Indeed, the analogy is an apposite one. In part, for one's moral character to be one's own is for one's powers of discrimination to be actively engaged in shaping its content.

The guiding idea of condition (2) is thus to impose a causal restriction on responsibility for character: the individual responsible for his character is the one who is active in a certain way in the shaping of it. It is important to be clear, however, about just what sort of activity engenders responsibility for moral character.

To begin with, given the nature of character, one's agency must of necessity be involved in its development and maintenance in a fundamental way, whether one is responsible for that character or not. The central elements of moral character are standing desires, attitudes, values, commitments, and emotions, as well as various abilities and capacities for voluntary action. Each of these elements, of course, essentially involves *will* in one way or another. For one thing, many of them essentially involve certain sorts of standing commitments. One decides to support conservative causes, to make the well-being of a lover one's own end, to promote the cause of justice, or to seek after and protect beauty or truth. For this reason, the acquisition and maintenance of political loyalties, loves, moral commitments, and personal values is to a significant extent a matter of *doing* and continuing to do certain sorts of things: choosing, deciding, endorsing, commitment, pursuing, accepting, and so on. This is not to say that the acquisition and maintenance of such desires, attitudes, and emotions can be done *at will*, if this is taken to imply at a moment's notice or in response to any passing fancy or whim. It is rather to say that acquiring and maintaining such elements of moral character is to some significant extent done *by will*, over time, perhaps despite many obstacles, and through much effort. It is in this sense that they are to a significant extent voluntary, for to continue to make such decisions over time just is in large measure to display the relevant trait.

Moreover, to say this is not to say that some continued exercise of will is *sufficient* to constitute (or indeed to maintain) desire, emotion, attitude, or valuation. Most of these traits are not *wholly* voluntary, even in the sense of being done "by will." We speak of being overcome by hate, of being forced to accept the need for social change, of discovering that one is in love, and of finding that one is attracted to beautiful things. Nonetheless, it seems clear that no congerie of affective or reactive elements can possibly constitute a desire, emotion, attitude, or valuation unless it is ordered and structured by the choice of some end or guiding principle.

Will is involved in a different but equally direct way in the case of those elements of moral character that are forms either of endurance or of self-control. These include courage, patience, determination, and industry. Some of these traits are abilities that are called into play at will. Others are capacities for voluntary action in the face of various sorts of recognized obstacles. Here, however, the acquisition of these traits of character is not voluntary to the same extent as it is with attitudes, commitments, etc., unless one thinks with the Victorians that can be self-controlled, say, simply by setting oneself to it.

It follows that at certain levels one's agency is always exercised when some element of one's character is *operative* in one's life and that one's agency is very often engaged simply in one's *having* a certain character as well. If one then supposes that condition (2) is satisfied by these sorts of involvements of agency in character, then it will follow (with minimal additional assumptions) that anyone who has a character will be responsible for it to a very great extent and that everyone who has a character will be more or less equally responsible for the character they have. This constitutes a kind of quasi-Aristotelian interpretation of condition (2).

However, the case of the malleable youth—call him "Wimpy"—undermines this quasi-Aristotelian interpretation. Wimpy, as I have described him, is not responsible for his character to any significant extent. It is precisely in this that he differs from most of us. Hence, the above-described involvement of one's voluntary action in the formation and maintenance of character cannot suffice to satisfy condition (2).

The way in which condition (2) must be interpreted to support our intuitions about Wimpy will be clearer if we acknowledge another figure who appeared in the above quotation from Kant's *Groundwork* (1964a). Unlike Wimpy, this figure is not charitable simply because he was taught to be. He is charitable because to be anything else goes against the grain of his natural temperament.

Parents often remark on the dramatic differences of temperament between very young children. Some are sweet and happy, some cranky and impatient. Some are docile, others aggressive. We may think of Kant as having asked us to imagine a child whose "innate" sweetness and cheerfulness persist throughout his adult life. Suppose that within the parameters of normal child-rearing practices it is highly unlikely that such a child will internalize any values inconsistent with a broadly open-handed, loving, and generous approach toward others.[3] To this extent he becomes the adult he now is because he is suited by nature to be so. He doesn't have it in him, as we say, to be small, narrow-minded, or suspicious. He need not be a Noble Innocent, although he could be. Either he may have very firmly entrenched and explicitly formulated moral beliefs, or he may have steady and well-developed natural affections. Call him "Sunny."[4]

Intuitively, the content of Wimpy's character is chosen for him, while Sunny makes his character for himself. (In neither case, of course, do these individuals make their *temperament*. This is a point to which I will return below.) Is there some deeper level at which we can spell out this idea that the one is passive and the other active in the development and maintenance of his character?

People's characters may be prone to develop, change, and stabilize in different ways and to different degrees. That is to say, people are inclined to act, choose, commit, endorse, and so on in different ways and to different degrees. To *do* these things is always, of course, to act voluntarily. Yet even so, the degree to which, and the manner in which one is disposed to make these changes is itself *largely a nonvoluntary matter.*[5]

Matters like these explain the nature and the stability of the dispositions to choose those ends the choosing of which constitutes so much of moral character. They thus explain to a large extent how, when, and in what directions a person's character is itself disposed to change or to remain the same.

There is, in short, a distinction between traits of moral *character* and underlying qualities of *temperament*. It is the difference in the nature of their temperaments that marks Wimpy as passive and Sunny as active, and which the interpretation of condition (2) should capture.

Wimpy may have a generous, kind, and just character. But when we ask how he got to be that way—why his character has *this* content rather than any other—the answer is that he was a malleable and uncritical youth receptive to whatever values his parents happened to have, one whose uncriticalness now operates to protect his acquired values from any real challenge. In this way Wimpy is and continues to be what others have made him.

The qualities of temperament forming Wimpy's character dispose him to discriminate among possible choices of ends, *but not at all according to their content*. To be malleable (or rigid, for that matter) is precisely to be in this sense *indiscriminate* about the content of one's values, ends, commitments, and motives.

The explanation for Sunny's having the character he does is quite different. He is "by nature" empathetic, open-handed, and—sunny. In his choice of ends, on this account, he is disposed to choose benevolent ends rather than malevolent or even morally insensitive ones. He could not easily have been made mean or ungenerous, given any normal child-rearing practices.

Sunny's case illustrates another class of qualities of temperament: those spontaneous and unreflective impulses toward others that are expressed in nonbehavioral ways as well as in behavior. These are the immediate but unsteady altruistic concerns that Rousseau called natural compassion: the impulse to prevent pain to another, the horror one feels at the sight of it, the immediate concern one has for the sufferer. These are all too primitive to be properly called emotions, motives, or attitudes. They are more properly classed as spontaneous reactions. And the tendency to have them is as much a matter of temperament as Wimpy's malleability, or the dourness and lack of empathy displayed by that notorious individual—call him "Grumpy"—whom Kant describes as "truly not . . . nature's worst product" (Kant 1964a, 398).

The tendency to such spontaneous reactions does not, of course, operate to modify the choices that constitute the content of one's character *in the same way* that gullibility or tentativeness would. Spontaneous sympathy is reinforced, shaped, and regularized so that it is transformed into those exercises of will centrally constitutive of the emotions, motives, and attitudes characteristic of a kind and generous person. Sunny takes up the ends distinctive of the virtuous person because to do so is *in this particular way* a natural outgrowth—given reasonable child-rearing practices—of the feelings and responses that he cannot help but have.[6]

Sunny's character, suitably trained, will thus take on the content it does because this suits his underlying temperament. A malicious and self-centered character would have "gone against the grain," as we say. To be explained are this resistance to evil character and the inclination to choose good character. The explanation is that Sunny's temperament is *discriminating* in just the way that Wimpy's is not. It moves him to select among sets of various possible ends on the basis of a certain content, and not merely on the basis of who else happens to favor them. There is thus a very special kind of activity characteristic of Sunny and absent in Wimpy: the activity of selecting in discriminating ways among various patterns of commitment to ends. It is not that Sunny's temperament explains why he chooses, e.g., to make helping those in need his end rather than making a great deal of money. Perhaps the explanation for that is to be found in his desires and beliefs, or in his reasons. But there is another explanation required in addition to all the explanations for particular choices of ends. What Sunny's temperament explains is why he persistently tends to choose or commit to ends of one sort rather than to ends of a different sort. Why is it that Sunny tends to choose altruistic goals or commit himself to benevolent ends? It is this *pattern* of choices or commitments that is explained by the activity of temperament.[7]

Selecting among various patterns of commitment is an activity or a congerie of activities because discriminating and selecting in these ways is something that we *do*. Yet it is not really something that is done voluntarily or by will. Rather, one finds oneself, like Sunny, drawn to characters who are kind and generous, impressed by their commitment to those in need, and inspired by their example. One may by horrified by malice, revolted by greed, repelled by dishonesty. Being drawn, inspired, impressed, and horrified, revolted, repelled are not things we do by will. And although they may be manifested in acts of will, to a large extent, to be drawn, inspired, ect., do not themselves involve the will.

That these things nonetheless constitute forms of discriminating or selecting, and so in some very broad sense "things that we do," reveals that the notion of agency, activity, or doing at work here must be at once much richer and more subtle than those found in the Kantian and indeed Aristotelian traditions.

The intuitive contrast between Wimpy and Sunny is expressed more abstractly in the interpretation thus suggested for condition (2). Although at certain levels both are necessarily active in the formation of their own characters, there is still a deeper level at which Sunny is active and Wimpy passive. It is this deeper difference in the extent to which each is discriminating that both explains and is in turn buttressed by the intuition that both are not equally responsible for the characters they have.

Condition (3) for a trait's being to an agent's credit requires that those very features of the trait that make it a virtue play some essential role in explaining why that trait in particular is developed and maintained. Intuitively, it seems clear that Wimpy's charitable concern also fails to meet this condition. What makes charity a virtue is the fact that it aims to meet the needs of others. It is one of the altruistic virtues. Yet it is not facts about the needs of others and about how charity aims to meet them that explain why Wimpy became and continues to be charitable. Instead, it is the fact that his parents happen to prize charity, and this latter fact, of course, is not at all what makes charity a virtue.

Now Wimpy's parents may have had very well-grounded moral beliefs. After all, charity obviously has "the right stuff." But here again, it is not this further fact about the groundedness of their beliefs that figures centrally in the explanation of why he is generous. If his parents, entirely without grounds, had perversely taken niggardliness to be a virtue and charity a vice, Wimpy, with equal facility, would have become niggardly and despised charity in new situations. (Here, as with the second condition, a great deal of refinement may be required to avoid counterexamples. I will not provide it, since its details here and above should not affect the points at issue.) Things are very different with Sunny. The fact that charity and love are traits that aim to benefit others is an essential part of the explanation for why his character comes to have the content that it does. The very facts that make these traits virtues also show why there was such an easy fit between those particular traits and his natural temperament.

The two examples we have been discussing are hypothetical. They are intended to illuminate two extremes. In reality, most of us are likely to fall somewhere in between. Precisely where is an important and difficult question in the psychology of moral education. Perhaps the truth is that most of us deserve only some of the credit for the noble traits we have acquired. Good fortune (the absence of temptation and of harsh circumstances) and good parenting deserve the rest. Correspondingly, perhaps Clarence Darrow was right at least to suggest that most of us deserve only some of the discredit for our vices.

The contrasting examples of Wimpy and Sunny and my discussion of them suggest that the three conditions I have proposed are not only necessary but jointly sufficient for the attribution of credit to the agent. Thus Sunny's traits are praiseworthy traits acquired because of the very features that make them praiseworthy, and in cases like Sunny's, the discriminating activity of the agent himself and no other explains his development and maintenance of those traits. What more could reasonably be required for the virtuous quality of one's character to reflect well on one's merit as a person?

4

We are finally in a position to see the errors in the Kantian argument against the virtuousness of the natural affections. To begin with, one crucial premise in that argument claims that moral virtues must be to the credit of their possessor. Now my account of credit makes it clear that praiseworthiness is only one precondition of credit. But moral praise, prizing, and encouragement are simply a family of external signs of moral virtue. Rightly given moral praise is simply an approving expression of the acknowledged moral value of a trait—its value from the removed and general perspective of the moral evaluator. Hence, the virtuousness of a trait is only one precondition for its being to one's credit and not by itself a sufficient condition. In this respect, virtue and vice are analogous to rightness and wrongness. Just as we can still ask of a wrong action how the agent came to do it and whether he is the one to be held responsible for it, so too we can still ask of a virtuous (or vicious) trait whether the possessor is the one responsible for his having it.

It follows that this crucial Kantian premise is false. Moral virtues need not necessarily reflect credit on their possessors. On the account I have given of virtue, credit, and praise, whether one's virtues in fact redound to one's credit depends on various facts about their genesis. Some do, and some don't.

The second important Kantian premise was that the natural affections do not and cannot reflect credit on their possessor. It is now easy to see why this premise too must be false. First, I assume that the natural affections may rightly be praised from the moral point of view. Second, the natural affections may be developed and maintained by the agent's own discriminating activity. Sunny may, for example, be equally the author of his own good character whether he becomes a Noble Innocent or a formally motivated benevolent agent. In either case, I have argued, it is his own temperament that shapes the content of his character.

Finally, even the Noble Innocent may satisfy the third condition. The development of one's character may be *responsive* to what is good and right, even if it is not informed by any articulated conception of, or concern for, rightness or goodness per se.[8]

5

I will end with a brief discussion of the role of moral luck in attributions of responsibility for character.

One might argue that on my account, responsibility for character is not really possible for anyone. After all, even for Sunny and Grumpy, what sort of temperament they have is not up to them. It is not a product of any discriminating or selecting on their part. To use Bernard Williams's (1981b) terminology, what traits constitute one's temperament is a matter of constitutive moral luck. But on my account the pattern of commitments that makes up much though not all of character is to be explained by the discriminative activity that is part of having a temperament. Thus if what temperament one has is a matter of constitutive luck, what sorts of patterns of commitment one is disposed to select will be a matter of luck as well. But character or any great portion of it cannot be something we are responsible for if it is a matter of luck whether we develop one character rather than another.[9]

This objection is an important one. One might reply simply by agreeing with Nagel (1979a) and Williams (1981b) that luck is in general a significant element in determining responsibility, whether for character or for action, and that this is a deeply puzzling and anomalous feature of commonsense moral thinking. But the importance of the objection lies not in its illustration of this general difficulty. It lies rather in what it reveals about the point of ascriptions of responsibility for character and, indeed, about the nature of character itself.

Notice first of all that I am discussing responsibility for character, not responsibility for actions or responsibility in general. The notion of action is the notion of something that emanates from the will. The notion of character is not. This is why character is not merely what Kant himself took it to be: the set of commitments to, or continuing endorsements of, moral principles by (rational) will. It is also the complex of attitudes, desires, emotions, and so on, in which commitments are situated. And although will plays a variety of significant roles in the development of character, as I have indicated, moral character is not simply the expression of an intention or volition in the way that action is. Once we have accepted some richer, non-Kantian conception of character, the question is whether there is any plausible account of responsibility for character so understood that avoids the charge of holding responsibility hostage to luck.

Aristotle's account is attractive but implausible. He holds that character understood in this richer way is or can be primarily the product of voluntary action. I have argued, however, that at least that the pattern of commitment, which is one central part of character, is instead the product of a nonvoluntary activity of discrimination among ends, whether in a way sensitive to their content or not. However much particular commitments may be the product of voluntary action (choosing), the pattern among one's commitments usually is not. Moreover, as I have pointed out, although one's attitudes, emotions, reactive capacities, and skills are or can to some extent be developed by will, no effort of will, however sustained, is *sufficient* for their development. Character is the product not only of voluntary action but also of the activity of temperament, along with upbringing, childhood experiences, social environment, peer expectations, and pure happenstance. And not only temperament but all of these things are not themselves the product of some exercise of agency, whether voluntary or nonvoluntary. Hence, no Aristotelian account of responsibility for character can succeed.

No realistic account of the nature of character and its origins can hope to avoid these conclusions. It follows that we have only one of two options: we can reject the notion of responsibility for character altogether as requiring too narrow a conception of character (along with a very powerful conception of the autonomy of the will), or we can accept some notion of responsibility for character that is compatible with a certain amount of constitutive moral luck in the genesis of character.[10]

Here the difference between judgments of character and judgments of action is central. First, Kantians make a powerful case for the proposition that in the very making of a voluntary choice or commitment, the agent must see himself as free, and so as responsible. If this is so, then perhaps Kant was right in thinking that to the extent that we as observers treat him as an agent, we too must regard him as responsible for whatever commitments he voluntarily undertakes, regardless of the details of the causal story we might tell when viewing his action as an event in the phenomenal realm.

Except to the extent that character involves voluntary action, however, the same sort of argument cannot be given for the development of character. The discrimination among patterns of commitment, which is the expression of temperament, is an activity. It is something that happens in us, it has an intentional structure, and it is both described and explained in psychological terms. But it is not and need not be a conscious activity, and so it need not involve the agent's deliberating or seeing himself in any particular way. Conversely, what must be present to the agent in deliberation is the question of whether to choose this end or that. The question of why his choice of ends reveals a certain pattern need not be. (To the extent that this question is present to him in deliberation, his pattern of choice will be a product not of temperament but of voluntary action.)

Thus a virtuous character does not simply constitute or express some voluntary choice. Instead, it is a species of excellence, and excellence is not in general equally within everyone's reach. Not everyone can be equally sympathetic, sensitive, devoted, or courageous, try as they might, any more than everyone can be equally intelligent, musical, strong, or graceful. This should not be a shocking conclusion, unless one remains wedded to the characteristically Kantian conception of virtuous character as consisting essentially in dispositions to choose. Moral character involves a tremendous variety of traits and qualities, most of which are not species of volition. Once we admit this, then barring an appeal to the Aristotelian account of the genesis of character, the antiegalitarian conclusion seems unavoidable. On the other hand, once we admit this, it does not follow from our antiegalitarian with respect to virtue that we must or should be antiegalitarianism with respect to the possibility of acting rightly. Here the Kantian perspectival argument I mentioned above may still persuade us.

Moreover, the point of responsibility ascriptions here is different than it is with respect to actions. In both cases we are attempting to address a question about origins. But the question with respect to action arises because of issues involving punishment, reward, and restitution. The question arises with respect to character because we wish to understand our lives. It is not a pragmatic question but a philosophical one arising in our everyday moral experience. To ask who deserves credit for Wimpy's character is to ask, To what extent is his life his own; to what extent, to use Mill's (1978) terminology, is he an individual, a person with character? To deserve credit for one's character is thus not to build up a positive balance in some cosmic bank account, as the medieval Church held one could do by performing supererogatory acts. It is rather to be the author of one's own character. It is ultimately for this reason that the fact of one's temperament not being within one's control does not threaten ascriptions of responsibility for character. The point of such ascriptions is not to establish that one formed one's character freely, or even that one could have "done otherwise," developed some other character instead. The point is rather to establish that of the various persons who might have authored your character, you were the one who did and not someone else. The content of your character is to be explained by the activity of your agency, and not by the activity of some other agent. It is for this reason too that faced with the ineliminable influence of constitutive luck on character, we find the option of abandoning ascriptions of responsibility for character altogether so unattractive. To do so is to abandon a significant portion of the attempt to understand one's life as one's own.

There is one other important reason for not abandoning the practice of making such ascriptions. To ask about credit for one's virtuous character is to raise an issue about what sorts of deeper-lying virtues and vices one displays. The qualities of temperament explaining Wimpy's character are *defects of temperament*, moreover, defects of a very special kind. They absolve him of responsibility for his defects of *character* because Wimpy's deeper-lying defects of temperament are *anchoring* vices. That is, they are traits that prevent his good motives and earnest resolve from being firmly anchored in an appreciation of what is good or right.

The metaphor of the anchor is good one. It highlights the thought that Wimpy's commitments to morality and moral values are shallow. Of course, a commitment may be shallow without necessarily being insincere. Shallow people are typically those who do make sincerely felt commitments but who also shed them easily. They develop strong views, but they are easily argued or cajoled out of them.

This means most obviously that Wimpy's commitments may not be completely reliable. Without a tether, to use Plato's version of the metaphor for a moment, Wimpy may gradually lose his active concern for the poor and downtrodden when he falls in with thieves and robbers, or wealthy Republicans, and moves to Washington to take a post in the Bush administration. One worries that his motives, attitudes, emotions, and values will serve the good only so long as Wimpy is in good company. In short, because Wimpy lacks the anchoring virtues of temperament, one fears that he, like Woody Allen's Zelig, may too easily take on the values, attitudes, etc., of those around him. Like Zelig, Wimpy may seem to lack not a character but a character of his own.

There is more to Wimpy's defects of temperament than this, however. To say that his concerns and values are shallow is also to say that they do not touch bottom. He is and remains, e.g., charitable (to the extent that he does) not because deep within himself he finds that he can be nothing else but only because he was taught to be so by significant others.

The traditional view of virtue is that it is a matter of responsiveness to what is antecedently right or good. If this is so, however, then Wimpy cannot be virtuous through and through. For at the level that is deepest, at least in the order of explanation, he does not respond to what is right or good at all. The goodness of his *character* is a consequence not of a *temperamental* response to moral values and reasons but of something else. Thus to the extent that Wimpy fails to satisfy condition (3), he must *ipso facto* fail to be thoroughly virtuous.

There are, of course, other defects of temperament that are not anchoring defects, like gullibility and uncriticalness. Such are the qualities of Kant's naturally dour and unsympathetic person, whom we have dubbed "Grumpy." Grumpy will probably be responsible for his character, on my account, although this is not at all likely to be to his credit. His temperament, like Sunny's, is a discriminating one, but it selects against virtues of character, like kindness, generosity, and benevolence.[11]

It is these temperamental defects of Grumpy's and the corresponding excellences of Sunny's that explain the contents of their respective characters. It is the values of others that explains the content of Wimpy's. This is why Grumpy's character is probably his own, while Wimpy's is not. Grumpy's and Sunny's characters are firmly anchored. Sunny is good through and through. Grumpy, if he is bad, is bad through and through. Neither will change with the whims of moral fashion or present company.

In short, to abandon talk of responsibility for character is to truncate the field on which judgments of virtue operate and to cripple the search for the identity of an agent. On the other hand, to retain that talk requires admitting that constitutive moral luck plays a significant role in the genesis of virtue. But this admission, I have claimed, is as unobjectionable as it is unavoidable.

I have argued for an account of credit for one's character that I hope is intuitively appealing and also illuminates the question of why attributions of credit matter. One may not agree with the "personalists" and their Romantic predecessors that the character of the noble innocent contains the whole of virtue. But if my account is plausible, then perhaps we may agree that an innocent altruism is as respectable a virtue as its more formal Kantian counterpart.

Notes

1. I have benefited from discussions with Thomas E. Hill, Jr., as well as from the comments of Thomas Wren and Michele Moody-Adams, both of whom served as commentators for various earlier versions of this paper.
2. In reality things are more complex because being this set in one's ways may well be psychologically incompatible with the flexibility one needs to recognize occasions on which new and different forms of charity are called for. Nonetheless, one may be genuinely and virtuously charitable on a wide variety of familiar and mundane occasions even if one is inflexible and unimaginative about the demands of charity. This is why not every doer of charitable deeds who is inflexible or close-minded need be a hypocrite as well.
3. Obviously, the notion of normal child-rearing practices is a morally loaded one.
4. See Ruth Benedict's (1934, p. 66) description of the Dobuan "of sunny, kindly disposition" in a suspicious and mistrustful society, whose "compulsion was too strong for him to repress it in favor of the opposite tendencies of his culture."
5. To say that gullibility, sensitivity, and other traits of temperament are nonvoluntary is, of course, not to say that they can't be altered by voluntary action. Voluntary action may alter them over time in something like the way it can alter an individual's weight, musculature, or other physical qualities that influence what one can do. Moreover, an effort of will can sometimes compensate for a temperamental defect, as Kant pointed out. So, for instance, if one is naturally gullible, one can decide to think twice before accepting any gossip as truth and can stick firmly, though with great effort, to this resolve.
6. It is important to emphasize that, unlike Rousseau himself, one need not hold that this process of moral development necessarily involves the acquisition and deployment of articulated moral concepts and principles. The Innocent can remain innocent and yet become genuinely noble.
7. One might hold that no additional explanation was required but that the explanation of the pattern of commitments was given by a conjunction of the explanations of the particular commitments constituting it. But this is to insist that the presence of a pattern must itself be regarded as merely a coincidence. To the extent that there really is some pattern, the question of what explains the persistent and repeated presence of certain features of one's commitments seems to be a legitimate one. Nor will it suffice to explain that pattern simply by appealing to the

persistence of certain facts (say about human suffering) whose presence always gives rise to commitment in the agent. My question then recurs as a challenge to discover what it is in that person that explains why he tends to respond to these facts in making his commitments rather than to others.

8. See Peter Railton's discussion of the causal role of the good of the individual in influencing the development of his motivation (1986, 179–180). Unlike Railton, however, I am not here presupposing the truth of moral realism in either a naturalistic or nonnaturalistic form. I am not claiming that the goodness of a trait can itself exert a causal role independently of the agent's conception of it. I am only pointing out that the very familiar and natural features in virtue of which a trait is good can have an important causal role independently of the agent's conception of goodness or rightness. The device of the Noble Innocent serves to dramatize this claim. Contrast Railton's stronger realist claims (e.g., p. 182).

9. I am grateful to Owen Flanagan for bringing the force of this objection home to me.

10. Nor will proposing some nongenetic account of responsibility for character avoid the problem. As a response to the problem under discussion, this move is familiar from the debates over free will. On such an account, the actual genesis of one's character would be largely or entirely irrelevant to questions about responsibility. One might hold, for example, that one is responsible for one's character if and only if one had some particular kind of reflective pro attitude toward them. But here again it will be matter of constitutive luck whether one is equipped properly to do this sort of reflective thinking or whether one's efforts at it are irretrievably warped by the luck of one's upbringing or, indeed, one's temperament. Here as for the Kantian account of responsibility, it would seem that the only way to avoid this difficulty will be to endorse too strong a conception of the autonomy of some faculty, whether it be will or reflective thinking.

11. As I indicated above, it is important to recall that strength of will and endurance can sometimes compensate for defects of temperament. Thus perhaps it is possible that Grumpy may manage to develop and sustain a good moral character in spite of himself. At least, it may perhaps be possible for him to take up the ends of morally good character requires. In this case he may satisfy the requirements for responsibility, as I have presented them. He will satisfy condition (2) if he adopts these ends as a consequence of reasoned reflection, for example, since such reflection can reasonably be seen as an exercise of agency. To be sure, his character is not the product of the discriminating activity of a sympathetic temperament, but I do not claim that only such activity counts as an expression of agency.

Chapter 5

On the Old Saw That Character Is Destiny

Michele Moody-Adams

The notion of character is indispensable in certain explanatory contexts—as when we account for a person's unenthusiastic responses to another's success by concluding that he is envious. There is no immediately obvious sense in which such explanations are incompatible with the practice of holding people responsible. Yet some philosophers argue that the circumstances in which we develop and exercise character traits reveal important ways in which we lack control over our actions and thus present a challenge to the doctrine that people are responsible for their actions. Thomas Nagel defends the most well-known and most extreme version of this view. He argues, first, that a moral assessment of a person's character amounts to a condemnation, not just of the actions that the person performs, but of what that person is "really like." But such condemnation is problematic, he claims, because what one is *really* like is a matter of "constitutive luck": luck in "the kind of person you are, . . . your inclinations, capacities and temperament" and in the virtues and vices as "states of character that influence choice but are . . . not exhausted by dispositions to act deliberately in certain ways" (Nagel 1979a, 28, 32). Thus, even when moral assessments concern actions, the qualities of character that influence our choices are largely "beyond the control of the will" (Nagel 1979a, 33). Nagel concludes that if ascriptions of responsibility are to be reserved for those matters within a person's control, then we cannot consistently hold people responsible for what is due to constitutive luck.

In effect, Nagel has revived Novalis's maxim that character is destiny. Against this view I will defend the following intuition: part of being human is having the capacity to act out of character—even in spite of one's character—should doing the morally right thing, or any other circumstance, require this. It is in virtue of this human capacity to act out of character that we can be justified in holding people responsible for their actions. I thus concede the existence of constitutive luck—at least in the initial structure of character—but deny that it undermines responsibility. Nagel's claims to the contrary rest on misconceptions about the practice of character assessment and about the relation between this practice and ascriptions of responsibility. Sections 1 and 2 show how these misconceptions underwrite Nagel's scepticism and how recognizing these misconceptions leads to a better understanding of both character and responsibility. In section 3, I consider a narrower scepticism about the compatibility of character and responsibility—one that acknowledges the importance of a capacity to act out of character but attributes possession of that capacity to constitutive luck. I contend that any such argument must fail and that such arguments fail because the sceptic either ignores or misconstrues the only point of view from which we can understand the practice of holding people responsible: the point of view of the agent. In section 4, I offer an account of that point of view that shows that it is possible to understand what justifies holding people responsible in spite of their initial constitutive luck.

1 Restoring the Connection between Character and Behavior

One of Nagel's most puzzling claims about the relation between character and the practice of holding people responsible for their actions occurs in his discussion of the "ordinary conditions" under which we make judgments about moral responsibility. One of Nagel's recent aims has been to identify a phenomenon that he describes as "moral luck"—the phenomenon of holding people morally responsible for what is beyond their control (Nagel 1979a). Character is a particularly problematic source of moral luck, he claims, for a bad character trait need not be "displayed" in order to be the object of disapproval: "Even if one controls the impulse, one still has the vice. An envious person hates the greater success of others. He can be morally condemned as envious even if he congratulates them cordially and does nothing to denigrate or spoil their success" (Nagel 1979a, 33).

Now what is puzzling about this example is that it is not clear *how* Nagel, or anyone else for that matter, could know that such a person is envious. A person might be envious and successfully disguise that fact, but surely one who does not display envy may simply not *be* envious. A skillful interpreter of demeanor is sometimes able to detect clues suggesting an effort at dissimulation: the hint of a sneer or a limp handshake may suggest that someone's congratulations are insincere. Yet such clues are outward *displays* (even if unintentional) upon which to base our disapproval. Envy that is not displayed simply cannot be the object of the moral disapproval of others. One may condemn *oneself* for envy that goes undetected by others. However, Nagel offers this special case not as an example of self-condemnation but of the "ordinary" circumstances under which we hold people responsible for what they are like. The problem is that our practices simply don't work as Nagel claims. An omniscient narrator in a novel has unobstructed access to the private sentiments of the characters in that novel. Ordinary human beings have no direct access to the private sentiments of other human beings, nor do our moral practices require such access.

Nagel's peculiar understanding of our ordinary character assessments is important for two main reasons. First, some of his most sceptical claims about moral responsibility turn out to violate his own well-known strictures against assuming that a full grasp of the subjective point of view is possible from the "outside" (Nagel 1979b).[1] If the person in Nagel's example is really as good at dissimulation as Nagel's description suggests, then only an omniscient moral judge, not a real human observer, could disapprove of that person's envy.

In another important example Nagel claims, "Conceit, likewise, need not be displayed. It is fully present in someone who cannot help dwelling with secret satisfaction on the superiority of his own achievements, talents, beauty, intelligence or virtue" (Nagel 1979a, 33). Conceit may be "fully present in" a person, but if it is successfully disguised, it cannot be the object of any moral disapproval but his own. Further, only through the outward expression of character in behavior can one have access to what another is "really like." It is precisely because our character assessments must be based on external behavior that people can frustrate our expectations about character: the quiet family man can turn out to be a mass murderer, or the shy neighbor may actually write torrid novels under a pen name. Of course, we can confidently assume that much of what we conclude about the character of others is true, but dissimulation, dishonesty, and secrecy are permanent possibilities of human behavior.

These possibilities for deception and secrecy, malevolent as well as benign, are not just incidental curiosities of human behavior. They show that we must at least revise, if not reject, a common presupposition about the nature of moral assessments. Oliver Wendell Holmes succinctly expresses that presupposition as a difference between law and morality: morality is concerned with the "actual internal state of the individual's mind," he claims, while the law cares only about the "external signs" (Holmes 1959, 424–425). But in making moral assessments, the moral judge cannot claim *direct* access to "internal states" any more than can a jury or judge in a court of law.

To be sure, assessments of character commonly include reference to various "internal" goings-on, such as motives and intentions. It is also true that while we accept strict liability in the law—legal liability without fault—most of us would reject the notion of strict *moral* liability. But lacking omniscience, a moral judge, even in her guise as a judge of character, must take as *fundamental* a connection between what is "internal" and its expression in conduct. In practice, various character traits are closely associated with certain kinds of emotional responses and certain patterns of thought. A shy person may experience physiological distress in unfamiliar circumstances, a cowardly person may feel such distress in certain risky situations, and an envious person may feel nausea at the thought of another's success. But there is no single "internal" phenomenon associated with all instances of envy, shyness, or cowardice—not even for one human subject. Most important, in order to acquire and use the concepts of envy, cowardice, or shyness, I do not need to be assured that some particular internal happening is taking place "inside" the people I learn to describe as envious, cowardly, or shy.

Only in a given *context* will it be appropriate to describe a pattern of behavior as envy, for example. But when we learn to use a concept such as envy, part of what we acquire is a capacity to recognize the complex range of settings within which various patterns of behavior are appropriately described as envious. In a good judge of character this capacity is highly developed, but even a good judge of character can be fooled by one who is skillful at frustrating expectations about the typical connections between a setting and a pattern of behavior. Further, even first-person judgments about one's own character traits can reveal insufficient attention to commonly recognizable connections between a setting and a pattern of behavior; judgments of this sort typically point to the existence of self-deception. Such self-deception is a central concern of Sartre's *No Exit*, for example, in Garcin's refusal to admit his cowardice. Garcin is unwilling to accept that engaging in certain patterns of behavior *in certain circumstances* is sufficient to constitute a display of cowardice. Even from the first-person perspective we do not understand character-trait concepts by appeal to internal happenings.

Concepts like envy, cowardice and conceit can be understood on an analogy with concepts like pain. Wittgenstein contends that our acquisition and use of such concepts as pain both depend upon taking as fundamental a connection between our inner life and its outward expression in behavior. In my view, the same kind of claim can be made about the acquisition and use of the concepts bound up with the language of character. In denying the connection between character and its outward expression in behavior, Nagel severs the very connection that makes talk about the character of real human beings possible and intelligible. Moreover, Nagel's severance of this connection also helps to fuel the notion that there might be an incompatibility between character and responsibility. But it is simply not the case that people are held responsible for sentiments, or "impulses" to use Nagel's term, that they never display. Of course, there can be envy, for instance, without envious behavior, but the concept of envy is intelligible only when we take the connection between envy and envious behavior as fundamental. Thus the first prong of Nagel's sceptical argument that the phenomenon of character undermines our ascriptions of responsibility simply won't stand up. A moral assessment of what a person is *really like* cannot rightfully be detached from what a person *really does*.

2 Character and Language: The Figurative Turn

I have argued that we can have access to what another is really like only through the outward expression of character in behavior. But what is it that we "have access to" in such outward expressions? And what are we doing when we claim to be able to make (moral or nonmoral) judgments about character? While an answer to the question about the nature of our discourse about character cannot provide an exhaustive answer to the question about what character really is, it can nonetheless prevent some more serious misconceptions about what character is. For some of the most common misconceptions about character in philosophical and nonphilosophical contexts result from a perhaps inadvertent but distorting acquiescence in an etymological understanding of the word "character."

In its root sense, a character is a distinctive mark that has been impressed, stamped, or engraved on the thing so marked. It is in this sense that the letters printed on this page are characters. When we use an expression such as "a person's character," however, the language takes a figurative turn: we commonly intend to refer to an aggregate, or collection, of more or less *enduring* qualities or traits of a person. Hume uses "character" in this sense when he insists that actions are, "by their very nature, temporary and perishing" and that unless they flow from "some cause in the character and disposition of the person who performed them, they can neither redound to his honour if good, nor to his infamy, if evil" (Hume 1975a, 98). A somewhat narrower sense of "character" figures in some of our moral assessments: the sense in which one is said to "have character," to display fortitude or consistency in the pursuit of one's ends. Though a judgment that one has character is most often a judgment about the manner in which one acts rather than about the kinds of things one does, such judgments certainly figure in moral discussions (Peters 1966, 271). But it is the concept of a character (a collection of enduring traits, whatever our consistency in the pursuit of ends) that is more fundamental in our assessments.

Two misleading assumptions about the concepts of a person's character are rooted in the notion of a character as something stamped or impressed on the thing marked with the character. It is assumed, first, that the primary function of our discourse about the character of *persons* is to pick out things. A character is then thought to be a thing—or more precisely, a set of things—somehow picked out by the language of character traits. Second, the set of traits allegedly picked out by the language of character traits is assumed to be somehow "impressed" or "stamped" on the person described in the language of character traits. Those who construe the concept of character in this way seem to think that this understanding best captures the sense in which character traits are enduring qualities of persons. The fact that people develop and display consistent patterns of emotional response, thinking, and acting seems, at least initially, to be captured quite nicely by the root sense of "character."

But acquiescence in this understanding of the word "character" turns out to be problematic for any account of moral psychology. First, there are some obvious ontological puzzles associated with the notion that character traits are entities that somehow endure "in" the persons who "possess" them. It simply is not clear how character traits could endure or even what they might endure in. It is especially puzzling that even Hume, who never relinquished his suspicions about the concept of personal identity, acquiesces almost completely in the etymological understanding of the notion of character. Hume claims not only that actions that flow from character traits proceed from something "in" the person that is "durable and constant" but also that they leave something "of that nature behind them" (Hume 1975a, 98). Hume believes that unless actions can be thought to leave "something of their nature" within the agent, we'd have to assume that "a man is as pure and untainted, after having committed the most horrid crime, as at the first moment of his birth." Indeed, he ridicules defenses of contracausal freedom on this very basis (Hume 1975a, 98).[2] But Hume's view of character is no clearer than the contracausal view that one is free from determination by one's character traits. It is particularly unclear how we are to understand Hume's view, especially in light of his rejection of the notion of a distinct and continuously existing self.

A second shortcoming of this understanding of character traits concerns our understanding of moral agency. Nagel, for instance, writes as if character traits were not only enduring things but also *unrevisable* things. To "possess" vices such as conceit, envy, or cowardice, according to Nagel, "is to be unable to help having certain feelings under certain circumstances, and to have strong spontaneous impulses to act badly. Even if one controls the impulses, one still has the vice" (Nagel 1979a, 32–33). Characteristics such as cowardice, conceit, or envy, he continues, are essentially "beyond the control of the will" (Nagel 1979a, 33). But it is at least intuitively plausible that people can change or revise their characters, or at least certain of their character traits. Indeed, several philosophers have tried to develop this intuition by suggesting that reflective evaluation of one's characteristic patterns of emotion, thought, and action may enable one to revise, even to relinquish, some of these characteristic patterns (Frankfurt 1971, Watson 1975, Taylor 1976). These analyses even suggest that the capacity to engage in reflective evaluation of one's "brute" desires, ends, inclinations, and traits is central to the concept of responsible agency.[3] Nagel accepts the possibility that one might control the tendency to act on some of the relevant feelings or emotions. One must then wonder why he assumes, without argument, that one cannot also control, revise, or even relinquish some of the "impulses" or emotions themselves.

More important, it is not clear why one would think that people "possess" character traits or that these traits "endure" in persons as entities, since the language of character assessment does not function primarily to pick out things of *any* kind. Statements concerning character traits are fundamentally elaborate inductive hypotheses rooted in the observation of patterns of behavior, and of the circumstances in which such behavior is displayed. In practice, claims about character are meant to be much more than inductive hypotheses—and of course, they are. We commonly intend such judgments as assessments of what people are like—not just of what they do. But I have shown that we go astray when we try to detach talk about what people are "really like" from what they really do. We are likewise misled when we ignore the varied ways in which statements about character traits embody elaborate inductive hypotheses based on the observation of behavior.

Some of these hypotheses are second- and third-person judgments embodying backward-looking generalizations about behavior. Moreover, experience constantly provides grounds for generally reliable claims of this sort. For instance, one who has repeatedly refused to stand up for causes he purports to think worth fighting for is justifiably described as a coward, barring unusual facts about circumstances. Further, such generalizations have an important place in a wide range of practices of assigning praise and blame, as, for instance, when they are used to assess the reliability of some accusation of wrongdoing. A character witness in a criminal trial may testify to the incompatibility of the accused's character with the offense he is alleged to have committed. Or a parent may appeal to character to express a conviction of a child's innocence: "He's a good boy. He wouldn't do such a thing." Such an appeal may simply express scepticism about the correctness of some attribution of physical agency; one may believe that even if *some* student broke a window, "It couldn't have been my Johnny." Or the appeal may be an elliptical expression of one's belief that even if physical agency can be established, the circumstances in which the person acted must surely excuse him from responsibility. But even when we make claims about the character of someone we know well, we can be wrong. Like all inductive generalizations, a judgment based on well-founded beliefs about character is not an infallible guide to what actually happened.

We also make primarily forward-looking uses of the language of character traits (in both second- and third-person judgments). We come to expect people to behave in ways consistent with their behavior in the past—and, of course, they often do. A friend's past generosity, especially when it has been extended without question and in difficult circumstances, makes it rational to expect that friend to be generous in the future. Moreover, as Hume skillfully argued, human beings in communities have so great a "mutual dependence" that the general reliability of human beings is central to survival (1975a, 89). Character is manifested in behavior as a more or less harmonious set of consistent patterns of behavior, and only on the basis of such patterns can we rationally plan our actions and interactions with others. But once again, even the most reliable beliefs about character are not infallible guides to what people will actually do.

I am going to argue that when we do make mistakes in prediction, those mistakes often reveal that people are sometimes capable of acting *out of character*. Moreover, the mere possibility of action that is out of character strongly suggests that character traits are *not* necessary determinants of action. But it has been argued that the fact that behavior sometimes frustrates expectations need not call into question the existence of necessary connections between character and action. According to Hume, for instance, "The most irregular and unexpected resolutions of men may frequently be accounted for by those, who know every particular circumstance of their character and situation. A person of an obliging disposition gives a peevish answer: But he has the toothache, or has not dined. A stupid fellow discovers an uncommon alacrity in his carriage: But he has met with a sudden piece of good fortune" (1975a, 88). Hume thus insists that we often deny any necessary connection between character and action when we simply don't know enough about the *circumstances* in which certain traits are likely to produce particular actions. Some actions appear resistant to this explanation, Hume acknowledges, though he thinks that he can explain them without relinquishing his theory: "Even when an action, as sometimes happens, cannot be particularly accounted for, either by the person himself or by others: we know, in general that the characters of men are to a certain degree, inconstant and irregular. This is in a manner the constant character of human nature" (1975a, 88). But Hume simply assumes that there are no significant "irregularities" in the realm of human behavior—claiming, with characteristic irony, that it is "the constant character" of human nature to be "to a certain degree, inconstant and irregular." Indeed, Hume's irony seems to be an attempt to mask his own sense that the explanatory role of the notion of character is limited. Further, he simply assumes that only when someone acts without any motive at all will an action even seem capable of undermining the claim of a necessary connection between character and action. Finally, as we have seen, he contends that it is unintelligible to hold a person responsible for an "action" of this sort; one cannot be "answerable" for an action, he believes, unless it proceeds from something "durable and constant" in the person. One cannot, in Hume's view, be responsible for an action that is out of character.

But if Hume is right, when a characteristically bad person does something good—say an extremely envious person triumphs over envy to offer cordial congratulations to a colleague—such behavior can't, in Humean terms, "redound to his honour," because he could not be held responsible for it. Or when a characteristically good person does something bad, on Hume's view, we cannot hold that person responsible for the action. But this is just implausible. Some central elements of moral practice, as well as of the nonmoral judgments we make about action, would be wholly unintelligible unless it made sense to hold people responsible for action that is out of character. Hume thinks that we can hold people responsible for only those actions that flow from character. That is, far from undermining our practices of holding people responsible, the concept of character, in Hume's view, is essential to the concept of responsibility.

But Hume fails to recognize an important *asymmetry* between judgments about character and ascriptions of responsibility. For ascriptions of responsibility are independent of judgments of character, even though judgments of character are dependent upon ascriptions of responsibility. A schoolboy with a previously spotless record, for instance, is no less responsible for breaking the school window than if he had been a consistent troublemaker. One can be responsible for actions that are out of character because responsible action need not reveal enduring character traits. Moreover, only if it is intelligible to hold people responsible for even just *one* action that is out of character can we make sense of the notion that a person's character can change. The schoolboy with the previously spotless record can become a troublemaker: a series of actions destructive of school property, for instance, would certainly suggest that such a change had taken place. But we can make such an assessment only if we can sensibly hold the young man responsible for the very *first* action in the series of destructive actions. We can understand the phenomenon of character change, that is, only if we accept that action that is out of character can be responsible action.

Ironically, despite the fact that Hume and Nagel come to diametrically opposed conclusions about the relation between character and responsibility, they both ignore this assymetry in the relation between assessments of character and assessments of responsibility. Nagel thinks, in contrast to Hume, that the phenomenon of character undermines the practice of holding people responsible for their actions. But while ascriptions of responsibility are conceptually independent of judgments of character, judgments of character are parasitic upon judgments of responsibility. That is, assessments of character are intelligible only as assessments of behavior—behavior that must first be intelligible as *responsible* action. The person who unknowingly purchases a bottle of aspirin that has been poisoned by a disgruntled employee of the manufacturer is surely not responsible for harm caused when she administers that medicine to a loved one. But neither could her action be taken to reveal any malevolent character traits. Only those actions for which one is responsible can be taken to reveal one's character. Nagel thus gets things the wrong way round. The phenomenon of character *doesn't* undermine the practice of holding people responsible; the practice of making assessments of character is undermined if we are unable justly to hold people responsible for their actions.

Moreover, Nagel, like Hume, virtually dismisses action that is out of character. He is likewise unable to recognize the relevance of this capacity to understanding the phenomenon of character change: he insists that character traits are essentially "beyond the control of the will." But the failure to appreciate the importance of the capacity to act out of character makes him equally unable to appreciate the very phenomenon capable of justifying our ascriptions of responsibility. The human capacity to act out of character justifies holding people responsible for their actions—whatever their constitutive luck. Once we reject the view that character assessments refer to enduring *entities* in the person that necessarily determine behavior, it becomes possible to see that the capacity to act out of character is a crucial feature of human psychology.

3 Constitutive Misfortune and Acting in Character

A skeptical response to my claims about character might argue that persons capable of acting out of character possess abilities that are themsevles a matter of constitutive good luck. It seems that only someone capable of taking an evaluative stance on his character is capable of breaking out of characteristic patterns of emotion, thought, and action. The ability to survey one's character from such an evaluative stance seems to require the ability to conclude that some of one's character traits are in need of revision and correction, that they are bad in themselves or likely to incline one toward wrongdoing. This ability, in turn, seems to presuppose the capacity to know right from wrong. The skeptic may charge that this ability is altogether too subject to constitutive luck.

Susan Wolf has recently defended such a view, arguing that some people never receive the sort of upbringing that could provide them with the "resources and reasons on which to base self-correction" (Wolf 1987, 58). The principal such resource, she argues, is the ability "to know right from wrong," and some people are "victims" of the sort of constitutive bad luck that deprives them of the ability. She identifies two classes of such victims. First, one may be a victim of an upbringing that renders one completely unable to avoid or revise deeply rooted ideals and convictions that consistently incline one toward serious moral violations. An abused child who grows up to commit violent crimes is an example of such a victim. Second, one may have lived in a society that "actively encouraged" mistaken values in such a way that one is rendered unable to know right from wrong relative to one part of one's character. In this group Wolf includes slave owners of the American south and Nazis in Germany of the 1930s (1987, 56–57).

But what might it mean to describe someone as a victim, and what connection might there be between someone's status as a victim and the question of that person's responsibility for wrongdoing? Deciding *what* a victim is seems fairly straightforward: a victim is someone

who suffers from some affliction or hardship due to human malevolence or neglect or to accidents of nature and disease. A victim is
also someone likely to need help, treatment, or protection, or sometimes simply to have the effects of her suffering treated seriously and
sympathetically. But deciding *who* is a victim is a difficult matter.
Wolf's account of victims of "misguided societies" is especially problematic. History reveals not only that these "victims" engaged in, or
actively supported, grievous wrongdoing but also that they actively
refused to entertain challenges to the morality of the contested actions. These refusals often extended to enacting or supporting legal
(and extralegal) meausures designed to suppress protest. Far from
providing evidence of an inability to know right from wrong, such
behavior suggests an unwillingness to entertain the possibility that
one might be wrong. To view as "victims" people who thus resist
scrutiny of entrenched convictions is barely plausible.[4] Indeed, if we
call a slave owner or Nazi a victim, then what are we to call the slave
or the concentration-camp inmate?

More convincing is Wolf's suggestion that people can be victims
of severely deprived or abusive childhoods. We are all familiar with
stories of the brutal crime committed by someone who turns out to
have had such a childhood and whose circumstances lead us to want
to suspend—even if only temporarily—our ordinary moral responses
to brutality.[5] But the status of such people as victims is not necessarily
relevant to assessments of their capacity to be responsible for their
actions. Though there is a connection between some kinds of character traits and difficult circumstances, similar (or even worse) circumstances may produce people not similarly possessed of bad
characters; there is no necessary connection between certain kinds
of circumstances and certain kinds of characters. Of course, the theorist of constitutive luck will say that the capacity *not* to emerge from
desperate circumstances with a profoundly bad character is itself a
function of constitutive luck (perhaps some "natural" temperamental
differences account for different responses to circumstances). Yet
even if one can be a victim of a deprived or abusive upbringing or
even of one's natural temperament, there remains the question of
the relevance of such facts to determinations of responsibility.

Sometimes, of course, the fact that one is a victim is quite clearly
relevant to concerns about responsibility and blame. In the case of
self-defense, in fact, one's status as a victim is thought by many to
justify (not simply to excuse) making a victim of another. At the very
least, most of us (except for the extreme pacifist) would agree that a
victim of violence who acts in self-defense against her attacker *and
with force appropriate to the circumstances* is not morally blameworthy

for any resulting harm to the attacker. In cases of self-defense we take the harm to have been required in order to prevent further victimization at the hands of one's attacker at the time of the attack. But only in such circumstances can the use of potentially harmful force against another bear a defensible and recognizable connection to alleviating one's status as a victim.

Quite a different connection almost invariably holds between the status of those offenders plausibly viewed as victims of their upbringing and the offenses they commit. In particular, the people who become victims of some manifestation of the bad character traits of such offenders are seldom the same people who were responsible for their abuse or deprivation. Moreover, in the case of people affected by severe economic or social deprivation, it is seldom clear how we could make an intelligible assessment of responsibility for the deprivation. Some cases of wrongdoing on the part of abused or deprived offenders may well be intelligible as manifestations of extreme anger or even despair *at their status as victims*. Moreover, the desperate circumstances in which some people must grow up may sometimes even justify their anger or despair. But anger and despair can be misdirected or simply vented in frustration with no particular direction at all. When the expression in behavior of (even justifiable) anger or despair bears no defensible and recognizable connection to actually alleviating one's status as a victim, one's status as a victim cannot excuse the wrongdoing. It may be unreasonable for us not to *mitigate* our ordinary moral responses once we understand that someone has been a victim of his childhood—much as we forgive a friend for being short-tempered when she suffers from severe toothache. Yet just as the fact that a friend is a victim of (presumably) undeserved pain cannot in itself excuse an angry outburst, the fact that one is a victim of an undeservedly desperate upbringing does not in itself excuse one from responsibility for one's actions. Appropriately mitigating our ordinary moral responses to offenses committed by victims of this sort involves extending mercy or forgiveness—not suggesting that no blameworthy offense was ever committed.

Further, even if one is a victim of one's upbringing, character traits simply do not necessitate action. The envious man who tries to sabotage the work of his recently promoted colleague may be powerfully drawn to the action, but a powerful impulse is not an irresistible impulse. As Feinberg has argued, "The psychological situation is never—or hardly ever—like that of the man who hangs from a windowsill by his fingernails until the sheer physical force of gravity rips his nails off and sends him plummeting to the ground" (1970a, 283). I would second Feinberg's concession (p. 284) that some desires may be so difficult to resist, given the circumstances of the agent, that it would be unreasonable to expect a person experiencing such desires in certain situations to resist them. A person who has been lost in the desert for several days will surely experience her thirst as overwhelming. But we have no reason to think that any of the emotional responses associated with a given character trait are phenomenologically like the thirst of a severely dehydrated person. Moreover, should this severely dehydrated person emerge from the desert and break into the first house she sees in an effort to quench her thirst, it is reasonable to forgive or to show mercy—not to deny that any offense was committed.

Still further, if the status of the victim of the deprived childhood is *in itself* an excuse, what is the proper moral response toward those who are harmed by a deprived or abused offender? Surely those whom they might harm are victims in a very different sense. More important, in many instances victims of deprived childhoods harm others whose childhoods (even whose current circumstances) may have been as bad as, or even worse than, their own. While this consideration does not show that the formative experiences of the offender are irrelevant to our judgments of responsibility, it should certainly give us pause.

But most important, we must reflect on the peculiar consequences of an assertion that the *way* in which someone is a victim is manifested in that person's character. What is peculiar about such an assertion can be understood by contrasting it with an assertion that initially appears to be similar. We describe people as victims of mental illness and think of mental illness as a class of afflictions manifested in the kinds of things a person does (as well as thinks and feels). Further, mental illness is often thought relevant to the question of responsibility, usually when it is believed to cause certain kinds of ignorance or (more controversially) to exert a kind of "irresistible" control over behavior. But mental illness disrupts one's normal patterns of functioning: it manifests itself in what one *does* (and often in what one thinks and feels) rather than in what one *is*. To describe someone's *character* as an affliction is to make a very different sort of claim. It is a claim that one's affliction manifests itself in one's characteristic patterns of functioning—not just in the kinds of things one does but *in the kind of person one is*. This is an extraordinary claim to make about another human being, particularly when combined with the claim that one's "affliction" is very likely incurable. It is a short step from this to the claim that the only thing that those not similarly afflicted can do with such a person is to try to treat, control, restrain, or perhaps simply tolerate him. To take this sort of attitude toward someone is to see him as no longer fully human.[6] To my mind, the consequences of such a view lend support to the Kantian intuition that (except for well-defined excuses like coercion and lack of knowledge) to exempt someone from responsibility and blame for wrongdoing is simply to deny that person's humanity.

This Kantian intuition looks even more plausible when we note an indefensible circularity in Wolf's argument. Wolf uses the fact of wrongdoing to try to prove the alleged inability to do otherwise, but then she attempts to explain (and excuse) the wrongdoing in terms of the inability. Without some evidence of an inability to avoid wrongdoing that is *independent* of the wrongdoing itself, Wolf's claim is simply unconvincing.[7] Moreover, she offers no reason for thinking that all cases of wrongdoing shouldn't be explained in terms of the same inability. That is, the logic of her account tends irresistibly toward Nagel's view of the matter: that *all* wrongdoers are victims of constitutive bad luck and that it is not clear how we can justify holding *any* wrongdoers responsible for their offenses (Nagel 1979a). Surprisingly, if we *reject* her reliance on the notion of constitutive luck, we can better understand why the wrongdoing in question seems to be in need of special explanation. The alleged victims of misguided societies seem to have actively feared and avoided self-reflection of the likelihood that it would undermine the contested values. Victims of abusive or deprived childhoods, in contrast, seem to fear and avoid self-reflection because it tends to intensify awareness of profoundly unhappy or desperate circumstances. Wolf is right to call attention to the lack of self-reflection in these cases, but in neither case can she show that such people lack the fundamental human capacity for self-reflection and self-correction.

To be sure, no evidence accessible to an observer "from the outside"—to adopt a phrase of Nagel's—could prove that the people whom Wolf describes actually do possess the abilities which justify us in holding them responsible for their wrongdoing. But that is a function of the fact that we ascribe responsibility on the basis of considerations accessible to us only from a very special perspective on persons and their behavior: the point of view of the agent. Looking at some action from the point of view of the agent does not require that we understand all that went on in the mind of an agent prior to action. The point is, rather, that in order to understand some happening as an action, not simply as an event, it must be reasonable to view that "happening" as the product of motives, intentions, or sentiments. But in asking what motives or intentions might have produced an action, we implicitly try to understand how things might have looked to an *agent*; that is, we look at the initiation of action "from the inside."[8] But Wolf's view requires that those whom she describes as victims take an unacceptable perspective on themselves. That is, her view requires them to acquiesce in a picture of themselves as incapable of self-evaluation and self-correction—as ultimately incapable of change. They would have to see themselves as susceptible of being acted upon but as unable to initiate self-corrective action, or even any real action at all. But for any agent, this would be an unacceptable self-conception. In fact, it would be a form of self-deception. I will develop the appropriate understanding of the first-person perspective on agency in the final section. At the very least, we already know that first-person uses of the language of character traits—just like the second- and third-person uses—do not commit one to viewing one's own traits as unrevisable and irresistible determinants of action.

4 *Understanding Action from the "Inside"*

We hold people responsible from what Nagel aptly labels the "internal perspective" on persons and their behavior: a perspective from which we try to see action from the "inside," to assess the merits of alternatives open to the agent as well as the merits of the choice itself. Of course, Nagel also thinks that when we consider the ways in which alternatives can be *in*accessible to the agent (including by virtue of the agent's character), we take up an external perspective on action that gradually excludes the internal perspective altogether. When this happens, he contends, we can no longer view the person as a responsible agent but must view him as merely "part of the world" (Nagel 1986, 120). In the remaining pages I will sketch an account of the internal perspective—of what it means to view action from the inside—that shows why we must reject Nagel's scepticism. While so brief an account cannot yield an exhaustive justification of our practices of holding people responsible, it does develop a central line of argument presupposed by any such justification.

First of all, although Nagel's scepticism requires a sharp boundary between the internal and external perspectives, seeing action from the inside simply does not exclude the external perspective, not even for the agent herself. In fact, the coherence of an agent's perspective on herself *as* an agent requires the compatibility of the internal and external perspectives. We are, after all, agents *in* the world. The vocabulary in which one learns to give expression to one's inner life and that shapes one's understanding of that inner life is a product of circumstances "external" to the agent: the linguistic conventions of the community. This fact, as I have shown, affects an agent's effort to understand how her own past behavior reveals her character. Self-understanding is thus dependent upon the compatibility of the internal and the external perspective on persons. Moreover, the nature of self-understanding is a function of the fact that the point of view of the agent takes shape largely with reference to circumstances external to the agent herself.

Second, the compatibility of the internal and external perspectives is crucial to the possibility of responsible agency itself. Constructive human purposes, unlike the constructive purposes of other species, are not given in any instinctual equipment. We can see this quite clearly when we reflect upon the distinctive feature of children "raised" in the wild by nonhuman animals or upon certain forms of autism (in which a child appears to be radically resistant to stimuli from social interaction). Radical social withdrawal, or the total absence of substantial interaction with other human beings, clearly hinders one's ability to form and pursue constructive human purposes and ends. I do not intend to deny that either the "wild child" or the autistic child has any ends. Rather, I contend that the sorts of ends likely to lead to the fullest development and enjoyment of human potential are beyond the reach of human beings deprived of social interaction. Thus many of our constitutive ideals and purposes, in so far as we develop them, will be unavoidably shaped by social interaction. Moreover, it is only because social interaction helps shape a character that human beings are capable of choice at all. For the formative experiences that tend to produce a certain kind of character also provide the parameters within which we can make meaningful choices. After all, if we never had any means of construing a problem of choice as being a selection from among a finite set of alternatives, we would never learn how to make choices at all. More important, with limited knowledge, finite memory, and a finite capacity for calculation, a person is just the kind of being who could never choose at all but for the fact that our constitutive ends preselect ways of framing problems of choice. Of course, we commonly encounter situations in which the parameters set down by our formative experiences prove unhelpful or inadequate. This, on my view, is when the capacity to act out of character comes into play. But the *initial* circumscription of alternatives (by means of formative experiences) is a condition of the possibility of responsible agency.

Now this claim might seem to play into the hands of the sceptic. I have conceded that many of an agent's constitutive ends and purposes are a function of circumstances not of her own choosing and that these circumstances help shape her understanding of what is even a possible alternative for her in many situations that require the exercise of choice. But similar limitations on alternatives are thought relevant to the question of responsibility. It is because circumstances such as ignorance of relevant facts or external coercion limit one's access to certain alternatives that they can thereby defeat attributions of responsibility. Why, then, the sceptic will ask, ought we to think any differently about the processes through which we become the kinds of people we are if they too limit access to alternatives in situations requiring choice? Yet there is an important difference between lack of knowledge or coercion, on one hand, and having one's constitutive ends shaped by formative experiences, on the other. In the case of lack of knowledge or coercion, the limitations on available alternatives cannot be overcome merely by changing oneself; in the case of the influence of character and the like, such limitations *can* be overcome by means of self-evaluation and self-correction. Sceptical resistance to my claim rests upon some serious misconceptions about the ways in which self-correction works.

The most common misconception arises primarily from within the internal perspective on action even before it is taken up into the sceptical view about responsibility. When an agent views action from the inside, it is all too easy to confuse the *difficulty* of altering, revising, or resisting characteristic patterns of behavior with an *inability* to do so. To be sure, this confusion has a perfectly intelligible explanation. For first of all, self-reflection is itself a complex phenomenon. Neurath's image of the mariner who must repair his vessel while at the same time staying afloat on the open sea is an instructive emblem of the process of self-reflection: because the evaluating self is always constituted, at least partly, by the ends and purposes under evaluation, one can examine one's constitutive ends only a plank at a time, so to speak. Secondly, a character is an interlocking set of relatively consistent patterns of thought, emotion, and action that develops and persists because of the role it plays in sustaining one in a way of life. Thus even when some aspect of a way of life proves detrimental to the person living that life, that person will find it difficult to relinquish even undesirable character traits if they help to sustain a settled existence. In such circumstances, the desires associated with any character trait one wishes to alter will seem recalcitrant. As some commentators suggest, these desires may even seem to the agent to be an alien power, some force other than his own, that seems to operate in opposition to resolutions of will (Frankfurt 1971, Fingarette 1988).

But the phenomenology of such experience does not show character traits to be beyond the agent's control. Rather, it reveals that self-correction is never simply a matter of resolving "once and for all" to be different. Changing an entrenched character trait requires a consistent *series* of efforts to avoid doing, feeling, or believing the things one characteristically does. It requires, in effect, an effort to revise a way of life. Revising a way of life is so difficult because one often needs the assistance of others in changing the *circumstances* that gave rise to the recalcitrant character trait. Indeed, one may sometimes need assistance even to recognize that one's traits help to sustain one in a way of life that is destructive. Once again, the compatibility of the internal and external perspectives proves to be indispensable to self-reflection. Character traits seem to be "beyond the control of the will," to adopt Nagel's phrase, only when we misunderstand what it means to attempt to change one's character. The sceptic incorrectly thinks that character change must be a kind of *conversion*. But for most of us, resolving to be different is not strictly a single "act of willing" to be different. It requires a series of attempts (over time) to think, feel, and act differently: one must take every occasion in which one would normally display a character trait as an occasion for understanding that one can now—on this occasion—act out of character, whatever one has done before.

To view oneself as incapable of acting on this understanding is to take a perspective on oneself that is ultimately incompatible with seeing action from the inside. Of course, it may be possible to see oneself as *nothing but* a "part of the world." Yet to do so is incompatible with respecting one's own worth, indeed one's very status, as a person. It is to see oneself as a thing—susceptible of being acted upon but incapable of action. A wrongdoer who acquiesces in the doctrine that he is a victim of constitutive bad luck internalizes the psychology of victimization; he will eventually *believe* that he can "diagnose" the symptoms of such an affliction in himself.[9] But to accept this view of oneself is to participate in one's own victimization. Ultimately, we cannot give up the practice of holding ourselves and others responsible, even if we cannot prove the existence of the capacity to act out of character from outside the internal perspective. Surprisingly, Nagel himself argues that important facts about what it is like *to be* a being of a certain kind can neither be described nor understood from a perspective that attempts to abandon altogether that being's "point of view." Indeed, he chides philosophers of mind for being tempted to deny the reality or the significance of such facts about persons (Nagel 1979b). Yet he mounts a sceptical challenge to the reality of a fact about *persons* (their capacity for responsible agency) from a perspective that totally abandons their point of view on action (the external perspective). But as Kant once suggested, we do not need to prove the capacity for responsible agency from the external perspective on human beings.[10] It is sufficient to show that we are the kind of beings who cannot act—or even conceive of ourselves as agents and persons—except when we believe that our characters do not contain our destinies.

Notes

1. By "subjective" here I mean something like from the point of view of the *individual* human being. Nagel also *uses* "subjective" to mean peculiar to all beings of a certain species or kind.

2. In his *Religion within the Limits of Reason Alone,* Kant insisted that we can hold the characteristically evil person responsible for his actions because at the moment of action it is *"as though"* the agent had stepped from a state of innocence into evil (1960a, 36). The presence of the phrase "as though" seems to render this passage from Kant immune from Hume's criticism.

3. In section 3 of this chapter I consider skepticism about the claim that one's capacity for reflective self-evaluation could be immune to luck.

4. For a somewhat different account of the blameworthiness of such persons, see Adams 1985, pp. 18–19. I do not claim to have *proved* that there is unwillingness at stake here rather than inability. But I show below that the attempt to prove that there is an inability is inherently circular. Even worse, it collapses into the stronger claim that all wrongdoers (indeed, all persons) are victims of constitutive bad luck. This leaves us with no reason to treat Nazis as any more blameworthy than their victims. The only way out of this impasse is to reject the argument that constitutive luck has anything like the import some theorists want to attach to it.

5. Gary Watson offers an illuminating and challenging discussion of such a case in Watson 1987a, pp. 268–277.

6. P. F. Strawson discusses the "moral reactive attitudes" and the circumstances in whch we are prone to suspend them in Strawson 1962.

7. The circularity problem is equally detrimental to Wolf's claim that the alleged inability constitutes a form of mental illness. I have treated the theory of constitutive bad fortune as *separable* from the claim of insanity—a claim actually referred to in the title of Wolf's 1987 article. My construal of the separateness of these two theses is justified by Wolf's own discussion. Wolf shows, implicitly, that she takes the theses to be separable when she argues that though Nazis and slave owners are victims of misguided societies, we can't intelligibly label them as *insane* (Wolf 1987, 57).

8. No justification of the practice of holding human beings responsible for their actions (and for themselves) is ultimately defensible unless the notion of an internal perspective on action (the perspective of the agent) can be made intelligible. More precisely, no justification bound up with a moral theory (addressed to persons whose behavior the theory aims to influence) can resist my claim about the importance of the internal perspective to our practice of holding people responsible. We treat persons as responsible for actions in a very different sense from that in which we treat hurricanes, earthquakes, or any other nonhuman force as "responsible for" damage. Among other things, this is because earthquakes, hurricanes, and so forth have no "point of view" on the harm they cause.

9. Berger and Luckmann (1966) have argued that when a psychology becomes "socially established, . . . it tends to realize itself forcefully in the phenomena it purports to interpret" (p. 178): "The rural Haitian who internalizes Voudun psy-

chology will become possessed as soon as he discovers certain well-defined signs. Similarly, the New York intellectual who internalizes Freudian psychology will become neurotic as soon as he diagnoses certain well-defined symptoms" (p. 179). Their claims about the central place of psychological theories in shaping the reality they purport to explain seems to be borne out by current experience. With the popular ascendancy of the psychology of addiction, all sorts of people who would once have described themselves as people who did potentially destructive things *to excess* (from sports stars engaged in extramarital affairs to people who consume too much chocolate) now describe themselves as *addicts*.

10. In the *Groundwork* (1964a) Kant insists that even if the problem of "having to prove freedom from a theoretical point of view" remained "unsettled, the same laws as would bind a being who was really free are equally valid for a being who cannot act except under the Idea of his own Freedom" (pp. 164, 116 n.).

Chapter 6

Hume and Moral Emotions

Marcia Lind

1 Introduction

In order to understand the role that emotions ought or ought not to play in moral theory, we must have an adequate idea of what an emotion is. In particular, we must do away with the idea that emotions consist entirely in feelings. On the view of emotion as a complex—as consisting in more than just feelings—it is possible to respond to the objection that allowing emotions to play an important role in a moral theory necessarily leads to a radically subjective moral theory.

In this paper I use David Hume's moral theory to begin working through the idea that analyzing emotion as a complex is indeed one way to avoid charges of radical subjectivity. I focus on Hume because his work represents a major investigation—and, I believe, still an underappreciated one (see, however, e.g. Baier, 1985b)—into emotions and their importance in moral theory. I am doing this because I believe that philosophers who claim that emotions cannot form an adequate grounding for moral theory are often working with a crude, simple view of emotion and that only once that view is changed will we be able to properly investigate the role emotions ought to have (Williams 1976a, de Sousa 1987).

Following the general line of thought laid out by philosophers such as Donald Davidson (1976) and to a more limited extent Pall Ardal (1966), I argue that emotion in Hume can be analyzed as a complex.[1] Most important for my ends in this essay, I focus on the "natural" connections that hold between the components of emotions. I then apply this particular idea of emotion as a complex to *moral* emotion in Hume and show that this analysis allows Hume to avoid at least the standard objection that he is committed to a radically subjective moral theory.

2 *The Received View about Hume on Emotions*

The standard atomist interpretation (Kenny 1963, Gardiner 1963, Foot 1978b) claims that for Hume, emotions consist only and entirely in feelings. Anthony Kenny, for example, argued that Hume believed that although passions have objects and causes, these objects and causes are not analytically connected to the passions (that is, in Humean language, through any kind of "relation of ideas"). Rather, the connection is only a causal one. It is therefore, Kenny argued, only a contingent connection, and thus the objects and causes of an emotion are not in any sense constitutive of the emotion.

Kenny's view was very influential. Following him, Patrick Gardiner and Phillipa Foot also interpreted passions in Hume's theory as consisting entirely in their feeling component. And as in Kenny's interpretation, Foot and Gardiner also claimed that this component was causally and therefore contingently connected to the object of the emotion.

Further, Kenny, Gardiner, and Foot all believed this (supposedly) Humean view of the passions was wrong. For passions, they argued, have an intentional structure, which could not possibly be captured by this Humean schema. Foot, for example, said that Hume was trying "to identify an action or quality [as] virtuous in terms of a special feeling" (1978b, 76). And her complaint about this, which was echoed by the others, is that "a feeling of pride . . . requires a special kind of thought about the thing of which one feels proud" (p. 76).

This reading has thus seen Hume as entirely missing the cognitive elements in an emotion, as entirely missing any thought involved. The emotion consists entirely in an atom of feeling. This view of emotion as an atom of feeling has problems making sense of parts— I believe important parts—of Hume's text.

The received view goes even further, telling us that Hume's view of emotion as an atom of feeling necessarily yields a (problematic) subjective moral theory. Phillipa Foot, for example, says that "this theory of Hume's about moral sentiment commits him to a subjective theory of ethics. He could not consistently maintain both that a man calls qualities virtues when he happens to feel towards them this peculiar sentiment, and that statements of virtue and vice are objective" (p. 77).

Since Hume has denied all logical connections—all connections of meaning—between moral approval and the objects of moral approval and would have to allow anyone to assert any kind of action at all to be virtuous on the strength of the supposed feeling of approbation, it follows that no one could get at an opponent who professed weird "moral views" (p. 77).

But claims that Hume's moral theory is radically subjective will, as we will see, run into difficulties with portions of Hume's text.

One important implication of the atomist view is apparent above. Foot claims that since emotions are atoms of feeling only contingently connected to their object and cause, it follows that we can have no (evaluative) standards for when something is the correct or incorrect object or cause of the emotion.

Hume does say the sorts of things the atomists attribute to him. But as others have noted (e.g., Davidson 1976), he also makes other claims that seem incompatible with the atomist interpretation, claims that seem at least to be telling us that he thought that the connection between, for example, the object and cause of an emotion was a very tight one and that there are evaluative standards for correct and incorrect objects and causes of emotions. Look at a passage like the following: "I find that the peculiar object of pride and humility is determined by an original and natural instinct, and that tis *absolutely impossible*, from the primary constitution of the mind, that these passions should ever look beyond self" (Hume 1978, 286). This passage certainly seems to be saying that there is some sort of very close connection between the emotion and its object and that for it not to hold would be at least very odd.

And if Hume were really a radical subjectivist about morals—or if, as Foot goes on to say, Hume "accepts this subjectivism with ease and even with relish," would we find him saying of Timon of Athens, when Timon is approving with what seems to be moral approval of enormous destruction and pain for many people, that Timon had "perverted" his "natural sentiment of humanity" (Hume 1957a, 53–54)? One would think a philosopher committed to subjectivism "with relish" would not be saying quite these sorts of things.

What is going on in these passages? What's wrong with the received interpretation? I believe that many things are wrong with the standard reading, but I want to focus on only one: emotions for Hume seem not to be the atoms of pure phenomenological feeling that the standard interpretation insists on but something much more complicated—parts that are somehow "glued" together in such a way that they are not one atom (that is, the parts are analytically connected) nor are they two or three atoms with only the weakest of contingent connections. Further, there does seem to be a reading on which Hume could have evaluative standards—a way to talk about appropriate and inappropriate parts for an emotion—while still believing the connection between the parts to be contingent. I will argue that one sort of connection that is a contingent connection, what Hume (1978, 280–281) calls a "natural" as opposed to a "capricious" connection, will allow us to understand how he can have a view of emotion other than the one standardly attributed to him. I will call this other view of emotion the view of *emotion as complex.*

But I will have to explain what Hume thought emotions were so that we can read Hume in a way that can yield an account of emotion other than the standard one, can avoid the claims of radical subjectivity commonly attributed to him, and in addition can explain the peculiar passages just cited, passages that tell us that it is "impossible" that pride, for example, not have self as its object and that it is "perverted" for Timon to have moral approbation in regard to enormous destruction and pain. In particular, I will have to explain the crucial role the idea of the natural plays in his analysis. What is this notion of natural?

3 Natural

In the seventeenth- and eighteenth-century theological tradition that had great influence on Hume (Burton 1846, vol. 1, p. 114), what was natural was normative in that what was natural was correct because God wanted us to do these things. We find Bishop Butler, for example, saying, "If the real Nature of any creature (that is, what is really natural to that creature) leads him and is adapted to such and such purposes only, more than any other, then this is a reason to believe that the author of that Nature intended it for those purposes" (Butler 1950, sermon 2, section 211).

One way to think of what Hume wanted to do—his project (Lind 1987)—was to detheologize the natural, that is, to keep the normative power of the natural but to do it without God.[2] For Hume too uses the notion of natural as normative. In various forms we find him saying, for example, that what is natural is correct. One of the clearest cases of this is where, as we just saw, he says that something not natural—a particular set of associations—is "perverted." What does "natural" mean for Hume so that he can get it to work normatively, and how does this help with this other view of emotion, emotion as complex?

Let us first canvas some of the things Hume says about what is natural. He says, for instance, that what is natural is

1. universal and inseparable from the species (Hume 1978, 225d; 1957b, introduction),

2. the foundation of all our thoughts and behavior and that without which human nature would crumble (Hume 1978, 225),
3. "requisite" that it hold and, even further, "absolutely impossible" that it not hold (Hume 1978, 278, 286),
4. (as I said above) correct, while the nonnatural is "perverted" (Hume 1978, 225–226; 1957a, 53–54).

Is it possible to come up with a satisfactory interpretation of all the above? Here I work through two interpretations.

Interpretation 1   Let us start with the claim that what is natural is "universal and unavoidable in human nature." We know what it is to say that something is universal. But what does it mean to say of a trait that it is "unavoidable"? Perhaps we can find a hint by looking at Hume's assertion that "by natural we understand what is common to any species or what is inseparable from the species" (1978, 484).

Suppose that what is unavoidable in human nature is what is inseparable from the human species. For something to be inseparable from the species is, literally, for it to be the case that the species could not remain the same species if we separated this trait from it. So it looks like we might say as a first approximation that natural traits and principles of human beings would be those without which creatures would not be human.

We might see this reading of what it means to say that something is natural as confirmed by Hume's characterizing of natural traits and principles as "principles which are permanent, irresistable, and universal. . . . [They] are the foundation of all our thoughts and actions, so that upon their removal human nature must immediately go to ruin" (1978, 255).

Barbara Winters (1981), for example, argues that "go to ruin" in the above quotation means that the species would no longer *be* the human species without these traits. These traits are, on her reading, seen as those that define human nature—that are, as she puts it, (metaphysically) "essential" to humans. So one possible interpretation is to say that if something is natural to humans, it is essential to humans. For something to be natural is thus for it to be essential.

Further, on this reading, it makes sense that Hume would say that such (natural) connections are requisite or that it is absolutely impossible that they not hold. On the above reading, such a connection must hold because without it the creatures would not be human, because its holding is essential to the kinds of creatures we are. And, of course, if these traits are essential to our being human, they would indeed be foundational.

This interpretation also accounts nicely for the claim that "natural" is a normative term. If what is natural is what is essential to us, then to do what is natural is to do what most expresses what we are. And that, it could be argued, is a good thing to do.[3]

However, there are problems with such a reading. These problems emerge if we look seriously at, for example, other claims Hume makes about what is natural—claims that would seem to indicate that any (metaphysically) essentialist reading of natural must be incorrect.[4] Hume says, for example, that emotions and their various "conditions" (as he puts it) are naturally connected. And yet whatever conditions surround the emotions for humans need not be the case for other creatures. This is because Hume believes that morality is a product of human sentiments. Rather, what constitutes the appropriate cause and object for an emotion is, for Hume, based "entirely on the particular fabric and constitution of the human species." He says, for example, "If morality were determined by reason, this is the same to all rational beings: But nothing but Experience can assure us, that the sentiments are the same. What experience have we in regard to Superior Beings? How can we ascribe to them any sentiments at all? They have implanted those sentiments in us for the conduct of life like our bodily sensations, which they possess not themselves" (Burton 1846, vol. 1, pp. 119–120).

Further, Hume also says that the thought of an emotion without its usually accompanying "conditions" produces no contradiction. When speaking of love and hatred, for example, he says, "This order of things, abstractedly considered, is not necessary. . . . If nature had so pleased, love might have had the same effect as hatred, and hatred as love. I see no contradiction in supposing a desire to producing misery annexed to love and happiness to hatred" (1978, 368).[5]

What are the implications of Hume's saying the above about those things that are natural? It seems that whatever interpretation of natural we come up with, these two quotations must act as a constraint. What do they tell us?

For one, they tell us that any essentialist reading of "natural" must be incorrect. By "essential" I mean that what is essential must hold for all creatures. For it seems that it is not the case that pride must have these components in order to be pride for all creatures if the gods could have different components for pride. Further, Hume believes that to imagine that the two propositions are separable without a contradiction is a test that proves that the two are not logically connected.[6] That is, the two need not be so connected for all creatures. Thus it need not be the case that emotions have the components for all creatures that they usually do for humans. Rather, the connections between components are "natural." So here, then, is our problem: What could it mean to say that the connection is a natural one, where this does not mean that there is a logical connection but still does mean that this connection somehow *must* hold, that it is, as we saw Hume say above, "absolutely impossible" that it not hold?

Interpretation 2   I will argue that we can get a satisfactory interpretation of natural as meaning something like a *law of nature*. Let's see how and whether such an interpretation can solve our problem.

Hume says at the end of his *Dissertation on the Passions* (1889) that he hopes he has shown the existence of principles of the mind parallel to the laws of thermodynamics. That is, "It is sufficient for my purpose, if I have made it appear, that, in the production and conduct of the passions, there is a certain regular mechanism, which is susceptible of as accurate a disquisition as the laws of motion, optics, hydrostatics, or any part of natural philosophy."

One might guess, then, that it is something like a law of nature that human minds operate in the way in which they do. This seems the most reasonable reading of the analogy with physical laws that Hume makes. Such laws do hold universally as far as our data base goes. But why is it "requisite" that they hold or, as I put it a moment ago, why *must* they hold? Perhaps it is requisite that emotion have a certain object in the same way that other laws of nature require things to occur. How might this help us here?

Let's start with an analogy with a current "law of nature" or physical law, for example, gravity. It is not unlikely that we would say something like, Objects whose weight is above x cannot fall upward. All we would mean by this is something like, Under the usual physical conditions in this world, gravity ensures that such objects must fall downward.[7] But notice that I only mean this "must" to hold in this world with these physical laws operating as they usually do. I believe we can explain Hume's thinking that emotions must have a certain sort of object or cause in much the same way: given laws of mind as Hume knew them and barring any extraordinary circumstances or various sorts of malfunctioning, it is absolutely impossible that emotions not have the sorts of objects they do. Indeed, Hume seems to indicate that some such reading is what he had in mind when he tells us that "it is absolutely impossible, *from the primary constitution of the mind* that it be otherwise" (1978, 286).

But Hume also says that we can operate in ways that are *not* natural, as when someone "is tormented, he knows not why, with the apprehension of spectres in the dark" (pp. 225–226) or when the "animal spirits" in the brain, "falling into the contiguous traces, present other related ideas in lieu of that which the mind desired at first to survey" (p. 61).

But if these laws of human nature hold universally, how can they also *not* hold? I believe the answer to this is to notice that in the gravity example it was very important that there be a *ceteris paribus* clause, that is, a claim that if everything was normal and nothing was unusual or malfunctioning, these laws held. Similarly here. These laws of human nature hold universally unless, that is, something, or more relevantly, as we will see, some*one* is *malfunctioning*. Therefore, these laws of mind do hold universally—but what I mean by that is that they hold universally for humans who are well functioning.

So I believe we can say on interpretation 2 that such laws of nature must hold. But why are these laws then "foundational" or "inseparable from the species"? Or even more perplexing on this reading, why are they the *correct* laws? I believe there are plausible answers to these questions.

What is natural is foundational for the following reason: a law of human nature, for Hume, is a regularity that has, as far as our observation shows, always been the case. Such laws of mind as the association of ideas, if they really do operate with the kind of regularity Hume describes form the basis of the patterns in which we think, perceive, and ultimately even behave. It is in this sense that they are the foundation of our being.

As to why these laws are inseparable from the species, as we will see, these laws of nature are those that, among other things, allow us to survive, that is, to at least get our ends satisfied. And if these laws are those by which we at least survive, then to take them away, to separate them from the species, would be to ensure the downfall of the species, or as we saw Hume say, without them the species would perish.

But why are these laws, the natural laws of mind, the *correct* ones as well? That is, why does Hume say that whenever we have an unnatural cause or object accompanying the feel of an emotion, we are malfunctioning? Why does Hume say, for example, "One who is tormented, he knows not why, with the apprehension of spectres in the dark, may, perhaps, be said to reason, and reason naturally too; but then it must be in the same sense that a *malady* is natural" (1978, 225–226). Why is this a *malady*, a way of *mal*functioning, rather than just a way of functioning *differently*? And why does Hume say, for example, that Timon "probably more from his affected spleen than any inveterate malice, was denominated the man-hater [and had] *perverted* sentiments of morals" (1957a, 53–54)?

If we understand this, we will understand how Hume managed to make "natural" be a normative term.

4 Natural and Normative

What is Hume's argument, if any, that when we have nonnatural patterns of mind, that is, whether we reason nonnaturally or have nonnatural components for an emotion, that we are malfunctioning?

First, let's look at what Hume's argument for this cannot be. He cannot say that to function unnaturally is to malfunction (and natural functioning is proper functioning) because functioning naturally is what most of us do most of the time. Saying this would render proper functioning a matter of according with what most others do. But the fact of others' doing it is not an argument for this behavior being proper. Whatever argument Hume gives for why the natural is proper and the unnatural wrong must be independent of what others do or don't do.[8]

Hume also cannot argue that unnatural inferences do not accord with the way we were designed (by, for instance, God or nature) to function. According to such an argument, there is a way we are supposed to work: it is the way we were designed to work. But Hume could never say these things, for he thought that only conclusions emerging from experience were legitimate. But from experience we can know only how we do in fact work, and that is not identical with how we should work. So he needs an argument that nonnatural functioning is malfunctioning that is independent of both what most people happen to do and any theological speculations. How might Hume provide such an argument?

One possibility is this: Start from the premise that an organism is not functioning properly if its ends, whatever they are, are constantly being frustrated. Hume argues that making unnatural connections of mind does result in frustrating a person's ends, whatever they may be.[9] Hume believes that a prerequisite for achieving whatever ends people can possibly have is stability and strength of belief and judgment. And he says that making only natural inferences gives us this stability and strength. Therefore, we can say to whoever is not acting naturally that they are acting in a way that will not promote whatever desires they may have. It is a good guess that such a person will not survive. So in nonnatural inferences the mechanism of mind is malfunctioning (and this is obviously some sort of normative term) in that whatever ends it has will be frustrated by this behavior. In addition, Hume points out that acting in accordance with natural laws of mind brings pleasure and happiness. And as I have argued in Lind, unpublished, Hume believes that if we act naturally, if—to use non-Humean terminology—our souls are well ordered, we will not only survive and have pleasure and happiness but will in addition "flourish."[10] Therefore, there appears to be at least some account, whether or not we think it is a good one, of why Hume thought there was an argument that to have our laws of mind unnaturally ordered was to be malfunctioning.[11]

So it seems that we can get a definition of "natural" that does indeed account for all the relevant citations. Also, the latest interpretation is in accord with the metaphysical biases, that is, the antiessentialism, that Hume demonstrates in book 1 of the *Treatise*. Therefore, there seems to be good reason to accept this interpretation of "natural." And so, interpreting what is natural as what is an instance of a law of nature does seem to be most satisfactory.

To review, I am saying of Hume's notion of natural that what is natural is what, according to our best evidence, has held universally in (well-functioning) humans and that what is natural plays a normative role—that is, when something is not natural, it is incorrect.

5 Emotions as Complexes

I now want to return to the alternative reading of emotion in Hume. Remember that my claim is that the notion of natural can account for the alternative view of emotion represented by the excerpts cited much earlier and that this alternative view of emotion can feed into a new understanding of *moral* emotion.

How can the notion of natural account for this alternative view of emotion mentioned earlier? The alternative view again, is that emotions are complex, that the parts are connected by a kind of connection of which we can say that "tis absolutely impossible that these passions should ever look beyond self." Does a natural connection explain why the relation between parts of an emotion *must* hold in the allowed way? That is, can we say a natural connection is a connection that is not analytic and yet nonetheless must hold?

To say the connection between parts of an emotion is a natural one is to say it is not an analytic connection. This is because unlike an analytic connection, a natural one does not follow from the idea or concept involved. A natural connection follows neither from the idea of the emotion nor from the idea of a human being. Therefore, to say a connection is natural is to say only that well-functioning humans must have the constituent parts for the relevant emotion.

If the connection between the parts of an emotion is natural, can we say that this connection must hold? To answer this question we must first determine what we mean by saying a connection must hold. Suppose there is a connection between A and B, and suppose we say that the connection must hold for well-functioning humans. We are making two interconnected claims: that in well-functioning humans, whenever A has appeared, B has appeared and that it is not possible in well-functioning humans for A to appear without B. Therefore, to say an emotion must have a particular object as a constituent part is to say (1) whenever this emotion occurs, it has had this object, and (2) the emotion can never occur as this emotion without this object in well-functioning humans. Can we assert both (1) and (2) of a natural connection?

Condition (1) seems to be easy to satisfy, given how a natural connection has been defined. That is, to say the connection between the feel of an emotion and its object is natural is to say humans are built so that when they are well functioning, whenever they have had the feel of this emotion, it has been accompanied by a particular object. That is, having this object is in accord with a built-in law of mind.

If the connection between the parts of an emotion is natural, can it satisfy condition (2) as easily? That is, can we say not only that the connection has always held but that it is impossible for it not to hold? For remember, one of the things we are trying to account for is Hume's saying "Tis absolutely impossible that . . . these passions should ever look beyond self." A natural connection explains why it is impossible. The reason is that if the connection is natural, then humans are constructed so that whenever they have the feel of the emotion, they have its associated object, and if humans don't have this associated object, they are broken. That is, the only conditions under which a well-functioning creature could have a different object or no object at all accompanying the feel of this emotion is if it were a creature with *different basic laws of mind*, in other words, a nonhuman creature. For humans, if a connection is natural and they are functioning well, then it is absolutely impossible that they have a different object for this emotion. That is the sense in which a natural connection is one that must hold.

Thus a natural connection is not an analytic one but is one of which we can say it is "absolutely impossible that it not hold." This is because for humans, if a connection is natural and the humans are well functioning, then it is absolutely impossible that we have a different object or cause for the emotion.

6 Moral Emotion and Subjectivity

Assuming that the definition I gave of "natural" does give us a way of claiming that emotions are complex, why does it matter for ethics that we are able to say that emotions are complex—complex in the way I have defined the term above. That is, what effect does it have on Hume's idea of a *moral* emotion? On the received view, the view, presented earlier, that emotions consist entirely in atoms of feeling that can attach to *any* object and can have *any* cause, the claim is that since Hume is an atomist about emotions, he must be a subjectivist about ethics.

But remember that in this case too the received view encountered textual difficulties. If Hume were such a subjectivist about morals, although it is *possible* that we might find him saying, as he does of Timon, that to morally approve of murder and destruction is "perverting his *natural* sentiment of humanity," it seems extremely unlikely. Rather, it seems more plausible that Hume's saying that Timon is perverted is an attempt to get at Timon in much the way Foot claims Hume cannot.

On the view of emotion as complex, with natural connections playing the role they do, Hume is not committed to radical subjectivity. So we can give an account of his saying that Timon is perverted as an attempt to get at him.[12] How is this?

Under the view of emotion as complex, if someone has an *unnatural* cause or object accompanying a feeling, it is an *incorrect* cause or object that they have because they are *malfunctioning*. Thus we are no longer in the position of having nothing to say to someone who happens to have, for example, the feeling associated with moral approval toward the murder of innocents. Rather, we can say to him, as Hume said of Timon, that there is something *wrong* with him, that he is perverted insofar as he has such unnatural connections of mind. Thus, seeing emotion as a complex does indeed allow us to avoid radical subjectivity while preserving the important role of sentiment.

To summarize, my claim is that when we move away from the received atomist view of Hume, we end up with a different view of emotion and moral emotion: the view that says emotion is a complex. Again, by that I mean that under normal conditions there must be other components to an emotion besides its phenomenological feeling. Further, this complex view of emotion avoids the problem associated with the standard reading of Hume on emotion, namely, ending up with a subjectivist moral theory.

I'd like to close with some thoughts about the usefulness of the material discussed above. David Hume thought of himself as an anatomist and not a painter, as someone who, as he put it,

> is admirably fitted to give *advice* to a painter; and 'tis even impracticable to excell in the latter art, without the assistance of the former. We must have an exact knowledge of the parts, their situation and connections, before we can design with any elegance or correctness. And thus the most abstract speculations concerning human nature, however cold and unentertaining, become subservient to *practical morality*; and may render this latter science more correct in its precepts, and more persuasive in its exhortations. (1978, 621)

I think it is critical to understand that those of us who, like Hume, reject purely cognitive models for moral theory, who reject being forced into a picture of moral psychology that does not describe us and indeed may not describe anyone, *are* those painters. I'd like to suggest, then, that Hume's work on the emotions is critical anatomy for those of us who wish to explore, or rather reexplore, the role of the emotions in a kind of understanding often disavowed in philosophy, an understanding through and with emotions. Maybe it's finally time to reexamine the prejudices that tell us of the evils of emotion: that emotion necessarily leads to radical subjectivity, that it cannot get us any sort of truth, in other words, that the poets should still be banned from the Republic.

On my reading of Hume, he has a story in which emotions are in part cognitive. In opposition to the standard reading, this view, even by itself, would be significant enough. But it is also an important step toward undermining the very reason-passion split Hume is most often accused of perpetuating. And maybe with this undermining can come the sort of understanding that we all know can happen through emotion. The painting has just been begun, but the anatomist has done his job well.[13]

Notes

1. I am not clear that Ardal would endorse the view that emotions are complex as I present it here, but he does argue that they have complex causal conditions.
2. John Rawls makes a similar point in his unpublished lectures on Hume's moral theory. Those lectures have been very influential in my thinking about Hume.
3. Although the reasoning underlying this move may not be immediately apparent, I take it to be a kind of neo-Aristotelian or neo-Hegelian reasoning in which acting morally is (somehow) expressing your essence (or function) as a human being. However, I don't mean to assert here that I have the key to making this kind of move work, for surely "natural" traits, when they are thought of as essential to

us in whatever way, are, as Owen Flanagan has put it to me, "a mixed bag" and are not clearly identical with virtues. I merely mean to indicate that this is a direction that others have thought could work in moral theory.

4. On this point, see also Baier 1978. I am not clear that I agree that the connection between pride and its object is bound by (as Baier wants to say) "closer than causal ties" *if* this means what I am here calling *analytic* connections. (I am also not clear this is indeed what Baier means.) But I do agree that (as she says) "the tie between pride and its object is special." Further, I agree with Baier that the relation is necessary *in a way*, namely, the way I lay out in this chapter.

5. Although neither "happiness" nor a "desire to producing misery" is an object or cause, it is still a usual condition of the emotion, that is, part of the causal complex usually making up the emotion. This is thus a broader claim, that is, a claim encompassing more than just cause and object, than I am in general making in this essay. However, I believe the example still supports my point.

6. See Hume 1957a, pp. 60–61. See also Barry Stroud's excellent discussion of the general argument in his book *Hume* (1977, 47).

7. Robert Brandon has pointed out to me that some readers will find this example needlessly complicated. All I mean to point to is that this is something that generally holds—and I am treating it like a law in the sense that it seems to imply some kind of natural necessity—but that we can also construct cases in which it doesn't hold.

8. See, e.g., Kydd 1964 for one sort of interpretation of Hume as not being a conventionalist moral thinker. See especially pp. 175–177.

9. Winters (1981) makes a version of the argument given in this paragraph. She cites Hume 1978, pp. 109–110, 225–226.

10. Owen Flanagan has pointed out to me that in a society where there is slavery, anger might be natural on the part of the slave but would not cause the slave to flourish. I think this is correct, and it raises all sorts of important questions about the extent to which the notion of natural is independent of social forces (on this, see Flanagan 1991, especially chapter 2). And I think this in turn raises questions about how culturally unbiased Hume's notion of natural really is. I take this issue up in my "Indians, Savages, and Women: Hume's Aesthetics" (unpublished). On this point also see B. H. Smith 1988, chapter 4.

11. Both Larry Blum and Alison Jaggar have said that this is unintuitive. I agree. But for the best account I have seen that makes it as plausible as it can be made, see Amélie Rorty's excellent paper "'Pride Produces the Idea of Self': Hume on Moral Agency," 1990.

12. I am grateful to Geoff Sayre-McCord for reminding me that because of the work that natural connections do for me here, there is another position besides that of emotions' being complex that could avoid radical subjectivity. And that is a kind of revised atomistic position where the objects and causes of an emotion are connected to the emotion—which consists in a feeling—through natural connections. I believe this is correct. I do not wish to commit myself here to saying that only a complex emotion is sufficient to ward off radical subjectivity. I do believe, however, that Hume's view was closer to emotion as complex than to revised atomism (although the difference between revised atomism and emotion as complex—as I have defined "complex"—is a bit blurry. But it is important to remember that Foot's atomism is *not* revised atomism.

13. This paper is a revised version of material in chapters 2 and 3 of my unpublished doctoral dissertation, "Emotions and Hume's Moral Theory," MIT, 1987. For helpful comments either on this version or on an earlier one, I would like to thank

Jonathan Adler, Ned Block, Larry Blum, Robert Brandon, Josh Cohen, John Deigh, Owen Flanagan, Alison Jaggar, Tom Kuhn, Geoff Sayre-McCord, Ted Morris, John Rawls, Wade Robison, Amélie Rorty, Jerry Samet, and audiences at MIT, the University of Cincinnati, and Bates College. I especially want to thank Josh Cohen for his repeated readings and numerous comments on the earlier versions. All remaining errors are, of course, fully my responsibility. The writing of this paper was supported in part by a Taft Post-Doctoral Fellowship at the University of Cincinnati.

Chapter 7

The Place of Emotions in Kantian Morality

Nancy Sherman

The image of the cold, heartless, duty-bound agent is yielding, in certain Kantian circles, to a portrait of an agent who values and cultivates the human gesture.[1] Similarly Kant's notorious impatience with Romanticism and his eagerness to expose the unreliability and natural lottery in the distribution of emotional temperaments finds itself poised against a view of the emotions as supporting moral interest. To a large extent I am sympathetic with this more congenial portrait and see my task in this chapter as one of surveying the evidence. The more humanistic picture emerges from *The Doctrine of Virtue*, as well as from less formal ethical writings, such as the *Lecture on Ethics* and *Anthropology from a Pragmatic Point of View*.[2] I believe the view can also find its way into the *Groundwork*, although I don't formally argue the point. Though sympathetic, I am cautious and well aware that concessions to the emotions are primarily a matter of moral anthropology for Kant—a way of applying the Categorical Imperative and its a priori motive congenially to the human case. This forces the question of just how tolerant Kant would be of human agents who act from the motive of duty but without appropriate affect or emotional comportment. The fact that for Kant nothing may be *morally* amiss may raise certain objections to his views and question the adequacy of his account in the human sphere. I raise these worries at the conclusion of this chapter.

The chapter divides into three sections. In section 1 I begin with some commonsense intuitions about the role of emotions in moral life. My hope is at least to make plausible the general claim that emotions often play a significant role in the expression and cultivation of moral character. In section 2 I turn directly to the place of emotions in Kantian morality. I suggest that Kant did not view the pathological emotions as necessarily beyond control or cultivation and that we can distinguish several interrelated claims regarding their supportive role in the expression of moral character. In the final section I assess these claims in the context of the general question of how heteronomous Kant's account becomes once we give ample room to the emotions. It may be that moral anthropology needs to be the central and "accepted" focus of Kantian ethics or, if it is already, that its boundary with an autonomous ethics be more sharply defined.

1 Emotions Matter in Moral Assessment

Before I can usefully talk about Kant's accommodation of the emotions, I need to become clearer about some basic issues, such as why emotions should play a role in morality. From the point of view of commonsense morality, it is plausible to suppose that the emotions have an important place in an account of moral character. Even if we think of morality as having primarily to do with the rightness of action, a necessary condition for acting rightly will include recognition of the morally relevant features of situations, or what has been called moral salience.[3] Often this will involve a sensitivity cultivated through emotional dispositions. Not only do we notice, but we notice with a certain intensity or impact that would be absent if emotions weren't engaged. We focus in a way we wouldn't otherwise. And once focused, we bring to bear further considerations that are relevant; we make inferences that would otherwise not have arisen or be thought of in as compelling a way. Sensitivity thus becomes more than a purely perceptual or cognitive matter. Of course, any notion of attending or noticing presupposes some degree of affective interest in the subject matter. It is no different in moral matters, but here specific sorts of emotions such as sympathetic sorrow or joy, indignation, fear, or anguish typically draw us in and help us to fasten onto matters where moral intervention may be required.

In addition to this perceptual role, the emotions play a role in communicating to others an agent's interest and concern. Even if action is to have a predominant role in moral theory, the emotional tone of one's action may make a moral difference. Action that is unfeeling may simply not be received in the same way as action conveyed through more gentle care. Of course, emotional tone is not always to the point. If someone is bleeding profusely, then helpful action might simply be action aimed at stopping the bleeding, whatever its emotional tone. The communication of emotion is neither here nor there. But there are clearly other cases where it matters, and matters a lot. It typically matters in how we comfort a child, how we volunteer services to a student, how we show our willingness to help a colleague who needs our resources. The point of helping in many of these cases is to reassure another that we care—

to show patience, loyalty, considerateness, empathy. Here the quality of the emotional interaction is inseparable from the act of helping. In the case of a parent or teacher, it is part of how we define the notion of assistance. Mutual aid is partly emotional tenor. (There may be an objection to the use of the term "tone" here in that actions with different tones are simply different actions, and that consequently, what we need to talk about is not the tone of the action but the different actions. I am not bothered by this correction. Even if we grant that it is more natural to say "the 'unfeeling' action was the wrong action" as opposed to "the right action with the wrong tone," the reason it is wrong, I am suggesting, is because of its emotional expression. It is the attitudinal aspect of action that we sometimes need to draw attention to and assess.)

In these ways, then, affective attitude appears to have something to do with the moral assessment of action. It seems to make a difference in how one helps but also in how one says "no." Suppose you decide not to help someone because you doubt their real need (you think they may be trying to take advantage), because you think ill of their cause, or perhaps because you just do not have time. Here whether the tone of your refusal is arrogant or civil, churlish or kind makes a difference to the moral assessment of your response. Even if your refusal is not objectionable, i.e., it is a permissible omission, the attitude that expresses it may be. *That* way of saying "no" is not acceptable. Again, whether we say a different action type is required or the same action with a different tone is for the moment not central. What is at issue is the attitude we convey when we act.

In some cases the presence or absence of regret may crucially affect the moral assessment of a response. Here what we evaluate is not so much what a person has done but what a person has *not* done and how she responds to not acting. Such cases are often conflict situations, where an agent is faced with two competing claims that contingently conflict. To do one is to leave something of equal moral weight undone. Though in such circumstances one may make a choice, the choice is not necessarily rational or justified. The sensitive agent is aware of a "moral remainder." And this moral remainder is experienced emotionally as regret, or in Bernard Williams's term, as "agent-regret" (1981b). It indicates that though one may not be at fault for failing to meet a claim, one nonetheless feels some degree of responsibility.[4] Its presence tells us something additional about the agent's moral character over and above how and what she chooses. It signals an awareness of the complexity of moral life and the difficulty of making wise choices in constrained circumstances.

In other cases of moral conflict what is required is not merely that a claim go unheeded but that an agent actively do something base in order to promote the competing claim. To free my family held hostage by a tyrant, Aristotle tells us, I may have to agree to perform a heinous act.[5] To allow the naval ships to set sail, Agammenon must violate his duty to his daughter. These are cases of dirty hands—cases where an agent must harm to help, kill innocents to save other innocent lives, violate one unqualified duty to fulfil another. The deontological considerations that might prohibit such actions are not my present concern. Rather, what interests me is the more limited point that if under certain conditions a dirty action *is*, practically speaking, required, the agent who experiences no regret or loss in performing such an action seems to lack an adequate moral appreciation of the complexity of the circumstances. This is not to say all agents must face these or lesser conflicts with a tortured soul. Even in conflict cases there may be no question in an agent's mind about what course of action must be taken. But still, though there is no ambivalence, there may be loss. And not to feel that loss is to fail to take seriously a moral claim. It is to assume that the claim can be wiped out by an act of mental balancing. But the point of regret is that it marks a cost that is not canceled out by a corresponding benefit. In this sense, conscientious deliberation and decision making do not exhaust everything that matters in the expression of moral character. To make a decision yet not to feel any residue from an unmet claim that tugs with equal moral force may be the sign of a morally deficient character.

Now it might be argued in reply that regret of this sort is morally commendable in only a secondary way insofar as it sensitizes an agent to the sort of claims that can typically be fulfilled by action. Though I may violate a duty in a conflict situation, my regret signals that I can typically fulfil that requirement and am aware of the force of the duty. As such the moral value of regret is ultimately parasitic upon action. It plays the role so many other emotions play of marking an occasion for moral action. The only difference is that it alerts us to a *type* of occasion, not a particular token. However, this reply does not go far enough. For even apart from the contribution to prospective action, there is a dimension of moral character revealed directly by the emotion. The presence of regret tells us that this claim matters here and now, however one goes on to formulate an appropriate intention next time round or even to make amends now. Just as those intentions to act will reveal character, so does the emotion. They both have their common source in character. Put another way, regret is a way of showing commitment (what you care about) when action is impossible. As such it is a mode of response valuable in its own right apart from any contribution it makes to future action.

In making this point, I do not wish to deny that there is a likely psychological correlation between recognizing a claim that must be left undone and acting on that sort of claim in the future when circumstances are more favorable. Moreover, even in the cramped circumstances of conflict, regret may issue in some measure of compensatory action here and now. Yet still, I want to make the stronger claim that even if the practice of regret led to no pay offs in present or future action, an agent who experienced regret at having to leave a claim undone because of competing claims is, other things equal, morally more admirable than one who does not. What is valuable is not that she loses sleep, feels tortured inside, or feels emotionally wrought on the outside. It is not sentimentalism that is at stake. Rather, it is that she is able to see and emotionally express concerns that are relevant here and now. She has a kind of moral vision. She is aware that the best one can do at a given moment does not always balance the claims on all fronts.

From this brief survey there appears to be intuitive evidence for the claim that emotions are relevant to our assessments of moral goodness. We are prone to find something morally lacking in the individual who acts from the right principles but with an inappropriate attitude or emotional comportment. The action is missing the right texture and tone. Other times we look to the presence of emotions, such as regret, not as something that enhances the action but as something that reveals the background choice and the moral compromise that has to be made. In this last case, to argue against the relevance of the emotion in moral assessment is either to eliminate the real possibility of moral conflict (as some have) or to argue that even if there are conflicts, what matters is that *one act and choose*, not that one also acknowledge the inadequacy of one's actions to reflect the moral demands. Yet to exclude this as relevant, I have implied, is to take too narrow a view of moral character.

I shall be assessing the Kantian position with these preliminary observations in mind. I should note now that I am not interested in the phenomenon of agent regret per se or in whether Kant can in fact allow for genuine conflicts of duties.[6] I mention regret as primarily a way of exposing the intuition that certain aspects of moral response (and moral character) are not easily conveyed by a decision to act. Granted, it may be that many emotions are actually captured by the complete description of the chosen action and that to look at the action is itself to look at emotional comportment. But regret is a case where the two seem to pull apart, where we can see more perspicuously that how we morally respond may not be exhausted by what we choose to do. I should also make clear that I by no means view these various judgments of commonsense morality as bedrock for moral theory. Nor, of course, would Kant. Still, I shall argue that there is a concerted effort on Kant's own part to accommodate the emotions in a way that is not fully at odds with our commonsense judgments about their role in the moral life and that there certainly is a wish and a hope on the part of neo-Kantians that he be able to do this. In what sense Kant can successfully do this within the rubric of his own rationalist theory is the question I will need to press.

2 The Kantian Accommodation

For Kant, what is of unconditioned moral value is the purity of a good will and its capacity to be determined by a motive unconditioned by inclination. Such a motive is duty. To act from duty is to act from the thought that one must act only on maxims that can be universalized by a will. It is to act from the idea of a will as legislating laws or to act from the Universal Law formula of the Categorical Imperative. That principle and the motive to act from it are said by Kant to be valid for all rational beings as such. Consequently, contingent inclinations and pathological motives are quite independent of the goodness of a will and indeed often appear to be its natural foe: "Virtue is the strength of man's maxims in fulfilling his duty.— We can recognize strength of any kind only by the obstacles it can overcome, and in the case of virtue these obstacles are the natural inclinations, which can come into conflict with man's moral resolution" (DV 54, cf. 114). "The impulses of nature, accordingly, are obstacles within man's mind to his observance of duty and forces (sometimes powerful ones) struggling against it. . . . Now the power and deliberate resolve to withstand a strong but unjust opponent is fortitude (fortitudo), and fortitude in relation to the forces opposing a moral attitude of will in us is virtue (virtus, fortitudo moralis)" (DV 37–38).

But though here and elsewhere an adversarial relation is often portrayed between the inclinations and a good will, we need conclude neither that all inclinations are obstacles to be overcome by a morally resolute will nor that a morally good will must have as a condition of its goodness the overcoming of inclinations.[7] An alternative reading is simply that a good will is most conspicuous in its struggle against inclination. It is in this confrontation that a good will shines forth most clearly. This is indeed the gloss Kant himself provides in the Groundwork: "The sublimity and inner worth of the command is the more *manifest* in a duty, the fewer are the subjective causes for obeying it and the more those against it" (*GW* 93).[8] But even if we limit the battle metaphor to heuristics, any notion that the emotions actually support the moral will is excluded by the above descriptions of virtue.

In the account of emotional affects and passions in the *Anthropologie* a similar picture of the recalcitrance of inclination is reinforced. Affects or agitations (*Affekte*) are emotional tempests; they come upon us unawares and just as suddenly subside. Passions (*Leidenschaften*), by contrast, are inclinations that root deeply, more like hatred than anger (*DV* 70). "An affect works like water breaking through a dam: a passion, like a stream that burrows ever deeper in its bed" (*Anthr.* 120). Both damage freedom and self-mastery.[9] "Emotional agitation does a momentary damage to freedom and self-mastery; passion abandons them and finds its pleasure and satisfaction in slavery." "The unhappy man" overtaken by passion "groans in his chains, which he cannot break loose from because they have already grown together with his limbs, so to speak" (*Anthr.* 134). "An agitation, even one aroused by the thought of the *good*, is a momentary and glittering phenomenon that leaves lassitude behind it" (*DV* 71).

On the basis of this sort of evidence, emotions traditionally come to be regarded as unstable and unreliable sources of moral motivation. Yet it is clearly not Kant's view that we are enslaved by all emotional experiences or are necessarily acted upon as victims. In a gamut of pathological responses, we experience emotions without necessarily being *overwhelmed* or *blinded* by their fury. The fact that the emotions are states of being acted upon (ways of being affected, *pathē* in the Greek), does not imply that they must be involuntary. That is, we need not deny the premise that emotions are passive states in order to argue that emotions are to a certain degree within the scope of our control. There is scope for responsibility, even if taking control does not amount to an automatic or immediate reversal of one's emotional dispositions.[10] There are roles we can take to influence how we are affected. "When an angry man comes up to you in a room, to say harsh words to you in intense indignation, try politely to make him sit down; if you succeed, his reproaches already become milder, since the comfort of sitting is [a form] of relaxation, which is incompatible with the threatening gestures and shouting one can use when standing" (*Anthr.* 120). These remarks suggest that there are strategies for influencing our emotional states. How a person postures himself—whether he sits or stands, is relaxed or tense—affects how he construes the circumstances and consequently how he emotionally reacts. The natural emotions can be cultivated and it

is suggested that there is a measure of responsibility in their cultivation. Similarly, Kant says, with implicit sexism, when a woman
practices smiling, the facial gesture helps to promote a spirit of benevolence.

The notion of taking an active role in controlling our emotional
responses emerges forcefully in a distinction Kant draws between
"sensitivity" (*Empfindsamkeit*) and "sentimentality" (*Empfindelei*) (a
distinction we seem to draw in our own moral vocabulary):

> Sensitivity is a *power* and *strength* by which we grant or refuse
> permission for the state of pleasure or displeasure to enter our
> mind, so that it implies a choice. On the other hand, sentimen-
> tality is a weakness by which we can be affected, even against
> our will, by sympathy for another's plight; others, so to speak,
> can play as they will on the organ of the sentimentalist; sensitiv-
> ity is virile; for the man who wants to spare his wife or children
> trouble or pain must have enough fine feeling to judge their
> sensibilities not by *his* own strength but by their *weakness*, and
> his *delicacy* of feeling is essential to his generosity. On the other
> hand, to share ineffectually in others' feelings, to attune our
> feelings sympathetically to theirs and so let ourselves be affected
> in a merely passive way, is silly and childish. (*Anthr.* 104)

Again, if we charitably overlook the sexism of this passage, Kant's
point seems to be this: there is a way of being affected by the welfare
of others that is compatible with cultivating a disposition to be concerned about certain sorts of circumstances ("it implies a choice"),
with a construal of circumstances not primarily according to one's
own sensibilities or tolerances but as best one can according to the
needs of those who are being helped (it is a kind of moral understanding or insight into how *they* feel and what *they* require in terms
of our help), and with an intention for effective action. There is the
further suggestion in all this that information is conveyed through
the emotions that would not be noticed otherwise. The husband
makes discriminations and sees nuances that would most likely not
catch his attention unless he attends affectively with certain interests
and wishes. Selection through the emotions facilitates action. Kant
adds that this sensitivity or "delicacy of feeling" is essential to generosity. It is worth noting here that though Kant describes sensitivity
as a "power and strength" (and sentimentality as "weakness"), this
needn't mitigate the suggestion that sensitivity may be to a certain
degree within our control. Strength may be cultivated, and though
we may not be strong merely "on demand," we can certainly decide
to do things that improve upon whatever natural strength we already

have. Similarly, though levels of natural sensitivity may vary, we can certainly undertake to do things to cultivate those dispositions.[11]

I shall return to this passage to ask how willing Kant is ultimately to acknowledge this sort of sensitivity as itself a kind of moral response. But in the meantime it is important to note that the passage shows clearly that emotions are not necessarily unruly disruptors of rationality. They can be controlled, cultivated, manipulated by the will. This is important if emotions are to be assigned some supporting role in Kantian morality.

More precisely, what is that supporting role? In what sense does Kantian morality include an *education sentimentale*? In what way is the expression of the emotions compatible with behavior by principles motivated? I shall distinguish several interrelated claims that arise from consideration of various texts, leaving aside more critical discussion of these positions until the next section. On the whole, the claims can be regarded as separating out different instrumental roles that the emotions play in the agent motivated by duty. Though the roles clearly overlap, Kant himself appears eager to note the variety.

To a certain extent the claims represent attempts to come to grips with the suggestive remarks Kant makes in the first chapter of the *Groundwork*:

> Some qualities are even helpful to this good will itself and can make its task very much easier. They have none the less no inner unconditioned worth, but rather presuppose a good will which sets a limit to the esteem in which they are rightly held and does not permit us to regard them as absolutely good. Moderation in affections and passions, self-control, and sober reflexion are not only good in many respects: they may even seem to constitute part of the *inner* worth of a person. Yet they are far from being properly described as good without qualification (however unconditionally they have been commended by the ancients). (*GW* 61)

The passage makes no specific mention of emotional dispositions. Under consideration in the extended text from which this is drawn are talents of mind (intelligence, wit), qualities of temperament (such as courage, resolution, and presumably moderation and self-control), and gifts of fortune (power, wealth, honor), all of which are described as conditional goods requiring the regulation of a good will, or will motivated by duty. But if we widen the class of goods to include the emotions, as Kant does in other works, then this opening passage of the *Groundwork* suggests what has often been denied on one reading of Kant,[12] namely that emotions can support the motives of duty and that they may be assigned conditional moral status. Though the *Groundwork* may not be the best place to find direct textual evidence to this effect, it is not implausible that evidence from elsewhere is compatible with the *Groundwork* view. I shall not argue the point but rather merely suggest that the claims I am about to outline could find their home in the *Groundwork*.

We can distinguish five claims.

1 For a start, there is the familiar *faute de mieux claim*. This is an eliminative-instrumentalist claim. According to it, the cultivation and appropriate expression of certain sorts of emotions constitute a kind of morality, but a provisional, *faute de mieux* morality. It is a morality of an inferior sort, a children's morality that will eventually be replaced in the progress of the individual. It is merely a stage along the way in a developmental process: "It was still wisdom on nature's part," Kant remarks in the *Anthropologie*, "to implant in us the predisposition to sympathy, so that it could handle the reins *provisionally*, until reason has achieved the necessary strength" (*Anthr.* 121). The claim gives a restricted and temporally contained role to the emotions and implies that any permanent conditional or constitutive role that they might enjoy is a sign of moral defect rather than of completeness. In principle, reason on its own is the author and implementor of mature, human morality.

2 Next, there is the *perceptual claim*. Certain sorts of emotions, such as sympathy, compassion, and love, enable us to apply moral principles by alerting us to circumstances that have a moral dimension and may require moral action.[13] According to my earlier discussion, emotions serve as perceptual modes of response. They are modes of discerning and attending to what is morally salient. We have a conditional duty to cultivate these emotions insofar as they support action from duty. Derivative moral worth will depend upon this relation. The point is brought out in *The Doctrine of Virtue*:

> We have an indirect duty to cultivate the sympathetic and natural (aesthetic) feelings in us and to use them as so many means to participating from moral principles and from the feeling appropriate to these principles. Thus, it is our duty: not to avoid places where we shall find the poor who lack the more basic essentials, but rather seek them out; not to shun sick-rooms or debtor's prisons in order to avoid the painful sympathetic feelings that we cannot guard against. For this is still one of the impulses

which nature has implanted in us so that we may do what the thought of duty alone would not accomplish. (*DV* 126)

If we have a practical interest in the moral law and and its spheres of justice and virtue, we still require the pathological emotions to know when and where these ends are appropriate. For a practical interest in the moral law to be truly practical, the interest must work through emotional (pathological) sensitivities. The emotions are part of·"the subjective conditions that . . . help man in *putting into practice* the laws given in a metaphysic of morals" (*DV* 14).

3 Related to this is a third claim, which I will call the *attitude claim*. The idea is that emotions have derivative moral status when they are seen as intentional expressions that appropriately fulfill some positive duty required by the moral law. The emphasis now is not on *locating* a moral problem through the emotions but on *performing* a required or recommended end (or subend) with the right sort of emotional attitude. The point has been developed by Marcia Baron:

> Part of what one morally ought to do is cultivate certain attitudes and dispositions, e.g., sympathy rather than resentment or re-pulsion for the ailing; a cheerful readiness to help and to find ways in which one can help out.
> If Smith's deficiency is that he lacks such attitudes and dis-positions and feels resentful, then whether or not he successfully masks it, it does not indict acting from duty as such. It shows there is something wrong with acting from a false conception of one's duty, a conception that overlooks the importance of the attitudes and dispositions one has when one performs certain acts, especially those which are intended to express affection or concern. Thus although it does not indict acting from duty as such, it points to certain parameters within which satisfactory ways of acting from duty must be located. (1984, 204–205)

These remarks are not intended as direct Kantian exegesis, though they find resonance in *The Doctrine of Virtue*:

> *Sympathetic joy and sorrow* (*sympathia moralis*) are really sensuous feelings of a pleasure or pain (which should therefore be called aesthetic) at another's state of happiness or sadness (shared feeling, feeling participated in). Nature has already implanted in man the susceptibility for these feelings. But to use this as a means to promoting active and rational benevolence is still a particular, though only a conditioned, duty. It is called the duty of *humanity*. (*DV* 125)

Kant's claim is that the imperfect duty of beneficence (or practical benevolence) requires as a derivative duty the cultivation of our natural susceptibility to feel sympathetic joy and sorrow. Though we cannot be obligated to have these inclinations, to the extent that we do already have them as part of our natural constitution, we are obligated to cultivate and manifest them in beneficent actions.[14]

Thus the duty of beneficence or *practical* love requires for its realization the cultivation of *pathological* love. In a somewhat misleading formulation, Kant says that duty becomes inclination: "The command to love our neighbor applies within limits both to love from obligation [practical love] and love from inclination [pathological love]. For if I love others from obligation, I acquire in the course of time a taste for it, and my love, originally duty born, becomes an inclination" (*LE* 197).

The claim is not meant to be a restatement of the principle that duty becomes second nature through practice, or more generally, that the more masterful one becomes at a given activity, the more one enjoys it.[15] Such an account of pleasure can be found in Kant, but not here, I believe. Rather, Kant's point here and in *The Doctrine of Virtue* is that duty "becomes" inclination to the extent to which we express duty through an appropriate range of natural emotions. Thus it is not an appreciation for duty (in the sense of a higher-order pleasure) that is his present concern but how we implement duty through the cultivation of appropriate subjective conditions. Practical love "becomes" pathological love not simply when it becomes easy but when one has cultivated emotional sensibilities that cooperate with and are regulated by duty. If we combine this claim with the previous one, sympathetic sensibilities are preconditions for acting morally (for recognizing the moral moment) as well as material constituents of (or attitudes manifest in) our morally motivated actions.[16]

4   A related claim is the *aesthetic claim*. Emotions are cultivated essentially as aesthetic ornaments that make morality more attractive to humanity. "They are a garment that dresses virtue to advantage":

> No matter how insignificant these laws of refined humanity may seem, especially in comparison with pure moral laws, anything that promotes sociability, even if it consists only in pleasing maxims or manners, is a garment that dresses virtue to advantage, a garment to be recommended to virtue in more serious respects too. The *cynic's purism* and the *anchorite's mortification of the flesh*, without social well-being, are distorted figures of virtue,

which do not attract us to it. Forsaken by the graces, they can make no claim to humanity. (*Anthr.* 147)

Note again that Kant does not speak directly of the emotions here. But an analogous point regarding them can readily be drawn. Affective attitude and gesture dress virtue, just as manners and etiquette do. They enliven the moral model and present virtue in a more agreeable way. They make more attractive a morality that in its purer form may gain few adherents. The educational dimension of this aesthetic is unmistakable. Virtue has an educative role. What is to serve as a model of virtue must be practically and pedagogically sound. As such it must be attractive to us, something we can admire and be encouraged to be like. It is clear that this claim runs very close to the previous one. It adds, however, that duty is to be conveyed through maxims that incorporate affect because duty is more effectively promoted that way. An attractive aesthetic of virtue recommends the life of virtue to both agent and beneficiary and stably reinforces its value within the community.

5   Cutting through these various instrumental claims is the view of duty as a *regulative constraint*—that reasons for an agent to act based on emotions such as compassion or friendship are permissible so long as they are constrained by a motive of duty. That is, inclinations can support acting from duty but only within boundaries set by duty. On Herman's and Baron's interpretations of these cases of regulative constraint, duty serves not as a primary motive but as a secondary motive that, as Baron says, "provides limiting conditions on what may be done from other motives." "It tells me that I may or that I should act as I wished" (1984, 207). In a similar vein, Herman speaks of a double acknowledgment, as when in acting from friendship, we recognize that in addition to having that motive, our action either satisfies a positive duty such as beneficence (that is, it is an instance of a required end) or is within constraints set by other duties. "What is required is that agents who act from emotion also act permissibly. And where there is an obligation to help, we are required to acknowledge this moral claim, even though we may give help out of compassion, etc." (1984a, 376). In Baron's phrase, the moral law represents a "counterfactual condition always at hand (though not always in one's thoughts): one would not do this if it were morally counter-recommended" (pp. 216–217). The idea is the familiar one that the morality of duty sets permissibility conditions on the pursuit of other motives as well as prescribes what is required whatever our

motives for action happen to be. The value of other pursuits is limited by the unconditional value of morality.

The overall evidence, then, is that emotions can promote morally interested action by alerting us to an appropriate range of occasions and by enabling us to realize required ends in affectively (and aesthetically) commendable ways. In turn, morality regulates emotions by conditioning what is permissible and required.

3 Evaluating These Claims

I want to press some of the above claims by asking if for Kant emotional expression is ultimately just a matter of optional aesthetics or is more central and constitutive of what we value in human morality. Put differently, are we to view certain emotions as optional (and eliminable) means for expressing duty? Or are we to view them as morally recommended ways of expressing human virtue so that it might make sense to say roughly that the *complete* (or composite) moral value of an action is compromised if it is motivated by an interest in being lawful yet lacks appropriate pathological constitution? This will take us to the question of how pure, after all, the moral laws are that guide our actions and behavior. The obligatory ends by which we are required to guide our lives, just like the emotions that help to realize them, may be peculiar to our contingent constitutions. But if this is so, then Kantian ethics seems more deeply heteronomous than Kant himself would have us believe.

I start with the perceptual claim. Here the work of emotions is purely instrumental, and any moral value they have is derivative upon their role in sensitizing us to the moral features of circumstances. Emotions are preconditions, but not constituents, of moral response. But sometimes we view the role of emotion as itself constitutive of moral expression and indeed, as Kant says, a matter of expressing practical interest (e.g., beneficence) through pathological or sensuous feelings. We regard the communication of emotion as itself intentional and practical and in its own right as an expression of the ends of moral character. Thus not only do we have some measure of control over how we are emotionally affected, but also we have some volitional control over how we express those affects in the world. Kant can meet this point under the third or fourth claim to the extent that emotions may be viewed at various times as capable of intentional expression and are formulatable within a maxim. Verbally making clear one's indignation when one is treated with malice or ministering to another with a deliberately upbeat, encouraging tone of voice or controlled body language (a smile rather than a scowl) may be thought of as part of the content of a maxim that realizes a more general end. Granted, such expression may not be under volitional control for all individuals alike, but this is true of other sorts of means by which individuals realize their ends. Similarly, that it is part of one's maxim may not become explicit until an individual reflects somewhat about how to describe a proposed intention and what to view as relevant to achieving one's ends. But again, this is so for maxims in general. The issue is part of a more general question of casuistry, of how we assess individual judgment about choice of means and subends in realizing a general policy. There is "play room" (*Spielraum*), Kant tells us, for perception and judgment. I am suggesting that how we emotionally comport ourselves may often be part of this "play room" and a legitimate part of the subject of casuistry.

Still, there are limits to how far Kant would go with this idea, and how much as action he would be willing to view the communication of emotion. He raises reservations in the *Doctrine of Virtue*: "The Stoic showed a noble cast of mind when he had his Sage say: I want a friend, not that he might help me in poverty, sickness, imprisonment, etc., but rather that I might stand by him and rescue a man. But the same Sage, when he could not save his friend, said to himself: what is it to me? In other words, he repudiated imparted suffering" (*DV* 125). And also in the *Lecture on Ethics*: "If in such a case there is no way in which I can be of help to the sufferer and I can do nothing to alter his situation, I might as well turn coldly away and say with the Stoics: 'it is no concern of mine; my wishes cannot help him'" (*LE* 199–200).

The question, of course, is whether communication of sentiment can "alter the situation," and Kant doesn't elaborate. But of course, sometimes displaying sentiment when more ameliorative action can't be taken is itself a way of actively sharing in another's ends. Tenderly telling an ailing parent at a nursing home who looks forward to the cheer of daily visits, "I know how important it is to you that I come visit, and I wish I could, but my work schedule is inflexible this week," seems something more than an ineffectual communication of feeling. Nor is one simply informing another of one's priorities. Rather, there is the intention of letting the other know one is sympathetic to their needs and supportive in a circumscribed way. Of course, the repetition of these sorts of phrases in a life that shows little else by way of altruism begins to ring hollow, but short of that wider assessment of an agent's track record, they ought not in themselves be ruled out as ways of responding to others' needs. They are sometimes ways of letting others know their needs have been recorded, even if one lacks the resources to help or chooses not to give priority to those needs now. In this respect, there may be an important difference between idly wishing another well and conveying sympathetic sorrow or joy. One can imagine cases in which volitionally expressing those feelings *is* showing kindness.

The aesthetic claim seems further to mitigate the idea that emotional comportment can be morally substantive and its lack a sign of moral deficiency. Recall here that emotions are ornamental trim, superficial garments that enhance the appearance of morality. But they are no more than an illusion of morality, shadow play of the real thing, something that brings us closer to morality but falls short itself. So Kant says at the conclusion of *The Doctrine of Virtue*:

> These are, indeed, only *outworks* or by-products (*parerga*), which present a fair illusion of something like virtue, an illusion which also deceives no one, since everyone knows how to take it. *Affability, sociability, courtesy, hospitality,* and *gentleness* (in disagreeing without quarreling) are, indeed, only small change; yet they promote the feeling for virtue itself by [arousing] a striving to bring this illusion as near as possible to the truth, . . . and in so doing they work toward a virtuous attitude in so far as they at least make virtue *fashionable.* (*DV* 145–146)[17]

We may agree with Kant that some of these particular qualities are not themselves moral; etiquette at the dinner party, a subject partial to Kant's heart in the *Anthropologie,* may be, as he suggests in the above passage, "small change," optional trim that enhances the overall packaging of morality but doesn't substantively affect its content. But should we regard the natural emotions in general in this way? Are the gentleness we show toward the suffering, the regret we feel at letting an innocent person die merely optional trim on our moral actions? To the extent that we have these sensibilities and fail to cultivate or express them, can we have an adequate moral response? In some cases it seems unlikely. To the beneficiary the action is not received in the same way, it doesn't convey the same *moral* qualities if it is lacking the appropriate tone or manner. And even when what we convey to others is not at issue, what we convey to ourselves (about ourselves) may be. We need a way of assessing the moral admirability of an action (and derivatively, moral character) that is thicker than whether or not it is motivated by an interest in what is lawful.

There is, as we might expect, a neo-Kantian rejoinder to this. In an already quoted passage Baron argues, "A conception [of duty] that overlooks the importance of the attitudes and dispositions one has when one performs certain acts, especially those which are intended to express affection or concern" is a "false conception of one's duty." What is required are "certain parameters within which satisfactory ways of acting from duty must be located" (1984, 204–205). The remarks are not intended to be Kantian exegesis. But still they are instructive for how Kant might pursue the sorts of objections we are raising. Kant might take "satisfactory ways of acting from duty" to mean ways that are not "forsaken by the graces." For otherwise, "they can make no claim to humanity" (*Anthr.* 147). But still, these modes of acting are only external packaging for morality, dispensible to those who know the true worth of virtue. They are a kind of outward ornament that ideally, in the community of mature moral persons, could be stripped without damaging the moral response. Those who can "behold virtue in her proper shape" would need none of these "spurious adornments" (*GW* 94 n).

Again, Kant might have a different sort of reply. The proper *temperament* of virtue must characterize above all the fully virtuous person's actions. A life devoted to duty doesn't entail, as Kant insists in his replies to Schiller's objections, a monastic cast of mind:

> Now if one asks, What is the *aesthetic character*, the *temperament*, so to speak, *of virtue*, whether courageous and hence *joyous* or fear-ridden and dejected, an answer is hardly necessary. This latter slavish frame of mind can never occur without a hidden *hatred* of the law. And a heart which is happy in the *performance* of its duty (not merely complacent in the *recognition* theoreof) is a mark of genuineness in the virtuous disposition. . . . A joyous frame of mind [is that] without which man is never certain of having really *attained a love* for the good, i.e., of having incorporated it into his maxim. (*Rel.* 19 n; cf. *K2* 121–123)

"All these things lose their value if we do or suffer them in bad humor and in a surly frame of mind" (*Anthr.* 104).

But I would argue that the *aesthetic character* of virtue in this passage no longer refers to the cultivated pathological emotions of compassion, amiability, gentleness, sympathy, regret, etc., whose expanded role I have been urging. Rather, what Kant has in mind is the gladness or acting from duty; this is a moral pleasure or contentment that is insurance of the genuineness of an agent's moral motive. Like the sense of respect, it indicates a wholehearted commitment to live a life from the motive or duty, that is, from an interest in acting only on maxims that can be willed as laws.[18] The pathological emotions are conceptually distinct from this sort of pleasure. For we can gladly act from duty without anguish or resentment in a kind of resolute and even joyous way and yet lack feelings of compassion or pity or friendliness toward the particular individuals we are helping.

My present claim is not that in acting from duty, we *overlook* individuals, priggishly caring more for duty (or in a sanctimonious way for our own moral achievements) than for the others whom we are helping. This sort of duty fetishism distorts the foundation of Kantian ethics. For duty requires that we respect individuals in their own right as ends worthy of being protected and promoted. As such, persons are not merely occasions for the promotion of duty or moral achievement but also objects we take an interest in for their own sake *because* of duty. We can agree with all this, however, and still argue that acting gladly from duty does not replace or make otiose these other emotions that reflect a diverse range of appropriate moral attitudes to persons. The fact that one acts from duty willingly and gladly does not ensure that one will express these other morally appropriate emotions. Sometimes an expression of confident reassurance is what is appropriate, at other times a tough, no-nonsense manner. Sometimes horror, sometimes grief. But certainly the range is more diverse and nuanced than Kant implies is requisite for acting from practical respect or gladness. Put another way, the absence of a kind of *akrasia* regarding duty and wayward inclination and its replacement with a kind of "temperate" or virtuous spirit seems too thin a characterization of moral sensitivity. The emotional palette is far too bland. The intrinsic pleasure of acting from a goodwill thus does not exhaust other, circumstance-specific emotions. Whatever the pleasure of realizing a commitment to virtue, there is a gamut of context-specific emotions that that pleasure stands in relation to. What the relation is, is not my present concern. That the emotions are something apart from the pleasure is the point. But equally, as conditional moral goods, they are something more than merely ways of accenting or adorning virtue. They are part of the fabric of the response. The moral response that lacks appropriate emotional expression lacks a means and mode of expression that for humans, at least, is morally significant. The motif of aesthetic embellishment seems to diminish this point about the constitution of human virtue.

But this brings me to a deeper point. It may not be just the way we *express* virtues (or moral ends) that is contingent upon human constitution. The virtues or moral ends themselves may be, and so in a sense the heteronomy of Kantian morality may be much more thoroughgoing than it appears at first glance. That is, assume Kantians reply that all I have said can be accommodated by talk about what is commendable and fine within *human* morality. Thus Kant can accommodate the emotions by talking about its special role in the *human* application of morality. But once we open the floodgates of moral *anthropology,* much more than emotions needs to be fitted in. For it is not just that we need a way of morally commending the emotional dimensions peculiar to human virtue. The virtues themselves and the principles that correspond to them are ways of realizing our rationality in human circumstances. Indeed, when we commend an agent for acting on the obligatory ends set by duty, we are commending them for an admirable *human* response. For the obligatory ends are themselves tailored to the human case.

Thus it is not insignificant that in justifying substantive moral principles or obligatory ends for human beings, Kant typically appeals to empirical premises that refer to the nature of human needs and *human* rationality.[19] Beneficence is not a moral principle for angels, but for human beings whose rational capacities happen to be finite and who therefore need the collaborative assistance and resources of others. A maxim that seeks to gain self-advantage by denying mutual aid is incoherent in the universalized world of that maxim only because the agent of such a maxim will be denied what she needs for effective human willing. It is because of our human condition that a policy of mutual disinterest is impermissible, and its opposite, benificence, morally required. Put differently, dependance is a contingent matter for us, and the obligation to be beneficent requires appeal to that empirical premise. We contradict our wills by a maxim of non beneficence insofar as we deny a standing fact about our wills.   Although I shall not argue the point here, I believe it can be argued that other substantive human virtues and the categorical imperatives that correspond to them are similarly justified by appeal to certain empirical facts. But if this is the case, then not only *how* we express what we are morally required to do is contingent upon our constitutions, but equally, *what* we are morally required to do. That is, substantive moral principles or ends depend upon empirical facts.[20] And though ultimately the ground of our obligation to be moral and our interest in morality may for Kant be a priori, resting on the fact of our rationality (and the fact that as rational, causal agents we must act lawfully), what principles we act on from that motive and how we apply and realize those principles appear deeply heteronomous. To the extent that we on earth aim to create a human, moral community, both the content of those principles and the ways they are realized matter morally. The regulative procedure given by the moral law in the pure metaphysics of morals cannot itself suffice to set obligatory ends without the addition of empirical facts.

Finally, by way of concession, even if this is the stuff of moral anthropology and not of the pure metaphysics of morals, the labels needn't prejudice us in a way they sometimes seem to for Kant. For even if we suppose that substantive moral principles are not objectively valid for all rational beings and that the moral estimability of our characters varies according to how well we express those principles relative to the resources, still an interest in morality as lawful agency may be independent of these contingencies. Just how substantive such a claim is, though, is another matter.[21]

Notes

1. I have in mind here recent writings of Marcia Baron (1984), Barbara Herman (1981, 1983, 1984a, 1984b, and 1985), and Susan Mendus (1984). For a portrait of Kant that emphasizes the concept of virtue in his writings, see Onora O'Neill (1985) and Robert Louden (1988).

2. Editions and abbreviations of Kant's texts that I cite are as follows: *Groundwork of the Metaphysics of Morals*, trans. H. J. Paton (Harper and Row, 1964) (*GW*); *Critique of Practical Reason*, trans. Lewis White Beck (Bobbs-Merrill, 1956) (*K2*); *The Doctrine of Virtue: Part II of "The Metaphysics of Morals,"* trans. Mary J. Gregor (University of Pennsylvania Press, 1964) (*DV*); *Anthropologie from a Pragmatic Point of View*, trans. Mary Gregor (Martinus Nijhoff, 1974) (*Anthr.*); *Religion within the Limits of Reason Alone* (Harper and Row, 1934) (*Rel.*); *Lecture on Ethics*, trans. Louis Infield (Hacket, 1963) (*LE*). In quoting Kant, I have kept the italics as they appear in these translations.

3. On the issue of moral salience, see Lawrence Blum 1980, Iris Murdoch 1970, Martha Nussbaum 1985, Onora O'Neill 1985, Barbara Herman 1985, Nancy Sherman 1989.

4. Marcia Baron explores Williams discussion of agent regret, arguing that the notion may help us to avoid too minimalist a conception of responsibility. See Baron 1988.

5. For a valuable discussion of moral conflict as it is treated by Aristotle in his notion of mixed actions in *Nicomachean Ethics* 3:1, see Stocker 1989.

6. See *DV* 23 for the denial of genuine conflicts of duty: "A *conflict of duties* . . . would be a relation of duties in which one of them would annul the other (wholly or in part).—But a *conflict of duties* and obligations is inconceivable. For the concepts of duty and oblgation as such express the objective practical *necessity* of certain actions, and two conflicting rules cannot both be necessary at the same time: if it is our duty to act according to one of these rules, then to act according to the opposite one is not our duty and is even contrary to duty."

7. The following passage from the *Groundwork* would seem to detract from the above claim: "Inclinations themselves, as sources of needs, are so far from having an absolute value to make them desirable for their own sake that it must rather be the universal wish of every rational being to be wholly free from them" (*GW* 95). But even this exhortation, reminiscent of Plato's *Phaedo*, can be seen as largely rhetorical and as urging not so much a policy of extirpation as one of cooperation. The point would be again that inclinations and needs are not valued in their own right apart from their service to a good will. Still, there is no positive note here to the effect that once they do support the moral motive, they become conditionally valued, and the moral motive somehow enhanced or morally more complete.

8. On this point I have been greatly influenced by Herman (1981).

9. So Carl G. Lange's famous essay on the emotions begins, "Kant, in a passage in his *Anthropologie*, qualifies the affections as diseases on the mind. . . . To a more

realistic school of psychology which knows no abstract "Ideal" man, but rather "takes men as they are," such a doctrine of the soul must appear strange. It must be but a meager conception of man's existence, to consider pain and pleasure, pity and anger, defiance and humility, as conditions foreign to normal life, or even as something from which one must turn away if one wishes to recognize the actual nature of man-kind (1922, 33–92).

10. I have profitted from the more general discussion of emotions and their voluntary aspects in Roberts 1988 and Gordon 1987.

11. See DV 59 for the suggestion that every person who is to be obligated by the moral law has sufficient natural (pathological) dispositions in virtue of which he can be obligated.

12. Compare, for example, the tone of GW 95, quoted above in note 7.

13. On this role, see Herman 1985.

14. "There are certain moral dispositions such that anyone lacking them could have no duty to acquire them. They are *moral feeling, conscience, love* of one's neighbor, and *reverence* for oneself (*self-esteem*). There is no obligation to have these, because they lie at the basis of morality as *subjective* conditions of our receptiveness to the concept of duty, not as objective conditions of morality. All of them are natural dispositions of the mind (*praedispositio*) to be affected by concepts of duty—antecedent dispositions on the side of feeling. To have them is not a duty: every man has them and it is by virtue of them that he can be obligated" (*DV* 59). Note that Kant equivocates within this passage between calling the feelings he lists "moral dispositions" and calling them "natural dispositions . . . to be affected by concepts of duty." Perhaps the thought is that when subjective or pathological conditions are properly cultivated, they themselves become moral.

15. Something like this is embodied in Rawls' Aristotelian principle (1971, 426 n). It is implicit in Aristotle's *Nicomachean Ethics*, 7:11–14, 10:1–5. I discuss the principle as it appears in Aristotle in Sherman 1989, p. 184–190.

16. Even the following *Groundwork* passage seems to be compatbile with this line: "Love out of inlination cannot be commanded; but kindness done from duty—although no inclination impels us, and even although natural and unconquerable disinclination stands in our way—is *practical*, and not *pathological*, love, residing in the will and not in the propensions of feeling, in principles of action and not of melting compassion; and it is this practical love alone which can be an object of command" (*GW* 67). I take Kant to be repeating the familiar claim that we cannot be commanded to have certain natural advantages. That is a matter of the external lottery. But we can be commanded to love out of inclination if this means to cultivate what by nature you already have.

17. Note that the passage does not directly refer to emotions (apart perhaps from the mention of gentleness), though it is similar enough to other passages that do to be relevant.

18. On respect, see GW 69 n.

19. For a clear exposition of this, see Buchanan 1977 and also Herman 1984b and O'Neill 1985.

20. Kant, of course, is by no means unequivocal about this. In the *Groundwork* he would seem to deny the above point: "We ought never—as speculative philosophy does allow and even at times finds necessary—to make principles depend on the special nature of human reason. Since moral laws have to hold for every rational being as such, we ought rather to derive our principles from the general concept of a rational being as such" (*GW* 79). Again, in the *Doctrine of Virtue*, substantive laws are viewed as valid a priori for all rational beings: "The counterpart of a

metaphysics of morals, the other member of the division of practical philosophy in general, would be moral anthropology. But this would concern only the subjective conditions that hinder or help man in *putting into practice* the laws given in a metaphysic of morals. It would deal with the generation, propagation, and strengthening of moral principles (in the education of school children and of the public at large), and other such teachings and precepts based on experience. This cannot be dispensed with, but it must not precede a metaphysics of morals or be mixed with it; for we would then run the risk of bringing forth false or at least indulgent moral laws, misrepresenting, as if it were unattainable, what has not been attained simply because the law has not been seen and presented in its purity" (*DV* 14–15). Thus the line between a pure metaphysics of morals and anthropology is not consistently drawn by Kant, with such terms as "categorical imperative," "practical law," "moral principles," and so on, failing to point to a decisive answer. On this, see Buchanan 1977.

21. I owe special thanks to Marcia Baron, Rudiger Bittner, Henry Richardson, and Michael Stocker for reading and commenting on some version of this chapter. Also, I am grateful to audiences at the University of Arizona, the University of California at Santa Barbara, and Georgetown University, before whom an earlier draft of this chapter was read.

Part III
Moral Psychology and the Social Virtues

Chapter 8

Vocation, Friendship, and Community: Limitations of the Personal-Impersonal Framework

Lawrence A. Blum

The conflict between personal projects and the impersonal demands of morality has been an important focus of recent moral theory. The writings of Thomas Nagel (1986), Susan Wolf (1982), Norman Care 1984, 1987), and others concern themselves with whether, and the extent to which, morality understood as impersonal, impartial, universal, and rational does, or ought to, constrain personal projects and satisfaction.[1] These writers appropriately question the unexamined presumption of traditional moral theories, especially of a Kantian or utilitarian stripe, that the impersonal demands of morality ought always and automatically to take precedence over personal pursuits. However, they also make the further assumption that ethical reflection must take place within a framework defined solely by the personal/impersonal dichotomy.

A second currently prominent issue is the communitarian critique of liberalism. An important strand of this critique is that because of its (alleged) bias toward individualism, liberalism cannot account for, nor can a liberal polity sufficiently foster, communalist social and political values such as a sense of community, citizen participation, the integrity of distinct cultures, specific shared goods as constitutive of political community, and the like.

The communitarianism/liberalism dispute has operated primarily in two philosophic domains—political philosophy and the "metaphysical" theory of the self. Regarding the latter, for example, Michael Sandel (1982) argues against John Rawls (1971) that the identities of selves are in part constituted by their communal attachments (to nation, ethnic group, family, class, and other such communal entities) and that this feature of the self is denied by Rawls's liberalism. Rawls (1985) replies that his liberalism requires no theory of the self at all and that the real question is whether a liberal polity can accommodate legitimate communitarian values. The dispute shifts back and forth between the metaphysical level and the political level.

Seldom is the liberalism/communitarianism dispute fought out on the turf of moral theory per se. Communitarians have not, by and large, attempted to develop a moral psychology for communitarianism. What kind of motivations, attitudes, sensibilities, and virtues are involved in the attachments, and the actions flowing from such attachments, to various communitarian entities? How do communitarian attachments in their various modes generate responsibilities and actions?

I will try to bring the communitarianism-liberalism debate into closer relationship with moral theory by arguing that the "personal-impersonal" framework that forms the context of the debate about the legitimate scope of the personal domain presents a substantial obstacle to developing the kind of moral psychology capable of illuminating the liberalism-communitarianism controversy.

I will suggest that while philosophers working on the personal-impersonal issue have, for the most part, rejected Kantianism as a moral theory, they have insufficiently broken with Kant's moral psychology—his portrayal of morally significant motivation as either the desire for personal happiness or respect for the impersonal demands of morality.

Against the moral psychology implied in the personal-impersonal framework (as exemplified in the work of Thomas Nagel, Susan Wolf, and Norman Care, described below), I will argue the following:

- There is a large range of types of action and motivation which fall neither on the side of the personal and nonmoral nor on the side of the purely impersonal and moral. I will be discussing in particular (1) actions of compassion for an individual outside a specific moral relationship, (2) actions stemming from one's social role, (3) actions of friendship, (4) actions issuing from one's understanding of one's vocation, and (5) actions stemming from one's attachment to a particular community. Actions in categories (3), (4), and (5) can in turn be broken down into three types: care, guidance by the general category of the relationship (friendship, vocation, or community), and guidance by the specific relationship.
- Although an attempt can be made to capture these nonpersonal, nonimpersonal actions within the personal-impersonal framework, this attempt distorts the phenomena in question.
- There are morally and psychologically distinct uses of "impersonal" that are also different from the notion of impersonality employed in the personal-impersonal framework.

• The personal-impersonal framework operates with a conception of personal good or flourishing that is excessively privatized and hence that fails to see how our personal good is bound inextricably to specific persons in personal relationships, to vocations, and to communities that give our lives meaning.

1

Thomas Nagel in *The View from Nowhere* (1986) sees "the central problem of ethics" as "how the lives, interests, and welfare of others make claims on us and how these claims . . . are to be reconciled with the aim of living our own lives" (p. 164). He characterizes the impersonal standpoint of morality as one from which all choosers can agree, as seeing oneself as merely one among others, and as seeing the world from nowhere within it. He looks forward to a world in which the impersonal demands of morality are met largely by impersonal institutions, leaving individuals "free to devote considerable attention and energy to their own lives and to values that could not be impersonally acknowledged" (p. 207).

Susan Wolf in her article "Moral Saints" (1982) expresses what she sees as the limitations of morality's hold over us and our practical deliberations, by speaking of two "points of view" from which choices and actions can be approached—the moral point of view, involving the impersonal demand that we consider other persons as "equally real" or equally important as ourselves, and "the point of view of individual perfection," in which the individual agent's making the most of herself, striving toward individual nonmoral perfection, is the salient consideration.

Wolf's distinction between these two perspectives is set in the context of a detailed criticism of a life centered on moral pursuits. While her rich and complex argument cannot be summarized briefly, one important overall strand in it is that the "moral saint" neglects the perspective of the point of view of individual perfection and tends to devalue it. (A fuller critique of Wolf's argument is given in Blum 1988b.) In this way the moral saint is importantly defective and unworthy of full (or perhaps even much) admiration and emulation.

A similar distinction between a purely personal good and the impersonal concerns of morality is put to a quite different use by Norman Care in his excellent and challenging book *On Shared Fate* (1987) and earlier article "Career Choice" (1984). Care notes great inequities within the world in regard to life chances and to the means to personal self-realization. Drawing on this empirical fact, Care argues that a reasonably advantaged person living in an advanced country such as the United States ought to sacrifice some (and perhaps a great deal) of her own self-realization for the sake of promoting the self-realization of others. Care discusses self-realization specifically in the context of career choice, which is the choice of a central project and mode of one's life. Care's argument is based on what he calls "shared fate individualism," in which securing the bases for everyone's individual self-realization is a task for each.

In this way Care gives the moral priority over the personal. This is denied by Wolf and partially denied by Nagel. Yet, like Nagel and Wolf, Care frames his concerns in terms of an opposition between two mutually exclusive and seemingly exhaustive desiderata—a personal good (of self-realization) and an impersonal morality.

2

To explore the large domain of actions and motivations that are neither personal nor impersonal, I begin with an example taken from Herbert Kohl's *Growing Minds: On Becoming a Teacher* (1984). Kohl, then a secondary school teacher, was asked by some parents in a school in which he was teaching if he would give special tutoring to their son. The boy was 14 years old and did not know how to read. He was a large boy, angry, and defiant; his teachers did not know how to handle him. Kohl agreed to work with the boy two days a week after class.

Kohl worked with the boy for several months. Kohl found him extremely difficult and never grew to like him personally. But eventually he helped the boy to begin reading. Kohl describes how he came to take a personal interest in the boy's progress as a learner and to find satisfaction in what the boy was able to accomplish under his tutelage.

This activity on Kohl's part does not come under the rubric of purely personal good as this is understood in the literature I have referred to. Kohl was motivated neither to undertake helping the boy nor to persevere in doing so by a desire to promote his own personal benefit or self-realization. The request from the boy's parents was essentially an unsought and quite probably unwelcome intrusion into, in Nagel's words, Kohl's "living his own life." And Kohl's inability to like the boy himself prevented the activity from being an enjoyable one for Kohl.

At the same time, the activity does not fall under the rubric of an accession to an impersonal moral demand either. For one thing, Kohl was not *required* to help the boy, and he does not describe himself as experiencing such a requirement. More important (since not all moral pulls from the side of the impersonal domain express themselves in the form of strict requirements), Kohl did not look at the situation, even implicitly, in an impersonal way. He did not step back to adopt a standpoint reflecting a universal, impartial perspective, figuring out what that standpoint urged on anyone situated similarly to himself, or looking at the situation from the viewpoint of any rational being. Rather, Kohl's motivation was of a more particularistic nature. He responded to, was moved by, the particular boy's plight, namely his being 14 years old and unable to read. Kohl experienced this as a terrible condition for the boy himself and was aware how damaged the boy would be if the schools system continued to be unable to teach him to read. Perhaps Kohl was moved also by sympathy for the parents' in their distress and despair. It is to the particular boy that Kohl responded, not to an impersonally derived value generating a reason for all.

The same could be said of many acts of compassion that presuppose no prior morally structured relationship between the agent and the sufferer. (In Blum 1986 I argue in greater detail that acts of compassion are typically neither "personal" nor "impersonal" according to the literature discussed here.) But it is significant in this situation that it is not simply as a human being or as an individual that Kohl takes on the tutoring, that he responds to the boy's plight, but specifically *as a teacher*. It is as a teacher that he sees the boy's need clearly, appreciates its significance, and is in a position to do something about it.

As Kohl is at pains to point out throughout his book, particularly in the chapter describing his interaction with the 14-year-old boy, Kohl's understanding of what it is to be a teacher is an important part of what meaning this particular activity has for him. In bringing this category (teacher) to bear on the situation, Kohl in a sense invokes the entire structure of social meaning and tradition within which the concept of teacher gets its significance. He sees that significance as involving certain values and ideals—promoting the intellectual growth of his pupils, teaching them habits of mind and a love for learning, which, as he sees it, will serve them in certain ways within society.

It is not that it would be *incorrect* to say that Kohl responds to the boy "as an individual." This could be a way of saying, for example, that he sees the boy as a whole individual person and not merely, say, as a member of a disadvantaged group or as a "problem case." And as a characterization of Kohl himself in this situation, to say that he acts "as an individual" could perhaps be to say that he is not acting merely from a narrowly circumscribed sense of his role. But in getting clear on the contours of the vast territory outside of the personal and the impersonal, there is an important distinction to be made between the kind of care, compassion, or concern appropriate to persons standing in no structured relationship to one another and those motives and sentiments as mediated by such structured relationships as teacher to student or parent to child.

3

I want to distinguish two forms of such structured mediating relationships. One draws on the idea of teacher as a role. Dorothy Emmet's account of this concept in her excellent book *Rules, Roles, and Relations* (1966) involves the imposition of a specific set of obligations on an occupant of the role—a set of obligations that applies in the same way to *anyone* occupying the role but not to those who do not occupy it. Thus the role obligations of a college professor might include holding a certain number of office hours, grading students fairly, teaching one's material in a professionally responsible way, and the like. This conception of role sees it as something like a job description. If you take on the job, such and such are your responsibilities.

The morality of a specific role in Emmet's sense is not wholly impersonal in the "view from nowhere" sense. It is not a universal morality but applies only to occupants of the role. It would be an impersonal morality in the sense of the personal-impersonal framework only if it could be further shown that the existence of that specific role with its specific responsibilities could be directly derived from (and not merely shown to be compatible with) such a purely impersonal point of view. Because of the historical contingencies bound up with the morality of virtually any given role in a particular society, this seems highly unlikely.

Thus action taken from a sense of role responsibility, even when done from obligation, is distinct from both personal and impersonal action. While in the Kantian morality the notion of duty or obligation is identified with the universal and impersonal standpoint of the categorical imperative, in fact, role duties are not impersonal in that sense.

Nevertheless, in a different sense, role morality *is* impersonal. It is impersonal in the sense that the morality in question applies to *any* occupant of the role, independent of the occupant's particular personal characteristics. The obligations of a role are set (if not totally fixed) and are externally placed upon anyone who comes to occupy the role. This is a familiar and significant sense of "impersonal" and is distinct from the view-from-nowhere sense.

4

If "role" is understood in Emmet's sense (as I will understand it from here on), then Kohl probably had *no* role obligation to help the illiterate boy, since doing so was not part of his specific job responsibilities as a teacher in the school. But for Kohl in this situation, the notion of teacher functions as a much richer concept than role does in Emmet's sense. It invokes a general place and purpose within society and carries with it certain values, standards, and ideals. In fact, one of the burdens of Kohl's book is to exhibit teaching *not* simply as a job with a job description (i.e., as a role in Emmet's sense) but as a *vocation*.

The notion of a vocation implies that the ideals it embodies are ones that speak specifically to the individual in question. There is a personal identification with the vocation, with its values and ideals, and a sense of personal engagement that helps to sustain the individual in her carrying out the activities of the vocation. These aspects are generally not present in the case of roles that are not also part of vocations. An individual needs to be in some way especially personally suited to a type of work in order for it to be a vocation, while this is not so for a role. Beyond this (since an individual could be suited to an occupation yet not experience it as a vocation) an individual with a vocation must believe deeply in the values and ideals of the vocation and must in some way choose or at least affirm them *for herself*.

(There are some wider issues about vocations that go beyond the scope of this chapter but that might be briefly mentioned. Not all vocations are service vocations in the way teaching and medicine are, i.e., serving, at least ideally, the good of individuals or of society as a whole. Science and art, for example, can certainly be vocations but are not necessarily service vocations in that sense. Perhaps there are even morally bad vocations, such as hit man or burglar. If so, then what would make a type of activity a vocation would be connected with the possibility of realizing various excellences, even if those excellences serve a countermoral end. This possibility implies that a paradigm vocation is one that both realizes excellences and also serves a good end or ends, even if these are not necessarily *moral* ends.)

The differences between roles and vocations yield a further sense in which vocations are nonimpersonal beyond the sense in which roles are nonimpersonal. Roles do not necessarily reflect the individual occupant's sense of personal value. This is why the moral pull exerted by role obligations as a moral requirement of the *position* can be experienced as entirely external to the person. In this sense the pull is impersonal. By contrast, when a vocation exercises moral pull—e.g., the moral pull which Kohl feels toward helping the illiterate boy—it is not in this sense impersonal, for it is experienced as implicated in the individual's own sense of personal values (as embodied in the vocation).

Related to this difference between role and vocation is that the particular way in which the individual agent understands the values, ideals, and traditions of her vocation yields what she experiences as its moral pulls. Perhaps another individual with a vocation for teaching would show her dedication to its values and ideals in what she did during class time but for various personal reasons might make a decision never to take on after-hours work. She might in some sense experience a moral pull in the kind of situation Kohl faces with the boy, but she would not experience it in the same way as Kohl does. What precisely *are* the values and ideals that inform being a teacher or any sufficiently complex and rich vocation and how to apply these values and ideals in a particular situation will be matters of some dispute. There is room for individual interpretation, though this possibility does not entail subjectivism. Arguments can be given for the superiority of some interpretations to others, and some interpretations can be ruled out as too far from what any reasonable person could take those values and ideals to entail.

The existence of such personal variability contrasts with the case of roles. While there is inevitably *some* room for interpretation with any set of definite rules or job specifications, this room is much less than in the case of vocations, partly because the statement of ideals and values is at a much greater level of generality than a statement of role responsibilities. (Note, however, that the line between strict role obligation and ideal cannot be firmly fixed. It is subject to alteration, so that what one individual regards as required by her conception of a given vocation beyond current role obligations can come to be generally accepted and institutionalized as constituting the actual role obligations of that vocation. For example, in a specific school or even in a school system a certain amount of after-class work could be or become mandatory as part of the role obligations of being a teacher in that school.)

We have, then, two distinct senses of "impersonal" of decreasing scope:

1. A sense that applies to all persons independent of personal characteristics or personal values (view-from-nowhere impersonality)

2. A sense that applies to a restricted group of persons (role occupants) independent of personal characteristics or values

Actions done from a sense of one's vocation are impersonal in *neither* of these senses, while role action is impersonal in sense (2) but not sense (1).

While vocational action involves the element of personal value and personal interpretation rendering it nonimpersonal in the two senses mentioned, neither is it personal in the senses given to the term by Care, Wolf, and Nagel. The vocational agent does not take herself to be pursuing a goal simply because of its value to *her*. It is not because it is part of her project that she is impelled to help the pupil, to give extra tutoring to the student, and the like. Rather, the vocational agent takes herself to be responding to a value outside of herself, following (what she takes to be) its dictates. She is not pursuing a merely personal value either in the sense of something unconnected with the claims of other persons or in the sense in which she sees the reason for its pursuit as being conferred by its place in her own personal goals.

It is true that the vocational agent perceives this external value, is sensitive to its force, is aware of its implications, and understands its dictates in the way she does *because* of her values, which she does not necessarily regard as incumbent upon all others similarly situated. This is what is involved in the concept of a vocation developed here. This means that acting from one's own values can precisely be a way of responding to the plight of others or of responding to the dictates of an "external" value. This point will be explored further below, but at this juncture I can say that part of what it means that Kohl (for example) has the vocation of a teacher and affirms its values (as he understands them) as his own is that he appreciates the damage caused by illiteracy and is moved by the plight of an illiterate boy. It is part of his identity as a teacher (as he understands it) that he possesses these sentiments, understandings, appreciations, and the like.

This analysis of vocational action as not personal and also not impersonal in the two senses above yields a third sense in which it *can* be said to be "impersonal," namely that it is and is regarded by the agent as a response to some external, objective, or real value. It has value transcending the merely personal.

Vocational action is not what Norman Care means by "self-realization," inasmuch as he counterposes that to "service to others," for a service vocation does involve service to others. It is not what Susan Wolf calls "individual perfection," since its aim and motivation is not to perfect the person as individual but to respond to the values one sees as implicated in one's understanding of one's vocation. It is not what Thomas Nagel means by "living one's own life," as that is counterposed to acknowledging the claims of others as setting limits on such pursuit, since service occupations do acknowledge the claims of others.

To summarize the argument up to this point, there are three dimensions of action and motivation—direct individual-to-individual care, Emmetian role action, and action from vocation—that fit neither the model of purely personal or private good nor that of purely view-from-nowhere, impersonal morality.

5

Though neither personal nor impersonal, vocational action itself is not all of one motivational type. I will distinguish three different types, or dimensions, of vocational action. (They often operate together and on many occasions are only analytically separate.) These differ in regard to the different ways that particularity and generality come into their characteristic motivational sets. I will argue also that the same trichotomy applies to communal action, actions stemming from the agent's involvement with (certain kinds of) communities.

I will explain the three modes by drawing an analogy between vocation and friendship, arguing that friendship (and personal relationships in general) lend themselves to the same trichotomy. Friendship shares with vocation the quality of being a social category involving values, norms, or standards of action, attitude, and sentiment. It also shares these features with roles that are not vocations, but it lacks the definite structure of roles and leaves room for and even requires personal variability and individuality. The latter quality makes friendship more like a vocation than a role.

I will refer to the three modes of vocation, friendship, and community as care, generality, particular relationship.

Care
A friend can act from a direct concern for her friend, without appeal to the norms of friendship, without a sense that the fact that the other is a friend renders her under an *ought* (which is not necessarily an obligation) to be helping her friend. She may simply be moved

by her friend's suffering, danger, or unhappiness to comfort her, to help her out, and the like.

Friendship care is not the same as the pure individual-to-individual compassion discussed earlier. The spontaneous unmediated act of friendship is not the act of a pure individual toward another individual but of a friend to another friend. The friend would not have that same spontaneous reaction to a nonfriend. This is partly because in general (though not always) one cares about one's friends more than about nonfriends. But it is also because one cares about friends in a different way than one cares about strangers. One notices different things about friends than about others (though one also notices different things about different friends). Friendship care is characteristically more bound up with intimacy and with trust than stranger-to-stranger caring or compassion.[2]

Like pure individual-to-individual care, friendship care is neither personal nor impersonal. Similarly, we can speak of a kind of care attaching to vocations, especially service vocations. Kohl exemplifies a kind of teacher caring in his dealings with the illiterate boy. He responds directly to the boy without consulting the norms of his vocation to see what they prescribe. (Nor does Kohl seem to be drawing on them implicitly either. Caring is often distinct from implicit guidance by norms or principles. On this, see Blum 1987.)

Yet Kohl's caring is a specific form of caring. It is different, for example, from the caring of one friend for another. And it is significantly different from the kind of caring appropriate to or characteristic of a nurse, a doctor, a therapist, an athletic coach, a lawyer, or a parent. One might say that these semispecialized carings involve focuses on different aspects of the other persons (whom I will refer to as "charges"—e.g., pupils, patients, clients, budding athletes, friends, children) party to the vocational, friendship, or parental relationship. They thus involve different kinds of sensitivities. And one might say they involve (to some extent) different virtues.

At the same time all carings have something in common. All involve, for example, caring about a person in her totality. So if the *only* object of a teacher's concern is making sure that a pupil understands a certain subject matter, then this teacher does not exemplify teacher caring. To be caring, the concern must involve some regard for the pupil's overall good and a sense of how the good of learning the specific subject matter fits into the pupil's overall good. Without this, one can infer that the teacher values her subject matter but does not seem to have a clear sense of the value of her pupils as persons in their own right.

Caring must involve more than merely taking into account other aspects of one's charge's life. For example, suppose a college athletic coach concerned herself with her charges' family lives but *only* because and insofar as it impacted on their playing ability. While this would be an improvement over having no concern for her charges' personal life, it would not count as caring in my sense, since the attention to the charge's family would be (for the coach) only a means to her sole ultimate concern, which is not for the athlete as a whole person for but only for her athletic prowess and accomplishment.

But caring for one's charge as a whole person, and in that sense having some concern for all aspects of her good, is not incompatible with a (semi)specialization of sensitivity and concern on only some aspects of her good. Caring doctors and nurses are particularly sensitive to aspects of a person's life that bear on her health; caring teachers are sensitive to aspects of person's life that bear on their learning; caring coaches, to athletic development. To some extent these semidifferentiated sensitivities can be learned, and some may be likened to skills. But they still constitute a kind of virtue. For however one arrives at the ability in question, there is a difference between teacher-caring abilities, such as knowing how to give respect while challenging the student to go further and how to recognize resistances to learning, and the caring sensitivities necessary for being a good doctor or good coach.

Different sensitivities and virtues are required for dealing with charges who are extremely vulnerable and dependent, such as therapy patients and some medical patients, than with charges who are (in general) much less so, such as college students and athletes. Vocations that deal with individuals in the context of groups, such as classroom teachers, require (for the associated caring) a sensitivity to the ways that charges' self-esteem and motivation are affected by the group and individuals in it and an ability to act within this group setting to foster that self-esteem. Vocations taking place on a more individual-to-individual basis (e.g., doctor, lawyer, individual therapist) do not require this kind of sensitivity. A sensitivity to issues of trust, confidentiality, and betrayal is also differently required in different vocations, depending partly on the intimacy of revelation by the charge (e.g., in therapy), though almost any service vocation will involve these issues to some extent.[3]

Perhaps in some of these cases the differences between the virtues and sensitivities involved in vocational caring is only a matter of degree. But the point still remains that the moral character of the caring itself within different vocations is to some extent distinct. Note that vocational caring (or vocations as loci of caring) will not be as distinct as on conceptions of professions as role definitions. Some such conceptions would justify a teacher, for example, in not concerning herself with a pupil's personal problems on the grounds that "that is for therapists, not teachers." Such rigid role definition is prevented by vocation as (in part) care, since the charge's whole good must be the object of care.

In fact, many of the divisions between vocations, while explainable historically, have the character of little more than pragmatic and provisional adjustments to human nature and time constraints. Teachers would in some ways be better *as teachers* if they were also (in part) counselors, therapists, friends—if they had the virtues, skills, and sensitivities involved. It is unrealistic to expect teachers (and similar points hold for other professions) fully to be all these things; the role would be too demanding for most people, and many people otherwise suited to teaching would not be able to take on these other sensitivities and their exercise. Nevertheless, it must also be kept in mind that the accepted definitions of vocations—with their specific norms, virtues, and ideals—are subject to contestation and change, and there are in fact currents afoot within teaching, law, and medicine to make them more caring and thereby to some extent to blur some of the divisions between these professions.

Recent discussion of a morality of care (see footnote 2), especially in the context of general talk of a morality of principle or morality of justice, has generally failed to explore the possibility that care can take significantly different forms in different contexts and thus can draw on significantly different virtues and sensitivities. But philosophical tradition—with its use of the very general and vague terms "beneficence," "benevolence," "altruism," "well-being," and the like—has been no better in this regard. Neither have appreciated the ways that caring about the good of others involves several distinct modes, sensitivities, and the like. Being able to perceive that someone is depressed and knowing how to bring her out of it is a different kind of quality than always being available to others when explicitly called upon. Yet both can be expressions of caring, and both count as benevolence. Generosity, kindness, and compassion are all distinct virtues concerning others' good, involving (perhaps clusters of) distinct sensitivities.

I mean my remarks here not primarily as a criticism of the notion of a morality of care but as a contribution to its further development. For seeing how caring can be different in different contexts actually gives a morality of care a greater power and scope than it has seemed to have (especially to some of its detractors, but to some sympathizers as well). That is, many have taken a morality of care to apply solely to the domain of personal relations and have thought that once one leaves this territory—moving to more "public" domains such as vocations, for example—another ethic will be necessary. It may be true in some sense that caring within personal relations is *less* specialized, and thus seemingly less restricted and more total, than vocational caring. But some degree of differentiation is present in personal relations as well. Caring for children is different from caring for friends. And anyway, caring for different friends can itself involve different sensitivities, depending on the particular friend and friendship. I may display some caring virtues with one friend and others with another friend; the two friends might need very different kinds of things from me. In any case, there are ways in which a teacher cares for a pupil and in which a parent does not for the child who is that pupil—virtues displayed by the teacher toward him that the parent does not need to display or has not the occasion to.

Recognizing that there can be caring in nonintimate relationships—less "personal" ones—thus can have the effect of broadening the scope of an ethic of care.

Generality
The next two modes of actions in friendship and vocation involve making explicit appeal to the existence of the friendship as a guide to action, trying to figure out what the norms of friendship bid of one in the particular situation. Thus these modes involve an ought—though not necessarily a *requirement* or an *obligation*—that is absent in the first mode of action of friendship or vocation (caring).

Not every such appeal will have the right to be called an act of friendship, however. The appeal has to be for the sake of the friend himself in order to count as a genuine act of friendship. Thus if I appeal to the norms of friendship as a way of ensuring that I am able to regard myself as a good friend, I am not really acting for my friend's sake. It can even be argued that appealing to the norms of friendship out of a genuine desire to *be* a good friend is too distant from a concern for the specific friend himself. The appeal to the norms of friendship must be a way of ensuring that I am doing what needs to be done *for, and for the sake of, that specific friend* in order to count as an act of friendship. When this is so, acting from the norms of friendship and friendship care can be genuine and authentic acts of friendship.

Yet within the category of the appeal to the norms of friendship there is a further distinction—that between the thought that friendship bids me to do a certain thing and the thought that *this particular friendship with this particular person* bids me to do a certain thing. The former thought—that of friendship in general—might for example restrain me from doing something incompatible with the very idea of friendship. For example, suppose a Chinese student, Da-Wei, studying in the United States at the time of the crackdown on the student democratic movement in China in spring 1989 is pressured by agents of the Chinese government to reveal the identities of Chinese student-movement activists in the U.S. If a friend of Da-Wei's is among those sought by the government, part of Da-Wei's motivation in not acceding to the pressures might well be the thought that one simply does not betray a friend in such a way. This is a type of action that the agent regards as prohibited by *any* friend toward any other friend.

This seems a case of a genuine act of friendship. However, appeal to the general category of friendship will sometimes be inappropriate to the situation and deficient as an act of friendship precisely *because* it abstracts too much from the particularity of the friendship.

Generality is like a role obligation in the respect that its moral pull applies to any occupant of the role (e.g., to any friend). But it is not really impersonal in the way that roles are (sense (2) in section 4). For the role obligation is generally spelled out explicitly as a rule (as part of the "job description"), while in friendship the norm the agent appeals to depends on his particular understanding of friendship and of the norms and values (which he need not ever have articulated before) that he sees implicit in it. He need not think of his interpretation as universal but can accept that others may interpret friendship differently. In this way appeal to the category of friendship itself is closer to the way that vocational action is "impersonal"—it involves responsiveness to a value external to the agent (see section 4).

Specific Relationship

The category of friend is invoked not only in general form but also explicitly as the specific relationship with a specific person. Each relationship has a unique, nonreplaceable value to its participants. Each has a unique history. And each involves the accumulation of specific understandings, both explicit and implicit, which reflect that value and that history. Because of this, I might feel that a certain action is called for on my part toward my friend Inez, an action that would not necessarily be appropriate to other friendships in similar circumstances. The thought here is not "friendship bids me to do *x*" but "*x* is what my particular friendship with Inez bids of me." An example might be of knowing that I should leave Inez alone during her current troubles but should make sure that she knows that my doing so reflects my understanding of what she does and does not want from me. I show my care for her by making sure that she realizes I am available should she feel she wants to call on me, but at the same time that (given our relationship and given who she is) she knows that I understand that she would not want my actively offering her comfort.

As mentioned above, people have different understandings of what they take to be involved in friendship per se, just as they do of vocations. So individuals have not only different and unique friendships but also individual (though not necessarily distinct) interpretations of friendship itself, which they do not necessarily expect that others share.

Friendship perhaps lends itself to the distinction between specific relationship and general category for the same reasons that Emmet is reluctant to call friendship a role, namely that it involves too much variability and individuality in comparison to such relationships as doctor-patient or teacher-student. And yet that distinction can be drawn to some (though generally much lesser) extent in vocational relationships as well. As a teacher one can, for example, take on a professional relationship with a student that is somewhat different from that with one's other students—giving extra tutoring, for example, or pursuing a certain topic further than with the rest of one's class. This is especially true of elementary school teaching in which the relationships are much more individualized than, say, in college teaching. The specificity of a particular relationship can generate a set of claims or norms that (to some extent) differ from those of one's other students (though not in a way that involves *violation* of general professional standards and norms), as in the case of friendship.

The more particularistic type of appeal to the norms within a specific relationship is a mode of motivation and action that is genuinely morally distinct from appeal to the type of relationship in general (friendship or vocational). It is not a mere application to a particular relationship of the norms of friendship in general (except perhaps in the formal sense in which acknowledging the specific understandings and values in a specific relationship in an exemplification of the general principle of acknowledging the individuality or particularity of specific relationships). For one thing, not every such particularistic appeal is governed by a statable principle that it is plausible to think the agent is (even implicitly) drawing on in her action. For another, even when one can find some principle that does seem applicable to an action—e.g., Be a comforting presence to one's friend—it is not clear that this principle is actually required by the very idea of friendship itself. It seems rather to be implied at best in certain sorts of, or certain understandings of, friendship. Finally, principles that *do* perhaps seem implied in the very concept of friendship and that are pertinent to this situation—such as, Support the well-being of one's friend—are pitched at such a level of generality that they clearly underdetermine the specific action appropriate to the situation. Thus even in cases in which there actually is an application relationship between a category principle and a particular friendship, moral attention to the particular friendship will often play a crucial role in the determination of the specific action chosen. (For further argument on the moral work done in applying principles, see Blum 1988a.)

In other circumstances the relationship between the appeal to the category of friendship and the appeal to a particular friendship seems to be that of a minimum standard to what goes beyond that minimum. Thus Da-Wei could well think that the mere idea of friendship tells him not to betray his friend to the government agents, but to know how else he might help his friend, he must appeal to the particularities of the friendship. (Remember, however, that some of his actions are prompted by neither of these motivations but by direct compassion or care for his friend. More generally, as mentioned earlier, the three modes of motivation will often not be readily separable in specific actions or activities.)

The existence of appeal to the norms of particular relationships suggests a fourth notion of impersonality, in which the value to which appeal is made is external to the agent's particular wants and desires in the situation (as in sense (3)) yet is internal to a particular relationship of the agent's.

6

Something like the same breakdown in types of motivations can also be seen in various types of communitarian actions, that is, actions stemming from one's sense of attachment to or implication in a communal entity. Corresponding to spontaneous care for a friend or charge is care for a member of one's group as a member of the group. In some cases such concern can have a morally suspect side to it, as when it is directly preferential (in relation to a nonmember) with no seemingly good reason beyond the group identification. (We seem to accept such direct preferential caring in the case of friends in a way we, or many of us, do not in the case of, say, ethnic-group identification). In other cases the communal care is not preferential but simply takes a specific form grounded in the shared identification. For example, if the carer and cared-for are both members of a socially vulnerable, disadvantaged, or neglected group, this can be a reason why the carer ought to be more concerned for members of her own group, for they are in special need of it and cannot count on getting that concern from others outside of the group.

In another case of communitarian care (which might overlap with the previous one), care for another individual member involves or implies a concern for the integrity of the group itself, as when a black's lending support to a particular black musician is seen both as helping that individual as an individual as well as preserving and advancing a shared heritage. (Some version of this motivation—concern for the preservation of a distinct culture—is available to those outside that cultural group as well. See Blum 1991.) Finally, as in the case of friends, membership in certain groups can imply a trust and confidence in the appropriateness and ability of one's helping the other, a trust and confidence that ground the caring response to the other person and make it not a preferential caring (or not a morally suspect one) but simply a specific form of caring.

As with friendship and vocation, there can be an appeal to the communal identification to guide action, and that appeal can take the form of direct appeal either to the communal entity itself or to one's particular relationship to it or particular interpretation of it. Thus as a Jew one can do what one regards as bidden or required of any Jew simply by what it means to be a Jew. Alternatively, one can appeal to the specific relationship one has oneself to Judaism. For example, one might feel that *any* or *every* Jew has a responsibility to do something to keep Jewish culture or heritage alive. But someone else might think that this is required only of herself, given her particular understanding of Judaism or Jewishness, and not necessarily of others who have (what one regards as not illegitimate) alternative relationships to or interpretations of that communal identification. (Of course, many communal identifications contain recognized subdivisions that mediate between the overall category itself, as Jew or African-American, and the purely individual level of interpretation, for example, Reform or Orthodox Jew, black nationalist or integrationist. There might also be a similar phenomenon within traditions that attach to vocations. For example, the notion of a general practitioner refers not only to a purely medical specialty but to a way of thinking about the practice of medicine itself.) Thus, as in the cases of friendship and vocation, communitarian action can take on a more or less impersonal, as well as a more or less individual and particularistic, character.

It should be noted that the focus of moral concern by members of communal entities is not always internal, toward members of the group. In this way the moral character of (certain) communal identifications is disanalogous to friendship, where to act from friendship is always to act in some way toward the specific friend in question. A good example of a noninternal communal focus is Miep Gies, the Dutch woman who helped to shelter the Frank family (Jewish, German refugees) during the Nazi occupation of the Netherlands. Gies regarded her rescue efforts as very much stemming from her Dutch identity. She thought of her Dutchness as requiring her to reach out to non-Dutch persecuted persons (Gies 1987). This kind of communal identification operates more like a service vocation, in which it is not the practitioners but the charges who are served. It is important to keep these cases in mind, since communitarian identifications are often portrayed as if they were necessarily exclusivist—promoting an inward and (sometimes therefore) parochial focus.

To bring together the discussions of sections 3 to 6, we have the following breakdown of five types of action and motivation distinct from *both* pursuit of personal good *and* the demands of impersonal morality.

1. Direct care or response to an individual by an individual, involving no other specific moral relationship
2. Action from role
3a. Direct caring action on behalf of friend, charge, or fellow (communal) member without (even implicit) appeal to the norms of friendship, vocation, or community
3b. Appeal to the general category of the *type* of relationship (friendship, vocational, communal)
3c. Appeal to a specific relationship (friend, vocational, or communal) with its specific history and character as a norm to guide action, or to an individual interpretation of vocation, communal values, or friendship, to guide action.

We have also found three senses or uses of "impersonal" distinct from the view-from-nowhere senses:

1. Independence of personal characteristics (as in a role)
2. Appeal to a value or norm that the agent personally identifies with but that is independent of the agent's desires in the situation (as in vocation)
3. Appeal to values or norms the agent identifies with that are independent of the agent's desires yet are internal to her individual relationship

7

So a framework for thinking about human motivations as they are relevant to morality (either as being themselves moral or as being separate from morality and potentially in conflict with it) that sees the only alternatives as wholly personal or wholly impersonal will miss a large territory of morally relevant forms of motivation and action.

But the damage that the personal/impersonal framework does to moral theory lies only partly in what it omits. What also tends to happen is that the omitted phenomena are taken up and squeezed into the framework itself, which thus preserves the illusion that personal/impersonal comprises an exhaustive dichotomy of morally relevant standpoints or classes of motives but actually distorts or misportrays the nonpersonal, nonimpersonal phenomena.

Let us look at friendship for an example. Friendship *can* in a sense be viewed as an example of "the personal." Indeed, friendships and close personal relations often show up on lists illustrating the personal domain in the writings of philosophers working with the personal/impersonal framework (Nagel, Wolf, and Care, for example).

It is actually possible to treat a friend and a friendship (at least for some period of time) primarily from the standpoint of its role in one's own good. This involves, for example, performing those acts of friendship most pleasant and enjoyable to oneself and in any case shunning as much as possible burdensome acts of friendship. It might also involve doing acts aimed at preserving the friendship when it seems to be threatened (e.g., by the friend's recognition that she is not really being valued for her own sake). It would also seem to imply a readiness callously to drop a friend as soon as the friendship stopped providing a balance of good to oneself.

It is evident that a friendship *entirely* in this mode is hardly a friendship at all. And one *primarily* in this mode is clearly a deficient sort of friendship. To treat friendship solely as a personal project, as something contributing to the good of the agent's life, is to distort what friendship is. In a genuine friendship, one must care about and value the friend for her own sake or good in life as an independent person separate from oneself, not for the sake of her role in one's own personal projects. And this caring will necessarily involve actions that one will not particularly want to be doing or that are in some way burdensome.

So while the personal-impersonal framework can attempt to encompass friendship, it succeeds only at the cost of robbing friendship of its true character and value.

Paradoxically perhaps, treating friendship only in terms of its good to oneself, only as personal project, actually prevents it from being the deep good to persons that friendship can be. Unless one fully appreciates and responds to the reality of the other person in her own right, to her particular needs, to her way of looking at things, and to her individuality more generally, one's relationship cannot have the depth of real friendship. But without that depth the friendship cannot constitute the deep good to the self that friendship can constitute. Thus, unless friendship is *not* seen on the model of the personal good, it cannot constitute the genuine good to the individual that philosophers (including some of those working within the personal-impersonal framework) have rightly wanted to recognize. (Illusory and superficial friendships can still provide certain kinds of goods—for example, companionship, admiration, connections, the ability to think of oneself as having (good) friends—though some of these depend on one's deceiving oneself and others are goods not specific to friendship.) The point here is like the paradox of hedonism noted frequently throughout the history of ethics, for example by Aristotle. The difficulty of finding a nonparadoxical language in which to state the paradox of friendship contributes, I think, to the hold that the personal-impersonal framework can have on our moral thinking.

Similar points can be made about vocations and communities. Being less private in their nature than personal relationships, they might be less likely to be construed on the model of a personal good. Nevertheless, like friendships, they can comprise profound goods in a person's life. Indeed, in the way I have defined "vocation" (and have assumed in my discussion of community), it is necessarily an important source of meaning and value in the life of the one who has the vocation. And it is a value that can conflict with a moral demand issuing from a more impersonal perspective.

Nevertheless, the distinctive values of vocation and community are lost once one treats them purely on the model of personal goods. That is, if one treats one's vocations and communities only as sources of good or meaning to oneself, one loses the essential point that vocations and communities present a set of values independent of the self, appreciation of which *as* independent of the self is required for the true meaning of vocation and community. If I attempt to view and treat my communities solely in light of their good to myself—for example, by putting in only the time necessary to do the minimum to maintain my inclusion in them, by focusing on how they give my life meaning but not really giving of myself to them as independent sources of value in their own right, by treating them as instrumental to my good—then in a sense I do not treat them as *communities*. And, again seemingly paradoxically, I cannot then derive from them the genuine and deeper good that communities (and vocations) can actually provide.

Thus it is certainly true that friendships, vocations, and communities can be important sources of good to the individual. Yet the way they are sources of good cannot be understood from within the personal-impersonal framework. To treat them as if they were personal goods in the sense of the framework is to deprive them—by failing to recognize them as having value in their own right independent of the person in question—of the substance that they must possess to constitute that good to the person.

The personal-impersonal framework can distort the phenomenon of friendship, communities, and vocations in the other direction as well, by treating them as a species of impersonal demand. A central dimension of this is the way in which the claims of other persons (e.g., the German Jews for Miep Gies, the illiterate boy for Kohl, the beleaguered community for a member of that community) are pictured within that framework as presenting themselves to the agent as a set of totally *impersonal* demands. While I have delineated three senses in which the claims of vocation, relationship, and community do present themselves as "impersonal," none of those involve the total impersonality of the view from nowhere. Indeed, sense (3) requires those claims to be *essentially* bound up with particular meaning-conferring commitments (friendships, vocations, and communities) of the particular individual self.

The nonimpersonal aspect of vocation is particularly striking. In fact, it is when an individual begins to experience the demands of her work as being entirely external—and in that sense (sense (2)) impersonal—that we feel she is losing her sense of vocation (though this may be only temporary). She no longer experiences the personal sense of value in her work that one does when one works from a sense of vocation.

8

It is in part this totally impersonalist conception of morality, and especially of the ways in which the claims of other persons present themselves to us, that prevents Wolf, Care, and Nagel from giving a serious or adequate hearing to the idealistic, socially engaged, and interpersonally caring individual. Wolf portrays such a character as obsessively dedicated to an impossible and wholly impersonal moral ideal that necessarily cuts the person off from personal and interpersonal satisfactions. The only satisfactions allowed to Wolf's moral saint are those of a pure devotion to morality itself, as in Kant, or of living out a totally impersonal benevolence toward all of humanity.

In contrast to Wolf, Care does want to recommend a life involving a high degree of dedication to the welfare of others. He calls this a life of "service" and sees it as embodied in career choice. It is thus particularly striking how the personal-impersonal framework constrains Care from making his best case for this worthy ideal. By pitting purely personal self-development against a purely impersonal moral mode of life, Care deprives himself of the resources to portray his morally serious ideal as a psychologically compelling and realistic one. Care seems to imply that the individual who would choose the path he recommends is to be sustained in her life of service by little more than a continual focus on the staggering inequities in access to resources for self-realization between persons, on the moral demands that these inequities yield, on her own responsibilities as a member of a world moral community, and on the reflective sense of "reconciliation" with the human condition in one's own time that stems from living out the "shared fate" perspective.

This individual is imagined to be conceiving of herself, by virtue of making this career choice, as greatly curtailing once and for all any hope of her *own* self-realization. For Care has conceived of self-development as a matter of purely private, "personal" concerns, such as the development of artistic or scientific talent, and it is this that the individual must forsake for the sake of a career of service to others. Care recognizes the psychological difficulties of his position in the preface to his book, where he says that what the argument of his book seems to recommend is a life that is in many ways quite unappealing and risks "important kinds of disappointment, frustration, or lack of fulfilment in our lives" (Care 1987, xiv).

What Care barely explores—and can hardly do so in view of his personal-impersonal framework—is the way that a career of service can itself be a form of something like what could be meant by "self-realization."

Herbert Kohl, for example, in many ways seems to exemplify Care's recommendation of a life of service. He helps to secure the conditions for the self-realization of many (such as the illiterate boy) who might otherwise be greatly hampered in their own life pursuits. Yet Kohl's life does not embody a systematic denial of personal realization. Rather, by drawing on a certain tradition of understanding and interpretation of what it means to be a teacher and by being able to root that understanding in his personal sense of values, Kohl has secured for himself a kind of self-realization precisely *in* serving others, within the vocation of being a teacher.

In this regard, it is significant that Care portrays the life choice between service and self-realization in terms of a "career." As Care brings out well, much is at stake for the individual in choosing a life work. A choice which does not suit the psychological makeup of the individual can have a seriously deleterious impact on her life. On the other hand, the notion of career speaks to choice of lifework only from the perspective of its impact on the purely individualistic, or personal, aspect of the person's good. When we speak of someone's career, we regard her mode of work primarily in terms of the values of stature, status, personal attainment, and advancement, which accrue to the person as an individual.

By contrast the notion of *vocation* that, drawing on Kohl's experience, I have explicated here places choice of lifework in the context of its social meaning and implies a meaningfulness and value to the individual that is bound up with the social significance of her particular vocation. In doing so, the notion of vocation allows one to see how there might be an intimate link between the service aspect of some lifework choices and the self-realization aspect. This is not to say that the notion of vocation is more *accurate* than that of career—both are entirely legitimate perspectives on individual life choice. The point is that the notion of career *taken by itself* (as Care does) meshes with the limited perspective of personal good as something to be *contrasted* with service to others, as implied by Care's personal-impersonal framework. Yet the perspective of vocations as neither personal nor impersonal allows us to explore how service to others can *be* an aspect of good to the person.[4]

It might be replied to this argument that Care does not really intend to address the question of what would make a person psychologically able to handle the career choice that Care recommends on purely moral grounds; his prime concern is only to show that morality does indeed recommend this choice. But if one's notion of morality is so severed from a broader notion of choice worthiness that takes into account the ways in which choice options bear on the identity and sense of personal good of individuals, then the *worth* of that notion of morality must be at least partly called into question. And my argument has been that by severing personal good so sharply from morality and from the claims of other persons, moral philosophers have helped to deprive us of the resources to address those questions of choice worthiness and moral psychology.

To summarize, then, I have argued that vast domains of human motivation do not fit into the category of *either* purely personal good *or* taking the standpoint of purely impersonal morality. And by showing how these motivations—specifically, vocation, friendship, and community—are bound up with the moral agent's sense of personal value and meaning, I hope I have suggested some directions for a communitarian moral psychology.[5]

Notes

1. Other philosophers dealing with the personal/impersonal dilemma include Bernard Williams, Owen Flanagan, Michael Slote, Samuel Scheffler, Peter Railton, and Harry Frankfurt.

2. The notion of care in this section is meant to be that of Gilligan (1982, 1988), of Noddings (1984), and of the many others who have further developed the notion of a "morality of care." My somewhat critical remarks are meant to apply to them as well. (The criticisms also apply to my own *Friendship, Altruism, and Morality* (1980).) While Noddings, Gilligan, and other writers show some recognition that caring means different things in different contexts, the implications of this for a theory of a morality of care are not developed, and the different virtues and sensitivities appropriate to the different contexts are not articulated. The criticisms made here echo Flanagan and Jackson's (1987) suggestion that there may be more than one distinct moral/psychological competency encompassed by Gilligan's notion of care.

3. See Churchill 1989 for an argument that medicine be seen as having distinctive (what he calls) moral ideals, values, and sensibilities not derivable from a universal ethic. This sort of argument also applies (though Churchill does not do so explicitly) to a distinctive form of medical caring, since medical caring can be seen as part of the general distinctive ethic of medicine.

4. The distinction between "career" and "vocation" (or "calling") is made and put to a good use by Sullivan 1988 and by Bellah et al. (including Sullivan) 1985, where both are contrasted with "job" (which is akin to what I have called "nonvocational role").

5. I wish to thank members and students of the philosophy departments of the University of Maryland (especially Michael Slote and Patricia Greenspan), Arizona State University, and Dartmouth College for their intelligent and sympathetic reactions to presentations of earlier versions of this paper; to Pauline Chazan for a very acute reading of an early draft, especially concerning the portions on friendship; to David Wong for a very helpful discussion of the relations between general category and particular relationship, especially in the context of friendship; to Judith Andre for a very helpful conversation concerning different forms of caring; to Susan Wolf for stimulating and clarifying conversations on the personal-impersonal framework; and to Owen Flanagan for excellent suggestions on late drafts.

Chapter 9

Gender and Moral Luck

Claudia Card

Pasts we inherit affect who we become.[1] As gendered beings in a society with a history of patriarchy, women and men inherit different pasts and consequently different social expectations, lines of communication, opportunities, and barriers. When these things influence character development, they make gender part of our "moral luck."[2] By "luck" I mean factors, good or bad, beyond the control of the affected agent: matters of chance and predictable results of social practice.[3]

I am interested in how gender-related moral luck illuminates biases in ethical theory. My special interest is character development under oppressive practices. In the present essay I question a view of women and care that proceeds as though women have no real damage to overcome, as though women's values and virtues need only to be appreciated and allowed to develop as they are, or at most, need to be supplemented by those more characteristically attributed to men. I then examine a more historically oriented view of women and ethics, preserving, without glorifying women's moral sensibilities, the idea that attention to women's lives can deepen and correct modern Western ethical thinking.

A number of feminist scholars are sympathetic to the idea, popularly associated with the work of Carol Gilligan, that an ethic of care is more characteristic of women or is more apt to be implicit in the experience and ideals of women and that an ethic of justice or rights, or abstract action-guiding principle, is more implicit in the experience of men.[4] If some such hypothesis were true, we might expect a bias in ethical theory toward justice or rights, or at least toward abstract action-guiding principles, given the history of sexism. Such a bias appears evident in the contractarianism and utilitarianism of modern Western ethics. Yet these theories have not always been dominant. A more modest hypothesis—less exciting, perhaps less romantic— also found in Carol Gilligan's work but often not distinguished from the "justice and care" hypothesis, is that *the responsibilities of different kinds of relationships* yield different ethical preoccupations, methods, priorities, even concepts.[5] Different kinds of relationships have been differently distributed among women and men in patriarchal society: a larger share of the responsibilities of certain personal and informal relationships to women, a larger share of the responsibilities of formal and impersonal relationships defined by social institutions to men. It is plausible that a result has been the creation of a significant difference in ethical orientation.[6] Putting it this way opens better to philosophical inquiry the questions of how good these relationships have been, what their virtues and vices are, their major values, their roles in a good life, in a good society. It allows us, for example, to explore the place of fairness in friendship and to note its absence as a flaw.[7]

The hypothesis in terms of *relationships* puts us into a better position than the justice and care hypothesis to identify moral damage resulting from and perpetuating sex oppression. We need to be sensitive to the possibility, easily disguised by the honorific language of "justice" and "care," that what often pass for virtues for both sexes are vices (see Houston 1987). Histories of oppression require us to read between the lines of what we say. The privileged are liable to arrogance with its blindness to others' perspectives. The oppressed are liable to low self-esteem, ingratiation, and affiliation with abusers ("female masochism"), as well as to a tendency to dissemble, a fear of being conspicuous, and chameleonism—taking on the colors of our environment as protection against assault. Histories of exploitation lead us to identify with service, to find our value in our utility or ability to please. Moral damage among both privileged and oppressed tends to be unselfconscious, mutually reinforcing, and stubborn. Where our identities are at stake, oppression is hard to face. Beneficiaries face guilt issues and are liable to defensiveness. The oppressed face damage to an already precarious self-esteem in admitting impotence.

It may also be our moral luck to develop special insights, even under oppressive institutions. I do not have in mind the *experience* of resisting oppressors. Temptations to romanticize resistance are sobered by the thought that so doing seems to glorify oppression (see Ringelheim 1985). Yet a priori, it seems plausible that divisions of responsibility divide opportunities for kinds of moral insight by unevenly distributing the decision-making experience that develops it. However, two cautions are in order. First, oppressive divisions of responsibility may encourage delusion more readily than insight. This suggests that insight is hard won. Second, the hypothesis that insights in the areas of *justice* and *care* might be unevenly distributed appears to assume uncritically that these are such different areas that insights in each are separable from insights in the other, assumptions that may be oversimple (Friedman 1987a, Stocker 1986, Flanagan and Jackson 1987). Both cautions are themes in the present chapter.

The remainder of this chapter has two main tasks. First, I sketch a tension between the two kinds of feminist critique represented by Carol Gilligan and Mary Wollstonecraft, the former flattering both sexes, the latter flattering neither, and both focusing on maternal and adult heterosexual relationships.[8] I argue that correcting misperceptions of women identified by a care perspective, such as Carol Gilligan's, is not enough to vindicate women's characters, nor, therefore, to lend much support to the hypothesis that women's values and aspirations can deepen and correct defects in modern ethical theory.[9] My second task is to explore what more is needed to make that "corrective hypothesis" more plausible. To do so, I examine the sense of responsibility attaching to informal, often personal relationships, contrasting it with that of formal and impersonal ones, and attaching to it independently of a contrast between justice and care. I argue that taking only formal and impersonal relationships as paradigms of obligation and responsibility has produced arbitrarily biased and probably superficial theory. This idea, suggested also in recent work of Annette Baier (1986, see also Flanagan and Jackson 1987), is not that *justice* is superficial. I do not find justice superficial. The idea is rather that the ethical significance of basic informal and personal relationships is at least as much of the first order as that of basic social institutions. To the extent that the personal and informal underlie and circumscribe formal institutions, they are *more* basic. I argue throughout that a focus on formality is not the only bias in modern ethical theory but that fairness has also been systematically ignored in personal and informal relationships, especially where women are involved.

1 Women and Care

Sigmund Freud (1961) criticized women as deficient in the sense of justice. As Carol Gilligan (1982, 18) observes, the behavior underlying this common criticism of women by men is also often cited under different descriptions as evidence of women's "special goodness"— caring, sensitivity, responsiveness to others' needs, and appreciation of the concrete particular. Both the criticism and the praise are part of the tradition of modern Western moral philosophy. "The very thought of seeing women administer justice raises a laugh," said Arthur Schopenhauer. He thought women "far less capable than men of understanding and sticking to universal principles," yet also that "they surpass men in the virtues of *philanthropy* and *lovingkindness* [*Menschenliebe*], for the origin of this is . . . intuitive" (1965, 151). On women and principles he followed Immanuel Kant, who exclaimed, "I hardly believe the fair sex is capable of principles," and speculated instead, "Providence has put in their breast kind and benevolent sensations, a fine feeling for propriety, and a complaisant soul" (1960b, 81). The contradiction is acute in Immanuel Kant, whose views on women and on morality seem to imply that good women lack moral character.[10]

I refer loosely to the above views from the academic canon as "the patriarchal view." Women criticize this view from different angles. Some, like Carol Gilligan, defend the moral responses attributed to women as "different but also valuable," arguing that theories by which women appear deficient are faulty. I call this "the rosy view" because it presents a fairly romantic picture of the insights of women and men. Everyone comes out looking good though not perfect; the insights of each sex, basically sound, need to be supplemented by those of the other. Other critics, like Mary Wollstonecraft (1982), reject so-called "women's goodness" as a euphemism for vices that make it easier for women to be controlled by men. Mary Wollstonecraft argued that women under sexist institutions become morally deformed, neither loving nor just. Noticing similarities between the vices of women and those of the relatively powerless men in military service, she disagreed with her contemporaries, Jean-Jacques Rousseau and Immanuel Kant, on the gender relatedness of virtues. Her view was that *duties* might vary but *virtues* are the same for everyone. She ridiculed the idea that powerless, abused, uneducated women have a special kind of goodness. I call this view, generously, "the skeptical view," for it suggests skepticism about the likelihood that the perspectives of oppressed women yield special moral insights. The correlative idea, that oppressors' perspectives are no wiser, is not developed by Mary Wollstonecraft, who was writing in 1792 to an audience of men without benefit of a supporting women's community. It is implicit in her approach, however. On this view, the problem with "women's ethics" and "men's ethics" is not that they are incomplete or underdeveloped but that they are warped from the start.

However mutually incompatible they appear, the protests of both Carol Gilligan and Mary Wollstonecraft initially seem right. I have wanted to find more truth in the rosy view. Yet the skeptical view refuses to let go of me. If the two views are to be reconciled, it seems to me utterly crucial not to deny the truths of the skeptical view.

An observation documented in Carol Gilligan's recent essays is that nearly everyone interviewed seemed readily able to adopt both the care and justice perspectives but, as with incompatible gestalts, not simultaneously, and that most found one perspective more comfortable than the other (Gilligan et al. 1988). To me, these observations suggest the presence of something *other* than justice and care—such as an oppressive relationship—skewing both perspectives. For how can we judge ethical conflicts between considerations of justice and care if we cannot hold them in mind without a priori subordinating considerations of one sort to those of the other?[11] By looking at cases, Marilyn Friedman (1987a) has convincingly argued that neither a priori ranking is plausible.

In friendship both fairness and caring are valuable. Although friendship does not usually center on formulating rules and applying them to cases, it typically does involve, as Marilyn Friedman (1987a) has pointed out, a division of responsibilities in a more or less extensive mutual support system. A good friendship is fair about such divisions. Such fairness may even be a requirement of caring. Fairness in friendship also requires responsiveness to personal deserts or worthiness.[12] If anything, to be a good friend one needs a *better* sense of fairness than to be a good citizen or soldier, an idea that makes good sense of Aristotle's report that people say that "When [we] are friends [we] have no need of justice, while when [we] are just [we] need friendship as well, and the truest form of justice is thought to be a friendly quality" (1925, 1155a). If "justice" here is meant to suggest enforcement, the idea seems sound. Responsiveness where enforcement is not forthcoming is a greater test of one's fairness than where there is possible recourse to sanctions. If the idea is that the values of justice are superficial, however, it seems confused. For what makes sense of friends not needing justice is that they have the relevant values so well internalized.

This interpretation suggests that it is *not* a mistake to evaluate the conduct of personal relationships by values associated with justice, such as fairness. Nevertheless, errors turn up in the patriarchal view of women and ethics, as Carol Gilligan has pointed out. Women's motives and intentions are often misperceived, misrepresented, oversimplified. The question arises whether righting these errors reveals virtues and values wrongly overlooked in patriarchal ethics.

In Lawrence Kohlberg's moral stages (Kohlberg 1981), for example, women may appear more concerned with approval, more conventional, when what they are actually doing is exhibiting a concern for maintaining relationships. In maintaining relationships, we respect points of view different from our own and attempt to empathize with them. Sigmund Freud found women to have "weak ego-boundaries," poor self-definition, problems with separation and autonomy, and a weaker sense of justice, at least a weaker "legal sense," and concluded that women were thereby deficient in moral reasoning. Carol Gilligan (1982, 43–45) responded that if women have a problem with separation, *men* have a problem with *connection*. She also responded that women judged deficient in justice may be resolving conflicts of interest by favoring inclusiveness over ranking or balancing claims. She illustrated the difference with the endearing story of "the pirate who lives next door."[13]

And yet despite the genuineness of such misperceptions and oversimplifications, disturbing facts remain. Women's political options in misogynist environments complicate the assessment of women's moral responses. Institutionalized dependence on men for protection against male assault, for employment, promotion, and validation, have given women reasons to seek "approval," usually *male* approval. This approval is granted for conventional affiliations with men, respect for their views, empathy with them, etc. Just as there is no need to suppose that women value approval or conventionality *for its own sake* or that we confuse "right" with "conventional" (or "approved"), there is no need to assume on the basis of women's empathy that women value these connections for their own sake. Many women are prudent. Many are convinced that this exchange is what heterosexual love is about, since, after all, convention requires women to affiliate with masculine protectors out of "love." How many attachments are the product of what Adrienne Rich (1980) called "compulsory heterosexuality," the result of orientations molded at an age when our powers of assessment are morally undeveloped?

Speculation that many women are basically prudent about heterosexual relationships may strike some as ungenerous to women. However, where women are not respected, prudence is necessary. It is less generous to assume our readiness to be basically moved by attachment to those who do not respect us. If the distribution of power in society's basic structure is a clue to its members' level of respect for others, as is argued by John Rawls (1971, secs, 67, 82), a pervasive gender-related imbalance of power is evidence of widespread social disrespect for women. If so, what is at stake in evaluating heterosexual relationships is not simply the uses of power by those with more of it but also what it means that they have more of it. In such a context, reciprocity of respect might be extraordinary.

The variety of motives from which women may affiliate raises ethical questions that both the rosy view and the patriarchal view tend to bury. Male "disapproval" commonly reaches the pitch of harassment. What are some ethically honorable ways of avoiding, resisting, and stopping harassment? Entering into heterosexual relationships to purchase "protection" may be not only risky but also unfair to other women in further entrenching women's need for protection rather than combatting that need. Women are often surprised to hear that *they* are *unfair* if they reject sexual advances from men and similarly, when they bring accusations of rape, that expecting anything else was *not fair* to under the circumstances. For patriarchy lacks a history of giving women *honorable* ways of invoking fairness to reject sexual overtures from men, especially from men from whom they cannot, or for various reasons do not wish to, sever connections altogether. Similar problems exist for the issues of self-definition and autonomy. Given women's inferior political position together with the lifelong message that a woman "alone" is "asking for it," who could be surprised that "studies show" women seeking to create and maintain affiliations? Again, cautions are in order: we need to look at why women affiliate and with whom. Women don't embrace just any affiliation. Many are terrified of lesbian connections and disdainful of interracial connections, for example. We who are women are taught that identifying ourselves in relation to certain men as sister, mother, wife, lover, etc., can reduce threats of assault. It does not follow that such a reduction amounts to *safety* or that women are under the illusion that it does. Nor does it follow that we do not know well where we leave off and men begin. We learn our places early.

Reciprocity is associated in modern ethics primarily with justice. Yet lack of reciprocity is probably a major cause of the breakup of friendships among peers. If, as Carol Gilligan noted early in her work (1982, 17), *at midlife* men come to see the value of intimacy, which women have seen all along, what does that say about the quality of heterosexual intimacy *prior to midlife,* and about the judgment of those who valued such relationships? Perhaps, as Phillippa Foot said of the villain's courage (1978c, 14–18), women's caring here is not functioning as a virtue. It is also doubtful that paradigms of relationship in which women's choices are less than free represent women's values fairly or well.

Women's connectedness is not always a good thing. When our *primary* relationships lack reciprocity of valuing, we risk losing (or failing to develop) self-esteem. Valuing others independently of their utility is at the core of both respect and love, and being so valued is important to self-esteem. In respect we appreciate others as like ourselves in certain fundamental ways; in love we also cherish their particularities. Identifying and valuing ourselves in terms of relationships to others who likewise identify and value themselves in relation to us can leave us with enriched self-esteem. But when our primary attachments are to those who define and value themselves by what they take to be their own achievements while they define and value us in terms of our relationships to them, we are encouraged at best to assimilate, not really to affiliate. We risk becoming extensions, tools. Our caring does not have the same meaning that it has when it is valued because it comes from us. It is not the same source of self-esteem.

Failure to appreciate the value of others independently of utility has not been the failure of only those with the lion's share of power. In military boot camps males of a variety of ages and political strata learn misogynist attitudes toward females in general.[14] Fear of the same phenomena seems to underlie Mary Wollstonecraft's opposition to boys' boarding schools, although she doesn't comment on military misogyny. When those who lack respect also come into the lion's share of power, affiliative relationships with them are not only impoverished but dangerous for those on the short end.

Recent work on women's conception of the self as rooted in relationships with others has led to speculations about men and violence. On the basis of fantasy studies, Carol Gilligan has suggested that violence in men's fantasies is rooted in men's fear of intimacy (Gilligan 1982, 39–45; Gilligan et al. 1988, chap. 12). She reported that in the studies in which subjects constructed stories in response to pictures, women tended to find safety in intimacy and danger in isolation while men tended to find danger in intimacy and safety in independence. We should be skeptical, however, about the conclusion that women find safety in intimacy. The conclusion about men's fears may clarify why, if it is amplified and made more specific.

Many relationships women construct are informal, even personal, but not intimate. Like the nets that women test subjects supplied in response to a picture of trapeze artists, women's relationships with women are often for safety and protection—they are *networks* of connections, not sexual unions. Thus they are not the same as the relationships men seem to fear. The fantasies of both sexes may be compatible with *both* sexes fearing intimacy, each for different reasons. Fear of isolation is compatible with fear of intimacy; fear of isolation may be stronger for women. Women's networks are often cushions against the violence of intimate relationships. Where men do not construct such networks, perhaps they do not have a similar need. When men fear heterosexual intimacy, they usually have the power to avoid it.

If we examine fantasies for clues to our senses of danger, what do women's infamous rape fantasies tell us? Women are reluctant to articulate them, and not always because they reinforce stereotypes of female masochism. Rape fantasies are not only of attack *by* rapists but also of responsive attack *on* rapists, killing rapists, maiming them, etc. Intimacy has not cured the violence in women's lives. It has given the violent greater access to their victims. Rape is one of the most underreported crimes because it is committed more readily by acquaintances and intimates than by strangers (Amir 1971). Battery of women by intimates is a serious issue in misogynist environments.[15] Men's fears of rejection and entrapment by women in this context are not altogether misplaced. Men's fantasy violence may betray an appreciation of the implications of misogyny. Perhaps what men fear is *women's* historically well-grounded *fears of men*, which predictably issue in the tangle of women's clinging to men for acceptability and protection (against other men) and at the same time in their withdrawing sexually, engaging in manipulation, daily resentful hostilities, and eventual fantasies of widowhood.

Women's failure to value separation and autonomy is a genuine problem. But the problem is political, not simply psychological. Women are systematically penalized for not being available on demand to children, relatives, spouses, male lovers. A good example of women's moral luck may be that as a result of our political inability to end bad relationships, we have not learned to discriminate well between good ones and bad ones but have learned instead to assume responsibility for maintaining whatever relationships "fate" seems to throw our way. The great danger, as well as the great strength, of the method of inclusion is its presumption that there should be a way to satisfy everyone. Women are afraid to say no. But separation can be preferable to inclusion.

Inclusion brings us again to the sense of justice. Why contrast the search for inclusive solutions with justice or with *fairness*? Fairness is not only a matter of ranking, taking turns, or balancing claims—ways of distributing power among competing parties—but also a matter of recognizing who deserves what from whom, and deserts tend to bring the affects of sympathy and antipathy into the picture. Sometimes everyone deserves to be included. Although inclusion is an alternative to balancing claims, it is not necessarily an alternative to justice. The *difference principle* in John Rawls's theory of justice as fairness could favor inclusion over competition or taking turns. This principle directs that basic social institutions be so arranged that those least advantaged are as well-off as possible (Rawls 1971, secs. 11– 12). If a more inclusive solution were more to the advantage of those least well-off, the difference principle would favor it. If methods of inclusion are *among* the methods of justice, women's reputation for a weak sense of justice may be undeserved in proportion to the accuracy of Carol Gilligan's observations. Where inclusion is unjust, it is unclear what can be said to recommend it.

Although women probably have more sense of justice than Freud thought, the truth that women are liable to misperception does not yet sustain the view that women's reasonings reveal virtues and values that can deepen and correct the ethics of those more privileged. Often our reasonings reveal survival strategies and, less flatteringly, vices complementary to those of the privileged. Still, I find the corrective potentialities of the data of women's lives to be genuine. To show how, I want to look at those data as giving us a domain of basic informal and personal relationships.

2 Women's Luck and Modern Ethical Theory

Women's care often takes the form of responsiveness to the needs of others. Thus in her 1982 writing Carol Gilligan naturally moved from "an ethic of care" to "an ethic of responsibility," understanding responsibility as a capacity for responsiveness. The Kohlbergian tradition from which she began took over the Rawlsian view that the business of justice is to distribute rights. Hence her easy move from "justice perspectives" to "rights perspectives." However, two different views are conflated by these equations, one of which is more plausible, if less sweeping or dramatic, than the other. The thesis that women develop an ethic of care and men an ethic of justice is not logically tied to the thesis that women develop an ethic of responsibility and men an ethic of rights. The "responsibility and rights" thesis, or something like it, is more promising than the "justice and care" thesis.

Justice is not exhausted by rights. Justice is a far older concept. Nor does caring exhaust the responsibilities of women's relationships. By "an ethic of responsibility" what was more specifically meant was the ethics of informal and personal relationships; by "an ethic of rights," the ethics of formal or impersonal relationships. Both involve responsibilities, however, just as both involve relationship—different kinds of responsibilities and different kinds of relationships. That we can hear a "different moral voice" in the ethics of informal and personal relationships is plausible, even if it is not always the voice of "care" or the voice from which it diverges, that of "justice."

Modern moral philosophy has been preoccupied with power and control—its uses, its distribution, its forms (Hoagland 1988).[16] Attachment, in the sense that suggests emotion or feeling, has been downplayed, underrated, dismissed. In her more recent essays (Gilligan et al. 1988) Carol Gilligan emphasizes that power and attachment are two ways of defining relationships, two ways of defining responsibilities. She no longer contrasts rights with responsibilities or presents only women as focused on relationships but sees women and men as often focused on different relationships and different responsibilities.

Contractarian and utilitarian ethics are preoccupied with control. They take formal and impersonal relationships as paradigms. Both kinds of theory reflect administrative practical wisdom. Ideal observers and veils of ignorance give versions of the perspective of an administrator (who may be a member of a board rather than a lone administrator). The data for these theories are drawn first of all from the public worlds of law and commerce, as are the concepts used in their analysis: *right* (or duty) and *good* (or interest). "Right" is rooted in law, the world of rights. "Good," in the relevant sense, suggests commerce, the world of goods. Ethics as normative theorizing about impersonal relationships is epitomized by John Rawls's theory of justice, by the current fascination with the prisoner's dilemma, and by consequentialist paradoxes concerning nuclear deterrence.

Responsibility in administration is a matter of supervision, management, accountability, and answerability. One who is responsible for something answers for it, takes whatever credit or blame is due. Those whose responsibilities go unfulfilled are expected to explain to others. This credit-and-blame sense of responsibility is the sense that figures in Nietzsche's obsession with the genealogy of morality as control. It is not at all what Carol Gilligan meant in attributing to women an ethic of responsibility. She had in mind responsiveness to needs, to situations. This is more congruent with the idea of *taking* responsibility *for* someone or something—committing oneself to look after its maintenance or well-being, preserve its value, even to make it good.[17] Here the focus is on well-being, not on control. When the focus is on well-being, responsiveness to needs comes to the fore. The administrative point of view is not noted for its responsiveness to needs.

The administrative point of view does not yield a theory of friendship. Philosophers in the last third of this century have begun remedying the relative lack of attention to friendship in modern ethics (Telfer 1970/1971, Stocker 1976a, Blum 1980, Raymond 1986). Friendship belongs to the larger area of personal relationships and informal practices—sexual intimacy, kinship, and a variety of networks loosely dubbed "friendships." As Annette Baier notes, historically, men have been able to take for granted a background of informal and personal relationships with women for the reproduction of populations and institutions, women have had less choice than men about participating in these relationships, and men have had material stakes in not scrutinizing such relationships morally (Baier 1986). It can be added that men also have stakes in not scrutinizing many informal relationships with one another underlying and circumscribing the formal ones on which attention is typically focused in their discussions of moral issues. If, as Annette Baier observes (1986), it has often been women's luck to have to make the best of involuntarily assumed personal relationships and to have to create networks of informal relationships in a world that denied women a voice in law, men also have recourse to networks and relationships of varying degrees of informality—the Ku Klux Klan, gentlemen's agreements—when they want to *circumvent* the law.[18]

We need theories of the ethics of informal and personal relationships at least as well developed as administrative ethics. Informal relationships tend to *underlie* formal ones, circumscribe them, come into play when formal ones break down. On the view developed by John Rawls, obligations (or, we might say, responsibilities) require for their analyses references to criteria formulated specifically for evaluating public institutions. Perhaps *personal and informal* responsibilities require for their analyses references to criteria formulated *specifically for evaluating personal relationships and informal practices.*

What are "informal" and "personal" relationships? The informal and the personal are not the same. An informal agreement need not be personal. An interpersonal relationship is *personal* when it matters to the parties who the other parties are and when this mattering is important to the nature of the relationship.[19] "Personal" suggests closeness, intimacy. The personal introduces issues of attachment and antipathy. Informal relationships are characterized by responsibilities that can facilitate relationships of attachment.

A relationship is *formal* to the extent that it is well-defined, limited, in ways that are publicly understood and publicly sanctioned. Formality facilitates control where there would otherwise be a lack of trust or simply an inability to predict and plan. Formality is not the same as legality; both legal and nonlegal relationships have varying degrees of formality. Spousehood, for example, is a formally defined status in law, but the obligations of spouses to one another tend to be highly informal. Those of outsiders to spouses, on the other hand, become more formal in consequence of marriage.

Within limits, formality and personality are matters of degree. *Very* formal relationships, however, involve rights, which one either has or lacks. Friendship is personal and relatively informal. We may have formal relationships, such as contracts, with friends. But that can also create problems for friendship. Personal relationships tend toward informality. The relationships of clients and patients to physicians and other caretakers become more formal as clients and patients insist upon rights, which creates tensions for those who find it desirable that such relationships retain personal aspects. The relationship of judge to defendant, on the other hand, is (supposed to be) impersonal, not merely formal.[20]

Relationships defined by what John Rawls calls "the basic structure of society" are institutional. Institutions define responsibilities, or obligations, closely correlated with rights; the relationships are thus formal. They are also impersonal; persons are repeatedly presented as competing for positions defined by basic institutions. The perspective from which such responsibilities are ultimately analyzed and evaluated—the "Original Position"—is thoroughly impersonal (Rawls 1971, chap. 3).

The ethics of basic *institutions* is the subject of Rawls's theory of justice. Basic informal and personal relationships, however, are *like* basic institutions in possessing the three major features he identifies to support his view of those institutions as basic to the structure of society. Basic informal and personal relationships should therefore also be recognized as belonging to the basic structure of society. Goodness here is at least as important as justice in basic institutions.

The points of similarity are as follows. First, personal relationships are at least as important to our "starting places" in life as the institutions constituting the basic structure. Second, self-esteem, especially the conviction that one's life is worth living, is contingent not only on basic rights but also on informal practices and primary personal relationships. Third, personal relationships and informal practices create special responsibilities (but ones that are not closely correlated with rights), just as impersonal relationships and formal institutions create special responsibilities (which are closely correlated with rights). If such considerations support the moral importance of basic institutions, they support that of basic informal and personal relationships as well.

Consider starting places. The importance of justice as the first virtue of basic institutions rests heavily, in Rawls's theory, on the fact these institutions determine our starting places in life. People born into different social positions have different expectations because these institutions work together in such a way as to favor certain starting points over others, and these inequalities, which tend to be deep, are not justifiable by appeal to merit or desert (Rawls

1971, p. 7). This is surely true. However, the profundity and perva-siveness of the effects of our personal and informal starting places is at least equal to those of our formal starting places. Our personal relationships with parents are a starting point. Parents who handle such relationships badly may leave us seriously disadvantaged for life. We have no more choice over these starting relationships than over participation in society's class structure or its basic economic institutions. Nor are they deserved or justifiable by appeal to merit. If involuntariness of participation and profundity of the effects upon health and well-being ground the ethical significance of social insti-tutions, they can likewise ground that of basic informal and primary personal relationships. Yet the latter are not defined by rights. They do not give us a "rights perspective," although they do give us a "responsibility perspective." Treating the monogamous family as an institution defined by rights does not adequately recognize the mo-rality of family relationships.

Second, consider the effect of such relationships on self-esteem. The basis of self-esteem in a just society, according to Rawls (1971, p. 544), is a certain publicly affirmed distribution of basic rights and liberties. However, self-esteem is also contingent upon primary per-sonal relationships, upon the sense we develop of ourselves in such relationships, our sense of ourselves as capable of faithfulness, un-derstanding, warmth, empathy, as having the qualities we should want in a personal affiliate, not only the qualities that it is rational to want in a "fellow citizen." Our sense of these things can be destroyed, warped, or undeveloped if our starting affiliations in life are impoverished, and it can be undermined later by abusive primary affiliations. If the connection with self-esteem explains part of the ethical importance of justice in institutions, it also explains part of the ethical importance of the responsibilities of informal personal relationships.

Third, like the relationships defined by basic rights, informal per-sonal relationships involve special responsibilities. They seem even to involve responsibility in a *different sense* from that of formal rela-tionships: responsibilities that are *not duties* closely correlated with *rights*. Immanuel Kant attempted to capture such responsibilities with the concept of "imperfect duties" (Kant 1948, chap. 2) and later "ethical duties" in contrast with "juridical duties" (Kant 1964b, 7–28). Intuitionists have also tried to cover them with the concept of duty (Ross 1930, chap. 2). To utilitarians, such responsibilities have seemed no more ethically fundamental than responsibilities corre-lated with rights, which also are not fundamental from the standpoint of utility (Mill 1957, chap. 5; Brandt 1984). What all of them have missed is the moral *relationship* between persons—literally, the *obligation* in its original sense of a *bond*—that grounds responsibilities.

The concept of obligation has paradigmatic use in two different contexts, as has been pointed out by Richard Brandt (1964): the context of promises or agreements and the context of accepting benefactions. The latter seems fundamental insofar as willingness to accept another's word manifests good will that does not itself rest on respect for contracts or promises. Such good will is, or can be, a benefaction. Promises and agreements ground duties correlated with rights, while accepting benefactions grounds responsibilities in relationships that are often highly informal. We commonly refer to both the responsibilities of carrying out duties and the responsibilities of informal and personal relationships as "obligations." But they differ from each other in *specificity* and in the *roles* they play in social relationships.

Formal obligations, like Immanuel Kant's "perfect duties," are to do some particular thing, often by a specified time and for or to some particular person. They are correlated with a right to that performance on the part of those to whom one is obligated. They are relatively well defined and often publicly sanctioned. They are the kind of obligation associated with the possible use of force or coercion, with a justification for limiting another's freedom. By contrast, as with "imperfect duties," when accepting a benefaction places us under obligation, there is often no specific thing we are obligated to do and no specific person to or for whom we are obligated to do it. There is consequently no correlated right to a specific performance on the part of the benefactor. We are typically responsible for determining what needs to be done (and when and how much), which requires initiative, imagination, and creativity. The most sympathetic way to interpret Carol Gilligan's method of inclusiveness is to see it as taking on a certain responsibility in this sense, the responsibility of *making it good* that everyone is included, of finding, creating, a *good* way to do that, thereby maintaining informal connections with everyone.

The different roles of the two kinds of obligation are suggested by differences in the consequences of fulfilling or failing to fulfill them. In fulfilling formal obligations, we *discharge* them, as in paying a debt. Discharging the obligation brings the relationship to a close, terminates that formal connection. Failing to fulfill responsibilities that are correlated with rights does not relieve us of the responsibility; it often makes us liable to penalties as substitutes for what we failed to do (sometimes in addition to making up what we failed to do). By contrast, with obligations incurred to a benefactor, we often think in terms of *living up to* them rather than of discharging them. Living up to them tends to *affirm* the relationship rather than to bring it to a close; the ties are extended, deepened. Putting pressure on those who are informally obligated to us can undermine the relationship on which the obligation depends. Failing to live up to an informal obligation likewise undermines the relationship in virtue of which the obligation existed. Formal obligations can thus facilitate good will between parties who are not intimate and perhaps have no wish to be, while informal ones can facilitate personal relationships.

Deontological ethics, especially contractarian, takes relatively formal, impersonal relationships as paradigmatic for moral theory, applying their metaphors and concepts to other relationships as well. This can yield farfetched results, as in Immanuel Kant's notion that ethical duties arise from a kind of contract with one's (bifurcated) self (Kant 1964b, pt. 1, secs. 1–4). Modern teleologies, on the other hand, drop the idea of obligation as a *relationship* in favor of a looser idea of "obligation" as what one morally ought to do. Utilitarianism thus assimilates obligations constitutive of personal and informal relationships to the theory of impersonal moral choice, focusing on abstract action-guiding principles, albeit without taking rights as a fundamental concept.

The promising idea I find in the hypothesis that "women's ethics" can deepen and correct modern Western ethical theory is that the informal and personal relationships salient in women's lives raise issues of the ethics of attachment that are not reducible to the issues of control that have preoccupied contractualist and utilitarian theorists. Informal, personal relationships are as basic as any relationships in our lives. Acknowledging this does not imply that women have more or better knowledge of the ethics of such relationships. What women more clearly have had is more than our share of the responsibility for maintaining these kinds of relationships and less than our share of the responsibilities of participating in and defining formal institutions.

3 Conclusions

I have argued that attachment to individuals is not sufficient to yield caring as a virtue. However, without the values of attachment, there can be no satisfactory ethics of personal relationships. Utilitarian and contractualist theories recognize at best general benevolence, impersonal goodwill toward others, and a kind of general faith in others' ability to reciprocate such goodwill. But they do not recognize as ethically significant the caring partial to individuals. Carol Gilligan observed in her discussion of the fantasy study that "women . . . try to change the rules in order to preserve relationships," while "men, in abiding by these rules, depict relationships as easily replaced" (1982, 44). The sense of relationships as not replaceable recalls Immanuel Kant's insistence that individuals have a value for which nothing can satisfactorily take the place (Kant 1948, chap. 2). Kant was thinking of human dignity, attributed to everyone alike. What is irreplaceable here is what is distinctive, what sets individuals apart from others, not something they have in common.

An ethic of attachment is not necessarily an ethic of care, any more than an ethic of principle—such as utilitarianism—is necessarily one of justice. To sustain the view that the capacity for love, like the sense of justice, is part of character, we need an understanding of this capacity comparable in sophistication to Immanuel Kant's understanding of the capacity for acting on principle. Not every passionate attachment to persons is valuable, any more than every passionate espousal of principles is. The nature and basis of the attachment matters. Immanuel Kant missed the differences in attachment to persons in his dismissal of "pathological love." Yet he appreciated the differences in acting on principle. In a little-known passage in the same essay in which good women are presented as morally characterless, he wrote, "Among men there are but few who behave according to principles—which is extremely good, as it can so easily happen that one errs in these principles, and then the resulting disadvantage extends all the further, the more universal the principle and the more resolute the person who has set it before himself" (Kant 1960b, 74). This danger did not deter him from searching for a devotion to principle having moral worth. Nor need present-day theorists be deterred by the danger of ill-founded personal attachments from recognizing the ethical value of others.

4 Postscript

I have cautioned against minimizing women's bad moral luck in a society with a history of sex oppression. I end with examples of moral damage that a rosy view of women and care may disguise and that a sound ethic of personal and informal relationships should reveal.

When people are affiliated with "protectors," their affirmations of those affiliations may have little to do with love, though the language of love be the language of their discourse. Women's caretaking is often unpaid or underpaid labor performed from a variety of motives.

More likely mistaken for a caring virtue is women's misplaced gratitude to men who take less than full advantage of their power to abuse or who offer women the privilege of service in exchange for "protection." Women have assumed caretaking responsibilities as a debt of gratitude for such "benefactions."[21]

Misplaced gratitude is a kind of moral damage women have suffered. There are others. Feminist thinkers are understandably reluctant to address publicly women's reputation for lying, cunning, deceit, and manipulation. (Arthur Schopenhauer did not have this problem.) But *are* these vices, one may ask, if they are needed for defense? They are surely not virtues, even if they are justified from the point of view of justice. Those who tell just the right lies to the right people on the right occasions may have a useful and needed skill. But it does not promote or manifest human good, even if needed for survival under oppressive conditions. Human good may be unrealizable under such conditions. Lying blocks the trust of friendship: though you are confident I lie only when justified, if you believe I am *often* justified, how can you know when to rely on me (Rich 1979b)?

I have supported a view of the moral luck of the sexes more specific and less romantic than the view that justice and care are gender-related. If informal practices and personal relationships are more salient in women's lives (and not only in women's discourse), women's characters may have a certain depth and complexity because of it. This does not imply that women are better; complexity is not virtue. Perhaps there *are* gender-related virtues, however, and perhaps they are best understood by the moral luck of the sexes. I have not argued that this idea is incoherent. My investigations suggest that some of our *vices* are gender-related because of a history of sex oppression. If so, we might expect to find, as Mary Wollstonecraft did, similar vices in relation to other forms of oppression—oppression by class and by race, for example—and perhaps more complex vices where oppression is compounded.

Then why use the language of *gender*-relatedness, one may ask, rather than that of *oppression*-relatedness? The answers are that gender is not incidental and that oppression is not everything. Those oppressed do not just happen to be female, brown-skinned, workers, or all of these. Social practices have made such aspects of our identities the bearers of fortune. Nor is all the fortune bad. Terms like "gender-related" enable us to call attention to these facts in order to clarify the myths and truths surrounding the moral luck of individuals.

Notes

1. This essay has benefited from critical readings by Victoria Davion, Owen Flanagan, Nel Noddings, participants in a University of Wisconsin Women and Legal Theory Conference, and Joan Ringelheim's colleagues in a New York City women's discussion group; from the encouragement of Amélie Rorty for more than a decade; and from discussions with audiences at the Philosophy Department of the University of Wisconsin at Madison, the APA Central Division Meetings, and a University of San Diego conference on virtues. Part of the work on it was supported by a sabbatical from the University of Wisconsin at Madison.

2. My interest is in what Bernard Williams called *constitutive* moral luck, which enters into one's character. He contrasts this with *incident* moral luck (on which he focuses in the essay introducing the concept "moral luck"), which affects the morality of particular acts (Williams 1981b).

3. In Card, unpublished c, I address the comaptibility of luck with moral responsibility. In this essay I do not treat moral luck as a problematic concept but plunge into what we can learn from recognizable examples.

4. Carol Gilligan reports that nearly all those tested could readily adopt both justice and care orientations, although not simultaneously, but that two thirds of each sex preferred one, and of these, almost all the men preferred the justice orientation, while half the women with a preference preferred the care orientation. Thus the care orientation might easily be overlooked in a study excluding women (Gilligan et al. 1988). Although she focuses on orientations rather than on their distribution, her recent essays describing testing across racial and class groups confirm her impressions about gender distribution. She sees a need for the care ethic where violence threatens but does not claim its superiority in all contexts.

Nel Noddings (1984) has defended a care-based ethic *against* a justice-based one, arguing that abstract action-guiding principles have at best a subordinate role in care-based ethics.

Sara Ruddick (1989) develops the idea of "maternal thinking" from ideals *implicit* in the practice of mothering and argues for their extension to international politics. Like Nel Noddings, she is not optimistic about the value of abstract action-guiding principles in general.

5. Focus on *differences in contexts and relationships* is more characteristic of the writings on women and care by Virginia Held (1984, 1987a, 1987b), Annette Baier (1985a, 1986, 1987a, 1987b), and Sarah Hoagland (1988).

6. If oppression were at the root of the differences in moral preoccupation attributed to the sexes, such differences should have a more complex distribution. Benefits of sex privilege can be diluted or counteracted and burdens of sex oppression overwhelmed by racial or class oppression, and women can have race and class privilege.

7. Marilyn Friedman (1987a), also concerned about underrating justice, urges similar shifts and likewise explores interconnections of justice and care.

8. I do not take up here, since I discuss in Card 1989, the lesbian care ethics developed by Sarah Hoagland (1988), which works from different paradigms, those of adult lesbians engaged in creating social alternatives to patriarchy.

9. I do not argue that women's development fares worse than that of men. My interest is more in women's characters than in such comparisons.

10. On the same page he says, "Women will avoid the wicked not because it is unright but, because it is ugly." Traits he calls women's virtues he called "merely adoptive virtues" in the preceding chapter, contrasting them with genuine virtues. That he

never reconsidered shows in his anthropology lectures published late in his life (Kant 1974a, part 2, B).

11. For extended critique of the "gestalt view," see Flanagan and Jackson 1987.

12. On justice and personal desert, see Feinberg 1970b and Card 1972.

13. The story, which I first heard from her at a conference in 1984, is this: "Two four-year olds—a boy and a girl—were playing together and wanted to play different games. . . . The girl said: 'Let's play next-door neighbors.' 'I want to play pirates,' the boy replied. 'Okay,' said the girl, 'then you can be the pirate that lives next door.'" Gilligan et al. write here of "comparing the inclusive solution of combining the games with the fair solution of taking turns" (1988, 9).

14. On military misogyny, see the first half (on U.S. Marine boot camp) of the film *Full Metal Jacket* (D. Stanley Kubrick, 1987).

15. Violence is also a problem for lesbian relationships in a homophobic society (Lobel 1986; Card 1988b, 1989), which creates situations for same-sex intimacy analogous to those misogyny creates for heterosexual intimacy.

16. On Hume as an exception, see Baier 1985a, 1987a.

17. I explore the concept of taking responsibility further in 1990 and further forward-looking senses of responsibility in unpublished c.

18. Laura Hobson's 1947 novel, *Gentlemen's Agreement,* portrays persistence of anti-Semitism in the U.S. despite formal equality of rights, by way of such things as "gentlemen's agreements" to exclude Jews from country clubs and other "friendly" organizations.

19. So-called "personal *obligations*" do not always involve personal *relationships.* Obligations may be called "personal" to contrast them with other obligations of the same person in an official capacity. My interest here is in the obligations of personal *relationships.*

20. For further discussion of paradigms of obligation, see Card 1988a.

21. On the ethics of friendships between parties very unequal in power, see Card 1988a.

Chapter 10

Friendship and Duty: Some Difficult Relations

Michael Stocker

Most every ethicist is a partisan of friendship, holding it to be a great good. But there is disagreement over how partisans of friendship should stand to duty. Those we might call the enemies of duty argue that duty is hostile to friendship and thus that a partisan of friendship must be an enemy of duty.[1] But those we might call the partisans of duty argue that friendship is good only if governed by duty and thus that a partisan of friendship must also be a partisan of duty.[2]

It is important to understand this issue. First, friendship and duty are of obvious moral importance, and we should try to see how they fit together or run up against each other. Second, as agreed by near enough all, friendship is clearly an important good. Thus, to ask about the relations between friendship and duty is to ask about the relative priority of goodness and rightness. And it is to ask this at a limited, moderately concrete level, rather than, as so often, as a matter of high and abstract theory. And thus it is to ask this at a level where we might reasonably hope to make some headway.

However, my arguments, even if well taken, may not satisfy either the partisans or the enemies of duty, nor therefore those who see the right as prior to the good or those who see the good as prior to, or at least independent of, the right. For I join the enemies of duty in arguing that friendship is hostile to various understandings of duty. But I join with the partisans of duty in arguing that the goodness of friendships and acts of friendship can be limited by duty. I also argue that duty in turn, or at least certain understandings of it, must be limited by friendship and that in still other ways the relations between friendship and duty, and thus between goodness and rightness, are more complex than commonly recognized.

1 Why Must and How Might Friendship Be Governed by Duty?

To help present some relations between friendship and duty, let us consider an attempted reductio of the claim that acts of friendship can be good even if not limited by duty. According to the reductio, if acts of friendship are not limited by duty, then friendship requires, or at least there is nothing within friendship to prevent, being committed to act immorally in the name of friendship. Thus, friendship could require "your friend to stick by you come what may, e.g., to lie for you on the witness stand or to assist you in a fraudulent business transaction" (Baron 1984, 216). If we agree that such acts are immoral, and thus not good, because they violate duty, we might naturally conclude that only an act of friendship limited by duty can be good.

This or a very similar argument is used by Kant at the start of chapter 1 of the *Foundations* (1962) to show that the eudaimonists are mistaken in thinking that courage and other virtues are absolutely or unconditionally good. They are mistaken because courage, for example, can be used in doing evil. And where it is, it is not good. To be absolutely or unconditionally good, courage must thus be limited by duty. Kant, of course, used this argument to try to show that courage is not absolutely or unconditionally good. But as I understand it, the reductio about friendship is used in an attempt to show both that friendship is not absolutely or unconditionally good and also that it is not good in itself.

Whatever its pedigree, the reductio argument seems to show too much. Its claim seems to be that in certain circumstances—in particular, the circumstance of not being limited by duty—acts of friendship can be bad, and thus such acts cannot be good either as such or absolutely and unconditionally. Correlatively, therefore, friendship too cannot be good as such or absolutely and unconditionally. But much the same might be thought about acts done from duty and correlatively about conscientiousness. In certain circumstances such acts are not good, or even immoral.

The circumstances I have in mind are those where we are mistaken—perhaps seriously, perhaps even egregiously—about what our duty is. In such a case we might think that a given act is our duty and do it out of duty but nonetheless do something quite seriously bad and even immoral. The act we do might be bad and even immoral in itself, and it might also be bad and even immoral to do because it prevents us from doing what is then and there really our duty. As is said, the road to hell is paved with good intentions.[3]

Partisans of duty might agree with this but reply along the following lines: The mistake needed to think that a bad act is one's duty is internal to duty. For the reasons that show the act to be bad also show that it is not a duty. In contrast, the reasons that show an act to be bad do not affect its being an act of friendship—acts of friendship can be bad. Thus, to see it as bad, one needs to see it from a standpoint outside of friendship—from duty.

In what follows, I will argue that duty is not so friendly to the good as claimed here, that goodness is internal to friendship, and that at least some acts of duty are good only if they are limited by friendship.

Let us start by noting what we must show to establish that the goodness of friendship depends on duty. We must first show that there is no inconsistency in the notion of an act of friendship governed by duty. We must show that an act of friendship can depend on duty. We must also show that only such acts of friendship can be good. And we must then show that acts of duty do not need to be similarly limited by friendship to be good.

A reason to worry about consistency is that there are some forms of governance by duty that are not available to acts of friendship. As I argued in "The Schizophrenia of Modern Ethical Theories" (1976a), an act of friendship is done for the friend, not for duty. Thus an act done for duty is not an act of friendship. And if acts of friendship are not done for duty, their goodness could hardly depend on their being done for duty. In "Values and Purposes" (1981) I modified my position in "Schizophrenia" to allow for overdetermination, to allow that an act of friendship could be done for duty provided that it is also done from friendship for the friend. But as I further argued, now in agreement with "Schizophrenia," an act is not one of friendship, nor does it have the value of an act of friendship, by being done for duty. (See also my 1986 paper.)

I make this point about friendship and acting *for* duty to help set the stage for the topic I want to consider in this chapter: friendship and acting *from* duty. Another way to set the same stage would be to note that Baron (1984) takes "Schizophrenia" to be arguing for a general repugnance in acting *from* duty, and more particularly for an incompatibility between friendship and acting *from* duty.[4] But in "Schizophrenia" I was not concerned with friendship and acting from duty, the topic of the present chapter. Rather, I was concerned with friendship and acting *for* duty.

However, Baron is absolutely right in thinking it vital to ask whether there is any repugnance in acting from duty, e.g., whether there is an incompatibility between friendship and acting with a sensibility informed by duty. Even if the goodness of acts of friendship does not depend on their being done for duty, it could depend on their being done from duty or from a sensibility informed by duty.

Further, concern with a sensibility informed by duty naturally leads to a correlative concern with whatever sensibility is essential to friendship, rather than just with *acts* of friendship. This is important for two reasons.

The first is simple but central to friendship. It is that character structure and sensibility, not simply acts, have central moral importance for friendship. After all, care is one reason friendship is so precious, both that one cares for another and also that one is cared for by the other. Of course, care motivates action. But even apart from their connections with acts, these ways of being and having friends and these forms of care are in themselves valuable and valued.

The agent's motivation and character are also important for acts of friendship. After all, acts of friendship are done from friendship. And to some large extent it is the thought and care in and behind the acts, not their results, that count. (See my 1981 paper.) In what follows, I will draw attention to this dual focus of friendship by talking of the complex composed of friendship and acts of friendship. (On the dual importance of friendship, see Aristotle 1983, Badhwar 1985, Baier 1986, Blum 1986, and Card, unpublished b.)

Second, it is important to see that the sensibility of friendship is itself deeply moral. Even if it develops out of natural instincts and likings, adult friendship is embedded in a context of moral concerns and indeed is itself a moral concern. It involves being concerned with the good of the friend. And as Aristotle and others argue, it has deep connections with justice, respect, and other moral categories and considerations. (See, of course, the *Nicomachean Ethics*, books 8 and 9. See also Badhwar 1985.) It does not have to do simply with evaluatively uninformed likings or "mere inclination." Thus a person without a conception of value—assuming this is possible—cannot be a friend.

So we might well agree with Baron (1984, 197) that we cannot "conceive of the perfectly moral person as someone who has all the right desires and acts accordingly without any notion that (s)he ought to act in this way." We might, of course, wonder which serious philosophers denied this. In any case, we cannot conceive of friends, much less perfectly good friends, who have the right desires and act accordingly without any notion of value or without any notion that they ought to act in various ways, including friendly ways.[5]

My question, then, is whether a sensibility informed by duty can also be informed by friendship. As I might put it, Is character capacious enough to allow both concerns? Partisans of duty may well reply, Yes, almost certainly; but if not, then so much the worse for friendship (see Baron 1984, 216).

However, I find these ethical and moral-psychological issues far from clear. For example, we must deal with the serious conflicts that Susan Wolf (1982, 1986) shows between friendship and the concerns of duty found in many of our ethical theories, e.g., maximizing the good and devoting oneself to fighting against great evils. To be sure, many of us think that those ethical theories are seriously mistaken about duty. But even in regard to other and better understandings of duty, it is unclear both how and even whether, for example, the trust needed for friendship is compatible with an overriding, or even a very strong, concern for duty.

It is, of course, possible, perhaps probable, that people with the concerns urged by contemporary ethical theories will be friendly and "make friends" while engaged in the appropriate moral enterprises. But it is unclear whether they would want to be, or whether they would have the time and emotional space to be able to be, centrally concerned with the friends and friendships. To this extent it is unclear whether it is humanly possible, or likely, to have a sensibility informed by both duty, as understood in our ethical theories, and friendships.

Further, it is unclear how showing that such a sensibility is possible or impossible would show whether particular demands of friendship and duty can conflict. And if, as seems obvious, they can conflict, then whether or not such a sensibility is possible, we must ask why we should join the partisans of duty in holding that where the two conflict, friendship is there not good.

Some might think that whatever is in conflict with duty cannot be good, because they think that the realm of values is harmonious, that there can be no real conflicts of values. But the realm of values is not harmonious. In both nonconflicting and conflicting situations indeed, in near enough all choices we need to choose which values to pursue and which to forgo. This is so both in regard morally problematic areas, such as moral conflicts, and also in far more pleasing areas. So, for example, in developing interests and abilities and in this way cultivating certain values, we cut ourselves off from others. The forgone values are not only forgone, they are also values.

To be sure, partisans of duty need not hold that the realm of value is harmonious. It is sufficient for them if in every clash between duty and friendship, duty holds sway and retains its value, while friendship loses its value. For then duty-violating friendships or acts of friendship could at most have merely prima facie value or some other lesser form of value.

In what follows, I will argue to the contrary: that duty-violating friendships and acts of friendship can be good in full-fledged ways.

2 *Moral Chauvinism*

Suppose we take seriously the claim that friendships and acts of friendship can be good only if governed by a sensibility informed by duty. Then presumably we must hold that those who do not act from such a sensibility cannot have good friendships or do good acts of friendship. Suppose further that we understand "duty" in one or other of the ways that our modern ethical theories understand it. Then presumably we must hold that those with a markedly different understanding of duty cannot have good friendships or do good acts of friendship. So too we presumably must hold that those with a morality in which duty, so understood, plays little role cannot have good friendships or do good acts of friendship.

Among the ethical theories excluded here are Aristotelian ones and many that are based on sympathy or benevolence, not to mention religion or group membership. Even if we have reason to reject these ethical views, I see no reason to think that those who embrace them cannot have good friendships or do good acts of friendship. To think that would be to think that only we, with our ethics understood in terms of a particular notion of duty, are able to have good friendships and do good acts of friendship. This seems unjustifiable ethical chauvinism.

Partisans of duty might reply that many non-duty-centered ethical theories do prohibit the sorts of things that we are warned friendships may involve unless governed by duty. Perhaps, then, the goodness of friendships and acts of friendship requires having and acting from a sensibility informed by duty *or alternatively* by some other appropriate moral concern that insures an extensional equivalence to a concern for duty. This latter would thus insure that one will do what one would do were one acting from duty. The suggestion here could be that the goodness of friendship and acts of friendship depends not on having a sensibility informed by duty but on a sensibility that insures acting in accord with duty.

Some might even suggest that any moral view that does this thereby deserves to be called a theory of duty. But this reveals such a syncretic and inchoate notion of duty that the suggestion, if even evaluable, is hardly worth evaluating.

I think it still excessively chauvinistic to hold that friendships and acts of friendship can be good only if they involve a moral sensibility that insures that they are extensionally equivalent to those involving a sensibility informed by duty, a notion from our ethics. Perhaps the goodness of friendship and acts of friendship requires only that they come from some appropriate moral sensibility. If so, we could allow that, say, Aristotelians could have good friendships and perform good acts of friendship even where these would not be allowed by duty.

But in allowing this, we would be denying that in order to be good, friendships and acts of friendship must be limited by duty. At most, they would have to be limited by morality. So it might be held that friendship is one good among others and that to be good it must fit well enough with the others. (Useful models of such conditioning are given by various doctrines of the unity of virtues.)

As should be clear, the moral conditioning of one good by other goods is significantly different from the moral conditioning of a good by duty—and this in two ways of central importance for us. First, ethics in which goods have pride of place are importantly different from ethics that accord duty that position. Second, friendship is one good among others. Thus, it is possible, and for reasons indicated below, it is in fact the case, that its goodness helps condition that of other goods. But the partisans of duty suggest that the goodness of friendship is conditioned by duty and does not also condition duty.

3 The Implications of Some Bad Acts of Friendship

Let us now return to our discussion of the relations between friendship and duty. One way to solve the problem of chauvinism is simply to avoid it—to declare that we should be concerned with ourselves and that since our ethics are an ethics of duty, our friendships and acts of friendship can be good only if we have and act from a sensibility informed by duty.

I would argue that this "since" exaggerates the point. Our ethics are also importantly not an ethics of duty. Many of their features are best understood in terms of Aristotelianism, religion, and sympathy, to name only some constitutive strands. There is no need to take up these issues here, however. For whether or not our ethics are an ethics of duty, our friendships and acts of friendship can be good even if we do not have, and act from, a sensibility informed by duty. To show this, I will turn to the reductio that if friendship can be good even when not limited by duty, it can be good, e.g., to murder or commit perjury from friendship.

Some of our hyperromantic thoughts about love have it that true love admits of no limits: "Unless you would kill, indeed murder, for me, you do not really love me." Even partisans of love can reject this. And partisans of friendship can deny that a friend must be willing to murder or kill or even commit perjury for a friend. This, however, does not give partisans of duty much aid in showing that quite generally, the goodness of friendship and acts of friendship depends on a sensibility informed by duty.

To see this, we can start by considering friendships and immoral acts of friendship. What shows that an act of friendship is bad need not show that the friendship is bad. A friendship does not become bad whenever the friend acts immorally or whenever the friendship would lead us to act immorally. Indeed, it would often be wrong, even immoral, to break off a friendship for such a reason. Here we could consider variations on the theme of the well-worn, trivial example of returning books. As the first variation, we all know, and perhaps have or are, perfectly wonderful friends who fail to return borrowed books.

Pursuing these thoughts would severely limit two other ways of taking the claim that to be good, friendship must be guided by duty: for a friendship to be good, our friends must have a sensibility informed by duty, and what we find attractive about the friend must be consonant with the values constitutive of a sensibility informed by duty (see Schoeman 1985).

Let us now turn from friendship to acts of friendship. Suppose we agree that the perjury done out of friendship is bad. We might also agree that acts of friendship can sometimes be bad because they violate a duty. But we can still deny what the partisans of duty claim: that quite generally, acts of friendship are good only if governed by a sensibility informed by duty.

The badness of the perjury done from friendship may be due to the moral enormity of the perjury. It remains to be seen whether in other cases of conflict, duty always takes precedence over friendship. We can no more conclude from this case that it always does than we can conclude from those cases where benevolence takes precedence over promise keeping that it always does.

Partisans of duty might reply that even if right, this misses the point: the badness of the act of perjury from friendship is constituted, not merely engendered, by lacking or not employing a sensibility informed by duty. But even if this is right, it still does not show what the partisans of duty require: that acts done by someone lacking or not employing that sensibility cannot be good. For in the perjury case, it is not merely that the agent lacks, or does not act from, a sensibility informed by duty. The agent violates duty, and insofar as this shows the agent's sensibility, it is a sensibility that is disrespectful or even contemptuous of duty. And there is an important differnce between not having a sensibility informed by duty and having a sensibility informed by disrespect or contempt for duty. An example might help. I think we can agree that it is wrong to endanger a friend's life. But from this it does not follow that a case of innocently talking with friends is all right only if we take care, or have a sensibility that takes care, that the talk does not endanger their life. Of course, it is easy enough to imagine circumstances where there would be a moral failure of negligence not to be alert to the dangers of telling a story to a friend. For example, the friend is in the hospital recovering from a near-fatal heart attack and the story concerns matters of great emotional moment, such as a rumor that the friend's child has been killed. But in more usual circumstances, our friends are more robust and our stories less charged. In such cases there seems to be no negligence in not having such concerns.

Similarly, we can imagine circumstances where it involves negligence not to use considerations of duty to temper, guide, or even preclude other acts done from friendship. So an official, such as a judge or the head of a department, must be alive to the moral dangers of favoritism. And a leader of a group on a dangerous mission may well have to put considerations of friendship aside for the sake of the group's success or even survival. But at least for many of us and at least often, our lives are not so morally charged and difficult. Our friendships and acts of friendship are not so likely to run up against our duties. And when they do, the outcomes are not likely to be so severe. Insofar as this is so, it is unclear why these acts cannot be good even where they are not done from a sensibility informed by duty.

Of course, it might well be better to make sure that acts of friendship do not violate duty and to have a sensibility that does this. Perhaps it would be best if here, as everywhere, one took into account all that is morally relevant. Perhaps, as Aristotle suggests about the best people, someone who does this might therefore have the best friendships and do the best acts of friendship. But taking everything of moral relevance into account goes well beyond taking duty into account. It also seems a counsel of perfection, not a condition for goodness.

4 The Importance of Duty

Partisans of duty might accept these general strictures but argue that their point has been missed. They could agree that in ethics, as in science, even conclusive reasons and arguments need not mention and deal with all possible conditions. They could insist, however, that duty is not just one consideration among many but is so foundational to our moral thought and life that not taking it into account is wrong and will make any moral reasoning or action suspect, if not actually wrong. So they might claim that it is our duty to take duty into account and that there can be no mere absence of a sensibility informed by duty: any absence is a violation.

Insofar as we are now concerned with our ethics—which, to some extent anyway, is an ethics of duty—we may well be unable to reply that this claim is chauvinistic. But if my suggestions above are correct, it is too strict. One need not be a perfectly good person, nor even a person whose sensibility is perfectly informed by duty, for one's friendships and acts of friendship to be good.

One way to proceed here would be to modify the claim of the partisans of duty to one of holding that if a sensibility were of this or that particular sort, then friendships and acts of friendship done from it would therefore involve a negligent disregard for what is morally important. For a person with such a negligent sensibility, it would simply be a matter of luck whether friendships and acts of friendship turned out well.

Investigating this claim involves the difficulty of specifying not only the relevant sensibilities but also the worlds of those who have the sensibilities. For, as suggested above, a sensibility adequate in morally simpler situations may be inadequate in more difficult ones.

Rather than confront these great difficulties, I will reverse Kant's method from chapter 1 of the *Foundations* (1962) and argue that friendships and acts of friendship can be good even if they violate duty and thus even if they are not done from a sensibility informed by duty.

Let us start by noting that there are duties of friendship. I think it unnecessary here to give a general characterization of duties of friendship—duties peculiar to, and constitutive of, friendship. It is sufficient to recognize—contrary to most modern ethical theories— that we have such duties. So I can have a duty of friendship to show special care to a friend. To treat a friend as just one person among all people may, as such, be to wrong the friend. Thus, insofar as the impartial point of view requires treating every person as just one among many, the impartial point of view can be incorrect and, in- deed, immoral. (See, e.g., Cottingham 1983, Annis 1987, Walker 1987, Blum 1988b, and Gewirth 1989.)

It is important for us that there are duties of friendship in at least two related ways. First, on the assumption of such duties, the exis- tence of conflicts between friendship and other duties cannot be taken as showing that friendship must be outside of duty (much less outside of morality). For the conflicts might be between duties (or other elements of morality). Second, suppose that we fail to see that an act of friendship is wrong, where it is wrong because it violates a duty. Our failure may well be due to our having given undue weight to an overridden prima facie duty. And clearly, this is quite different from a failure due to giving weight to nonmoral, morally irrelevant, or immoral considerations.

It is also important for us that there is no lexical ordering between duties of friendship and the duties usually considered. Duties of friendship are not lexically stronger than all other duties. Thus, because of the way they violate other duties, it can be wrong to maintain a friendship or do an act of friendship.

But also, the duties of friendship are not lexically weaker than all other duties. Thus, it can be morally right, perhaps even obligatory, to do an act of friendship even though this involves not doing what most modern ethical theories designate as our duty. So I might have to miss a department meeting in order to help a friend in need.

As this shows, by focusing so exclusively on duty, as understood by them, our theories of ethics make mistakes both about morality in general and also about duty itself. And as this also shows, serious mistakes are also made by those who think that our ethical theories, though mistaken about morality in general, are right at least about duty. (See, e.g., Wolf 1982, p. 435, and Williams 1985, passim.)

Were we to follow the reductio that since there are bad acts of friendship not governed by duty, an act of friendship cannot in itself be act good, we could now offer the following riposte to the argument of the partisans of duty: As just seen, it can be wrong to do what is recognized by our present ethical theories as one's duty. In particular, this can be wrong when it involves failing to recognize and act on a stronger duty of friendship. Thus, "do your duty," at least as understood by those theories cannot be a sound principle. But as I already said, I think that we should rather conclude that duty has been misunderstood by those theories. At the very least, it needs to be augmented by duties of friendship.

It might seem that duties of friendship should be welcomed, if not seized upon, by partisans of duty. For these duties show that friendship should not be hostile to duty as such and that at least some aspects of friendship must be guided by considerations of duty. But on deeper reflection this seems like renaming a defeat a strategic withdrawal and then, almost without pause, renaming that a victory. For here friendship shows what duty is and in this sense takes precedence over it. (See Blum 1988b, p. 490.) Or somewhat differently, friendship helps constitute duty. Partisans of duty, who hold that the goodness of friendship depends on duty, cannot accept either of these.

Further, friendship and its value clearly go beyond duty. The duties of friendship are hardly the whole of friendship. So it would be surprising if the only way friendship shows contemporary moral theories mistaken is by showing their failure to acknowledge duties of friendship.

And indeed, there are other important ways that friendship shows those theories mistaken. To mention only two, first, as mentioned above, central to the value of friendship is the spirit and feelings constitutive of it. These motivational and affective structures, and of course their value, have been omitted—on principle, I think—from our ethical theories, and not only from their accounts of duty. Second, friendship and its value helps us see that duty is not the whole of morality, nor even always the paramount moral consideration.

This last is also shown by supererogatory acts and some self-regarding acts. It is not my duty to act supererogatorily. But I may do so. If the supererogatory act includes the duty—as in going the second mile, where the first is required—I have an option either to do just my duty or to do it and also the supererogatory (part of the) act. We might call this a simple option to contrast it with a contrary-to-duty option—a moral option not to do one's duty. Some supererogatory acts also create contrary-to-duty options: my running into a burning building to rescue someone can be supererogatory, even if it makes me unable to do what is my duty, e.g., attend a department meeting. (Whether "is my duty" should be "otherwise would be my duty" is taken up below.)

We also have moral options generated by some self-regarding acts. For example, there are simple options where I would not violate a duty by allowing someone to take my share of some goods, even though I would be completely justified in taking my share. There are also contrary-to-duty self-regarding options. In certain cases, at least, I am entitled to save myself from being harmed even if in so doing I will violate my duty not to cause or allow harm to another.[6]

Friendship also creates simple options. I may well not violate a duty either by seeing or not seeing a friend. But it also creates contrary-to-duty options (and not simply because of their self-regarding or supererogatory aspects). Consider a case where an old friend is about to leave town for several years. It may well not be my overall duty to visit with the friend. Speaking on the phone might be sufficient. Or if I really should visit the friend, I may do nothing wrong if I stay for only a short while. Nonetheless, I do not think it excessively lax to hold that it can be all right to stay the entire afternoon, even if this involves not doing what is my duty, e.g., attending the department meeting.

If I am right about these and similar contrary-to-duty cases, even acts that are not governed by duty can be good. Indeed, even acts that violate duty can be good.

Some may suggest that these acts are good but do not violate duty. They could hold that in these cases what was thought to be one's duty, e.g., to attend the department meeting, is shown not to be one's duty, and this is in fact shown by its being all right not to do the act in question. This claim, however, is no help to the partisans of duty. On the contrary, it tells importantly against their claim about duty and its predominance. For what it really says is that friendship, supererogation, and considerations of self-regard have precedence over duty. For it says that there are acts that it would be one's duty to do but for the fact that they conflict with acts of friendship, supererogatory acts, or self-regarding acts.

Many of these points can be usefully summarized by taking note once again of Baron 1984 and its criticism of "Schizophrenia." Baron says that her claim about the repugnance of acting from duty "could be couched in aretaic rather than deontic terms. It is important to clarify that nothing hangs on my use of deontic terms. I use 'duty' and 'ought' repeatedly, partly in the hope of convincing readers that much of the opposition to acting from duty is nothing but a dislike for the word 'duty'" (Baron 1984, n. 3). Further, she says that by "duty" she does not follow what she acknowledges as the common understanding, which allies duty and requirement. Rather, she uses "duty" to cover both what morality requires and also what it only recommends (Baron 1984, p. 201).

We have, I think, three choices of how to interpret her position: (1) as an example of the syncretism discussed above, (2) as an expression of the view that duty covers all of moral value and thus as a rejection of imporant and hard-won distinctions between duty and other moral notions, (3) as indicating a concern to integrate friendship into morality, not simply duty.

My views come close to (3). However, Baron's stated claims point to (2). This, however, presents a problem. She takes "Schizophrenia" to be arguing that friendship and acting from duty are incompatible. But then either she takes "Schizophrenia" to be flatly contradictory, or she must take it as arguing that friendship is not a duty. And to follow her usage, that would mean that friendship is not even recommended by morality.[7]

Yet, one of the central points of "Schizophrenia" is that our moral theories are defective as moral theories precisely because they fail to recognize the moral value and importance of friends and friendship. To quote two representative passages, both from p. 455, "Duty, obligation, and rightness are only one part . . . of ethics. There is the whole other area of the values of personal and interpersonal relations and activities." "It is not possible for moral people, that is, people who would achieve what is valuable, to act on those moral theories."

Perhaps the explanation of how Baron might have thought "Schizophrenia" was arguing against the value—indeed, the morally important value—of friendship is her taking duty as the central part, if not the whole, or morality. This is (2) above. For (2) may help us see how one might fail to understand as a moral recommendation, or simply fail to understand, the claim that friendship is good even if independent of duty and even if not required or even recommended by duty.

Conclusion

My goal has not been to show that a concern for duty can play no, or no important, role in a good character. Of course, it can. But much else is also important. So good character can require a sensibility informed by morality, including duty, and also by friendship.

This was shown above in regard to duties of friendship. These showed that just as friendship should be limited or augmented by duty, so duty should be limited or augmented by friendship, and of course by many other moral considerations as well. A perfect sensibility will be informed by everything of moral importance, and by these in the proper ways. An imperfect but good sensibility will be informed by good, even if imperfect, forms of at least some of these.

These, of course, are easy and programmatic points to make even though they must be made to allow for an adequate account of friendship. What is difficult is what is still needed: detailing how the various elements of morality and moral psychology, including duty and friendship and thus rightness and goodness bear on each other.[8]

Notes

1. See, e.g., Lawrence Blum 1980, 1986 (which has influenced this work), and 1988b.
2. See, e.g., Marcia Baron 1984. Baron disputes this interpretation of her work, claiming that she wanted to argue not that acts of friendship are good only if governed by duty but only that acting from duty is nor morally repugnant, not even for acts of friendship. I discuss this below. For now it is sufficient to say that even if the attribution is incorrect, the position is worth discussing in order to help clarify relations between friendship and duty.
3. I owe thanks to Justin Oakley (1988) for his discussion of this problem with acting from or for duty.

4. I find it difficult to see the basis in "Schizophrenia" for this interpretation. But others also make it. See, e.g., Wolf 1982, Flanagan 1986, and Piper 1987. (Still others, however, such as Card (unpublished b) do not make it.) These philosophers were, I suggest, interested in issues closely related to those dealt with in "Schizophrenia" and thus found it easy not to see that our concerns are importantly different, even though related.

5. It has been suggested to me that Baron rejects this, or thinks "Schizophrenia" rejects this, and that she holds or thinks "Schizophrenia" holds that even good friendships are a matter of mere likings and inclinations. I reject this view and, so far as I can see, "Schizophrenia" gives it no support.

6. On some aspects of the optionality of self-regarding and supererogatory acts, see my 1976b paper. In the same journal number as Baron's piece, Michael Slote (1984) argues similarly about self-regarding and other-regarding harms. On contrary-to-duty supererogatory acts, see my 1966 book, especially chap. 6, "Duty Precluding Supererogatory Acts"; Kamm 1985; and Wolf 1986.

7. This interpretation and criticism of Baron are developed independently in Hudson 1986, p. 126, n. 12.

8. My thanks are owed to the philosophy departments of the University of Minnesota and La Trobe University for their help with earlier versions of this work. I also wish to thank Marcia Baron, John Campbell, Norman Care, Pauline Chazan, Norman Dahl, Owen Flanagan, Graeme Marshall, Justin Oakley, Amélie Rorty, Laurence Thomas, and Robert Young.

Chapter 11

Trust, Affirmation, and Moral Character: A Critique of Kantian Morality

Laurence Thomas

Living morally—to hear some philosophers tell it—is very much a rational enterprise: it is in virtue of having rationally grasped the precepts of morality that one is moved to act morally.[1] Ideally, one's will to live morally is anchored in nothing other than a rational grasp of the precepts of morality. On this view, it is rationality, and not people, that grounds morality. That others should turn out to play a more central role is attributed to human frailty. Comenting upon the awareness of philosophers that in their moral behavior human beings do not always act for (and only for) the sake of duty, Kant approvingly wrote, "They have spoken . . . with deep regret of the frailty and impurity of human nature, which on their view is noble enough to take as its rule an Idea so worthy of reverence, but at the same time too weak to follow it" (407).[2] Well, I believe that love and concern for others play a very central role in our living morally and that this has no more to do with human frailty than does the fact that human beings are unable to fly of their own powers. My aim in this essay is to offer an account of that role and to reject the ideal of the wholly rational moral self—an ideal clearly anchored in the Kantian legacy (about which I say more at the end of these introductory remarks). Let me bring things into sharper focus.

It has been said that a house is divided against itself will fall. Yet a self that is a divided house is what much of moral philosophy often presupposes, owing in large part to the influence of Plato and especially Kant. There is the self of reason and the self of emotion (feelings, passions, desires, whims, and so on). To be sure, the former is supposed to rule the latter. But the self is no less a divided self on that account, for although it is the self of reason that rules the self of emotion, the latter is generally not construed as a part of the former. This is so even in the case where (following Plato) we have a well-ordered soul and reason always rules the emotions. What is more, implicit in this conception of the divided self is the view that the self really would be better off if only the self of rationality did not have to contend with the self of emotion.[3] Accordingly, the less dependent a person is upon the emotions for living morally, the better.[4] Having the self of emotion is more like having to take the bad with the good rather than being provided with an asset, whereas the self of rationality is viewed as an asset pure and simple.

Many sympathetic to the thought of Plato and Kant think along these lines, along with many sympathetic to the contract tradition. The difference between the two is that for the former the rational self discovers morality, whereas for the latter the rational self creates it. In either case, however, the thought is that persons should be moved to act in accordance with principles that recommend themselves to wholly rational individuals. What is more, persons should be so moved in virtue of knowing what these principles are. On this view, if one can count upon people to be wholly rational, then one can count upon them to be moral, and ideally, at any rate, one should always be able to count upon people to be wholly rational. In the case of human beings we presumably cannot on account of the emotions, and that we cannot is deemed a pity. We all want to be wholly rational moral selves, or so it is in our rational heart of hearts, as such a self is superior to our divided selves in all moral respects.

I want to contest this superiority by looking at an aspect of a theme that has been developed by Baier (1986), Stocker (1976a), Williams (1981a), and Wolf (1982). The last three have drawn attention to the difficulty of being a wholly rational moral self in the context of such important interpersonal relationships as loves and friendships. The first has drawn attention to the importance of trust by, among other things, drawing attention to how little importance the contract tradition places upon trust. I want to make a more sweeping indictment, namely that the conception of the wholly rational moral self, whether in the Kantian or the contract tradition, has no space at all for the invaluable good of trust, and thus we could not be such selves without incurring a considerable loss.

Kantians are, of course, well aware that human beings are not wholly rational moral selves and that the emotions sometimes result in human beings' acting other than as they ought to act.[5] All the same, the wholly rational moral self is held out by Kantians as an ideal in the shadow of which human beings live, since humans are not strictly what Kant calls "rational beings as such."[6] Indeed, Kantians maintain that it is because of the emotions that human beings will invariably miss the moral mark. For, as Kant himself insisted, even if human beings should always perform the right act, their motivations will certainly be suspect upon occasion, or at any rate, there is no way in principle to rule this out:

In actual fact it is absolutely impossible for experience to establish with complete certainty a single case in which the maxim of an action in other respects right has rested solely on moral grounds and on the thought of one's duty. It is indeed at times the case that after the keenest self-examination we find nothing that without the moral motive of duty could have been strong enough to move us to this or that good action and to so great a sacrifice; but we cannot infer from this with certainty that it is not some secret impulse of self-love which has actually, under the mere show of the Idea of duty, been the cause genuinely determining of our will. We are pleased to flatter ourselves with the false claim to a nobler motive, but in fact we can never, even by the most strenuous self-examination, get to the bottom of our secret impulsions. (407)

So for Kantians, the mere fact that the emotions are part of the nature of human beings makes it impossible that living morally could receive its fullest expression in the lives of human beings, since their existence make it impossible for us to be certain that we act for (and only for) the sake of the moral law. By contrast, I maintain that it is precisely because of the emotions that living morally has the possibility of receiving its fullest expression in our lives. One aspect of the Kantian legacy, I believe, is that the ideal of the wholly rational moral self should be the yardstick against which we should consider the moral frailty of human beings. In this chapter I wish to reject this aspect of the Kantian legacy, because I wish to reject the very ideal of the wholly rational moral self. I believe that the moral ideal for human beings should be anchored in a conception of the human self as it is actually constituted rather than a conception that is merely a philosophical fiction.

1 Prediction and Trust

A wholly rational moral self would act morally, which means that such an agent would always act in accordance with morality, the moral law, as Kant would say. There can be no doubt about that, just as a there can be no doubt that a glass of water would freeze if put at temperatures below 0°C or that a human body would be weightless if put in outer space or that a metal object (in Earth's gravitational force field) would fall if simply dropped. The idea is that a wholly rational moral self would act morally in a way that mirrors the conformity of inanimate objects to the laws of nature. Recall Kant's observation, "Everything in nature works in accordance with laws. Only a rational being has the power *to act in accordance with his idea* of laws" (413, italics in translated text).[7]

Because of the laws of nature, each one of these outcomes is inevitable if the antecedent conditions obtain. There is no room for either hope or trust here. To be sure, one can hope that one got both the laws and the facts right, and in this regard, one can either trust one's own judgment or the judgment of others. But if one takes it to be a settled matter that both have been correctly ascertained, then there is no place for hope and trust in regard to these outcomes. One does not check in on the laws of nature to make sure that they are operating smoothly! What we get with the laws of nature is enormous predictive power: water *will freeze* when its temperature is lowered below 0°C, a metal object *will fall* when dropped, and so on. A natural law ranges over a set of conditions and objects, say, and it tells us that when certain antecedent conditions obtain for an object covered by the law, then certain other conditions *will obtain* as a consequence. One can predict with certainty that they will.

In what follows, I shall intuitively distinguish between prediction and trust. I do so with an eye toward bringing out the untoward implications of the view that wholly rational moral selves follow the moral law rather as objects obey the laws of nature.

A prediction, obviously, is a statement about what will occur in the future. Both prediction and trust share this feature in common, as trust entails a species of prediction, although the converse is not true. In fact, as I shall illustrate in the penultimate paragraph of this section, prediction can render trust unnecessary. Paradigmatically, trust may be defined as (1) having both the expectation and the desire (want) that another will, without ill motive, behave favorably toward one, although the person could act otherwise, where the basis for this expectation is the nondissimulating self-presentation of the other intended to generate precisely this expectation on one's part and (2) the willingness to rely on the other to behave favorably toward one in the relevant respect on account of the person's non-dissembling self-presentation, where one would be worse off in some nonnegligible way if the individual failed to live up to one's expectations.[8] Expectations exceeded in a favorable way do not constitute a violation of trust.

Trust is distinguishable from a number of related concepts. Reliableness is particularly worth mentioning. With trust comes reliability, but not conversely. The laws of nature are reliable but not trustworthy. A car can be reliable but not trustworthy. And one may be able to rely upon the subway driver to pull into the station at 9:00 A.M. each day without this being a matter of trust. For it could be that the train has been scheduled to arrive in that station at 9:00 A.M., drivers are given bonuses for maintaining an excellent schedule, and it is in the hopes of securing bonuses that the driver pulls into the station promptly at 9:00 A.M. each day. Reliability has to do with consistency in performance over time, and that consistency can be assured in ways that have nothing to do with trust. Hence, a person can be reliably late or belligerent in certain social contexts or ostentatious in formal attire.

Now because the predictions involving trust are tied to nondissembling self-presentation on the part of the other, we may think of them as intentionally manifested predictions. It is this feature that sets predictions involving trust apart from typical predictions. The prediction that such and such horse will win the race, while no doubt based upon a myriad of facts about that horse, is not based upon any socially calculated self-presentations on the part of the horse intended to generate the expectation (in its rider, trainer, or anyone else) that it will win the race. Likewise for the prediction that it will rain tomorrow. In general and very much to the point, predictions involving natural laws are intentionally unmanifested predictions.

Needless to say, there can be typical predictions—that is, intentionally unmanifested predictions—about human behavior, even predictions of quite favorable outcomes. The prediction that Smith will give a million dollars to the charity for children can be an unmanifested one if it is based upon, say, her wealth, the aims of the charity, and the recent discovery that a sibling she never knew was lost to sickle cell anemia at the age of three. That there can be typical and quite favorable predictions about human behavior has no doubt obscured the fact that there are two species of prediction: intentionally manifested and intentionally unmanifested predictions. Trust entails the former kind of prediction. And most important, unmanifested prediction does not entail manifested prediction; hence, unmanifested prediction does not entail trust. Throughout, the claim that prediction does not entail trust is elliptical for the statement that typical (intentionally unmanifested) prediction does not entail trust, since it does not entail intentionally manifested prediction, which is an essential feature of trust. (So when prediction is left unmodified, typical (unmanifested) prediction is meant, though as a reminder of the distinction and to insure clarity, I shall use the modifiers "typical (unmanifested)" and "manifested" from time to time.)

With the above observations in hand, the primary differences between trust and typical prediction can be put as follows: (1) Prediction, unlike trust, does not presuppose any awareness on the part of the object of prediction that a prediction has been made about it, any relationship between the predictor and the object of prediction, whereas an object of trust must be aware at some level or the other that it is being trusted or at any rate that it is regarded by others as trustworthy on account of its nondissembling self-presentation. (2) Equally irrelevant is whether the object of prediction wishes to have predictions made about it. A prediction is not more or less reasonable depending upon the wishes of the object of prediction. The wishes of the object of trust, however, can render trust very unreasonable. Suppose an individual utters the remarks "I just don't want to be trusted with that sort of information. It is too much responsibility." The person can thereby make it less reasonable to trust her or him. Accordingly, given these observations and (1), predictions can range over animate and inanimate objects as well as over creatures with or without the capacity for higher-order intentions, desires, and so on. (3) The desirability of what occurs is completely irrelevant to the enterprise of predicting. One hardly has to want an event to occur in order to be able to predict successfully that it will do so. This is the case even when a successful prediction is itself desirable, as with storms, earthquakes, and so on. One wants to be able to predict these things successfully. One does not want their actual occurrence. It is said that one could set one's watch by Kant's daily walk. But for all we know, some may, alas, have found Kant's predictability rather maddening. (4) Whereas the necessity of an event's occurrence, far from rendering prediction otiose, enhances the likelihood of a successful prediction, such a truth renders trust quite unnecessary. The knowledge that God will bring it about (cause it to happen) tomorrow that it will rain makes for an extremely successful prediction about tomorrow's weather. The knowledge that God will bring it about (cause it to happen) tomorrow that Esther will go before the king makes it quite unnecessary to trust Esther's claim that she will obey her father and go before the king.

Trust, as I said above, entails (manifested) prediction. So it might be thought that if a person is trustworthy with respect to a given form of behavior, then successful predictions with respect to that behavior thereby constitute trust. Not so, however. True enough, if one knows (for example) that a person is honest, then one can predict that she will tell the truth in the appropriate context. But as a thoroughly despicable person, one need not want this, since her truthful report will reveal one's ignominious motives in offering to care for a child. We have here prediction, not trust. By contrast, to trust an honest person is not just to predict that she will tell the truth in the appropriate context but to want her to do so. And from the fact that one knows that a person is honest it does not follow that one wants her to be honest. I can know that you will not accept a bribe even as I very much wish that things were otherwise. Thus from the fact that one knows that a person is trustworthy, it does not follow that one actually trusts that person.

Naturally, if a series of predictions warrant the belief that a thing (including a person's behavior) will occur with regularity and its occurrence is beneficial, then one may come to rely upon its occurrence. The letter carrier shows up everyone morning at 9:30. Being a lover of mail, one allows the arrival of the mail to mark the beginning of one's day. One found it almost unbearable when the letter carrier's delivery varied. There need not be any trust here. In fact, the letter carrier may change from day to day. It is just that the carrier's supervisor expects her to have delivered the mail to your apartment complex by 9:30 A.M. Here is a different example. The neighbor, with whom one shares an adjoining wall, is never home between 2:00 and 5:00 P.M. Even when she is not working, she is not home during these hours. As a lover of music and of playing it very loudly, one finds this to be very convenient, as it makes it possible to listen to one's music as loudly as one wishes without disturbing anyone. Rather than play one's music loudly at other times, then, one does so during these hours. In fact, because one prefers not to disturb the neighbor, one generally makes a point of being home between the hours of 2:00 and 5:00 P.M. Again, there need not by any trust here; indeed, aside from polite greetings there is no social interaction between the two of you. And you both prefer it that way. But having been her neighbor for six years, one is able to detect patterns, and her being away from home daily between the hours of 2:00 and 5:00 is one of them.

The point here, of course, is that it simply does not follow from the fact that one can predict a regularity in a person's behavior to the point that one can rely upon that person to so behave, and one actually does rely upon the person in this way, that any trust on one's part is involved. I have been talking about predictable behavior that is beneficial. But needless to say, not all such behavior is.

Suppose, for instance, that during the summer, starting with Memorial Day, a gang of motorcycle youths ride through a quiet working-class residential street every night at 9:00 P.M., the noisy procession lasting some 10 minutes. There is no legal recourse available to the residents, since people are allowed to ride their motorcycles, and the hour is early enough. So at 9:00 P.M. people just steel themselves for 10 minutes of very unwelcome noise. It would be absurd to say that there is any trust going on here. Again, it could be predicted that those running Nazi concentration camps would murder the Jews in them, and it could be predicted that racists of the antebellum South would discriminate viciously against blacks. Yet is would be an abominable use of the language to claim that with regard to these forms of treatment Jews and blacks were trusting, respectively, of the officials of concentration camps and white racists of the antebellum South.

I hope it is clear now that from that fact that we can predict a human being's behavior and even rely upon that prediction it hardly follows that we trust the individual (that we have an intentionally manifested prediction in such instances). This is so even though the prediction pertains to a matter about which the person is actually trustworthy. For as we saw, we do not trust an honest person to tell the truth just because we can predict that the person will do so, since we may not want the individual to tell the truth at all. Not only does (intentionally unmanifested) prediction not entail trust (because it does not entail the intentionally manifested prediction essential to trust), but prediction can actually make trust unnecessary.

Consider the following scenario. I extend a dinner invitation to Jones, which, as in the past, he gladly accepts. My friend remarks, "Surely you don't believe that Jones is actually going to show up, since he has never attended a single dinner party of yours, although he has accepted each invitation and promised to attend." I respond, "Oh, Jones will be there this time but not because he accepted my dinner invitation. As it turns out, the reason that I believe that Jones will show up is that one of the dinner guests will be Lena Horne, Jones's idol and a long time friend of the family. She will call him later this afternoon to ask him to pick up a bottle of French wine. Once he finds out that she will be at the dinner, then it is no longer an issue of whether he will show up; for nothing short of death could prevent him from doing so." In this instance, it is quite unnecessary for me to trust Jones to keep his word to attend my dinner party. It is unnecessary precisely because I can predict that he will do so. This example is, of course, yet another illustration of claim (4) above.

In this section I have sought to distinguish between prediction and trust in order to bring out that only prediction and not trust is applicable in the case of natural laws. The relevance of these considerations to morality is this: since prediction does not entail trust and can actually render trust unnecessary, a moral theory according to which persons can predict that persons will act morally is not, on that account alone, one according to which persons can trust that persons will act morally. As I shall now try to show, because it embraces the notion of a wholly rational moral self, ideal Kantian moral theory is a case in point.

Before moving on, however, a caveat is in order. I should like to think that Kant or someone defending Kant would come, upon reflection at any rate, to accept the account of trust offered because the account is seen as constituting a philosophical explication and refinement of what is generally referred to as trust. I offer no argument to this effect. If I am right, then at least with regard to the nature of trust, no questions will have been begged against Kant in the argument that follows. If, on the other hand, I am wrong, then from the very start the argument is much less meritorious than I would like for it to be. Annette Baier (1986) has observed that the good of trust has been much overlooked by philosophers writing in the contract tradition, as Kant himself did. Her observation is very much vindicated if this should prove to be a most costly oversight for, at any rate, Kantian moral theory.

2 Prediction and Kantian Moral Theory

Although it is certainly true that a wholly rational moral self always obeys the moral law, Kant held a much stronger claim, namely, that *necessarily* a wholly rational moral self always obeys the moral law. Kant held the stronger claim because, on his view, it is not a mere contingent truth and feature of the world that a wholly rational moral self always obeys the moral law. For Kant, being a wholly rational moral self and disobeying the moral law is as much of a synthetic a priori conceptual impossibility as is a fly that is human or water that is gold. On Kant's view, a wholly rational moral self always chooses to do what is morally right, and necessarily so. It is a constitutive feature of such a creature that necessarily it always chooses to do what is morally right, in contrast with human beings who miss the moral mark often enough, their best efforts notwithstanding.

Of course, obeying the moral law is said to be in keeping with, indeed, the most profound expression of, the very nature of wholly rational moral selves. Accordingly, the reality that wholly rational moral selves necessarily obey the moral law is hardly incompatible with their being free, any more than the fact that humans must breath in order to live is incompatible with their being free or (better) any more than having to hold that "2 + 2 = 4" (and not 6 or 10) is incompatible with being free. The idea is that if following the Good or accepting the True is a deep feature of the very nature of a set of beings, then their freedom is in no way diminished in virtue of being constituted so that they necessarily choose do these things (Wolf 1980).

Whether or not we have genuine free choice here is a matter that I do not wish to settle. Rather, (on the assumption that we do) what I wish to draw attention to is that what we have here is a conception of free choice for which the notion of prediction as understood in the case of natural laws can be applied *salve veritate*. Precisely what Kant wanted, it seems, is a conception of choice such as this. But if so, then what we have is a conception of freedom that is incompatible with trust, for as I have argued, trust and hope are out of place with respect to the natural laws. To be sure, Kant did not want obeying the moral law to be a matter of cause and effect. However, he did want conformity with the moral law to have the same immutable regularity characteristic of the natural laws. It is just that he wanted the immutable conformity to be imposed from wtihin rather than from without: "Thus a kingdom of ends is possible only on the analogy of a kingdom of nature; yet the kingdom of ends is possible only through maxims—that is, self-imposed rules—while nature is possible only through laws concerned with causes whose action is necessitated from without" (85). The kingdom of ends and nature are disanalogous with respect to the explanation for the immutable conformity of the objects subsumable under their respective laws; they are completely analogous from the standpoint of immutable conformity. Kant thought that the analogy in this respect could be exploited to his favor. I am suggesting that he is mistaken, since what we get is a world that is incompatible with trust.

To make things somewhat perspicuous, imagine a wholly rational moral self, whom we may call Spock, in a world of divided selves—people like you and me—whose lives are influenced by both rationality and emotion. Everyone, let us suppose, knows the identity of this wholly rational moral self; further, everyone knows and fully undersands what it means to be a wholly rational moral self. Hence, it is known that no matter how wrongly a divided self treated Spock, he would of necessity always act morally, and that favoritism and partiality are utterly impossible for him. It would make no more sense to wonder whether Spock would go on telling the truth and treating others morally after having been lied about and ridiculed by everyone than it would make sense to wonder whether a jar of water would freeze at $-25°C$ after having been tossed about endlessly for several hours.

In general, there could be no such thing as making oneself vulnerable to Spock in the hopes that he would in the end do the right thing. This is so for two related reasons. One is that Spock cannot help but do the right thing. The other is that we make ourselves vulnerable to others in terms of trust only if it is possible for them to act in exactly the ways in which we trust that they will not act. Trust is anchored in the belief that a person will choose *not* to perform the action that he has been trusted not to perform, rather than in the belief that he *cannot* perform it. Trust is unnecessary if the person is incapable of performing the action (or if it is highly improbable that he could perform it) and this is known.[9] Only as a form of humor would someone say, "Can I trust you to go on breathing tonight, if you should be alive?" It will be recalled from my account of trust in the preceding section that we do not have trust in virtue of having reliability.

Of course, as habits and addictions reveal, the boundary between what a person cannot and what a person will not do is not always a tidy one (Greenspan 1978). However, it is worth noting that for the purposes of predicting behavior, habits and addictions are in some cases regarded as if they are genuine instances where a person cannot refrain from engaging in the behavior in question, at least not without tremendous psychological preparation. The habitual coffee drinker, smoker, and drug addict come readily to mind. These habits are thought to be anchored in deep cravings, which great effort is required to extinguish and the nonsatisfaction of which can be very disruptive, and these habits are thought to render a person predictable in a way that makes trust unnecessary. Accordingly, although cravings exemplifying habits or addictions can be extinguished or gotten control of, we do not normally speak of trusting a person to satisfy such cravings (as opposed to a fleeting craving, say, for ice cream today) when he is in their grip. Only as a crude form of humor would one speak of trusting a drug addict to get a fix. (Of course, one can, out of desperation, hope this, and trust is sometimes used synonymously with hope, as in "I trust that everyone had an enjoyable visit."

To be sure, not all habits are to be viewed in this way, as we say that some habits are commendable. But this matter need not detain us. For the moral behavior of wholly rational moral selves is grounded in a motivational structure that has less contingency to it than that of habit, since the view is not only that wholly rational moral selves always act morally but that this is necessarily so. Habits, by contrast, can in principle be broken, and in any case one does not necessarily have this or that habit, whereas wholly rational moral selves necessarily act morally.

Typically, when we think of instances where prediction in the lives of creatures capable of moral agency especially renders trust unnecessary, no doubt cases of manipulation first come to mind: *A* wires *B*'s brain (implants a device in it or whatever) so that she can bring it about that B will perform the action that she wants performed—by, say, causing him to have an overwhelming desire to do so—if B should choose not to perform the action on his own, A being an excellent judge of such matters.[10] But alas, prediction can also render trust unnecessary when the (correct) explanation for the prediction is a creature's metaphysical constitution, which I should like to distinguish from a creature's personally wrought constitution. The latter, while presumably supervenient upon the former, is not uniquely determined by it. The former refers to the way a creature is in virtue of being an instance of its kind; the latter refers to the way a creature turns out to be with certain habits, idiosyncrasies, and the like. Accordingly, it may be true that a creature's personally wrought constitution is such that it could not lie or harm a fly or whatever even if its very life depended on it, and yet be quite false that the creature cannot do these things because of its metaphysical constitution.[11] The personally wrought constitution of individuals may change, but not their metaphysical constitution. It makes perfectly good sense to say that ten years ago one could not imagine so-and-so attending a party without getting rip-roaring drunk, whereas today the person does not touch the stuff. Once more, sexist, anti-Semitic, and racist attitudes are surely not determined by the metaphysical constitution of human beings. The personally wrought constitution of firm racists can surely change. Consider George Wallace, the late and former Alabama governor. By the time of his death the distance he had traveled in terms of attitudes to toward racial harmony from that time when he stood on the steps of a university in opposition to its being integrated is absolutely mind-boggling.

Needless to say, I maintain that wholly rational moral selves are metaphysically constituted so that they necessarily choose to do what is moral. As I remarked, for Kant, being a wholly rational moral self and disobeying the moral law is as much a synthetic a priori conceptual impossibility as is a fly that is human or water that is gold.

Now if human beings were metaphysically constituted so that they always told the truth at 20°C and above, we would surely find ourselves much more interested in the temperature of the environment in which a person spoke rather than whether the individual said, with a straight face, such things as "I am being perfectly honest with you." For this statement is nothing other than a way of claiming to one's listener that one is trustworthy, whereas if people could not help but tell the truth at above 20°C, there would be no need to trust a person who spoke in an environment at that temperature. By the same token, then, a wholly rational moral self just is a self that is metaphysically constituted in such a way that there is no need to trust it to act morally, since a wholly rational moral self is conceptually unable to act otherwise. True enough, wholly rational moral selves presumably find great satisfaction in their being so constituted. But this has no bearing upon the matter whatsoever. In particular, wholly rational moral selves do not become proper objects of moral trust (so to speak) on that account.

It may very well be that a fully realized metaphysically constituted self will not want to be other than it is. And it may very well be that a kind of freedom consists in wanting through and through to be the way that one is (Frankfurt 1971). This, however, should not blind us to the reality that even down to the choices determined by its metaphysical constitution, such a self cannot be other than it is. Perhaps freedom is compatible with not being able to do otherwise (Frankfurt 1969). I do not know. What I do know, though, is that if a person cannot but act as she does owing to her metaphysical constitution and this is countenanced as genuine knowledge about her, then with respect to the behavior in question it cannot be possible to trust her to act as she does.

Whether or not I have convinced you that wholly rational moral selves are not proper objects of moral trust, I have perhaps gone on in this vein long enough. In any case, one naturally wonders, So what if they are not? As I hope to show in what follows, much is lost in a world without trust. However, first I should like to bring out an interesting implication of what has been said thus far concerning trust.

3 One Thought Too Many

The thesis that it is not necessary to trust wholly rational moral selves gives us another way to express the "one thought too many" criticism raised by Fried (1970) and later echoed by Williams (1976b), Blum (1980), and others.

It goes without saying that out of moral duty a wholly rational moral self would, if she could, save any person from drowning, be it a perfect stranger, a spouse, or other family member or friend. The by now familiar objection is that while it is better that a wife should save her spouse out of moral duty than not to save him at all, surely the relationship between a wife and husband ought to be such that the thought that she has a moral duty to save her husband from drowning is not necessary to get her into the water. She should be motivated by love alone to do so. Kantians like Darwall (1983) may respond that saving one's spouse has (full) moral worth only if that is what one ought to do, all things considered. While in all likelihood it will be, this must first be ascertained; herein lies the significance of the thought that it is one's moral duty to save one's spouse.

My response to this Kantian line is this. Trust is deeply constitutive of flourishing ties of affection, and affectional trust, so to speak, is not transitive: if *A* trusts *B* and *A* knows that *C* is as good as *B* in all of the relevant respects, it simply does not follow that *A* trusts *C*. Accordingly, where there is affectional trust between individuals, they look to one another for support in ways that they would not look to others for support, though others are able and willing to provide the support and, moreover, even if others should provide that support. There is the deep-seated trust on the part of each that they can look to the other to diminish the misfortunes they suffer. It is irrelevant whether the misfortune is such that from a universal and objective standpoint anyone else in the position to help would incur a moral obligation to do so. In these instances the trust shared by those with flourishing ties of affection is not put on hold. Its character is not altered.

Consider the case of a person having difficulty staying afloat in the water and screaming for help. A perfect stranger whom he knows to be an excellent swimmer from having seen him swim is walking by. Also walking by, but on the other side, is another excellent swimmer who is a friend of the person in the water. Neither the friend nor the stranger can see one another. Both have on tuxedoes and are on their way to the President's ball, and for this reason neither makes an attempt to rescue him. The person in the water survives, however, because a large a piece of wood floats by just in time. No doubt he will be rather upset that the perfect stranger made no attempt rescue him, but he will surely be outraged and extremely disappointed that his friend did not. The survivor would undoubtedly view the friend's not attempting a rescue as an extraordinary breach of implicit trust: "If ever I needed you, I needed you then. And all you can say is that you didn't want to ruin your tuxedo." As a satisfactory response, the friend cannot point to the truth that the stranger too should have made the attempt.

Let us assume that, all things considered, both morally ought to have made an attempt to save the survivor. While this assumption can explain the feelings and attitude that the survivor has toward the stranger, it cannot begin to explain the very different feelings and attitude that he has toward the friend. These, obviously, are ineluctably tied to (unmet) expectations generated not by the moral point of view but by the presumed love and trust between them. And they entail the belief on the part of the survivor that even when it comes to doing what morality calls for, the friend should be motivated to act on his behalf by considerations other than moral ones. For as I have said, when there is affectional trust between individuals, then they look to one another to diminish the misfortunes that they suffer, and it is irrelevant whether the misfortune is such that from an objective and universal standpoint anyone else in the position to help would incur a moral obligation to do so.

Affectional trust does not and cannot end where morality begins. The explanation for this is due to the nature of such trust and not to the fact that from a universalized perspective trust thus extended is deemed commendable. Herein, I believe, lies the important kernel of truth that underlies Fried's one-thought-too-many criticism. Even in moral matters, friends look to one another out of trust. That trust would be betrayed if it were possible for one friend to respond to the misfortune of another as if the only relevant considerations were moral ones. A friendship between a wholly rational moral self and a divided self would invariably run afoul (see Stocker 1976a, 1981), for time and time again the wholly rational moral self would betray the trust of the divided self by not allowing trust to be a relevant consideration in the context of morality. The fountain head of this trust is, of course, affection itself.

4 The Value of Trust

In a basically moral society, trust is an integral part of the social and moral fabric of life. We trust people to be honest with us and with others about us. We trust that people will not desire our harm or death or the harm or death of others generally, that the reason why it does not occur to people to kill someone is not because they generally have too much on their minds but because they do not in fact want to be murderers. We would scarcely order a meal in a restaurant or ask a stranger for the time or walk down the street without wearing a bullet-proof vest if we thought for a moment that every stranger in life was out to kill us. To be sure, there are legal sanctions that are roughly directly proportional to the harm that a person intentionally does to another. Therefore, it might be held that we do not much have to trust people not to murder us, because the explanation for why most people do not murder is simply that they desire to avoid the undesirable legal consequences that attend to committing a murder. The view, then, is that because of this desire and the legal consequences of murdering someone, our not having to worry about being murdered can be attributed to prediction pure and simple, and not trust. Anyone who thinks this should think again.

For one thing, the thought that one's murderer will be duly apprehended and punished hardly inspires one not to worry about being murdered, any more than the horror of an automobile accident that leaves one paralyzed from the waist down is diminished by a handsome jury award. For another, as Lon L. Fuller (1964) and H. L. A. Hart (1961) have amply demonstrated, if most people did not refrain from murdering because they deemed murder to be a bad thing, the laws against murder would not do much good. The laws of a society's legal system can be efficacious only insofar as the overwhelming majority of the members of the society willingly comply with them, and this is incompatible with everyone's chaffing at the bit to commit a murder but, being mindful of the legal ramifications of murder, refraining from doing so. As Hart ever so ably demonstrated, John Austin (1873) was absolutely wrong in supposing that the law is a set of commands backed up by threats.

In a basically moral society, most of us do not return home after each venture out feeling lucky to have survived yet another occasion on the streets. With rare exception, dinners are not usually spent recounting the close calls of the day and going over strategies for avoiding being killed. Nor, on the other hand, are most of us experiencing pent up frustration on account of having been thwarted in this or that attempt to commit a murder. With rare exception are any of us disappointed in ourselves for not having committed a murder. For most of us, the thought of murdering another is extremely abhorrent. Of course, there is a connection here. Most of us do not worry about being killed when we leave our houses precisely because killing is so abhorrent to most of us. A society wherein trust abounds is deeply satisfying and comforting.[12] I want to bring out why this is so in what follows.

In a word, my thesis is this: a world where trust abounds—and so one where trust prevails between people across differences in ethnic and religious heritage and differences in phenotype—is one where people contribute to one another's flourishing by affirming each other's moral worth. We could not want for greater evidence that those whom we do not know, and thus with whom we have no personal ties, nonetheless regard us as having worth, or as being deserving of respect, than that they do not make us worse off although they are well aware that they have the opportunity to do so and, of course, are able to do so. We do not expect to be robbed when we have everything under lock and key. And a person who tries and fails has not shown us any respect. We do not feel that our worth is affirmed by their failure. By contrast, when a person with every opportunity to rob us nonetheless *refrains* from doing so, our worth is very much affirmed. Again, a person does not show us any respect in telling us the truth if he does so only because he believes that we already know the truth, whereas a person who tells the truth although she could have prevaricated without detection very much does. A gain need not be in the offing at all. Those who simply do not cause us harm when they are easily able to do so with full or near full impunity—for example, the very strong person who is not a bully—also affirm our worth.

A world where trust abounds affirms our moral worth because the very best measure we could have of the value that individuals attach to objects—be they inanimate or animate, including those capable of self-consciousness—is the way in which individuals freely and regularly choose either to treat or to behave toward the objects in view of a vast array of options in terms of what they can do. What is more, we as human beings naturally and inevitably draw inferences and form judgments about the value that people attach to various objects on the basis of having observed their behavior toward others. We need not become entangled in the issue of whether or not a thing can have value regardless of what individuals think of or do to it. For the claim just made is true in any case. If in the year 2000 people start hoarding, going out of their way to acquire, and getting extremely excited about finding 1969 nickels, then to some extent such nickels are valuable to people, whatever else may be true. And if given the choice between a 1969 nickel and a 1969 penny, people invariably prefer the former, get more excited about it, and so on, then nickels of that vintage are more valuable to people then 1969 pennies. It does not matter why in the year 2000 people suddenly have this fondness for 1969 nickels, be it learned that Neil Armstrong left a 1969 nickel on the moon or that the Beatles always recorded and performed concerts with 1969 nickels in their pockets or whatever. Further, it goes without saying that what is valued can be relative to a group. All the world could watch with utter disbelief at the sudden obsession that Americans have for 1969 nickels.

Insofar as our free and voluntarily performed actions have meaning to us and, moreover, bear upon the lives of others, then they necessarily have a normative structure to them, because they are indicative of the value that we attach to objects (Adams 1975, Gewirth 1978). Of course, in an imperfect world we can be mistaken in our assessment of what is important to a person, because we can be mistaken about why a person is doing what she is doing or about the extent to which she is acting freely. However, the point being made is not vitiated on that account, for the claim is not that people are always correct in their judgment of others' actions but that free and voluntary actions necessarily have a normative structure to them, and the truth of this claim is compatible with people always being mistaken in their judgments of others' actions. In that case what would follow is that people would not be warranted in having much confidence in their judgments of the things that are valuable to other people. Let me assume here that such wholesale skepticism about the character of other people's actions is unwarranted.

As one has no doubt surmised, the connection between what has just been said in the past several paragraphs and my thesis about trust is this: it is because free and voluntarily performed actions that bear upon the lives of other individuals necessarily have a normative structure to them that trust is morally affirming, that trust affirms the moral worth of individuals. When we trust others, we believe that they have freely and voluntarily chosen not to have our harm as their aim.

If I am right in this, on the assumption that we can only be either wholly rational moral selves or selves possessing both a self of reason and a self of emotion, then what follows, quite astonishingly, is that it is only in virtue of selves possessing both reason and emotion that we, *qua* human beings, are able to affirm one another morally, for only then can our moral behavior be truly an expression of choice. I am not here making the very strong conceptual claim that moral affirmation is possible only as an expression of choice but rather the much weaker claim that among human beings, choice is the route to moral affirmation.

Among human beings it is precisely because we know that the hurt that comes from losing out to another can blunt the cooperative spirit of people that we are deeply moved and affirmed by someone who in such an instance continues to be cooperative with an abundance of good will. It is precisely because we know that phenomenal arrogance can be a by-product of phenomenal success that we are deeply touched by the successful who continue to value our company. And again, it is precisely because we know that the most well meaning of people can fall prey to some temptation or other that we are deeply grateful, and so affirmed, when a person does not yield to a temptation that would have caused us hurt, although it would have been understandable if the person had, the temptation being what it was.

Suppose, for example, that Tom is a very attractive seventeen-year-old male who has acknowledged his homophilia. One evening Tom makes rather overt and provocative sexual overtures to John, a seventeen-year-old gay male who is a very close friend of Tom's family. While Tom's parents are more than accepting of their son's homophilia, they nonetheless think that it would be best if he not have his first sexual experience at seventeen, although they realize that they really cannot prevent him from doing so. Tom and John both know this. Though John finds Tom enormously attractive and is sorely tempted, he resists Tom's advances out of love for Tom's parents, as they have been like second parents to him. Several months later in a heart-to-heart conversation with his parents, Tom relays the experience to them. It is not necessary to point out how appreciative they are of John's behavior, even if quite surprised that he managed to resist, nor to point out that their appreciation is owing to their knowledge that John resisted what was for him a considerable temptation. Clearly, if John had been an utterly uptight homophobic male who just gives the impression of being gay and this were known by all, he would have found Tom's advances not in the least tempting but very off-putting. In this case his not responding to Tom's advances simply could not have meant the same thing to Tom's parents. Specifically, John's not responding affirmatively to Tom's sexual advances could not in this latter instance rightly elicit appreciation and admiration on the part of Tom's parents. Likewise if Tom had been a wholly rational moral self and thus as a matter of metaphysical constitution had been incapable of any form of inappropriate temptation.[13]

The example of John and Tom is rather complex. Some personally wrought constitutions are born of deep fear. This is presumably the case with homophobia and is presumably not the case with the personally wrought constitution that comprises living morally. Choices that affect us and that are owing to personally wrought constitutions born of deep fear cannot be affirming. This is because as an explanation for a person's behavior, fear resembles an external constraint, and an individual's choices that are owing to external constraints are nonaffirming.

Now the fact that creatures capable of both reason and emotion, namely human beings, are able morally to affirm one another on account of being able to choose not to do what is wrong—a choice that would not be there but for the emotions—does not in the least strike me as some kind of human frailty. The emotions, then, far from interfering with our capacity to regard others as members of the moral community, are what make it possible for us to give expression to this conception of others if, as I have claimed, we affirm others in choosing not to harm them.

But, it might be asked, would it not be better if human beings did not need to look to one another for affirmation? Well, nothing is without a price. If human beings did not look to one another for affirmation, then there could not be a moral community among human beings. For a community is not just a body of individuals all of whom either have the same ideas or would reach the same conclusions and perform the same actions if similarly situated. No, a community is a body of individuals who can be both positively and negatively affected by the deeds of others. A community just is a whole that can be profoundly affected by its parts. This is why trust is indispensable to community. And once again, if community is important in the lives of individuals, as I believe it is, it is far from obvious that this constitutes a frailty on their part.

I believe that in the right social context, doing good can be contagious, and thus, having a good moral character is mutually reinforcing. That context, quite simply, is a community of individuals where each member has very good reason to believe that she or he can trust others to do good. Multiple instances of trust—that is, trust here, there, and everywhere one turns—creates a deep moral climate of trust. We may very well be able to predict that people will treat us in accordance with the precepts of morality. Perhaps being a constrained maximizer (Gauthier 1986) and the like will ensure this, though I very much doubt it (Thomas 1988). However, it is only when we can trust individuals to treat us so that our moral worth is affirmed by their doing so.

I do not believe that we have a community thus conceived represented in the ideal that Kant calls the kingdom of ends. For wholly rational moral selves do not need one another for moral support and affirmation. Since all are metaphysically constituted so that of necessity they act in accordance with the moral law, there can be no sense in which their moral endeavors sustain one another. Indeed, if their moral endeavors did, then they could not be members of the kingdom of ends, since in that case they would not be acting for (and only for) the sake of the moral law. With wholly rational moral selves we have absolute autonomy, but we lack moral community.

I cannot see why human beings should embrace this moral ideal. For it is an ideal that tells us that *human* life at its very best nonetheless misses the moral mark. The good life, if only we could achieve it, is one where individuals are mutually supportive of one another and trust abounds, where individuals find strength in one another's moral victories and learn from one another's moral shortcomings, and where in general the biological capacity for love (Thomas 1989b) and the good will anchored in it give morality a foothold in our lives that it would not otherwise have. I can see nothing frail or imperfect in life thus lived. Nor can I see that we should want to think of life thus lived as at best a limited expression of what living morally is all about. Given the choice between an ideal that characterizes human life at its very best and one that characterizes the best for human beings in terms of what, as a matter of metaphysical constitution, they cannot possibly be, it seems imminently more reasonable to embrace the former rather than the latter. There are virtues and values available to human beings that are not available to beings who are wholly rational moral selves, not least among these being trust itself.[14]

Notes

1. In writing this essay, I am grateful to many: my Subjectivity and Reality class (Oberlin College, Spring 1989); audiences at the University of Pittsburgh, the University of Texas at Austin, and SUNY at Albany; the audience at the Eastern Pennsylvania Philosophical Assoc., where this paper was presented as the Keynote Address; Catherine Elgin, Patricia S. Greenspan, Joel Kidder, William G. Lycan, Terrance McConnell, J. B. Schneewind, and especially Jennifer T. Parkhurst for instructive comments and criticisms; and finally both editors of this volume. This essay builds upon the account of trust offered in *Living Morally: A Psychology of Moral Character* (1989b, chap. 6), where trust is distinguished from such related notions as counting and relying upon. The account in the text of the difference between trust and prediction, which is central to this essay, is new here but is hinted at in Thomas 1989a. I have been much influenced by the writings of Annette Baier (1985a, 1986), Carol Gilligan (1982), Iris Murdoch (1971), Michael Stocker (1976a), and Gregory Trianosky (1988).

2. Unless otherwise noted, all parenthetical references are to Kant's *Groundwork of the Metaphysic of Morals*, and all quotations from the *Groundwork* are from H. J. Paton's translation (New York: Harper and Row, 1964a). Pagination is that of the Royal Prussian Academy.

3. Recently Patricia S. Greenspan (1988) has challenged the dichotomy between reason and emotion, maintaining that "emotions *are* reasons" (p. 175). But the emotions are claimed by her to have a "rebellious tendency." And although this tendency is said to have a valuable side effect, this sort of statement about the emotions invites the thought that we would be better off without them. By contrast, reason is not characterized as that out of which something good can be squeezed in spite of itself.

4. In "Themes in Kant's Moral Philosophy" (1989), Rawls writes, "Our consciousness of the moral law discloses to us that we can stand fast against the totality of our natural desires; and this in turn discloses to us our capacity to act independently of the natural order. Our consciousness of the moral law could not do this unless that law was not only unconditional and sufficient of itself to determine our will, but . . ." (p. 112).

5. Kant tells us, "Hence for the *divine* will, and in general for a *holy* will, there are no imperatives: 'I ought' is here out of place, because 'I will' is already of itself necessarily in harmony with the law. Imperatives are in consequence only formulae for expressing the relation of the objective laws of willing to the subjective imperfection of the will of this or that rational being—for example the human will" (414, italics in translated text).

   Let me here acknowledge the important work of Barbara Herman (e.g., 1981, 1985). She and others have argued convincingly that Kantian moral philosophy is sensitive to the restraints of human nature in ways that have often gone unappreciated. And H. J. Paton, writing well before the present debate between impartialists and personalists, observes "[Kant] never wavers in his belief that generous inclinations are a help in doing good actions, that for this reason it is a duty to cultivate them [i.e., generous inclinations], and that without them a great moral adornment would be absent from the world" (Kant 1964a, 19–20). But even if Kant's views are more congenial to human nature than has been supposed, this is compatible with the view that Kant regarded the wholly rational moral self as the moral ideal, of which moral existence could at best be a distant approximation. This chapter argues against the very ideal itself. It leaves untouched the extent to which Kant's views can accommodate human nature, his moral ideal notwithstanding. It does not speak to whether we should reject what I refer to in the text as the Kantian legacy.

　　I have resorted to the expression "Kantian legacy" in response to the comments of Elgin and Schneewind. I do not know whether Kant himself ever meant for the ideal of the wholly rational moral self to serve as a yardstick against which we judge the moral frailty of human beings, though it does not seem implausible to suppose that he can be read in this way. But in any case, much of the debate between personalists and impartialists (or neo-Kantians) makes very little sense if Kant is not often thus understood.

6. For Kant distinguishes between pure moral psychology, which he calls metaphysics, and applied moral philosophy. The former gives us a priori moral principles "not grounded in the peculiarities of human nature," and from "such principles it must be possible to derive practical rules for human nature as well, just as it is for every kind of rational creature" (410, the first n.).

7. For a conception of the nature of laws that I am supposing Kant to have had in mind, see Nagel 1961, chap. 4. He writes, "A law [of nature] is often held to express a 'stronger' connection between antecedent and consequent conditions than just a matter-of-fact concomitance. Indeed, the connection is frequently said to involve some element of 'necessity,' though this alleged necessity is variously conceived and is described by such adjectives as 'logical,' 'causal,' 'physical,' or 'real' " (p. 51). It is the element of necessity, obviously, that I mean to draw attention to.

8. For this way of formulating the notion of trust, in addition to Annette Baier (1986), I am indebted to Julian B. Rotter (1980). I am grateful to Jennifer T. Parkhurst for bringing this article to my attention. Interestingly, his definition of trust does not fully capture the way in which he uses it, since his definition is shorn of the positive connotations that he clearly associates with trust. He writes, "As distrust increases, the social fabric disintegrates." This quote suggests that trust must make reference to expectations regarding favorable behavior. As will become clear from the text, this is surely right.

　　I say "paradigmatically" for two reasons: (1) I want to allow that a person may be trustworthy but have a sufficiently low opinion of herself that she is unable to believe that she is trustworthy. Oppression tends to be conducive to its victims' not seeing themselves as trustworthy in fundamentally important ways. I am much indebted here to Horney (1942) and Wescott (1986) and to conversations with Glenn Kramer, Jennifer T. Parkhurst, and Alan J. Richard. (2) We are disposed to trust individuals when they have been warmly recommended by those whom we regard as very trustworthy.

9. It goes without saying that there are various ways in which it can turn out that a person is incapable of performing an action. It may be that no human being is

capable of performing the action, e.g., seeing through lead with the natural eye, or it may be that a person is incapable of performing an action owing to a specific psychological or physical difficulty, e.g., a blind person cannot see, or it may be that a person is temporarily incapable of performing an action, e.g., a person under the full influence of a heavy drug may be incapable of distinguishing his body from other objects in his immediate environment, or a person may be incapable of performing an action because some other agent successfully prevents him (temporarily or permanently) from doing so. For a fuller discussion of these matters, see Thomas 1989b.

10. I have in mind here Harry G. Frankfurt's (1969) example of Black and Jones (reprinted in Fischer 1986). Frankfurt is concerned not to distinguish between prediction and trust, of course, but to show that "a person may well be morally responsible for what he has done even though he could not have done otherwise" (Fischer 1986, 143). In the example Black will bring it about that Jones performs a certain action if Black detects that Jones will not of his own volition choose to perform it. See also Fischer's important introductory essay in Fischer 1986.

11. The wording here is meant to be sensitive to evolution. A species may evolve. Each member of a species has the biological constitution it has and will not come to have another (genetic engineering aside), but owing to evolution, each member of a species need not have the same constitution. I have been much helped by Rorty 1976a.

12. Over the years I have been struck by the number of people who have denied the claim that we generally trust people not to kill us. I have been told that no trust is involved here because we can simply predict that most people will not kill us owing to the legal consequences or that it simply will not occur to most people to kill anyone, and hence we can take it for granted that they will not murder anyone. I have spoken to the former in the text. As to the latter, suffice it to say that one can take the trustworthiness of another for granted in the same way that one can take another's kindness or generosity for granted. The norm may be that I spend hours with students, and so students naturally expect me to do so. That this is the norm, however, hardly entails that I am being any less generous with my time. Likewise, in a basically moral society, the norm would naturally be that most people give no thought to killing another. But since the explanation for this would be that most people have a good moral character, we have an explanation that is expressible in terms of trust, namely, that the moral character of most people is such that they can be trusted not to kill anyone. Here I am very appreciative of the work of Norman S. Care (1987).

13. I am grateful to Glenn Kramer and Alan J. Richard for very helpful discussion of this example.

14. It has been brought to my attention, by Christine Korsgaard and members of the audience at the Eastern Pennsylvania Philosophical Association that a most untoward consequence of the conception of trust that I offer is that it is not possible to trust God. Surprisingly, perhaps, I accept this, if it were possible to know how God should behave and what God would deem right. But clearly, whatever relationship there might be between God and human beings, it is surely one of radical uncertainty owing, presumably, to the inability of human beings both to fathom the will of God and to determine whether they measure up to it.

Chapter 12
Why Honesty Is a Hard Virtue
Annette C. Baier

Hume prefaces book 3 of A *Treatise of Human Nature* with a quotation from Lucan exhorting the lover of severe (*durus*) virtue to search for an exemplar of honesty in order to discover what virtue is. Does he himself do much in what follows to tell us what this harsh virtue consists in, or does what follows at most exemplify rather than do much to analyze honesty? The conclusion of the book shows that Hume did think that he had shown brutal honesty rather than engaging guile in his general portrayal of morality—he had presented the bare anatomy of virtue, not draped her agreeably to make us love her (Hume 1975b, 621). Does he give us a candid discussion or at least an honest sketch of honesty? Honesty includes truthfulness, and metatruthfulness is particularly hard. "Perhaps nobody yet has been truthful enough about what 'truthfulness' is" (Nietzsche 1966, sec. 177). How truthful is truthful enough?

The Latin *honestas*, perhaps best translated as "probity," is a broad-ranging virtue, but then so is English honesty. Honesty comprises both veracity, a virtue of speakers, and also uprightness in matters of property. Dishonesty is shown by the liar, by the cheat, by the thief. In the *Treatise* Hume has tried to give us the straight story about theft and fraud. Virtually nothing, however, is said about what is wrong with deceit or lying. In An *Enquiry Concerning the Principles of Morals* both "veracity" and "truth" get included in lists of virtues, truth being singled out as one of the virtues that have complicated sources (Hume 1978a, 238). The *Treatise* is indeed striking for its failure to analyze the vices of either the liar or the murderer, two of the traditional paradigms of moral vice. Hume glances at the liar (1975b, 461) and the parricide (1975b, 446–468) in the negative preliminaries to his theory to show the poverty of the traditional accounts of vice, but in parts 2 and 3, when he is supposedly giving us the true story about the virtues, he ignores the two most familiar exemplars of vice.

In this Hume follows Hobbes, whose laws of nature forbid neither violence nor any form of false speech except convenanting without the intention to keep the convenant and bearing false witness. The Ten Commandments too limit the prohibition on lying to a prohibition on bearing false witness. Hobbes's only variants of the Sixth Commandment, not to kill, are his first and second laws, requiring us to seek peace and to be willing to disarm ourselves when others are also willing (*Leviathan* chaps. 14 and 15). Hume mentions danger to life and limb from the assault of other persons in his discussion of the circumstances that give rise to the need for government (1975b, 540), but the only threats to life that he mentions when he describes the circumstances of justice are weather and natural accidents (1975b, 485). Nor does he discuss any general obligation or duty to refrain from violence against others. Presumably, magistrates will make some forms of such violence crimes, and respect for the authority of magistrates is an artificial virtue. But for all Hume says about the matter, violence is not vicious until forbidden by magistrates. Charity, clemency (Hume 1975b, 578), and humanity (Hume 1975b, 603) are, of course, natural virtues, and gentleness is a virtue in masters (Hume 1975b, 606). They will put some limits on the sort and degree of danger to life and limb we can properly impose on others, but in Hume's versions of morality we find no real equivalent of the Sixth Commandment and very little about lying.

The omission of a discussion of moral restraints on violent or murderous human desires is a real weakness in Hume's theory, and one not so easy to patch up for him. Gentleness may be in a sense an easier virtue than honesty, but it is not so easy to know exactly where it ends and the vice of undue nonassertiveness begins, any more than it is to know where honesty in speech ends and brutal frankness begins. Hume's own disposition, that combined gentleness with due self-assertion, may have led him to underestimate the threat of normal human aggression and its need for some redirection or "moral equivalent."

What of mendacity? Even if Hume was over optimistic about the naturalness of gentleness to human persons, surely he was not unaware of our natural proclivity to deceive. Even if, both as a child and an adult, he found himself subject to no temptations to assault and murder and so gave too little attention to the social control of aggressive and murderous impulses, it is implausible to suppose that he found no childhood occasions to fib, nor any adult temptations to deceive. So what would a Humean moral theory say about control of the inclination to resort to lying and deceit? Is it harmless? Hume cheerfully tells us that poets are "liars by profession" (1975b, 121), but surely he is not proposing to transfer mendacity to the column of the virtues. There presumably is a vice of mendacity, even if poets' "lies" do not display it. What sort of vice is it? I shall argue that mendacity is an artificial vice not so very different from the other sort of dishonesty that Hume did analyze, the dishonesty that consists in a disposition to take or to keep the property of others. After a Kantian detour I shall eventually propose a unified Humean account of honesty as an artificial virtue. But I shall also argue that there is a virtue (one that Hume calls "truth," whose sources are more complicated) that crosses the natural/artificial boundary and may give us good reason to blur that distinction. In brief, I shall argue that there is a natural tendency to candor in expression of current emotion, a tendency we have every reason to welcome and encourage, but I shall also argue that once we have language, then cover-up and deceit become second-nature abilities. Speech gives us the means for concealment and deceit about what we really think, believe, feel, and want. "Truth," as a virtue of those who have acquired language, is best construed as a regulation of our understandable tendency to use our acquired abilities to conceal and deceive, a tendency and an ability that are themselves superimposed on prespeech involuntary candor. Candor in an appropriate degree and form will indeed be a virtue with complicated sources, but honesty as veracity will be a bit less complicated to analyze, both because its scope is narrower and because it is more wholly artificial.

Veracity is a virtue of talkers, and to understand it, we need to understand talk and its relation to our other, more primitive means of expression. With nonlying speech we make our fellows aware of states of mind, such as our opinions, that would be well nigh impossible to convey nonverbally even if we suppose that we could acquire them without relying in some way on our linguistic competences. Talk is used to tell others what we tend to think and what we believe, as well as what we want, plan, and intend. For the latter purposes, nonlinguistic indicators sometimes suffice, but if we are to know what our fellows believe about, say the strengths and weaknesses of the government, as distinct from whether they are for or against it, talk or its written equivalent is essential.

Kant, famous for his refusal to condone any lies, also taught that "no man in his true senses is candid." Our own good sense, backed by the will of Providence, directs us, Kant finds, to cultivate "reserve and concealment . . . that the defects of which we are full should not be too obvious" (Kant 1963b, 224). Only Momus, the god of mockery and censure, would want all the contents of human hearts to become open to view. Reserve and reticence are our protection against mockery and censure. Mockery and censure, however, are not the only ills we dread; isolation is also an evil.

> Man is a being meant for society (though he is also an unsociable one) and in cultivating social intercourse he feels strongly the need to reveal himself to others (even with no ulterior purpose). But on the other hand, hemmed in and cautioned by fear of the misuse others may make of this disclosure of his thoughts, he finds himself constrained to lock up in himself a good part of his opinions (especially those about other people). He would like to discuss with someone his opinions about his associates, the government, religion, and so forth, but he cannot risk it—partly because the other person, while prudently keeping back his own opinions, might use this to harm him, and partly because, if he revealed his failings while the other person concealed his own, he would lose something of the other's respect by presenting himself quite candidly to him. (Kant 1964b, 143)

Kant thinks that some "exchange of sentiments" with others is required by the duty of humanity, but not at the cost of mutual respect, which apparently would be put at risk by total mutual candor. As he says in the *Lectures on Ethics*, "Fellowship is only the second condition of society" (1963b, 224). Better, if need be, that we keep our hearts' shutters permanently closed than that we open them so wide in the hopes of fellowship that we sacrifice mutual respect. Mutual respect, it seems, not only is threatened by too much candor but can subsist without any. We are to respect other human persons simply because of their presumed rational personhood, not because we have gotten to know them, talked with them, and *found* them to be rational and worthy of respect. So selective "disclosure" in an occasional "exchange of sentiments" is the most that is required of us to satisfy the duty of humanity. Intimate friendship, with its fuller mutual disclosure, is permissible but risky, and its moral gains are not so great. "Friendship develops the minor virtues of live" (Kant 1963b, 209). Better, it seems, for a man to risk regrettable isolation and be "*alone* with his thoughts, as in a prison" (Kant 1964b, 144) than for us to "place ourselves in a friend's hands completely, to tell him all the secrets that might detract from our welfare if he became our enemy and spread them abroad" (Kant 1963b, 208).

In all of these homiletic pronouncements, Kant assumes that it is within our power to keep our thoughts and sentiments "locked up" in the secrecy of our own hearts. There may be both a natural impulse and a duty to some "disclosure," but disclosure is what it will be, a making public of what is inherently private. Yet Kant's metaphors of shutters, prison rooms, and locks, invite the question of who or what made the shutters, the locks and the fortress-prisons that shut each man up within himself, alone with his own sentiments. If indeed, as Kant says in the *Doctrine of Virtue*, when we occasionally get out of our solitary confinement with our own sentiments, we "enjoy a freedom" rather than suffer from agoraphobia, then the solitary con-finement itself must be contrived, not altogether natural to us. Shame, fear of mockery and hurt, and a wish to retain respect are what make us *want* to shut ourselves away from others, on his story, but what is it that enables us to do this when we wish to? Kant seems to assume that reserve, restraint in expressing one's mind, is the easiest thing in the world. We need merely keep quiet and then no one will get to know our possibly shameful thoughts. And we need do nothing in order to keep quiet.

But Kant knows that this is not so, at least for half of us. He remarks in the *Lectures on Ethics* that "the person who is silent as a mute goes to one extreme; the person who is loquacious goes to the opposite. . . . Men are liable to the first, women are talkative because the training of infants is their special charge, and their talkativeness soon teaches children to speak, because they can chatter to it all day long. If men had the care of children, they would take much longer to learn to talk" (Kant 1963b, 226). Women, as Kant understands them, do not shut themselves up in themselves but open their minds at least to the children in their care, and presumably both male and female children may come to "chatter to it all day long," like their mothers and nurse maids, until shame, caution, and male dignity teach the boys to censor their utterances. "Loquaciousness in men is contemptible, and contrary to the strength of the male" (Kant 1963b, 226).

So should the "shutters," "locks," and "prison walls" that enclose a person, shut him in with his own thoughts, be seen as the result of a sort of enclosure of what was in childhood more open, more automatically expressed to those around him? Those who follow Plato and Ryle in seeing thought as silent speech, so that speech proper becomes the natural expression of thought, thought liberated back into its own home range, postulate a time in childhood when all our thought was "thinking out loud," when "candid avowal" of our state of mind came naturally. We might combine this view with Kant's and suppose that it is mainly the boys who somehow learn silent thought. (They might first think aloud something like this: "Maybe I'd get into less trouble if my thoughts were less noisy. Let me see if I can have the next one under my breath." Or they might imitate their strong, silent fathers, who will be models of *sub voce* thought.) The girls will not be encouraged to lose the habit of constant chatter, for that habit will prove functional once they become child minders. By this graft onto Kant's theory we could accommodate both Kant's conviction that reticence is second nature to sensible (and well brought-up) men and his realization that this sensible reticence is also a "prison," occasional escape from which counts as freedom.

But *is* it plausible to suppose that mothers and the children learning to talk from their chatter are all engaged in candid verbal communication of states of mind? A lot of mothers' "chatter" to the children will usually consist in songs, nonsense rhymes, nursery rhymes, fairy stories, white lies about birth, sex, and death, whitewashed versions of family and national history, attempted cover-ups of parental quarrels, utopian ideals of sibling love, and so on. If a child does engage for a time in candid talk, that will not be because the child has learned candid talk by example, if to speak candidly is to tell the truth and the whole truth as one sees it, to ask all and only what one wants to know, to try to utter all one's real and full wishes, all one's true and uncensored feelings. Talk, as we teach and learn it, has many uses. It is not unrelievedly serious—it is often an extension of play and fun, of games of hide and seek, of peekaboo, where deceit is expected and enjoyed, of games of Simon says, where orders are given to be disobeyed, of games of tag, where words have magic power, of skipping games, where words are an incantation. Speech, as we teach and learn it is not just the vehicle of cool rational thought and practical reason but also of fun and games and of anger, mutual attack, domination, coercion, and bullying. It gives us a voice for our many moods, for deceit and sly strategy, as well as for love and tenderness, humor, play and frolic, mystery and magic. The child is initiated into all of this and gradually learns all the arts and moods of speech. Among these are the arts of misleading others, either briefly and with the intent soon to put them straight again ("I fooled you, didn't I!") or more lastingly to keep deceit going for more questionably acceptable purposes. If loquacious women are the ones who transmit the arts of speech, and their verbal arts are the arts that are transmitted, then in all honesty we should add guile to loquaciousness as the imitable attributes of those entrusted with transmitting them. Nietzsche said, "From the very first nothing is more foreign, more repugnant, or more hostile to women than truth—her great art is falsehood" (1966, sec. 232). If there is some truth in this, then the arts of speech that are transmitted to children are guileful arts—they empower the natural will to the guile that is an integral part of many infantile games and extend the power to demand, to coerce, and to protect and defend oneself. The constant chatter in the nursery need not always be candid chatter, unless shameless guile can count as a form of candor (as perhaps it can, but it also counts as a form of harmless and temporary deceit).

Speech enormously increases our ability to mislead others, at least for a while. Our ability to mislead is coextensive with our ability to pretend, to put on a convincing show. Pretense becomes false pretense when guided by the intent to seriously misled rather than the intent simply to participate in a game of "let's pretend," where all concerned are led into imaginary states of affairs, so no one is misled (or if one is carried away by the game, one is as much misled by oneself as misled by others). We all have pretty good ability at pretense of intentions and feelings that we do not really have, an ability honed by all the playing we did in childhood. By the time we learn to talk, we are already actors, and speech merely increases the means we have for pretending to be in those situations and states we choose to enact, or to try on for size.

What speech adds is the ability to pretend to *beliefs*. Intentions, feelings, and some desires can be acted out without speech, but beliefs can only be indirectly faked before we have speech as the vehicle of pretense. What speech does is enable us to directly communicate, truly or falsely, what it is that we take to be the case, to say straight out what without speech we could only indirectly indicate. Speech enables us to tell the truth and to lie, to make public and to cover up what, without speech, had to remain only inferred from the version of our intentions and our feelings that was made public. For these latter naturally do tend to get expressed and do not depend upon speech for their communication.

Darwin's classic *Expression of Emotions in Man and Animals* (1916) explores the means by which our emotions and associated desires get expressed and recognized by our fellows. Both the expression and its recognition are universal and unlearned. What we learn, and learn variously, is when and how to inhibit natural expression, to try to fake it, or to replace or supplement it with culturally variant gestures and with speech. This universal body language, the language of eyes, face muscles, shoulders, and hands, of cries and voice quality, expresses primarily emotions along with associated desires and intentions. Candor about our emotions comes naturally to us, since reticence and faking take effort and training. But there is no such thing as natural candor in respect of the beliefs that inform our expressed emotions, desires, and intentions. Until we learn to speak, we cannot express our beliefs, and even after we have learned to speak, we may still not yet have learned candid avowal of what we

believe. For our "true beliefs" do not automatically distinguish themselves from our self-deceptions and our fantasies in the way in which
our true emotions make or made themselves evident. (For those, like
women, whose duty it was to smile and be pleased by their masters,
true spontaneous emotions may be a distant memory and acquired
factitious ones the norm.) Our true emotions are the ones that express
themselves without our trying to express them, without control. But
there are no such "true" beliefs, since the only vehicle for the expression of belief is a learned language and self-controlled sentences.
Everything we say is what we choose to say, but very little that we
show in our eyes is what we choose to show. Even when we blurt
out words and give away secrets, what we blurt and let out are will-
mediated forms of expression, sentences we form, and learned to
form, in a way we never form or learned to form a lighting up of the
eyes in welcome or the glazed look of boredom. Our natural nonverbal expression of emotion often gives us away, but what our
blurted-out sentences give away are only our artifacts, sentences we
accept as adequate representations of what we believe. Our control
over speech is unlike our control over body language in that the latter
is primarily the acquired ability to inhibit and to fake, the former the
acquired ability to produce the real thing. Once we are speakers, of
course, speech becomes second nature to us, and the chatterers may
have to learn to inhibit their second-nature loquaciousness. But beliefs, requiring speech for their most direct expression, will still get
controlled expression even in what Ryle called the most "unbut-
toned" talk. Normally, we select which beliefs to express and how
to express them. And unless we select them, they stay unexpressed.
This is not the case with our emotions. They may remain without
verbal expression unless we select them for attempted articulation,
but they do not stay unexpressed. Expression is the norm for emotions, the exception for beliefs. Even with the greatest possible will
to candor, we would be hard put to express our version of "the whole
truth" on any matter, let alone to express "everything we believe" at
any one time. Our beliefs must outrun their expression, but our
emotions, desires, and intentions need not. They usually *do* outrun
their expression, especially if we have long term intentions and desires for goods in the distant future, but they do not outrun expression as inevitably as our thoughts do.

Both reticence and deceit concerning our beliefs, then, are quite
different from reticence and attempted deceit about our emotions,
intentions, and desires. For one thing, the chances of success are
much greater, since what we say we believe does not, to be credible,
have to square with what we otherwise directly show we believe in

the way that what we say or refuse to say we feel has to square with what we more reliably show we feel. Even lie detection by polygraphs depends not on a perceived misfit between what is said and what is shown to be believed but only on revealed discomfort during the saying of it or a misfit between *actual intention* (to deceive) and *apparent intention* (to speak the truth). Bare-faced lying about one's beliefs can be carried off much more easily than bare-faced lying about one's emotions, since the face is naturally bare when it comes to beliefs. A bare face *is* the face for cool fact reporting. It is bare of the expressions faces have evolved to have: shock, delight, disgust, horror, amazement, fear, tenderness, anger. Faces can, of course, also show disbelief of what others are saying, and there are pious believing faces put on while reciting some credo, but ordinary facts are parlayed without expression. When we try to conceal or feign any expressive face, we have not only to *produce* some suitable expression, verbal or nonverbal, we also have to inhibit the spontaneous expression of what we really feel. Since there is no spontaneous expression of ordinary belief states, there is at least nothing to suppress, only something to produce, when we try to conceal or deceive others about our matter-of-fact beliefs. The only suppression needed will be of guilt or anxiety, if we feel it. Glib liars and those practiced at cover-ups will not feel it and so will have nothing to suppress. Since all talk is second and not first nature and since reporting talk has no natural belief expression constraining it, lies and silent closure can come as naturally to human lips as truths, as far as factual beliefs go. Factual truth is no more the telos of speech than fairy tales are.

I have been arguing that there is neither a natural urge to accurate reporting of what we take to be the case nor any natural prelinguistic constraint on our powers to use words to deceive and conceal our belief states but that our natural spontaneous nonlinguistic expression of emotion does put constraints on our ability to deceive about what we feel. Our thoughts and beliefs are "shut up" within us, unless we choose to let them out, in a way our emotions and sentiments are not. So Kant was half right, right about thoughts, wrong about emotions. What is more, our experience of natural candor in our emotional life, along with the involvement of thought in emotions, explains why it may feel like liberation to share our thoughts as well as our feelings. Candor becomes an understandable ideal for us, since we are in a position to feel nostalgia for the candor we had before we learned the concealing and complicating arts of speech, and we might hope for conditions in which we can extend to belief states the candor that is present, unless we inhibit it, for emotional states. Candor is natural for feelings, but Kant is right in seeing controlled expression or silence as quite natural for thoughts.

Darwin emphasized the mutual advantage there is in the mutual awareness we have of each other's changing emotions, through their natural expression. We need to keep up to date with what our neighbors feel and intend, to adapt our activities to theirs, both to take advantage of their good will and to protect ourselves against any ill will. Do we not need for the same reasons to keep up to date with what they are thinking and what they take to be the case? Often we can infer that from communicated emotion, but much that they currently think and believe will not inform any currently expressed emotion. However, if we share the same environment and have the same sense organs, we can usually assume that our fellows' belief states will largely duplicate our own, so we will not need any "readout" of their belief states in the way we do need a readout on their individual emotion and intention states. We can often fairly safely assume that most knowledge is common knowledge. (It is significant that we have no parallel concept of "common emotion," nor of "common intention.") So we can often assume that our fellows believe what we believe—their opportunities for special knowledge will not be so frequent. But occasionally we will want to find out what they have done in our absence or have found out that we could not find out, and so truth telling will then be welcome. For there will be no other way that we can tell what our fellows know or believe except by their telling us and our accepting what they tell us. The twin virtues of veracity and due credulity are the virtues needed when it matters to our fellows what we personally know or believe on a given question and where our fellows have some sort of need and right to find that out. These virtues, I want to suggest, are highly "artificial," in Hume's sense. They presuppose agreement on what rights we have to a kind of knowledge that is not automatic, to mutual knowledge of one another's cognitive states. The honesty of virtuous truth telling, and with it due trust in what others say, is at least as convention-dependent as the honesty of respect for others' property, along with proper trust in others' honesty. Honest speech is a special case of respect for rights—namely respect for another person's right to occasional access to one's own naturally private states of mind. This is as complex a right as the right to have a debt paid. It is the right to get from another what is currently in their secure possession.

Among the circumstances of justice that Hume lists are limited generosity with scarce goods and prior experience of the benefits of conformity to agreed rules regulating the distribution of scarce goods. Hume thought that our childhood experience of family life gives us this knowledge that recognition of rights (or protorights) can improve life for all. The recognition that occurs in the family is spontaneous and needs no conventions. Are rights to know, to share knowledge, also spontaneously recognized in the natural family? Hume himself emphasized that between friends and between loving parent and trusting child there can be total openness, complete candor, when a "being like ourselves . . . communicates to us all the actions of his mind, makes us privy to his inmost sentiments and affections, and lets us see in the very instant of their production, all the emotions that are caused by any object" (1975b, 353). This is candor about sentiments, affections, and emotions, and so about such thoughts and beliefs as are implied by these. It is not candor about beliefs as such. Nor is there any implication that it is specifically verbal candor. Presumably, the acquisition of language does usually occur in such an intimate circle, so verbal candor may be included in the mutual mind sharing of intimates that Hume describes. But if what I have argued is correct, it cannot be so total. "All the emotions" one feels one may well express to an intimate, but what would it be to communicate all one's thoughts? The "actions of the mind" involved in belief, as Hume himself had analyzed them in book 1, include all its past actions as remembered and as influencing current associations. Even if one wanted to, one could not put all of that into words—one would have to be constantly condensing and expressing and updating one's intellectual autobiography. Even on a specific "limited" topic, say what one now believes about the character of a mutual acquaintance, one's beliefs outrun one's ability to confide them. Time constraints alone ensure that. One *cannot* make others privy to all one has learned and all that feeds into one's belief on any one topic. The only way others would be privy to that is by sharing one's life path, along with one's interests, and so by having had the same experience. So candor about belief is always limited. It is not so much that we *dare* not, as Kant suggested, as that we *cannot* tell the whole truth about our thoughts and beliefs even on any one topic. We can try to give truthful answers to specific questions when cross examined. We can relax watchful internal censorship when talking to friends, but even then we cannot "let it all hang out"; there just is far too much of it. If I accept the offer of "a penny for your thoughts," I still must select which ones to give you and may deceive myself as much as you as to which were in the foreground of my attention. If I try to deceive others about my current feelings, I may or may not be caught out. If I deceive myself about my current feelings, others will soon put me straight—they may well recognize my irritation for what it is more readily than I do. But if I deceive myself about the focus of my mental attention, it will not be easy for others to correct me. For others have no access to my current thoughts except what I choose to give them, and if I am deceived, then even when I speak frankly, I may speak falsely. The truth about one's beliefs is not so accessible to oneself or to others as one's current feelings. (Even if they are to some extent artificial, cultivated by cultural pressure, they may still be truly felt on a given occasion.)

So what is it that we expect of the person with the virtue of veracity? How is the virtue of truth telling possible? Our best way to understand it, I suggest, is as a form of the artificial virtue of being true to an understanding, often to one's word. Just as one has to *give* one's word, to renounce a natural liberty to adapt one's intentions to changing desires or circumstances, in order to be in a position to be true or false to one's word, so there must be a certain understood renunciation of one's normal liberty to use speech for any of its normal purposes, including harmless or strategic deceit and concealment, for veracity or the lack of it to be a possibility. When we are under oath or oath equivalent, the truth is expected of us. It takes a certain solemnity of occasion for anything to count as a lie. If you ask me "How are you?" and I reply "Fine thanks, and you?" although in fact I take myself to be far from fine, I have not lied. Even a white lie requires a more seriously fact-finding context than that. To respond to the casual greeting "How are you?" with a detailed accurate account of one's troubles is not to be veracious but to tell what one might call "black truths," unwanted, inappropriate revelations. It is to fail to have proper reticence. Whereas Kant sees reticence as primarily a self-protective necessity, a protection against public shame and mockery, on the Humean alternative I am suggesting, it should rather be seen as a form of consideration for others, a protection of them from undue embarrassment, boredom, or occasion for pity. Truth, let alone "the whole truth," is something we very rarely want told to us. We prefer to see it or ignore it for ourselves, to select for ourselves which truths to attend to. Children have a quite natural and proper resistance to the sort of schooling that consists in being sat down and *told* things purveyed as truths. Teachers in that sort of school system are professional truth tellers, but that does not make veracity their professional virtue. For veracity is knowing *when* one is bound to speak one's mind and then speaking it as best one can. Even then, fallible judgment will be involved, snap decisions concerning how most helpfully to speak it, what sentences to produce.

As it takes special circumstances for promise breaking to be a theoretical option for us, so it takes special circumstances for us to have an occasion when a lie is possible. One such circumstance is when we are "put on the mat," or in the witness box, under oath. Lying is then always tantamount to a form of perjury. Other circumstances of veracity are the cases where there is a clear but informal mutual understanding that truth is expected. Unless we understand what it is to have such an understanding or to have made a solemn undertaking, then whatever counter-to-fact things we say will count merely as polite conversation, "just kidding," fictional narrative, reconstruction of the past, or imaginative play. Children with vivid imaginations often have difficulty recognizing when play ends and "real life" begins. They learn the truth-telling game usually through being accused of lying. The solemn or angry faces of their accusers teach them the limits of the freedom to protect and to pretend, limits that they need not have realized from any exemplary behavior on the part of the adults who now accuse them. (Children are not expected to call adults liars, even when they come to disbelieve the stories those adults tell them about Santa Claus, storks, heavenly homes where grandparents have gone to, and so on.) Learning what counts as a lie is like learning what counts as a debt or a broken promise. Complex rules are involved, and fairly subtle contextual clues have to be picked up. It is not just a matter of telling a serious or solemn face from a merry one, for serious and solemn faces are often assumed in games. It is a matter of telling real solemnity from pretend solemnity, the rules of real life from the rules of the games that partially fill it. This is a matter of coming to recognize what authority can overrule other more limited authorities, what concerns can preempt other concerns. It is not that real life in adult society is structured by an overarching will to have only the truth spoken; it is rather that for our multiple uses of speech to go well, we need to be fairly confident of at least some of one another's intentions, and this may lead to an occasional check on beliefs, and so to inquisitions, cross-examinations aimed at verbal revelation of states of mind. We assume that if any statement of intent can be relied on, that made in a vow can, in part because it incorporates acceptance of a conditional threat. So we take it that if a person has vowed to tell the truth, she is more likely to do so than if she had not so vowed. Of course, if the vow is made without any conviction, as with "so help me God" spoken by the atheist, then it will be ineffective—a lying promise not to lie will scarcely ward off lies. But we do the best we can and use what verbal and other magic we hope works best.

If it is harder to deceive about intentions and feelings than about beliefs, because the former are expressed in nonlinguistic as well as linguistic ways, then it is understandable that we bootstrap our way to reliable communication to belief via the more reliable communication of feeling and intent. We bully others into swearing to tell the truth, trusting their solemn oath in part because they trust our threat to punish oath breakers. They must tell the truth to carry out their expressed agreement and must keep their agreement if they are to avoid the threats we convincingly make. Or we lure others into truthful confidences with expressions of assurance of love and reciprocal candor. We use the more secure reliability of expressed feelings and immediate intentions to secure the reliability of expressions of belief when it matters enough to us that they not be false. The truth of what we say and tell piggybacks on the truth of what we show in other ways.

The obligation not to lie, as I have construed it, is conditional on a clear understanding that the truth is then to be spoken. A lie is false pretences, an untruth where truth was offered, perhaps even promised. But we are under no permanent duty to deliver the truth about our states of mind to others, and it would be an intolerably inquisition-prone society that would force us to take on such a duty, say by a promise. It would bring the artifice of promise into disrepute for it to be so employed, and truth telling would share in the degradation. If revelation of our states of mind on request were a duty, voluntarily offering them to selected intimates would lose value—we would come to offer our best deceits, rather than our "confidences," as free gifts for our friends. We would then perhaps dare to conceal our states of mind from them in ways too risky with others, engage in a sort of intimate mental game of hide and seek. In our actual society, which does tend to find implicit vows all over the place and to deceive itself about its will to truthful disclosure, our special relations with our intimates are probably a mix of these two extremes—some candid confidences are reserved just for them, and some special cover-ups are also kept for them alone, covers that are not expected really to conceal but rather to drape agreeably or to tantalize a little, to create some pretend mystery. It is not, after all, just anyone that we would bother deceiving or bother going through the motions of deceiving.

Information about some of others' states of mind is something we get used to having, because when those states are emotional states, they are spontaneously expressed to us. It is understandable that we want more than we easily get—we sometimes want to know our fellows' cognitive states as well as their emotional and conative states. So we sometimes try to get that information, by quizzing and cross-examining them. We meet with proper resistance, and language, the medium of the asking and the answering, is a wonderful screen and camouflage. It enables us to mislead nosey people, to mislead them about our cognitive states and sometimes about some of our emotional states too. Outwitting becomes the name of the game, but success in it is hard to recognize, especially if we take ourselves in. "Lively natures lie only for a moment: immediately afterwards they lie to themselves and are convinced and honest" (Nietzsche 1982, sec. 391). Is this success or failure at the outwitting game?

Kant in his ethics links the wrong of lying very closely with that of promise breaking. To lie is to break an implicit agreement to speak only the truth, an agreement that he takes to be made in the very act of speaking at all. To make an explicit promise, then, will be to make a lying promise if the will to keep it is not firm. On this theory, we make ourselves retrospectively into liars whenever we break a promise, and we make ourselves into promise breakers whenever we lie. I have accepted the close Kantian link between speaking the truth and being true to a mutual understanding, perhaps to one's word, but have resisted the suggestion that this understanding is in permanent effect, that the *telos* of speech is disclosure. On the contrary, its special contributions are to make story telling possible and to give us the means of superior camouflage of what *is* naturally disclosed, namely our current emotions. Still, there are occasions when that special speech artifact, the oath, is used to commit a speaker to truth telling. On those solemn occasions the point of speech becomes disclosure, and truth telling becomes a solemn duty. But these occasions are rare, and rightly kept rare. At the other extreme from the cases where lying amounts to perjury are the cases where it amounts to treachery, where what one's false words make one false to is not some formal or quasi-formal vow to tell the truth but rather to a personal loyalty, an understanding with friends or comrades. In such close associations there is an expectation not just of truthful responses in serious talk but also of some freely offered disclosure of known facts and of thoughts. We expect more candor of our friends than of strangers, not just in the form of less inhibited expression of feeling but also in the form of shared thoughts, shared knowledge, shared opinions. If in the guise of offering voluntary disclosure, making the gift of greater candor, one in fact offers deceitful words, then one is not merely a liar but a false friend. One's false words in this context make one false not so much to one's word (unless one has taken a vow of friendship) as to something more fundamental than one's word—to one's trusted gestures of friendship. It is one's open arms and open face, the show of friendship, that is false. False confidences are like gifts of poisoned chocolates— the lie, that which harms or violates the other's right, is masked as a special treat to a special person, and one that is trustingly accepted only because of the special relationship. Between these two extremes of answering under oath and free offerings to friends lie all the cases where misinforming is disappointing a reasonable expectation and so, unless one has a good excuse, malicious and wrong. It may be a breach of a special professional responsibility voluntarily entered into. Scientists publishing faked data, reporters making up the news, bureaucrats falsifying official records, all clearly fail to deliver the goods it is their job to deliver—the facts as they know them. But it is a bit harder to say what we demand in the way of truth in medical care of the dying, in advertising, in sermons, in editorials, in politicians' speeches, in bargaining, in high school (or for that matter, in college) teaching, or in philosophy essays. (Could I be lying in this essay?) Saying what one does not oneself believe is sometimes a breach of one's professional responsibilities, but it can also become a professional responsibility (in a defense lawyer, in an official spokesperson, maybe in a national leader in times of national danger—"We shall never surrender").

Knowingly false or misleading statements made in contexts where those statements are tantamount to neither perjury, treachery, malice, nor breach of professional responsibility are not lies but normal purposeful talk, verbal ploys made to others who understand the games we speakers play and realize that inquisition, informing, reportage, mutual revelation are only a few of our many forms of talk, all structured by rough mutual understandings and mutual acceptance of multiple purposes of talk. It takes rather special contexts for veracity to be a possibility, more special ones for it to be obligatory, and even more special contexts for verbal *candor* to be welcome. The O.E.D. tells us that candor in its oldest sense is "dazzling whiteness," and we tend to shield ourselves from what dazzles. To have candor is for one's mind to show itself with a pure white light, to kindle or candle in others an awareness of one's own total mental state. As Kant recognized, it is less discriminating than veracity. It is more than sincerity, since sincerity can coexist with reticence. The O.E.D. cites Johnson's 1751 use: "He was sincere, but without candour." Johnson, in his dictionary, notes the Latin etymology (which links candor with candy) then gives this entry: "sweetness of temper, purity of mind, openness, ingenuity, kindliness." The sweetness seems an accidental addition to the whiteness. It may, however, take a certain sweetness, trust, and innocence of temper to be willing to open one's mind freely to others, so that the person with aggressive intentions will sensibly avoid candor. In principle, but rarely in practice, could we be as candid about schemes to harm others as about our good intentions. The Darwinian story, which makes nonverbal candor come naturally to us, makes the evolutionary point of natural expression lie as much in "fair warning" of evil intentions as in reassurance of sweetness and light. Were candor a virtue, its circumstances would be a need to adapt to others' intentions, along with the unlikelihood of successful deceit. Once we have language, we are not in these circumstances. Our deceiving tongues combine with our grabbing hands to create the circumstances of the virtue we *do* recognize, namely honesty, a willingness to let others have some of what we might have seized from them and some knowledge of what we might have concealed from them. In both cases complex conventions tell us exactly what others have a right to in what specific conditions. Honesty in both its main forms is an artificial virtue. As a virtue of speakers, it is indeed an artificial virtue needed to regulate the workings of what is itself an artifice, natural language. Honesty regulates the mutual deceit that language makes possible by allowing language occasionally to work with, not against, natural expression, to reveal rather than conceal states of mind.

The honesty of veracity is more like the second artificial virtue that Hume discusses in the *Treatise* than it is like the first. The first was willingness to accept and respect rules fixing individual possession, to put a stop to the insecurity and instability of possession of scarce goods. Hume construes this agreement as one that created property rights that were not yet rights to voluntary transfer but rights only to entailed property, as it were. Each gets something and can keep it to himself, but as what each gets depends very much on chance, "persons and possessions must often be very ill-adjusted. . . . The rules of justice seek some medium between a rigid stability and this changeable and uncertain adjustment" (Hume 1975b, 514). In the state of nature there was uncertain adjustment when each simply tried to grab what he thought he needed. Transfer by consent is the medium that restores to possessions some of their previous mobility, but without the violence and insecurity that property rights were invented to cure. Orderly voluntary exchange of property is the civilized replacement of the state of nature, a state where everyone tried "to seize by violence what he judges fit for him." The second artifice restores the human condition to something closer to the state of nature than the hypothetical condition of "rigid stability" existing after the first artifice. If we adapt this highly artificial story of a sequence of agreed artifices, the later correcting the excesses of the earlier, from property rules to language rules (encouraged by Hume's own analogy at 1975b, p. 490, between conventions "fixing" private possession and conventions "fixing" word meanings), then we can see the acquisition of language as bringing as great a change to human life as the acquisition of the first property rights and as bringing as dubious an advantage, the advantage of denying others access to what earlier they might have had access to. Now each can fence off and enclose something as all her own, her own property, her own thoughts, posting No Admittance signs and setting traps for would-be trespassers. There will still be some unenclosed "commons"—we may still be free to grab what fresh air we can, what rain water we can. Similarly, we may still have some access to the states of mind of others. The arts of language, while giving us thoughts we can keep to ourselves, may not give us the ability fully to camouflage the natural expression of our emotions, so we will not be able to stop sometimes giving ourselves away. Just as unprevented transfers of air and water from one owner's place to another will still occur, which reminds the right holders of the old natural instability, so unprevented expression will still occur, which reminds the wily speakers of the lost candor of prespeech communication. And as the disadvantages of the new ways become evident to all, some medium will be sought between old and new ways, some reform that will enable us to keep what was advantageous in the old ways without losing the powers that the new ways have given us. Hume presents "transfer by consent" as such an additional artifice, one enabling property owners to make gifts and exchanges, to transfer and trade their rights. We have no special word for the honesty that shows itself in completing agreed transfers, as distinct from refraining from trying to transfer what there has been no agreement to transfer, and Hume simply uses "justice" to cover both. He has a special word, "fidelity," for completing those agreements to transfer that take the special form of promises or contracts, and we might extend this to cover respect for any agreement, whether or not secured and solemnized in the way promises are. If we did this, then we could say that veracity is parallel to fidelity in that each consists in conformity to an artifice that counteracts the effects of a previous artifice and does this by a social agreement giving force to individual agreements, to acts of consent and of vow, enabling them to create new obligations and new rights. Whereas the effect of the new virtue of fidelity is to restore some beneficial *instability* to private possession of "external" goods, the effect of the invention of the virtue of veracity will be to restore not so much mobility as some publicity to what language had enabled us to make into private possessions, namely our states of mind.

At the start of his account of the artificial virtues, when Hume describes the circumstances that give their invention some point, he

lists "three species of goods we are possess'd of; the internal satisfactions of our mind, the external advantages of our body, and the
enjoyment of such possessions as we have acquired by our industry
and good fortune. We are perfectly secure of the first. The second
may be ravish'd from us, but can be of no advantage to him who
deprives us of them. The last only are both expos'd to the violence
of others, and may be transferr'd without suffering any loss or alteration; while at the same time there is not a sufficient supply of them
to supply everyone's desires and necessities" (1975b, 487–488). Are
our states of mind goods (or ills) of the first sort, perfectly secure?
Some of them, our cognitive states, may be possessions like the third
sort, "acquired by our industry and good fortune," and they can in
a sense be transferred to others without alteration and be of advantage to them. The alteration they will undergo if "transferred" will
be from private to public, from secret to shared knowledge, and that
may be an alteration significant to their value to the original possessor. That is why it may take a "ravishing" to get that knowledge. But
once the knowledge is "transferred," it is not *lost*, even if it is deval-
ued, to the one from whom it was taken. In Ben Zipursky's term
(1987), it is "replicated" and strictly not transferred at all. It comes
to be in a "place" it was not before, but not by leaving the place it
was in. It becomes less scarce by becoming fertile. Knowledge can
be and come to be in many places at once and does not always have
to be exclusively possessed to be valuable. Hume's division of goods
ignores those privately possessed goods that can replicate without
thereby devaluing themselves, and it altogether ignores public goods,
ones available as easily to many as to one. We can either regard
knowledge of an individual's state of mind as a fertile private good,
one that can be "spread" to others without being lost to its original
possessor, or as a possible public good. Naturally expressed emotions
provide public and common knowledge, and awareness of this sort
of state of mind is best treated as a (perhaps impure) public good.
An individual's conscious knowledge is a replicable private good. It
is fairly "secure" in any possessor of it in that it would take memory-
destroying interference to take it from a knower, but it is not perfectly
securely kept from others. Hume divides the private goods he considers by cross-cutting criteria: degree of security from loss by sei-
zure, degree of "externality" from the possessor, degree of scarcity
(demand in excess of supply). He assumes that mental states are all
internal and that only the most external of goods can be transferred
"without suffering loss or alteration." Both assumptions are false.
Emotional states are as external as they are internal, as much a matter
of the eyes as of the brain. Awareness of them is internal, but both

it and awareness of an individual's cognitive states can be transferred (in the weak sense that does not imply their ceasing to be where they were) without suffering any loss or alteration except loss of secrecy, an alteration from being private to becoming more public. Whether that alteration is of consequence will depend upon other factors.

In conditions where the dominant game is mutual deceit and outwitting, secrecy and nonreplication of many cognitive states will be valued. We will *want* others to share with us at least knowledge of the language we speak, since we can outwit them better with a common language than we could without one, but much other information that we have we will prefer to keep to ourselves, since keeping it from others may give us competitive advantage. Veracity as an artificial virtue requires us sometimes to replicate what we might have kept infertile, to make public what could have been private and exclusive. It creates a duty to increase supply, to tackle scarcity not just by a distributive scheme but by a distribution of duties to allow the scarce goods to replicate themselves.

Hume's initial account of the advantage of social cooperation in adoption of agreed rights and duties was that thereby three "inconveniences" of the hypothetical state of nature would be remedied: insufficiency of power, insufficiency of ability, and lack of security against "fortune and accident." "By the conjunction of forces our power is augmented: By the partition of employments, our ability encreases: And by mutual succour we are less exposed to fortune and accidents" (Hume 1975b, 481). The odd thing about the first artifice he describes, recognition of individual rights to fixed possession, is that the only "conjunction" of forces it involves is the conjunction of all right holders in recognition of the distribution of property rights, the only "partition of employments" whatever might accidentally follow from the fact that different employments might be needed to make the best of different initial lots. Until there is the right to exchange, there will be no impetus to the partition of employments. Clearly Hume does think that when rights to trade and to have contracts kept are added to property rights, increase of goods will in fact occur. The need for the artifice of government is said to arise "long after the first generation" of property owners and only when the first three artifices (property, transfer by consent, promise) had led to "an encrease of riches and possessions" (Hume 1975b, 541). No particular artifice is directed at facilitating this increase—the artifices Hume describes are all concerned with allocation of what is already somehow there. However, point of social coordination is not just security of possession but decrease of scarcity through conjunction of forces and partition of employment. If we are to adapt Hume's account to cover the immaterial goods of information and intelligence, it seems pretty clear that the role of "conjunction of forces" will not be restricted to conjoining to protect rights to private exclusive possession or to transfer by consent (let increase take care of itself) but will include conjoining forces and perhaps partitioning employment to *increase* available information, to pool and replicate individual knowledge states. (Hume's later interests in the cultural impact of the printing press and in freedom of the press of course acknowledge this.) Although it takes no cultural contrivance for there to be some sharing and replication of awareness of emotional and intention states, knowledge and belief states are directly replicable only through the cultural contrivance of language, which is as good at preventing as at faciltating replication. It will take normative rules to introduce a sharing of knowledge states, to allow them to replicate. Veracity is respect for those rules, giving others a right of access to what we are in a position to block access to. As rules of property regulate without completely immobilizing our grabbing hands, so rules of truthfulness regulate our wily, secretive, deceitful tongues without outlawing all deceit. Veracity is the just or adjusted medium between the natural candor and easy access of prespeech states of mind and the natural secrecy and deceit of human speakers.

Kant is by no means the only philosopher who takes there to be the opposite presumption, the presumption that if we speak at all, we naturally speak the truth. Those who link thought itself very closely to language as its vehicle take the first thinking to be thinking aloud and "candid avowal" of thoughts to be an ever present possibility, a simple lifting of the acquired inhibition of the vocal chords. On such a view, the only artifice that truth telling requires will be that of language itself. Speaking deceitfully will be "unnatural" in a way that speaking truthfully is not. David Gauthier postulates, in those who are to bargain their way into a morality, a natural "translucency" to one another, an incapacity for sustained deceit (1986, 173–178, 266). If what I have said in this essay has any truth in it, then all these philosophers are deceiving themselves about our capacity for deceit. "Translucency," for those who have acquired language, takes some social and moral contrivance and will be only intermittent. Only if we can *already* keep agreements are we likely to speak the truth (as we see it) about what we know. Veracity cannot be supposed to be already in place before we can expect to have fidelity to mutual understandings. Veracity is part of the artificial virtue of honesty, not part of its "natural" foundation. The foundation, I have suggested, is an inevitable degree of nonverbal candor about current emotion and immediate intention states, combined with a natural reticence about belief states and a tempting verbal capacity for both benign and less benign deceit. The circumstances of veracity include the ability and the temptation to deceive along with prior experience of the advantages to be gained from some reliable mutual expression (of immediate intentions and emotions) and of our proven capacity for some mutual trust and mutual coordination.

Veracity is a form of the aritificial virtue of honesty, a virtue consisting in conformity to conventions allocating rights, in this case rights to get straight answers to questions one has a right in certain circumstances to pose. Hume lists truth as a virtue, as well as veracity, and seems to mean it to include a *natural* virtue shown by friends and lovers who are true to one another in more than verbal or verbally mediated ways. "Truth: see also troth," says the *Oxford English Dictionary*. There is even an obsolete verb "to truth," which was to trust. The first senses of "truth" and "true" that the *O.E.D.* gives are "truth" and "true" as applied to persons, "truth" as faithfulness, fidelity. Clearly, we do not need troths and truth for candor, except where spontaneous candor has already been interferred with by the new means of deceit that language brings. But veracity may indeed involve reliance on the natural virtue of *truth to* fellow cooperators, a virtue of which both it and fidelity to promises are artificial extensions. Truth telling or veracity is fidelity to an intermittently operative linguistic troth, consent to share on some occasions what we might have tried to keep secret. It is a social linguistic remedy for a linguistic condition, an excess of mental camouflage, of bluff or double bluff. The hard thing is to recognize which times are the times to which this consent applies. That makes honesty as veracity a hard virtue.

There is one last question that needs to be addressed to complete my Humean account of veracity as an artificial virtue. That is the question of what passion it is, if indeed it is only *one* passion, that is in the long run better satisfied by the discipline or regulation that veracity imposes than it would have been if left unregulated. Hume cites avidity, the desire to accumulate material goods, as the desire that the kind of honesty that he analyzes satisfies in a superior, nonviolent, and civilized way. Is it avidity that both tempts us to deceive and also motivates us to accept restraints on our proclivities to deceive? Avidity for what? The power to protect ourselves from others who pose a danger can be what motivates deceit as well as the reticence that Kant sees it to motivate. This can be danger to the relatively powerless from those who would dominate and control them or danger to the dominators from those who would be less docile if not systematically deceived. So there can indeed be an interested passion that motivates deceit, the passion for defensive and aggressive power. It might in some conditions control itself the better to further its ends. Could honesty in speech serve our self-protective and self-assertive ends better than lying and deceit? In what conditions? Those are hard questions to answer. Nietzsche wrote, "The demand for truthfulness presupposes the knowability and stability of the person. In fact it is the object of education to create in the herd member a definite faith concerning human nature. It first invents the faith and then it demands truthfulness (1967, 227). Must we make ourselves into herd members to get any general benefits from truthfulness? It may be as hard to invent the "right" detailed version of veracity as it is to invent the "right" property rules.

Deceit is sometimes motivated by a less interested passion, namely the wish not to hurt those we love. Some white lies are loving and tender lies, not bullied or bullying lies, and so some self-regulation of the impulse to deceive could be motivated by the hope of avoiding inflicting the worst hurt, the realization that our loved ones have not trusted us to be able to share hard truths with them. Love and friendship themselves can be the values invoked both to excuse deceit and to justify the self-regulation of the impetus to resort to it. But again, it will be only in some conditions that we really hurt our loved ones less by frankness than by judicious deceit, by a few secrets and silences. In what conditions? The hard questions remain. Honesty in friendship, as much as honesty in politics and in public life, remains a hard virtue and a matter of fallible judgment.

Hume assumed much too blithely that *any* version of private-property rights was better than none, that honesty is always worth its social and individual costs. Honesty, in both its main manifestations, is not just a hard virtue to exhibit but also a hard one to design. Because of its fluid and changing design in our culture, every display of honesty will also be an exercise of good (but contestable) judgment, perhaps of creative redesign. It will not be easy to recognize honesty when we encounter it, to distinguish it from false or brutal frankness. Even with Diogenes' lamp to help our search, we may well not agree in selection of any exemplar of this hard virtue.[1]

Note

1. I am very much indebted to Rob Shaver and to Ben Zipursky for ideas explored in this paper—so indebted that I have lost track of exactly which ideas these are. Claudia Card made very helpful comments on the first version, comments that led

me to modify many of my original claims and to realize that the concept of one's "true" feelings is much more difficult than I had blithely assumed. I have not fully faced up to these complications even in this revised version. Its baroque complexities, as much as its over simplifications and repetitions, may be a defense against rethinking that central point. (Am I not truthful enough with myself in this essay?)

Part IV
Rationality, Responsibility, and Morality

Chapter 13
Higher-Order Discrimination
Adrian M. S. Piper

This discussion treats a set of familiar social derelictions as consequences of the perversion of a universalistic moral theory in the
service of an ill-considered or insufficiently examined personal
agenda.[1] The set includes racism, sexism, anti-Semitism, homophobia, and class elitism, among other similar pathologies, under the
general heading of *discrimination*. The perversion of moral theory
from which these derelictions arise, I argue, involves restricting its
scope of application to some preferred subgroup of the moral community of human beings. Those who try to justify rejection of the
stringent requirements of universalistic moral theory on the grounds
that it is too demanding, distant, or alienating properly to govern
our behavior often mean to restrict its scope of application to one's
friends, family, colleagues, and loved ones without regard to whom,
in particular, such a subgroup includes. The following analysis of
higher-order discrimination suggests that we often select the individuals who constitute such subgroups for reasons that we ourselves
would reject on moral grounds were we to examine them carefully,
but that we choose instead to put our rational resources in the service
of avoiding any such examination at all costs. The implication is that
arguments that truncate the scope of moral theory in fact justify
bestowing the gift of moral treatment on a select few who deserve it
no more than the many from whom we withhold it. Therefore, it
would be precipitous to conclude that universalistic moral theory can
be legitimately restricted in its practical scope of application in any
way at all.

1 Reciprocal First-Order Discrimination

By *first-order discrimination* I mean what we ordinarily understand by
the term "discrimination" in political contexts: a manifest attitude in
which a particular attribute of a person that is irrelevant to judgments
of that person's noninstrumental value or competence, e.g., her race,

gender, sexual orientation, class background, or religious or ethnic affiliation, is seen as a source of disvalue or incompetence, in general, as a source of inferiority.[2] I shall call an attribute so perceived a *primary disvalued attribute*, and a person perceived as bearing such an attribute the *disvaluee*. Conversely, I shall call any such arbitrary attribute seen as a source of value or superiority a *primary valued attribute*, and a person perceived as bearing such an attribute the *valuee*.

Instances of first-order discrimination are familiar targets of moral condemnation because they disvalue individuals for having attributes perceived as primary disvalued attributes that are not in actuality sources of disvalue. But how should we evaluate what I will call *reciprocal first-order discrimination*, in which the attribute is perceived as a primary *valued* attribute and its bearers elevated accordingly? Are such attributes ever relevant to judgments of a person's noninstrumental value or competence? Take the case in which we are particularly drawn to befriend a valuee with whom we share a similar ethnic background because we expect to have more in common (lifestyle, tastes, sense of humor), share similar values, or see the world from a similar perspective. In this kind of case the primary valued attribute is not, say, being Jewish but rather having the *same* ethnic background, whatever that may be. Is similarity of ethnic background an attribute that is relevant to our judgments of how valuable the valuee is as a friend? No, for it does not form any part of the basis for such a judgment. That a friendship is better, richer, or more valuable in proportion to the degree of similarity of the friends' ethnic backgrounds is a judgment few would be tempted to make.

In these cases it is not the valuee's similar ethnicity itself that is the source of value but rather the genuinely valuable attributes—for example, similarity of values or worldview—with which we expect similar ethnicity to be conjoined. Rather than making a *normative* judgment about his value or competence as a friend in this case, we in fact make an *epistemic* judgment about the probability that because of the valuee's ethnic identity, he will bear attributes susceptible of such normative judgments. These epistemic rules of thumb are defeasible and may have disappointing consequences for personal relationships. For they ascribe primary value to a kind of attribute at the expense of others that are in fact more important for friendship— like sensitivity, similarity of tastes or experiences, and mutual respect—with which that kind of attribute is only contingently, if ever, conjoined. (Presumably something like this may explain the malaise of someone who has chosen all the "right" friends, married the "right" spouse, and landed the "best" job yet feels persistently un-happy, disconnected, and dissatisfied in his social relationships.)

If similarity of race, gender, sexual orientation, class background, or religious or ethnic affiliation are in themselves irrelevant to judg-ments of a person's noninstrumental value or competence, primary valued attributes such as being of a *particular* race, gender, etc., are even more obviously so. At least it has yet to be demonstrated that any particular racial, ethnic, gender, class or religious group pos-sesses the attributes necessary for, e.g., friendship to an outstanding degree.[3] Epistemic probability judgments about the concatenation of any such primary valued attributes with genuinely valuable traits, such as sensitivity or similarity of interests, may also bias our ability to perceive clearly the attributes a particular individual actually has, as when a wife minimizes the reality and seriousness of her hus-band's physical abuse of her because of the weight she accords to his class background. This would be a case of reciprocal first-order discrimination, according to the above definition, because she sees as a (compensating) source of superiority a primary valued attribute, class background, that is irrelevant to judgments of the valuee's noninstrumental value or competence as a spouse.

It might be objected that we need such epistemic rules of thumb, however irrational or poorly grounded, in order to survive in a world of morally opaque others. How *ought* we behave, for example, alone in a subway car with four black male teenagers carrying ghetto blast-ers and wearing running shoes? However, while we may need rules of thumb to get along in the world, it is fairly obvious that we are not getting along all that well in the world with the rules of thumb we have. Even if it were true that most muggers were black male teenagers in running shoes, it still would not follow that most black male teenagers in running shoes were muggers. It might be a mistake on quite a large scale (as self-fulfilling prophesies often are) to react to every such person we encounter as though he were. The conse-quences of acting on the rules of thumb on which we now tend to rely do not inspire sufficient confidence to warrant our continued unquestioning allegiance to them.

Alternately, one may make a judgment of value about some such attribute abstractly and independently considered. One may value being black, or of working class origins, for its own sake. Or one may choose a partner from the same religion because one views that religion and its traditions themselves as intrinsically valuable, inde-pendently of one's partner's compatibility with respect to lifestyle, values, or worldview. Here the judgment of value is directed not at the valuee's value or competence but rather at the attribute he bears, to the preservation of which one's choice of him is instrumental. Nothing in the following discussion addresses or precludes such judgments, although there is much to say about them. My target is judgments of noninstrumental value about individuals, not about attributes of individuals abstractly and independently considered.

Is it humanly possible to value a person just because she bears some such primary valued attribute—not because of the further attributes with which we expect that one to be conjoined but just for the sake of that attribute in itself? It is difficult to make sense of this. Suppose that I value Germanness because the Germans I have known tend to have deep passions and an amusingly fatalistic sense of humor and that I then meet a shallow and phlegmatic German with no sense of humor at all. In the absence of other, unexpectedly attractive personality characteristics I may appreciate, just what is it about being German *in itself* that is supposed to confer worth on this particular individual? Either we must be able to spell out an answer to this question in terms of other attributes that are only contingently connected, if at all, to this one—e.g., having been socialized within a certain culture "from the inside," being part of a certain historical tradition, etc.—or else we are appealing to a mysterious and ineffable, nonnatural quality of Germanness.[4] Then suppose that there are such qualities and that we may arguably appeal to them. To what degree might Germanness outweigh the person's other attributes that, by hypothesis, I deplore? Surely, the mere fact of Germanness can provide no consolation at all, in practice, for other attributes of the person that offend me. It will not compensate, for example, for a failure to laugh at my jokes or a tendency to discuss the weather at excessive length or to fall asleep at the opera. And then it is hard to see in what its purported value consists.

Independently of the other, genuinely valuable attributes with which they are only contingently, if at all, conjoined, attributes such as race, gender, sexual orientation, class background, and religious or ethnic affiliation are in themselves always irrelevant to judgments of a person's noninstrumental value or competence. This holds whether they are considered as primary disvalued *or* valued attributes and even where they are used as epistemic rules of thumb for detecting such attributes. We may, in fact, feel compelled to make such judgments, in the service of expediency or what we imagine to be our self-interest, and screen our circle of associates accordingly. But it is nothing to be proud of. In what follows, I will focus primarily on some consequences of cases in which these and other, similar attributes are seen as sources of disvalue, i.e., on first-order discrimination rather than reciprocal first-order discrimination. My thesis will be that we have reason to scrutinize our social behavior even in situations in which we sincerely believe ourselves to be above both types of discrimination.

2 Higher-Order Political Discrimination

By *second-order discrimination* I will understand the attitude within which a primary disvalued attribute in turn confers disvalue respectively on further attributes of the disvaluee. I shall refer to these latter as *secondary disvalued attributes.*

Second-order discrimination works in the following way. A disvaluee's primary disvalued attribute, say, being a male homosexual, causes the second-order discriminator to view some further attribute of the disvaluee, say, being an eloquent speaker, in a negative light. The *respect in which* this further attribute is seen as negative depends on the range of possible descriptions it might satisfy, as well as the context in which it appears. Thus, for example, the second-order discriminator might view the disvaluee's eloquence as purple prose, as empty rhetoric, or as precious, flowery, or mannered. These predicates are not interchangeable for the second-order discriminator. Nor are they taken to be arbitrarily applied. The second-order discriminator will choose from among them to express his disvaluation in response to contingencies of the situation and individuals involved. The second-order discriminator may, in all sincerity, explain his disvaluation with reference to impartially applied aesthetic standards or to his ingrown, native suspicion of big words. But the crucial feature of second-order discrimination is that the actual explanation for his disvaluing the person's eloquence, *in whatever respect he disvalues it,* is the person's primary disvalued attribute of being a male homosexual.

Does second-order discrimination as thus defined ever actually occur? Some familiar examples of it include attaching disvalue to a person's having rhythm by reason of its putative connection with her being black, or attaching disvalue to a person's being very smart by reason of its putative connection with his being Jewish. Both of these cases are examples of discriminatory stereotyping in which some arbitrary attribute is falsely taken to be characteristic of persons of a particular race or ethnic or religious affiliation. But I mean to call attention to a slightly different feature of these examples. Someone who practices second-order discrimination regards a black person who has rhythm as vulgar, salacious, offensive, or at the very least, undignified. Similarly, such a person regards a Jewish person who is very smart as sophistical, glib, crafty, subversive, ungentlemanly, or at the very least, untrustworthy. In both cases, attributes that are in themselves salutary, or at least neutral, are castigated by the second-order discriminator by reason of the disvalue conferred on them by the primary disvalued attribute. This is what makes them examples of second-order discrimination.

These familiar, stereotypic examples of second-order discrimination do not exhaust the repertoire of higher-order discrimination for many reasons. First, orders of discrimination can, in theory, be multiplied indefinitely. So, for example, a case of *third-order discrimination* would involve what I shall call *tertiary disvalued attributes:* The primary disvalued attribute (being black, say) confers disvalue on a further, secondary disvalued attribute (having rhythm), which in turn confers disvalue on yet a further attribute of the person (being a good dancer, say). Having rhythm is seen as vulgar by reason of its association with being black, and being a good dancer is then seen as exhibitionistic (say) by reason of its association with having rhythm. In any such case the primary attribute is in fact irrelevant to judgments of a person's value or competence. Hence, the value or disvalue it confers on secondary, tertiary, etc., attributes is bogus.

The *n*-order disvalue relation is *transitive* in that, for example, if being black confers disvalue on having rhythm and having rhythm confers disvalue on being a good dancer, then being black confers disvalue on being a good dancer. The *n*-order disvalue relation is also *inclusive* in that the primary disvalued attribute poisons the higher-order discriminator's evaluations of all further attributes of the disvaluee. For example, the primary disvalued attribute of being black may confer disvalue, alternatively, on a dancer's classical styling: classical styling in a black dancer may be seen as inappropriate or as an obscene parody of traditional ballet.[5] The primary disvalued attribute also confers disvalue on other, unrelated attributes of the disvaluee: her appearance, accent, mode of dress, etc.[6]

The inclusiveness of the *n*-order-disvalue relation underscores a second reason why stereotypical cases of second-order discrimination do not exhaust the repertoire of higher-order discrimination: nonstereotypical traits are also recruited to receive disvalue from primary disvalued attributes to suit particular occasions. We do not ordinarily think of classical styling in dance as an attribute about which discriminators might have any particular attitude. But this may be mistaken. Higher-order discrimination is not concerned solely with *stereotypical* secondary, tertiary, etc., disvalued attributes. It may be concerned with *any* further attributes of the person on which the primary disvalued attribute itself confers disvalue. Thus, for example, being Jewish (or black or a woman) may confer disvalue on being smart, which in turn may confer disvalue on being intellectually prolific. A person's intellectual prolificity may be seen as evidence of logorrhea, or lack of critical conscience, and may thus poison the evaluation of those intellectual products themselves. We do not ordinarily think of intellectual prolificity as an attribute about which discriminators have any particular attitude, either. But this too may be mistaken. A first test for ascertaining whether the disvalue of some attribute of a person is to be explained as a case of higher-order discrimination is to ascertain whether or not that attribute is disvalued uniformly across individuals, regardless of anything that might count as a primary disvalued attribute for a higher-order discriminator. If someone is just as contemptuous of Fred Astaire's having rhythm as they are of Michael Jackson's, or just as contemptuous of intellectual prolificity in Balzac as in Isaac Asimov, then the charge of higher-order discrimination may be defeated.[7]

A third reason why stereotypical cases of second-order discrimination do not exhaust the repertoire of higher-order discrimination is that stereotypes change in accordance with changes in the objects of discrimination as different populations seek access to the goods, services, and opportunities enjoyed by the advantaged, and primary and higher-order disvalued attributes change accordingly. For instance, the anti-Semitic response to the attempts of Jewish intellectuals to achieve full assimilation into the institutions of higher education in this country frequently found expression in the disvaluative description of assertively ambitious Jewish academics as pushy or opportunistic. Now similarly situated blacks and women frequently enjoy that title. Conversely, those with such primary disvalued attributes who attempt to substitute diplomacy for assertion are characterized by higher-order discriminators as manipulative, obsequious, or sycophantic. A second test for ascertaining whether or not the disvalue of some attribute of a person is to be explained as a case of higher-order discrimination is to ascertain whether there is any alternative attribute, conduct, or manner directed toward the same goal of gaining access to unjustly withheld social advantages that avoids or deflects the disvalue conferred by the primary disvalued attribute. If there is not—if, that is, whatever your strategy, you're damned if you do and damned if you don't—then the charge of higher-order discrimination is *prima facie* justified.

3 Nonstereotypical Higher-Order Discrimination

A fourth reason why stereotypical cases of second-order discrimination do not exhaust the repertoire of higher-order discrimination is that other arbitrary attributes, not just the familiar political ones, can function as primary disvalued attributes to a higher-order discriminator. Physical appearance, style of diction, social bearing, familial, educational, or professional pedigree, circle of associates, and manner of dress are among the more familiar, if less widely acknowledged, objects of higher-order discrimination. Some of these attributes are often assumed to go hand-in-hand with, or even to be partially definitive of, more widely recognized primary disvalued attributes. For example, higher-order discriminators may tend to assume that ethnic identity is inherently connected with a certain physical appearance (Jews have dark, curly hair and long noses), that racial identity is connected with a certain style of diction and class background (blacks speak Black English and come from the ghetto), or that gender identity is connected with a certain social bearing (women are sympathetic, passive, and emotional). This is how a stereotype is formed. But again, I mean to call attention to a slightly different point: these attributes themselves may be seen as sources of disvalue *independently* of their possible connection with such stereotypically primary disvalued attributes. Someone who has all of the valued race, ethnic, religious, class, and gender attributes but lacks the valued style of diction, mode of self-presentation, or educational or professional pedigrees may be subject to higher-order discrimination just as fully as someone who lacks all of the former attributes but has all of the latter. In both cases this means that their other attributes—their personality characteristics, interests, or achievements—will be seen as higher-order disvalued attributes by reason of their association with these equally arbitrary primary disvalued attributes.

This shows that the first-order political discrimination with which we are familiar is merely a special case of a more general psychological phenomenon that is not limited to first-order *political* discrimination at all. However, higher-order discrimination usually includes it, for it would be psychologically unusual, to say the least, to find an individual who is in general corrupt in his evaluations of a person's other attributes in the ways just described, yet impartial and scrupulous in his evaluations of blacks, Jews, women, gays, etc., and *their* attributes. Someone who is apt to dislike a person because of her hair texture or accent or family lineage or mode of dress can hardly be expected to be genuinely judicious when it comes to judging her gender, race, sexual orientation, class background, or ethnic or religious affiliation. Hence, we can expect that first-order political discrimination and higher-order discrimination in general are to be found together.

4 Reciprocal Higher-Order Discrimination

A fifth reason why familiar, stereotypic examples of second-order discrimination do not exhaust the repertoire of higher-order discrimination is that higher-order discrimination as so far described implies a companion phenomenon, which I shall call *reciprocal higher-order discrimination*. This is what occurs when attributes irrelevant to judg- ments of a person's competence or worth are seen as primary *valued* attributes, as sources of value that then confer value on the person's secondary, tertiary, etc., attributes. Any one of the primary attributes enumerated so far may have this function. For example, a person's gender may be perceived as conferring value on secondary attributes, such as his competence to hold a certain professional position. Or a person's familial lineage may be perceived as conferring value on her admissibility to an institution of higher education. Or a person's class background may be perceived as conferring value on his manner of dress. Or a person's educational pedigree may be perceived as conferring value on her political pronouncements, which in turn confer value on her personal lifestyle, and so on. Each of these examples have an arbitrary and irrational quality to them. That is because reciprocal higher-order discrimination, like higher-order discrimination itself, is an arbitrary and irrational attitude.

Higher-order discrimination and reciprocal higher-order discrimination are materially interdependent. If a person's having a particular racial identity is a source of disvalue for a higher-order discriminator, then if someone lacks that racial identity, they are not seen as tainted by that disvalue. For example, if a person's being Oriental confers disvalue on his attempts at tact, i.e., if he is therefore perceived as particularly evasive and inscrutable, then if he were white, he would not be perceived as similarly evasive and inscrutable. For if a higher-order discriminator recognized that one can be just as evasive and inscrutable without being Oriental, say if one has a hidden agenda or lacks social skills, then it would have to be recognized that those attributes, *rather* than his being Oriental, might be conferring disvalue on his attempts at tact. Conversely, if a person's having a particular racial identity is a source of value for a higher-order discriminator, then someone who lacks that racial identity is not blessed by that value. For example, if a person's being white confers value on his attempts as tact, i.e., if he is therefore viewed as sensitive and rea- sonable, then if he were Oriental, he would not be perceived as similarly sensitive and reasonable. For if a higher-order discriminator recognized that one can be just as sensitive and reasonable without being white, say if one has no personal investment in the issue or has thought hard about it, then it would have to be recognized that those attributes, rather than his being white, might be conferring value on his attempts at tact.

The two tests for higher-order discrimination apply analogously to reciprocal higher-order discrimination: (1) Ascertain whether or not the higher-order valued attribute is valued uniformly across individuals, regardless of anything that might count as a primary valued attribute for the discriminator. If a person's perceived competence to hold a certain professional position would not be in any way diminished if she were black (if, that is, blacks with comparable competence have been hired to such positions) or if the perceived value of a person's political pronouncements would not be in any way diminished if he had a different educational pedigree (if, that is, comparable political pronouncements on the part of others who lack that educational pedigree are similarly valued), then the charge of reciprocal higher-order discrimination may be defeated. (2) Ascertain whether there is any alternative attribute, conduct, or manner directed toward the same goal of gaining access to some social advantage that avoids or deflects the value conferred by the primary valued attribute. If there is not—if, for example, whether you are assertively ambitious or carefully diplomatic, intellectually prolific or intellectually fallow, you can do no wrong—then the charge of reciprocal higher-order discrimination is prima facie justified.[8] Henceforth I will take higher-order discrimination to include reciprocal higher-order discrimination. These two phenomena demonstrate that one need not be a blatant racist, sexist, anti-Semite, snob, or homophobe—let us describe such an individual as a *simple first-order discriminator*—in order to practice political discrimination. Higher-order discrimination is given fullest expression indirectly, by implication, in seemingly unrelated tastes, preferences, and behavior.

5 Higher-Order Discrimination: A Species of Pseudorationality

So far I have used locutions like "seen as conferring value/disvalue on" and "by reason of its association with" to describe the relation between primary and higher-order disvalued or valued attributes without saying in any detail in what I take that relation to consist. It does *not* consist in the set of beliefs held by the higher-order discriminator to the effect that

(1)   a. agent A has primary disvalued attribute P,
      b. agent A has n-ary attribute N, and
      c. P confers negative value on N.

The set (1) is faulty because of (c): only the most perverse and unrepentant higher-order discriminator would admit, even to herself, that it is P that confers negative value on N. On the other hand, only the most absurdly consistent higher-order discriminator would affirm the belief that, in virtue of (1a) and (1b),

c′. N is of negative value, period.

This would be the plight of the higher-order discriminator who, in virtue of his contempt for Isaac Asimov's intellectual prolificity, would feel compelled to abjure Balzac as well. Instead, (c) must be replaced by

c″. N, in the way in which it is borne by A, is of negative value.

Condition (c″) is better because it incorporates that locution that scrupled higher-order discriminators are so reluctant or unable to further define. For the higher-order discriminator, there is *just something about the way in which* a person dances rhythmically that is vulgar, something about the way in which a person manifests their intelligence that is glib or sophistical, something about the way in which they attempt to gain access to social advantages that is unctuous or opportunistic. The higher-order discriminator would vehemently reject the suggestion that this "something" might have anything to do with the person's race, gender, sexual orientation, class background, or ethnic or religious affiliation. But in fact, it is precisely this primary disvalued attribute from which the blemish spreads. Let us, then, take the set of beliefs that

(2) a. agent A has primary disvalued attribute P,
   b. agent A has n-ary attribute N, and
   c″. N, in the way in which it is borne by A, is of negative value,

plus the stipulation that

(3) For the higher-order discriminator, A's possession of P is what in fact confers negative value on N

as characteristic of the typical (i.e., scrupulous) higher-order discriminator.

What makes higher-order discriminators so scrupulous? What, that is, explains the higher-order discriminator's tendency to suppress (3)? Part of the answer lies in the nature of first-order discrimination. First-order discrimination can be understood as a species of *pseudorationality* that relies heavily on the mechanisms of rationalization and dissociation (Piper 1985, 1988). In *rationalization* we apply a concept to something too broadly or too narrowly, magnifying the properties of the thing that instantiate the concept and minimizing those properties that fail to do so. The perception of someone's race, gender, sexual orientation, class background, ethnic or religious affiliation, etc., as a source of disvalue or value is the consequence of applying value concepts like "person," "human being," "citizen," "member of the community," "rational and responsible agent," etc., too narrowly to include only those individuals who have the primary valued attribute and to exclude those individuals who lack it. In *dissociation* we identify something in terms of the negation of the value concepts in question: identifying Jews as subhuman, blacks as childlike, gays as perverts, working class men and women as animals, or women in general as irrational, for example, are ways of obscuring one's identification of these individuals as fully mature, responsible human beings and thereby of obscuring one's recognition of these individuals as full members of the community with which one identifies.[9]

These habits of thought indicate that first-order discriminators have a *personal investment* in the perversion of moral theory that results from restricting its scope of application to individuals viewed as relevantly similar to themselves (Piper 1987, 1988). Agent A is personally invested in some state of affairs t if the existence of t is a source of personal pleasure, satisfaction, or security to A; the nonexistence of t elicits feelings of dejection, deprivation, or anxiety from A; and these feelings are to be explained by A's identification with t. A *identifies with t* if A is disposed to identify t as personally meaningful or valuable to A. The first-order discriminator identifies as personally meaningful a truncated moral theory that identifies only individuals of the same race, gender, sexual orientation, class background, or ethnic or religious affiliation as rational and responsible human beings and as full members of the moral community. Such a discriminator gets personal satisfaction and a sense of security from delimiting the moral community in this way and feels deep anxiety at the suggestion that this theory is false or inadequate (or, even more terrifying for the discriminator, that he or she may in fact violate it).

Higher-order discrimination then adds to this constellation of habits of thought the pseudorational mechanism of *denial*, in which we suppress recognition of an anomalous thing or property altogether in order to preserve the internal consistency of our beliefs or theory about the world, ourselves, and other people. I have already argued that typically, higher-order discriminators are likely to be first-order discriminators as well, that is, that they have the same prejudices that incline them to view individuals with the primary disvalued attributes as inferior, not fully members of their community. The simple first-order discriminator experiences no conflict in categorizing disvaluees as inferior beings to be suppressed and exploited. Therefore, she has no need to exercise denial, either of her own discriminatory responses or of the disvaluees' existence. By contrast, higher-order discriminators must deny both in order to preserve the consistency of their beliefs. Because they are deeply affected, but not fully reformed, by arguments and experiences that suggest that first-order discrimination is unjust, both their own discriminatory responses and the objects of those responses are anathema to higher-order discriminators. Because they do not want to believe that their responses are discriminatory, they deny them altogether. The higher-order discriminator may deny, for example, that the primary disvalued attribute in question is a disvalue at all and yet helplessly deplore the "fact" that nevertheless there are no competent or worthy candidates bearing this attribute to be found, or he may hold any such candidate to a much higher standard of acceptance or performance than that which he ordinarily applies, relative to which her secondary attributes can be disparaged. He may denigrate her intelligence as cleverness or ridicule her for working too hard when she exhibits energy and commitment to her work or disparage her professional recognition as achieved through hustling or connections.

Thus the higher-order discriminator's personal investment is in not merely the truncated moral theory embraced by the first-order discriminator. In the higher-order discriminator this is conjoined with an equally genuine personal investment in the more comprehensive moral theory that includes all human agents within its scope. The higher-order discriminator is too intellectually sophisticated to avow explicitly, say, the view that blacks are childlike or that Jews are subhuman. Even to admit privately to herself that she held such a belief would be a source of embarrassment. Yet she does. Naturally, this conjunction engenders an inconsistent worldview in which, on the one hand, the truncated moral theory endorses the exclusive superiority of individuals relevantly similar to the discriminator but in which, on the other, the more comprehensive moral theory to which the higher-order discriminator also subscribes condemns discrimination against those in fact perceived—in accordance with the truncated theory—as morally inferior. In this funhouse worldview, first-order discrimination is rightly viewed from the perspective of the comprehensive theory as not only morally reprehensible but also vulgar. But as such it is, from the perspective of the truncated theory, of a piece with other perceived signs of inferiority, such as being of a different race, gender, sexual orientation, class background, or ethnic or religious affiliation, from any of which the higher-order discriminator views herself as exempt. The inconsistency of this worldview often results in a corresponding, detectable inconsistency in behavior: The higher-order discriminator often vacillates in her treatment of disvaluees between denial of their existence on the one hand and an exaggerated paternalistic attitude of *noblesse oblige* toward them on the other. Because the higher-order discriminator has a deep personal investment in a perversion of moral theory that flatly excludes disvaluees from its scope of application, she is, despite her best efforts, without the psychological resources for recognizing and treating a disvaluee as an equal or even clearly understanding what would be involved in doing so.

Thus, like the first-order discriminator, the higher-order discriminator in fact categorizes such members of the disvalued group themselves in similarly demeaning terms with respect to their primary attributes but, unlike the first-order discriminator, experiences a conflict of conscience about doing so. Faced with the conflict between first-order discriminatory habits of thought and the dictates of conscience, the higher-order discriminator exercises denial, above all in order to avoid this conflict by eradicating its source from awareness. The higher-order discriminator often fails to acknowledge the very existence or presence of members of the disvalued groups in order to circumvent his own first-order discriminatory responses to them.[10] For instance, he may ignore or fail to acknowledge a disvaluee's contribution to a general discussion or respond to that contribution as though someone else had made it. Or he may relegate a disvaluee to marginal or peripheral tasks in a professional setting. Or he may simply ignore the disvaluee altogether, avoiding all social interaction not strictly required by social or institutional obligations. In behaving in this fashion, the higher-order discriminator does not give vent to any sort of malevolent impulse. His aim is not to insult or injure the disvaluee in any way. Rather, his aim is to avoid the painfully conflicting feelings—of disgust or contempt on the one hand and the pangs of conscience on the other—that acknowledgement of the disvaluee provokes.[11]

When social or institutional obligations make denial of the disvaluee's presence impossible, denial of (at the very least) her primary disvalued attribute or of its perceived disvalue supplies a second-best resolution to this conflict of conscience: denial of the disvaluee's primary disvalued attribute suppresses from awareness the discriminatory habits of thought elicited by it and so preserves consistency by placating the requirements of conscience. This is why the higher-order discriminator tends to suppress (3). Unfortunately, to suppress habits of thought from awareness is not to eradicate their influence, any more than to suppress the disvaluee's existence from awareness is to eradicate her influence. Higher-order discrimination is characterized by that attitude in which a certain habit of thought, namely first-order discrimination, poisons one's evaluations and behavior, whether one acknowledges this or not.

The higher-order discriminator is inclined, moreover, *not* to acknowledge this, no matter how obviously incriminating his evaluations and behavior may be to a disinterested observer. For this would expose the painful conflict of conscience that the higher-order discriminator's behavior attempts to suppress. To acknowledge this conflict would be to acknowledge the need to resolve it, i.e., the need to work through and overcome the first-order prejudices that gave rise to it. But it is precisely in virtue of those first-order prejudices themselves that such a project of self-improvement stands very low on the higher-order discriminator's list of priorities. Unlike the resolution of Oedipal conflicts, emotional problems, tensions in one's personal relationships, and career dilemmas, coming to terms with one's prejudices and learning not to inflict them inadvertently on others just is not, in the last analysis, seen as terribly important by the higher-order discriminator. That is part of what makes him a discriminator in the first place.[12]

As I have painted it, then, higher-order discrimination is peculiarly the sickness of thoughtful, well-intentioned, and conscientious individuals who nevertheless have failed adequately to confront and work through their own prejudices or perhaps have been too quickly satisfied by their ability to marshall arguments on behalf of doing so. Such individuals are being neither disingenuous nor hypocritical when they deny that a person's race, gender, sexual orientation, class background, or ethnic or religious affiliation affects their judgment of her competence or worth. They vehemently insist that this is so, they want it to be so, and they genuinely believe it to be so. They are, nevertheless, mistaken. Their efforts to explain away each manifest expression of higher-order discrimination on different and inconsistent grounds are unconvincing. And their behavior exhibits a degree of otherwise inexplicable arbitrariness and idiosyncracy that severely strains our attempts to apply the principle of charity in making sense of it. Hence, in order to understand the behavior of higher-order discriminators, we must watch what they *do*, not what they *say*.[13]

6 *Some Familiar Examples of Higher-Order Discrimination*

These attitudes may find expression in an expectation of greater deference or genuflection from a member of the disvalued group. The simple first-order discriminator expresses his anger at the violation of this expectation in certain familiar stereotypes: the "uppity nigger" whose refusal to behave subserviently is seen as impudence or disrespect, or the "Jewish American Princess," whose assertiveness, presumption of self-worth, and expectation of attention and respect is seen as a sign of being spoiled, selfish, or imperious. But for the higher-order discriminator, such anger is displaced into more subtle but similar reactions. Such an individual may just feel angered or personally affronted by a woman's presumption of equality in personal, social, or intellectual status or in professional worth or as a competitor for social or professional rewards, or he may feel unduly irritated by her failure to defer or back down in argument. She may be viewed as forward in conversation, when in fact she contributes no more and no less than anyone else, or stubborn, unresponsive, or impervious to well-intentioned criticisms, when in fact the only acceptable response to those criticisms, in the eyes of the higher-order discriminator, would be for her to concur with them whole-heartedly and apologize for her dereliction. Or, to take another example, the higher-order discriminator may feel invaded or compromised by a black person's jocularity or willingness to trade friendly insults that one accepts as a matter of course from those considered to be one's peers. The black person may be viewed as overly familiar, insolent, or presumptuous. In all such cases the disvaluee's behavior is seen as a *presumption*, not a right or an accepted practice.[14] The higher-order discriminator is tortured by the suspicion that he is somehow being ridiculed or shown insufficient respect or that the disvaluee's conduct bespeaks contempt.

In a recent compelling analysis of anger (1984), N. J. H. Dent suggests that anger is based ultimately on feelings of personal inferiority. These lead one to overestimate the importance of others' expressions of regard and esteem for one, which in turn multiplies the number of occasions in which one feels slighted when such expressions are not forthcoming or are of insufficient magnitude relative to one's importunate requirements. This oversensitivity to being slighted in turn provokes in one the desire to rectify one's situation through retaliation by lashing out at the offender. This analysis by itself does not, I think, cover all cases of anger, nor does it explain the origins of simple first-order discrimination. But it does provide insight into why higher-order discriminators, like simple first-order discriminators, are apt to become so angry so often at imagined slights from seemingly arrogant disvaluees. The more inferior one feels, the more expressions of esteem one requires. And the more inferior one perceives a disvaluee to be, the more elaborate the disvaluee's expression of esteem of one is required to be. Whereas a friendly nod from a perceived superior is sufficient to transport one to a state of bliss, anything less than a full-length obeisance from a perceived inferior appears to be an insult.[15] In all such cases, irascibility regularly directed at particular members of disvalued. groups should not be dismissed as simply an idiosyncracy of character, even if it is not intentionally directed at members of disvalued groups *as such*. It is nevertheless an overt expression of higher-order discrimination.

A second, related example of behavior and judgments distorted by higher-order discrimination is the treatment of disvaluees in a way that would constitute a clear insult or *faux pas* if the person so treated were one of one's recognized peers. For example, a white Gentile may privately make an anti-Semitic remark to a black colleague in a misguided effort to establish rapport, whereas such a remark would be seen as a serious social lapse even among other white Gentiles. Or a heterosexual may make gratuitous disparaging remarks to a gay colleague about her work or job performance of a sort designed to "cut her down to size" rather than to provide constructive criticism. Or a man may make offensively personal remarks to a woman colleague about her physical appearance, personal life, or manner of dress, of a sort that would be highly inappropriate if they were made to another man. Or he might expect from a woman colleague extra forbearance for fits of temper or irresponsible conduct, or he might expect extraordinary professional demands that he would not from a man. The higher-order discriminator, in other social contexts, may be acclaimed quite rightly as a "prince among men." To disvaluees, however, he reveals himself as Mr. Hyde.[16] Yet unlike President Lyndon Johnson, who conferred with his cabinet through an open bathroom door while uninhibitedly and indiscreetly performing his morning ablutions, the higher-order discriminator cannot be supposed to commit these boorish excesses with any offensive intent. Rather, he regards his response to a person's disvalued attributes as socially innocuous, as an acceptable variation in social etiquette keyed to the variations among the personality traits of different individuals.

A third example of judgments and behavior poisoned by higher-order discrimination is the kind of arbitrariness in evaluating a person's assets and liabilities as a member of one's group or community mentioned earlier: attributes that would qualify as assets in a valuee or impartially considered individual are liabilities in a disvaluee, and attributes that would qualify as liabilities in a disvaluee or impartially considered individual are assets in a valuee. For instance, a disvaluee being considered for a creative writing instructorship may be belittled on grounds that she is merely "clever," "bright," or "a hard worker," whereas a valuee showing the same traits may be congratulated on his resourcefulness, intelligence, and drive. Or a potential law partner who is a valuee and is "long on ideas but short on argument" may be praised for her creativity, while a similarly situated disvaluee may be suspected of underlying incompetence.

A fourth example of such distorted behavior is the implicit treatment of disvaluees as being obligated by different rules of conduct than those that govern oneself and those considered to be one's peers. Among one's peers, humor or irreverence at the expense of some sacred relic—a work, personage, or achievement in one's field—may be an acceptable source of entertainment, while such humor on the part of a disvaluee is a sacrilege, personal affront, or iconoclasm that expresses the same lack of respect as that manifested in the "presumption" of equality. Or one may apply different criteria of interpretation of the behavior of disvaluees. Whereas enigmatic behavior by valuees is excused, overlooked, or given the benefit of the doubt, similar behavior on the part of disvaluees is interpreted as proof of vice or malevolence. This interpretation motivates the higher-order discriminator not only to avoid but also to justify the avoidance of direct interaction with the disvaluee and thus to avoid the conflict of conscience described earlier. Or one may apply rules of honor, loyalty, and responsibility only to those considered to be one's peers but may have no scruples about betraying the trust or confidentiality of a disvaluee, who is implicitly viewed as unentitled to such consideration. Alternatively, one may hold disvaluees to far more stringent moral standards than the members of one's own community in fact practice among themselves. Any violation of these standards by the disvaluee then creates an irradicable moral blemish to which the valuees are not vulnerable by reason of their status as valuees. These cases express quite clearly the conviction that disvaluees just do not have quite that same status, and hence are not to be subject to the same standards of treatment, as members of one's recognized community. And at the same time the higher-order discriminator vehemently and in all honesty denies that any such discrimination is taking place. Indeed, in all of these examples the higher-order discriminator may sincerely deny that the person's race, gender, sexual orientation, class background, ethnic or religious affiliation, etc., arbitrarily influences his evaluations when his behavior shows patently that they do.

7 Abettors of Higher-Order Discrimination

There are many forces that may intensify higher-order discrimination and its social consequences. Among them are, first and foremost, complicitous institutional practices. Individuals in positions of responsibility often rank their personal and social allegiances ahead of their professional obligation to protect disvaluees from the pernicious effects of higher-order discrimination. Or they effectively reward higher-order discrimination by regularly interpreting instances of it as expressions of professional autonomy and refusing in principle to scrutinize suspected instances of it on the grounds that doing so would be unwarranted interference in an organization's internal affairs. These institutions often comply with the letter of antidiscriminatory policies by hiring members of disvalued groups to temporary positions of high public visibility. Since such individuals are regularly replaced by other, equally competent but equally transient members of the same disvalued group, that group's visibility within the institution can be maintained without dismantling the entrenched system of discrimination through permanent or seniority status. This is to abdicate the responsibility for enforcing those antidiscriminatory policies to which such institutions publicly claim to be committed.

Second, there is the intellectual resourcefulness of the higher-order discriminator. Someone who is in fact deeply invested in the disvaluational status of some primary attribute may always recruit some further, equally irrelevant attribute to explain her seemingly irrational judgment and thus deflect the charge of higher-order discrimination. It may be said, for example, that the disvalued attribute is not a person's race, gender, sexual orientation, class background, or ethnic or religious affiliation but rather his inability to "fit in," "get along with others," or "be a team player." This is a particularly familiar and dependable response because the evidence for ascribing this attribute may be materially coextensive with the evidence for disvaluing the primary attribute at issue. Since the disvaluee is in theory held to the same standards of conduct that govern others in the community but is in fact expected to conform to different ones tailored to his disvalued status, his inability to "fit in" can be guaranteed at the outset.[17]

A third force that intensifies higher-order discrimination is the repressive, pseudorational habits of rationalization, dissociation, and denial already discussed. Earlier I suggested that higher-order discriminators were generally well-intentioned individuals who had failed to come to terms with their own prejudices. I also mentioned some possible reasons for this failure, among them first-order discrimination, avoidance of conflicts of conscience, and feelings of personal inferiority. Another reason that should not be neglected is that higher-order discriminators tend to rationalize, dissociate, or deny the very existence of higher-order discrimination itself. They might claim, for example, that the phenomenon I have described is in truth simple sensitivity to subtle variations and qualities among individuals, all of which might be relevant to questions of value or competence in a sufficiently broad sense. Or they might agree that higher-order discrimination exists but dissociate it from their own motives and behavior as an anomalous phenomenon that is too rare to merit further scrutiny. Or they might just flatly deny the existence of anything like what I have described as higher-order discrimination and deny as well the undeniably familiar instances of it that I have invoked to anchor the foregoing analysis. These tactics reinforce the tendencies of higher-order discriminators to deny their own collusion in the practice of higher-order discrimination and to deny or minimize their need to come to terms with it. Higher-order discriminators are adept at the tactics of pseudorationality because they have so much self-esteem to lose by modifying their beliefs. But *we* need not be taken in. For above all, higher-order discriminators need to understand that no one is fooled by their tactics. With the aid of this understanding, they may someday learn to stop fooling themselves.

8 Higher-Order Discrimination: A Case of n-Level Pseudorationality

Higher-order discrimination is an identifiable moral vice that is generically related to, but essentially unlike, such familiar moral vices as self-deception, hypocrisy, deceit, and weakness of will. It is related to the latter in involving an obfuscation of the self and of reality in ways that are simultaneously destructive and self-serving. But higher-order discrimination is unlike these in that it is a moral vice of a purely intellectual kind. In hypocrisy and deceit, for example, we speak or behave in ways that communicate falsehoods to others for reasons of self-interest. And in weakness of will our rational beliefs are corrupted and overridden by illicit emotions. In each of these familiar cases our rational capacities are corrupted or distorted by some other motivational component of the self—our desires, interests, or emotions.

First-order discrimination is similar to self-deception, hypocrisy, and weakness of will in this respect. The first-order discriminator perverts the purpose of her moral theory by treating it as conferring honorific status on people like her. So she truncates the scope of her moral theory by confining its application to people like her. Thus she views others who are not like her as anomalies that threaten it. Involved in this perception of others are fear and anger, in addition to the feelings of personal inferiority earlier discussed. The first-order discriminator then eradicates these anomalies by pseudorationally dissociating or rationalizing them, and this too can be best understood as involving deep emotions that would require a separate paper to explore. For my purposes here the point is simply that these emotions and reactions subvert the capacity to think clearly and rationally about the situation at hand.

By contrast, in higher-order discrimination, rationality is superveniently self-subverting. Having perverted the scope of her moral theory in the service of irrational fears of another's appearance of difference, the higher-order discriminator is now beset by the reproaches of her moral theory itself for having done so. Her personal investment in the truncated version of the theory explains away her first-order discrimination against the disvaluees that theory excludes, while her higher-level personal investment in the comprehensive moral theory compels her to deny her own first-level violation of it. Therefore, what motivates higher-order discrimination is ultimately the discriminator's pseudorational application of her moral theory to her own first-level pseudorationalization of that theory. She becomes a higher-level pseudorationalizer by denying her own first-level pseudorationality at increasingly removed intellectual levels. Call this *n-level pseudorationality*. I think that *n*-level pseudorationality is the kind of thing we have in mind when we say of a person that he is "out of touch with his feelings."

Higher-order discrimination is not the only example of *n*-level pseudorationality. As an alternative, consider self-deception, in which a person pseudorationalizes her perceptions of herself and her relations to others because she is personally invested in a truncated theory of who she is, i.e., in a *personal self-conception*. By itself this is a case of first-level pseudorationality. But if her personal self-conception includes the trait of being particularly committed to self-knowledge, she may pseudorationalize her first-level pseudorationality, for example, by rationalizing her first-level denial of unpleasant facts as an instance of merely refusing to dwell what is unimportant or irrelevant and then dissociating her rationalization from her theory of self-scrutiny as an isolated and atypical mental glitch. And so on. We might describe this as *higher-order self-deception*. Higher-order self-deception would be an instance of *n*-level pseudorationality. The differences among cases of pseudorationality and among cases of n-level pseudorationality have to do not with differences in the strategies deployed but rather in the particular theories perverted by it. Whereas self-deception perverts a theory of who one is as an individual, first-order discrimination perverts a theory of who persons are and how they are to be treated. And whereas higher-order self-deception pseudorationalizes one's pseudorational theory of who one is, higher-order discrimination pseudorationalizes one's pseudorational theory of who persons are and how they are to be treated.

So higher-order discrimination is but one instance of a perfectly general tendency, first, to attempt psychologically to explain away anomalies that intrude into, disrupt, or disconfirm our most favored theories and then, having done so, to explain that away as well. We see the workings of n-level pseudorationality as clearly in theory-building in the social and natural sciences as we do in human interaction in the social and political sphere. In all such cases it is not difficult to imagine the survival value such a tendency may once have had and may still have under certain conditions.[18] Because of our limited cognitive capacities, prereflective higher-order discrimination and first-order discrimination as well are probably unavoidable. Only those who have a deep personal investment in a comprehensive moral theory will feel obliged, on reflection, to modify them.

Notes

1. This paper is excerpted from chapter 12 of *Rationality and the Structure of the Self*, work on which was supported by an Andrew Mellon Postdoctoral Fellowship at Stanford University and a Woodrow Wilson International Research Fellowship. Earlier versions were delivered to the Philosophy Department at George Washington University, the Kennedy Institute of Ethics of Georgetown University, Howard University, the University of Mississippi, the City College of New York, the University of Maryland, and the Boston Area Conference on Character and Morality, hosted by Radcliffe and Wellesley Colleges (Nancy Sherman commenting). I have benefitted from these discussions and particularly from the remarks of Nancy Sherman and Kenneth P. Winkler on the issues addressed in section 1. Laurence Thomas provided extensive comments on an earlier draft.

2. I restrict the discussion to consideration of *noninstrumental* value or competence as determined by principles of justice and equality. The contrast is with *instrumental* value or competence in furthering some specified social or institutional policy of the sort that would figure in arguments that would justify, e.g., hiring a black person to provide a role model in a classroom or to provide a unique and needed perspective in a business venture or court of law, refusing to sell real estate in a certain neighborhood to a black family solely because doing so would lower property values, hiring a woman to a professional position solely to meet affirmative action quotas, or refusing to serve Asians at one's family diner solely because it would be bad for business.

3. The thesis that women make better friends is often supported by arguments to the effect that they *become closer confidants more quickly*. But there are many other attributes that contribute to friendship—e.g., trustworthiness, loyalty, dependability, honesty, mutual respect, etc.—that such arguments do not address.

4. For purposes of this discussion I ignore the range of cases in which my valuation of, e.g., Germanness is rooted in the status or worth I expect my choice of German friends to confer *on me*. This kind of case occurs both in situations in which the valued attribute is one shared by oneself and in those in which it is not. Thus it may happen that one's choice of a white, Anglo-Saxon Protestant spouse is made in part with an eye to reinforcing the value of one's own status as a white, Anglo-Saxon Protestant, or alternately, that one's choice of a black spouse is made with an eye to highlighting one's rejection of the policy of "remaining with one's own kind." These are all cases in which the attribute is valued as a source of *instrumental* value or competence, i.e., its ability to confer value on the evaluator. Therefore, they are irrelevant to my argument.

5. Of course, there are other, more convoluted cases of higher-order discrimination that represent epicyclic variations on the straightforward cases I shall be examining. For example, being black may wildly exaggerate the value attached to classical styling in a black dancer if classical styling is perceived as something the person had to overcome great innate and cultural obstacles to achieve. In either case, being black functions as a primary disvalued attribute because it carries a presumption of inferiority into the evaluation of further attributes of the person.

6. Is it perhaps too strong to claim that a primary disvalued attribute poisons the higher-order discriminator's evaluation of *all* of the disvaluee's other attributes? Can't a higher-order discriminator respect a disvaluee's traits of character in a certain restricted area *despite* his disvalued status? I am inclined to think not. For this seems to occur almost exclusively when the "valued" attribute itself conforms to the higher-order discriminator's stereotypes. For example, a black man may be admired for his athletic prowess but encounter hostility when he runs for political office. In such cases the higher-order discriminator's admiration and respect for the stereotypical trait is not unalloyed. It is tempered by a certain smug complacency at the disvaluee's confirmation of his disvalued status in the very cultivation and expression of that stereotypical trait. To sustain the above objection, we would need to see a higher-order discriminator exhibiting *unalloyed* admiration and respect for *non*stereotypical traits in such a way that *these positive feelings did not, in turn, positively reform the higher-order discriminator's prejudicial attitude toward the person's primary disvalued attribute*. Someone who sincerely respects and admires a disvaluee for nonstereotypical reasons without feeling threatened or invaded has already begun to weaken the psychological edifice on which her discriminatory evaluation of the person as a disvaluee is based.

7. It might be thought that this first test is inherently self-limiting for the case in which the person happens to dislike, e.g., just the attribute that is most typically associated with a certain race (dark skin) but nevertheless passes the first test in that she disvalues it uniformly across individuals, whether it occurs in blacks, East Indians, Jews, Arabs, Aborigines, or Coppertone-soaked Californians. I think what we should say about this kind of case is that it does not present a problem. The fact that someone is acquitted of being a racist doesn't imply that her evaluations are therefore admirable or enlightened. Any predicate or combination of predicates that *fails* the first test is either a rigged definite description of a particular disvalued group, e.g., "ova-producing featherless bipeds," or else describes a discriminatory stereotype, e.g., "dark-skinned, dark-eyed, woolly haired individuals with

rhythm." Of course, a person might just happen to disvalue only individuals who fit such a stereotype and not those who violate it. But since this disvaluation would not be independent of anything that might count as a primary disvalued attribute for such a person, it would not defeat the charge of higher-order discrimination.

Note, however, that the first test does *not* work for identifying a distinct but related attitude, which we might call *generalized higher-order discrimination*, in which a person comes to disvalue some constellation of higher-order attributes across the board *specifically because of its original association with* a primary disvalued attribute stereotypically ascribed to a certain group. Someone who finds having rhythm vulgar in any dancer, regardless of racial or ethnic affiliation, *because* he associates having rhythm with blacks, whom he fears and despises, would exemplify such an attitude.

8. Here it might be objected that the second test is inadequate to ascertain the existence of reciprocal higher-order discrimination, since the explanation for why "you can do no wrong" may be not that all such higher-order attributes receive value from primary valued attributes but rather that all such higher-order attributes are in any case irrelevant to judgments of a person's competence. However, remember that the second test applies specifically to attributes directed toward the goal of gaining access to some social advantage. This includes not only attributes irrelevant to the question of one's entitlement to that advantage, such as those pertaining to the manner or quality of one's self-promotion, but also attributes directly relevant to that question, such as those pertaining to one's status, potential, training, experience, etc. The second test sifts out those cases in which irrelevant higher-order attributes are made the basis for conferring the advantage, e.g., one's manner of self-promotion, and in which relevant higher-order attributes are discounted as the bases for conferring the advantage, e.g., one's previous professional experience. In both kinds of cases, higher-order discrimination is marked by the *relaxation or modification* of the criteria of competence for receiving the advantage in order to accommodate the particular attributes of the valuee.

9. The irony in the case of racism is that there is a substantial literature in biology and the social sciences that indicates that almost all purportedly white Americans have between five and twenty percent black ancestry and hence are, according this country's entrenched "just one trace" convention of racial classification, black. See Williamson 1974; Cavalli-Sforza and Bodmer 1971; T. E. Reed 1969; Workman, Blumberg, and Cooper 1963; Glass and Li 1953. For these references and discussion on this matter I am indebted to Professor Monro S. Edmonson of Tulane University's Department of Anthropology.

10. This may contribute to an explanation of the researched phenomenon (Schuman, Steeh, and Bobo 1985) that in the last twenty years, white support for the *principles* of equality and fairness for blacks have increased concurrently with white opposition to the *implementation* of those principles.

11. Here the joke characterizing the difference between first-order racism in the South and in the North is relevant: in the South, it is said, whites don't mind how close a black person gets, as long as he doesn't get too big, while in the North, whites don't mind how big a black person gets, as long as he doesn't get too close. Only the higher-order discriminator of either region feels compelled to deny the existence of the black person altogether.

Denial of a person's presence as a way of avoiding conflicting feelings about him is fairly common. A very handsome man may be the object of denial when others' feelings of attraction to him conflict with their conviction that these feelings are inappropriate. A very fortunate or charismatic person may be the object of denial when others' feelings of envy or resentment conflict with a similar conviction. Or a homely person may be the object of denial when others' feelings of repugnance conflict with their kindness or social good will. Higher-order discrimination is most analogous to this last case.

12. Here I think it would be wrong to interpret the higher-order discriminator as concerned only with personal problems and not with social ones. Rather, the higher-order discriminator belittles the importance of addressing a certain *personal* problem.

13. One implication of characterizing higher-order discrimination as a sickness rather than as a fault is that higher-order discriminators are, in the last analysis, not morally responsible for their behavior. This conclusion seems unpalatable in many respects. Nevertheless, I am reluctantly pessimistic about the efficacy of appeals to reason in higher-order discriminators. Because their reason, or rather their dogged pseudorationality, is so inherently a part of the problem, I am inclined to think that the solution should be sought in the adoption of some version of Strawson's "objective attitude" toward them, i.e., that higher-order discriminators must be *managed*, perhaps psychotherapeutically, rather than *addressed*. I suggest an explanation for this kind of intractability in Piper 1985 and 1988.

14. The view of the disvaluee's assumption of equality as a *pre*sumption may explain the higher-order discriminator's otherwise inexplicable umbrage at being complimented by a disvaluee: an inferior is in no position to confer favors of any kind.

15. In the deep South up to the mid 1960s, for example, for a black person to meet the gaze of a white person was perceived as an offense, and for a black man even to look at a white woman was to invite lynching.

16. This often creates additional difficulties in identifying cases of higher-order discrimination for what they are. The testimony of a disvaluee suffers a credibility problem at the outset. This problem is severely exacerbated if the testimony concerns a higher-order discriminator whom others have every reason to regard as a saint. Under these circumstances any charge of inconsistency—whether it comes from others and targets the disvaluee or comes from the disvaluee and targets the higher-order discriminator—is in the eye of the beholder. For higher-order discriminators regard coarse, tasteless, or brutal behavior toward disvaluees as called forth by them and so as warranted and hence as fully consistent with highly refined manners and courtly civility toward others.

17. Under these circumstances the disvaluee too may be rightly accused of pseudorationality if his personal investment in the theoretical standards of equal treatment is so great that he rationalizes, dissociates, or denies the facts of discrimination that blatantly confront him. But I argue in Piper, unpublished, that self-preservation *requires* that although such ideals must ultimately die, they must not do so without a long and painful struggle.

18. In Piper 1988 I argue that the internal consistency of our theories about ourselves and the world are necessary conditions for what I call *literal self-preservation*, i.e., the theoretically rational unity and integrity of the self, and that we are often prepared to sacrifice the integrity of those theories themselves to achieve this.

Chapter 14

Obligation and Performance: A Kantian Account of Moral Conflict

Barbara Herman

Conflicts of duty pose practical problems for agents and theoretical problems for philosophers. The theoretical problems track the practical less than one might hope: the extensive discussion of such moral dilemmas in the literature is not about the dilemmas—about their resolution, occasion, or cause.[1] What are of concern to philosophers are the theoretical difficulties that the mere possibility of practical dilemmas introduce.

This essay is also not really about conflicts of duty. Its subject is the philosophical discussions of conflicts of duty insofar as they present one of those nodal points at which seemingly benign shared assumptions reveal the strains they impose on theory. In explications of occasions when we are said to have more than one obligation or duty without being able to act to satisfy each of their conflicting claims, routine assumptions about the application of theory to its domain (here, practice) make this conflict a sign of theoretical inconsistency.[2] One then has a dilemma *between* theory and practice. If one accepts that there are conflicts of duty, then moral theory lacks consistency insofar as it allows them. If, giving priority to consistency, one denies the possibility of conflicts of duty, then one must explain away the phenomena of conflict in moral experience. Either choice imposes fairly large costs as it has been worked out—one to morality (to its ambitions of deliberative authority), the other to the integrity of moral experience. The question is whether we must accept that these are the alternatives. I think we do not.

Of first importance is the fact that conflict of duty is not a theory-neutral phenomenon. To produce conflicts, morality must contain (or set) independent moral requirements that can apply simultaneously in circumstances of action. But it is not a necessary feature of morality that it generate duties or obligations (plural), even when the account of morality is deontological. Indeed, morality as I believe Kant understands it does not impose duties or obligations (plural) and therefore, as he claims, *cannot* generate conflicts of duties. The frequent accusations to the contrary mistake the nature of Kantian moral requirement.

What the Kantian requirement of obligation is and how it supports Kant's claim that "conflict of duties and obligations is inconceivable" are the central concerns of this essay. But they are not the only ones. There are reasons to welcome the Kantian concept of obligation that go beyond its resolution of difficulties associated with conflicts of duty. Chief among them is its effect on the structure of moral experience. I want to argue that it introduces greater narrative coherence into the life of a moral agent than does either the view of obligation usually imputed to Kantian morality or the view that is taken for granted in most conflict-of-duty discussions. The idea of narrative coherence is in turn a vehicle for an interpretation of autonomy and self-legislation that can counter criticism of Kantian ethics as incompatible with values of agential integrity (having a life that is one's own, that one can care about in a human way). Because such criticism relies on a conception of obligation foreign to Kantian ethics, it has the effect of an alien species brought into a friendly environment, driving out the native inhabitants. This essay is to be seen, then, as part of a project of rehabilitation.

1

If you survey the literature on conflicts of duty, it is clear that these conflicts disturb moral theory insofar as they cannot coexist with two basic moral postulates. Generically, a conflict of duty involves two moral requirements applying to an agent in circumstances that do not permit the satisfaction of both. If failure to satisfy a valid moral requirement implies wrongdoing, then agents can be in circumstances in which wrongdoing is unavoidable. But "unavoidable wrongdoing" does not sit well with the "Ought implies can" postulate. Normally we say that if you cannot do X, then it is not the case that you ought to do X. However, if we appeal to this postulate, it is hard to say what remains of the phenomenon of conflict of duty. For if it must be possible for an agent to negotiate the moral terrain without fault (because agents must be able to do what they are morally required to do), then either there are no conflicts of duty, or in violation of the second postulate, moral requirements do not obligate (where being obligated to do X implies that one may not omit doing X). Yet if moral requirements do not obligate, "conflict of duty" would seem to signal no more than the presence of a hard moral question. The tension is thus between the claim for the phenomena and the moral postulates. Something needs to be abandoned or modified.[3]

There are some who would deny the phenomena. They do not dispute that we experience conflicts of duty, nor that we have feelings of guilt and remorse that we believe appropriate to having failed to meet a moral requirement. What they deny is that the experience of conflict implies any actual conflict of duties (McConnell 1978, Conee 1982). Concerned to defend the consistency of morality or the possibility of determinate moral reasoning, they explain the experience by appeal to agents' lack of full moral awareness or their lack of knowledge (moral and empirical). Guilt and remorse are justified because they support useful character traits, even though, or even because, they reinforce the false belief that there are conflicts of duty. Indeed, the experience of moral conflict *as* conflict of duty and the attendant feelings are sometimes thought to be necessary to secure reliable performances in difficult circumstances.

These are recommendations for "indirection" in morality. One says that if we must permit agents to do things that are generally wrong (and possibly very wrong), we risk making them able to do what is truly wrong too easily unless they suffer guilt based on their belief that they have done something wrong (even if unavoidable). The moral character of ordinary agents cannot withstand knowledge that such actions are even moral possibilities (for them or for others); moral psychology requires the conventional distinctions and prohibitions. Guilt and the belief in wrongdoing keep them sensitive to the awfulness of what they might do. But since it does not follow from these beliefs and feelings that an agent acting for one of the requirements in a conflict-of-duty situation does anything wrong (or does any wrong thing) in failing to act for the other, we do not, in our theory, admit the reality of moral conflict.

The cost of saving the consistency of morality in this way is the competence and the integrity of character of the moral agent. This joins a recurrent tendency in moral theory to divide theory and practice in a manner that demeans most moral agents (particularly those ordinary moral agents who are not privy to the indirectness arguments). Though we are not now tempted to see morality as Plato saw justice, or Aristotle virtue—as a way of life suited to the few— we often share with them the belief that although moral behavior is socially necessary (and so legitimate to impose on people through law or socialization), people (people in general, that is) cannot be expected to (really) understand morality or to be motivated by such understanding. Indeed, it is often argued that for many people, understanding morality would defeat its authority for them. Because people cannot internalize or work with "true morality," they must be given a different version of morality that will cause them to act (approximately) as they would act if they could act in accordance with an understanding of the dictates of true morality.

I do not dispute the claims about our character and situation on which the indirectness theses rest. What I object to is the program of holding morality apart from the very features of human character that make morality necessary. The danger sign in indirectness arguments is the fact that the morality they most often recommend for "us" is "commonsense" morality. (If agents cannot act as "direct" moral theory would dictate, it is hard to know what could command assent in practice other than commonsense morality. Any other practice would require indirect (false) justification and false content.) If one is at all worried about what may be enshrined in commonsense morality, one should be all the more sensitive to arguments that depend on the supposed incapacity of people, especially ordinary people, to act according to "true moral principles." It is anything but obvious that the content of commonsense morality is neutral to the interests of those whose lives it regulates. The very thing that gives commonsense morality its authority—the accumulated wisdom of the ages—should ground skepticism and suspicion.

There are good grounds to accept a presumption against a moral theory if it requires indirectness to work. And if one is friendly to morality, there are especially good grounds to reject any theoretical account that imposes indirectness *without regard to the content of moral requirements*.

Independent of theory, we would say that the phenomenon of moral conflict is an ordinary part of moral experience. You don't need Agamemnon or stories of Third World bandits to establish that agents may be faced with situations (brought on by themselves or by the actions of others) that leave them with no choice that does not also involve apparent wrongdoing. To the contrary, one might hold that moral conflict is the stuff, the data, that moral theory ought to be about. If we started from experience instead of supposing that we have in place moral theory whose principles ought to yield consistent results (if they are any good) but do not (and so fail), we might take it that the determining data for theory is the experience of conflict and the need for its resolution. Our understanding of what moral principles are (or do) ought to accommodate that.

If we are hesitant to accept the phenomenon of moral conflict because it sets off theoretical disorder, we should look again at the two postulates that set the engine of disorder running. We need not accept without question that they are the fixed points around which everything else in moral theory must circulate.

Rejection of the idea that obligations necessitate may seem the most appealing strategic move, especially since it is less than clear what kind of necessitation could be involved. If, as one might first suppose, it were the practical necessitation of "best reasons," we would have reason to reject the idea that obligations necessitate if only to accommodate the unexceptionable fact that there are cases of moral conflict where one has better reasons to act for one duty rather than the other. On the other hand, if obligations do not necessitate, we do not generate the phenomenon of conflict of duty. Without a better account of the necessity obligation introduces, we cannot make this move. There is greater opportunity with the usually sacrosanct "Ought implies can" postulate.

In the sense that enters conflict-of-duties discussions, the "Ought implies can" postulate is implausible. Consider a simple case. If I am obligated to repay a debt on Wednesday but I squander the money on Tuesday, it seems reasonable to say that my inability to repay my debt does not remove my obligation. Surely, it is not the case on Wednesday that I have no obligation to repay my debt. So we need to see what it is about the way we are reading the postulate that has got to be wrong.[4]

The intuition that supports the "Ought implies can" postulate is that morality, or the possibility of the moral ought, requires that we must be able to do what we are obliged to do. The intuition is sound enough. But there are narrow and wide interpretations of what the intuition represents. The narrow reading requires an ability to perform whatever is in the scope of the ought (or obligation).[5] The wide view holds that we can be obliged to do actions only of a *kind* that it is possible for us to do. So we cannot be obliged to know what someone else is thinking or to alter a past event. Rather than determining the conditions of moral responsibility (what an agent can legitimately be obliged to do), one might say that "Ought implies can" in the wide sense establishes the necessary condition for the *possibility* of responsibility. Knowing what *kinds* of things morality can require, we are then able to consider in a given case whether it is reasonable to hold someone responsible for an action he could not, at the time of the action, avoid.[6]

This is Kant's point in the *Critique of Pure Reason*. He argues that obligation (the possibility of moral ought) would be unintelligible if we (as moral persons) were fully determined—if we did not have in any sense a free will (Kant 1933, 469 ff.). Free will is the condition of our ability to act on moral principle. It does not follow from *this*

"Ought implies can" that there will be no limitations to our ability to act to satisfy moral requirements, though it does follow, Kant thinks, that we cannot be unable to *will* as we ought.

If we accept the wide interpretation of "Ought implies can," there is no particular tension generated by moral conflict. Each of the moral requirements is, if valid, a kind of thing the agent is able to do. That the circumstances are such that the agent is unable to satisfy both requirements sets a practical problem that a good theory will have a way to resolve. There is no theoretical problem, since it does not follow from "Ought implies can" that a given agent in particular circumstances must be able to satisfy all moral requirements that apply.

2

At this point one might object that it has become hard to see what is involved in the very idea of moral requirement or obligation. On the one hand, I want to insist that obligation necessitates, and on the other, I speak of the possibility of moral requirements obtaining even when agents are unable to act as they direct. Surely, to say that obligation necessitates is to say that if one has an obligation (or duty) to X, nothing could be a reason justifying not Xing. (The sense of "necessity" here is not logical or physical but *practical*.) But if it is possible that one may (even faultlessly) be unable to satisfy moral requirements, then it would seem that at the least, one is "not unjustified" in not Xing. To explain why there is no inconsistency here, I want to reset the problem of the conflict of duties through close attention to the one passage in which Kant discusses them and declares their impossibility. We can find in it the lineaments of an account of obligation and moral requirement that saves both phenomenon and theory.

The text is the (in)famous passage in the *Doctrine of Virtue* in which Kant argues that conflict of duties is impossible.

> A conflict of duties would be a relation of duties in which one of them would annul the other (wholly or in part).—But a conflict of duties and obligations is inconceivable. For the concepts of duty and obligation as such express the objective practical *necessity* of certain actions, and two conflicting rules cannot both be necessary at the same time: if it is our duty to act according to one of these rules, then to act according to the opposite one is not our duty and is even contrary to duty. But there can be, it is true, two *grounds* of obligation (*rationes obligandi*) both present

in one agent and in the rule he lays down for himself. In this case one or the other of these grounds is not sufficient to oblige him (*rationes obligandi non obligantes*) and is therefore not a duty.— When two such grounds conflict with each other, practical philosophy says, not that the stronger obligation takes precedence (*fortior obligatio vincit*), but that the stronger *ground of obligation* prevails (*fortior obligandi ratio vincit*). (Kant 1964b, 23)

Alan Donagan provides a more literal translation of the key sentence: "When two such grounds of obligation are in conflict, practical philosophy does not say that the stronger obligation holds the upper hand (. . .), but that the stronger ground of obligation holds the field (. . .)"[7] (Gowans 1987, 274).

The crucial claim is this: If there were conflicts of duty, one duty would "annul" the other (wholly or in part). But since the concept of duty expresses practical necessity, there can be no "annulling." The necessity that comes from the concept of duty makes it the case that failure to act for either duty is "contrary to duty." An un-acted-upon duty does not lose its necessity; it is not annulled.

We can see why Kant talks about "annulling" a duty if we look at how one resolves conflict between Kantian pragmatic oughts. When, because of two ends I pursue, I find that I am in circumstances in which what I must do for one end conflicts with what I must do for the other, I resolve the conflict by backing off from (at least) one of the ends. The object of some want or desire can, at that time, no longer be an end of action. One could say that my choice to act for one end "annuls" the ought set by the other (wholly or in part, as circumstances permit). It is part of the concept of the moral ought that I cannot annul its requirement by choice or by abandoning an end. From this it would seem to follow that a system of pragmatic oughts that allows conflict is possible, but a system of moral oughts that allows conflict is not.

Although Kant appears to agree with those who deny the possibility of conflict in order to save the consistency of morality, he does not adopt their secondary "indirectness" arguments to explain the experience of moral conflict. The shift from conflict of obligations (or duties) to conflicting *grounds* of obligation "saves the phenomena" directly.

The easiest reading of "grounds of obligation" is by analogy to Ross's prima facie obligations (Ross 1930). Grounds of obligation would provide reasons for action but no necessity. Conflict between grounds of obligation would be possible and resolved by having the stronger ground (reason) obligate. This strategy preserves the experience of conflict without producing a conflict *of duties*. (One could only have duties when the grounds did not conflict.) The necessity of the resulting obligation would be the necessity of best reasons.[8]

Kant's metaphors suggest that something else is going on. He says that if conflicts of duty *were* possible, the stronger duty would "hold the upper hand." That is, it would have compelling power, defeating or controlling the conflicting duty. This fits with a "balance of reasons" story. Conflict resolution through a balance of reasons is possible if the reasons (duties) present have different weights. One goes with the best or strongest reason, the duty that holds the upper hand. But the metaphor governing conflicting grounds of obligation is different: the stronger ground "holds the field." The metaphor is exclusionary and suggests that the weaker ground of obligation cannot gain the field at all—it has no effective weight in these circumstances.[9] There is no balance of reasons in the resolution of conflicting grounds of obligation. So we need to think again about what a ground of obligation could be.

If obligation marks moral requirement (practical necessity), then a ground of obligation ought to be that in virtue of which one is obliged. In Kantian ethics, the ground of obligation would be that which constrains what can be willed a universal law (under the rules of the two tests of the CI [categorical imperative] procedure).[10] Consider the duty (or obligation) of mutual aid. Because we cannot will a maxim of nonbeneficence a universal law—we are dependent rational beings for whom a law of mutual neglect cannot be rationally willed—we are directed by the CI procedure to acknowledge the needs of others as a possible moral reason for action.[11] The ground of the obligation is the fact that we are dependent beings, a fact that is salient in an agent's circumstances of action through the claim of need.

The ground of the Kantian prohibition on deceit is the integrity of the rational will itself.[12] Deceit is a means of controlling the will of another. A universal law of deceit is not possible, because it is not consistent with the integrity or separateness of agents. There is thus a prohibition on deceit (strictly, on maxims of deceit as a routine means). The ground of obligation in the circumstances of action is the conditions of the integrity of the will.

What these argument sketches are meant to suggest is that grounds of obligation are *facts* of a certain sort. They have moral significance because they are defining features of our (human) rational natures that limit what we can rationally will (as defined by the CI procedure). These facts enter moral deliberation, carrying with them the deliberative presumption that they will generate decisive reason for action (obligation) unless other "moral facts" in the circumstances of action rebut the presumption.[13] For example, if I am faced with someone who has a valid claim of need, I cannot appeal to facts of self-interest in deliberating whether I should offer help, because self-interest per se cannot rebut a moral presumption. I may consider (i.e., include in deliberation) any danger or risk to my life that may be involved in helping; these are morally salient facts. If there is no danger and I have the resources to meet the need, I must help.

Because grounds are facts, they cannot conflict. Facts may occasion conflict, given certain theoretical or practical constructions. The potential for moral conflict occurs when an agent must take account of more than one ground of obligation and she cannot directly take care of (act for) both. Moral conflict occurs when there are "two *grounds* of obligation (*rationes obligandi*) both present in one agent and in the rule he lays down for himself." Moral conflict, then, is *in the agent*, in her maxim of action. In other words, if an agent recognizes more than one moral fact (ground of obligation) in her circumstances of action, she *may* adopt a maxim of action that brings them into conflict. Recognizing both that her friend needs help and that she has a promise to keep, an agent may set herself to act on both grounds of obligation only to discover that acting on one will make acting on the other impossible. "In this case one or the other of these grounds is not sufficient to oblige." Conflicting grounds of obligation so understood are not the mark of inadequate deliberative procedures but indicate an occasion in which deliberation is necessary.

There are two things to note here. (1) The location of the conflict in the agent's rule or maxim provides the strongest sort of evidence that Kant does not restrict the idea of autonomy to the metaphysics of morals. This treatment of moral conflict suggests a quite literal understanding of autonomy as self-legislation. There is conflict because of the rule an agent *lays down for herself*. (2) Resolution of conflict in an agent's maxim requires a principle of deliberation. It is not a matter of weighing reasons. The question is whether the claim of need (of friends) rebuts the presumption (whatever it is) against promise breaking. If it does, then she ought to aid her friend and break her promise. If not, then she may not help her friend in these circumstances. (I am, of course, assuming here and in what follows that the CI procedure is or provides a principle of deliberation able to deliver results. It is not the point of the present project to show this. The task here is the more limited one of describing the kind of moral results the Kantian deliberative principles were intended to produce.)

The *result* of deliberation is obligation. The practical necessity that is the core of Kant's view of morality arrives as the agent determines which of the grounds of obligation present "binds to duty." Guided by the CI procedure, deliberation takes up grounds (plural) of obligation and determines obligation (singular). So we can say that a ground of obligation "holds the [deliberative] field" when it is not rebutted by the other relevant facts in the agent's circumstances of action *as* determined by the principle of deliberation (the CI procedure). Grounds of obligation by themselves do not give reasons for action at all. They are reason-giving only in the sense that they set terms of moral deliberation. The ought that Kantian deliberation yields is a moral ought, the ought of obligation and practical necessity.[14] In holding that moral deliberation issues in a requirement of practical necessity, one might say we have offered Kant's interpretation of the idea that the conclusion of the practical syllogism is action.

Whatever merits this kind of account may have in negotiating conflicts of duty, as an interpretation of Kant it seems incompatible with his commitment to juridical duties and duties of virtue (both plural). If there are such duties, they would surely seem to undermine the account of obligation I have just described as Kant's and make conflicts of duty, in the traditional sense, unavoidable.

Conflicts of duty are unavoidable when duties (or obligations) are conceived of as *performance* requirements, that is, as obligations to *do* certain actions (or kinds of action). What we must show, then, is that, understood as *moral* duties, the Kantian duties of virtue and justice are not "performance obligations."[15]

This is easiest to see with the duties of virtue. They do not constrain the agent to specific actions or courses of action but require the agent to take certain ends as her own (as "obligatory ends"). Actions that will promote one obligatory end can conflict with actions that support another. But since one has no obligation (or duty) to any particular action in support of an obligatory end, the incompatibility of actions promoting obligatory ends does not constitute moral conflict. This is not to say that these duties are "imperfect" in the sense that one is in any way free to determine when the duty applies. (The *spielraum* of obligatory ends leaves one to determine how, not whether, one will act.)

The necessity that comes with an obligatory end constrains not action but the will. The obligatory end of mutual aid requires that I attend to need. I am to acknowledge its claim on my actions and resources and accept a deliberative constraint or presumption on my maxims where there is a valid claim of need. Other duties of virtue require sensitivity to different facts and impose different deliberative constraints. One can think of the duties of virtue as elaborating the parameters of a single deliberative obligation: we must attend to a set of moral facts and give them deliberative standing in practical judgment. While it may be impossible to pay attention to some different sets of things at once, this possibility does not generate dilemmas: attention always has circumstantial limits. What is required is that we *not ignore* what is there.

Let us compare this account with a traditional conflict-generating one. Suppose that the lives of identical twins are in jeopardy and that through force of circumstance I am in a position to save only one. (The example is from Ruth Marcus; following her, I think of this and similar examples as "Buridan cases."[16]) Conflict of duty can seem unavoidable if we assume that there is an obligation to save each and that there are no moral grounds for choosing to save one twin over the other. No matter which twin I save, I had an obligation to the other that I did not meet.

Something blocks the natural thought that in such a case where the claims of the twins are of equal weight, where it makes no moral difference which of the twins I save, morality can underdetermine outcomes. I believe this option is rejected because the traditional account is committed to something like the following. If I have an obligation to help A, then there is no reason that could justify not helping A (if I can and the means are not impermissible). But if I also have an obligation to help B, and I can only help A or B, then I will necessarily act in a way that cannot be justified. In such circumstances the underdetermination of outcomes is unacceptable. One cannot honor both obligations, and morality gives no grounds for choice.

These difficulties do not arise for the Kantian obligation to aid in the Buridan saving case. One is obliged to acknowledge claims of need and to be prepared to help as and if one can. This obligation can be met for *both* twins. It remains true that if one acts to save A, one cannot act to save B (and vice versa). But in not saving B, one has *not* left one's obligation to B unfulfilled. One had no obligation to save B (or A). Having acknowledged the claim of both twins' needs and with no moral reason to prefer saving one twin over the other, everything that ought to be done is done in saving either one. (Acknowledgment plus preparation is not just idle talk; if one is ready to help both and circumstances change—the current suddenly sweeps the twins together—one is *already* committed to saving both.)

The Kantian account of the Buridan twins directs us through a set of problem cases. If someone's life is in jeopardy but we are separated by a deep river gorge, I can do nothing beyond acknowledging need and being prepared to act. I must act if I can; if I cannot, that is (morally) the end of it. This is also the case when we judge that I do not fail to act as I must if, having acknowledged a claim of need, I defer to someone better situated to save (another's help is preferable or more safely given). No obligation is left unfulfilled in these cases, though there is no action taken.

Performance obligations cannot manage these cases without strain. If I have no obligation where I cannot act to save, shifting circumstances may make my obligations come and go. In the river gorge, when I discover a bridge around the bend I then, for the *first time*, can have an obligation to save. (This makes it hard to explain any obligation to seek means that are not at hand.) In the "defer to the better saver" case, if we think I have no obligation when my help is not necessary (or preferred), then an obligation will once again "pop up" if it turns out that the better saver falters. (If we think I do have an obligation, then since only one of us can help, there will be an unmet obligation. Would this give us reason to compete to avoid this demerit?)

The Kantian model has no suddenly appearing or disappearing obligations. The cases are situational variants of the same obligation to aid. In each case I am obligated throughout: I acknowledge need and am prepared to act. I do not become obligated only as there is opportunity to act. In each case, whether I act or not, I can have fulfilled my obligation. This is equally so when I am unable to act (the gorge and the twins) and when I have good reason to refrain from acting (the better saver). As circumstances change (action becomes possible, etc.), the obligation that I *already* have is sufficient for action.

Since it may seem that the Kantian account depends on features special to the duty to aid, let us also look at the obligations associated with promises. They certainly seem to involve performance requirements and so to be occasions for conflicts of duty.

Take a second Buridan case, again from Marcus. "Under the single principle of promise-keeping, I might make two promises in all good faith and reason that they will not conflict, but then they do, as a result of circumstances that were unpredictable and beyond my control. All other considerations may balance out" (Gowans 1987, 192). The conclusion is that conflict is both possible and unresolvable. As before, the assumption behind this conclusion has to be that if I have an obligation to do X (here, keep a promise) and I am able to do X, I am not justified in not doing X.

Let us look at the obligation-generating "single principle of promise-keeping." To support the conclusion, it must give an agent an obligation to do what she has promised to do. This is a performance obligation: in promising to do X, I incur an obligation to do that thing. But if obligation carries practical necessity, this is at odds with the fact that we frequently think we have good reason not to do what we have promised to do.

There is no evidence that Kant believes we have a perfect duty of promise *keeping*. There are three grounds of obligation relating to promises. They concern making, keeping, and breaking promises. (One breaks a promise when one believes one has sufficient reason not do the promised thing; failure to keep a promise does not involve belief that one's action is justified, as when one has forgotten.) It is implausible to think we are obliged never to break a promise or never to fail to keep a promise. Insofar as we have a perfect duty to do anything, it is *not to make* a deceitful promise.[17]

Having made a promise, I have constrained my future deliberations in certain ways. This constraint on deliberation is in fact the content of the promising obligation. (I take this to be part of the elaboration of the claim that what is constrained in Kantian ethics is not deeds but willings, where will is the active face of practical reason.) I know that not wanting to keep the promise (or wishing I had not made it) is not a deliberative ground that rebuts the presumption that I am to act as I promised. On the other hand, if at the time when the promise is to be kept, I have good (moral) reason to do something else, then the deliberative presumption can be rebutted, and I am not required to do what I promised. Since the obligation in promising is a deliberative constraint, it is possible to be unable to do what one promised without failing one's obligation.[18]

In the Buridan promising case, whichever promise I keep (and it makes no moral difference which of the two it is), it follows that I will not be able to keep the other promise, but it does *not* follow that I have not done what I ought to have done *with regard to the promise I have not kept*. I can have satisfied the obligation (in the sense of deliberative constraint) imposed by both promises.

Furthermore, since among the deliberative constraints that reasonably come with making a promise is that we not knowingly do what will make keeping the promise impossible, we can explain why, if I have promised to repay a loan on Wednesday but squander the money on Tuesday, I have violated the obligation incurred by promising. Indeed, even if the cause of my not having the money on Wednesday is not my own doing (bank failure, theft, etc.), I do not cease to have the obligation. What will change is what I am to do in these new circumstances. It also does not follow that the promisee who failed to get what she was promised has no claim. That is a question for the casuistry of promising: the moral fact of an unkept promise may require some further action.[19]

For Kant, all obligation set by the duties of virtue and of justice issues from moral judgment or deliberation. When grounds of obligation conflict (they cannot both be taken up into an agent's maxim of action), one's obligation follows one's deliberative determination of the ground that "holds the field" or, when the grounds are the same, one's choice of action. There remain, of course, many differences between duties of virtue and duties of justice in the particulars of their deliberative requirements. What I have argued is that insofar as Kantian duties necessitate, they do not do so directly. Necessitation (obligation) is always the outcome of deliberation.

The Kantian concept of obligation protects the idea of practical necessity without generating dilemmas by not placing us under multiple standing or voluntary performance obligations. Moral conflict is experienced by an agent in circumstances where she is responsive to more than one ground of obligation and at least one of them cannot bind to obligation if the others do. There is no moral dilemma, because the grounds of obligation do not each obligate. The experience of conflict, of there being a moral problem, sets the agent a deliberative task, the resolution of which reveals her obligation. Although procedures of deliberation do not always dictate what to do, they (in principle, at least) resolve the status of competing moral claims. If the agent still needs to choose, even if the choice is hard, it will not be one horn of a moral dilemma.[20]

3

Although this way of understanding obligation saves the experience of conflict without introducing moral dilemmas, it does not resolve the issue entirely. There are those who argue that there are certain basic facts of morality that we must preserve even if they force acceptance of moral dilemmas. I think of this as the problem of the three Rs: remorse, restitution, and remainders. Each of the three Rs includes something that an adequate moral theory must address, but each also carries dilemma-generating assumptions about conflict and obligation. The question is whether we can preserve the basic facts they contain within the Kantian account of obligation. First, let us see why the three Rs in their customary presentation do not fit in the Kantian account.

Remorse When an agent is unable to meet a moral demand or requirement present in her circumstances of action, we take it to be a
good thing that the agent does not act without compunction (a feeling
of moral concern and caution, an awareness of moral danger). But
some hold that she ought to feel remorse (not just regret) for the
action not done, especially when the consequences of not acting are
grave. (It would be odd to think that one should feel remorse for
breaking a promise that puts the promisee in the way of some great
good fortune.) Eschewal of indirection arguments leaves the conclusion that if it is morally good for the agent to feel remorse, she has
done something wrong.[21] If remorse is the correct or good response
to situations of conflict, we cannot accept the Kantian account. The
Kantian agent does nothing wrong in acting as deliberation directs.

Restitution It is often held to be the case that the agent owes something in virtue of the un-acted-upon obligation, from as little as an
apology to as much as damages for harm incurred. We would not
owe unless we had done wrong: the very idea of restitution implies
repair of wrongful damages. An apology does moral repair work too.
It averts the damage to moral stature that would be incurred if one's
valid moral claims were left unacknowledged. (Some repairs are
necessary for maintenance: their omission lets a damaging condition
progress.) It is hard to see how the Kantian account could accept the
appropriateness of restitution if it denies that the agent has done
(any kind of) wrong in resolving a dilemma situation.

Remainders Remainders support the claims of restitution. It can
seem that if there were not moral remainders, there would be no
grounds to claim that something more needed to be done after the
"right" choice was made in a dilemma situation. Then, one will
conclude, if there is to be restitution, something of the unfulfilled
obligation must remain. But the Kantian resolution of the situation
of moral conflict leaves no unfulfilled (or un-acted-upon) obligations.

There is no good argument that justifies remorse or guilt in the
absence of wrongdoing. If I am unable to do what I think I ought to
have done, I often do feel guilty, even when I know my action is
justified. But I also often feel guilty when I am unable to bring
something about (say, a good thing for my child) that is neither mine
to bring about nor something that is a matter of obligation or wrongdoing. I do not think we are clear enough about guilt—about its role,
its place, its cognitive and affective content—to have much confidence in our guilt responses as foundations for theoretical claims.

And surely the myriad psychological accounts of the etiology of guilt should make us hesitant to read guilt feelings literally.

Perhaps confidence in the suitability of guilt to circumstances of conflict comes from hard cases. We are unable to imagine a moral agent who would not feel guilt at leaving one of the twins to drown. And we do take the inability to feel guilt about certain kinds of action as a sign of moral pathology, if not insanity. But this does not show much. The power of guilt to move and define us is so strong as to make it unlikely that these feelings are not co-opted by all sorts of private purposes and cultural projects (if it is not morality itself that has done the co-opting). There are many reasons that it should be hard to do certain kinds of action. Some actions should be impeded by inertial forces; others need to stay behind the barrier of a taboo. These limits, held in place by negative moral feelings, are appropriate constraints for imperfectly rational beings, for rational agents who have a character.

Even so, I think that we unnecessarily spread the occasions of guilt beyond wrongdoing. There are other morally more precise feelings to do the required instrumental work (compunction, repugnance, regret) that can, in addition, withstand "the dissolving force of analysis." So if we do not need guilt to secure a strong negative reaction in the face of the normally forbidden, it is hard to see how it could be morally good for an agent to feel guilt when she has done nothing wrong. *If* Agamemnon acted as he ought, whatever feelings he should have had (horror, a sense of pollution), guilt would not be called for.[22]

Some seem to think that guilt is simply a mark of good character in the face of those actions normally forbidden. No further purpose would need to be served by guilt any more than there is purpose served by the joy we feel at something gloriously beautiful. We might think that guilt, like joy, is constitutive of a certain sort of experience, the appropriate occurrence of which is the mark of a certain kind of character. Guilt is a retrospective feeling; prospectively, it works as a form of fear. To encourage a guilt response independent of wrongdoing would create a certain sort of moral character, to be sure. But it seems a dubious thing to encourage dissociation of a moral feeling held to be constitutive of good character from correct moral belief.

There is a better case for the other two Rs. We want the agent to do *something* in the face of unmet obligation. And if restitution brings things morally back to a former condition, it is appropriate only if there is something for which we need to make amends. While remainders per se do not imply wrongdoing (actions leave all kinds of things behind), if the thought is that there is remaining unmet obligation, something that ought to have been done but was not, then of course remainders do imply wrongdoing (even if excused or justified wrongdoing). The claim of restitution is easiest to make if there are such remainders.

The problem is that the three *R*s, as customarily presented, are basic terms in a particular theory of moral failures. If they seem natural to us, it is because we accept the performance theory of obligation that makes them necessary. When one holds that obligations require performances, the unmet obligation in a conflict situation is a justified nonperformance, an omission. It could not be the ground of any (further) moral requirement unless the unmet performance obligation leaves a remainder (the limiting case being the wrong done by leaving the obligation unmet). Only then is there something substantial to proceed from (and something to feel guilt about when restitution is not possible).

Accepting an account that depends on performance obligations brings costs beyond the theoretical difficulties that attend conflicts of duty. There are also serious practical consequences in the way performance obligations construct a certain kind of moral life. This is most easily seen by following the economic metaphors that are often used in accounts of these obligations. Take the Buridan promises again. If we hold that an agent acting to meet the obligation of the first promise fails to meet the other obligation, we find it natural to say that because of the unmet obligation, there is a balance due, a debt that is owed. It is incumbent upon a responsible agent to discharge the remaining obligation, to clear her balance. Because it is inefficient not to have clarity and finality about the balance due, a likely demand on the casuistry of promising will be for clear determinations of the appropriate response to various kinds of broken promises. To have made a promise is to have set oneself to a certain performance. If justified promise breaking leaves remainders, then one is in the wrong unless one clears this up. The second performance wipes the slate clean. (This sort of thinking can lead to the view that promise keeping and promise breaking plus restitution are morally equivalent.[23] Making a promise opens an account that either action can close.)

These metaphors extend beyond promises to other forms of obligation: to our families, to the state, even to friends. Obligations are burdens to be discharged, interfering with the real business of our lives. If we are good or better than good, we discharge our obligations cheerfully. If we are not so good (and far from bad), we just do what we have to do. Whichever we are, with this understanding of what it is to have an obligation, it is irrational not to want them to be over and done with.

I suspect that this view of obligation is one of the reasons that a recent strand of moral theorizing has been so opposed to accepting obligation as the basic category of morality (Blum 1980, Williams 1976b). It is argued that thinking of the moral relations between persons in terms of obligations produces estrangement from one's actions and from others. So an obligation to help others leads us to view their needs as demands on our resources, and the morality of obligation requires only that the need be met, not that one care. Of particular concern are special relationships such as friendship. If one wants to regard friendship as a moral relationship (or a relationship having moral components), then it is ill described in the language of obligations. It is because we view friendship as an ongoing affective relationship that the metaphors of "discharging what is owed" or "clearing one's balance" are not only inappropriate but destructive. The needs of friends are not to be thought of as burdens (though they may come to be burdensome), and acts of friendship are not discrete required performances but expressions of a continuing friendship.

The mistake in this critique is not in the view of the morality of aid or friendship but in the uncritical acceptance of the performance conception of obligation.

One of the reasons we hang on to this conception, I believe, is the need to support the three Rs, especially remainders. Without remainders it is not clear how an agent could be further obligated (to apologize, make restitution, etc.) in cases of moral conflict, especially when her nonperformance is justified. But with remainders we have to accept the theoretical consequences of unavoidable wrongdoing.

The deep attractiveness of the Kantian conception of obligation is that it can both do the work assigned to remainders and be free of the real defects of the performance conception.

The Kantian conception of obligation does not need to leave remainders to provide a basis for ongoing moral requirement. In circumstances of moral conflict, the agent is presented with a deliberative problem whose resolution leaves her obliged to act as deliberation directs. With Buridan promises, having done one of the things promised, the agent's circumstances change; they now contain the fact of the unkept (or broken) promise. This is a new situation, setting a new deliberative problem. If restitution is in order, it will be because of the circumstances the agent comes to be in having acted as she ought. Restitution does not require remainders.

Because the unkept promise in the Buridan case does not mark an unmet obligation, there is no wrong done. And if there is no sense in which the agent has left anything morally required undone, there are no remainders. There is nothing to feel remorse or guilt about.

The language and metaphors of obligation are different too. If what it is to be obliged is to be under the practical necessity of acting as moral deliberation directs, obligation is not a matter of required performances but of commitment to a way of determining how one is to act. The Kantian agent lives in a very different kind of moral space than that created by "performance obligations." It is direct (as opposed to indirect) in its requirements, morally transparent in a sense, and, as I will argue, able to integrate morality more intimately into an agent's life. When an agent acts as Kantian deliberation directs in conflict situations, it is not the case that she is meeting one obligation while failing to meet another (that is, she does not do two things—one good, the other requiring justification and leaving remainders, wrongs done, etc.). She acts as she ought on the ground of obligation that is sufficient in these circumstances to oblige her. She does one thing. Because of what she does, it may turn out that she must later do something else, since in acting, she moves from a situation in which she faces two grounds of obligation to one in which she faces a new one, or more than one, according to what is morally present in her new situation.

In changing the understanding of obligation, one also changes what particular duties are about. On the performance model of obligation, making a promise commits one to a performance or, upon failure, remainder management. Continuity of obligation across nonperformance was secured by remainders. On the Kantian model, the commitment is to a procedure of deliberation that not only includes concern with performance but is equally and from the outset responsive to the full moral features of the agent's changing circumstances of action.

Having made a promise, the agent has initiated an ongoing deliberative commitment to take into account the particulars of the promise, the conditions and opportunities of successful performance, as well as the deliberative significance of an unkept promise, justified or unjustified. (These need not be the only things she has committed herself to.) There is no guarantee that her obligation will be closed-ended. While it does not follow from the fact that not keeping a promise causes some harm that the agent who causes it thereby has responsibility for relieving, responsibility is possible—even when not keeping the promise is justified—as neither fault nor remainders are required to sustain continuing obligation. The point of a casuistry for promises is not to produce an account of what one owes (the "alternatives" to keeping one's promise), but to provide a method of determining what is morally salient in the making, keeping, and breaking of promises. Casuistry does not settle the issues in advance; it gives deliberative guidance.

One might say that regarding promises as deliberative commitments does not so much give you a future task that you must perform (or else . . .) as it alters to a greater or lesser degree the way your life will go on. As rational agents with autonomy, we make plans and prepare to create a future. Of course, our creative powers are limited and affected by the activities of others (thus the insistence in the *Rechtslehre* on enlarging external freedom compatible with like freedom for others).[24] But to acknowledge our autonomy is to refuse passivity (the practical denial of determinism); we view ourselves as making our lives. To make a promise is to introduce new deliberative considerations that carry weight against our other projects. We may need to alter present activities to prepare for doing what we promised; we know that we cannot guarantee performance and so may be responsible for events beyond the scope of the actual promise. And so on. The casuistry of promising describes the deliberative constraints an autonomous agent accepts in making a promise. Analogous deliberative constraints constitute our other moral requirements (the "duties" of justice and virtue).

Morality shapes—perhaps codefines—what our lives will look like. If morality were about obligations, performance obligations, it would be reasonable to regard it as external to us, introducing limits and constraints from outside the course of our activity. It would then be natural to think of morality as something imposed, something we wish to be free of. Such a picture of morality makes it hard to explain attachment to morality; it is not obvious why one should want to increase one's burdens.

It might look this way: since we already have a variety of things limiting our activity—natural forces, physical limitations, the activity of others—why should we volunteer to further decrease our effective freedom? It will then seem that the only possible answer is that the very limits morality imposes actually increase our freedom—*if* enough others also accept them. This introduces indirectness and ambivalence at the outset. The burdens imposed by the obligations do not correlate with the conditional good produced. Even the agent who accepts this morality will, insofar as she is rational, experience it as external and estranging, as something she would elude if she could.

One cannot care for something when what you primarily want to do is discharge it at reasonable cost. A normal moral agent will feel morality separate from her life. She will accrue a goodness score and perhaps value herself on its scale of performance success. But her moral obligations take her away from her life and she pursues them with a different structure of concern and care than the projects which she takes to make her life worth living.

By contrast, the Kantian account of morality does not work from a set of constraining obligations. Its central notion is the agent as rational deliberator. Accepting morality involves deliberative commitment both to a way of thinking about one's life and choices and to acting as deliberation directs. One's deliberative frame no longer locates one's life at the center nor places morality along with other constraints at the boundaries as external, confining, limiting one's possibilities. The basic field of deliberation contains not only my interests and private projects but also the interests of others as possible sources of claims on my actions and resources. The grounds of obligation partially create the practical world I live in.[25] Moral requirements are part of the fabric of the practical world and require attention independently of my wishes.

This is why I believe the Kantian model of obligation is not destructive of friendship or of other care-based moral relations. If friendship is a moral relationship (or has a moral dimension), then there will be alterations in one's deliberative field as one has friends (and different elements introduced as one has different kinds of friends). Morality does not cause the needs of friends to be regarded as burdens or in competition with the needs of strangers. If among the moral features of friendship is a more stringent duty of mutual aid, then the needs of one's friends will occupy higher ground in the deliberative field. One will be open to the needs of friends in a way that one is not to the needs of strangers. There is not only commitment to giving friends' needs some kind of deliberative priority, one is committed to being more attentive to the possibility and occasions of their need. There need be no separation between morality and caring.

The charge that Kantian impartiality requires that one gives no precedence to friends' needs, that it requires rigid even-handedness, just assumes that there is no distinctive moral dimension to friendship. It may well be that Kantian ethics challenges some assumptions about the content of obligations of friendship, but that would be as deliberation directed and not because the very idea of obligation excludes the value of special commitments. "That she is my friend" may be a very good moral reason to provide help. This does not preclude there being some circumstances in which attention to the complete deliberative field shows that giving preference to friends is not justified.

Many of the examples in the philosophical literature tell a story of moral requirement as an intrusion or interrupting errand. I am on my way to meet a friend for lunch, as promised, when I see an accident occur. I deliberate, May I (or must I) break my promise to rescue the accident victims? Walking across a bridge, I see a child struggling in the water. Must I go out of my way, risk my health, be late to a very important meeting, to try to save her?

These moral tales have me on my way in morally neutral territory when something "outside" my narrative happens. Morality intrudes. Moral inquiry determines the nature and degree of this interference with my story (my "business"). The metaphor embedded in this narrative structure practically makes it the case that I must most want to be on my way, to get on with what I was doing. Interruption is bad enough; absence of closure is intolerable. So, concluding that I must stop to save the child, we do not even ask, in the philosophical story, "What must I do next?"

It is understandable that we should want what morality requires of us to be finite. We have our lives to live. And even when we are prepared to live our lives within the confines of morality, we expect our engagement with morality's positive requirements to be something we can negotiate and go on from, like a necessary errand in the middle of the day. We are thus somewhat more comfortable with the omnipresence of negative moral requirements, for they introduce limits on means rather than detours away from our ends.

Different moral conceptions carry different narrative models. How we think about the fit of morality with our lives affects what the narrative of a life looks like. Performance obligations yield narrative interruptions. Kantian obligation yields ongoing, narratively central, deliberative commitment. And not surprising, each narrative structure offers different possibilities of integration into a self-conception, or a conception of oneself as a particular kind of moral agent. The hero of Kantian narrative has a conception of herself as an autonomous agent among others. The hero of the conventional morality of performance obligations is well described by the individual of liberal theory: triumphant in the face of obstacles (including morality) in the pursuit of private goals.

The different narrative models bring with them different views about closure. The agent who views herself as attentive to the moral features of the deliberative field has no special reason to wish for closure. As need is a sign of distress, she must wish for the end of need; as an unkept promise may cause hurt or loss, she has reason to respond. In neither case is her interest in closure per se. That moral requirement may be open-ended is the nature of moral requirement. Sometimes circumstances may be such that moral demands exhaust the deliberative field; at other times it may be easy to attend to what morality presents but exhausting to care for oneself. In living a moral life the agent knows there is uncertainty about the different demands that will be made on her resources. Some of these demands will be out of her control. (In this regard morality is not badly modeled by our view of the good parent: one simply cannot know in advance what having a child will do to one's life. It may be that life goes on much as before, amplified in some areas, restricted in others. But it may equally be that one's life is utterly altered in ways that have nothing to do with choice because of the actual needs of one's children. One then lives a different life.)

By contrast, the agent whose life narrative is constrained and interrupted by morality cannot be sanguine about open-ended requirements. One may accept that one's life has to be within the moral frame, but as with most practical matters, excessive interruption undermines the possibility of successful activity. Some individuals may be able to accept high levels of moral demand under perceived conditions of emergency. But we talk then of "putting one's life on hold" to deal with the tasks at hand.

We are not free to think about the place of morality in our lives any way we want to. The narrative fit of morality is dependent on the kind of moral requirement that is central to the moral conception we accept. This is not a matter of theory—something we can ignore "for practical purposes." Our self-understanding, our appreciation of our lives (what we do, what we have accomplished) is very much a function of how we understand our connection to morality.

It may seem that in my account of the different ways one might look at obligation, I have located deliberation in only one kind of moral theory. That, of course, is not the case. Every moral conception requires that agents deliberate about what to do. What distinguishes the Kantian conception is the idea of a unified deliberative field.[26] What matters, what is of value, including both the agent's preferences (her interests, in the traditional sense) and the moral features of her circumstances, is presented in the field. (Attention to all of the elements of the field is not automatic and may not even be possible. But this is not a special problem for the moral elements of the field. We are equally familiar with difficulties there can be in attending to some kinds of needs and deeper interests.) Because the field is unified, the agent does not engage in multiple courses of deliberation: what I want to do, what would be good for me, what morality requires, etc. We do not determine what, on the one hand, morality requires, and what, on the other, one ought to do "all things considered." It is incumbent on the agent to perceive the grounds of obligation and the grounds of other concerns that are present. The presence of the former may determine the deliberative status of the latter. One might say that there are differences in value *in* the deliberative field. Making a promise, for example, introduces a deliberative presumption against reasons of mere self-interest. An interest that gave sufficient reason to act before the promise was made may no longer do so. The mere fact of interest may not now be reason enough to occasion deliberation. The promise alters the terrain of the deliberative field.

A deliberative presumption introduces value considerations whose effects are not correctly described in terms of greater weight. Their presence may exclude some sorts of considerations altogether and give others authority in the deliberative field. This contrasts with the usual view of reasons and deliberation. When "X is a reason" (or "X is of value") implies that X has a certain practical weight (either in itself or relative to other sorts of reasons), then X must be counted in deliberation. For most X, some sum of other reasons (values) will be equivalent in weight. This kind of arithmetic is not implied by the concept of value itself; it is a particular conception of value with strong normative consequences. It not only makes us think of deliberation as a kind of summing; it suggests that there must be some kind of currency of value in which value weight can be expressed. Indeed, it can seem that unless this is so, the heterogeneity of value would make deliberation impossible.

Kantian deliberation protects the heterogeneity of value by excluding nothing from the deliberative field. The principles of obligation regulate what will be salient in deliberation in view of the facts of the agent's actual circumstances of action. An autonomous moral agent sees a complex world containing physical, social, and moral limits *and* possibilities. Some of what the agent finds is unalterable. Other features are reflections of contingent circumstances and structures. The principles of deliberative morality introduce practical order, making the world a human one.

Notes

1. For the purposes of this chapter there is no need to distinguish conflicts of duty and moral dilemmas. In the literature with which I am concerned, the latter is of interest only as it appears to be an instance of the former.

2. Whatever important differences there may be between "duty" and "obligation" in some moral theories, in discussions of moral dilemmas they do not function differently: each carries a moral requirement, an ought, that is not cancelled by the fact of conflict and that cannot be set aside at the discretion of the agent. Because I am most concerned with this fact of our being obligated, with the "practical necessity" or morality, I will sometimes talk about conflicts of duty as involving competing obligations.

3. There are some (e.g., Bradley (1927) and Nagel (1979c)) who do not think morality contains, even in theory, a consistent set of requirements. If the requirements are not internally ordered and there is no set of principles that can sort them, then moral agents are left with the practical task of developing a kind of character that can withstand the effects of moral indeterminacy without collapse into cynicism.

4. This problem could be elicited directly from cases where it may seem that one ceases to have an obligation to do X once one chooses to do Y, even if one chooses to do Y in order to avoid doing X. There are, of course, solutions to such cases, but they too undermine any simple inference that inability shows absence of obligation.

5. If the narrow reading is defensible, it is hardly self-evidently so. Perhaps I have no obligation to pay my debt on Wednesday when I cannot, but a theory that accepted this could plausibly do so only if it had other resources to account for the obligations I do have in virtue of the reasons why I no longer have the obligations I did have.

6. Perhaps confusion about the wide and narrow readings of "Ought implies can" explains our puzzlement over Aristotle's insistence on responsibility for parts of our character we cannot now change.

7. "Wenn zwei solcher Gründe einander widerstreiten, so sagt die praktische Philosophie nicht: daß die stärkere Verbindlichkeit die Oberhand behalte (. . .), sondern der stärkere Verpflichtungsgrund behälte den Platz (. . .)."

8. Ross is not always consistent in what he understands a prima facie obligation to be. At times he presents prima facie obligations as reason-giving, and conflict is resolved through the balance of reasons (what one is obliged to do emerges only after the balancing of reasons). At other times what it means to have a prima facie obligation is that it is an obligation one would have had except for the presence of another, weightier, obligation. Then conflict is not between two duties or obligations, nor between two prima facie obligations. There are two instances of duty kinds, one of which is prima facie my duty, the other is my duty. I think this second picture of conflict is much closer to Kant, though Ross's view of obligation is hardly the same as Kant's.

9. Owen Flanagan reminded me that what is kept off a field may exact some toll in its exclusion. It does not follow, however, that it therefore has weight in the "balance of reasons" sense.

10. It is now customary to refer to the two tests of the categorical imperative for determining the permissibility of agents' maxims of action as the "CI procedure." The first test asks whether it is possible to conceive of your maxim as a universal law without contradiction; the second whether it is possible to will your maxim a universal law without your will contradicting itself. (See Rawls 1989; O'Neill 1975, 1985.)

11. See Herman 1984b, where the argument that a law of mutual neglect cannot be rationally willed is spelled out.

12. See Herman 1990 for a fuller sketch of this argument.

13. This account of moral deliberation is developed in Herman, unpublished.

14. It does not follow from the claim that deliberation resolves conflict that the ground of obligation that does not "bind to duty" is to be ignored. It can occasion *further* deliberation. This and related issues are taken up in section 3.

15. Moral duties are here contrasted with juridical duties in a public order. Such duties are identified as actions that can be legitimately coerced by public authority. Treating promising as a duty that also belongs to ethical theory, in the sense of having a derivation independent of law, may not be something Kant would have accepted. However, because of the recent habit of regarding promises as canonical examples of ethical duties and because nothing in this discussion depends on promising being an ethical duty, I will proceed as if it were.

16. In Gowans 1987, p. 192. Marcus uses this example to show that no single-principled theory can avoid conflict. It is therefore quite suitable to our purpose here of explaining how Kantian theory is both single-principled *and* conflict-avoiding.

17. This is not quite right, for it suggests we may never make a deceitful promise. I think the perfect duty that Kant has in mind is more restricted: one may not make a deceitful promise for reasons of self-interest. The argument for this is to be found in Herman, unpublished.

18. Even Nietzsche does not think that it is our ability to perform the action we promised that makes promising defining of moral nature—we have no such ability. What promising signifies is our ability to stand guarantor for ourselves for what we will.

19. This argument is elaborated in Herman 1990.

20. Faced with the prospect of having to let one twin drown, one would feel a deep sense of conflict at the prospect of having to choose where no reasoned choice is possible and where the costs are so large. This is wholly compatible with the absence of moral dilemma.

21. If we *excuse* the untaken action because of the circumstances of conflict (as with the Buridan cases), we are thereby committed to the thought that the agent did something wrong. In such cases some are tempted to say that the agent did not "act wrongfully" in "doing something wrong." Embedding the excuse in this way does not clarify the question of whether remorse is an appropriate response.

22. I find it hard to believe that our sense that he ought to have felt guilt is not rather a sign that we believe his action was horribly wrong. We would do better, I think, to avoid Agamemnon (and like examples) in seeking either illustrations or evocations of our moral intuitions. The power of these stories is in their complexity and ambiguity, a feature all the more exaggerated by their role in the purposes of the classical dramatists.

23. There is a view of contracts where what one has agreed to is *either* the performance of the terms of the contract *or* nonperformance and a payment that meets the original value of the agreed to performance. This view is justified as giving protection to the parties when changing costs make staying with the terms of the contract unfairly burdensome.

24. One does not want to exaggerate the claims for autonomy. Although as a rational agent with autonomy I view my life as a kind of creative activity—the expression of my causality and plans in the world—it may be that my actual circumstances of living do not permit effective activity and may even undermine my capacity for conceiving a life. Such facts can be grounds for the moral criticism of oppressive social institutions.

25. The claim that moral facts alter the world is a claim within the domain of the practical, not a gambit in the metaphysics of moral realism. The world a rational

agent lives in contains moral facts, features that demand attention and that carry deliberative significance.

26. John Rawls (1989) develops a similar interpretation of Kant in the idea of a moral framework through which the autonomous agent constructs a complete conception of the good.

Chapter 15

Rational Egoism, Self, and Others

David O. Brink

Commonsense thinking about the nature of morality and the role of moral considerations in practical reasoning is, I think, ambivalent. On the one hand, most of us regard moral considerations as important practical considerations. We are sensitive to moral criticism, and we expect our moral advice and argument, if accepted, to influence the action of others. One explanation of these attitudes and expectations is that we think that moral considerations, for instance moral obligations, give agents reason—indeed, especially strong reason—for action.

But many of us are also prepared to entertain serious doubts about the justifiability of morality. Commonsense views about the content of morality and philosophical moral theories typically agree in representing morality as impartial in important respects. Morality asks each agent to see herself as one point of value among others in a moral universe in which the lives of others make certain claims upon her. She has negative obligations to refrain from harming others' interests in certain ways and positive obligations to help others in living decent and interesting lives. But these other-regarding aspects of morality can seem to constrain the agent's own pursuit of a valuable life. Especially when the constraints imposed upon the agent by other-regarding moral demands are substantial, we see an apparent conflict between living well and living right or morally. To this extent many of us wonder and perhaps doubt whether moral behavior and moral concern are always or even generally rationally justifiable.

I share this ambivalence; I take these doubts about the justifiability of morality seriously, but I'm committed to seeing to what extent these doubts can be resolved. Because these doubts are motivated by *egoist* assumptions about rationality, I want to explore egoist attempts to justify morality.

1 A Skeptical Challenge

We might reformulate the source of these worries about the justifiability of morality as the following argument for *amoralist moral skepticism*—skepticism not about the existence of moral requirements but about their rational authority.[1]

> 1. An agent has reason to do x just insofar as x contributes to his interests, welfare, or happiness.
>
> 2. An agent's happiness or welfare can be specified independently of the happiness of others, for instance, in terms of his pleasure or in terms of the satisfaction of his desires.
>
> 3. Morality often requires agents to benefit others or refrain from harming them.
>
> 4. These patterns of benefit and restraint often fail to promote the agent's own independent good (e.g., his pleasure or the satisfaction of his desires).
>
> 5. Hence, being moral often detracts from an agent's own happiness or welfare.
>
> 6. Hence, agents often fail to have reason to be moral.

It's clear that a justification of morality requires the denial of (6); it's less clear how much, if any, more the justification of morality requires. Some believe that we haven't vindicated the authority of moral considerations or their importance in practical deliberation unless we can show that they provide every agent on every occasion with not only strong but overriding reason for action. Others doubt that this sort of justification of morality is either possible or necessary. They allow that we may not always have conclusive reason to be moral; they think it a sufficient vindication of the authority of morality if we can show that people generally have sufficient reason to be moral. Rejection of (6), they think, is a sufficient justification of morality. In what follows, I will discuss various issues about the scope and weight of different justifications of morality, but I won't try to settle this debate about the exact standards for a successful reply to the skeptic. Because (6) is trouble enough, we might begin by focusing on it. Reconstructing the skeptical argument in this way allows us to see different methods of response.

One response would be to deny (3), to revise common conceptions of the demands of morality by dropping its other-regarding aspects so as to eliminate conflicts between morality and the agent's rational self-interest. This strategy might be plausibly employed as a supplement to some other strategy, but as the sole ground for resisting (6), this cure seems as bad as the disease. Our commonsense moral views should be revisable. But the injunctions to help others and refrain from harming them are not peripheral features of our conception of morality; they are central to it. The conception of morality with which this strategy would leave us would be so emasculated that we should not recognize this as a strategy for justifying morality. This way of denying (6), therefore, represents a *skeptical solution* to this skeptical argument and so represents only a Pyrrhic victory over the skeptic.[2]

Premise (1) states *egoist* assumptions about the nature of reasons for action.[3] Rational egoism is an *agent-relative* theory of rationality, because it makes an agent's reasons for action depend only upon how her actions might affect *her* welfare, interest, or happiness. An *agent-neutral* theory denies this; it takes an agent's reasons for action to be a direct function of the value her actions would produce, whether this value accrues to the agent or not (e.g., to others instead). Agent-relative theories of rationality seem to assume that *sacrifice requires compensation,* that is, that an agent has reason to make a sacrifice, say, to benefit another, if and only if the agent receives some (sufficient) benefit in return. Agent-neutral theories, by contrast, deny that sacrifice requires compensation.

One reply to the skeptic, therefore, would be to reject (1) and justify agent-neutral theories of rationality. Then there would seem to be little difficulty justifying morality's other-regarding demands, because on agent-neutral assumptions about rationality, the rationality of sacrifice does not require compensation and an agent's reasons for action are directly proportional to the good she can do. Once we realize that the welfare of others provides the agent with equally strong and equally direct reasons for action, we seem to remove doubts about the justification of morality.[4]

This is a perfectly appropriate strategy. But it is the proponent of agent-neutrality who bears the burden of proof *here.* Agent-relative assumptions are an important part of the worry about the justifiability of morality. For it is only if we assume that the rationality of sacrifice requires compensation, as the agent-relative theory claims, that we can explain why it should seem hard to explain why I have reason to sacrifice my own interests to benefit others, as morality seems to require. So by taking this skeptical argument seriously, we assign rational egoism the "default setting" (as it were); we need to justify the adoption of agent-neutral assumptions about reasons for action.

This is not the strategy that I shall pursue here. Instead, I want to explore the resources available to the rational egoist to respond to moral skepticism. Friends of rational egoism can regard one or more of the remaining methods of reply as the preferred line(s) of response to the skeptic, while friends of agent-neutrality can regard these remaining methods as interesting ad hominem strategies of response.

The skeptical challenge to the egoist is, of course, to explain how benefiting others and refraining from harming them in the ways that morality requires is in one's own interest. There are two general methods of response available to the rational egoist, corresponding to the two remaining premises in the skeptic's argument. The first method accepts the common assumption in (2) that an agent's happiness can be specified independently of the happiness of others (e.g., in hedonistic or desire-satisfaction terms) but denies (4); it argues that the patterns of benefit and restraint characteristic of morality are in fact the most reliable means for advancing the agent's own, independent good. The second method denies (2). It claims that there is a noncontingent relation between the agent's good and the good of others; it tries to justify the sort of other-regarding concern characteristic of morality by arguing that the good of others is *part* of the agent's own good in the appropriate way. In the rest of this paper I'd like to explore the resources available to these two sorts of egoist methods and assess their prospects of success.

2 A Subjective Egoist Justification of Morality

Consider egoist justifications of morality that accept (2). Premise (2) claims that the good of the agent can be specified independently of the good of others. This premise is satisfied on two familiar theories of value: hedonism and the desire-satisfaction theory. According to hedonism, the simple, qualitative mental state of pleasure is the one and only intrinsic good, and the simple, qualitative mental state of pain is the one and only intrinsically bad thing. According to the desire-satisfaction theory, the satisfaction of desire is the one and only intrinsically good thing, and the frustration of desire is the one and only intrinsically bad thing. We might call these theories of welfare *subjective*, because they make a person's welfare consist in or depend importantly upon certain of the person's contingent psychological states, and we might call any version of rational egoism that incorporates a subjective theory of welfare a form of *subjective egoism*.[5] My question is whether the subjective egoist can justify morality's other-regarding demands.

Some individuals may experience pleasure as a result of causing pleasure or preventing pain for others, and some may have desires that others do well that will only be satisfied if they contribute to the satisfaction of others' desires. (Of course, there will be a problem if everyone has exclusively other-regarding desires.) The egoist might appeal, as Hume does in his claims about sympathy (1978, II, i, 11/ 316–318, III, iii, 1/575–591), to the psychological facts that people have the capacities for personal and social relationships that involve mutual respect and concern and that they derive pleasure from the exercise of these capacities.

However, it's just not clear that the relevant psychological claims are *universally* true. It does not seem to be true that everyone enjoys or desires being related to others in ways that satisfy our obligations to others. Those who don't may be deviants (e.g., sociopaths), but it's not clear that subjective egoism can expose any irrationality in them. Moreover, even if it turns out that everyone has some such desires for the welfare of others and takes pleasure in satisfying these desires, this fact does not itself justify this sort of other-regarding concern. Even if I do desire the well-being of others and derive some pleasure from benefiting them, doing so consumes resources that might have produced at least as much good for me had I consumed them myself. Why shouldn't I, as a rational egoist, cultivate these more self-confined attitudes and allow these other-regarding attitudes to wither? Or to put the same point another way, we can see why I will have subjective-egoist reason to benefit others if I already have other-regarding desires, but why should I cultivate or maintain such other-regarding desires? The appeal to the psychological fact that people often have such desires does not explain why they are rationally appropriate. Finally, even if we concede that these other-regarding concerns do provide us with reasons for action, this tells us nothing about the *comparative strength* of these other-regarding attitudes in people's psychology or of the reasons for action that they support. A convincing justification of morality should show that people typically or at least often have *compelling* reason, and not just *a* reason, to be moral. And while it is implausible that everyone always has such other-regarding attitudes, it is even more implausible that these other-regarding attitudes are always or even usually stronger than more self-confined attitudes. But then an appeal to the existence of these other-regarding attitudes will not establish that people have sufficient or conclusive reason to sacrifice their interests for the sake of others, as morality sometimes seems to require.[6]

The subjective egoist can also appeal, as Sidgwick does (1981, 136, 403), to the paradox of hedonism (see also Butler 1950, sermon xi, pars. 1, 9). The paradox of hedonism is that an agent will likely fail to maximize his own pleasure by consciously attempting to do so and is much more likely to promote his own pleasure by cultivating concerns for activities and other people for their own sakes.

But there's no obvious reason why the projects and relationships that fulfill this function should cover all of other-regarding morality. My projects might just be hobbies (e.g., stamp collecting), and my relationships may include only a few intense friendships. This may give me the sort of false targets necessary to promote my own pleasure more effectively, but it won't give me the full range of concerns that a moral agent must have.

3 A Strategic Defense

One familiar subjective-egoist method of justifying morality concedes the existence of a conflict between the agent's own immediate good and the good of others but attempts to provide a justification of morality's other-regarding components by arguing that for strategic reasons the agent can maximize his own good in the *long-run* by forgoing his immediate good to some extent in order to benefit others. This reply promises to be explanatory in a way that the mere appeal to other-regarding attitudes is not; if successful this reply will explain why a rational agent should cultivate and maintain such attitudes.

My subjective good depends to a large extent upon other people: either upon their cooperation in projects of advantage to me or upon their refraining from interference in my solitary pursuit of projects and plans. The subjective egoist can try to show why it is in an agent's own interest to cooperate with others in projects of mutual advantage and to refrain from harming others in various ways, even on the assumption that cooperation and restraint are costs that the agent would otherwise prefer to forgo. We might call this reply a *strategic defense.*[7]

Consider the case of cooperation with others. I make an agreement with you to exchange services in a mutually advantageous way. If I could get your help without giving mine in return, on the assumption that cooperation is a cost, I would be better off by not giving mine. If ours is a single transaction and you have already given me your help, I would be better off, it seems, to withhold mine. This won't be true if this is the first of many transactions with you from which I would like to benefit; if I fail to keep my part of the agreement this time, you are likely to refuse to offer me any more help. In fact, this won't be true even if this is our only transaction if you are likely to inform others, whose services I desire, that I am noncompliant.

Strictly, all this gives me reason to do is to maintain the *appearance* that I have complied. But, the strategic egoist might argue, the easiest way of maintaining the appearance of compliance is by the *fact* of compliance. This is clearly demonstrated by my agreement with you. If I agreed to give you a gallon of moonshine in exchange for viola lessons, then in order to sustain our system of cooperation, I must maintain the appearance of fulfilling my part of the deal. But, of course, the easiest way to do that is to give you a gallon of moonshine. Moreover and more generally, because it will clearly be in others' interests that the agent be cooperative and restrained, we can see how communities will tend to reinforce compliant behavior and dispositions and discourage noncompliant behavior and dispositions. Community pressure and education will, therefore, foster the development of fairly coarse-grained other-regarding sentiments, and these psychological mechanisms will help ensure that the easiest way of maintaining the appearance of compliance is by the fact of compliance.

The strategic defense of cooperation (or restraint) has three main parts:

a. It is in the agent's interest to receive the benefits of a system of cooperation (or restraint).

b. The benefits of a system of cooperation (or restraint) are only available to those who maintain the appearance of cooperation (or restraint).

c. The easiest way to maintain the appearance of cooperation (or restraint) is by being cooperative (or restrained).

The egoist maintains that because the sort of cooperation and restraint characteristic of the other-regarding aspects of morality satisfies conditions (a) through (c), compliance with these other-regarding features of morality represents the best strategy for promoting the agent's own long-run good.

4 Problems with the Strategic Justification of Morality

There are a number of problems, or at least serious limitations, in this egoist justification of morality (cf. Sidgwick 1981, 164–170, 499–503).

One limitation is that there are systems of cooperation (or restraint) from which the agent can benefit, where cooperation (or restraint) is or can be a moral obligation, but that fail to satisfy condition (b). These situations concern what social theorists call "public goods." Roughly, a public good is any object or state of affairs such that, if available to some member(s) of a group, it is available to all others, including those who have not shared in the costs of producing it (e.g., clean air, energy conservation, population control, political participation, the rule of law, and national defense).[8] When these conditions are met, the public good is threatened by free-riders. A rational individual will reason as follows:

1. Whether I contribute or not, either (a) enough others will contribute to produce the good or they will not (if the provision of the good is all or nothing) or (b) my contribution will have a negligible effect on the amount of the good available to me (if the provision of the good is continuous).
2. My contribution is a nonnegligible cost to me.
3. If enough others will contribute, either (a) the good will be provided and my contribution would be a waste or (b) the good will be produced and my contribution would have a negligible impact on the amount of the good available to me.
4. If enough others won't contribute, either (a) the good will not be produced and my contribution would be a waste or (b) a very small amount of the good will be produced and my contribution would have a negligible impact on the amount of the good available to me.
5. Hence, either way, my contribution would be either (a) a waste or (b) cost-inefficient in terms of my own independent good.
6. Hence, I should not contribute.

Public goods and the free-rider problem raise a number of issues. The public-good problem is usually understood as one of *provision*. The free-rider problem seems to present an *n*-person prisoner's dilemma. For any rational individual, noncooperation strictly dominates cooperation. Every rational individual will reason in this way, with the result that rational individuals cannot in principle secure public goods.[9]

I'm not interested here in the difficulties that the free-rider problem raises for the provision of public goods. Rather, I'm interested in the situation where there is a system of cooperation in place that is producing the public good. The free-rider problem shows that an egoist for whom cooperation is a cost will not have reason to cooperate, as fairness to others presumably requires (at least in the case of public goods whose provision is continuous). The egoist can enjoy the benefits of public goods without having to maintain even the appearance of cooperation.

Moreover, it is not clear that, as condition (c) claims, the fact of cooperation (or restraint) is always the least costly way of securing the appearance of cooperation (or restraint). There are two distinct points here, one empirical and one counterfactual.

The empirical point is that (c) does not always hold, especially where, among other things, there are a number of cooperators, it is difficult to determine the burden that each cooperator should bear, it is difficult to trace contributions to contributors, or record keepers are easily bought off. If any one of these conditions obtains, an individual agent may be better off by maintaining the appearance of cooperation and restraint without being cooperative or restrained.

The counterfactual point is that we can imagine circumstances in which (c) would not obtain and we should not assume that it obtains. This is one way of stating Plato's point in *Republic*, book 2. If there were only one ring of Gyges and I had sole access to it, then (c) would be false as applied to me; I could maintain the appearance of cooperation and restraint without being cooperative and restrained (*Republic* 359b6–361d4). This shows that this strategic egoist justification of morality is not counterfactually stable. It is at best a contingent fact that cooperation and restraint are in the agent's interest. In those (perhaps only counterfactual) circumstances in which cooperation and restraint are not the least costly means of securing the appearance of cooperation and restraint, the strategic egoist will have no reason to be cooperative and restrained.

The strategic egoist might reply to these objections by insisting that it is sufficient for her purposes if (1) most schemes of cooperation (restraint) satisfy conditions (a) through (c) and (2) agents cannot reliably discriminate for exceptions to (1). She might claim that we are sufficiently coarse-grained both in our dispositions and our cognitive abilities that we cannot dispose ourselves to be cooperative (restrained) only in those situations in which conditions (a) through (c) are satisfied. To be cooperative (restrained) here, we must be cooperative (restrained) in the other situations as well. Compliance simply cannot be fine tuned so as to pick out all and only cases where (c) does not obtain (cf. Hume 1983, IX, ii/81–82). Because most such schemes satisfy (a) through (c), the egoist can explain why an agent should be cooperative (restrained) in all such schemes.

This reply does extend the scope of cooperation and restraint that admit of strategic justification, but it has serious problems and limitations.

First, resting as it does on further empirical claims, this reply fails to address the counterfactual objection that if I could maintain the appearance of compliance (restraint) without being compliant (restrained), I would have no reason to be compliant (restrained), as morality presumably requires. For a strategically rational agent, moral behavior (e.g., compliance) must always remain a second-best choice behind undetected immorality (e.g., noncompliance), even if the first choice is in fact psychologically inaccessible.

The strategic egoist might respond that we should be content with an extensional justification of morality's other-regarding features and not demand counterfactual stability. After all, the moral skeptic's claim, as I formulated it above, is that people fail to have reason to be moral, not that there are merely possible circumstances in which they would fail to have reason to be moral. So if the strategic reply were empirically adequate, the egoist would have a reply to the skeptic.

But I think that this response dismisses the requirement of counterfactual stability too quickly. It's one thing to claim that there are some counterfactual circumstances whose bearing on our reasons for action should not interest us (e.g., if every agent was a disembodied and self-sufficient intellect and interpersonal interaction was impossible). It's another thing to allow as part of a justification of morality that the sort of cooperation characteristically required by morality would turn out to be irrational if only I could be more selectively deceptive or noncompliant than I am in fact able to be. Indeed, because the possibility of successful deception will render my cooperation irrational, this strategic justification of morality will, in these circumstances, allow *the rationality of my actions to vary inversely with their morality*. It hardly seems a vindication of the authority of morality if its rationality rests in this way on our psychological and cognitive infirmities. The particular counterfactual instability that infects this egoist strategy, therefore, represents a limitation in this sort of egoist justification of morality that many of us will find seriously troubling.

Second, the empirical claims about our discriminatory infirmities seem implausible, and so the strategic reply does not seem even extensionally adequate. Though there's certainly some truth to this sort of psychological claim, it seems overstated as a matter of empirical fact. It's just not clear that all of us are this psychologically undiscriminating. Some people, even if only a few, seem remarkably good at being noncompliant only when noncompliance is unlikely to be detected (e.g., cheating only when fellow cooperators are not looking) or at being noncompliant in the production of public goods.[10]

Third, this strategic defense simply fails to cover a significant portion of morality's other-regarding aspects. The strategic defense justifies other-regarding action and concern only for those with whom one strategically interacts.[11] But the scope of our obligations to others does not seem to be limited to instances of cooperation or restraint that admit of these strategic justifications (cf. Sidgwick 1981, 168).

We seem to have obligations to do things for others where benefactor and beneficiary are not participants in some system of mutual advantage, for instance, duties of mutual aid. For example, the billionaire presumably has (perhaps imperfect) obligations to help destitute people with whom he has, and will have, no cooperative interaction.[12]

Fourth, even if this strategic defense could justify morality's insistence on other-regarding *conduct* (e.g., cooperation and restraint), it seems unable to justify morality's insistence on other-regarding *concern*. In particular, even if the egoist can justify the moral demand that I benefit others, he seems unable to account for the moral demand that I benefit others out of a *concern for their own sakes*. Since this egoist justification of beneficial action defends it as a reliable means for securing a good of the agent that can be specified independently of the good of others, there seems little reason to suppose that the rational agent will base these benefits on a concern for the others' own sakes. On the contrary, it looks as if the strategic egoist's benefits will be conferred out of a concern for the benefactor's own good rather than the beneficiary's own good.

Now perhaps these sorts of limitations in an egoist justification of morality are not defects but represent limitations in the rational authority of morality. But they are limitations in the defense of moral conduct and concern that many will find disturbing.

5 An Objective-Egoist Justification of Morality: A Neo-Aristotelian Approach

Given the apparent limitations in these subjective-egoist justifications of morality, the egoist might try to answer the moral skeptic by denying the claim of premise (2) that an agent's happiness or welfare can be specified independently of the happiness or welfare of others. The version of rational egoism that I would like to discuss incorporates an *objective* theory of happiness or welfare, one that claims that the value of a person's life consists in the exercise of certain capacities and the possession of certain relationships with others and to the world and that the value of these activities and relationships is more or less independent of the pleasure that they produce for the agent or of their being the object of the agent's desire.[13] If this version of egoism is to respond to the moral skeptic, its theory of value must not only be objective but also explain how an agent's welfare depends upon the welfare of others and how the other-regarding action and concern required by morality will promote the agent's own well-being. These claims are not uncommon; the trick is to provide a reasonably satisfactory explanation of them.

The egoist strategy that I wish to explore derives its inspiration, as well as some of its details, from Aristotle's justification of friendship in *Nicomachean Ethics* (*NE*) ix, 4–12. For this reason I think it deserves to be thought of as a neo-Aristotelian view, whether or not it is Aristotle's own.[14] Aristotle, as I understand him, wants to justify concern for one's (best or complete) friends and concern for one's family members (e.g., children and siblings) as cases of, or on the model of, *self*-love (*NE* 1161b15–1162a5, 1166a10).

> For it is said that we must love most the friend who is most a friend; and one person is most a friend to another if he wishes goods to the other for the other's own sake, even if no one will know about it. But these are features most of all of one's relation to oneself; and so too are all the other defining features of a friend, since we have said that all of the features of friendship extend from oneself to others. (1168b2–6)

> The excellent person is related to his friend in the same way as he is related to himself, since a friend is another self; and therefore, just as his own being is choiceworthy for him, the friend's being is choiceworthy for him in the same or a similar way. (1170b6–9)

One way to understand these claims is as a proposal to model the *inter*personal relationship between "other-selves" (e.g., virtuous friends) on the *intra*personal relationship between a self and its temporal parts. I have reason to regard my (best) friends and family members as other-selves of mine, because they bear approximately the same relationship to me as my future self does to me, and this fact provides me with reason to care about them for their own sakes in much the same way that I have reason to care about my future self for its own sake.[15] Aristotle's general ground for regarding the good of these other people as part of my own could then be extended to my relationship with other members of the right sort of political community so as to provide the basis for an egoist justification of more general other-regarding moral and political commitments (e.g., justice) (*NE* 1155a24–28, 1167a25–28). I think that this basic egoist strategy is promising but needs to be set out more carefully.[16]

In the normal case of self-love I am concerned about and make sacrifices for future stages of myself. The rational egoist thinks that such concern and sacrifice for one's own future are rational: concern for my own future is concern for me, and I am compensated for sacrifices of my present self on behalf of my future self, because my future self is a part of me.

But how must a future person stage be related to my present self in order for both to be parts of me? A common and plausible answer that I shall explain and employ, without strictly defending, is *psychological continuity*.[17] On this view, a particular person consists of a series of psychologically continuous person stages. A series of person stages is psychologically continuous just in case contiguous members in this series are psychologically well *connected*. And a pair of person stages is psychologically connected just in case (a) they are psychologically similar in terms of such states as beliefs, desires, and intentions and (b) the psychological features of the later stage are causally dependent upon the earlier stage. So far, self-love would seem to imply that I should be concerned about future person stages that are psychologically connected with my present self by these causal ties, because these stages are part of me (cf. NE 1166a14). And, indeed, this justified concern for my future self will itself reinforce the psychological connections and continuity among the stages of my life (cf. Whiting 1986).

6 The Problem of Fission

But psychological continuity, unlike identity, can be a one-many relationship. Consider a case of fission. A, B, and C are identical triplets. B and C have suffered from degenerative brain disorders and are now brain-dead, but their bodies are intact. By contrast, A's brain is fine, but she suffers from a special disease that produces rapid bodily degeneration. Assume that it is possible to transplant A's brain into B's body and that this preserves psychological continuity with A. If we do this (case 1), we regard A as the surviving recipient and B as the dead donor (C is simply dead). Now assume that half the brain is sufficient to sustain psychological continuity. If half of A's brain is seriously damaged and we transplant the healthy half into B's body (case 2), A again survives. If, however, A's entire brain is healthy and we transplant half of it into B and half into C (case 3), then the logic of identity seems to prevent us from regarding either of the recuperating patients as A. This is the fission case. Call the recuperating patient in B's body D and the one in C's body E. D and E have exactly equal claims to being A. So it seems that if A is identical to D, A must also be identical to E. But identity is transitive, and D is definitely not the same person as E. Therefore, neither D nor E can be A.[18] But there is just as much psychological continuity between A and D and between A and E as there was between A and the recuperating patient (i.e., A) in cases 1 and 2. Because A survives transplants 1 and 2, she has good egoist reason to be concerned for the recuperating patient in both cases. Because A does not survive fission (case 3), it looks as if she can have no egoist reason to be concerned about D or E; it looks as if she could not be compensated for any sacrifice that she might make for D or E. But she should be just as concerned about D and E as she is about her recuperating self in cases 1 and 2, since she bears exactly the same relationships to D and E in case 3 as she does to her recuperating self in cases 1 and 2. What really seems to matter for the rationality of concern is psychological continuity, not personal identity per se, though psychological continuants will normally be single persons (cf. Parfit 1984, chap. 12). And this fact seems to undermine rational egoism, because the egoist seems unable to justify concern for all selves that are psychologically continuous with the agent's present self.

7 An Egoist Account of Fission: The Base Case for Extending Egoist Concern to Others

This assessment of the implications of the fission case for rational egoism seems premature. In fact, the fission case seems to me to provide the resources for a much more extensive egoist justification of other-regarding action and concern.[19]

We have to agree that the fission products are not identical with the subject of fission. But the egoist can still justify concern by the subject of fission for her fission products if we can represent the goods of the fission products as part of the good of the fission subject. The egoist can explain why A should be concerned about D and E, even though neither D nor E is the same as A, if D and E extend A's interests and D's good and E's good are part of A's good.

In the normal, nonbranching case, psychological continuity extends both the agent's interests and the agent.

$$P(A)$$

$$\overbrace{\hspace{4cm}}$$

$p_1 \ldots p_2 \ldots p_3 \ldots$, at
$t_1 \ldots t_2 \ldots t_3 \ldots$

A is a person who consists of a nonbranching series of psychologically continuous person stages p_1 through p_n. Stage p_2 has a certain psychological profile (it has certain beliefs, desires, and intentions). Stage p_3 has a similar psychological profile (it has similar beliefs, desires, and intentions and acts according to intentions like those found in

p_2 so as to satisfy desires like those found at p_2), and this profile causally depends upon the profile at p_2. This psychological continuity from p_2 to p_3 extends A's interests in the sense that p_3 inherits the projects and plans of p_2 and carries on and carries out the projects and plans of p_2. In this nonbranching case it also extends A's life.

In the fission case, however, psychological continuity does not literally extend A's life.

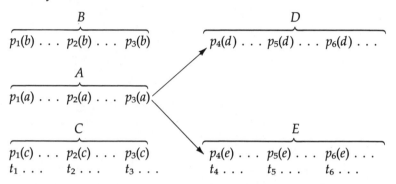

Neither D nor E is the same as A, though each is fully psychologically continuous with A. So neither D nor E literally extends A's life. But by virtue of being fully psychologically continuous with A, D and E will each inherit, carry on, and carry out A's projects and plans (though presumably in somewhat different directions over time). This seems to be a good ground for claiming that D and E extend A's interests even if they do not literally extend A's life. In this way A can regard D and E as extending her interests in the very same way that her own future self would normally extend her interests, and so A can regard D's good and E's good as part of her own good. If so, then we can explain how A could be compensated for benefits she might bestow on D or E and how the egoist could justify A's concern for D and E. This means that the rational egoist can, after all, claim that an agent should be concerned about selves that are psychologically related to his present self by the appropriate causal ties, because the good of such selves is part of his good.[20]

8 Intimates: Extending Egoist Concern Further

But this opens up the possibility for the egoist to justify more general other-regarding commitments. Recall that a psychologically continuous series of selves or person stages is made up of selves or stages such that (a) temporally contiguous pairs of selves or stages in this series are psychologically similar and (b) the psychological features of later selves or stages are causally dependent upon the earlier ones. The fission case shows us that stages of other people can in some cases be so related to my present self; the relationships between A and D and between A and E satisfy conditions (a) and (b). But there seem to be other, more familiar cases in which the relationships between different people satisfy synchronic analogs of conditions (a) and (b) to a significant extent. I will be related to others in this way whenever (a) we share important psychological traits and (b) we share these traits as the result of our causal interaction. In particular, I can be and often am related in these ways to those with whom I stand in intimate relationships, for instance, my close friends, my spouse, my children, and my siblings (*NE* 1159b25–33, 1161b17–1162a1, 1166a1–12, 1170b10–17, 1171b30–1172a6). The causal dependence between the mental lives of intimates takes the form of mutual interaction (e.g., sharing projects, discussion, and cooperation). As a psychological matter, my regular interaction with another naturally generates concern between us; concern develops as our relationship develops. This concern has two relevant features: it is rationally appropriate, given our shared mental life and interaction ((a) and (b)), and it further establishes our shared mental life. This parallels the intrapersonal case where psychological dependence of my later self upon my present self (psychological continuity) justifies my concern for that future self, and this concern reinforces connectedness and continuity. These relations give me reason to regard my intimates as extensions of myself—as other-selves of mine—and to regard their interests and welfare as part of my own, and these facts make our welfares interdependent.

So, for example, in many parent-child relationships, the child's physical and psychological nature are to a significant degree a causal product of the parent's physical and psychological nature and activities. This is how we can explain the common view that the parent's interests are extended to the child's welfare and that the child's welfare is part of the parent's good. The parent will benefit by the child's benefit and so will be compensated for her sacrifices for her child. This helps us see how the parent's interests extend beyond her own existence. Because her child's good is part of her good, she will be concerned about how her child fares after her death and will have reason to make sacrifices before her death so that her child will fare better. And because the child's good is part of hers, these sacrifices will not be uncompensated, and the egoist can justify them.[21] And these sacrifices and other forms of concern further cement the psychological continuity between parent and child and so reinforce the extension of the parent's interests through the child's welfare.

In some cases (e.g., the fission cases and some parent-child relationships) selves connected by relations (a) and (b) are asymmetrically connected. However, I shall focus on the symmetrical relationships more common among close friends, spouses, and siblings. In these relationships there will be psychological similarity (e.g., common values, aims, and beliefs), and this similarity will be produced and/or sustained by their mutual interaction (e.g., common experiences and discussion). In relationships of these kinds each self can regard the other as another-self: the other will extend the self's own interests, and so the other's good will be part of one's own good. This means that one will be compensated for sacrifices that one makes for the other and that the egoist can explain why one can have justified concern for the other.

9 Why Cultivate Other-Selves?

If we are to justify the full range of morality's other-regarding commitments, then we will have to see if the scope of egoist concern can be extended from those to whom the agent stands in fairly intimate relationships of the sort we have been considering to those to whom she stands in less intimate relations. But there is a prior worry that applies to the egoist justification of concern for intimates.

The egoist may be able to explain why I should be concerned about my other-self for his own sake once I have such another-self, but can she explain why I should cultivate other-selves? Why not just spend my financial, emotional, and intellectual resources directly on myself rather than cultivate another-self?

The egoist might claim that having another-self *extends* and *protects* my interests in ways not available to me on my own (cf. Irwin 1988, 393–395).

Another-self extends my interests. An objective conception of welfare can reasonably claim that it is in my interest to exercise those capacities that are central to the sort of being I am and that these capacities importantly include capacities for practical deliberation of the sort exercised in the formation, assessment, and pursuit of projects and plans. Having another-self allows me to engage in more complex and more diverse activities than I could on my own (*NE* 1169b5–6, 1170a5–7). I can engage in more diverse projects, because my other-selves have time and resources to pursue projects that promote my interest but that I do not have the time and resources to pursue myself. Thus through my other-self I can pursue careers or avocations that I have had to forgo in order to pursue the ones I've chosen for myself. I may have had to choose between a career as a professional philosopher and one as a veterinarian and may have chosen philosophy, but I can pursue my interest in veterinary medicine vicariously by watching and discussing your work as a vet. More generally, I can enjoy and benefit from the greater range of experiences that my other-self brings to me and can broaden my sphere of deliberation by my deliberative interaction with my other-self. I can also engage in more complex projects requiring intimate cooperation among like-minded people (e.g., rational articulation of my beliefs, desires, and values through discussion with people who know me). In these ways my other-selves increase both the complexity and the diversity of projects that I can pursue and the capacities that I can exercise.

It is worth noting that these aspects of the way in which another-self extends one's interests constrain the degree of psychological similarity one has reason to seek in such a relationship. My activities will be more diverse and more complex if my other-self is no mere clone of me. Clearly, I will diversify my experience more by interacting with someone who has somewhat different interests and experiences. And cooperation in complex projects will often be enhanced when participants have different strengths and talents. For instance, the project of rationally articulating my beliefs, desires, and values through discussion with another who knows and understands me depends upon the other person being willing to disagree with me and force me to consider matters from another perspective. This critical role for the other-self may be easier to perform if the other-self does not share all of my beliefs, desires, and values.

On the other hand, there must be limits on the degree of psychological differences between two people if they are to stand to each other as other-selves. Indeed, if we are very different psychologically, it will be difficult for me to absorb someone else's experiences; I will absorb her experiences better if we have a common system of past experiences, beliefs, desires, and values with which to interpret these experiences. And cooperation in complex projects is likely to be more reliable if cooperators are in agreement about the general point and terms of cooperation. This suggests that the egoist will have most reason to seek interaction with people that are not mere clones of herself but with whom she nonetheless shares important structural beliefs and aims.

Another-self also protects my interests. On reasonable views about happiness or welfare, whether subjective or objective, my happiness will depend in part upon goods that are not completely within my control—what Aristotle calls "external goods" (*NE* i, 8–12). Because my happiness is subject to fortune in this way, my other-selves secure my happiness more firmly, because they afford me some protection against misfortunes that I would not otherwise possess. For my other-self cares about me as she cares about herself and will share her resources with me.

Of course, other-selves also make me more vulnerable. Since the good of my other-self is part of my good, harms to my other-self will be harms to me. But, while this is true, it cannot be a good or sufficient reason not to cultivate other-selves. First, the fact that my other-self herself has another-self in me will moderate the impact of many harms to her: what would otherwise be a severe misfortune to her will typically be less of a misfortune to her, because my activities and resources are available to her.[22] Second, the impact on me of a severe misfortune to my other-self will also be moderated by how many other-selves I have. If I have a number of other-selves, my life will not be ruined (though, of course, it will be made worse) by serious harms to one of my other-selves. Finally, even ignoring these two ways of moderating the vulnerability that my other-self intro- duces, it would seem that I have sufficient reason to cultivate another-self as long as her life realizes net value, and it seems plau- sible that this condition is almost always satisfied.

10 Justifying Morality: Extending Egoist Concern Further Still

So far I've argued that the egoist has reason to cultivate other-selves and to regard the good of other-selves as part of his own good. In this way the egoist can justify concern for the other-self. But my examples of other-selves have been people to whom I stand in very special and intimate relationships (e.g., my fission products, my children, my spouse, and my closest friends). But surely this won't take us very far in justifying morality, because morality requires that I benefit and be concerned about a wider net of people than my friends and family. Won't this egoist justification of other-regarding concern fall far short of a decent reply to the moral skeptic?

The egoist might profit from seeing how Aristotle can try to use his justification of the best sort of friendship (where the friend is another-self) to justify (general) justice. The best sort of friendship can't hold on the sort of scale involved in a political community that is just (NE 1158a11–12, 1171a18–20), and political communities are associations for mutual advantage (NE 1160a11–15). Nonetheless, friendship is the virtue appropriate to communities or associations in general and includes the perfection of justice (NE 1155a22–28, 1159b25–1160a8), and Aristotle's justification of friendship applies to the justification of justice.

Political communities that are just have to a significant degree the two features that are crucial to the egoist justification of concern in general and friendship in particular: (a) there is commonality of aims and aspirations among members of the political association, and (b) this commonality is produced by members of the association living together in the right way (e.g., defining aims and goals consensually) (*NE* 1167a25–28, 1155a24–28). So on Aristotle's view, members of a just community will be psychologically and causally related to each other to a significant degree in ways that justify each member in regarding other members as other-selves. Justice, Aristotle claims, aims at the *common good* (*NE* 1129b15–30), and this presumably means the good that community members share by virtue of conditions (a) and (b). But then Aristotle's claims allow him to explain why it is in the agent's interest to promote the common good as justice requires.

Moreover, I have reason to become a member of such a community, because by cooperating with other members of my community in this way, I both extend and protect my interests (*Politics* 1253a12–18, 25–30). I enlarge my experiences still further, and their input improves my deliberation about even the more self-confined aspects of my life. Moreover, participation in community projects exercises new deliberative capacities and provides me with security against misfortunes to which I am vulnerable on my own.

But it's one thing to think that this sort of egoist justification of concern with other-selves might be carried over to concern among members of cooperative communities and associations the size of the Greek city-state (e.g., trade unions, universities, and professional associations), who can be expected to have common aims and regular interactions. It's quite another thing, it may seem, to try to carry this sort of justification over to large, modern, pluralistic nation-states.

The relevant question is whether conditions (a) and (b) are met in an appropriate way in large nations. Though this is a serious challenge to the scope of the egoist's justification of other-regarding concern, it does not seem obviously unanswerable. We saw that the egoist's reasons for cultivating other-selves argue for a certain amount of psychological diversity among such selves. My experiences will be enlarged and my own practical deliberations will be enhanced by the input from people with different experiences, values, and perspectives, and larger groups with more diverse membership will typically make possible more complex forms of social cooperation and hence the exercise of new kinds of deliberative capacities. Moreover, these considerations also argue for certain kinds of social and political organization. A society will extend and protect the interests of its members roughly in proportion to the extent of its democratic equality, where democratic equality is understood to involve democratic institutions against a background of personal and civic liberties and comparative social and economic equality (cf. Rawls 1971, chap. 9, esp. sec. 79). Democratic decision making affords the opportunity for widespread participation in a process of mutual discussion and articulation of ideals and priorities; democratic processes thus establish psychological continuity more widely, and in so doing, they exercise new deliberative capacities in the members of such a society. A background of personal and civic liberties with comparative social and economic equality makes possible more widespread development of individual talents and capacities, and this will expand the range of experiences, values, and perspectives that individuals can enjoy vicariously and draw on in their own deliberations.

We also saw that there are limits on the amount and kind of psychological diversity that can exist between people if they are to stand to each other as other-selves to some significant extent. In particular, it seems reasonable for the egoist to require certain kinds of abstract, structural agreement in beliefs and aims. We stand some hope of explaining why an egoist should regard other members of a large pluralistic community as other-selves that extend her interests if we can identify important kinds of agreement in beliefs and aims.

Underlying the psychological, cultural, and political differences and disagreements in large, more pluralistic cultures one can typically find agreement on certain abstract values and aims. For instance, within a democratic culture we share a commitment, among other things, to public debate of political issues, democratic legislative processes, religious toleration, individual autonomy, and fair equality of opportunity. Of course, people hold quite different conceptions of these abstract values, but it's precisely this abstract agreement that makes our disagreements possible. Without these shared concepts, our differences would be mere differences, not disagreements. These shared democratic commitments include the public and rational articulation and interpretation of these shared values and the public and rational resolution of interpretive disputes over the extension of these values (cf. Dworkin 1986, esp. chaps. 2, 6–7). This commonality of moral and political aims also satisfies causal condition (b). Agreement on these abstract values flows from a common intellectual heritage and is sustained by intellectual debate among current members of the society and by the interaction between members of the society and existing institutions that reflect this heritage. (Similar claims could perhaps be made about less political aspects of shared cultural psychology.)

Moreover, there are ways in which this abstract agreement is psychologically more important than the more concrete disagreements. In cases where an agent acts from several motives, we often would like to know which motive was dominant. We usually answer such questions by appeal to counterfactual considerations. Suppose Zach kept his promise to Zenobia in circumstances in which this was profitable for him. I may want to know whether it was Zach's concern for Zenobia and his desire to keep his promise to her or his concern for his own (self-confined) interest that was dominant. It would be natural for me to try to decide which motive was dominant by asking what he would have done if the situation and his collateral beliefs about it had been somewhat different, in particular, if Zach would have kept his promise if doing so had required a greater sacrifice on his part and he had recognized this. It may sometimes be difficult to answer these counterfactual questions confidently, but answers to them seem to be our best guide to dominant intention and motive. Appealing to such a counterfactual test seems to support the dominance of the abstract concepts on which there is agreement over the more specific conceptions of those concepts over which people disagree (see Brink 1988, 125–129). Because specific conceptions result from abstract values together with collateral beliefs about the extension of those values, the appropriate change in one's collateral beliefs would change one's specific conception. This shows that the abstract value that one shares with others is more important than one's specific conception of that value. Suppose that you and I share an abstract aim of prohibiting cruel and unusual punishment. If we disagree in our collateral beliefs, either in our beliefs about the nature of justified punishment or in our beliefs about the nature of the death penalty (e.g., the way in which it is judicially administered), we will disagree in our specific conceptions of cruel and unusual punishment. Assume that you oppose the death penalty as cruel and unusual punishment and that I think it's permissible. Which is more important here, our agreement in abstract concept or our disagreement in conception? If I were to come to think that capital punishment is morally indefensible or cannot be administered fairly, would I (a) come to believe that the death penalty is cruel and unusual punishment and ought to be prohibited or (b) cease to want to prohibit cruel and unusual punishment? If I can really imagine what it is like to change my collateral beliefs in this way, the answer seems clear: (a). But this answer to my counterfactual question supports the dominance of my abstract value over my specific conception of that value. I think that this conclusion generalizes fairly well, so that the agreement in pluralistic societies on abstract aims and values is structurally more important than the specific conceptions of a good life over which citizens often disagree or diverge.

Because these abstract aims are dominant and because, moreover, one of the abstract values is a commitment, within certain parameters, to abide by the results of public debate and democratic processes, particular political decisions and particular interpretations of the abstract values can typically be seen as common particular commitments that have been produced by a process of mutual interaction among members of the society. Insofar as other members of my society share these aims and goals with me and participate with me in their maintenance, articulation, and application, I can regard them, to an interesting degree, as other-selves of mine, and so I can see them as extending my interests and see their good as part of my good. If so, we could perhaps claim that a morally acceptable articulation and application of these common aims would represent a common good and that justice, interpreted as the promotion of this common good, is something that is in the agent's interest to realize.

11 Degrees of Egoist Concern

However, even if we agree that members of a large community possess a significant amount of psychological similarity with one another as the result of their causal interaction, surely their psychological connections with each other are not as great as those between, say, A and her fission products D and E. Psychological connectedness is a positive function of (a) degree of overall psychological similarity and (b) strength of causal connection. Overall psychological similarity will itself be a function of the degree of similarity of specific psychological states (e.g., beliefs, desires, and intentions), the number of psychological states shared, and the structural importance of the states shared to the overall psychological profile of the self (e.g., centrality of the shared beliefs or desires). Since (a) and (b) can hold to different degrees, psychological connectedness can vary greatly. Indeed, the cases we have been considering have involved selves that have been successively less connected psychologically. At the most connected end of the spectrum are the temporally contiguous intrapersonal cases and the fission cases. Here psychological similarity and causal connectedness hold maximally. With intimates (e.g., spouses, friends, and siblings) we have selves who are somewhat less psychologically connected. Members of small communities of like-minded people (e.g., members of a *polis*) are still less connected, and members of pluralistic, nation-states are even less connected. Because, according to the neo-Aristotelian justification, psychological relations extend one's interests and justify egoist concern, this depreciation of connectedness must affect the amount of concern that the egoist can justify. Isn't this an important limitation to this egoist strategy of justifying moral concern?

But notice that similarity of aspirations and aims is not necessary for establishing psychological continuity. In the intrapersonal case we can have psychological continuity between two stages of the person without psychological connectedness between them. Because the similarity relation in psychological connectedness is not exact similarity, my distant future self need not be psychologically well connected with my present self in order to be psychologically continuous with my present self, and in fact it won't be if temporally contiguous stages of me are psychologically well connected with each other but are not psychologically (qualitatively) identical. So too in the interpersonal case. As we have been seeing, distinct selves can nonetheless be significantly psychologically connected. But as in the intrapersonal case, selves might be psychologically continuous without being psychologically well connected. If I am well connected to X, X is well connected to Y, and Y is well connected to Z, then Z can be continuous with me even if Z is not herself well connected with me. So distinct selves with quite different aims and aspirations might nonetheless be significantly psychologically continuous. As long as psychological continuity is sufficient to extend one's interests and justify concern, the egoist can explain why I have reason to benefit and be concerned about other members of my community with whom I am only psychologically continuous (and not necessarily well connected).[23]

No doubt this is only a partial response to the worry in question. This might be an adequate reply if more distant other-selves (e.g., fellow citizens) were simply further along from me in a causal-psychological chain of equally strong links than closer other-selves (e.g., my spouse). This would be similar to the way in which my distant future self might just be further along in a causal-psychological chain that connects temporally contiguous person stages by equally strong links. For then more distant other-selves would be just as continuous with me as closer other-selves, just as my distant future self is just as continuous with my present self as my nearer future selves are. And insofar as continuity is sufficient for concern, I should have just as much reason for concern about these distant other-selves as for closer other-selves. But the links within chains of other-selves will not be as strong as those within chains of stages of a single self. After all, the proponent of psychological continuity presumably wants to be able to distinguish (in nonbranching circumstances) between future selves that are stages of me and other selves. Presumably the greater spatial and physical separation to be found among other-selves than is found between temporally contiguous stages of a single person will, at least in part, normally explain why there is less psychological connectedness among other-selves than among temporally contiguous stages of a single self and so will allow the proponent of psychological continuity to distinguish between future selves that are stages of me and those that are stages of other people, even if these other people are other-selves. Similar facts will also affect the degree of psychological connectedness to be found between me and different sorts of other-selves. Just as spatial and physical separation will help account for the greater connectedness between temporally contiguous stages of myself than between myself and my spouse, so too geographical and cultural differences will help account for the fact that there is greater connectedness between my spouse and me than there is between some of my fellow citizens and me. But if the links of psychological connectedness in the chains of psychological continuity can vary in strength, then, arguably, psychological continuity itself can vary in strength. If so, then the chain of psychological continuity connecting me with ever more spatially distant selves will typically grow weaker as the chain extends further. More distant other-selves will not be other-selves to the same degree that closer ones are. So, for example, mere fellow citizens will be more weakly continuous with me than intimates of mine will be because they are more weakly connected. And this will mean that though their interests extend mine, they extend mine somewhat less than, say, my intimate's interests do and I will have somewhat less reason to benefit them and to be concerned about their welfare than I do for an intimate of mine.

Neo-Aristotelian rational egoism seems, therefore, committed to a *discount rate of rational concern* for others that tracks the degree of psychological continuity between the agent and others. In the normal, intrapersonal case continuity holds between all aspects of the psychological profile of the earlier and later selves. This is equally true of the relation between the fission subject and both of her fission products. In these cases all interests of the later selves seem to be part of the interests of the deliberating agent (i.e., the temporally extended person in the intrapersonal case, the fission subject in the fission case). But as we pass along the continuum of relationships to others (e.g., from that between fission subjects and fission products to that between intimates to that between neighbors or coworkers to that between fellow citizens), continuity begins to hold along fewer dimensions of the psychological profile. This means that common interests begin to narrow, and parties to these relationships begin to acquire progressively larger independent or self-confined interests. As the interests that I have in common with others decreases, my egoist reasons for other-regarding concern weaken, and as my self-confined interests increase, this makes possible conflicts between my self-confined and other-regarding reasons for action. These limitations in the neo-Aristotelian justification of morality may seem like defects.

But I'm less sure. The fact that you and I share only some interests need not greatly affect the *scope* of my concerns for you. (Here the issue concerns the scope of my concern among the different interests of a single person rather than the scope of my concern among persons.) If you and I are coworkers, there are important but limited psychological dimensions along which we are continuous; we have common interests in our work environment and our collaborative enterprises. If we are other-selves to each other only to this extent, I may seem to have egoist reason to be concerned only about quite narrow aspects of your life. But notice that if I am entitled to be concerned about you insofar as your interests and mine are common, about you *qua F*, then I have reason to provide you with those necessary conditions of ϕing (where ϕing is part of being *F*) and those extrinsic goods that will enhance your ϕing. But this will extend my concern to broader aspects of your life, including your material and psychological well-being. Indeed, often my concern for you *qua F* will lead me to become interested in those aspects of your life that affect your ϕing, and this will lead me to interact with you along other dimensions (e.g., *G* and *H*), and this will expand our psychological continuity (e.g., we will become friends), and this will provide egoist justification of still broader concern for you on my part.[24]

However, the fact that narrow continuity can justify concern with wider scope does not seem to affect the fact that the *weight* or *degree* of concern must remain hostage to the degree of continuity, and this will vary along a continuum (as I have indicated). Isn't at least this a defect in the neo-Aristotelian justification of morality?

Not obviously. After all, most moral theories recognize *special obligations* that the agent owes to those to whom he stands in different relationships. The extent of one's moral obligations to others is commonly thought to be a function not simply of the amount of benefit that one can confer or harm that one can prevent but also of the nature of the relationship in which one stands to potential beneficiaries. In particular, many moral theories recognize stronger obligations to family and friends than to comparative strangers and again to partners in cooperative schemes (e.g., coworkers and promisees) than to third parties. This is true, of course, of agent-relative (e.g., deontological) moral theories that build these differential obligations directly into their theories of obligation. But even defenders of agent-neutral moral theories, such as utilitarianism or consequentialism, typically try to justify recognition of special obligations and the legitimacy of differential concern for those to whom the agent stands in special relationships (Sidgwick 1981, 432–434; Railton 1984; Brink 1986). We might think of the scale of stringency among our moral obligations to those to whom we stand in different relationships as forming a *moral discount rate*. It remains to be seen whether the moral discount rate and the egoist's discount rate of rational concern are exactly isomorphic. Without settling this difficult question, we can, I think, still make two claims on behalf of neo-Aristotelian rational egoism. First, it is not a defect per se of its justification of other-regarding concern that it embodies a discount rate of concern, because there is a moral discount rate. And second, the neo-Aristotelian discount rate will be a positive virtue to the extent that it accommodates and indeed explains the existence and shape of the correct moral discount rate.[25]

12 The Scope of Egoist Concern: Still Too Narrow?

Another worry for this strategy concerns the scope, rather than the weight, of concern. In fact, worries about the scope of the neo-Aristotelian justification of other-regarding concern are arguably more serious than the worries about its weight to the extent that we are more confident in our views about the scope of morality itself than we are in our views about moral weight. I am somewhat uncertain about precisely how much sacrifice morality requires of me in various contexts.[26] By contrast, I am more confident in my belief that morality has wide scope, in particular, that we have some moral obligation, whatever its exact strength, to benefit those who need our help and whom it is in our power to benefit—regardless of our relationship to them. This claim about the wide scope of moral obligation is a common claim reflected, for example, in the story of the Good Samaritan (Luke 10:29–37). But this belief in the wide scope of moral obligation raises a worry about the scope of the neo-Aristotelian justification of other-regarding concern. One such worry is that there will be persons with whom we have no causal interaction and hence no psychological continuity (whatever psychological similarity there might or might not be) and yet for whom morality can demand our concern and on whose behalf morality can require us to make some personal sacrifices. Won't this egoist strategy be unable to justify these moral requirements? The problem for this egoist strategy is not in defending sufficient concern for these distant selves but in providing any justification at all.

One reply relies on features of psychological continuity that we have already noticed. It is not necessary for me to have had direct causal contact with Z in order for me to have some psychological continuity with Z. If I have direct causal-psychological contact with X, X has direct causal-psychological contact with Y, and Y has direct causal-psychological contact with Z, then Z will have some psychological continuity with me. Z can thus extend my interests to some extent, and so I can have some egoist reason to benefit Z even if Z and I are separated by significant geographical and cultural boundaries. In this way the egoist might try to extend this justification of other-regarding action and concern beyond national boundaries.

But surely there are individuals—even if only nonactual, possible individuals—with whom I am not in the least psychologically continuous and to whom I nonetheless would have certain moral obligations. Consider my relationship to Max, who is an inhabitant of Lotusland, a strange hot planet in a distant galaxy. Of course, Max and I have never interacted, and we are quite different psychologically. Suppose our causal isolation ends: at a certain point he is teletransported into the street next to me with his back to an oncoming truck. Surely, I have a moral obligation to pull Max out of the path of the truck even if the process poses the threat of minor injury to me. Our previous causal isolation and our psychological differences ensure that we are not psychologically continuous. And this seems to imply that the egoist cannot justify my moral obligations toward Max.[27]

If Max's relocation is permanent or of any significant duration, then he holds out the prospect of becoming one of my other-selves. In these circumstances, the egoist can appeal to *future continuity* to justify other-regarding action and concern for those with whom I have as yet no psychological continuity.

Suppose, however, that Max's visit will be very brief: if I rescue him, he will then be instantaneously teletransported back to Lotusland. Here there seems no prospect of ongoing future continuity, yet my moral obligation presumably remains. Is there any way for the egoist to offer a justification of my obligation to rescue Max under these rather bizarre circumstances? Two kinds of justification seem possible.[28]

Even if the egoist is unable to offer a direct justification of rescue in these circumstances, she might still offer an *indirect* justification of my moral obligation. If the general egoist strategy has succeeded, then my own welfare is implicated, to varying degrees, with everyone with whom I come in direct contact and with most of those with whom I never have direct contact. This will justify me in developing general other-regarding sentiments (e.g., kindness and compassion) that will induce me to make various sacrifices for others. But these sentiments are not infinitely fine-grained. We cannot develop and maintain concern for all the disparate individuals with whom we are or will be psychologically continuous (to varying degrees) without also caring about those individuals, should we ever meet them, whom it was in our power to benefit but with whom we were not and never would be psychologically continuous. This indirect egoist justification of my obligations toward Max is not as satisfying as I would like; in particular, it is counterfactually unstable. But this form of counterfactual instability seems less general and less invidious than that which afflicts subjective egoist justifications of morality (sec. 4). On its own it might seem to be a rather small imperfection in an otherwise promising egoist story.

Better yet, the egoist may have a *direct* justification of rescue, even if there is no prospect of ongoing future continuity. For the egoist can claim that the act of rescue *itself* establishes a psychological connection between Max and me and thus establishes limited continuity that can provide an egoist ground for my reason to rescue. Indeed, though a limited connection, the act of rescue is, of course, a significant event (especially for Max), and such events are often supposed to establish special bonds between benefactor and beneficiary. The limited character of the continuity thus established will presumably limit the weight of my reason to rescue Max. But it will vindicate the claim that I do have reason to rescue, and the weight of this reason will presumably be sufficient to justify the sort of small sacrifice that morality clearly requires and that I envisioned in the example. It may not be sufficient when the sacrifice in question is great, but then it's also less clear how substantial a sacrifice morality requires toward people to whom one stands in no special relationship.

13 Is the Egoist's Concern for Other-Selves Too Mercenary?

It is a general worry about egoist justifications of morality that they cannot justify moral demands, because morality requires not just that we perform the actions it demands of us but also that we fulfill its demands from the right sort of motives. The objection I have in mind was raised in section 4; it claims that even if egoism can justify morality's insistence on other-regarding *conduct* (e.g., cooperation and restraint), it cannot justify morality's insistence on other-regarding *concern*. In particular, even if egoism can justify the moral demand that I benefit others, it may seem that it cannot account for the moral demand that I benefit others out of a *concern for their own sakes*. The problem arises because our strategy justifies personal sacrifice on behalf of another by representing the other's good as part of the agent's own good. This seems to base the agent's other-regarding action not on concern for the other's own sake but instead on self-love.[29]

However, the egoist strategy developed here seems to allow us to justify both concern for the other's own sake and other-regarding action.[30] We need to distinguish the two stages of the neo-Aristotelian argument: (i) the justification for cultivating other-selves and (ii) the justification for concern for those that are one's other-selves.

Stage (i) addresses the question of why I should begin to care about those to whom I do not yet stand in any special relationship. The extension and protection arguments purport to supply the answer. Part of this justification for the initial concern for the other does seem instrumental. According to the protection argument, my reason for acquiring other-selves is to secure myself against vulnerability that I would have on my own. It's less clear that the extension argument has this instrumental character. According to that argument, cooperative relationships with others afford me opportunities to exercise more diverse and complex deliberative capacities. It's true, of course, that this argument justifies acquiring another-self by appeal to how that relationship affects my capacities, but the capacities in question are ones that involve, among other things, one's relation to another in cooperative and beneficial ways. So if I'm justified in entering such relationships because they exercise *these* sorts of capacities, my justification does not obviously reflect a purely instrumental attitude toward those with whom I'm entering such relationships. So it's not clear to me that (i) is thoroughly instrumental.

Once we distinguish (i) and (ii), it is also not clear that there's anything objectionable about (i)'s being instrumental. It would perhaps be objectionable if (ii) were instrumental, that is, if my justification for caring about those who are *already* other-selves to me (e.g., family and friends) were instrumental. But it's much less clear that there's anything untoward in supposing that one's justification for caring about those with whom one does *not yet* stand in any special relationship is partly instrumental; *initial* concern may have these instrumental properties.

Once my relationship with others is under way, psychological continuity begins to get established, and I can begin to regard them as other-selves and to see their welfare as part of my own. According to the egoist, this last fact provides my justification for being concerned about them. Does this make (ii) mercenary?

One of the central features of the neo-Aristotelian form of rational egoism is to reject the popular contrast between self-love and concern for others; self-love is not inconsistent with, and indeed requires, other-regarding concern when the other's good is a *component* of the agent's own good. The crucial claim here is that if x is a constituent part of y, then x can be desirable both for its own sake and for its role in, and contribution to, y (*NE* 1094a18–19, 1097a27–b6).

Consider again the (purely) intrapersonal case of self-love. When I undergo a present sacrifice for a future benefit, I do so because the interests of my future self are interests of mine; the rationality of my present sacrifice is not conditional on my present self having desires for my future self. In this way I make present sacrifices out of a concern for my future self. Of course, the rationality of the sacrifice depends upon its promoting my overall good, that is, the good of my temporally extended self. And in this way my concern (e.g., my willingness to make sacrifices) for my future self is not unconditional. But because the good of my future self is part of this overall good, concern for my overall good requires, as a constituent part, a concern for the good of my future self. In this way concern for my future self for its own sake seems compatible with, and indeed essential to, self-love.

But the fission case, which introduces the notion of another-self and helps explain how the egoist can justify other-regarding demands, is, for present purposes, isomorphic to the (purely) intrapersonal case. Just as in the intrapersonal case the agent's future self is a part of her, so too in the fission case the interests of the fission products are part of the interests of the subject of fission. And so just as egoism explains why the agent should be concerned about her future self for its own sake, so too it explains why the subject of fission should be concerned about her fission products for their own sakes. In making sacrifices for them (e.g., in investing her savings before the transplants, if she anticipates her fission), she acts out of a concern for the sake of her fission products because their welfare is part of hers. Similar claims will apply *mutatis mutandis* to the relationship between the agent and other other-selves to whom she is related by different degrees of psychological continuity (e.g., intimates, neighbors, fellow citizens). Her concern for them individually or collectively (e.g., the sacrifices she is willing to make) will not be unconditional, but insofar as they are psychologically continuous with her, she should regard their interests as parts of hers, and insofar as their welfare is a part of hers, she should be concerned about their welfare for its own sake (just as she should be concerned about her future self for its own sake).

14 Prospects for an Egoist Justification of Morality

There are different egoist methods for responding to amoralist skepticism. Subjective versions of egoism, which conceive of the agent's good independently of the good of others, can employ various forms of strategic reasoning to justify morality's other-regarding demands (e.g., those concerning cooperation and restraint). However, there seem to be serious limitations to these strategic justifications of morality. They seem to hold the justification of morality hostage to exaggerated empirical claims, they are counterfactually unstable in inappropriate ways, they do not apply to other-regarding obligations in nonstrategic contexts, and they have a difficult time justifying other-regarding concern as well as action.

By contrast, the justification of morality's other-regarding aspects in terms of psychological continuity looks more promising. It is worth distinguishing two aspects of my argument here: (1) the claims that psychological continuity, whether diachronic or synchronic, justifies concern and that this allows a justification of morality's other-regarding aspects, and (2) the neo-Aristotelian egoist interpretation of (1). Someone might accept the appeal to psychological continuity as a justification of rational concern and its ability to establish the authority of morality without accepting the egoist interpretation of this project, that is, without thinking that psychological continuity extends the agent's own interests. This too offers a reply to the moral skeptic. But, of course, I have tried to defend (2) as well as (1). If the extent of our interests is determined by psychological continuity, as the neo-Aristotelian justification claims, then the egoist can justify sacrifices made on behalf of selves who are psychologically continuous with the agent. In this way, I have tried to argue, neo-Aristotelian rational egoism holds the promise of supplying an account of the scope and weight of our reason to benefit and be concerned about others that meshes fairly well with plausible moral claims about our other-regarding duties.

My argument for this claim has been highly programmatic and exploratory. For instance, I have focused on the justification of other-regarding aspects of morality and special obligations. A more adequate assessment of the neo-Aristotelian justification would, among other things, explore its implications for a more varied range of moral considerations.[31] But my focus has not been arbitrary. Other-regarding duties and special obligations are central parts of morality, and other-regarding duties pose the most obvious problem for an egoist justification of morality, as the skeptical challenge reflects. So while much work remains to be done to establish the adequacy of this egoist justification of morality, I hope to have shown at least that neo-Aristotelian rational egoism is an interesting position whose resources to justify moral conduct and concern merit further exploration.[32]

Notes

1. *Internalists* about morality and reasons for action do not distinguish these two forms of moral skepticism, because they assume that to be under a moral obligation simply is to have a reason for action (Prichard 1912; Harman 1975; Mackie 1977, chap. 1). I have argued against this internalist assumption elsewhere (Brink 1989, chap. 3). Here I shall make the externalist assumption that we can first (defeasibly) identify our moral obligations and then ask whether we have good and sufficient reason to fulfill our moral obligations. It is worth noting, though, that the internalist who also accepts agent-relative assumptions about rationality (see below in the text) and so embraces *ethical* egoism (and not simply rational egoism) could accept most of my argument in the rest of this paper, suitably reinterpreted. My primary concern will be to see to what extent other-regarding moral requirements can be justified to the rational egoist. An agent-relative internalist could reinterpret this as the project of seeing to what extent conventional views about the other-regarding aspects of morality can be accommodated by the ethical egoist.

2. This is basically the position of Callicles in Plato's *Gorgias*. Callicles resolves the apparent conflict between virtue and the agent's own benefit by arguing that "real" or natural justice, as opposed to merely conventional justice, does not require the agent to help others or forbear from harming them (482de, 483ab, 488b–490a). And precisely because the revision in ordinary moral views that he makes is so drastic, Callicles is usually thought of as a moral skeptic, even though he accepts the justifiability of real virtue.

3. As such, *rational* egoism should be contrasted with *psychological* egoism (the view that agents act only so as to promote their own real or perceived interests) and *ethical* egoism (the view that an agent's one and only moral obligation is to promote his own interests).

4. However, this appearance may be misleading. An agent-neutral account of rationality will provide a perfect justification of moral demands only if morality is itself agent-neutral. If morality is not fully agent-neutral, then agent-neutral assumptions about rationality may not provide the best justification of morality. I will return to this issue briefly in section 11.

5. Perhaps it is worth noticing that theories of value that are subjective in this sense need not be subjective in the further sense of claiming that a person's welfare is whatever he takes it to be. In *this* sense, hedonism and some desire-satisfaction theories are objective.

6. Similar remarks seem to apply to Parfit's use of the "present-aim" theory of rationality to justify moral concern (1984, 131). This should be no surprise in view of the Humean pedigree of the present-aim theory.

7. I think that this justification of morality is clearly expressed in Epicurus' defense of the instrumental value of justice on hedonistic grounds (*Kuriai Doxa*, 31–38). (For a different reading of Epicurus, see Mitsis 1988.) A variant of this strategy is vigorously defended by Gauthier (1986). Gauthier's strategy is a little different from the one I shall be discussing, because he wants to derive the content of morality from this kind of strategic reasoning ("constrained maximization"), whereas the strategy that I am considering assumes that we can identify the content of morality independently of our attempts to justify it rationally and then tries to justify morality, so understood, by certain patterns of strategic reasoning. But Gauthier's discussion is parallel to my concerns, because his strategy of constrained maximization is the sort of strategic reasoning that my egoist employs and he takes the ability of his theory of morals by agreement to sustain other-regarding action to be a constraint on the adequacy of his moral theory. So the worries about the problems and limitations of this egoist justification of morality that I express below should apply to Gauthier's project as well. Cf. also Axelrod 1984 and M. Taylor 1987.

8. There are (I count) five conditions that are individually necessary and jointly sufficient for a good to be a public good. (1) Widespread, but not universal, contribution is both necessary and sufficient for the good to be produced (in the case of goods whose provision is all or nothing) or for large quantities of the good to be produced (in the case of goods whose provision is continuous). (2) If the good is produced, it is available to all, even to noncontributors; it is impossible or impractical to prevent noncontributors from enjoying the good. (3) Contribution is a nonnegligible cost. (4) The effect of individual contributions on securing the good or on the amount of the good available to individual contributors is negligible, or if some possible contributions have nonnegligible effects (say because of threshold phenomena), then it is the antecedent likelihood of an individual's contribution being one of these that is negligible. (This condition includes the assumption that behavior is not interdependent.) (5) The amount of the good that each individual would gain from widespread contribution outweighs the costs of his share of contribution.

9. See Olson 1965. Taylor (1987) discusses public-good problems that are better modeled as chicken or assurance games rather than as prisoner's dilemmas and argues that the voluntary cooperative provision of these various kinds of public goods is *possible* if certain special conditions obtain: the model must be dynamic, actors must not discount future payoffs too much, the environment must include a sufficiently large number of conditional compliers, and conditional compliers can reliably monitor the compliance and noncompliance of others (this last condition tends to be more easily satisfied in small groups).

10. In a similar way Gauthier's argument for constrained maximization depends upon the assumption that people are psychologically "translucent" (1986, 173–174). But, while the assumption of translucency is psychologically *more* realistic than the notion of "transparency," which he attempts to do without, the assumption is not realistic enough (i.e., it is far from universally true).

11. Cf. Gauthier 1986, 16–17, 232. Notice that for Gauthier, unlike the strategic egoist, this is not just a limitation in the scope of the rational authority of morality but actually a limitation in the scope of *morality itself* (see note 7 above).

12. The egoist can try to justify other-regarding concern in nonstrategic situations by appeal to her justification of other-regarding concern in strategic situations and by insisting that our capacities for benevolence are so coarse-grained that we can maintain benevolence in the strategic situations only by extending it to nonstrategic situations as well. But while this will extend the scope of the other-regarding behavior that the strategic defense can justify, it seems inadequate. As before, the crucial psychological claim seems overstated, and the justification of other-regarding behavior that it provides in nonstrategic cases is counterfactually unstable.

13. I am not saying that no value attaches to pleasure (or disvalue to pain) or to the satisfaction of desires (or disvalue to their frustration). I am assuming only that these are neither the sole nor the primary components of a valuable life (see Brink 1989, chap. 8, sec. 2).

14. Here I owe a great debt to Terry Irwin's published and unpublished writings on this subject (see, e.g., Irwin 1988, chap. 18). However, it should not be assumed that he endorses all of my claims about neo-Aristotelian rational egoism or its Aristotelian pedigree. This strategy bears comparison with other views also. First, Plato claims (a) that the virtuous person will have love for others (*Republic* 402d–403c, 412d), and (b) that love (i) involves concern for the beloved's own sake and (ii) is for the lover the next best thing to immortality (*Symposium* 206e–212c and *Phaedrus* 243c–257b; see also Irwin 1977, 241–243). Plato's grounds for accepting (ii) seem very similar to Aristotle's reasons for regarding one's friend as "another-self" (see below). Claims (a) and (b) allow Plato to argue that the virtuous agent will be concerned about others for their own sakes and will necessarily benefit from benefiting them. Second, Green (1969, secs. 180–191, 199–203, 232–239, 286) and Bradley (1927, 69–81, 163, 166–192, 203–206, 219–225) argue that (a) my good includes the good of others because I am essentially part of a social whole and, hence, (b) in promoting the good of others as duty requires, I promote my own good. I'm not sure that I accept or even understand all of the metaphysical claims on which their defenses of (a) (especially Bradley's) rely.

15. There are some who are unhappy with a metaphysics of temporal parts (see, e.g., Thomson 1983, esp. 210–213). They accept talk of temporal parts as only a *façon de parler*; talk of temporal parts is legitimate if and only if it can be translated, without loss, into talk about enduring objects and their properties at particular times. I don't share these scruples. I see no reason why we shouldn't allow into our ontology objects whose criteria of individuation include temporal properties; on one such view (Heller 1984), temporal parts are four-dimensional objects. However, I don't see that my claims here require me to take a stand on whether temporal parts are respectable entities; I think that all of my claims about temporal parts can be translated, without loss, into claims about persons at times.

16. Cf. Whiting 1986, esp. 557, 572–573. On the surface, her position is just the reverse of mine; she wants to model the justification of self-concern on concern for one's friends, whereas I want to model the justification of concern for one's friends (and others more generally) on self-concern. I'm less clear that our different routes to this comparison between self-concern and concern for one's friends require us to disagree on the substance of the comparison.

17. See, e.g., Perry 1976, Lewis 1976, Parfit 1984, Shoemaker 1984. For some evidence that such a view appeals to Aristotle, see NE 1159a5–14, 1165b21–23, 1166a20–24 (see also Irwin 1988, 241–255, 284–286, 345, 376–378). Because I shall not be explicitly defending psychological-continuity accounts of personal identity, readers may want to accept my conclusions about neo-Aristotelian rational egoism only conditionally as claims that are true *if* psychological continuity is the correct ac-

count of personal identity. However, I do think that the implications of such an account for fission cases (see below) and the uses to which the neo-Aristotelian justification puts such an account provide some indirect evidence for the plausibility of such an account and so some reason for affirming the antecedent in the conditional statement of my conclusions.

18. Consider two objections to my description of the problems in the fission case. (1) The description of the fission case does not *entail* that neither D nor E is A. Even though D and E seem to have equal claims to being A, it could just be true that one of them, but not the other, is A. The question is, of course, in virtue of what would one of them, but not the other, be the same person as A. The answer that it's just a brute fact is no answer at all (because it is no explanation). And even if we accepted the brute fact "answer," the fact that D and E are equally continuous with A might still make us think that rational concern should be divided equally between D and E, and *this* seems to be the crucial claim for my purposes.

(2) My description of the fission case may seem to presuppose three apparently incompatible claims: (i) half a brain is sufficient for personal identity, (ii) two half brains in different bodies are different people, and (iii) two half brains in one body make one person. If (i) and (ii) are true, shouldn't we reject (iii) and conclude that two brains in one body make two people? Or if (iii) is true, shouldn't we deny (i) and (ii) and conclude that two half brains in two bodies still make just one person? No. We can map numbers of brains (and brain parts) onto numbers of people when we know whether the brains (or brain parts) are *functionally integrated*. When two (fully functional) half brains are functionally integrated, they represent one person; when they are not, they are two people. So we can rewrite the triad in such a way as to avoid paradox: (i') half a brain is sufficient for personal identity, unless it's functionally integrated with some other brain (part), (ii') two half brains in different bodies are different people if they are not functionally integrated, and (iii') two half brains in one body make one person if they are functionally integrated.

19. This is one way in which I do not agree with Parfit, who thinks that such "reductionist" accounts of personal identity undermine rational egoism (cf. Parfit 1984, chap. 14 and Brink 1991).

20. Three comments on this egoist account of fission are in order. First, the egoist *cannot* claim that (1) what justifies my concern for my fission products and their pursuit of my projects (after I am gone) consists simply in the fact that these projects are worthwhile. Thus, for instance, the egoist cannot think that my justification for wanting my fission products to complete my search for a cure for cancer is simply because that would be a good thing, say, for the rest of mankind. The egoist must claim that (2) my justification for wanting my fission products to pursue and complete my projects is that this would in some way improve the significance or value of my life. Since my purpose here is not directly to defend rational egoism against rivals (e.g., against agent-neutral theories), I'm not now concerned to defend (2) as superior to (1). Rather, I want to show that the egoist can justify concern on the part of the fission subject for her fission products in a way that opens the door to the justification of wider other-regarding concern. It is interesting to note against (1), however, that I seem to have special reason to be concerned about the completion, after I'm gone, of those projects that I pursued during my life and not just any worthwhile project. (Cf. Perry 1976, 78–85; Whiting 1986, 561–563, 576–580.)

Second, I am claiming that a self's being appropriately psychologically connected with my present self is a sufficient condition for its good to be part of mine and for my having egoist reason to be concerned about it. However, I do not claim that the good of a future self that is appropriately psychologically related to my present self is part of the good of my *present* self; this would commit me to what we might call egoism of the present. Rather, the egoist's justification of concern for my own future self or for my fission product is that the good of that future self is part of *my* good, that is, part of the good of a temporally extended being. (I am grateful to Nick Sturgeon for showing me the need to distinguish these two readings of my claims.) What justifies this claim in the normal, intrapersonal case is that my present self and my future self are both parts of the psychologically continuous series of selves that constitutes me. In fission cases (and more generally with other-selves) there are selves that are not part of me but that are, to varying degrees, psychologically related to selves in the series that I am. This is the reason to regard the welfare of my fission products and other-selves as extending my welfare even if they do not literally extend my life.

Third, there is a more metaphysically revisionary version of rational egoism that I will mention here but not pursue. This version of egoism defines "continuants" as maximal series of psychologically continuous selves and then takes continuants, rather than persons, to be the bearers of reasons for action. This suggestion is similar to Lewis's view (1976), though he seems to want to identify persons and continuants, whereas I do not. Thus in the fission case we would identify two continuants, F and G (where F represents the sum of A and D and G represents the sum of A and E). The justification, say, for A's sacrifice for D's greater benefit is to be understood and explained, according to this form of rational egoism, as F's sacrificing its earlier good for the sake of its later, greater good. Since D is a part of F, F will benefit D for D's own sake and for D's role in F. This proposal may seem metaphysically revisionary in comparison with neo-Aristotelian rational egoism, which takes persons to be the bearers of reasons for action, because it allows the subjects of deliberation to overlap (F and G share A's body and mind) and it seems to recognize many more subjects of deliberation than neo-Aristotelian rational egoism does.

21. Here, of course, I commit myself to the possibility of posthumous interests (benefits and harms) (cf. *NE* i, 10–11). Here and more generally in the neo-Aristotelian justification of other-regarding action and concern, I also commit myself to denying a certain interpretation of the common claim that there is no such thing as *inter*-personal compensation (Nagel 1970, 142; Rawls 1971, 23–29, 187–188, 191; Nozick 1974, 31–34). If there can be interpersonal compensation, this would weaken a standard argument against teleological moral theories (e.g., utilitarianism). Unfortunately, I can't pursue this issue here (I hope to pursue it elsewhere).

22. Of course, this won't be true in asymmetrical cases (e.g., in some relations between parents and children and in that between a fission subject and fission products). This may constitute some reason to prefer cultivating symmetrical other-self relationships.

23. Consider the intrapersonal case. Even views according to which both continuity and connectedness matter (e.g., Parfit 1984, 298–302) claim that each matters. According to these views, continuity by itself matters but is not the only thing that matters. Such a view might be sufficient for my present purposes. But I believe that continuity, rather than connectedness, is what matters. Briefly, it seems to me that we need to believe this if we are to be able to explain why people have strong agent-relative reason (as they surely do) to improve themselves in ways that involve significant psychological changes. For if connectedness matters, then it can become difficult to explain why Fred should undergo such a change

even if it is conceded that the person who has the new psychological profile (Fred*) is much better off than Fred was. (For a fuller discussion of these issues, see Brink 1991.)

24. This discussion of what aspects of a person's life can justify concern raises an interesting and, I find, difficult question about the temporal scope of the egoist's concern. Is the egoist primarily concerned for other selves (fully temporally extended people) or for temporal parts of persons? The interest of the question is brought out in cases where one's relation to another changes, in particular, in cases where it erodes or terminates over time. The form of egoism I have been developing seems committed to taking temporal parts of a person to be the primary objects of concern. I am justified in being concerned about a future self insofar as it is psychologically continuous with the temporal series of selves that I am. So, for example, I have reason to be concerned for you insofar as we are coworkers. If we will not remain coworkers in the future, I will not at that time have as much reason to be concerned about you, and I presumably do not now have as much reason to be concerned about your future welfare (your welfare when we will no longer be coworkers) as I do about your current welfare. Nonetheless because of the continuity between your present self and your future self and my connections to your present self, I presumably do and will have more reason to be concerned about your future welfare than I do and will have reason to be concerned about the welfare of a mere fellow citizen.

25. Thus, recognition of special moral obligations may actually provide some support for this version of rational egoism. An agent-neutral theory of rationality implies that an agent has reason to do something insofar as that action would make people better off, independent of any special relationship that the beneficiaries bear to the agent. There might, therefore, be cases in which an agent-neutral theory of rationality would represent an action as rationally required, because it would produce a significant benefit to comparative strangers, that was incompatible with the actions required by the agent's special moral obligations. If so, we would have to conclude that the neo-Aristotelian version of rational egoism is actually *better* able to justify moral demands than the agent-neutral theory is.

Of course, agent-neutral theories of *rationality* have resources with which to try to give an indirect justification of the stringency of special obligations parallel to the resources of agent-neutral *moral* theories (e.g., consequentialism and utilitarianism) to accommodate special moral obligations. But even if this is true, it might still be a feather in the rational egoist's cap if his justification of these special obligations is more direct or stable.

26. My moral uncertainty here reflects uncertainty both as to the ordinal issue about the precise shape of the moral discount rate (e.g., How much more do I owe a friend than a colleague?) and as to the cardinal issue about precisely how large a sacrifice any one of my other-regarding obligations demands (e.g., Morally, what costs should I bear to provide a certain amount of help to my colleague?).

27. Max is presumably a person, if not a human. So there will be some limits to our psychological differences. A somewhat different problem concerns the justification of our moral obligations toward beings that are neither humans nor persons. I think the egoist treatment of Max's case can probably be adapted to these other cases with plausible results, but I cannot pursue the issue here.

28. Of course, I will have *subjective* egoist reason to rescue Max, even if in fact he will be whisked back to Lotusland before I can establish psychological continuity with him, if I won't be in a position to know this fact about his return. My concern in the text (on this point and others), however, is with the *objective* reasons for action

that rational egoism assigns to agents (i.e., the reasons an agent has in virtue of what the facts are or will be, regardless of whether she is, or should be, in a position to realize what these facts are).

29. This objection is similar to, but distinct from, one based on the Kantian claim that morality should be independent of the agent's own interests. Insofar as this is a different worry from the one I discuss in the text, it raises issues that I cannot properly address here. But I can sketch the outlines of a reply. There are at least three possible Kantian themes here: Kant believes (1) that a good will requires us not only to act in conformity with duty but also to act out of a sense of duty and not because doing so contributes to our own interests (1981, 393–398, 442), (2) that moral obligations apply to agents independently of their antecedent interests or desires (1981, 405, 408, 411, 414–416, 427, 432, 434, 442), and (3) that moral obligations provide agents with reasons for action independently of their antecedent interests or desires (1981, 405, 408, 411, 414–416, 432, 434, 442). As far as I can see, neo-Aristotelian rational egoism is incompatible only with (3); it need deny neither (1) nor (2).

Claim (1) is about the *motivation* characteristic of a good will. But rational egoism is a theory about the grounds of reasons for action, not a theory of motivation or of how agents do or should reason. So egoism places no constraints on the kind of motivation that a good will may require; it says only that if an agent is to have reason to display a good will, whatever that may require, then doing so must contribute to her own good. Since, as we have seen, the egoist can insist that a rational agent have intrinsic concern for things other than herself, I see no reason of principle why the egoist cannot justify a concern to do as morality requires *because* morality requires it.

Rational egoism is a theory about the grounds of reasons for action: it makes reasons for action dependent upon the agent's interests; it does not make moral obligations dependent upon the agent's interests (as *ethical* egoism does). So rational egoism is compatible with (2). Indeed, this is an assumption of our egoist justification of morality. We identify the content of moral requirements independently of their relation to the agent's own welfare, see that many of them are other-regarding, and then ask whether these moral requirements can be rationally justified on egoist grounds.

Though neo-Aristotelian rational egoism does not make an agent's reasons for action directly dependent upon the agent's antecedent desires and though it is capable of rationally justifying a number of familiar moral obligations (whose content and application are not themselves dependent upon the agent's antecedent interests or desires), it does make an agent's reasons for action dependent upon her objective interests. This is simply a way of stating its agent-relativity. So neo-Aristotelian rational egoism does seem committed to denying *this* Kantian theme, but it's not clear that this is any embarrassment.

30. One might question whether morality really makes this additional demand. Does morality require more of me than that I be a reliable benefactor in the appropriate circumstances? Does it also require that my benefaction be based on a concern for others for their own sakes? Or is this concern something that goes beyond one's moral obligations? Is it perhaps something supererogatory? If this sort of concern is not part of moral obligation but at most something supererogatory, then it would arguably be no defect in egoism if it were unable to justify such concern. For while we may hope to be able to show that most of morality's requirements are rationally justifiable, supererogatory acts and character seem to represent precisely that dimension of morality that we don't expect to be rationally required. Fortunately,

I do not think that we need to resolve this problem about the moral status, if any, of this sort of other-regarding concern, because the egoist seems able to justify such concern.

31. One natural question is whether the neo-Aristotelian rational egoist can justify agent-centered moral restrictions or side-constraints, for example, the moral claim that it would be impermissible for one to cause certain sorts of harms even as a means to minimizing a greater number of such harms caused by other people. There may be room for a direct justification of fairly robust restrictions and constraints. Suppose A can prevent B from causing harm to C and D by herself causing a comparable harm to E. X represents A's causing E harm in order that C and D may each be spared comparable harm from B; Y represents A's refusal to harm E even as a means of preventing harm to C and D. If X would establish a stronger or more direct causal-psychological connection between A and E than Y would establish between A and either C or D, then, according to neo-Aristotelian rational egoism, A will have more reason to refrain from causing harm to E than she has to prevent B's harming either C or D. And this will imply that her reasons for action here are not directly proportional to the good she can do or the harm she can prevent (see my discussion of special obligations in sec. 11). While this may be sufficient to accommodate fairly robust restrictions and constraints, it seems insufficient to accommodate the sort of *absolute* restrictions and constraints that some have assumed morality contains. But I think it is very unclear that morality does contain restrictions and constraints that are absolute and not merely robust. So it's not obvious that a direct justification of reasonable agent-centered restrictions or side-constraints is beyond the reach of rational egoism. Moreover, though these are interesting issues that deserve fuller discussion, agent-centered moral restrictions and side-constraints are themselves puzzling enough moral claims (cf. Scheffler 1982, chap. 4; Nagel 1986, 175–185) that it would not obviously be a defect of the neo-Aristotelian justification if it could not fully accommodate them or if its justification of them took an indirect form.

32. I am grateful to audiences at Stanford University and the University of Iowa for helpful discussion of distant ancestors of some of this material. A more recent version was read at the 1989 APA Central Division Meetings; Nick Sturgeon provided extremely valuable comments. I would also like to thank Joshua Cohen, David Copp, Stephen Darwall, Owen Flanagan, Michael Hardimon, Brad Hooker, Diane Jeske, Scott MacDonald, Derek Parfit, Paul Pietroski, Amélie Rorty, Sydney Shoemaker, Walter Sinnott-Armstrong, Judy Thomson, Jennifer Whiting, and my colleagues in a Cambridge-area moral psychology study group for helpful discussion of these issues. Special thanks go to Terry Irwin and Alan Sidelle for especially helpful discussion and support.

Chapter 16

Is Akratic Action Always Irrational?

Alison McIntyre

---

1 Why Is Continence Rational and Incontinence Irrational?

We act akratically when we judge a course of action to be the best for us to pursue and yet, without relinquishing the original judgment, voluntarily pursue some other course of action.[1]

Many have thought that the chief philosophical question to ask about this phenomenon concerns its possibility: Can an agent really make a judgment, keep it in mind, continue to accept it, and yet act against it by doing something else? Or must the judgment have been in some way defective, the agent less than clear-headed, or the action not entirely voluntary?[2]

If we concede that agents can act against their better judgment, a more fundamental question can be raised about akrasia: Why would it be rational for an agent to act in accordance with his judgment about what he ought to do, and why is it irrational of him to abandon it? The answer to this question has seemed obvious. Akrasia is a form of inconsistency, since the agent's action is not of the kind specified in his practical conclusion. Thus, since inconsistency is a form of irrationality, akrasia is necessarily irrational. It might even be thought that continent action is the paradigm for rationality in action, as opposed to rationality in thought or reasoning, while incontinence is our paradigm for practical, as opposed to theoretical, irrationality.

I will try to show that this simple explanation is inadequate, and in doing so, I will address two questions: When is it irrational to act against one's better judgment? Why is it irrational (when it is irrational) to do so? I reject the view that explains the irrationality of akrasia as a form of inconsistency. I will also defend the view that akrasia is not necessarily irrational.

The simple account of the irrationality of incontinence fails to give two features of deliberation and practical reasoning their proper weight. First, practical reasoning is defeasible. Sometimes the most rational response for an agent to make after drawing a practical conclusion is to revise the line of thought that led up to it. Thus, an agent does not have to comply with and execute a practical conclusion in order to be rational. Second, incontinence is not the only form of irrationality in action and deliberation that can occur. Rationalization (of the Freudian sort) is a form of irrationality, as is the failure to revise one's practical conclusion in light of new information that undermines it.

Of course, akratic action is *often* irrational. Perhaps it is usually irrational and even typically irrational. Furthermore, the usual examples of akrasia involving, e.g., smoking, gluttony, drinking too much are irrational in some sense. But if I am right, it is not the case that akrasia as such, as action that meets the rather formal definition of action against one's better judgment, is necessarily irrational.

I will not argue that incontinence is ever rational as such. I believe that the principle enjoining us to be continent is a prima facie rational requirement. However, I will argue that in certain situations, incontinence may be more rational than continence and at the very least is no less rational than continence. I will try to show that the principle of continence is a defeasible rational requirement, that there are other principles that govern practical reasoning, and that their recommendations can conflict with those of the principle of continence.

Consider the situation of Mark Twain's character Huckleberry Finn, brought to the attention of philosophers by Jonathan Bennett (1974). Having helped Jim, a slave, run away from his owner, Huck experiences what he identifies as pangs of conscience, and he decides to turn Jim in. But when he has the opportunity to do this, Huck finds himself incapable of carrying out his resolve, and castigating himself for his weakness, he lies to some bounty hunters in order to protect his friend. We might well think that Huck should revise the line of thought that produced his decision to turn Jim over to the authorities in light of the considerations that made that decision impossible to carry out: Huck's friendship with Jim, his awareness of Jim's trust and gratitude, his sympathy with his desire for freedom. It would be irrational of Huck to ignore these considerations entirely, having found them so compelling. Equally, it would be irrational of Huck to achieve continence simply by rationalizing his failure to turn Jim in by telling himself that *this* was not the time to do so and that a better time would come up later. Such a move would not respond adequately to the considerations that prevented Huck from carrying out his original plan.

Given all of this, why might one say that it is irrational of Huck to act against his better judgment by not turning Jim over to the slave hunters? Three different ways in which this question might be answered come to mind:

- Incontinence is irrational because it involves the overcoming of reason by desire or emotion and so has an irrational or nonrational source. Huck allows feelings of sympathy to overcome what he takes to be his moral principles. This seems to be Bennett's view about the nature of Huck's conflict. He characterizes Huck's dilemma as one in which general moral principles and reasons conflict with "unreasoned emotional pulls" (p. 127).
- Rationality in action is an *internal* affair that concerns how an agent acts in light of what he believes. Huck fails to do what he believes he has most reason to do. Hence, he fails to do what he has (in the internal sense) most reason to do. Our justified approval of his action should not obscure the fact that it was irrational of Huck to perform it in light of *his* moral principles. The judgment that was violated in his akratic action was one that took more into account (e.g., that Miss Watson had done no harm to Huck and so didn't deserve to lose a valuable slave) and so represented a superior assessment of what course of action Huck had most reason to pursue. Thus the akratic action is better only from a more limited perspective, a perspective that is not his best or most rational one and perhaps not the perspective that is most stably or most consistently his own.
- Huck believes that morality requires him to turn Jim in and that his resistance to doing so is a form of weakness, perhaps a form of squeamishness. Huck values acting on moral principles more than he values responding to whatever emotional tugs he happens to experience, so in acting akratically, he fails to satisfy his higher-order desires concerning his own agency. In doing what he most desires to do, he fails to do what he most values doing or alternatively what he thinks it is most important to do.

I think it can be argued that each of these claims is false about Twain's character, though it would be difficult to settle the matter in any conclusive way. What I want to show is that there can be cases of akrasia much like Huck's that are not irrational in any of these three ways, that is, that akratic action does not necessarily have an irrational or nonrational source, that it is not necessarily the course of action that the agent has less reason to pursue in view of his beliefs and desires, and that in acting akratically, an agent does not necessarily pursue a course that he evaluates as less important or less valuable than the continent alternative. Thus these three kinds of irrationality are not necessarily present when an agent acts against his better judgment. The correlative thesis is that continent action is not always more rational in these three respects than the incontinent alternative.

If we take a highly idealized view of our rational capacities as agents, these claims may seem especially hard to accept. Two idealizing assumptions in particular will be identified as supports for the view that akrasia is necessarily irrational. The first is the assumption that through introspection and reflection, agents can become fully aware of what motivates them to act and what factors influence them in deliberation. Researchers in social psychology (e.g., Nisbett and Wilson in 1977, Ross and Anderson in 1982) have challenged both the assumption that agents are generally aware of their reasons for changing their evaluations and beliefs and the assumption that agents are generally aware of changes in their evaluative judgments and motivational states that influence their behavior. Within philosophy, attacks upon doctrines of transparency and privileged access concerning the mind have become commonplace, yet their effects have not penetrated fully into philosophical discussions of practical reasoning. I will argue that agents are not always aware of the factors motivating their actions that could also serve to justify them. Thus, even on an account of reasons for action as internal reasons, one shouldn't assume that agents are fully aware of the considerations that count, for them, as reasons.

The second idealizing assumption concerns the appropriate standard for judging the rationality of agents. To assume that deliberating agents have at their disposal unlimited memories, unlimited time, and unlimited attention is to fail to acknowledge the important role played by the practical constraints imposed on agents in deliberation. Deliberating well, and thus rationally, is a matter of making the best trade-offs between competing demands for thoroughness and efficiency. Models of belief revision and inference that take into account the opportunity costs of expending attention and processing time and the limits imposed by human memory have been put forward (e.g., Harman 1986, Cherniak 1986). I will introduce a related consideration that bears more directly upon the constraints we encounter in practical deliberation: that traits of character that do in fact constitute deliberative virtues may not, when exercised, lead the agent to make choices that would be considered optimal from the perspective of ideal rationality.

In the next three sections I will discuss in greater detail the three different charges of irrationality that could be brought against akratic action and the ways in which akratic action could fail to fall under them.

2 The Irrationality of the Sources of Akratic Action: Emotion and Desire

It may well be that akrasia has been thought to be essentially and necessarily irrational because it has been thought to involve the usurpation of reason by desires that are at best nonrational and at worst irrational. The failure of the agent's motivations to conform to his practical judgment could be taken as evidence of the irrationality of their source: the motivations don't recognize the proper authority in questions of action. Since reason was not in charge of action motivated by the agent's recalcitrant desires, it was irrational action.

Such claims are probably true about akrasia as Aristotle defined it. In book VII of the *Nicomachean Ethics* he distinguished what he considered to be genuine akrasia, or akrasia simply speaking, from other phenomena called akrasia only by resemblance. Genuine akrasia is caused by an excessive concern for satisfying bodily appetites (1148a5–12). Akrasia "by resemblance" is prompted by emotion or by excessively strong desires for wealth, victory, profit, or honor—things choice-worthy in themselves—and was strongly distinguished by Aristotle from akrasia prompted by appetite (1147b24–33, 1148a23–b14). Akrasia by resemblance is not considered to be blameworthy, Aristotle argues, because what is pursued to excess is something that is good and worthwhile, but it is to be avoided, since such action conflicts with correct reason.

Aristotle's criteria need not be our own. Though he was concerned to distinguish the two kinds of akrasia according to their causes and proper objects, his insightful comments about akrasia by resemblance bear witness to the fact that if akrasia is defined as action against the agent's better judgment, not all cases of akrasia will involve a conflict between reason and appetitive desires.

It is common now for philosophers to discuss examples of akrasia that fall under this broader definition (Davidson 1969, Jackson 1984). Not only may akrasia be prompted by any kind of motivation on this view; the judgment that is flouted need not be the morally or prudentially correct one. Furthermore, cases of nonappetitive akrasia need not have a nonrational or irrational motivational source. As Aristotle observes about cases of akrasia caused by emotion (which he classified as nonappetitive akrasia), we perceive that "we are being slighted or wantonly insulted; and emotion, *as though it had inferred that it is right to fight this sort of thing*, is irritated at once" (1149a32–b2). Emotion responds to the justificatory force of a consideration, while appetite is moved by the mere prospect of pleasure.

3 Does the Akratic Choose the Less Rational Course of Action?

It could be argued that by acting against his better judgment the akratic agent does what he has less reason to do, given his beliefs and desires, and does what he believes he has less reason to do, since he abandoned his practical conclusion. Thus akratic action is irrational on purely internal grounds.

It would be relatively easy to show that an akratic agent might be doing what he has more reason to do if one appeals to reasons of the external sort—reasons that can be attributed to an agent whether or not the agent is in any way motivated to act in accordance with them (see Williams 1981c for an account of this distinction). Perhaps this is what one is led to conclude about Huck Finn's failure to betray Jim: Huck does what we believe he has most reason to do, since we believe that slavery is wrong. But if one appeals to reasons in this external sense to show that in some situation the akratic course was the one that the agent had most reason to pursue though she didn't see this, then it will seem to be an accident that the agent took the course that there were more reasons for her to take, and in her ignorance of what reasons she has, she will appear irrational. Hence, this strategy would provide no defense of the claim that an akratic agent may not be irrational.

I will take a very different tack. I will try to show that the akratic course of action may be one that the agent has more reason to pursue, where reasons of the internal sort only would be appealed to in justifying this claim.

I will assume that drawing a practical conclusion about what it would be best for oneself to do involves corresponding beliefs about what reasons one has to act.[3] Thus, if you judge that it is *better*, all things considered, to speak your mind than to remain silent on some occasion, then you believe that you have *more* reason to speak your mind than to remain silent. If you judge that speaking your mind is *best*, all things considered, then you believe that you have *most* reason to speak your mind. According to this it would be incoherent for an agent to say, "I judge this best, all things considered, but I have most reason to do something else."

The same need not be true about the content of the judgments or intentions that prompt or accompany action. When an agent acts akratically, what she does is not what she believes that she has most reason to do. What I want to show is that even though the akratic agent does not believe that she is doing what she has most reason to do, it may nevertheless be the case that the course of action that she is pursuing is the one that she has (in the internal sense) most reason to pursue.[4]

Akrasia would be impossible if the connection between an agent's evaluative judgments and her motivations were both finely calibrated and perfectly reliable. So to be plausible, an account of internal reasons must be weak enough to allow that what an agent is most motivated to do may not be what she has most reason to do. An agent might believe that she has more reason to do x than to do y, while at the same time being more motivated to do y. Here is a candidate: some consideration constitutes an internal reason for an agent to act in some way at a particular time only if that consideration has motivational force for the agent at that time or the agent is not aware of the fact but would see it as a reason if the agent were to become aware of it. As Bernard Williams points out in "Internal and External Reasons" (1981c), this can also give us grounds for disqualifying from counting as a reason for the agent some consideration that the agent thinks is a reason when the agent's belief is based on some factual mistake. (For example, he thinks that he has a reason to feed this stuff to the zebra because he thinks it's hay, but he's wrong, it's bedding straw, so he does not have a reason to feed it to the zebra.)

This additional disjunct requires the immediate assent of the agent: some unknown fact constitutes a reason for the agent to act in a certain way only if the agent would be motivated accordingly if that fact were brought to the agent's attention. Following Williams (1981c), I propose a weaker additional condition that allows that if the agent could come to see, as a result of deliberation, that this consideration is a reason for her, then it might be a reason for her. This allows that an agent might be aware of some fact or consideration but not see it as a reason for her even though it is a reason for her: she could see it as one if she were to reflect or deliberate further.

This is still an internalist view in that the limit on what constitutes a reason for an agent is set by what reasons the agent herself could derive or come to see that she had, through deliberation, from her more basic motivations. It is only by bringing her tastes, preferences, values, dispositions, desires and commitments to bear on particular circumstances that an agent can see what reasons she has to act in one way rather than another.

The coherence of describing someone as *discovering* that something constitutes a reason for her to remain silent, say, just by reflecting and not by learning any situational facts seems to require that a reason for her to remain silent might exist without being so recognized. Thus, even on an internalist view, agents may not always see what their basic motivational set, as Williams calls it (p. 110), gives them reasons to do in particular circumstances. Now, Williams claims that an adequate theory of practical reasoning will have to acknowledge and account for the fact that there are no clear limits on what an agent might arrive at by rational deliberation. He observes that "practical reasoning is a heuristic process, and an imaginative one, and there are no fixed boundaries on the continuum from rational thought to inspiration and conversion" (p. 110). He concludes that there is an appropriate vagueness about just what an agent has reason to do because this depends on how ambitiously one conceives the deliberative processes that can lead from an agent's present motivations to his acquiring the belief that he has some previously unappreciated reason for action.

Even if one makes very modest assumptions about the deliberative capacities of an agent, so that these are clearly on the side of rational thought as opposed to inspiration and conversion, it can be argued that agents might not see what reasons they have for acting in a certain way.

If one accepts this, then a possibility opens up that seemed to be foreclosed by standard accounts of the irrationality of incontinence. If an agent is not necessarily clear-sighted about what reasons she has on a particular occasion to act in one way rather than another, then when she deliberates, taking into account all the reasons she sees as relevant, the practical judgments that she arrives at will express what she *believes* that she has most reason to do, but they might fail to express what she actually *has* most reason to do or what it would be most rational for her to do. She might have reasons to act that she doesn't acknowledge but could acknowledge if she were to deliberate better in those circumstances. Perhaps she could have deliberated better because she didn't see the relevance of certain considerations to the issue, because there is more in her motivational set than she sees, or because she didn't make the connection between her more fundamental desires and projects and their relevance in the situation at hand.

4 Renegade Reasons versus New Considerations

Donald Davidson (1969, 37–41) has argued that the akratic break in the agent's practical reasoning occurs when an agent goes from an all-things-considered evaluative judgment to an unconditional judgment. The contrast he draws is between a judgment that some course of action is best relative to a set of considerations—the all-things-considered judgment—and a judgment that some course of action is simply best—the unconditional judgment. For example, suppose that you are at a contentious meeting and you consider whether you should remain silent about a certain topic or speak your mind. There are reasons for and against each course. Suppose that after considering everything that seems relevant, you judge that all things considered, it would be best to remain silent. This is what Davidson calls, in what has become a technical term in his writings and in the work of those who follow him, a *best judgment*. It is your judgment about what would be best. If you then akratically stand up and speak your mind, that is, if you stand up, perhaps thinking to yourself, "This is *not* a good idea," and speak your mind, you will be acting against your best judgment. Now according to Davidson, the akratic course of action, speaking your mind, was prompted or at least accompanied by an unconditional judgment that it would be best to speak up. Typically (that is, in continent action), the unconditional judgment that accompanies action corresponds to the previous all-things-considered, relative judgment, though it is not logically implied or entailed by it. But as Davidson sees it, this inferential link is broken when someone acts akratically and the two judgments endorse different courses of action. The akratic agent shows evaluative inconsistency, but no logical inconsistency, in reasoning in this way.

Instead, the akratic's irrationality could be characterized as a violation of a principle of continence according to which an agent should "perform the action judged best on the basis of all available relevant reasons" (Davidson 1970, 41). An agent who accepts this second-order principle is irrational by his own lights when he violates it. Davidson says, "What is wrong is that the incontinent man acts, and judges, irrationally, for this is surely what we must say of a man who goes against his own best judgment." But note that the agent's judgment that some option is best might not be the expression of the best judgment that the agent could have made in the circumstances. Philosophers who have followed Davidson in using the technical term "best judgment" to describe the agent's judgment that some course of action is best (e.g., Charlton (1988, 136)) will find it easy to miss this point because their choice of terminology makes it so hard to state. A Davidsonian best judgment is a judgment about what is best, but a judgment about what is best might not be arrived at by exercising one's judgment in the best way possible given the considerations that matter to the agent.

On this view, assessing practical judgments in terms of their relation to the considerations that were in fact taken into account is assumed to be equivalent to assessing practical judgments in terms of the agent's reasons. Davidson assumes that the "best judgment" in his technical sense is the best possible judgment in the circumstances because it takes more into account. As Davidson describes the akratic's reasoning, a consideration figures first in a set of reasons relative to which the agent makes an all-things-considered judgment. Then this consideration escapes from its subordinate position as one consideration among many and triggers action on its own by giving rise to an unconditional judgment.

A well-known example of Davidson's can be used to illustrate this. A man realizes, while already lying in bed, that he hasn't brushed his teeth. He decides that it is best, all things considered, not to bother: decay is slow at his age, and he'll have trouble getting to sleep if he gets up now. Nevertheless, prompted by some sort of overly conscientious urge, he gets up and brushes his teeth anyway, and so he brushes his teeth akratically.

His action is not necessarily irrational in the other respect that I have described: what motivated him is not some blind, nonrational appetite but something more cognitive in nature. It is irrational for the second kind of reason: in making the unconditional judgment that it's best to brush, the agent takes less into account than was taken into account in making his all-things-considered judgment that it was best not to get up.

The agent's reason for forming that final unconditional judgment is, according to Davidson, something that was treated as one consideration among many, and so was overridden, in forming the all-things-considered judgment, but it manages to escape from this subordinate position and motivate action on its own despite this fact. It is a kind of renegade reason (this is not Davidson's term; it is my characterization of it).

Davidson takes this to be part of the definition of incontinence, not merely a description of a typical case. An action x is incontinent, he suggests, if "the agent has a better reason for doing something else: he does x for a reason r, but he has a reason r' that includes r and more, on the basis of which he judges some alternative y to be better than x" (1970, 40). According to Davidson, the reasons that motivate the akratic action must therefore be a proper subset of the reasons that were taken into account in forming the all-things-considered judgment. This is a commonly accepted diagnosis of what has gone wrong when an agent is akratic. Christopher Peacocke says in a similar vein, "The akrates is irrational because although he intentionally does something for which he has some reason, there is a wider set of reasons he has relative to which he does not judge what he does to be rational" (1985, 52).

Akrasia is necessarily irrational on such accounts because the agent really has a better reason, a more inclusive reason, not merely a reason thought to be better, for performing the continent action. So it is argued that the irrationality of incontinence as such depends on this defect in the agent's deliberative procedure, a defect that consists in letting a reason count, as Davidson describes it, "twice over."

The supposition that the unconditional judgment (the one that led to the akratic course of action) must have been prompted by a renegade reason of this kind can reasonably be made when cases of Aristotelian or appetitive akrasia are in question. When an agent's judgment caves in to one of his appetites, then the psychological insistency and urgency of the appetites ensure that this appetite was seen to constitute at least a reason for seeking to satisfy it when the agent was deliberating to form his all-things-considered judgment. Thus it makes sense to assume that the appetite in question was one of the things considered in forming the all-things-considered judgment not to satisfy it.

If we want to consider akrasia more broadly than Aristotle did, as most of us believe we should, we shouldn't carry over this assumption uncritically. If it is possible that akratic action be prompted by something other than the considerations that the agent has already treated as relevant in making his all-things-considered judgment and that he has given proper weight to, then the irrationality of akrasia may not be as deep or as universal as is generally thought.

In fact, there are at least three ways in which an episode of akrasia might not fit Davidson's description. First, the reason that motivates the akratic action might be one that the agent had previously taken into account but without giving it sufficient weight. That is, it might be a reason that has assumed its proper role in motivating action, rather than a renegade reason that has escaped from its properly subordinated position. Second, the akratic action could be motivated by an entirely new consideration that had not been taken into account initially. Third, it could have been the subtraction of a consideration that was previously treated as a reason that provoked the akratic action. The circumstances of Davidson's toothbrushing akrates could be understood in any of these three ways.

Aristotle considers the sophistical argument that foolishness combined with akrasia yields virtue in *Nichomachean Ethics* VII. The foolish person thinks that what is bad is good, but if he is akratic, he avoids what is bad anyway and so does what is virtuous (1146a27–31). What I have suggested may seem equally sophistical: is it just that two kinds of irrationality, a bad initial judgment and akrasia, can cancel each other out? In Aristotle's example, the foolishness and the incontinence have separate sources, but this is not so with the examples I wish to consider. In these it is because the agent has almost attained the deliberative perspective from which the more rational judgment could be made that he departs from the less rational all-things-considered judgment. Such an akratic action would not be irrational in the first two ways I have discussed.

If the agent is sensitive to something that constitutes a reason for him but he doesn't see that it does, and if this consideration is what motivates him to perform the akratic action, then these are not two separate errors cancelling each other out; they are two different ways in which the justificatory force of this consideration can be manifested.[5]

What I want to suggest is that an agent's sensitivity to considerations that are reasons might on some occasions outstrip his more intellectual ability to see that they are reasons and are such as to justify a course of action. If such a sensitivity is what causes him to choose the course of action that is more rational, then his akratic action is not irrational in the second sense that I have discussed: it is not caused by a renegade reason and it is not what he has less reason to do.

5 Rationality in Action as Evaluative Consistency

So far I have suggested that akratic action may not be irrational if the agent is motivated by some consideration that could also have led her to revise the reasoning that led to her practical conclusion. Perhaps if she had had more time, more information, more insight, or greater powers of self-observation, the agent would have been able to justify performing the action that was done akratically. But how can we or the agent distinguish considerations with justificatory force from considerations that would merely rationalize an action without really justifying it? After all, even if a motivating factor could have produced a revision in the agent's practical reasoning, this does not show that such a revision would have been rational or justified.

We generally assume that to rationalize not performing an action in the face of recalcitrant motivation is to fail to justify it. Sidgwick eloquently describes a person in this familiar situation:

> Having sat down to a hard and distasteful task which he regards it as his duty to do—but which can be postponed without any immediate disagreeable consequences to himself—he finds a difficulty in getting under way; and then rapidly but sincerely persuades himself that in the present state of his brain some lighter work is just at present more suited to his powers—such as the study, through the medium of the daily papers, of current political events, of which no citizen ought to allow himself to be ignorant. (1893, 185)

In this case the agent actually revises his practical conclusion: he decides that it would be best to spend his time with the newspapers. We can equally well imagine an akratic outcome in such a situation: the man with the disagreeable task doesn't relinquish the judgment that he really ought to be starting it, but his recognition of a new consideration, the difficulty of beginning in the present state of his brain, leads him to read the newspaper nonetheless. What distinguishes the cases of akrasia that interest me from this akratic outcome? Furthermore, what distinguishes the situations in which an agent would be justified in revising his reasoning from situations in which this kind of rationalization occurs?

Part of the answer has already been suggested: akrasia (or a revision in the agent's practical conclusion) will not be irrational if the agent really has more reason to perform the action done akratically (or the newly decided upon action) and the recognition of some consideration that has this justifying force motivates the action (or the revision). But this is not enough. The kind of rationality that is in question here is supposed to be an internal matter: what matters is what the agent was able to justify given what he knew, believed, or wanted *then*, not what could have been justified from some other perspective that he did not at that time have.

It could be argued that what is irrational about the decision to read the newspapers made by the man in Sidgwick's example is that his judgment doesn't cohere well enough with all of his other beliefs, desires, and evaluations. Perhaps he values carrying out the disagreeable task expeditiously more than he values keeping up with world affairs on a daily basis. Similarly, the akratic counterpart of Sidgwick's man could be said to be acting irrationally because he is responding to a new consideration that prompts him to do what he does not want himself to do: perhaps he believes that in general it is more important to persist in these situations than to succumb so easily to distraction.

The point could be expressed in terms of higher-order desires or preferences (Frankfurt 1971). The akratic in fact wants to read the newspapers more than he wants to start the disagreeable task. However, he wants himself to act on his desire to perform the task, and he doesn't want himself to act on his desire to read the newspapers (see Jeffrey 1974, Schiffer 1976). It's not clear that this is the best way to characterize akrasia. Why should we think that an agent's fundamental evaluative judgments are best expressed as desires about his own desires or as preferences about his own preferences? Not only is it implausible to construe our deepest commitments as preferences concerning our own psychology, it is also not clear why a desire should derive greater authority simply from the fact that it is a higher-order one (see Watson 1975, 1987b). Furthermore, not every action motivated by a desire by which one desires not to be moved will count as akratic. If you prefer not to act out of a desire for revenge but seek vengeance on some occasion nevertheless, you will have failed to live up to one of your ideals, but your action need not be akratic. You may have been unhesitating in your choice when you made it. The peculiar irrationality of akrasia involves evaluative inconsistency between one's judgment about what it is best to do on a particular occasion and one's action; inconsistency between one's practical judgments and one's more general values is another matter.

David Charles has suggested that incontinent action is irrational because it violates the practical principle that enjoins agents to aim at maximal satisfaction of their most *important* desires (1983, 209–211). One desire is more important than another, on this view, if it is better supported by an agent's (intention-based) practical beliefs and by his other commitments. "They provide one element in an explanatory backdrop against which certain desires can be conceived of as more fundamental, independent of the sum of satisfactions they bring individually" (p. 209). This proposal would explain the irrationality of akratic action as a failure on the part of the agent to satisfy the more important of two conflicting sets of desires. The akratic counterpart of Sidgwick's man satisfies the set of desires that supports reading the newspapers but not the (more important) set that supports starting the disagreeable task. The latter is more important because it is the set of desires that the agent's long-term plans aim to satisfy and that will provide the rationale for his future plans and projects.

Is akratic action always irrational in this respect? In particular, does the following case of akrasia necessarily manifest this kind of evaluative inconsistency? Mary is an impatient and excessively critical person, and she has realized that her manner offends her employees in a way that is counterproductive. She has adopted the policy of prefacing her critical comments to her employees with an appreciative remark. She finds this extremely difficult to carry out since she finds it difficult to think of anything appreciative to say to someone who has exasperated her, but she perseveres and forces herself to stick to the policy. One day Mary sees a newly hired trainee making a mess of an extremely simple task (the daily mail is about to go out with insufficient postage), and it is necessary to say something to him immediately to remedy the problem. She decides that, all things considered, it would be best to follow her policy and to preface her criticism of him with an appreciative comment about his punctuality, which is all that she can think of to appreciate. Nevertheless, with an uneasy feeling she akratically launches directly into her criticisms.

Suppose that what Mary did is what she had most reason to do in the circumstances. If she had fumbled through an appreciative comment, it would have sounded so insincere or so condescending that it would have insulted the employee; hence, it really was better for her to have omitted it.

Suppose also that Mary didn't fully see that as a reason for departing from her policy. It seemed to her to be best, all things considered, to stick with her policy. She was akratic because she responded to the consideration that it just didn't seem right to add the appreciative comment without fully taking in its force as a justification for her action. In such a case, by akratically omitting the appreciative comment, Mary performed the action that it was more rational for her to perform. Furthermore, this was no accident. What motivated her akrasia was a response to just the consideration that makes her action the more rational one: the fact that the appreciative comment would not have had its intended effect. This time it was not irascibility or impatience that made her depart from her policy.

Still, it might be objected, wasn't her act irrational, because she didn't act on the judgment that would satisfy the set of desires that *she* thought most important? After all, we are assuming that her policy was instigated in order to ensure that her feelings did not interfere with her carrying out her job effectively. Thus *she* thinks that her desire to be diplomatic is more important than her desire to express her honest opinion.

Mary's situation is most plausibly understood quite differently. What deterred her from making the appreciative comment was not the impetuousness that her policy was designed to suppress. Rather, it was her sense that a lame appreciative comment would have seemed too transparently insincere and so condescending. Her desire to deal effectively with her employees is the desire that it is most important for her to satisfy. A more adequate policy would take this into account, so Mary would also have been justified in revising her practical conclusion in light of this. Perhaps she would have changed her mind if there had been more time to reflect before acting. Mary's akratic action is not irrational, then, in this third way: it does not reveal an evaluative inconsistency. Although Mary did not, at the moment of action, fully see the importance of leaving out a patently insincere compliment, it doesn't follow that avoiding such insincerity was not important to her. In fact, the general rationale for her policy—avoiding counterproductive interactions with employees—would cover this new kind of case as well.

6 Revise or Be Continent

I have argued that an akratic action need not involve a rebellion against reason on the part of desire, need not be a course of action that the agent has less reason to pursue, and need not manifest a certain kind of evaluative inconsistency: the set of desires that were acted on need not be less important to the agent than the set of desires that support the agent's judgment about what it would be best to do.

It could be conceded that akrasia is not irrational because it is a form of inconsistency or contradiction or a case in which reason is overthrown, and yet maintained that it is nevertheless an option that is always second best for an agent and thus irrational. That is, incontinence is irrational because the agent always has some alternative to incontinence that it is more rational for the agent to choose. For instance, it might be argued, if we find it difficult to act as we think best, we should consider whether we should change our practical conclusion, and if we don't end up revising the reasoning that supports it, we should carry it out. We should be like Socrates as he is portrayed in the Crito: obligated either to persuade the city of the wrongness of a judgment or, failing that, to obey it. Civil disobedience is not an option for a pious citizen. Equally, one might argue, akrasia is always a less desirable course for rational agents than attempting to revise their practical judgments or, failing that, carrying them out.

This objection changes the terms of the inquiry about the irrationality of akrasia. Instead of locating its irrationality in some practical analogue of the formal notion of inconsistency, it bases the charge on a claim about what it is most rational for a deliberating agent to do in the face of a perceived reluctance to act on his judgment about what it would be best to do. I believe that this is the right perspective to adopt in exploring the question. Whether akrasia is necessarily irrational will then depend on how one understands the practical constraints on deliberation and how an agent ought to deal with them.

I will now argue that even when an agent's akratic behavior is not irrational in any of the three respects previously discussed, continent behavior might violate other principles that express norms of rationality in deliberation and action. Or to put the point less abstractly, some dispositions that it is rational for an agent to have and to exercise in deliberation can work against continence. Principles governing rational deliberation can exclude the continent alternatives to akrasia and so give akratic action some indirect rational support. Along with the principle that enjoins continence, there are principles advising us against deliberative stolidity or obstinacy, against the deliberate suppression of countervailing motives, and against hasty changes of mind that rationalize a perceived reluctance to act in the way we judge best.

Recall the case of Mary, the impatient employer. We could characterize Mary's alternatives to akratic action in this way: she could be continent and stick to her original judgment, or she could revise her judgment so as to justify her reluctance to act on her policy. Each of these options could take more than one form.

1. Continence might take (a) the mild form of choosing to set aside the new consideration that challenged her decision to adhere to her policy or (b) the stronger form of actively suppressing the thoughts that undermined her resolution. It could also take (c) the ideal form of resolving to follow her policy now and to reflect later on whether the new consideration justified a revision of it.

2. She could revise her judgment about what course of action would be best. This also could be done in many ways: (a) She could merely rationalize doing what she felt tempted to do, without clearly grasping what justified this feeling. Or (b) as an ideal and attentive deliberator, she could, in a flash of insight, revise and improve her policy on the spot by recognizing an exception to her policy. There is an intermediate possibility here as well: (c) Mary could maintain her belief that it would be best to act according to her policy but decide, in the face of her reluctance to act on it, that she wasn't capable of doing what would be best and so should revise her practical aspirations

downward. That is, she could reject the policy on the grounds that it was not feasible for her, without doubting that it would be better if she were able to do what it recommended.

One of these alternatives (2b) is clearly better than akrasia. It would be better for Mary to revise her policy sensitively and accurately before speaking to the employee. But in the circumstances as we have imagined them—Mary has little time to deliberate—the ideal course may not be open to her. Alternative (1c) too is arguably a better course than akrasia: perhaps it would be best for her to stick with the old policy of doing what she could to avoid sounding insincere and for her to rethink the policy immediately after her encounter with the employee. This is the objection now under consideration. Isn't an agent better off being continent when revision of this clear-sighted sort is not an option? No. There are good reasons for a rational agent not to be disposed to be continent in circumstances like those in which Mary found herself. Let me explain why.

7 Obstinacy and Continence

David Wiggins has observed in the course of a discussion of Aristotle's treatment of akrasia that "when one sticks by the decision even where the original deliberation and judgment stand in need of review (e.g., in the light of new perception), that is *obstinacy* [not continence]" (1980, 243). Aristotle himself distinguished continence from superficially similar but undesirable states, like obstinacy and inflexibility: it is not the mark of a continent person to be hard to persuade, for the continent person will be easily persuaded to change his mind when it is appropriate to do so (*NE* 1151b5–17). Aristotle's claims suggest the view that a disposition that supports continence is a kind of deliberative virtue, one that involves keeping to one's decision in the right way, at the right time, and for the right reason (because the decision is right (*NE* 1151a32–b4)), while obstinacy, persistence, and inflexibility regarding one's decisions are merely traits of character. The latter are merely traits of character and not virtues, because they could lead an agent to persevere with any decision, whether right or wrong.

If one understands continence and incontinence as Aristotle does, as concerned with an agent's susceptibility to temptation specifically from bodily desires and appetites, then it may be possible to show that continence is psychologically distinct from a trait like perseverance. Aristotelian continence is specifically concerned with the rational control of one's physical appetites and with the successful defense of the stands of reason that oppose these appetites. But a broader view of the scope of continence and incontinence has been taken here: continence can involve overcoming recalcitrant motivation of many different types in order to uphold a decision that may or may not be a good one. On this sort of view, if there is anything that could be called a disposition toward continence, it consists in just being resolute. If we were to assume, as Aristotle did, that the exercise of a deliberative virtue always leads to right action, then this kind of persistence or resolution would not count as a deliberative virtue. Since it is a disposition that it may or may not be a good thing for an agent to exercise on a particular occasion, it would not necessarily lead to the right result in every case. But such a standard for what counts as a deliberative virtue is simply too high to be a useful one. It may even not be useful as an ideal.

Agents work with limited information about themselves and their situation, and they must decide how to act upon this information in a limited amount of time by exercising limited cognitive capacities. There is nothing that guarantees that an agent who has functioned well within these constraints will choose and pursue the course that she has most (internal) reason to pursue. It may well be the case that to be resolute, to be disposed to be continent, to a very high degree would inevitably involve being disposed to be obstinate (in Wiggins's sense) at least some of the time.

To be the sort of agent who *could* be continent in every situation in which continence would, in fact, be the most reasonable course is to be the sort of agent who would lack a different deliberative virtue: alertness or acuity. An agent with alertness or acuity would be disposed to recognize the need to revise her practical reasoning and to do so for the right reason. One should expect that one's plans and the facts that one registers about the world, one's capacities, and one's motivational resources might not mesh perfectly. And one should cope with such situations with flexibility and even imagination. Therefore, being alert and perhaps also being on guard against deliberative obstinacy will make continence more difficult than it would otherwise be.

A capacity for alertness is presupposed by many of the plans that we actually make. It is rational for planning beings like ourselves to recognize the defeasibility and inconclusiveness of some of our planning and so to recognize at crucial junctures that something not allowed for in one's current plan is not necessarily disallowed by one's deeper reasons. There are plans the force of which depends on the presence of sufficient motivation at a later time. A plan to go swimming this evening if you feel like it is such a plan: in making it you have committed yourself to assessing your motivational state this evening before carrying out the plan.

We are also constantly forced to acknowledge the loose texture of our plans and the fact that the conditions for abandoning them often remain unspecified when our plans are formulated. This deliberative norm is especially important when we are acting on some ideal to which we want to hold ourselves where it is part of the ideal that the actions in accord with it are motivated by appropriate and genuine feelings (e.g., some compliments, vows, solemn promises). Other sorts of plans may depend on there arising no defeating external circumstances, where the list of such defeating considerations is not specified in adopting the plan, through no deliberative fault or shortcoming on the part of the agent.

In order to reconsider and revise a judgment, there must be time to reconsider, and even where there is time, there may not also be the opportunity to do so. Perhaps people are staring at you, making you nervous, or you don't trust your judgment (you've just had your third glass of champagne in an hour, or you're tired, stressed, or depressed). Or perhaps, like Mary, you're in a situation in which you are inclined, because of past experience, to distrust your usual impulses. Then you might be in a situation where a revision to a plan or abandoning it would actually make sense but you (quite rightly) don't feel confident about your ability to judge that this is the case.

These observations about the dispositions of a rational planner can now be put together: there can be situations where deliberative caution or a resistance to rationalization will make it harder to revise a plan when one should, but at the same time a tendency to resist deliberative obstinacy will make it hard for the agent to continue resolutely on his original course. A preference for continence no matter what would make the alternatives to continence easier to reject, but a rational planner would not have such a preference. On one hand, to be disposed to prefer a plan just because we have made it and to resist reconsideration even where this is appropriate is to manifest a kind of deliberative weakness. On the other hand, we want to be disposed to avoid neurotic indecision, endless reconsideration, the impulse to rationalize, self-doubt, and vacillation. This suggests that when resolute continence is the right deliberative course, it is valuable because it enables one to resist changing one's mind for the wrong reason, e.g., hastily or from the urge to rationalize. It is not valuable just because it preserves the fit between evaluation and action.

Our aspiration as deliberators is that the judgment that we see the most reason for making will select the action that we have most reason to do, but there is no guarantee that this will happen. When this doesn't happen, it may still happen that the agent will see that some consideration has been left out without seeing how to take it into account. In such a case, where the all-things-considered judgment has been made and where time is short or where it is not appropriate to reconsider, the agent may have dispositions that constitute her as a rational agent but that make akrasia hard to avoid. It is not that there is a disposition for akrasia itself, but akrasia can function like a safety valve when the agent is rightly disposed not to carry out any of the continent alternatives.

It is in this sense that akrasia can be at least as rational as hastily and perhaps recklessly revising one's judgment, suppressing the contrary motivation, or ignoring the new consideration. When there is no clear way to choose between these conflicting higher-order principles, akrasia may be a reasonable course, the course a reasonable person would take. Therefore, an appropriate humility about our deliberative capacities would be expressed by our willingness to allow that even our more carefully formulated justifications may be only a rough guide to what we have reason to do, and that what actually moves us may, on some occasions, be evidence about what we could be moved to understand and justify through further reflection.[6]

Notes

1. I will be using the terms "akrasia" and "incontinence" as synonyms throughout this paper.
2. Philosophers who have asked this question include R. M. Hare (1952, 1963) and Gary Watson (1977).
3. There are good reasons to doubt that all practical conclusions are necessarily evaluative in form (see Bratman 1985, Charles 1983), but I will restrict my discussion to cases in which the agents' practical conclusions do involve evaluative judgments.
4. In what follows I will be speaking of facts or considerations that constitute reasons for agents (following the usage of John McDowell in 1979) instead of speaking of reasons as belief or desire states that explain the occurrence of an action, as Davidson (1963) does. Thus I do not assume that a reason is necessarily a mental state, a belief, or a desire. The mental states that figure in action explanations might involve an agent's being motivated by reasons, but on this usage, reasons are the contents of mental states, not the states themselves. Facts about the agent's circumstances or about what might be brought about by acting in a certain way may also constitute reasons to act. It should also be clear now that I am not describing reasons for action as propositions that have the form of rules or function as rules. A reason need not be a full-blown justification for an action.

5. When Aristotle responds to the sophistical puzzle about akrasia at *NE* 1151a29–b4, his solution is similar. The continent person abides by his decision not simply because it was his decision but because it was the correct decision: what makes it correct is what makes him abide by it. The foolish person may do what is right in the end, but what makes this action right is not what leads him to perform it. Here I am following T. Irwin's notes on this passage (1988, 355–356).

6. I would like to thank audiences at the University of New Hampshire, the University of California at Berkeley, the University of Illinois at Chicago, and Wellesley College for helpful comments on an earlier version of this paper.

Chapter 17

Rationality, Responsibility, and Pathological Indifference

Stephen L. White

1 Pathological Indifference

Imagine you are about to enter SoHo. You are retracing the only route you know to an address below Canal Street, and a detour would make you lose at least an hour. Unfortunately, you have offended a ruthless criminal, C., whose power inside SoHo is absolute. Should you enter the district, C. will obtain his revenge by having you tortured. C.'s busy schedule, however, would not permit him to devote more than half an hour to making you suffer. All told, if you decide to enter SoHo, you will be delayed forty-five minutes, fifteen minutes less than if you take the detour. The time saved, of course, is at the cost of a period of intense pain. Pains you will experience in SoHo, however, are completely discounted in your calculations. Given the opportunity to avoid pain or displeasure that will be experienced *outside* SoHo by choosing to experience more pain or more displeasure *in* SoHo, you always prefer (while you are outside SoHo) to do so. And this preference remains even if you anticipate experiencing much more pain as a consequence. Similarly, you always prefer (when you are outside SoHo) to sacrifice very great pleasures available to you *in* SoHo for much smaller pleasures available elsewhere. As a result, you ignore the detour and pursue your original route into the district.

Let us call the attitude that discounts pleasurable and painful experience in SoHo *SoHo indifference.*[1] Derek Parfit has considered a similar motivational makeup in which one discounts pleasures and pains that will occur on future Tuesdays (1984, 124). If one is *future-Tuesday-indifferent*, one will accept the prospect of great suffering that will fall on a future Tuesday in order to save oneself even the smallest amount of suffering on other days. And one is similarly indifferent to pleasures that one will experience on future Tuesdays. This is not to say that one is indifferent when Tuesday actually arrives. On Tuesday pleasures and pains are experienced and assessed in the normal way; it is only the pleasures and pains of *future* Tuesdays that are discounted. Parfit claims (p. 124) that future-Tuesday indifference is irrational. And he would clearly make the same claim about SoHo indifference. I shall argue that this is not necessarily the case.

This disagreement with Parfit is not a disagreement about the psychology of future-Tuesday indifference or any of its analogues. Rather, it is a disagreement over fundamental issues concerning the nature of rationality. And these issues are not likely to be settled without at least some suggestion of what an adequate theory of rationality would involve. In what follows, I shall mention briefly three points concerning future-Tuesday indifference on which Parfit and I can agree in order to bring the more fundamental disagreement into focus. I shall then sketch an argument for an account of rationality that has the consequence that future-Tuesday indifference and SoHo indifference need not be irrational.

Point 1   Parfit can agree that to someone in the grip of future-Tuesday indifference or SoHo indifference, there may be nothing we could say to show that person the error of his or her ways. Imagine we are trying to reason with a person who is indifferent to pain on future Tuesdays. We argue that by trading off smaller pains on Mondays or Wednesdays for greater pains on Tuesdays, he needlessly increases the total amount of pain he experiences.

The person who is future-Tuesday-indifferent, however, claims that this begs the question. "Whether this disposition increases or decreases the total amount of pain," he points out, "depends on whether the pain experienced on Tuesdays *counts*." "Bear in mind," he continues, "that I simply don't *care* about pain that will occur on a future Tuesday. So, to compute the total pain (in any sense that is relevant), the pain that will fall on a Tuesday must be ignored. If it is, then my disposition will have *decreased* the amount of pain I experience."

We object, naturally, that he *will* care about the pain. And we remind him that when Tuesday arrives he will bitterly regret his decision.

"The relevance of that," he replies, "depends on when the regret occurs. If it occurs on Tuesday, then since I am indifferent to the pain, I surely have no reason for concern about my feelings of regret. If it occurs on any other day, of course, it will figure in my calculations in the same way that any other negative consequences of choosing the greater pain on Tuesday will. Only if the feelings of regret (as well as the other negative consequences of the choice that occur on days other than Tuesday) are outweighed by the pain that I avoid (on days other than Tuesday) will I choose the pain on Tuesday."

We suggest that he must, then, believe that it will not be he who suffers or believe that in some sense he does not really exist on Tuesdays.

He replies as follows: "Consider the anthropologically sophisticated psychopath. Suppose such a person is asked whether his willingness to see others suffer rather than have his slightest whim frustrated is immoral. If he is candid, he is likely to admit that in relation to the standards of the society in which he finds himself, such a characterization would be correct. These standards, however, mean nothing to him. Thus it would be misleading of him to use the term 'immoral,' except in scare quotes, to describe his own disposition. Such a description would suggest an endorsement of the prevailing standards. However, in offering such a description, he would be giving nothing more than the anthropologically correct account of the application of these standards to his own case.

"I am like the psychopath," we can imagine the person who is future-Tuesday-indifferent going on. "I am fully aware that by all the criteria that prevail, it will be I who suffers on Tuesday. The person stages that suffer on Tuesday can be as physically and psychologically similar to the Monday person stages as is possible given the discontinuity between my present lack of concern for what happens on Tuesday and the concern that will be felt when Tuesday arrives. And my lack of concern now for what will happen on Tuesday is not based on the belief that I have a Cartesian soul that will be gone before Tuesday comes. There is no further fact, over and above the physical and psychological facts, in which the question of personal identity could consist. The physical and psychological similarities between the Monday person stages and the ones that exist on Tuesdays, however, are a matter of indifference to me. I can admit, then, that *I* will suffer only using the word 'I' in scare quotes. Like the psychopath's admission, mine describes an anthropological fact that, because of my motivational makeup, has no bearing on my disposition to express sincere evaluations."

Given this analogy between the person who is future-Tuesday-indifferent, or SoHo-indifferent, and the psychopath, I shall call such indifference *pathological indifference* without prejudice to the question whether or not such a disposition is rational. The first point on which Parfit and I can agree, then, is that if we are, or have become, pathologically indifferent, that indifference may be stable in the following sense: just as we will be indifferent when we are not in the relevant circumstances to the pain we will experience when we are, we may be indifferent to all those considerations that are thought to establish that our indifference to the pain is either irrational or unjustified. Facts about psychological continuity or about the regret that will be felt when the pain occurs may have no more significance for us than the pain itself. In this sense we can say that there are circumstances in which pathological indifference will be in equilibrium.

Point 2   Parfit, in fact, can agree to something stronger. There are circumstances under which it would be rational for us to make ourselves future-Tuesday-indifferent if we could do so effectively and at reasonable cost (say by taking a pill). Suppose that we were faced with the prospect of a number of unavoidable and extremely painful experiences each week and that our only control over the situation lay in our ability to schedule the experiences in any way we chose. And suppose we had a similar control over the timing of the pleasurable experiences open to us. In such a case it would seem perfectly rational to schedule all the pains on Tuesdays, all the pleasures on other days, and then to take the pill.

It is necessary, however, not to overstate the amount of agreement with regard to this kind of case. For Parfit, it is rational to take the pill only if the following condition is met: taking the pill must increase the expected utility of one's future experiences, where the utility is assessed from the perspective of an impartial concern for all of one's future person stages. This condition is likely to be met in the present case if, for example, one nearly always suffers the same amount of pain regardless of when in the week one schedules it. And this latter condition is not obviously unrealistic. Except in emergencies, cases in which one suffers more pain as the result of postponing it are usually ones in which the pain is postponed for a significant period of time. In the case of the person who is future-Tuesday-indifferent, however, there is no incentive to postpone the pain any more than a week. Moreover, not only must Parfit require that his condition be met if the decision to become pathologically indifferent is to be rational; he must also hold that the benefits of such indifference are extremely limited. For Parfit, the gain in becoming future-Tuesday-indifferent lies in saving oneself the pain and anxiety of anticipating future pains that one has no way of avoiding. The significance of the pains themselves, once they occur, is in no way diminished by one's indifference to them before the day on which they are experienced.

For those who do not assume that rationality requires impartiality regarding one's future person stages, however, Parfit's condition need not be satisfied. Any partiality in one's concern for one's future person stages would be reflected in one's decisions about whether to make oneself pathologically indifferent. And it is difficult to see what we could say to someone who made such a decision on grounds which were not fully impartial (on the basis, for example, of a preference for future person stages that were closer in time merely because they were closer). At least it is difficult to see what we could say that would convince the person that he or she had made an irrational decision. In addition, for those who do not share Parfit's assumptions about rationality, the benefits of pathological indifference may involve more than eliminating the anticipation of pain. For the person who is future-Tuesday-indifferent, the pain experienced on Tuesdays may, as he or she would maintain, simply not count.

It does not follow, however, that one would be likely to make oneself pathologically indifferent if there were a significant chance that in doing so one would be led to accept a great deal of suffering one could otherwise avoid. It seems very unlikely, for example, that one would make oneself SoHo-indifferent if one could foresee the possibility that one would make oneself undergo torture merely to save time. This is because from the perspective one must assume in deciding for or against SoHo-indifference, the person stages in SoHo are just as important as those in other locations. And this will be true even though from the perspective of the person who would be SoHo-indifferent, the pains felt in SoHo could be completely discounted.

Point 3   A final point about pathological indifference, and again one with which Parfit can agree, is that the possibility of acquiring such an attitude might have genuine explanatory significance in psychology. The explanation most commonly offered by clinical psychologists for the phenomenon of multiple personalities is that splitting the self represents a rational response to a situation in which one anticipates that one will suffer intolerable pain over which one has no control. Splitting the self represents a rational strategy, however, only if one can withdraw one's present concern from one or more of the future selves. This is evident if one imagines the possibility in which two future selves that are psychologically discontinuous with each other will alternate in control and only one will experience the pain. The fact that the future selves are psychologically discontinuous with *each other* is no improvement from one's perspective in the present if each one remains continuous with one's *present* self. From one's perspective in the present, the future self that experiences the pain is just as much a matter of concern as it would have been if it and the future self that avoids the pain had been psychologically integrated. Thus it is only the ability to withdraw concern from a part of one's own future that provides the strategy of splitting the self with the rationale that was intended.[2]

Parfit and I can agree, then, not only that pathological indifference may represent an equilibrium from which one has no motivation to depart, but also that it may be an equilibrium at which one has good reason to aim. In the sections that follow I shall sketch the argument that pathological indifference may not only be in equilibrium, but that when it is, it is not irrational.

2 Ideal Reflective Equilibria

General accounts of rationality are notoriously controversial. As an alternative to assuming the truth of some conception of rationality, I propose to look at a dilemma for our practice of assessing some actions as *irrational* that arises if such assessments are to play the role they seem to play in our ordinary practical decision making. The dilemma about ascriptions of irrationality (and rationality) is a special instance of a dilemma concerning our ascriptions of blame more generally (and hence of responsibility). I shall describe the dilemma concerning the ascription of responsibility and blame in section 3 and the dilemma regarding rationality in section 4. In order to state the two dilemmas, however, I shall develop in this section the notion of equilibrium involved in the claim that when pathological indifference is in equilibrium, it need not be irrational.

The concept of equilibrium in question is the one that would result if we had complete control over our own motivational makeup. Imagine that we had a pill that would allow us to add or eliminate any noninstrumental desire that we chose and with which we could increase or decrease the strengths of any of our noninstrumental desires. Many of us have desires of a persistent or possibly even addictive sort, which we would happily eliminate. There are also desires, such as the desire for more exercise, whose strengths we would seriously consider increasing. Those with serious emotional or motivational conflicts would be likely to make far more extensive changes. In order to characterize the notion of equilibrium that I have in mind, however, I require that all such changes should be subject to the following proviso: one must be reflectively aware of the basic facts about one's motivational makeup. One cannot, for example, be so thoroughly in the grip of an obsessive desire, say for revenge, that one is unaware that one has other desires, such as the desire to retain one's freedom, with which that desire is in conflict or is likely to be in conflict. It is not required, however, that one know anything more than the facts of this basic kind.

With this proviso, one's addition and elimination of desires, as well as one's adjustments of their strengths, will satisfy the following conditions:

- What motivates one to add or subtract desires must be other desires that one has. I assume that the idea of stepping back from all of one's noninstrumental desires *simultaneously* and choosing which to keep is incoherent. Rather, the process is one of increasing the overall coherence of the set of desires with which one starts. This is not to say that one has a non-instrumental second-order desire that all one's first-order desires should be coherent and that this second-order desire takes precedence over all one's other desires. One need have no such noninstrumental desire, and those who do happen to have it might have good reason to eliminate it or to see that its strength is decreased. Few of us, after all, would want to devote the rest of our lives to increasing the coherence of our noninstrumental desires. What will motivate one to eliminate (from an otherwise normal set) the desire to drive at twice the legal limit, to gamble with one's life savings, or to brawl in pubs is not an abstract commitment to the coherence of one's desires. Rather, it is the recognition that such desires threaten to frustrate most or all of the others, together with the motivational force of those other desires.
- The strength of a noninstrumental desire alone is irrelevant to whether it will be retained or eliminated. The desire for heroin might be the strongest desire one has in terms of one's tendency to act on it, but it will still be eliminated from an otherwise normal set.
- Whether a noninstrumental desire is retained depends on the amount of support it receives from other noninstrumental desires and does not depend on its content. Very general desires may be eliminated for their failure to cohere with very specific desires, just as specific desires may be dropped because they fail to find support from other specific desires and general desires. This process has obvious analogies to the process that Rawls describes as arriving at reflective equilibrium. Since the pill that defines the equilibrium achieved produces an idealization of what we could achieve without it, I shall call this outcome an *ideal reflective equilibrium* (IRE).
- The coherentist and holistic character of the process of arriving at an ideal reflective equilibrium has one important limitation. Let us define an *unconditional desire* as a desire for a state of

affairs that one wants to be realized whether or not the desire for it persists. One's desire for luxuries, for example, is ordinarily a desire that one have them only if one continues to want them. One's desire that one should be honest, however, is ordinarily unconditional. Even if one knew now that in the future one would cease to have any noninstrumental desire to tell the truth, one would ordinarily prefer now that one continue to tell the truth, even if one does so out of habit, fear of punishment, or superstition. To say that one's desire to tell the truth is (likely to be) unconditional, however, is not to say that it is unqualified. One's desire to be truthful may be unconditional, even though one has no desire to insist on the truth when to do so would cause suffering and when the issues involved are trivial. Indeed, a desire to tell the truth may be qualified in indefinitely complex ways while remaining unconditional. Moreover, the claim that one's desire for honesty is unconditional does not entail that its existence is independent of the nature of one's upbringing or the character of one's society. Nor does it entail that one would prefer to remain honest regardless of how much suffering one would experience if at some time in the future one came to desire not to be honest and that desire were frustrated. All that follows from the claim is that if one contemplates now a time in the future in which one's present desire to be honest no longer exists, one prefers now, all other things being equal, that at that future time one should be honest.[3]

Given this definition of an unconditional desire, we can note the following relation between conditional and unconditional desires. In a competition between an unconditional noninstrumental desire and a conditional noninstrumental desire, the unconditional desire will always survive, regardless of how well supported the conditional desire is by other conditional desires. The reason is that eliminating either desire makes it less likely that one will bring about the state of affairs that corresponds to that desire and thus less likely that it will come about. In the case of a conditional desire, this represents no loss from the perspective of the choice situation. If the desire is conditional, then if one will not have it in the future, that fact completely compensates for the fact that the state of affairs that is its object is less likely to come about. For an unconditional desire, this is obviously not the case. Thus there is a two-tiered structure within the set of one's noninstrumental desires in that unconditional desires play a foundational role relative to conditional desires. But within each tier, considerations of coherence are decisive.

• One's ideal reflective equilibrium is relative to one's *actual* beliefs. Whether the desire for heroin supports and is supported by an otherwise normal set of desires, depends on whether one believes that it is addictive, that it is illegal, that it is likely to shorten one's life, that its use is likely to force one into criminal activity, and so forth. With a sufficiently bizarre set of beliefs, both the desire for heroin *and* one's more normal desires might remain in one's ideal reflective equilibrium.

3 The Dilemma Regarding Responsibility

Once we have the notion of an ideal reflective equilibrium, the dilemma regarding our ascriptions of responsibility and blame can be explained as follows. Suppose we contemplate making someone suffer for an act of harm that the person has committed. There are two possible explanations of the action if one assumes it was not performed in ignorance of some of the relevant facts. The person in question may have produced the harm on the basis of a desire in IRE (i.e., a desire that would have remained had he or she had access to the pill in terms of which an IRE is defined) or on the basis of a desire out of IRE. (I shall assume that in explaining the action, we presuppose a picture of the underlying causal connections that is not strictly deterministic. But I shall also assume that whatever indeterminacies the picture involves, it is no better than determinism as far as the prospects of making sense of ascriptions of responsibility are concerned. In other words, I am making the familiar assumption that indeterminism raises the same problems for ascriptions of responsibility and blame that determinism does.)

In the case in which the person acts *in IRE*, the person knew he or she was acting so as to cause harm and did so on the basis of a desire the person was perfectly content to have. That person, of course, either miscalculated the chances of being caught or was simply unlucky. In either case, the harm did not figure prominently enough in the person's motivational makeup to deter the action. The preference, then, for the action over refraining from the harm was in equilibrium for that person. Hence, our blame of the person finds no footing in the person's motivational makeup. Though the person might feel guilt or remorse, these sentiments themselves would be eliminated were the person in IRE. Thus in the internal sense in which what is justified for us must have some connection with what would actually motivate us (under suitably idealized circumstances), such a person would be unjustified in retaining any disposition to feel guilt or remorse for the harm in question. Since the person's lack of concern over the harm in question is in equilibrium, there is nothing we could appeal to in the person by condemning the action and making the person suffer. Our making the person suffer could, of course, work as a deterrent or as a restriction on the person's freedom, but the connection between punishment and the possibility of genuine guilt or remorse would be broken.

Imagine, for example, that Martians had the ability to punish people for stepping on insects. (Assume that there is no disagreement between the Martians and us over the psychology of insects. They may simply find the analogy between pain and its closest analogue in insects more striking than we do.) And suppose you continued to step on insects whenever the possibility of being caught was remote and the cost of avoiding doing so was significant. If you were caught and made to suffer, you would certainly regret your misfortune. You might also change your assessment of the Martians' surveillance techniques. You would not, however, find guilt or remorse appropriate, nor would you regard your suffering as punishment. You would be to the Martians what the psychopath is to us. Though they could manipulate your behavior and exercise power over you, they could not do so in a way that would constitute genuine punishment.

Similarly, if you lived in the vicinity of a tribe whose taboos you considered superstitious but who had the power to make you suffer for breaking them, you would not regard such suffering, if it were inflicted, as genuine punishment. And what is essential to this example is not that the norms you violate are superstitious but that, as in the previous example, they incorporate values so alien to yours that you could not be internally justified in acquiescing in your suffering. The same considerations would apply if you were a political prisoner whose values differed radically from those of your captors. In all three cases, though you might recognize that your suffering was intended as punishment, you yourself could only regard it as the exercise of superior force. Thus in the sense in which I am using the expression "genuine punishment," none of these cases in which you suffer are ones to which that term applies.

The person who causes harm on the basis of a desire in IRE, then, is in an important respect like the psychopath. And there is fairly wide (though hardly universal) agreement that the psychopath cannot be the object of genuine punishment or blame (Haksar 1964; Fingarette 1967, chap. 2; Feinberg 1970c; Murphy 1972, 288–289). Let us call *unreachable* those subjects who, for lack of the appropriate motivational makeup, are beyond the reach of genuine punishment. It is not the psychopath's lack of sympathy for others that makes him or her unfit for punishment. Someone who lacked sympathy for others but was rationally motivated to avoid actions involving harm to people for other reasons *would* seem to be blameworthy if he or she intentionally caused such harm to occur. It is the psychopath's lack of any element in his or her motivational makeup in which our blame could find a foothold, that is, his or her unreachability, that makes such blame inappropriate. And it is this feature that the person who acts on the basis of a desire in IRE so as to produce harm shares with the psychopath.

Thus someone whose harmful action stems from a desire in IRE is not an appropriate candidate for punishment or blame. This is not to say, of course, that we would be unjustified in protecting ourselves from the harm that such an unreachable subject might cause. It is merely to say that in so doing, we would be doing something more akin to protecting ourselves from the victim of a contagious disease or a mental illness than to administering genuine punishment. Unreachable subjects include, besides the psychopath and the subjects who live under the sway of the Martians or the local tribesmen, subjects with radically different conceptions of the good from ours and subjects with radically different conceptions of responsibility.

In the second case the person we contemplate making suffer has committed an act of harm on the basis of a desire *out of IRE*. Since the desire was one on which the person actually acted, it follows trivially that it was that person's strongest desire in the motivational sense. Let us contrast, then, the *motivational strength* of a person's desire, which is a measure of the person's tendency to act on it, and its *evaluational strength*, which is the tendency it has to survive (or to survive undiminished) the person's acquisition of the pill that defines IRE. Since the desire from which the harm stemmed was out of IRE, its motivational strength was out of proportion to its evaluational strength. In this respect, however, the person is not relevantly different from the compulsive. Of course, the person who acts on a desire out of IRE need not exhibit the kind of recognizable and repetitious pattern often associated with compulsive behavior. Nor must the desire that was acted upon have been any more than marginally stronger than its nearest competitor. Thus just as the action done from a desire out of IRE may lack the external marks of compulsion, it may lack the phenomenology as well. The person may have acted on a desire that he or she had chosen not to act on many times in the past. And the person may have felt perfectly capable of choosing not to act on it on this occasion even as he or she did choose to act upon it. This is just to say, however, that if the desire had been weaker, the person would not have acted on it. And this is equally true of the compulsive. The fact that in this case, in contrast to the case of the compulsive, the desire acted upon was not over-whelmingly greater in strength than its nearest competitor does not seem to be a morally significant difference. Thus, like the person who acts on a desire in IRE, the person who acts on a desire out of IRE seems an inappropriate candidate where punishment and blame are concerned.

It is possible, of course, that the person who caused harm did so as the result of ignorance of the consequences of his or her actions. If this is the case, then again blame seems unjustified. There is a puzzle, then, in seeing how ascriptions of responsibility and blame could ever be justified.[4]

Such an argument might seem to support a utilitarian account of responsibility and blame. The puzzle we are considering was generated in large part, however, by the following intuition: that guilt and remorse should have an internal justification for those to whom responsibility and blame are ascribed. For those who take this intuition seriously, the utilitarian account of responsibility is unlikely to have much appeal. In the next section I shall argue that ascribing irrationality is a special case of ascribing responsibility and blame. I shall then argue that there is an account of responsibility that does satisfy the intuition that the appropriateness of punishment and blame and the internal justification of the suffering involved are necessarily connected.

4 The Dilemma with Regard to Rationality

Given the dilemma about responsibility, an analogous puzzle emerges concerning rationality. This is because to call a person's action irrational is to ascribe a certain kind of blame to the person, and such ascriptions of blame may have serious consequences for the person's future interests. This blame that we ascribe to a person for the irrationality of his or her *acts* must be distinguished from an ascription of irrationality to the *person*. In what follows I shall be concerned with ascriptions of irrationality where *particular acts* of a subject are concerned and in which the subject is not excused on the grounds that he or she is irrational in general. Both kinds of ascriptions are likely to have an adverse effect on the interests of the person to whom they are made, and thus both may cause the person to suffer. But only for ascriptions of the first kind are resentment in the case of another's action and guilt and remorse in the case of one's own action appropriate. And only in these cases does the suffering that ascriptions of irrationality impose involve genuine punishment and blame.[5]

The question, then, like the question in the general case of responsibility, is how the suffering involved in ascriptions of irrationality is to be justified. Since this puzzle is a special case of the earlier one, it has exactly the same structure.[6] Suppose that we contemplate making someone suffer for an act we describe as irrational. Let us assume that the stakes are relatively high and that the action resulted in harm, either to the person who performed it, to some other person, or both. As in the general case of responsibility, if the person did not act out of ignorance or on the basis of some other cognitive defect, then he or she either acted on the basis of a desire in IRE or on the basis of a desire out of IRE. And as in the general case of responsibility, the problem is to see how the blame and suffering that ascriptions of irrationality involve can be justified.

Let us consider, then, each of the alternatives where blame for irrationality is concerned. In the first case the person knowingly acts in a way that is likely to cause harm, as harms and benefits are ordinarily assessed, either to himself or herself, to others, or both. Moreover, the person acts on the basis of a desire that he or she is perfectly content to have. One such case is similar to an example of Harry Frankfurt's (1971, 12). I shall use the term "integrated addict" to refer to someone whose addiction to a drug is not in serious conflict with the majority of his or her other desires. The integrated addict would not mind, for example, that as a result of the addiction, he or she could not hold a conventional job, maintain normal human relationships, or count on a normal life expectancy. Such a person could also be expected to enjoy associating with other addicts, to find excitement in selling illegal drugs, and to derive meaning and significance from the drug subculture. Thus if offered the pill that defines IRE, the integrated addict would be unmotivated to eliminate the desire for the drug. The integrated gambler is another example of the same type. A third example might be the person whose desire in IRE is to fulfill a promise at enormous personal cost even though it is to someone who will benefit only slightly, if at all, from its fulfillment. Other examples include the person whose commitment to an apparently frivolous goal, such as being in the *Guinness Book of World Records*, is in equilibrium and the person whose willingness in IRE to sacrifice himself or herself for others seems wildly extravagant by ordinary standards.

Would the actions typical of such subjects be irrational? Viewed from the outside, the drug addiction, the gambling, the promise kept at enormous cost, the trivial pursuit, and the extravagant self-sacrifice are quite plausibly regarded as irrational and self-destructive. One's judgment is likely to change, however, when the stories are spelled out in enough detail to make it clear that the actions stem from desires in IRE. Terms like "compulsive," "ill-considered," or "obsessive" would be regarded as appropriate by the person in question (and would in fact be appropriate) only on the assumption that we could appeal to those normal goals and desires that we ordinarily possess and that make these terms appropriate in our own cases. For such a person acting in IRE, these normal goals and desires that we ordinarily take for granted do not exist. Guilt and remorse over the harm that such an action might cause to oneself or to others would be equally unjustified for such people on the assumption that the action stems from a desire in IRE.

For the person who is not in IRE but who acts on an apparently self-destructive desire that would be in IRE if the appropriate drug were available, this need not be true. Such a person will necessarily have conflicting desires, which might well make the person vulnerable to feelings of guilt, remorse, self-directed anger, or shame. But such a person still differs from most of us in that if the person were given the choice, it would not be the apparently self-destructive desires, but the desires with which they conflict and the emotions such as guilt and remorse that they generate that would be eliminated. For such a person, then, it is the guilt and remorse that would be unjustified, as would any suffering caused by being blamed for irrationality. Therefore, as in the case of the psychopath, it is difficult to see how genuine blame could be justified and thus difficult to see what could justify calling such a person irrational.

The second case is analogous to the second case of the puzzle about responsibility. The person to whom we are tempted to ascribe irrationality and on whom we would impose the adverse consequences that such ascriptions involve has acted on a desire out of IRE. Suppose, for example, that faced with an intruder threatening one's family, one reacted with anger, thereby subjecting the family to more danger than if one had remained calm. One may well have known, even while evincing them, that the angry reactions were not the ones that maximized the chances of survival. Had one been able to change one's motivational makeup on the spot, one would have eliminated the desires underlying the dangerous reactions. (That is, one would have eliminated the token desires that resulted in the angry reactions on that occasion. One would not, of course, necessarily have eliminated the types of desires of which they were tokens.) Other cases that involve harm to oneself as a result of acting on a desire that is out of IRE include gambling or taking drugs when the desire to do so is not integrated with one's other desires. Unusual fear that prevents one from saving someone's life or from saving one's own is another case. One's fear of heights, for example, might prevent one from jumping into a net from a burning building even though if one had an appropriate pill, one would eliminate the desire not to jump and thereby survive.

Unlike the case of acting in IRE, acting out of IRE, when it produces harm, *is* likely to produce feelings of guilt or remorse as well as feelings of self-directed anger or shame. This is clearly true in the case in which one's irrational reaction to the threat to one's family results in harm that could have been avoided. But even if no one else is harmed, one's irrational reactions may well inspire guilt or remorse. Gambling or taking drugs on the basis of a desire out of IRE, for example, may result in guilt or remorse even if one only harms oneself. This would be particularly likely if one had been made painfully aware of the consequences by past experience and had vowed never to use drugs or to gamble again.

Although one's feelings of guilt or remorse would be natural in such a case, it is hard to see how they could be justified. In acting on a desire that is *out of IRE*, one is acting on one's desire that is motivationally strongest, even though one would not be motivated to keep it if one had the means available for its elimination. In this respect, one does not seem relevantly different from the compulsive. Of course, one would have acted differently if the desire on which one acted had had a different relative strength. But in this respect too the compulsive is no different, and we do not hold the compulsive responsible or ascribe blame to such an individual. Though one might be blamed for causing harm by one's irrational action and one might blame oneself, it is unclear what grounds the distinction between this case and the case in which ascriptions of responsibility and blame seem obviously unjustified.

Another possibility is that an action we are tempted to regard as irrational is the result of a cognitive rather than conative failure. Again, however, ascriptions of responsibility and blame seem to lack any justification. Suppose that one of one's actions appears irrational and worthy of blame but that one has lacked some crucial piece of information that would have altered one's decision to act. If at some earlier stage one irrationally declined to acquire the information, then one is, presumably, in some respect blameworthy. But in this case the question is simply pushed one step back. Since one failed to acquire the information because of a desire in IRE, a desire out of IRE, or some cognitive defect, the question of how one could be responsible and worthy of blame remains open. If, on the other hand, there was nothing blameworthy in the failure to acquire the information, it is not immediately apparent how there could be anything blameworthy in acting without having access to it. The same argument applies if one acts on the basis of a false belief.

Suppose, however, that one has all the relevant information but that under the pressure of stress, time constraints, or distractions one acts on the basis of an obviously bad inference. Here again, responsibility and blame for one's irrationality seem in place only if one found oneself in the situation as a result of some earlier act that one was irrational in performing. If one was not to blame for being in the situation, how could one be blamed for the limitations on one's computational capacity?

Finally, consider cases in which one might be faulted for inattention, for insufficient effort, or simply for a slack performance. If one had known in advance that one was prone to such failures of performance and one was blameworthy in not preparing for such contingencies, then blame for the performance might be appropriate. If, however, one had had no prior warning of one's tendency toward inferior performances in the kinds of circumstances in question or no warning that such circumstances were likely to occur, then the justification for one's being blamed remains obscure.

5 Internal Justification and Rationality

Unless there is some solution to the puzzle about rationality, then whatever other role they play, ascriptions of rationality and irrationality will lack the practical force we ordinarily attribute to them. When we accuse someone of acting irrationally, what we do goes beyond stating that the person exhibits a particular psychological mechanism. We are not, for example, simply claiming that he or she possesses a certain set of desires or that he or she is prone to computational or performance failures. And it is not enough to add that by pointing to one or more of these facts, we may be warning others of their possibly detrimental effects. Not even the fact that such ascriptions may have beneficial consequences by deterring harmful behavior on the part of those to whom they are being made is enough to capture their full force.

In order to have the full force that we ordinarily take such ascriptions to have, they must justify not only the adverse reactions of others toward our irrational actions but also our own attitudes of self-directed anger, shame, guilt, or remorse. To see how this is possible, recall that the notion of an ideal reflective equilibrium leads naturally to an internal conception of justification. A noninstrumental desire that is in IRE for a subject is justified for that subject by its coherence with, and hence its support by, that subject's other non-instrumental desires. But how could the blame that ascriptions of irrationality involve have an internal justification in this sense? And how would such an internal justification solve the puzzle of rationality?

Given this notion of internal justification, one of the claims that generates the puzzle of rationality can be stated as follows: there is no internal justification of self-directed anger, guilt, or remorse where actions stemming from desires in IRE are concerned. But if the notion of internal justification cannot help in the case of actions stemming from desires in IRE, it is difficult to see how it could help at all. In the case of actions stemming from desires out of IRE or from cognitive defects, the actions are not relevantly different from those of the compulsive or those of the person who is ignorant. Since we do not blame those who are ignorant or compulsive for their actions, we seem, even given the notion of internal justification, to be saddled with an arbitrary distinction. Another way of putting this is to say that if we are blamed when we are not relevantly different from those who are ignorant or those who are compulsive, we seem to have been blamed for our bad moral luck, and this seems clearly unacceptable.

Whether the dilemma regarding ascriptions of rationality, and more generally of responsibility, is really intractable, however, depends on whom we count as relevantly different from those who are compulsive or ignorant. Our ordinary assumption is that the distinction between those who are responsible and those who are not should depend only on properties that are intrinsic in the sense that they satisfy the following two conditions. First, they are determined by the psychology of the individual agent alone. For example, they are independent of facts about the utility of punishing the agent. Second, they are independent of the attitudes, values, commitments, and beliefs about responsibility that are held by the agent in question. Not even the fact that a person has a set of values as radically deviant as those of the psychopath is relevant to whether the person is genuinely responsible. Similarly, whether the person lives in a society in which the medical model is the sole model of social deviance is irrelevant.[7] Even if in such a society the concepts of blame and punishment (as opposed to therapy or behavior modification) are held to be incoherent, the assumption is that the facts about responsibility and blame are independent of such facts about social practice. That is, either our social practices including punishment or the practices of those in the society where punishment is excluded get things right. The assumption is, in other words, that the social arrangements regarding who is punished and blamed and who receives therapy instead must answer to the facts about responsibility. The same is true of the attitudes and values of individuals that determine whether they are willing to accept blame and whether they regard guilt and remorse as justified. Thus such social and psychological facts could not constitute the facts about responsibility. On this assumption, the claim that there is any relevant difference where responsibility is concerned between those who act compulsively or in ignorance and those who act out of IRE is difficult to support.

Corresponding to the assumption that the facts about responsibility depend only on the intrinsic properties of the agent is the following constraint. Any justification of our practices of ascribing responsibility and blame must be grounded in properties that are intrinsic in the sense described. Call this the *intrinsic-property constraint*. Suppose this constraint is unjustified. Suppose that whether we are responsible for an action depends on whether, if the action were harmful, we would be justified in feeling guilt and remorse and in acquiescing in the suffering entailed by our being punished and blamed. And suppose that the justification in question is internal justification. Then whether we are responsible will depend on just those facts about our attitudes, values, and practices that the intrinsic-property constraint rules out as irrelevant. Now consider the claim that actions stemming from a desire out of IRE or from a cognitive failure are not relevantly different from compulsive actions or actions done out of ignorance. The reply would be that they *are* relevantly different. It is quite possible that for many cases of actions stemming from desires out of IRE, guilt and remorse would be justified, even though for many other such cases they would not be. In cases of weakness of the will, for example, we accept responsibility for the action that results when our strongest desire (in the motivational sense) is out of IRE. And we are apparently justified in doing so, even though compulsive actions, for which we do not accept responsibility, are also ones that are caused when a desire that is out of IRE is the strongest. If we are in fact justified in accepting responsibility in such cases, then abandoning the intrinsic-property constraint and appealing to internal justification will provide a solution to the dilemma where ascriptions of responsibility are concerned.

In order to see what is involved in abandoning the intrinsic-property constraint, consider the following distinction between two kinds of compatibilism (see Glover 1983, 461–465). Let us say that *indirect compatibilist theories* are those according to which punishment and blame are justified by appeal to one or more intermediate facts. These typically include the fact that the agent in question was responsible for what he or she did. This ascription of responsibility in turn is ordinarily justified by reference to the claim that in some sense the agent acted freely. And this claim itself is frequently supported by appeal to the alleged fact that in some relevant sense the agent could have done other than what he or she did. Compatibilist theories of this kind contrast with those that it is natural to call *direct compatibilist theories*. According to these theories, punishment and blame are justified directly without reference to an independent notion of responsibility. Moreover, they are justified without appeal to the claim that the agent could have done otherwise. On a direct compatibilist account, the agent is responsible for harm in virtue of the fact that the agent's being punished or blamed and the agent's feeling guilt or remorse are justified.

Dropping the intrinsic-property constraint means opting for a direct rather than indirect form of compatibilism. This is because dropping the constraint means giving up the assumption that for any person we might contemplate punishing, there is an intrinsic property in virtue of which punishment is justified, if it is justified at all. But such notions as an agent's having acted freely or having been able to do otherwise, as used by the indirect compatibilist, have clearly been intended to pick out just such intrinsic properties. Thus, dropping the intrinsic-property constraint means abandoning the attempt to provide the kind of justification of punishment that the indirect compatibilist envisages.

Direct compatibilists, of course, need not hold that the justification of punishment and blame is internal justification. P. F. Strawson (1962), Jonathan Glover (1983), and Daniel Dennett (1984) are all direct compatibilists who differ in the accounts they offer of the justification of punishment and none of whose accounts is internalist in the sense I have sketched.[8] Among the direct compatibilist accounts, however, the internalist version does seem to do the least violence to our pretheoretical intuitions. Noninternalist versions either leave no room for guilt or remorse or provide no guarantee that if the punishment of some subject is justified, that subject's feeling guilt or remorse could be justified from his or her own point of view. Thus it is direct compatibilism in its internalist form that, I shall claim, provides a solution to the dilemma for ascriptions of responsibility and blame.

Such a solution to the dilemma regarding responsibility and thus to the dilemma with regard to rationality will be convincing, of course, only if it is possible to supply some content to the notion of an internal justification of our accepting blame and feeling guilt and remorse. But before we can see that such a justification might be possible, we must be clear about what it would entail. To be internally justified in accepting genuine blame or in accepting punishment or liability, one would have to be justified in doing so even when it could *not* be justified by reference to one's interests, including one's long-term interests. One would also have to be justified in accepting punishment or liability or feelings of guilt or remorse even when such acceptance could not be justified on utilitarian grounds. To be genuinely blamable, it is neither necessary nor sufficient that one be the most useful instrument of a social policy geared toward producing the best outcome. What is required is that one should be justified in accepting the blame (over some range of cases) for what one has *done*, regardless of the consequences of doing so. In order for the desire that one accept such blame to be internally justified, it must be part of one's IRE and hence must cohere with, and be supported by, the other desires in which that IRE consists. Moreover, we can assume that the IRE of any normal individual contains the desire that no one suffer unnecessarily and assume that that desire is unconditional. Since the desire to accept the blame (even when doing so will not produce the best consequences) may conflict with the desire that no one suffer unnecessarily, the former desire must also be unconditional. The question, then, is what other desires might exist that could support an unconditional desire of this kind.

The most promising way to approach this last question is to ask what would be lost to a person for whom, or a society for which, responsibility and blame were unintelligible. The answer, though complicated, seems to have two basic components. First, if one cannot be blamed for what one does, neither can one be credited. The desire, then, for authorship in the widest sense—the desire that one's creations, talents, and efforts be regarded as one's own and deserving of praise—is a desire that supports the desire to be blamable if one's actions cause harm.

Second, one's desire for a sphere in which one's own decisions carry authority and in which one cannot be second-guessed supports the desire to be blamable. Consider a society in which one could not be blamed for some class of actions because, for example, they were regarded as compulsive. In such a society one would lack an important type of internalized motivation to avoid such actions, and as a result, one would be less likely to do so. Also, in such a society one would lack any belief in one's ability to control the actions in question and would again be less likely to avoid them. In this case, however, it is difficult to see what grounds one could have for objecting to interventions by others when these were aimed at preventing such actions when they were likely to prove harmful. Consequently, one's desire for a sphere in which one has authority supports the desire that there be a class of actions for which one is blamable. Moreover, suppose one unconditionally desires not to harm others without justification. Then one's desire for a sphere in which one has authority supports the unconditional desire that one acquiesce in punishment and blame if an action for which one is blamable causes harm. This amounts to saying that if in IRE one desires *autonomy* (in one natural sense of the term), then one's desire to accept blame under some range of circumstances will be in IRE as well.

To say that the desire to accept blame for a certain range of actions would be supported in IRE is one thing. It is another thing to say what the principles would be like that distinguish the circumstances in which we could desire to accept blame from those in which we could not. We have already seen that the principles could not rest on intrinsic distinctions, but this tells us almost nothing positive about them. I am inclined, however, to think that there is room here for a great deal of variation. There seems to be nothing in the notion of an internal justification that rules out a society of super Sartreans who allow scarcely any excuses at all. The members of such a society could desire in IRE to accept blame for their actions under a far wider range of circumstances than we do. By the same token, there seems to be nothing to rule out a society in which even the man or woman on the street accepts as broad a range of excuses as would be accepted if most instances of deviance were understood in medical rather than judicial terms.

The solution to the dilemma regarding moral responsibility, then, lies in the fact that those who suffer may be internally justified in acquiescing in their suffering. Thus the solution justifies the punishment of those who act on desires out of IRE but not those who act on desires in IRE. It follows that we cannot blame the psychopath when his or her actions are motivated by desires in IRE, even if these actions result in serious harm. And this consequence raises two apparent difficulties. First, while we cannot blame the psychopath, it is essential to the account of the internal justification of blame that we can blame those who desire to be blamable. Furthermore, there is no reason why the psychopath should not desire to be blamable, in virtue of desiring the authorship of his or her creations. The conflict here, however, is merely apparent. In order to be blamable, there must be *some* class of actions for which the psychopath would be justified in feeling self-directed anger, guilt, or remorse. But these actions need not be the ones in which he or she knowingly and deliberately causes harm to others. They might instead be actions that, because of the psychopath's motivational makeup, are weak-willed and thus not motivated by desires in IRE. The psychopath might be blamable, for example, for failing to act with sufficient ruthlessness in advancing his or her own interests. Thus there are two conditions for being justified in feeling guilt and remorse for one's actions and in acquiescing in the reactive attitudes, punishment, and blame that those actions elicit in others. The actions must belong to a class of actions for which one is blamable, and the actions must be performed on the basis of desires that are out of IRE. And whereas the actions of the psychopath that cause harm to others may well satisfy the first condition, they will not in general satisfy the second.

The second difficulty for this account of responsibility is that the consequence that we cannot punish the psychopath may seem to be in conflict with our pretheoretical intuitions. This may be the case despite the reservations about such punishment that many theorists have expressed on independent grounds. And the analogy between the psychopath and the person with normal moral commitments living among a tribe governed by superstitious taboos may not dispel the doubts concerning this consequence. But the fact that we cannot punish the psychopath for harming others will seem less implausible if we recognize that some of the consequences it may appear to have do not actually follow. As we have seen, the fact that punishment cannot be justified in these cases does not entail that we cannot protect ourselves from the psychopath. What does follow is that the justification of such protection will be of a different kind from the one that supports genuine punishment. The justification of punishment will involve notions like guilt and remorse and will appeal to the values of the subjects being punished and to the fact that these values justify their acquiescing in the suffering that their punishment entails. In contrast, we justify protecting ourselves from the psychopath on consequentialist grounds that need not involve the notion of desert. Just as we may quarantine a person without supposing that the person is responsible for his or her condition, so we may minimize our risk of being harmed by the psychopath without supposing that genuine blame is appropriate. In the case of the psychopath who is blamable for at least some actions, it is not even ruled out that we should enforce the full range of legal penalties on purely deterrent grounds. And in such a case all that would be missing is the connection between the enforcement of the penalties and any form of blame in which the person being penalized could acquiesce. This is sufficient, however, for saying that the penalties cannot constitute genuine punishment.

The account of rationality I have outlined is one according to which ascriptions of irrationality are a special case of ascriptions of responsibility and blame. Thus it is natural on such an account to address the dilemma where ascriptions of irrationality are concerned by appeal to this treatment of the dilemma regarding responsibility. The account of rationality, then, will involve the direct justification of ascriptions of irrationality and the ascriptions of blame that constitute them, and the justification will be an internal one. And as in the theory of responsibility, only those whose actions are out of IRE (or stem from ignorance or computational failures) will be open to genuine blame. Since we cannot genuinely blame those who are in IRE, it follows that those who are in IRE are not acting irrationally.

That this theory solves the puzzle about rationality (and it is difficult to see how a noninternalist theory could do so) is a strong point in its favor. But such an internalist approach to rationality has the consequence that we originally sought to establish. To say that SoHo indifference and future-Tuesday indifference might each be in equilibrium is to say that each might be part of a motivational makeup in IRE. And this is to say that such desires are not irrational. It was, after all, the desires out of IRE (as well as one's cognitive failings) for which one could be justified in accepting blame and feeling guilt or remorse. For the desires in IRE, this would not be possible. Hence, it is a consequence of an account of rationality, and an account supported on independent grounds, that the kind of indifference that I have called pathological need not be irrational.

The account of rationality I have presented is, of course, one version of what Parfit calls the present aim theory—the theory that "tells each to do what will best achieve his present aims" (Parfit 1984, 92). And by arguing for the rationality of future-Tuesday indifference, I have blocked the claim, strongly suggested by Parfit's account, that any theory that has the consequence that future-Tuesday indifference is not irrational is unacceptable for that reason. And this is, in fact, the only objection that Parfit offers to the present aim theory. The possibility that future-Tuesday indifference is rational, however, is a consequence of a theory of rationality that is justified on independent grounds. Thus any argument that it must be irrational, if it is to be convincing, must be founded on an alternative treatment of rationality that we have at least as much reason to accept.[9]

Notes

1. The example of SoHo indifference was suggested by Jerrold Katz.
2. This is not to say that there are not other ways of explaining how making oneself a multiple-personality subject might constitute a rational response to the anticipation of unavoidable pain. For example, by making it the case that the different parts of one's future are not psychologically continuous with each other, one could anticipate now a *part* of one's future in which one would not anticipate the pain and suffering that one now anticipates. This seems, however, to be a much less powerful strategy for dealing with unavoidable pain than the one that involves withdrawing one's concern for those person stages that undergo the pain.
3. The role that the unconditional desires that survive in one's IRE are intended to play is analogous to that played by Harry Frankfurt's higher-order desires (1971). Both the notion of a desire's being unconditional and in one's IRE and Frankfurt's notion of a desire's being appropriately endorsed by a desire of second (or higher) order are intended to capture the intuitive idea of a desire's being one with which one identifies. And the desires with which one identifies are the ones that represent one's deepest values and commitments. I discuss these issues in more detail in "Self-Deception and Responsibility for the Self" (1988). The notion of an unconditional desire in IRE, however, is designed to sidestep the most obvious problem with Frankfurt's analysis: the fact that one's higher-order desires may be as alien to one as one's first-order desires and that the analysis therefore leads to an infinite regress.
4. The dichotomy that results if we put aside cases of ignorance is in one respect seriously oversimplified. (This was pointed out to me by Annette Baier.) Consider the case of genuine moral dilemmas. Suppose, for example, that before one has access to the pill that allows one to realize one's IRE, one has an unconditional desire not to betray one's friend, come what may, and an unconditional desire not be betray one's country under any circumstances. It seems at least conceivable that both desires might be well supported and that in forming one's IRE one might opt to keep both. Moreover, one could opt to keep one's desires to accept blame and to feel guilt and remorse if one were to act in such a way that either desire were unfulfilled. And it seems conceivable that one could do this knowing full well that it would have the following result. There would be possible circumstances (those in which not betraying one's country would mean betraying one's friend and vice versa) in which one would be motivated to acquiesce in punishment or blame and in feelings of guilt and remorse regardless of what one's choice under those circumstances turned out to be. Suppose such an IRE is not inconceivable. Then it will *not* be the case either that we act in IRE without remorse (or without remorse that would survive in IRE) and are not relevantly different from the psychopath or that we act out of IRE on the basis of a desire that we prefer not to have and are not relevantly different from the compulsive. We may act in IRE and still feel remorse that is itself fully supported in IRE. Such a possibility, however, contributes nothing toward the solution of the dilemma for ascriptions of responsibility and blame. The possibility of such an IRE simply makes the dilemma a trilemma. Suppose one actually faced the situation in which one was forced either to betray one's friend or one's country. And suppose that in fact one betrayed one's friend. In this case one would be motivated in IRE to accept any blame ascribed by others in addition to one's own guilt and remorse. But it is even less obvious how one could be justified in doing so in this case than it is in the case in which one acts on a desire out of IRE.

5. P. F. Strawson makes the connection between genuine punishment and the appropriateness of these attitudes (which he calls other-reactive and self-reactive attitudes) when he says, "So the preparedness to acquiesce in that infliction of suffering on the offender which is an essential part of punishment is all of a piece with this whole range of attitudes of which I have been speaking. It is not only moral reactive attitudes towards the offender which are in question here. We must mention also the self-reactive attitudes of offenders themselves. Just as the other-reactive attitudes are associated with a readiness to acquiesce in the infliction of suffering on an offender, within the 'institution' of punishment, so the self-reactive attitudes are associated with a readiness on the part of the offender to acquiesce in such infliction *without* developing the reactions (e.g., of resentment) which he would normally develop to the infliction of injury upon him; i.e. with a readiness, as we say, to accept punishment as 'his due' or as 'just'" (1962, 207).

6. The similarities between the puzzle about responsibility and the puzzle about rationality, however, raise the following question. The puzzle about responsibility was generated by our taking as basic the problem of justifying our practice of blaming those who cause harm for which we regard them as responsible. The problem is generated, that is, by our taking as basic the problem of justifying such reactive attitudes as resentment and indignation where others are concerned and guilt and remorse in our own case and the suffering they entail. Similarly, the problem of rationality is generated by our taking as basic the problem of justifying a similar set of reactive attitudes toward those who cause harm by acting in ways we consider irrational. How, then, can we distinguish within this framework between irrationality and immorality?

   It seems implausible to suppose that immorality and irrationality can be distinguished by a special set of reactive attitudes specific to each. It seems perfectly possible, for example, to feel guilt and remorse for one's actions that are irrational as well as those that are immoral. This seems especially true when an irrational action causes serious harm. It also seems implausible to claim that morality rather than rationality is involved if the interests of others are at stake. One can easily cause harm to others, as well as to oneself, by actions that are irrational but not immoral. Consider, however, a clear case of irrationality. Someone performs an action that leaves the whole group of people affected (including himself or herself) far less well off than some other action would have that was readily available. If we assume the agent bears the others no ill will but rather has a genuine interest in their welfare, this seems to be a case of irrationality but not immorality. On the other hand, someone willing to gain an advantage by causing harm to others will ordinarily count as immoral. In what follows, I shall not try to refine this distinction any further, since it is sufficiently clear in the paradigm cases, and nothing I shall say turns on a more precise formulation.

7. For proposals that treat social deviance in medical terms, see Menninger 1968 and Wootton 1959, part 2; 1963.

8. In Strawson's case the need to justify our reactive attitudes is apparently denied, though some of Strawson's remarks might point in the direction of a theory like the one I suggest. For Dennett, the justification is a consequentialist one, and such a justification makes it difficult, as I have argued, to capture the distinction between punishment and blame on the one hand and manipulation and the exercise of power on the other. Glover suggests that we interpret our reactive attitudes as aesthetic attitudes. But our aesthetic attitudes may themselves fail to cohere with our desire not to cause others to suffer by blaming them for their actions when we have no justification for doing so. As a result, Glover seems to fall back on what is

426 Stephen L. White

a consequentialist (and essentially utilitarian) justification of our reactive attitudes. Thus the possibility of an alternative approach to the justification of these attitudes is worth exploring.

9. An earlier version on this paper was read to the Society for Philosophy and Public Affairs at the Eastern Division meeting of the American Philosophical Association, December 29, 1986. I am grateful to the commentators, Annette Baier and George Sher, for their discussion of these issues and to Amélie Rorty for her comments and suggestions.

Part V
Virtue Theory

Chapter 18

Some Advantages of Virtue Ethics

Michael Slote

Act utilitarianism and act consequentialism more generally are frequently said to require too much of moral agents. Such views standardly demand that one produce the best overall results one can, and if they express a valid conception of morality, then in most individual cases, one will have to sacrifice one's interests or one's deepest personal concerns in order to comply with the demands of morality. Frequently it is defenders of commonsense, intuitive moral thinking who criticize consequentialism for making unreasonable demands on moral agents, and it has often been taken to be an advantage of commonsense morality that it treats our most fundamental and most important form of act evaluation as in most cases requiring nothing like the kind of self-sacrifice entailed by a utilitarian or consequentialist form of morality. To be sure, there are occasions when even common sense seems to require an agent to sacrifice her deepest concerns, even perhaps her life, but as a rule, commonsense moral thinking seems to permit the individual to pursue her own good or well-being as long as she refrains from harming, and does a certain amount on behalf of, other people. And this is precisely what act consequentialism, with its requirement that one always do what, in impersonal terms, is considered best for mankind, seems not to allow.

In this essay, however, I want to argue that, for reasons somewhat different from the familiar ones just mentioned, commonsense and Kantian morality can likewise be said to give insufficient weight to the interests or well-being of moral agents and thus in an important sense to slight, devalue, or downgrade such agents. By contrast, a properly conceived virtue ethics does not slight us as moral agents in the way that consequentialism is commonly thought to do or in the less familiar way that ordinary and Kantian morality can, I think, be shown to do. And this constitutes a major advantage of virtue theory that may help to add impetus to the recent revival of virtue ethics. Much of the recent interest in virtue ethics has focused on the analysis and comparison of particular virtues and on the ways in which talk of virtue may importantly supplement what ethics needs to say about the rightness and wrongness of actions. But the virtue-theoretical advantages to be argued for in what follows support virtue ethics in a deeper sense. If (utilitarian) consequentialism, Kantianism, and commonsense morality all give insufficient weight to the interests of the individual agent, then perhaps a virtue-theoretic approach that avoids this sort of difficulty may in fact turn out to offer the best way of *grounding* our ethical thinking.

1 Moral Asymmetry

In the past few years a great deal of energy has been expended on the critical evaluation of so-called commonsense morality, and much of what I have to say in criticism of ordinary and Kantian moral thinking is based in these recent discussions though in important ways it seeks to go beyond them. It has frequently been pointed out, for example, that commonsense thinking about right and wrong is permissive in the personal sphere in ways and to a degree that act consequentialism and, most familiarly, act utilitarianism are not. (Henceforth I shall use "consequentialism" and "utilitarianism" in place of these longer designations.) Just above I spoke of our commonsense permission(s) to pursue our own personal projects and concerns even at a cost to overall or impersonally reckoned good. And in recent work the distinction in this respect between consequentialism and ordinary morality has been expressed by saying that the latter grants agents a moral permission to pursue innocent projects and concerns in ways that are not optimific, not productive of the greatest overall balance of good.[1] These moral permissions allow the agent to favor herself to some extent over other people, to seek her own good on some occasions when she could do more good by trying to help others, and this, of course, is precisely what standard utilitarianism does not allow one to do. In the present context I shall also refer to such permissions as *agent-favoring* permissions, because I would like to draw a contrast between this familiar category of commonsense moral permission and a less familiar form of moral permission that treats it as morally permissible for agents to neglect their own projects and concerns and even, in fact, to thwart them.

Our intuitive moral thinking seems to regard it as entirely permissible, though of course hardly advisable or rational, for an individual to deny herself the very things she most wants or to cause herself unnecessary pain or damage. (Here common sense diverges from Kantian ethics—criticism of the latter will come in later in my discussion.) Even if no one else stands to benefit from such self-sacrifice, even if there is no reason of moral deontology for it, such an act of self-sacrifice does not seem morally wrong.[2] It is appropriate to refer this new class of permissions as *agent-sacrificing* in order to mark the contrast with the agent-favoring permissions that are already so well known in the ethics literature. Both sorts of permission allow for nonoptimific action, but in addition the agent-sacrificing permissions allow for nonoptimific behavior that doesn't even serve the interests or concerns of the moral agent. So if, as we might put it, agent-favoring permissions allow the substitution of the agent's good for the larger overall good that consequentialism uses as the standard of right action, then agent-sacrificing permissions morally allow for action that cannot be justified by any appeal to what is good or best and indeed allow for action that must inevitably seem stupid, absurd, or irrational by comparison with agent-favoring behavior. However, we should not immediately assume that commonsense morality itself cannot sensibly make moral accommodation to behavior that itself is not sensible, and for the moment, at least, we need only focus on the fact that commonsense morality does seem to permit such senseless or stupid behavior.

Consider, then, what our ordinary moral thinking seems to allow and to forbid with regard to our treatment of *other people*. Negligently to hurt another person intuitively seems to be morally wrong in a way or to a degree that it does not seem wrong to hurt oneself through negligence. (It can be wrong to hurt oneself if one thereby makes it impossible for one to fulfill certain obligations, but I am speaking of less complex situations.) Similarly, if one could easily *prevent* pain to another person, it is typically thought wrong not to do so, but not to avoid similar pain to oneself seems crazy or irrational, not morally wrong. And so given the agent-sacrificing commonsense permissions we have described, we may now also speak of an *agent-sacrificing* (or *other-favoring*) *self-other asymmetry* that attaches to what is commonsensically permissible. Various ways one may permissibly act against one's own interests or well-being are ways in which one is commonsensically not allowed to act against the interests or well-being of others.[3]

But isn't there, then, another side to this coin in virtue of the familiar agent-favoring permissions that we have also attributed to our commonsense moral thinking? We ordinarily think that people have a right to neglect their own interests, but don't we also believe that one may to a certain extent permissibly favor one's own interests over those of other individuals, and doesn't this latter give rise to some sort of agent-favoring self-other asymmetry? If so, don't we

then also face the considerable problem of explaining how our commonsense permissions can simultaneously yield agent-favoring *and*
agent-sacrificing asymmetries?

These difficulties can be avoided if one only recognizes that our
agent-favoring permissions provide no obvious footing for asymmetry. I may be permitted to act against overall optimality in the
pursuit of my own concerns, but this yields an agent-favoring asymmetry only if the analogous claim with respect to *other* people seems
commonsensically suspect and in fact it isn't. Just as one may favor
one's own interests or special concerns, there seems to be nothing
intuitively wrong with helping *another person* in an overall nonoptimific fashion. In commonsense terms, there is no obligation always to
do what is best overall for people, and just as the person *p* who
chooses a lesser benefit to himself in preference to some greater
benefit for another person may not do anything wrong, someone *g*
who chooses a lesser good for another rather than a greater good for
himself also does nothing wrong. In fact if we intuitively compare
these last two choices, *g*'s nonoptimific agent-sacrificing choice seems
morally more meritorious than *p*'s nonoptimific agent-favoring
choice. And in that case, far from leading to an agent-favoring self-
other asymmetry, our permission to favor ourselves actually takes us
right back to the agent-sacrificing asymmetry we started with.

However, there is a great deal more to be said about the agent-
sacrificing self-other asymmetry that I have located in commonsense
morality. I have thus far largely concentrated on the asymmetry of
our commonsense moral permissions, but I have also briefly indicated that such asymmetry is also to be found in our views of (positive or comparative) moral merit. It is time now to focus our attention
on the way in which agent-sacrificing self-other asymmetry applies
outside the area of permissions. Moral theorists tend to assume that
moral evaluation is our most fundamental and/or important form of
ethical evaluation. But the aspects of self-other asymmetry that I shall
now focus on force us to question whether either commonsense or
Kantian morality can properly fulfill such a role.

The point I wish to make about both these forms of morality is
perhaps best approached by means of a contrast with a well-known
aspect of (utilitarian) consequentialism. The latter allows for neither
agent-sacrificing nor agent-favoring permissions of the sort I have
described because it is entirely agent-neutral: no one may be treated
in any way fundamentally different from the way any other person
is treated, and this uniformity of treatment crosses the boundary
between self and other as well as that between different others. In
consequentialism, if something is permitted with respect to one in-

dividual, it is acceptable with respect to any other individual as long as the causal-evaluative facts on which moral judgments are based remain otherwise the same. If, for example, it is wrong for me to hurt another person when by not doing so I can create more overall good, then it is wrong for me to hurt myself in similar circumstances. Even if I hurt myself in order to help others, my act will count as wrong if I could have done more overall good by favoring myself more and benefiting others less.[4] Furthermore, if the agent's sole choice is between helping herself and helping another person to exactly the same extent, the two possible acts are of equal moral value, are equally good morally, according to any recognizable form of consequentialism. But if the agent has to choose between helping herself more and helping another less or between helping another person more and helping herself less, the morally better action according to consequentialism will always be the one that does the most good.[5] And this also holds for choices exclusively concerned with the good of the agent or exclusively concerned with the good of others. As a result, I think we may say that consequentialism treats the good of the agent and that of any given other as counting equally toward favorable moral assessment.

Note the contrast with egoism. The latter presumably regards what helps the agent more as automatically morally better than what helps the agent less but makes no similar comparative judgment about effects on other people. Only when the agent's good is (contingently) tied to that of other people can effects on others make a difference to egoistic moral evaluation. And so in respect to its comparative moral judgments, egoism is asymmetric in a way that consequentialism clearly is not. Where, then, does commonsense morality fit into this picture?

Unlike egoism, our ordinary thinking tends to regard giving more rather than less to another person as morally better or more meritorious, other things being equal. But when we turn to situations in which the agent is in a position to affect himself in some way, a different picture emerges. We earlier saw that commonsense morality allows or permits the agent to hurt or fail to help himself. But when comparative moral judgments are at issue, the agent's own good also appears to be irrelevant. If I have to choose between helping myself a little or a great deal, the latter choice would not normally be regarded as morally better—wiser, more rational, more prudent perhaps, just not *morally* better. Here there is a marked contrast with both consequentialism and ethical egoism, but not just here. Where both the agent's and another person's good are at stake, our ordinary moral thinking seems to assign the former no positive weight whatever. It may be more rational to choose a great good for oneself in preference to a lesser good for another person, but for commonsense, it is not morally preferable to choose one's own greater good, and it even seems morally better to seek the *lesser* good of another in preference to a greater benefit for oneself. Here again there is a contrast with both egoism and consequentialism.[6]

Of course, what helps the agent would ordinarily be taken to be capable of indirect moral value. It may be morally better for me to be careful about my health than to be indifferent about it if a family's or a nation's welfare depends on my keeping healthy, but if in order to make a case for the moral value or merit of some agent-beneficial action, we ordinarily have to say something to tie that action and that benefit to the well-being of others, that fact only serves to underscore the asymmetry of comparative evaluations I have just been calling attention to. It is now time to see whether our ordinary understanding of virtue and virtues is subject to any similar asymmetry and whether, if such understanding turns out to be relatively free of such asymmetry, we can use this difference to argue in favor of a virtue-theoretic approach to ethics.

2 The Symmetry in Virtue

In her ground-breaking article "Moral Beliefs" (1978a) Philippa Foot assumes that if a trait of character does not benefit or serve the needs of its possessor, the trait cannot properly be regarded as a virtue. She notes that in the *Republic* Plato takes it for granted "that if justice is not a good to the just man, moralists who recommend it as a virtue are perpetrating a fraud," and she points out that Nietzsche, unlike present-day moral philosophers, seems to accept a similar view.[7]

Foot herself, however, has subsequently retracted this assumption. In some of her later work she has separated the issue of what counts as a virtue from issues concerning what the agent has reason to do and has treated it as intuitively unobjectionable to hold that traits that fail to benefit their possessors may properly be regarded as virtues.[8] For present-day commonsense thinking it might be enough, for example, that a trait be one by which *other people* generally benefit. (As Foot herself notes, what counts as a virtue in functional objects like knives doesn't benefit the knives themselves, only those who use them.)

To the extent that Foot's retraction constitutes a concession to our ordinary thought about virtue and virtues, I think Foot was correct to retract her earlier assumption and recognize that virtues may not benefit their possessors. But it would be a mistake to conclude from this that our ordinary thinking about the virtues is subject to a self-other asymmetry similar to what we have found in commonsense morality. My assessment of whether a given character trait counts as a virtue (and of whether a given act in exemplifying a certain character trait also exemplifies a virtue) is favorably affected by the consideration that the trait in question benefits people other than its possessor. But it is no less favorably affected by the consideration that a given trait benefits, or is useful to, its possessor(s). In our ordinary thinking it may not be *necessary* to status as a virtue that a given trait be beneficial (more or less generally) to its possessors, but it certainly *helps to qualify* any given trait as a virtue that it is useful or beneficial to those who possess it, and in fact I think it is entirely in keeping with commonsense views to suppose that both helpfulness to its possessors and helpfulness to others are independently and in fairly equal measure capable of conferring virtue status. To consider the issue first on a fairly abstract level, if I hear that people generally need a given trait of character and benefit from possessing it, I will normally think I have been given excellent reason to regard that trait as a virtue.[9] But by the same token, if I learn that a certain character trait is generally useful to people other than its possessors, I will also naturally or normally think I have been given reason to regard that trait as a virtue.

When, furthermore, we look at the whole range of traits commonly recognized as virtues, we once again see that self-regarding and other-regarding considerations are both capable of underlying the kind of high regard that leads us to regard various traits as virtues. Justice, kindness, probity, and generosity are chiefly admired for what they lead those who possess these traits to do in their relations with other people, but prudence, sagacity, circumspection, equanimity, and fortitude are esteemed primarily under their self-regarding aspect, and still other traits—notably self-control, courage, and (perhaps) wisdom in practical affairs—are in substantial measure admired both for what they do for their possessors and for what they lead their possessors to do with regard to other people.[10]

It is also worth noting that traits admired for other-regarding reasons do not have any sort of general precedence over predominantly self-regarding virtues that might be taken to entail a self-other asymmetry of the sort I have discussed in connection with commonsense morality. (I think the opposite problem of precedence for self-regarding virtues need not concern us.) The other-regarding traits mentioned above lack any (implicitly) recognized status as greater or more important virtues than the self-regarding traits also mentioned above, and neither does a mixed virtue like courage, self-control, or wisdom seem inferior to, or less of a virtue than, such predominantly other-regarding virtues as justice and kindness. We greatly admire probity and fair dealing, but we also have enormous admiration for many self-regarding and mixed virtues. So I think our ordinary thinking in this area gives rise to nothing like the marked or extreme self-other asymmetry that characterizes commonsense morality.

Yet consider the view of Hume, who says that "when a man is called *virtuous*, or is denominated a man of virtue, we chiefly regard his social qualities."[11] I have no wish to deny what Hume is saying here, but I think that we must distinguish between virtue and virtuousness, on the one hand, and what constitutes something as *a* virtue, on the other. Both "virtue" (without the qualifying article) and "virtuous" are sometimes used in a restricted sense to refer to certain sorts of sexual conduct, or nonconduct, especially on the part of women. But no similar connotation arises when we say that a certain trait is a virtue or speak of various virtues. And even when "virtuous" and unarticled "virtue" are used in a more general sense or way, they have a moral significance that doesn't automatically attach to our talk of particular virtues. It has often been pointed out that in its broader usage, "virtuous" is roughly equivalent to "morally good," and in a similar way a phrase like "a man of virtue" is typically used as roughly equivalent with the notion of a (morally) good man.[12] Hume is certainly right if he assumes that our talk of virtuousness lays a special emphasis on social virtue, on other-regarding traits and dispositions. But that is because these notions are fundamentally moral, even if the word "moral" and its cognates do not always appear when they are employed. (As Ross points out, even "a good man" is normally understood to mean a morally good man.)[13] By contrast, the notion of a virtue lacks such an automatic connection with morality and other-regarding considerations. When we say patience, circumspection, or prudence is a virtue, we are not committed to saying that it is morally better to have than to lack that trait. Of course, these traits can be useful to morally good individuals and so help such individuals do morally better things than they otherwise could have, but prudence and the other traits we have just mentioned can also be used for morally neutral or nefarious purposes, and (unlike Kant, as we shall see) we commonly regard these character traits as virtues independently of any implicit judgment of how selfishly or altruistically they are likely to be used. It is enough that the person with patience or prudence (or fortitude or circumspection) have a trait needed to get on well in life. And so until now I have quite deliberately been talking about given virtues and what counts as *a* virtue precisely in order to avoid the self-other asymmetry that attaches to moral notions and to terms like "a man of virtue" and "virtuous" in common usage. Our common understanding of what it is to be or to exemplify a virtue (or an admirable character trait) is unburdened with agent-sacrificing moral connotation, and I hope to show in what follows how this enables virtue theory to gain an important superiority over the familiar sort of moral view that employs terms like "right," "wrong," and "morally good."

Our ordinary thinking about virtues is symmetric in a way that ordinary thinking about morality is not. But we have also seen that other possibilities exist in the field of morality, with egoism embodying an agent-favoring self-other asymmetric conception of morality and consequentialism a strictly symmetric form of moral thinking. And it turns out that similar variation with respect to self-other symmetry is also possible in the sphere of the virtues. Even if most of us would intuitively reject the notion that only what helps its possessor(s) is properly regarded as a virtue, that assumption is arguably common to Plato, Stoicism, Epicureanism, and Nietzsche, and such a fundamentally egoistic understanding of virtue, like egoism about morality, is self-other asymmetric in an agent-favoring manner.

Furthermore, even if our ordinary thinking about virtue(s) fails to exemplify the agent-sacrificing (or other-favoring) asymmetry we find in commonsense morality, such self-other asymmetry is clearly *possible* in the realm of virtue, and in fact, I believe that we have a good example of such asymmetry in Kant's views about what counts as an estimable character trait. Kant's doctrine of virtue is fundamentally a doctrine of moral virtue, but more important in the light of what I said above, his views about what counts as *a* virtue entail the same agent-sacrificing asymmetry we find in his view of morality. In the *Fundamental Principles of the Metaphysics of Morals* Kant says that character traits like moderation, perseverance, judgment, self-control, courage, and the ability to deliberate calmly have value and are praiseworthy only conditionally. In the absence of a good will, these traits are not estimable and presumably do not count as virtues. Having a good will, in turn, is understood by Kant (roughly) as a form of conscientiousness, of doing one's duty out of respect for the moral law, of doing one's duty because it is one's duty rather than from any other motivation.[14] So the Kantian conception of virtue will turn out to be asymmetrical if Kantian morality is asymmetrical, and in fact, Kantian morality is asymmetrical in some of the same ways in which commonsense morality is. On Kant's view, for example, we have an obligation to benefit or contribute to the happiness of other people but no parallel obligation to seek our own well-being or happiness. We have a duty to develop our natural talents, a duty not to *harm* ourselves, and a duty of self-preservation that derives from our other duties. But except insofar as it is necessary to fulfill those other obligations, we have no moral reason to make ourselves *happy* or *well-off*. (By contrast our obligation to seek others' happiness is nonderivative, is independent of our other obligations.)

But (roughly) if the status of moderation or perseverance as a virtue depends on its being accompanied by a Kantian good will and such a will is fundamentally more concerned with the well-being of others than with the well-being of the moral agent, then the agent-sacrificing asymmetry of Kantian moral obligation will translate into a similar asymmetry in Kantian views about what properly counts as a good trait of character, as a virtue. Our commonsense views of what counts as a virtue escape this asymmetry, despite the self-other asymmetry of commonsense moral obligation because, unlike Kant, we ordinarily regard some of the character traits mentioned above as admirable or estimable independently of their accompaniment by moral goodness or virtue. We may have an unfavorable moral opinion of a colleague who mistreats his friends and his family yet have a high regard for that colleague's devotion to some academic subject or his coolheadedness or his fortitude in the face of (deserved or undeserved) personal tragedy.[15]

And so in the area of virtue the same three possibilities exist as exist in morality, but we find commonsense views occupying a different position among these possibilities. With regard to personal happiness or well-being, commonsense and Kantian morality are agent-sacrificingly self-other asymmetric in contrast with the agent-favoring (other-sacrificing) asymmetry of egoism and the self-other symmetry of (utilitarian) consequentialism. But in the field of the virtues it is common sense that occupies the symmetric position (along with utilitarianism, but I am ignoring some complications here), whereas egoism is once again agent-favoringly asymmetric and only the Kantian view, among those I have mentioned, is agent-sacrificingly asymmetric.

Of course, I have not yet explored the significance, the theoretical implications, of these varying symmetries and asymmetries. To the extent that symmetry is a favorable characteristic of an ethical view, I could perhaps on that basis alone argue for the superiority of either consequentialism or a commonsense ethics of the virtues over a commonsense or Kantian ethics of right, wrong, and obligation. But in fact, the symmetry in consequentialism and in commonsense virtue ethics has a significance that far outstrips the desirability of symmetry as such. However desirably symmetrical consequentialism may be, it still is subject to the complaint of being too demanding, of requiring too much individual sacrifice. And I am now in a position to show that the agent-sacrificing asymmetry of commonsense and Kantian morality subjects them to the rather similar complaint that they downgrade or deprecate the importance of the moral agent, a charge that, as we shall also see, the particular symmetry of our ordinary view of virtue allows the latter to escape.

3 How Ordinary Morality and Kantian Morality Devalue Moral Agents

How can commonsense morality be guilty of devaluing or deprecating the importance of the moral agent? After all, it is itself the source of the criticism that consequentialism and utilitarianism ride roughshod over the particular concerns and projects of the individual by demanding that she sacrifice them whenever they interfere with her production of impersonally reckoned best results. Is commonsense or Kantian morality perhaps more demanding than its adherents have realized? Is that the basis for the objection I wish to make to such morality?

I do want to claim that these forms of morality downgrade the (actual) importance of moral agents and their individual concerns, projects, even desires. But the argument for this claim will not be that like consequentialism the ordinary and/or the Kantian standard of right and wrong make an insufficient concession to the moral agent's welfare. On the contrary, it will involve, rather, the claim that commonsense and Kantian morality *do* make concessions to the well-being and happiness of agents *but make them only as concessions*.[16]

Commonsense and Kantian ethics permit the moral agent to seek and find her own happiness at the expense, at least to some extent, of overall, or impersonally judged, optimality. But this does not mean that they treat such usefulness to the agent as a source of *positive moral value*. Other things being equal, if an agent has to choose between two actions and one of these would (probably) be more helpful to the agent, then the more helpful action would typically be regarded as one that it is more rational for the agent to perform and, in the appropriate reasons-related sense, as a better option from the standpoint of the agent. But from the ordinary or Kantian point of view, such an act would usually not be considered morally better or morally more praiseworthy or meritorious than the act that would do less good for the agent. The point simply recaptures some of what I was saying earlier: for ordinary or Kantian moral thinking, how morally good or meritorious an act is will depend in part (and especially in the absence of deontological factors) on how much it does for the well-being of other people but not on how much it does for that of the agent.

So in cases where someone helps herself at the expense of overall best results and of the potential good of other people, commonsense morality may maintain the moral permissibility of what the (utilitarian) consequentialist would standardly regard as a violation of moral obligation but will nonetheless share with consequentialism the judgment that such action is morally less good than what would have achieved greater overall good and greater good for other people. And in such cases, therefore, common sense makes moral concessions to the agent's personal good but attributes positive moral value only on the basis of what the agent does for the well-being of others. (Again, I am assuming an absence of deontological considerations.) And if you wish to object that our ordinary thinking here accords positive moral value to what the agent does solely on her own behalf but simply refuses to assign *greater* moral value to what is *more* self-beneficial, then consider what we think about purely self-regarding cases where someone has to choose between having or not having something nice. Intuitively speaking, if someone decides to have a nice lunch rather than not eating at all, then other things being equal, what that person does is neither morally better than the alternative nor, intuitively, the sort of action we would praise as morally a good one. And Kant's conception of morality likewise provides no basis for assigning positive moral value to actions to the extent they merely promote the happiness or well-being of their agents.

By contrast, the utilitarian and the consequentialist more generally (but remember we are talking about act-utilitarianism and act-consequentialism only) will treat the preference satisfaction or well-being of the agent as a basis for positive moral assessment. In self-regarding cases the consequentialist holds not only that the agent has a moral obligation to do the best she can for herself but, in addition, that it is morally better for her to do so than for her to perform some less self-beneficial alternative action. Moreover, where an agent has to choose between on the one hand, doing x amount of good for others and y amount for himself, and on the other, simply doing x amount for others, consequentialism regards the former act as morally superior, but our ordinary thinking about morality seems to lack this tendency. We don't normally regard someone who could have benefited himself at the same time he helped others but chose only to help the others as morally less meritorious for having done nothing for himself. Indeed, there may be some tendency to regard such action as morally better or more praiseworthy precisely because the agent *sought nothing for himself* in the process.[17]

In summary, then, it would appear that over a large range of cases our ordinary thinking about morality assigns no positive value to the well-being or happiness of the moral agent of the sort it clearly assigns to the well-being or happiness of *everyone other than the agent*. For such thinking, the fact that an act helps its agent cannot provide any sort of basis for the favorable, as opposed to the merely non-unfavorable, evaluation of that action. And harm to the agent seems similarly irrelevant to an unfavorable evaluation of an act. I believe that this aspect of commonsense morality is and can be shown to be ethically objectionable.

Defenders as well as opponents of an intuitive or intuitionist approach to ethics typically regard morality as the central concern of ethics and treat the moral assessment of acts and agents as our most fundamental, our most important, form of act and agent evaluation. (This fact is reflected, for example, in the familiar use of the expression "moral philosophy" to refer to the area of philosophy that people in ethics are interested in.) I believe it is objectionable to suppose that our most central (or fundamental or important) mode of ethical evaluation treats facts about whether and how an act is (or is intended to be) helpful or harmful to its agent's interests as at best irrelevant to favorable and unfavorable evaluation of that act. If at the most fundamental level or in its most central concerns, our ethics is in this way indifferent to whether the agent is helped or hurt by his actions, then our ethics devalues the interests of the agent and the agent himself as agent and imposes or entails a kind of self-abnegation or selflessness in regard to the *agent's own* assessment of the ethical value of what he is doing. And I believe that such considerations give us as much reason to be suspicious of commonsense or Kantian morality, considered as our most central or fundamental form of ethical evaluation, as consequentialism's supposedly exorbitant demands for self-sacrifice give us reason to question the validity of consequentialism.

I should point out, however, that it is hardly objectionable that *some* form of act evaluation should fail to concern itself with the interests of the agent. The existence of such a mode of evaluation is entirely consistent with a proper concern for the interests of agents as such, because it is entirely consistent with the existence of important forms of evaluation that *do* positively take the agent's interests into account. What seems to deprecate and devalue the moral agent, to rob her of her actual importance, is rather the assumption that *at the most fundamental level*, or *in its most central concerns*, substantive ethical thinking gives no positive evaluative weight to the interests of agents as such. Of course, when a person is viewed as a recipient of the acts of other agents, commonsense and Kantian morality regard the well-being of every person as having a positive and fundamental valuational significance. But at the same time they assign no such significance to the effects of an act on the well-being of the agent of the act. It is the latter fact that lies behind the charge that I am bringing against commonsense and Kantian morality.[18] If morality is to function as the centrally important part of our ethical thinking that most of us think it is, then both commonsense and Kantian morality are unfitted for such a role because of the way they depreciate the interests of moral agents both from the standpoint of those agents' evaluation of their own actions and more generally. They each require the agent to be valuationally selfless or self-abnegating with respect to her own actions—though not with respect to other people's actions—and in effect, they alienate the agent from her own self-interest or welfare when she evaluates the ethical significance of her own actions. But even from a more general standpoint of evaluation, both views regard all effects on the agent's well-being as fundamentally irrelevant to the favorable or unfavorable evaluation of a given action, whereas that well-being is taken into account when anyone else's actions are being evaluated. Clearly, commonsense and Kantian morality, if seen as concerning themselves with the most central or fundamental questions of ethics, can each be criticized for deprecating or devaluing the welfare of the moral agent as such.

Of course, the *way* in which these two conceptions of morality can be regarded as devaluing the moral agent and her interests is not precisely the way in which utilitarian consequentialism can be thought and is commonly thought to devalue agents and their interests. By the same token, the way in which ordinary and Kantian moral thinking impose self-abnegation or self-alienation upon moral agents is to some extent different from the way in which utilitarian consequentialism imposes these constraints. These differences, as I have already mentioned, have something to do with the difference between conditions of permissibility and conditions of (positive or comparative) moral goodness. But even if we grant that such differences exist (and that more needs to be said about them), it nonetheless seems highly significant that the very same charges may be levelled at consequentialism, Kantianism, and commonsense morality and in addition ironic that commonsense morality, at least, has in recent years been directing such charges at consequentialism and using them in an attempt to demonstrate its own superiority over consequentialism.

However, when we turn to our commonsense views about what counts as a virtue, we get an entirely different picture. Nothing in our usual understanding of (major) virtues like probity, generosity, prudence, benevolence, and courage requires us to assume that the person who has such virtues will invariably act for the greatest good of the greatest number whenever such action importantly conflicts with his own interests. And furthermore, the fact that a certain trait of character enables its possessor to advance his own well-being is not treated as irrelevant to a positive evaluation of that trait. Indeed, many of our most significant commonsense virtues—e.g., prudence, perseverance, foresight, caution, fortitude, courage, sagacity—are to a considerable extent admired for their usefulness to those who possess them. So our ordinary thinking about the virtues treats both self-regarding and other-regarding usefulness as bases for the favorable evaluation of traits of character and the actions, feelings or thoughts that exemplify them. And the same holds, *mutatis mutandis*, for traits actions, etc., that harm either their possessors or people other than their possessors.

4 The Incoherence of Commonsense Moral Thinking

For some view or set of views to function adequately as our most fundamental or central form of ethical evaluation, it should not devalue agents by treating their happiness as irrelevant to the positive or negative ethical assessment of their own actions. We have seen that Kantian and commonsense morality both fail to meet this condition of adequacy in a way that commonsense virtue ethics does not. (By virtue ethics I here mean an ethics that deals with what counts as admirable or as a virtue but does not speak of moral virtue as such. The latter is part of commonsense morality and shares its problems.) But none of this shows that commonsense or Kantian morality is mistaken or invalid. It may only show that neither can function on its own as the foundation or most central part of our ethical thinking, and this leaves open precisely the possibility that commonsense or Kantian morality might function *together with* commonsense virtue ethics as the foundational or most central part of our ethical thinking. And it also leaves open the alternative possibility that commonsense or Kantian morality might be a valid but merely superficial part of ethics, with virtue ethics then exclusively taking on the central or foundational role that morality is often assumed to have.

Each of these results would demonstrate the importance of virtue theory and vindicate its recent claims to be taken seriously rather than shunted to the side, as has so often happened in the past, in favor of an almost exclusive ethical preoccupation with moral right and wrong, with moral obligation, duty, and permission. And we could certainly remain content with such results if we could be reasonably sure that the above criticisms were all that could be said against commonsense and Kantian morality.

However, both commonsense and Kantian morality can be additionally faulted from the standpoint of their own implicit assumptions. The more or less commonsensical intuitions that underlie commonsense morality and Kantianism lead, in fact, to incoherence and paradox in such a way as to render both forms of morality inherently problematic and objectionable quite apart from the question of morality's uniquely central or foundational character within substantive ethics. Some of these difficulties arise at least in part from the asymmetric character of ordinary and Kantian moral thinking; others arise from aspects of common sense that may be unrelated, or at least are not obviously related, to the issue of symmetry and asymmetry. And at this point I think I should briefly mention why I think that even if supplemented or relegated to a minor role by virtue ethics, neither commonsense nor Kantian morality is acceptable.

To begin, let me just allude to the incredible problems that surround the issue of moral luck. As Nagel and others have argued, the judgments we make of individual cases where luck plays a role in determining the outcome are out of keeping with the commonsense and Kantian intuition that our moral attributes are not subject to the influence of factors of luck beyond our control or knowledge. Someone who through inattention swerves into the lane of oncoming traffic but meets no oncoming car is not commonly regarded as culpable to the extent or degree to which we would ascribe culpability to someone who with similar inattention swerves into an oncoming car and kills all its occupants. Yet the two cases may differ only in factors of luck, and so our intuitions in this area turn out to be at odds with one another, and no one has proposed any satisfactory way of softening or undercutting this apparent inconsistency in commonsense thinking.

But I don't want to dwell here on the subject of moral luck, whose problems and paradoxical character at least for commonsense morality have been well documented by others.[19] The ways in which self-other asymmetry creates philosophical difficulties are far less familiar, and so I would like to explore these in what remains on this essay. It is obvious that self-other asymmetry seems irrational and unmotivated from an impersonal standpoint. But I shall now argue that it is difficult to reconcile the self-other asymmetry of commonsense and Kantian moral views with *other aspects of these same views*.

Unlike act utilitarianism, both ordinary and Kantian morality treat our obligations to others as dependent on how near they stand to us in relations of affection or special commitment: obligations to our immediate family (other things being equal) being stronger than those to our relations generally, obligations to friends and relations being stronger than those to compatriots generally, and obligations to the latter, in turn, being stronger than those to the people of other countries.[20] To that extent, ordinary and Kantian morality reflect the normal structure of an adult's concerns. We are naturally more concerned about, and have more reason to be concerned about, the well-being of friends and relations than of more distant others, and commonsense morality seems to build such differences into the varyingly strong duties it assigns us to concern ourselves with others' well-being. However, by means of its agent-sacrificing self-other asymmetry, commonsense and Kantian morality both also superimpose an absolute moral discontinuity on the structure of concern in which each agent is normally situated. They encourage the idea that the strength of obligation weakens as one gets further from the agent, but paradoxically and in seeming opposition to the first idea, each also assumes that there is no moral obligation whatever (except indirectly) for the agent to benefit *himself*. Once one leaves the agent behind, the agent's obligations of beneficence vary in proportion to his reason for concern, but where he has greatest reason for concern in the natural course of things, he has no direct obligation whatever. This appears odd and unmotivated even apart from a utilitarian or consequentialist perspective (though the latter provide a way out of the oddness, the seeming inconsistency or discontinuity).

In fact, there is one very obvious way in which one might attempt to justify the self-other asymmetry (or some aspects of it), but in the light of what has just been said, such justification makes the picture appear even bleaker for commonsense and Kantian morality by making it appear impossible to make sense of the above-mentioned discontinuity in their thinking. Let me explain.

Kant claims that one can account for the lack of moral duties to provide for one's own well-being in terms of normal human desires and instincts and plausible assumptions about their influence on our actions.[21] We can be expected to take care of ourselves most of the time, and that, according to Kant, is why there is no need for morality to impose obligations or duties to do so. But such an explanation immediately gets into trouble if we consider the facts about our relations to other people that we mentioned above. (Kant is aware of these facts but doesn't see the problems they raise for his explanation of why we have no duty to provide for our own well-being or happiness.) We can normally be expected to take better care of our spouse and children than of distant others, yet our obligations to the former are stronger than to the latter, and this is just the opposite of what one would expect if the above account correctly explained the absence of any duty to seek one's own well-being. Yet it is commonsensically very natural to try to explain and justify agent-sacrificing self-other moral asymmetry and more particularly the absence of duties to seek one's own well-being in terms of what is normal and expectable, and I think that this is additional proof of how much commonsense is at odds with itself in this general area. The explanation used by Kant seems like the only possible and sensible explanation of self-other asymmetry, yet that explanation makes nonsense out of another aspect of commonsense morality, and these internal difficulties of ordinary thought about right and wrong gives us some reason to conclude that neither commonsense nor Kantian morality is acceptable as it stands, even as an outlying province of our considered ethical ideas.[22]

In that case, if we continue to regard consequentialism as too unreasonably demanding to be an acceptable ethical view of things,[23] we are left with as yet untainted virtue ethics and in particular with a commonsense or intuitive approach to virtue ethics that is not obviously asymmetrical in either an agent-favoring or an agent-sacrificing way. The question then immediately arises whether ethics can make do with such a limited and/or specialized form of evaluation. I am inclined to think that theoretical ethics can and even should proceed on an exclusively virtue-theoretic basis, but therein lies a much longer tale to be told on other occasions.

In any event, we have seen that commonsense, intuitive virtue ethics has some significant advantages over its major competitors. Nowadays egoism is not even regarded as a moral view but is seen rather as a controversial claim about our reasons for action, about practical *rationality*.[24] And consequentialism, Kantianism, and commonsense morality all slight the moral agent and her concerns in ways that seem philosophically or ethically objectionable. Earlier in this century and possibly as a result of lingering Victorian, and more generally Christian, high-mindedness, the selflessness of commonsense morality went largely unnoticed and entirely uncriticized.[25] But in recent years many moral philosophers have advocated a healthy self-assertiveness on the part of moral agents.[26] And although much of this recent thinking has been directed against Kantianism and consequentialism rather than against commonsense morality, a climate of opinion has nonetheless been created in which it is easier to make and perhaps to sympathize with the broader defense of virtue ethics that has been offered here.[27]

Notes

1. On these points see, e.g., Scheffler 1982.
2. I am not talking about masochism, where what seems like self-sacrifice may in some way or degree not be, but of cases where a person could, but won't actually, sacrifice her own dearest projects, etc. In such cases self-sacrifice is permitted, but would be irrational. (It would be a mistake to say of such a person: if she sacrificed the projects, she wouldn't have them as projects and so wouldn't be acting irrationally. This counterfactual claim cannot be defended. See Slote 1978.)
3. It has been suggested to me that the reason why we are allowed to harm ourselves or avoid some benefit where we would not be permitted to harm another person or prevent her from receiving similar benefit lies in the consent implicit in actions we do to ourselves. If I harm myself or avoid a benefit, I presumably do this willingly, whereas the agent whom I refuse to benefit does not consent to this neglect (and when she does, there is nothing wrong with what I do). It might then be thought that agent-sacrificing asymmetry is not a deep feature of commonsense morality but rather is derivative from, and justifiable in terms of, the moral importance of consent. But such an explanation will not do. It makes a significant difference commonsenseically whether I negligently cause another person unwanted harm or negligently do so to myself. Yet consent seems *equally absent* in these two cases. More persuasively, perhaps, if I can either avoid an enduring pain to myself or avoid a short-lived one to you, you and I might both agree that it would be foolish of me to prevent the shorter one to you. So you might not consent to my taking the longer pain upon myself in order to save you from the shorter pain. Yet there would be nothing morally wrong, commonsensically, in such a sacrifice. But when positions are reversed and I can avoid a short-lived pain to myself or a longer one to you and it is morally right that I should do the *latter*, you will presumably not consent to my doing the former, and it will be wrong if I do so. Again, consent/lack-of-consent seems not to make the relevant commonsense moral difference. The agent-sacrificing moral asymmetry eludes the distinction between consent and nonconsent and is thus not easily accounted for.
4. On agent neutrality, see Parfit 1984, p. 27. Note that nonoptimizing forms of utilitariansim and consequentialism are also strictly agent-neutral. If, for example, one accepts some form of "satisficing consequentialism," one's criterion of right action will be whether a given act has *good enough* consequences (relative, perhaps, to its alternatives). But such a form of consequentialism will in no way distinguish among agents in its ultimate determinations of what counts as good enough consequences. On this point, see Slote 1985.
5. Even nonoptimizing forms of consequentialism have the feature just mentioned. And because of this feature, such views allow for moral supererogation in a way that a more standard utilitarianism and consequentialism do not.
6. See Ross 1930, 168; 1939, 72ff., 272 ff.
7. See Foot 1978a, 125f.
8. See Foot 1978a, pp. 159 f., 168. In more recent and as yet unpublished work Foot seem to be moving back toward her earlier ideas.
9. I am leaving it open whether we want to emphasize the distinction between character traits and personality traits and so argue, for example, that charmingness, however desirable or admirable, is not a virtue.

10. On this point, see Foot 1978a, p. 119, and H. Sidgwick 1981, pp. 327 f., 332, 356.
11. Hume 1983, book 4, sec. 262.
12. See Ross 1930, p. 161.
13. Ross 1939, p. 271.
14. For more on the conditional character of certain virtues both in general and in Kant's ethics, see Korsgaard 1983, pp. 169–195, and Slote 1983, chap. 3.
15. See Slote 1983, chap. 3.
16. In speaking here of the concerns and well-being of moral agents, I am leaving *simple desires* out of account. But commonsense morality arguably makes concessions to less than deep, less than serious desires (or intentions). It is not entirely clear how far commonsense agent-favoring permissions extend in this direction. See Slote 1985, pp. 141 ff.
17. For what I take to be an example of such thinking, see the final two pages of H. James 1973.
18. Even if Kantianism can treat prudence and prudential actions as (nonmorally) valuable and admirable, such evaluations will presuppose the moral goodness of the agent's or trait possessor's will and will thus be conditional, e.g., on whether the individual in question is doing what he should in regard to other people's happiness. To that extent, prudential action will lack the *fundamental* value of moral action (although this doesn't mean that the agent is a mere means to other people's happiness). Clearly, this view devalues the moral agent and makes him play second fiddle in relation to other people.
19. See Nagel 1979a. Many of these ideas are also to be found in Smith 1976.
20. See Sidgwick 1981, p. 246, and Kant 1964b, pp. 118 ff.
21. See the introduction to Kant 1964b, pp. 44 ff., and also Butler 1859.
22. Even if commonsense moral thinking is incoherent in the manner just suggested, there may be reason to advocate or hold onto commonsense views for everyday practical purposes, e.g., as useful rules of thumb. This is a line that utilitarians typically take about commonsense morality, but the present point is that there may be nonutilitarian reasons, reasons generated by an incoherence *within* commonsense morality, for treating the latter in the way in which utilitarians so often say it should be treated. I also wouldn't want to deny the possibility of altering commonsense or Kantian morality so that it can avoid the just-mentioned criticisms, but that whole issue is best left to another occasion.
23. Utilitarianism can seem too demanding when regarded from the standpoint of actual human motivation. But *even utilitarians* have some reason to regard it as too demanding. From the standpoint of utilitarianism's historically familiar foundational moral psychology and general methodology, there is no reason to accept an optimizing form of utilitarianism over a satisficing or scalar (i.e., purely comparative) version. An argument for this conclusion can be found in Slote 1989, chap. 7.
24. See Parfit 1984, p. 129.
25. Ross in 1930 and 1939 is clearly aware of the selflessness of commonsense morality but in no way sees this as a limitation or defect.
26. See, for example, important recent work by Philippa Foot, Samuel Scheffler, Michael Stocker, Bernard Williams, and Susan Wolf.
27. Perhaps the recent revival of virtue ethics as against moral theory narrowly construed represents some sort of implicit or dim recognition of the attractions of its greater assertiveness on behalf of rational/moral agents.

   I would like to thank David Brink, Georges Rey, Amélie Rorty, and Ernie Schlaretzki for helpful suggestions.

Chapter 19

On the Primacy of Character

Gary Watson

1

John Rawls taught us to think of moral theory as treating primarily three concepts: the concept of right (wrong, permissible), the concept of good, and the concept of moral worth. Of these concepts, however, he takes the latter to be derivative: "The two main concepts of ethics are those of the right and the good; the concept of a morally worthy person is, I believe, derived from them. The structure of an ethical theory is, then, largely determined by how it defines and connects these two basic notions."[1] Thus Rawls recognizes two types of theories: those that "define" the right in terms of the good and those that do not. Rawls's own theory illustrates the second type. An example of the first is classical utilitarianism, which "defines" right action as maximizing human happiness (or the satisfaction of rational desire), which is taken to be the intrinsic or ultimate good.

On either of the types of theory that Rawls recognizes, the concept of moral worth (which includes that of virtue) will be subordinated to one of the other concepts. For example, on Rawls's theory (as well as on broadly Kantian theories generally), virtues are construed as "strong and normally effective desires to act on the basic principles of right" 1971, p. 436). Some versions of utilitarianism may accept this construal as well, or else define virtues directly in terms of the good that certain traits or dispositions will do.

Recently a number of philosophers have expressed dissatisfaction with this kind of scheme on the grounds that it precludes from the outset views that give to virtue a more central place (such as those by and large of the ancients). My aim is to investigate whether or not this dissatisfaction is well grounded. The alleged alternative has not, in my opinion, been sufficiently, or even roughly, articulated. I wish, then, to explore the structure of "ethics of virtue," as they are usually called, to determine whether they indeed constitute theories of a third kind.

2

Rawls's twofold scheme corresponds to another prevalent division of theories into "teleological" and "deontological." These theories are ways of relating the two concepts that Rawls takes to be basic. In teleological views "the good is defined independently from the right, and then the right is defined as that which maximizes the good" (1971, p. 24).[2] Teleological theories are, in a word, consequentialist. The contrasting conception is defined negatively as what is not teleological. As a result, all moral theories are construed as either consequentialist or deontological.

The awkwardness of this taxonomy can be seen by applying it to the case of Aristotle. Rawls considers Aristotle a teleologist (of the perfectionist variety). This classification would have us think of Aristotle's view as differing from utilitarianism only in its conception of what is to be maximized. But that is very doubtful. For Aristotle, the virtuous person is not one who is out to maximize anything, nor is virtue itself defined as a state that tends to promote some independently definable good (these being the two ways in which virtue can be treated in a broadly consequentialist theory).

So Aristotle's theory is deontological if that just means nonconsequentialist. But this classification seems equally inapt.[3] For a concept of good *is* primary in Aristotle's view. Thus if teleological theories are those in which the (or a) concept of the good is primary, then Aristotle's theory is rightly said to be teleological. It is a mistake, however, to think that the only way of asserting the primacy of the good is consequentialism. We should recognize the possibility of a view that is at once teleological and nonconsequentialist. An ethics of virtue, I shall suggest, is a theory of this kind.[4]

We can avoid some unfortunate conflations by replacing this distinction as Rawls draws it with the threefold distinction that his discussion originally suggests: an ethics of requirement, an ethics of consequences, and an ethics of virtue or character. This classification enables us to observe that while both ethics of consequences and ethics of virtue are teleological insofar as they are guided fundamentally by a notion of the good, Aristotle is nonetheless closer to Kant than to Bentham on the question of consequentialism. It also enables us to consider what it means to take the concept of virtue as fundamental.

3

Before I go on to consider this question more fully, I should note that the phrase "ethics of virtue" is often used in a different way from the way in which it will be used here. Some writers use this phrase to indicate something to live by (Frankena 1970), a certain moral outlook that calls for exclusive moral attention to questions about character and the quality of one's whole life. The contrast here is supposed to be with an "ethics of duty or principle," in which the fundamental moral questions are about what one's duty is and how to do it.

This is not at all the contrast that concerns me in this chapter. In the sense that concerns me, an ethics of virtue is not a code or a general moral claim but a set of abstract theses about how certain concepts are best fitted together for the purposes of understanding morality. To claim that we should give exclusive moral attention either to questions of duty or to questions of character seems to me a very special and suspect position. A morally admirable person will, for example, acknowledge her duties as a teacher to read her students' work carefully and promptly, acknowledge her obligation to repay a loan, and acknowledge the principle never to take bribes as a juror. No doubt we will disagree in some cases about what duties there are and what they involve (whether a democratic citizen has a duty to vote, for instance) and about the importance of certain duties relative to one another and to other considerations. Nonetheless, to say that questions of duty or principle never take moral precedence (or always do) seems morally incorrect.

To think that an ethics of virtue in my sense is opposed to duty is a category mistake. Duties and obligations are simply factors to which certain values, for example, fidelity and justice, are responsive. They do not compete with virtue for moral attention.

4

While it might have implications for how one lives, an ethics of virtue is not, like an ethics of love or liberation, a moral outlook or ideal but a claim that the concept of virtue is in some way theoretically dominant. On an ethics of virtue, how it is best or right or proper to conduct oneself is explained in terms of how it is best for a human being to be. I will call this the *claim of explanatory primacy*.

Explanatory primacy can be realized in different ways by different theories. One straightforward way, for example, is to explain right conduct as what accords with the virtues.[5] To be explanatory, of course, virtue must be intelligible independently of the notion of right conduct. That requirement would be violated by the Rawlsian definition of the virtues as attachments to the principles of right.

But I have formulated the thesis too narrowly, for it should also encompass terms of appraisal besides "right." It should include more generally the concepts that fall under the heading of "morally good conduct." An ethics of virtue is not a particular claim about the priority of virtue over right conduct but the more general claim that action appraisal is derivative from the appraisal of character. To put it another way, the claim is that the basic moral facts are facts about the quality of character. Moral facts about action are ancillary to these.

Indeed, some recent writers have been deeply distrustful of the general notions of moral right and wrong; they question whether there *are* any facts about right and wrong of the kind that moral philosophers want to explain. They recommend the *replacement* of talk about moral right and wrong with talk about the virtues. As G. E. M. Anscombe puts it, "It would be a great improvement if, instead of 'morally wrong,' one always named a genus such as 'untruthful,' 'unchaste,' 'unjust.' We should no longer ask whether doing something was 'wrong,' passing directly from some description of an action to this notion; we should ask whether, e.g., it was unjust; and the answer would sometimes be clear at once."[6]

I shall extend the interpretation of the thesis of explanatory priority to accommodate replacement views. This is admittedly a stretch, since on the most radical view, virtue concepts achieve priority by default. (Unless otherwise noted, when I speak of the claim of explanatory primacy hereafter I mean to include both the reductionist and the replacement interpretations.)

5

If "right" and "wrong" are contrary predicates, then the thesis of explanatory primacy commits ethics of virtue (in their nonreplacement versions) to a kind of harmony among the virtues. If it were possible for someone to act in accordance with one virtue while acting contrary to another, one's conduct would in that case be both right and wrong. This implication can be avoided if no virtue can be exercised in a way that is contrary to another. In this way, ethics of virtue is naturally led to embrace a historically controversial thesis.[7]

The controversy is avoided altogether by rejecting the idea that "right" and "wrong" are contraries. It might also be avoided by a sufficiently radical replacement view. The view would have to replace not only "right" and "wrong" but also "proper" and "improper," "licit" and "illicit," for these too seem to be contraries.

6

Another tenet often associated with ethics of virtue is uncodifiability, that is, that there are no formulas that can serve as exact and detailed guides for action. Aristotle expresses this idea in the following passage: "How far and how much we must deviate to be blamed is not easy to define in an account; for nothing perceptible is easily defined, and [since] these [circumstances of virtuous and vicious actions] are particulars, the judgment about them depends on perception" (*Nicomachean Ethics* 1109a21f). I shall confine myself to three general remarks on this idea.

First, this thesis is difficult to evaluate because codifiability seems to be a matter of degree. On the one hand, there are true moral generalizations about conduct, as even the proponents of uncodifiability should agree; on the other hand, the most rigid codifiers should concede that judgment is necessary for interpreting and applying any rules and principles. The uncodifiability thesis is supposed to be opposed to classical utilitarian and Kantian formulas, although these are far from exact and detailed. So it is unclear what counts as too much codification.

In the second place, uncodifiability is not strictly a corollary of an ethics of virtue. It is not incompatible with explanatory primacy to suppose that right action could be determined according to a clear and definite general criterion. If it could be shown that some principle of right action could somehow be derived from and explained by the conditions for being a virtuous human being, then the resulting view would still deserve to be called an ethics of virtue. Such a derivation would be perfectly consistent with the claim of explanatory primacy. Right action is acting in accordance with the virtues, but it might turn out that some principle(s), even the principle of utility or the categorical imperative, characterizes what the virtues would lead a person to do.

In this connection, it is sometimes said that in an ethics of principles or duties, it is the principles or duties that tell you what to do, whereas in an ethics of virtue, it is virtue that tells you what to do. So it might be supposed that if such principles were available (if morality were codifiable), virtue would lose this distinctive role. This thought seems to me to be somewhat confused. In the sense in which a principle can tell one what to do, namely by expressing or implying a prescriptive conclusion about action, a virtue cannot tell anything. A virtue is not a proposition one can consult or apply or interpret; it does not in the same sense prescribe any course of action. Only something like a principle can do that. On the other hand, one's virtues may enable one to endorse, apprehend, correctly apply, or disregard some principle of action. But they will also have this role in an ethics of consequences or requirement. The principle of utility may tell agents what to do, but it is their virtue that leads them to listen, interpret, and to follow.

I conclude that the uncodifiability thesis is not something to which every version of an ethics of virtue is committed. Nonetheless (and this is my third point), the relation between uncodifiability and ethics of virtue is not merely an accidental association. One of the main impetuses for the recent resurgence of interest in ethics of virtue, I suspect, is the sense that the enterprise of articulating principles of right has failed. On the Rawlsian view, that failure leaves the concept of virtue (as attachment to the right) altogether at sea. The content of virtue, if it has any, would have to come from somewhere else. One of the appeals of ethics of virtue, I conjecture, is that it promises a nonskeptical response to the failure of codification.

7

An alternative response to the failure of codification is traditional intuitionism. We have just seen that uncodifiability is not necessarily a tenet of an ethics of virtue. Since that thesis is compatible with the right being prior to the good, it is even more clearly not sufficient for an ethics of virtue. Some intuitionists may think of virtue(s) as attachment(s) to right conduct, as intuitively apprehended in particular circumstances, or perhaps better as capacities for discernment and commitment to right conduct. More generally, if intuitionism is defined as any nonskeptical view of right conduct that rejects codifiability, then some ethics of virtue are species of intuitionism.[8] More familiar members of the genus would be distinguished by their acceptance of a different direction of priority between the concepts of right and virtue.

Because of the preferred direction of priority of an ethics of virtue, its theoretical power clearly depends upon its theory of virtue. Once more, the concept of proper or right conduct will be well understood only if the concept of virtue is. Though some will hold that we can understand what the virtues are and how they are expressed without the benefit of any general theory,[9] the thesis of explanatory primacy will then be quite gratuitous. If the alleged priority cannot be established by an account, in this case a theory of virtue, then the distinction between virtue intuitionism and act intuitionism seems merely to be nominal. I question whether "prior" has any sense here whatever.

To be interesting and, I suspect, even to be meaningful, the priority claim has to occur as part of a theory of virtue. I shall take it, then, that an ethics of virtue will have two components:

    a. Some version of the claim of explanatory primacy
    b. A theory of virtue

My aim in the remainder of this essay is to explore some of the difficulties of developing (b) in a way that does not compromise the distinctive character of an ethics of virtue.

8

The most familiar versions of (b) are theories of an Aristotelian kind.[10] An Aristotelian ethics of virtue will look something like this:

(1) *The claim of explanatory primacy* Right and proper conduct is conduct that is contrary to no virtue (does not exemplify a vice). Good conduct is conduct that displays a virtue. Wrong or improper conduct is conduct that is contrary to some virtue (or exemplifies a vice).

(2) *The theory of virtue* Virtues are (a subset of the) human excellences, that is, those traits that enable one to live a characteristically human life, or to live in accordance with one's nature as a human being.

I shall not pause to consider the content of (2). It is, of course, the merest gesture toward a certain type of naturalism. What interests me at this point is the contrast with another theory in which (2) is replaced with (2'):

(1) As before

(2') A virtue is a human trait the possession of which tends to promote human happiness more than the possession of alternative traits.

As with (2), this formulation is oversimplified. The view it oversimplifies is often called *character utilitarianism*.[11] This theory has the same structure as the Aristotelian one. The only difference comes from the second component. Is it too an ethics of virtue?

9

But if character utilitarianism is an ethics of virtue, we have not succeeded in identifying an ethics of a third kind. To see this, recall my earlier suggestion that the three central concepts of moral philosophy correspond to the three distinct types of theory that take one of these as basic: ethics of requirement, ethics of consequences, and ethics of virtue or character. Plainly, character utilitarianism belongs in the second category.[12] Even though character utilitarianism differs from its cousins in not taking the consequences of actions as the direct standard of appraisal for those actions—and hence is not consequentialist in Rawls's sense[13]—the value of the outcome of possessing and exercising certain traits is the ultimate standard of all other value. It shares with act utilitarianism the idea that the most fundamental notion is that of a good consequence or state of affairs, namely, human happiness. For these reasons, it seems better to call this general class of theories *ethics of outcome*.

In these terms the problem will be to see how to avoid classifying ethics of virtue as a species of ethics of outcome. For will not the ultimate standard of appraisal on Aristotelian theories be the idea of living properly as a human being, that is, flourishing, from which the value of virtue is derived?

The three types of theories are distinguished by what they take the fundamental moral facts to be: facts about what we are required to do, about the intrinsic or ultimate value of possible outcomes, or about people's desires, ends, and dispositions. An ethics of virtue, at least of the Aristotelian kind I have considered, will have a theory that explains the significance of various constituents of character by reference to certain necessities and desiderata of human life, in which case the basic moral facts would be facts about what is constitutively and instrumentally needed for that way of life, facts, in short, about flourishing.

The problem, then, appears to be this: any ethics of virtue that lacks a theory of virtue will be nonexplanatory,[14] but any ethics of virtue that has such a theory will collapse into an ethics of outcome. If that is so, then Rawls's classification has not been seriously challenged.

The independence of an ethics of virtue as a type of theory distinct from character utilitarianism and other ethics of outcome must depend on the special character of its theory of good. I shall consider two proposed accounts of this special character. On the first explanation, what distinguishes the Aristotelian view from character utilitarianism is its conception of virtues as constitutive of, not merely instrumental to, flourishing. This difference is conspicuous, but on the second account the difference is deeper. It is not merely that an ethics of virtue employs a different theory of what is ultimately good from that of character utilitarianism; it is that an ethics of virtue does not have that kind of theory of good at all.

10

On the first account, what distinguishes an ethics of virtue from character utilitarianism is that it takes human excellence to be at least partially constitutive of flourishing, not just instrumental. Now if there were other constituents of flourishing, it would be arbitrary to make the theory the namesake of virtue. (It should then be called an ethics of virtue plus whatever else constitutes flourishing.) Thus virtue must be construed as the sole or somehow primary constituent of flourishing, as it was by Socrates. The resultant theory construes the basic moral facts to be facts about virtue.

Here the proposed contrast turns on the theory of value rather than on the claim of explanatory primacy. As I have construed it so far, the claim of explanatory primacy asserts the primacy of virtue over action appraisal. The theory as a whole must also establish the primacy of virtue over other values. On character utilitarianism, virtues are so identified because of their relation to independent values such as happiness. According to the first account, then, an ethics of virtue must imply, in all of its components, that human excellence is the sole or at least primary constituent of what is intrinsically valuable.

11

This is an appealing account of the difference. And such a view is naturally called an ethics of virtue. Nevertheless, I doubt that this account succeeds in identifying a theory of the third kind, that is, of a kind that contrasts with both an ethics of requirement and an ethics of outcome.

Character utilitarianism is disqualified as an ethics of virtue because the facts it takes to be morally basic are not facts about virtue. However, it is not enough just to meet this qualification. For consider a restricted version of what Rawls calls perfectionism, which enjoins us to promote the development and exercise of virtue, these being intrinsically good.[15] This view meets the above qualifications, but if it is an ethics of virtue, it is so only in the way in which utilitarianism is an ethics of happiness or welfare. What fills in the blank in "an ethics of ＿＿" merely indicates the kinds of intrinsically valuable facts or states of affairs that are taken as basic. Different terms yield different versions of ethics of outcome.

Thus if the view I have been investigating is an ethics of virtue because it takes virtue as the ultimate value, then so is perfectionism, which is an ethics of outcome. To be sure, perfectionism differs from what I have been calling an ethics of virtue in its rejection of the claim of explanatory primacy. And so it might be suggested that both an "areteic" theory of value and an "areteic" theory of right are necessary and sufficient for an ethics of virtue. According to this suggestion, an ethics of virtue stands to perfectionism as character utilitarianism stands to act utilitarianism: each pair has the same theory of good but a different theory of right.

To disqualify perfectionism as an ethics of virtue because it does not hold the claim of explanatory primacy is superficial. For unlike character utilitarianism, which in its theory of virtue goes against the grain of the primacy of virtue, the perfectionist theory of right and theory of good both hold virtue supreme. Taken together, they enjoin the fullest realization of virtue in character and action. A consequentialist theory of right is only a schema without a theory of good. When that theory is areteic, so is the theory of right. Questions of classification are, of course, relative to purpose. But for the reasons just mentioned, the kinship of perfectionism and Aristotelianism (as conceived on the first account) seems to me much closer than the relationship of character utilitarianism to either.

12

Unlike perfectionism, of course, an ethics of virtue as so far conceived is not consequentialist (in the prevalent narrow sense). But nor, as we have seen, is character utilitarianism. Consequentialist theories in the narrower sense belong to a wider class of theories that share a certain scheme of value according to which the ultimate standard of appraisal is provided by states of affairs or outcomes deemed to be intrinsically good or desirable on their own. I have been calling this wider class of theories ethics of outcome, which are characterized neither by their theories of right (which may or may not be consequentialist) nor by the specific content of their theories of good (which may range from pleasure to excellence of character) but by their appeal to this kind of scheme.

The first account of an ethics of virtue makes it a kind of ethics of outcome that is like perfectionism in its appraisal of outcomes but like character utilitarianism in the form of its conception of right conduct. I now turn to the second account, which holds that an ethics of virtue is not an ethics of outcome at all.

13

We may depict the appraisal of conduct on an (Aristotelian) ethics of virtue with the following schema:

1. Living a characteristically human life (functioning well as a human being) requires possessing and exemplifying certain traits, T.

2. T are therefore human excellences and render their possessors to that extent good human beings.

3. Acting in way W is an accordance with T (or exemplifies or is contrary to T).

4. Therefore, W is right (good or wrong).

Here there is an appeal to several notions of good: to functioning well as a human being, to being a good human being, to being a human excellence (perhaps also to being good for one as a human being). But at no stage need there be an essential appeal to the idea of a valuable state of affairs or outcome from which the moral significance of everything (or anything) else derives.

To be sure, a concern for outcomes will be internal to certain virtues. For instance, the benevolent person will be concerned that others fare well. But the moral significance of this concern stems from the fact that it is part of a virtue, not from the fact that misery and well-being are intrinsically or ultimately bad and good respectively. To put it another way, it will follow from an ethics of virtue that virtuous people care about certain things (and outcomes) for their own sakes (as final ends in themselves). There is no further commitment, however, to the idea that these concerns are virtuous ones because their objects are inherently valuable or desirable for their own sakes.[16]

Nor, more generally, is there a foundational role for the idea that living a characteristic human life is intrinsically good. Perhaps it will follow from the theory that the virtuous person *will* desire to live such a life for its own sake, and in that sense such a life can be said to be desirable for its own sake (the virtuous person being the standard), but that will be because such a desire is part of human excellence, rather than the other way around. That appraisal is made from the standpoint of virtue and is not its basis.

It may be useful to compare a theory of excellence for a nonhuman animal. The judgment that a lack of attention to her cubs is an imperfection in a mother tiger (though not in the father) is based upon a notion of a good specimen of tiger. This idea in turn depends upon what is normal for or characteristic of tigers. None of these judgments is mediated by any notion of the value of a tiger's living a life characteristic of its species. On an ethics of virtue, the same goes for people. The specific excellences will be different, of course. Moreover, for us but not for tigers there may be a point to a distinction between virtues and other excellences.

What is liable to be confusing on this account is that faring well, for example, plays a double role in this view, first in the theory of virtue, where virtues are identified in part by their contribution to a characteristic human life, and second in the theory of good, where living such a life may be among the final ends of morally admirable individuals. The distinctive feature of an ethics of virtue on the second account is that the evaluation of such a life as a final end is derivative from, rather than foundational to, the theory of virtue. On the first account, the theory of virtue is dependent on a theory of the ultimate good. On the second account, the theory of ultimate good is dependent on the theory of virtue.[17] (Hence, the fact that virtues are identified as such by their "instrumental" properties does not make them of instrumental value.)

Whatever one may think of the prospects for an ethics of virtue, this last point seems to me to be of some importance for moral philosophy. For it shows how one can assert a systematic connection between virtues and other goods without undermining the autonomy of virtue. In an outcome ethics that recognizes these goods, it is notoriously difficult to explain satisfactorily why they should not be of paramount moral concern (at least ideally), that is, how there can properly be restrictions on consequentialist reasoning. On an outcome ethics, such restrictions can never seem fully enlightened. (Hence the appearance of paradox or irrationality in "indirect" forms of consequentialism.) On an ethics of virtue, however, there is not even the appearance of a problem. For the value of virtue is not said to come from the value of anything else at all. Although it is a teleological view, an ethics of virtue can acknowledge "deontological" reasons without paradox, because it is not an ethics of outcome.[18]

In summary, on the first account, an ethics of virtue is a species of ethics of outcome, distinguished from character utilitarianism by the fact that it takes virtue and its exercise to be the sole ultimate value and from perfectionism by the fact that it does not give a consequentialist definition of right action. On this view, Rawls is right in the end to think that moral theories come in two fundamental kinds, namely (in my terminology) ethics of requirement and ethics of outcome. What his scheme overlooks is that ethics of outcome can take both a consequentialist and nonconsequentialist form.

On the second account, what Rawls's scheme overlooks is more significant. Ethics of virtue contrast importantly with both ethics of outcome and ethics of requirement. The first two are teleological in that the primary notion is a notion of goodness, but they differ in the kind of theory of good that is employed. On the first account, act utilitarianism, character utilitarianism, perfectionism, and ethics of virtue are merely structural variations of an ethics of outcome. But on the second account, it is not that ethics of virtue have a different view of what outcomes are good but rather that they do not employ this notion at the foundation of the theory. The result is a teleological theory that has not received much attention or even recognition. For this reason, only the second account seems to me to identify a distinctive, third kind of moral theory.

Furthermore, only the second account yields a theory that is at bottom truly naturalistic. Admittedly, what is valuable on the first account is the natural (what belongs to human nature). But so long as the theory relies upon a primitive idea of the intrinsically or ultimately valuable outcome, the conception of value remains ungrounded. In contrast, valuable outcomes are understood on the second account by reference to the concerns of those who exemplify human nature.

14

By rejecting outcomes as the foundational standards of appraisal, ethics of virtue are, of course, allied with ethics of requirement. I complained in section 2 that the identification of teleological and consequentialist theories forces us wrongly to classify ethics of virtue as deontological. What we have now seen is that if teleological theories are those in which appraisals are guided ultimately by some notion of the good, then there are (at least) two kinds of teleological theory: those based on the notion of a good outcome and those based on the notion of good of (and for) a kind.

As I have remarked, ethics of virtue will, of course, be deontological on Rawls's negative characterization, namely, as nonconsequentialism. But if a deontological view holds more positively that "it is sometimes wrong to do what will produce the best available outcome overall,"[19] then it will not do to think of an ethics of virtue as deontological. For on this characterization, deontological views share with consequentialism the assumption that there is a coherent and acceptable way of defining "best available outcome overall" independently of the notion of right and wrong action. But an ethics of virtue is not committed to this assumption.[20]

Nor need an ethics of requirement accept this assumption. Kant, for one, would have rejected it, though he is the first to come to most people's minds when they think of "deontologists." For Kant, it may indeed turn out to be wrong to do what would in the circumstances produce the greatest overall satisfaction of desire (or to maximize any specified kind of effect), but that will not be, for Kant, a case in which acting wrongly would produce the best overall outcome. The satisfaction of desire has no value whatever when it conflicts with the moral law.

Instead of defining "deontological theory" in either of the ways just considered, it seems best simply to use it synonymously with "ethics of requirement," a useage that is in accordance with its etymology. This type of theory, as I have said, is one that takes the notion of requirement as primary to the concepts of virtue and valuable outcome. But what this means more precisely remains to be clarified. Presumably, Kant's moral philosophy, which attempts to understand moral phenomena in terms of the requirements stemming from the conditions on free agency, is to be included, as is the minimal theory of Prichard, according to which we intuitively apprehend facts about duties and obligations. One would also expect contractualism to fall under this heading. It construes moral phenomena in terms of the requirements implicit in the conditions for mutually acceptable social life. But perhaps all that these views have in common is that they are *not* teleological in either of the two ways I have identified. Is there another way? Until we understand these theories better, we cannot say.[21]

15

Despite a renewal of interest in Aristotelian ideas, ethics of virtue continue to prompt a lot of resistance. Perhaps it is worthwhile briefly to indicate why.

Many of our modern suspicions can be put in the form of a dilemma. Either the theory's pivotal account of human nature (or characteristic human life) will be morally indeterminate, or it will not be objectively well founded. At best, an objectively well-founded theory of human nature would support evaluations of the kind that we can make about tigers—that this one is a good or bad specimen, that that behavior is abnormal. These judgments might be part of a theory of *health,* but our conception of morality resists the analogy with health, the reduction of evil to defect. (This resistance has something to do, I suspect, with a conception of free will that resists all forms of naturalism.) An objective account of human nature would imply, perhaps, that a good human life must be social in character. This implication will disqualify the sociopath but not the Hell's Angel. The contrast is revealing, for we tend to regard the sociopath not as evil but as beyond the pale of morality. On the other hand, if we enrich our conception of sociality to exclude Hell's Angels, the worry is that this conception will no longer ground moral judgment but rather express it.

A related but distinct complaint concerns moral motivation. Even if we grant that we can derive determinate appraisals of conduct from an objective description of what is characteristic of the species, why should we care about those appraisals? Why should we care about living distinctively human lives rather than living like pigs or gangsters? Why is it worthwhile for us to have those particular virtues at the cost of alternative lives they preclude? There are two sorts of skepticism here. (1) Can an objective theory really establish that being a gangster is incompatible with being a good human being? (2) If it can, can it establish an intelligible connection between those appraisals and what we have reasons to do as individuals?

To answer (2) by saying "Because we are human beings" is obscure. For we are (or can be) these other things as well. "Our humanity is inescapable," it might be replied, "whereas we can choose whether or not to be a Hell's Angel."[22] The force of this reply is unclear, however, for we *can* choose whether to live a *good* (that is, characteristic) human life.

However, the point might be that we are human beings *by nature* and not these other things, and our nature determines what descriptions are essential. A good gangster is a bad human being and for that reason fails to fare well. Defective or nonvirtuous human beings are worse off for that. They are not merely bad human beings but *they* are badly off as individuals, and if they acquired virtue, they would not only be better human beings but also be better off than they would have been otherwise. Whether we are flourishing depends on who (what) we are by nature. Since we are essentially human, the description "bad human being" dominates the description "good gangster" in appraisals of well-being.

Such evaluational essentialism does not sit well with modern notions. Just as God is dead, it will be said, so the concept of human nature has ceased to be normative. We can no more recover the necessary-world view of the ancients than we can revitalize the Judeo-Christian tradition. But an ethics of virtue need not take this essentialist line. It could say instead that we care about being good human beings because or insofar as we are good human beings. Insofar as we are not, we don't (at least in the virtuous way). If we don't, then we will not flourish as human beings, though we might do very well as thieves. There is no further question to be answered here about well-being.

These seem to me to be the main worries and issues that must be faced before we can determine the prospects for an ethics of virtue. There is much to be said about what an objective account of human nature is supposed to be, as well as about the supposed disanalogies with health and about issues of motivational internalism.[23] In this section I have tried merely to indicate some of the more troublesome questions.[24]

16

I began this essay with a complaint about one of Rawls's distinctions. I shall conclude by endorsing another. In "The Independence of Moral Theory" Rawls characterizes moral theory as the systematic comparison of moral conceptions, in other words, "the study of how the basic notions of the right, the good, and moral worth may be arranged to form different moral structures" (1975, 5). He rightly emphasizes the importance of such a study quite independent of the question of which moral conception is correct. He believes that "the further advance of moral philosophy depends upon a deeper understanding of the structure of moral conceptions" and urges that "all the main conceptions in the tradition of moral philosophy must be continually renewed: we must try to strengthen their formulation by noting the criticisms that are exchanged and by incorporating in each the advances of the others, so far as this is possible. In this endeavor the aim of those most attracted to a particular view should be not to confute but to perfect" (1975, 22).

This essay is intended to be a contribution to "moral theory" in Rawls's sense. My complaint has been that Rawls's twofold classification stymies the recently renewed examination of ethics of virtue by obscuring its distinctive character. We should not be indifferent to this consequence, even if we suspect that nowadays an ethics of virtue is not something that we are going to be able to live with philosophically. For the distinctive features of this moral conception (or set of conceptions) might reveal theoretical possibilities that will help us eventually to fashion something in which we can feel more at home.[25]

Notes

1. Rawls 1971, p. 24.
2. If maximizing is understood causally, as Rawls pretty clearly construes it, then the independence clause is implied by the definition. E cannot be said to maximize or produce G unless G is definable independently from E.
3. I agree with John Cooper: "In Aristotle's theory, human good *consists* (partly) in virtuous action, so his theory, while decidedly not teleological in the modern [consequentialist] sense, is also not deontological either" (1975, 88). See note 24 for a further discussion of Aristotle.
4. Rawls's treatment of the three main concepts of moral theory might seem infelicitous in another way. The concept of moral worth is the concept of a kind of goodness of persons. If it is derivative at all, how could this concept fail to be derived from the concept of the good, since it is an instance of that concept? The answer, I think, is that here Rawls is thinking of the concept of the good needed for consequentialist theories, the concept of a good state of affairs or outcome. See note 17.
5. At least the negative half of the primacy thesis—that wrong action is to be construed as behavior that exemplifies a vice or is contrary to a virtue—is endorsed by James Wallace: "It is a plausible thesis generally that the faulty actions philosophers lump under the heading of 'morally wrong' are actions fully characteristic of some vice" (1978, 59.)

   The relation between action appraisal and character appraisal is complicated and is different for different terms of appraisal. My formulations of the primacy claim suggests that the rightness or wrongness of an action depends upon its explanation (in the person's motive or character). However, we often appraise a prospective action as the right or wrong thing to do without appraising anyone's character. We need not refer to someone's motives or character to judge that it would be wrong for her not to return a lost wallet. This observation indicates the oversimplications of the formulations of the primacy thesis in the text. An adequate formulation would distinguish, for example, between the appraisals "P acted rightly or wrongly in doing *a*," and "It would be wrong (for P) to do *a*" or "What P did was the right (or wrong) thing," and it would show how all of these appraisals are implicated with standards of virtue. It might show, for example, that the standard for the right thing to do is what the morally good person would do but also that whether one acts rightly or wrongly in doing the right thing depends on one's reasons and hence on the explanation of one's behavior (or what it displays about one's character). When particular formulations of the primacy thesis are given in the text, the reader should bear these complications in mind.

   A mixed view is also possible here: that priority holds in the case of some virtues and not others. I shall ignore this possibility.
6. Anscombe 1981, p. 33. I do not assert here that Anscombe is adopting an ethics of virtue. One could hold a version of the replacement thesis—that "right" and "wrong" should be replaced by "unjust," "cowardly" etc.—without holding that the latter terms can be explained by terms of character. In several forums Richard Taylor has recommended a radical version of the replacement thesis. He advanced

this view in his lecture at the Conference on Virtue at the University of San Diego, February 1986. See also Taylor 1985.

7. This commitment is not peculiar to ethics of virtue. If the explanatory relation between virtue and right conduct were reversed, if, for example, a virtue were a kind of sensitivity to proper conduct within a certain sphere, then arguably the harmony thesis would follow as well. For this kind of argument, see McDowell 1979.

8. Radical replacement theories neither accept nor reject codifiability, since this question presupposes the applicability of the concepts they wish to abandon.

9. In the lecture referred to in note 6 Taylor opposes theory of this kind.

10. For the most part my discussion will be confined to roughly Aristotelian versions. See note 24 for a brief discussion of a non-Aristotelian alternative.

11. See Adams 1976. One glaring oversimplification is this. Virtues are obviously only a subset of optimizing traits. Another point is that optimizing traits cannot be determined in isolation from other traits possessed by the agent. This last point is not so easily met.

12. My concern, of course, is not with utilitarianism in particular but with consequentialism in general. There are as many different theories of this kind as there are kinds of valuable consequences that virtue(s) might foster.

13. The limits of Rawls's taxonomy is further revealed in its application to this case. Because of (1) and because character utilitarianism does not define the right as what maximizes the good, Rawls's scheme counts that view (along with all nonact forms of consequentialism) as deontological.

14. To charge intuitionism with being nonexplanatory is not an honest objection to this view, for the "objection" is precisely what intuitionism asserts: that there are no explanations of the kind we seek. This is no problem for the theory if the theory is true. So the charge begs the question. It is a "problem" only for those who wish more. So this charge (as a charge) has to be seen as an expression of one's conviction that this assertion is unreasonable. The burden will be on one who makes this charge to produce the relevant account.

15. Rawls's scheme cannot accommodate perfectionism as readily as Rawls supposes. The theory that we are to maximize excellence (where virtues are understood as human excellences) is clearly a teleological view. But it is not one in which the concept of moral worth is derived from the other concepts of the good and the right. Unlike other forms of consequentialism, perfectionism cannot accept Rawls's definition of virtues as "normally effective desires to act on the basic principles of right" (1971, 436). To avoid circularity (virtue is a commitment to maximize virtue) and to yield a teleological theory, virtues must be independently defined. On the other hand, perfectionism is not a view in which the concept of virtue is derived from the good. On this view, virtue *is* the good.

16. Christine Korsgaard (1983) has pointed out the importance of the difference between the concept of the intrinsically good and the concept of what is desirable in itself. For my purposes here, however, I do not think it matters which way I put it. An ethics of outcome may be stated either way. On the second account, an ethics of virtue has no use for the former and explains the latter by appeal to the desires of the virtuous person.

17. This constitutes my reply to a problem posed at the end of section 9 above. Insofar as virtues must in the end be characterized by their contribution to the good for human beings, that notion of the good will be primary relative to virtue. But there would still be a point to thinking of the theory under consideration as an ethics of virtue, since virtue remains basic relative to concepts of right and a good state

of affairs. In the classification to which I refer at the beginning, I suspect that Rawls understands the concept of the good in that context as what is ultimately worth choosing, aiming at, seeking—that is, in effect, as the finally good outcome. So understood, on the theory I am trying to describe, virtue is prior to *that* notion, and so the priority claim is maintained. See note 4.

18. For more on deontological reasons, see the next section. My discussion here is obviously influenced by the work of Philippa Foot (1985). Foot urges that the basic feature of consequentialism is that it employs the idea of "the best overall state of affairs." While I know of no work in which she characterizes the distinctive features of ethics of virtue as I suggest here, this characterization fits well with the writings I have seen.

19. Scheffler 1982, p. 2. This is his initial characterization of "standard deontological views." He goes on to say, "In other words, these views incorporate what I shall call 'agent-centred restrictions': restrictions on action which have the effect of denying that there is any non-agent-relative principle for ranking overall states of affairs from best to worst such that it is always permissible to produce the best available state of affairs so characterized." What follows "in other words" is not equivalent to what precedes it. An ethics of virtue will be deontological in the former sense but not in the latter.

20. See once again Foot 1985.

21. It follows from my discussion that one cannot tell whether a theory belongs to one of these types by consulting the content of its requirements or proscriptions. Conceivably, a particular version of an ethics of virtue may conclude that there is but a single virtue, the concern to produce the greatest good for the greatest number or to act only on maxims that could become universal laws for all rational beings. The same goes for contractualism; it could be argued that utilitarianism or Kantianism gives the content of the basic agreement. Moreover, many an ethics of outcome has argued for a role for "deontological constraints" in vouchsafing their favorite states of affairs. What makes these theories what they are is not their practical implications but their premises.

22. For this reply, see Wallace 1978, pp. 43–44.

23. Foot has recently explored these questions in an illuminating set of lectures, which remain, as far as I know, unpublished.

24. Did Aristotle have an ethics of virtue in the sense I have been after? The text intimates in several places that he did have, that since his theory does not comply with Rawls's scheme, it is a model for the third kind of theory I have been seeking. Surely my formulation of the second component of the theory is rightly named after Aristotle, but there is textual evidence that he did not countenance the first component, that is, the claim of explanatory primacy. The evidence I have in mind comes from the doctrine of the mean. That doctrine is a thesis about what a virtue is, namely, a state of character that is "a mean between two vices, one of excess and one of deficiency." The trouble arises when Aristotle goes on to say that this state is a mean "*because* it aims at the intermediate condition in feelings and action" (*Nicomachean Ethics* 1109a22–32). Again, "Virtue is a mean insofar as it aims at what is intermediate" (1106b28).

Such passages as these show how an intuitionist such as W. D. Ross could have found Aristotle's views so congenial. If these remarks on the mean are put together with Aristotle's remarks on uncodifiability, we get the basic intuitionist picture. If Aristotle held an ethics of virtue, one would have expected him to have said that action and desire are "intermediate," when they are, in that (because) they manifest a medial disposition. (So Aristotle is construed by Urmson, who does not consider these contrary texts.) What he said instead implies that states of character are virtues, when they are, because of the qualities of the actions and desires in which they issue.

In view of the complexity of Aristotle's texts, I do not find these passages to be conclusive. The issue must be discussed in the context of a reading of Aristotle's work as a whole. The bearing of Aristotle's treatment of *eudaimonia* in *Nicomachean Ethics*, book 1, and of the discussion of practical reason in book 6 are also important to consider. It is not clear, for instance, how to think of the aim of practical reason on an ethics of virtue. Doesn't the practically wise individual *get it right*, and can we make sense of this without reference to a standard independent of virtue? What does the individual get right, according to an ethics of virtue? (I am grateful to Gloria Rock for pressing this point in conversation.)

Meanwhile, it is somewhat disconcerting not to be able to adduce here a single clear instance of a historically important ethics of virtue in the sense I have identified. (Of course, Aquinas should be considered in this connection as well.)

My second question is this. In view of the problems endgendered by the appeal to human nature, are there alternatives to Aristotelian versions of ethics of virtue? Aristotelian formulations are most familiar, but there are also hints in contemporary discussions of the possibility of a *tradition-based* theory, a theory in which the concept of tradition somehow does the work that the concept of human nature does in the Aristotelian view. (See, for example, Larmore 1987, MacIntyre 1981, and Wallace 1988. As far as I can tell, none of these writers explicitly adopts the view I sketch below.) Let me consider briefly some of the questions raised by this idea.

The idea of a tradition-based view might be expressed as follows. Morality is radically underdetermined by the abstract and universal notion of human nature employed in Aristotelian views. To be sure, nature places boundary conditions on culture, but by itself it yields no definite content for the moral life. That content can come only from particular cultures and traditions. (Although they are clearly not synonymous, I will use "culture" and "tradition" interchangeably here.) To put it another way, what is characteristically human is to be initiated into a shared way of life. Human nature must be made determinate by socialization.

So far these ideas do not suffice for an ethics of virtue. To do so, they have to be conjoined with something like the following thesis: that proper behavior (acting, feeling, and thinking properly) is acting in accordance with the virtues as these are specified and interpreted in a person's ideals that are implicit in the culture.

I am not prepared to pursue this matter further here. I shall confine myself to two observations. First, most obviously, culture-based and nature-based views need not be exclusive. Nature might determine the sorts of things that are virtues for human beings, while culture determines the specific content. This conception would allow for cultural variation within a general nature-based ideal of the human being. (See Hampshire 1983.)

The second observation is this. It may be illuminating to subsume ethics of virtue, in either a culture-based or a nature-based version, under "self-realization" ethics. That is to say, acting properly is acting in accordance with those traits that express or realize one's self, nature, or identity. Whether one is faring well depends, as I said, upon what one is. Nature-based and tradition-based views can be seen at the extremes as giving different answers to the question of what is central to human identity. On a nature-based view, one's identity is cast by one's "species-being," so to speak, whereas on the tradition-based version, the self is more particular to its culture. As I just suggested, however, this is a false opposition on the sensible view that human nature is bound up with culture. If human nature is to live in and in accordance with a tradition, then tradition-based ethics of virtue is a form of nature-based ethics of virtue.

25. This paper originated in a brief panel presentation at a conference on virtue theory at the University of San Diego in February 1986. I am grateful to the director, Lawrence Hinman, for inviting me. I am also grateful to members of the Moral and Political Philosophy Society of Southern California and to the Philosophy Department at the University of California at Riverside for helpful discussions of earlier drafts of the paper, in particular, to David Estlund, Craig Ihara, Gloria Rock, Gerry Santas, and Paul Weithman. Thanks are also due, finally, to Owen Flanagan and to Amélie Rorty.

Bibliography

Adams, E. M. 1975. *Philosophy and the Modern Mind*. Chapel Hill: University of North Carolina Press. (Reprinted by University of Press of America, Washington, D.C., 1985.)

Adams, R. M. 1976. Motive utilitarianism. *Journal of Philosophy* 73:467–481.

Adams, R. M. 1985. Involuntary sins. *Philosophical Review* 94:3–31.

Amir, M. 1971. *Patterns in Forcible Rape*. Chicago: University of Chicago Press.

Annis, David B. 1987. The meaning, value, and duties of friendship. *American Philosophical Quarterly* 24, no. 4:349–356.

Anscombe, G. E. M. 1981. Modern moral philosophy. In *The Collected Philosophical Papers of G. E. M. Anscombe* (vol. 3). Minneapolis University of Minnesota Press. (First published 1958.)

Ardal, P. 1966. *Passion and Value in Hume's Treatise*. Edinburgh: Edinburgh University Press.

Aristotle. 1925. *Nicomachean Ethics*. Translated by W. D. Ross. London: Oxford University Press.

Aristotle. 1962. *The Nicomachean Ethics*. Translated by M. Ostwald. New York: Library of Liberal Arts.

Aristotle. 1963. *Nicomachean Ethics*. Oxford: Oxford University Press.

Aristotle. 1984. *Politics* (revised Oxford translation). Princeton: Princeton University Press.

Aristotle. 1985. *Nicomachean Ethics*. Translated by T. Irwin. Indianapolis: Hackett.

Austin, J. 1873. *Lectures on Jurisprudence*. London: John Murray.

Axelrod, R. 1984. *The Evolution of Cooperation*. New York: Basic Books.

Badhwar, N. K. 1985. Friendship, justice, and supererogation. *American Philosophical Quarterly* 22:123–131.

Baier, A. 1978. Hume's analysis of pride. *Journal of Philosophy* 75:27–40.

Baier, A. 1985a. What do women want in a moral theory? *Noûs* 19:53–63.

Baier, A. 1985b. *Postures of the Mind: Essays on Mind and Morals*. Minneapolis: University of Minnesota Press.

Baier, A. 1986. Trust and antitrust. *Ethics* 96:231–260.

Baier, A. 1987a. Hume, the women's moral theorist? In E. F. Kittay and D. T. Meyers (eds.), *Women and Moral Theory*. Totowa, N.J.: Littlefield, Adams.

Baier, A. 1987b. The need for more than justice. In M. Hanen and K. Nielsen (eds.), *Science, Morality, and Feminist Theory*. Calgary: University of Calgary.

Baier, A. 1988. Critical notice of C. Taylor, *Philosophy and the Human Sciences: Philosophical Papers*, vol. 2. *Canadian Journal of Philosophy* 18:589–594.

Baron, M. 1984. The alleged moral repugnance of acting from duty. *Journal of Philosophy* 81:197–219.

Baron, M. 1988. Remorse and agent-regret. In P. A. French, T. E. Uehling, and H. K. Wettstein (eds.), *Midwest Studies in Philosophy*, vol. 13, *Ethical Theory: Character and Virtue*. Notre Dame: Notre Dame University Press.

Bellah, R., Madsen, R., Sullivan, W., Swidler, A., and Tipton, S. 1985. *Habits of the Heart: Individualism and Commitment in American Life*. Berkeley: University of California Press.

Benedict, R. 1934. Anthropology and the abnormal. *Journal of General Psychology* 10:59–82.

Bennett, J. 1974. The conscience of Huckleberry Finn. *Philosophy* 49:123–134.

Berger, P. L., and Luckmann, T. 1966. *The Social Construction of Reality: A Treatise in the Sociology of Knowledge*. New York: Doubleday.

Blum, L. 1980. *Friendship, Altruism, and Morality*. London: Routledge and Kegan Paul.

Blum, L. 1986. Iris Murdoch and the domain of the moral. *Philosophical Studies* 50:343–367.

Blum, L. 1987. Particularity and responsiveness. In J. Kagan and S. Lamb (eds.), *The Emergence of Morality in Young Children*. Chicago: University of Chicago Press.

Blum, L. 1988a. Gilligan and Kohlberg: Implications for moral theory. *Ethics* 98:472–491.

Blum, L. 1988b. Moral exemplars: Reflections on Schindler, the Trocmes, and others. *Midwest Studies in Philosophy*, vol. 13, *Ethical Theory: Character and Virtue*. Notre Dame: University of Notre Dame Press.

Blum, L. 1991. Altruism and the moral value of rescue: Resisting persecution, racism, and genocide. In L. Baron, L. Blum, D. Krebs, P. Oliner, S. Oliner, and Z. Smolenska, *Embracing the Other: Philosophical, Psychological, and Historical Perspectives on Altruism*. New York: New York University Press.

Bok, S. 1978. *Lying: Moral Choice in Public and Private Life*. New York: Pantheon Books.

Bowen, M. 1978. *Family Therapy in Clinical Practice*. New York: Jason Aronson.

Bradley, F. H. 1927. *Ethical Studies* (2nd ed.). Oxford: Oxford University Press.

Brandt, R. B. 1964. The concepts of duty and obligation. *Mind* 73:373–393.

Brandt, R. B. 1984. Utilitarianism and moral rights. *Canadian Journal of Philosophy* 14:1–19.

Bratman, M. 1985. Davidson's theory of intention. In E. LePore and B. McLaughlin 1985.

Brink, D. O. 1986. Utilitarian morality and the personal point of view. *Journal of Philosophy* 83:417–438.

Brink, D. O. 1988. Legal theory, legal interpretation, and judicial review. *Philosophy and Public Affairs* 17:105–148.

Brink, D. O. 1989. *Moral Realism and the Foundations of Ethics*. New York: Cambridge University Press.

Brink, D. O. 1991. Sidgwick and the rationale for rational egoism. In B. Schultz (ed.), *Essays on Sidgwick*. New York: Cambridge University Press.

Bruch, H. 1988. *Conversations with Anorexics*. Edited by D. Czyzewski and M. A. Suhr. New York: Basic Books.

Buchanan, A. 1977. Categorical imperatives and moral principles. *Philosophical Studies* 31:249–260.

Burton, J. H. 1846. *Life and Correspondence of David Hume* (2 volumes). Edinburgh: William Tait.

Burton, R. 1977. *The Anatomy of Melancholia*. New York: Vintage.

Butler, J. 1859. *Bishop Butler's Ethical Discourses and Essay on Virtue*. Edited by J. T. Champlin. Boston: J. P. Jewett & Co.

Butler, J. 1950. *Fifteen Sermons Preached at the Rolls Chapel.* New York: Bobbs Merrill. (Reprinted in S. Darwall (ed.), *Five Sermons,* Hackett, Indianapolis, 1983. First published 1749.)

Butler, S. 1970. *Characters.* Cleveland: Press of Case Western Reserve University.

Card, C. 1972. On mercy. *Philosophical Review* 81:182–207.

Card, C. 1988a. Gratitude and obligation. *American Philosophical Quarterly* 25:115–127.

Card, C. 1988b. Lesbian battering. *American Philosophical Association Newsletter on Feminism and Philosophy* 88:3–7. (Review essay on Lobel 1986.)

Card, C. 1989. Defusing the bomb: Lesbian ethics and horizontal violence. *Lesbian Ethics* 3:91–100.

Card, C. 1990. Intimacy and responsibility: What lesbians do. In Martha Fineman and Nancy Thomadsen (eds.), *At the Boundaries of Law: Feminism and Legal Theory.* London: Routledge and Kegan Paul.

Card, C. Unpublished b. Virtues and moral luck. Read at the 1985 Western Division Meetings of the American Philosophical Association.

Card, C. Unpublished c. Responsibility and moral luck: Resisting oppression and abuse. Read at the 1989 Eastern Division Meetings of the American Philosophical Association.

Care, N. S. 1984. Career choice. *Ethics* 94:283–302.

Care, N. S. 1987. *On Sharing Fate.* Philadelphia: Temple University Press.

Cavalli-Sforza, L. L., and Bodmer, W. F. 1971. *The Genetics of Human Populations.* San Francisco: W. H. Freeman and Co.

Charles, D. 1983. Rationality and irrationality. *Proceedings of the Aristotelian Society* 83:191–212.

Charlton, W. 1988. *Weakness of Will: A Philosophical Introduction.* Oxford: Basil Blackwell.

Chaucer, G. 1985. *Canterbury Tales.* Oxford: Oxford University Press.

Cherniak, C. 1986. *Minimal Rationality.* Cambridge: MIT Press.

Chodorow, N. 1978. *The Reproduction of Mothering: Psychoanalysis and the Sociology of Gender.* Berkeley: University of California Press.

Churchill, L. 1989. Reviving a distinctive medical ethic. *Hastings Center Report* 19, no. 3: 28–34.

Conee, E. 1982. Against moral dilemmas. *Philosophical Review* 91:87–97. (Reprinted in Gowans 1987.)

Cooper, J. 1975. *Reason and Human Good in Aristotle.* Cambridge: Harvard University Press.

Cottingham, J. 1983. Ethics and impartiality. *Philosophical Studies* 43:83–99.

Darwall, S. L. 1983. *Impartial Reason.* Ithaca: Cornell University Press.

Darwin, C. 1916. *The Expression of Emotion in Man and Animals.* New York: D. Appleton. (First published 1872.)

Davidson, D. 1963. Actions, reasons, and causes. *Journal of Philosophy* 60:685–700. (Reprinted in Davidson 1980.)

Davidson, D. 1969. How is weakness of the will possible? In J. Feinberg (ed.), *Moral Concepts.* Oxford University Press. (Reprinted in Davidson 1980.)

Davidson, D. 1976. Hume's cognitive theory of pride. *Journal of Philosophy* 73:744–756.

Davidson, D. 1980. *Essays on Actions and Events.* Oxford: Oxford University Press.

Dennett, D. 1984. *Elbow Room: The Varieties of Free Will Worth Wanting.* Cambridge: MIT Press.

Dennett, D. 1988. Why everyone is a novelist. *Times Literary Supplement* 4, no. 459.

Dent, N. J. H. 1984. *The Moral Psychology of the Virtues.* Cambridge: Cambridge University Press.

De Sousa, R. 1987. *The Rationality of Emotion.* Cambridge: MIT Press.

De Vos, G. 1973. *Socialization of Achievement*. Berkeley: University of California Press.

Dewey, J. 1960. *Theory of the Moral Life*. New York: Holt, Rinehart and Winston. (Original version, 1908; revised 1932.)

Dworkin, R. 1986. *Law's Empire*. Cambridge: Harvard University Press.

Earle, J. 1811. *Microcosmography*. London: White and Cochrane.

Emmet, D. 1966. *Rules, Roles, and Relations*. New York: St. Martin's Press.

Epicurus. 1988. *Kuriai Doxa*. In *Hellenistic Philosophy: Introductory Readings*. Translated by B. Inwood and L. Gerson. Indianapolis: Hackett.

Erikson, E. H. 1968. *Identity: Youth and Crisis*. New York: W. W. Norton.

Feinberg, J. 1970a. What is so special about mental illness? In *Doing and Deserving*. Princeton: Princeton University Press.

Feinberg, J. 1970b. Justice and personal desert. In *Doing and Deserving: Essays in the Theory of Responsibility*. Princeton: Princeton University Press.

Feinberg, J. 1970c. Crime, clutchability, and individual treatment. In *Doing and Deserving*. Princeton: Princeton University Press.

Festinger, L. 1965. *Theory of Cognitive Dissonance*. Stanford: Stanford University Press.

Fingarette, H. 1967. *On Responsibility*. New York: Basic Books.

Fingarette, H. 1988. *Heavy Drinking: The Myth of Alcoholism as a Disease*. Berkeley: University of California Press.

Fischer, J. M., ed. 1986. *Moral Responsibility*. Ithaca: Cornell University Press.

Flanagan, O. 1986. Admirable immorality and admirable imperfection. *Journal of Philosophy* 83:41–60.

Flanagan, O. 1991. *Varieties of Moral Personality: Ethics and Psychological Realism*. Cambridge: Harvard University Press.

Flanagan, O., and Jackson, K. 1987. Justice, care, and gender: The Kohlberg-Gilligan debate revisited. *Ethics* 97:622–637.

Foot, P. 1978a. *Virtues and Vices*. Berkeley: University of California Press.

Foot, P. 1978b. Hume on moral judgment. In Foot, 1978a.

Foot, P. 1978c. Virtues and vices. In Foot 1978a.

Foot, P. 1978d. Morality as a system of hypothetical imperatives. In Foot 1978c.

Foot, P. 1985. Utilitarianism and the virtues. *Mind* 94:196–209.

Frankena, W. K. 1970. Prichard and the ethics of virtue. *Monist* 54:1–17.

Frankfurt, H. 1969. Alternate possibilities and moral responsibility. *Journal of Philosophy* 66:828–839.

Frankfurt, H. 1971. Freedom of the will and the concept of the person. *Journal of Philosophy* 68:5–20. (Reprinted in H. Frankfurt (1988), *The importance of What We Care About*, Cambridge University Press, Cambridge. Also reprinted in Watson 1982.)

Frankfurt, H. 1982. The importance of what we care about. *Synthese* 53:257–272. (Reprinted in H. Frankfurt, *The Importance of What We Care About*, Cambridge University Press, Cambridge, 1988.)

Freud, S. 1961. Some psychical consequences of the anatomical distinction between the sexes. In *The Standard Edition of the Complete Psychological Works of Sigmund Freud* (vol. 19), translated by J. Strachey. London: Hogarth. (First published in 1925.)

Fried, C. 1970. *An Anatomy of Values: Problems of Personal and Social Choice*. Cambridge: Harvard University Press.

Friedman, M. 1987a. Beyond caring: The de-moralization of gender. In M. Hanen and K. Nielsen (eds.), *Science, Morality, and Feminist Theory*. Calgary: University of Calgary.

Friedman, M. 1987b. Care and context in moral reasoning. In E. F. Kittay and D. T. Meyers (eds.), *Women and Moral Theory*. Totowa, N.J.: Littlefield, Adams.

Fuller, L. L. 1964. *The Morality of Law*. New Haven: Yale University Press.

Gardiner, P. 1963. Hume's theory of the passions. In *David Hume, A Symposium*. London: MacMillan.

Gauthier, D. 1986. *Morals by Agreement*. Oxford: Oxford University Press.

Geertz, C. 1973. Person, time, and conduct in Bali. In *The Interpretation of Cultures*. New York: Basic Books.

Geertz, C. 1984. From the native's point of view: On the nature of anthropological understanding. In R. Shweder and R. Levine (eds.), *Culture Theory: Essays in Mind, Self, and Emotion*. Cambridge: Cambridge University Press.

Gewirth, A. 1978. *Reason and Morality*. Chicago: University of Chicago Press.

Gewirth, A. 1989. Ethical universalism and particularism. *Journal of Philosophy* 85:283–302.

Gies, M., with Gold, A. L. 1987. *Anne Frank Remembered*. New York: Simon and Schuster.

Gilligan, C. 1982. *In a Different Voice: Psychological Theory and Women's Development*. Cambridge: Harvard University Press.

Gilligan, C., Ward, J. V., and Taylor, J. M., with Bardige, B., eds. 1988. *Mapping the Moral Domain: A Contribution of Women's Thinking to Psychological Theory and Education*. Cambridge: Harvard University Press.

Glass, B., and Li, C. C. 1953. The dynamics of racial admixture—An analysis of the American negro. *American Journal of Human Genetics* 5:1–20.

Glover, J. 1983. Self-creation. *Proceedings of the British-Academy* 69:445–471.

Gordon, R. 1987. *The Structure of Emotion*. Cambridge: Cambridge University Press.

Gowans, C. W., ed. 1987. *Moral Dilemmas*. Oxford: Oxford University Press.

Green, T. H. 1969. *Prolegomena to Ethics*. New York: Crowell (First published 1883.)

Greenspan, P. S. 1978. Behavior control and freedom of action. *Philosophical Review* 87:225–240.

Greenspan, P. S. 1988. *Emotions and Reasons*. New York: Routledge, Chapman and Hall.

Haksar, V. 1964. Aristotle and the punishment of psychopaths. *Philosophy* 39:323–340.

Hampshire, S. 1983. Two theories of morality. In *Morality and Conflict*. Cambridge: Harvard University Press.

Hare, R. M. 1952. *The Language of Morals*. Oxford: Oxford University Press.

Hare, R. M. 1963. *Freedom and Reason*. Oxford: Oxford University Press.

Harman, G. 1975. Moral relativism defended. *Philosophical Review* 84:3–22.

Harman, G. 1986. *Change in View: Principles of Reasoning*. Cambridge: MIT Press.

Harrison, R., ed. 1979. *Rational Action*. Cambridge: Cambridge University Press.

Hart, H. L. A. 1961. *The Concept of Law*. Oxford: Oxford University Press.

Held, V. 1984. *Rights and Goods: Justifying Social Action*. New York: Free Press/Macmillan.

Held, V. 1987a. Feminism and moral theory. In E. F. Kittay and D. T. Meyers (eds.), *Women and Moral Theory*. Totowa, N.J.: Littlefield, Adams.

Held, V. 1987b. Non-contractual society. In M. Hanen and K. Nielsen (eds.), *Science, Morality, and Feminist Theory*. Calgary: University of Calgary.

Heller, M. 1984. Temporal parts of four dimensional objects. *Philosophical Studies* 46:323–334.

Hendel, C. W., Jr. 1925. *Studies in the Philosophy of David Hume*. Princeton: Princeton University Press.

Herman, B. 1981. On the value of acting from the motive of duty. *Philosophical Review* 90:359–382.

Herman, B. 1983. Integrity and impartiality. *Monist* 66:233–250.

Herman, B. 1984a. Rules, motives, and helping actions. *Philosophical Studies* 45:369–377.

Herman, B. 1984b. Mutual aid and respect for person. *Ethics* 94:578–602.

Herman, B. 1985. The practice of moral judgment. *Journal of Philosophy* 82:414–436.

Herman, B. 1990. What happens to the consequences. In P. Guyer and T. Cohen (eds.), *Pursuit of Reason*. Lubbock: Texas Tech University Press.

Herman, B. Unpublished. Moral deliberation and the derivation of duties.

Hoagland, S. L. 1988. *Lesbian Ethics*. Palo Alto, Calif.: Institute for Lesbian Studies.

Hobson, L. 1947. *Gentleman's Agreement*. New York: Grosset & Dunlap.

Holmes, O. W. 1959. The path of law. In C. Morris (ed.), *The Great Legal Philosophers*. Philadelphia: University of Pennsylvania Press. (First published 1895.)

Horney, K. 1942. *Self-Analysis*. New York: W. W. Norton.

Houston, B. 1987. Rescuing womanly virtues: Some dangers of reclamation. In M. Hanen and K. Nielsen (eds.), *Science, Morality, and Feminist Theory*. Calgary: University of Calgary.

Hudson, S. 1986. *Human Character and Morality*. Boston: Routledge & Kegan Paul.

Hume, D. 1846. Letters, Hume to Hutcheson, Hume to Henry Home. In Burton (ed.), *Life and Correspondence of David Hume* (2 volumes). Edinburgh: William Tait.

Hume, D. 1889. *A Dissertation on the Passions*. In T. H. Green and T. H. Grose (eds.), *Essays Moral, Political, and Literary*. London: Longhan, Green and Co. (First published 1757.)

Hume, D. 1957a. *An Inquiry Concerning the Principles of Morals*. Edited by C. Hendel. New York: Library of Liberal Arts. (First published 1751.)

Hume, D. 1965. *Of the standard of taste*. In *Of the Standard of Taste and Other Essays*. Indianapolis: Library of Liberal Arts. (First published 1757.)

Hume, D. 1975a. *Enquiries Concerning Human Understanding and Concerning the Principles of Morals*. Edited by L. A. Selby-Bigge. Oxford: Oxford University Press. (Reprinted from 1777 edition.)

Hume, D. 1975b. *A Treatise of Human Nature*. Edited by L. A. Selby-Bigge and P. H. Nidditch. Oxford: Oxford University Press. (First published 1739.)

Hume, D. 1977. *An Enquiry Concerning Human Understanding*. Edited by E. Steinberg. Indianapolis: Hackett. (First published 1748.)

Hume, D. 1978a. *Enquiries*. Edited by L. A. Selby-Bigge and P. H. Nidditch. Oxford: Oxford University Press. (First published 1748, 1751.)

Hume, D. 1978. *A Treatise of Human Nature* (2nd ed.). Edited by L. A. Selby-Bigge and P. H. Nidditch. Oxford: Oxford University Press. (First published 1739.)

Hume, D. 1983. *An Enquiry Concerning the Principles of Morals*. Edited by J. Schneewind. Indianapolis: Hackett. (First published 1751.)

Irwin, T. H. 1977. *Plato's Moral Theory*. Oxford: Oxford University Press.

Irwin, T. H. 1988. *Aristotle's First Principles*. Oxford: Oxford University Press.

Jackson, F. 1984. Weakness of will. *Mind* 93:1–18.

James, H. 1973. *The Ambassadors*. Harmondsworth: Penguin Books. (First published 1903.)

James, W. 1950. *The Principles of Psychology*. New York: Dover Publications. (First published 1890.)

James, W. 1978. *Pragmatism: A New Name for Some Old Ways of Thinking, and The Meaning of Truth: A Sequel to "Pragmatism."* Cambridge: Harvard University Press. (First published 1907 and 1909.)

James, W. 1979a. *The Will to Believe and Other Essays in Popular Philosophy.* Cambridge: Harvard University Press. (First published 1897.)

James, W. 1979b. The dilemma of determinism. In *The Will to Believe and Other Essays in Popular Philosophy.* Cambridge: Harvard University Press. (First published in 1897.)

James, W. 1979c. The moral philosopher and the moral life. In James 1979a. (First published in 1891.)

James, W. 1983. *Talks to Teachers on Psychology and to Students on Some of Life's Ideals.* Cambridge: Harvard University Press. (First published 1899.)

James, W. 1988. *Manuscript Essays and Notes.* Cambridge: Harvard University Press.

Jeffrey, R. C. 1974. Preference among preferences. *Journal of Philosophy* 71:377–391.

Kagan, J. 1984. *The Nature of the Child.* New York: Basic Books.

Kagan, J., Reznick, J. S., and Snidman, N. S. 1988. Biological bases of childhood shyness. *Science* 240:167–171.

Kahneman, D., Slovic, P., and Tversky, A., eds. 1982. *Judgment under Uncertainty.* Cambridge: Cambridge University Press.

Kamm, F. M. 1985. Supererogation and obligation. *Journal of Philosophy* 82:118–138.

Kant, I. 1933. *Critique of Pure Reason.* Trans. N. Kemp Smith. London: Macmillan.

Kant, I. 1934. *Religion within the Limits of Reason Alone.* New York: Harper and Row. (First published 1795.)

Kant, I. 1948. *The Moral Law: Kant's Groundwork of "The Metaphysic of Morals."* Translated by H. J. Paton. London: Hutchinson. (First published 1785.)

Kant, I. 1956. *Critique of Practical Reason.* Indianapolis: Bobbs-Merrill. (First published 1788.)

Kant, I. 1960a. *Religion within the Limits of Reason Alone.* Translated by T. M. Greene and H. H. Hudson. New York: Harper and Row. (First published 1795.)

Kant, I. 1960b. *Observations on the Feeling of the Beautiful and Sublime.* Translated by J. T. Goldthwait. Berkeley: University of California Press. (First published 1764.)

Kant, I. 1962. *The Moral Law: Kant's Groundwork of "The Metaphysics of Morals."* London: Hutchinson University Library. (First published 1785.)

Kant, I. 1963a. *Lecture on Ethics.* Indianapolis: Hackett.

Kant, I. 1963b. *Lectures on Ethics.* Translated by L. Infield, New York: Harper & Row.

Kant, I. 1964a. *Groundwork of "The Metaphysics of Morals."* Translated by H. J. Paton. New York: Harper and Row. (First published 1785.)

Kant, I. 1964b. *The Doctrine of Virtue: Part II of "The Metaphysic of Morals."* Translated by M. J. Gregor. New York: Harper & Row. (First published 1797.)

Kant, I. 1969. On a supposed right to lie from benevolent motives. Translated by L. W. Beck. In L. W. Beck (ed.), *Kant's Critique of Practical Reason and Other Writings in Moral Philosophy.* Chicago: University of Chicago Press. (First published 1797.)

Kant, I. 1971. *The Doctrine of Virtue: Part II of "The Metaphysics of Morals."* Philadelphia: University of Pennsylvania Press. (First published 1797.)

Kant, I. 1974. *Anthropology from a Pragmatic Point of View.* Translated by M. J. Gregor. The Hague: Nijhoff. (First published 1797.)

Kant, I. 1981. *Grounding for "The Metaphysics of Morals."* Translated by J. Ellington. Indianapolis: Hackett. (Prussian Academy pagination. First published 1785.)

Kemp Smith, N. 1941. *The Philosophy of David Hume.* London: MacMillan.

Kenny, A. 1963. *Action, Emotion, and Will.* New York: Humanities Press.

Kohl, H. 1984. *Growing Minds: On Becoming a Teacher.* New York: Harper and Row.

Kohlberg, L. 1981. *The Philosophy of Moral Development.* San Francisco: Harper & Row.

Korsgaard, C. 1983. Two distinctions in goodness. *Philosophical Review* 91:169–195.

Kydd, R. 1964. *Reason and Conduct in Hume's Treatise.* New York Russell & Russell.

La Bruyere, J. D. 1891. Les caractères. In H. Morley (ed.), *Character Writings of the Seventeenth Century*. London: G. Routledge.

Lange, C. G. 1922. *The Emotions*. Baltimore: Williams and Wilkins Company.

Larmore, C. 1987. *Patterns of Moral Complexity*. Cambridge: Cambridge University Press.

LePore, E., and McLaughlin, B., eds. 1985. *Actions and Events: Perspectives on the Philosophy of Donald Davidson*. Oxford: Basil Blackwell.

Lewis, D. 1976. Survival and identity. In A. Rorty (ed.), *The Identities of Persons*. Los Angeles: University of California Press.

Lind, M. 1987. *Emotions and Hume's Moral Theory*. Unpublished doctoral dissertation, MIT.

Lind, M. Unpublished. Hume and neo-classicist moral theory. Paper read at the Fourteenth World Congress in Philosophy of Law and Social Philosophy, Edinburgh, Scotland, 1989.

Lobel, K., ed. 1986. *Naming the Violence: Speaking Out about Lesbian Battering*. Seattle: Seal.

Louden, R. 1988. Can we be too moral? *Ethics* 98:361–78.

McConnell, T. C. 1978. Moral dilemmas and consistency in ethics. *Canadian Journal of Philosophy* 8:269–287. (Reprinted in Gowans 1987.)

McDowell, J. 1979. Virtue and Reason. *Monist* 62:331–350.

MacIntyre, A. 1981. *After Virtue: A Study in Moral Theory* (1st ed.). Notre Dame: University of Notre Dame Press.

MacIntyre, A. 1984. *After Virtue: A Study in Moral Theory* (2nd ed.). Notre Dame: University of Notre Dame Press.

MacIntyre, A. 1988. *Whose Justice? Which Rationality?* Notre Dame: University of Notre Dame Press.

Mackie, J. L. 1977. *Ethics: Inventing Right and Wrong*. New York: Penguin.

McLaughlin, B., and Rorty, A. 1988. *Perspectives on Self-Deception*. Berkeley: University of California Press.

Marcus, R. B. 1980. Moral dilemmas and consistency. *Journal of Philosophy* 77:121–136. (Reprinted in Gowans 1987.)

Mendus, S. 1984. The practical and the pathological. *Journal of Value Inquiry* 19:235–243.

Menninger, K. 1968. *The Crime of Punishment*. New York: Viking Press.

Merleau-Ponty, M. 1963. *The Structure of Behavior*. Boston: Beacon Press.

Mill, J. S. 1957. *Utilitarianism*. New York: Bobbs-Merrill. (First published 1861.)

Mill, J. S. 1978. *On Liberty*. Indianapolis: Hackett. (First published 1859.)

Miller, D. 1981. *Philosophy and Ideology in Hume's Political Thought*. Oxford: Oxford University Press.

Milne, A. A. 1974. *Winnie-the-Pooh*. New York: Dell Publishing Company.

Mitsis, P. 1988. *Epicurus' Ethical Theory: The Pleasures of Invulnerability*. Ithaca: Cornell University Press.

Molière, J. B. 1869. *L'Avare, Le Malade Imaginaire, Le Misanthrope*. In *Œuvres Complètes*. Paris: Charpentier.

Mossner, E. C. 1980. *Life of David Hume* (2nd ed.). Oxford: Oxford University Press.

Murdoch, I. 1970. *The Sovereignty of Good*. London: Routledge and Kegan Paul.

Murdoch, I. 1971. *The Sovereignty of Good*. New York: Schocken Books.

Murphy, J. G. 1972. Moral death: A Kantian essay on psychopathy. *Ethics* 82:284–298.

Nagel, E. 1961. *The Structure of Science: Problems in the Logic of Scientific Explanation*. New York: Harcourt, Brace & World.

Nagel, T. 1970. *The Possibility of Altruism*. Princeton: Princeton University Press.

Nagel, T. 1979a. Moral luck. In *Mortal Questions*. Cambridge: Cambridge University Press.

Nagel, T. 1979b. What is it like to be a bat? In *Mortal Questions*. Cambridge: Cambridge University Press.

Nagel, T. 1979c. The fragmentation of value. In *Mortal Questions*. Cambridge: Cambridge University Press.

Nagel, T. 1986. *The View from Nowhere*. New York: Oxford University Press.

Nietzsche, F. 1966. *Beyond Good and Evil*. Translated by W. Kaufmann. New York: Vintage Books. (First published 1886.)

Nietzsche, F. 1967. *Will to Power*. Translated by W. Kaufmann and R. J. Hollingdale. New York: Random House. (First published 1901.)

Nietzsche, F. 1982. *Daybreak: Thoughts on the Prejudices of Morality*. Translated by R. J. Hollingdale. Cambridge: Cambridge University Press. (First published 1881.)

Nisbett, R. E., and Wilson, T. D. 1977. Telling more than we can know: Verbal reports on mental processes. *Psychological Review* 84:231–259.

Noddings, N. 1984. *Caring: A Feminine Approach to Ethics and Moral Education*. Berkeley: University of California Press.

Norton, D. F. 1982. *David Hume*. Princeton: Princeton University Press.

Nozick, R. 1974. *Anarchy, State, and Utopia*. New York: Basic Books.

Nussbaum, M. 1985. The discernment of perception: An Aristotelian conception of private and public morality. In J. Cleary (ed.), *Proceedings of the Boston Area Colloquium on Ancient Philosophy*, pp. 151–201. New York: University Press of America.

Nussbaum, M. 1988. Comment on Paul Seabright. *Ethics* 98:332–340.

Oakley, J. 1988. Morality and the emotions. Unpublished doctoral dissertation, La Trobe University, Bundoora, Victoria, Australia.

O'Flaherty, W. D. 1978. The clash between relative and absolute duty: The dharma of demons. In W. D. O'Flaherty, J. Duncan, and M. Derrett (eds.), *The Concept of Duty in South Asia*. New Delhi: Vikas Publishing House.

Olson, M. 1965. *The Logic of Collective Action*. Cambridge: Harvard University Press.

O'Neill, O. 1975. *Acting on Principle*. New York: Columbia University Press.

O'Neill, O. 1985. Consistency in action. In N. Potter and M. Timmons (eds.), *Morality and Universality*. Reidel Publishing Company.

Parfit, D. 1984. *Reasons and Persons*. Oxford: Oxford University Press.

Peacocke. C. 1985. Intention and akrasia. In B. Vermazen and M. Hintikka (eds.), *Essays on Davidson: Actions and Events*. Oxford: Oxford University Press.

Pears, D. 1980. Courage as mean. In Rorty 1980b.

Pears, D. 1984. *Motivated Irrationality*. Oxford: Oxford University Press.

Perry, J. 1976. The importance of being identical. In A. Rorty (ed.), *The Identities of Persons*. Los Angeles: University of California Press.

Peters, R. S. 1966. Moral education and the psychology of character. In I. Scheffler (ed.), *Philosophy and Education: Modern Readings* (2nd ed.). Boston: Allyn and Bacon.

Piaget, J. 1932. *The Moral Judgment of the Child*. New York: Free Press.

Piper, A. M. S. 1985. Two conceptions of the self. *Philosophical Studies* 48, no. 2: 173–197.

Piper, A. M. S. 1987. Moral theory and moral alienation. *Journal of Philosophy* 84:102–118.

Piper, A. M. S. 1988. Pseudorationality. In A. Rorty and B. McLaughlin (eds.), *Perspectives on Self-Deception*. Berkeley: University of California Press.

Piper, A. M. S. Unpublished. The meaning of 'ought' and the loss of innocence. 1989.

Plato. 1963a. *Phaedrus*. Translated by R. Hackforth. In E. Hamilton and H. Cairns (eds.), *Collected Dialogues of Plato*. Princeton: Princeton University Press.

Plato. 1963b. *Symposium*. Translated by M. Joyce. In E. Hamilton and H. Cairns (eds.), *Collected Dialogues of Plato*. Princeton: Princeton University Press.

Plato. 1974. *Republic*. Translated by G. Grube. Indianapolis: Hackett.

Plato. 1979. *Gorgias*. Translated by T. Irwin. Oxford: Oxford University Press.

Prichard, H. 1912. Does moral philosophy rest on a mistake? *Mind* 21:21–37. (Reprinted in *Moral Obligation*, Oxford University Press, Oxford 1949.)

Railton, P. 1984. Alienation, consequentialism, and the demands of morality. *Philosophy and Public Affairs* 13:134–171.

Railton, P. 1986. Moral realism. *Philosophical Review* 95:163–207.

Rawls, J. 1971. *A Theory of Justice*. Cambridge: Harvard University Press.

Rawls, J. 1975. The independence of moral theory. *Proceedings and Addresses of the American Philosophical Association* 48:5–22.

Rawls, J. 1989. Themes in Kant's moral philosophy. In E. Forster (ed.), *Kant's Transcendental Deductions*. Stanford: Stanford University Press.

Rawls, J. Unpublished. Lectures on the ethics of Butler, Hume, and Kant and handouts from a course on social and political philosophy. Harvard University, Cambridge, 1979, 1980.

Raymond, J. 1986. *A Passion for Friends: Toward a Philosophy of Female Affection*. Boston: Beacon.

Read, K. E. 1955. Morality and the concept of the person among the Gahuku-Gama. *Oceana* 25:185–230. (Reprinted in J. Middleton (ed.), *Myth and Cosmos*, Doubleday, New York, 1967.)

Reed, T. E. 1969. Caucasian genes in American negroes. *Science* 165:762–768.

Rich, A. 1979a. *On Lies, Secrets, and Silence: Selected Prose, 1966–1978*. New York: Norton.

Rich, A. 1979b. Women and honor: Some notes on lying. In *On Lies, Secrets, and Silence: Selected Prose, 1966–1978*. New York: Norton.

Rich, A. 1980. Compulsory heterosexuality and lesbian existence. *Signs* 5:631–660.

Ringelheim, J. 1985. Women and the holocaust: A reconsideration of research. *Signs* 10:741–761.

Roberts, R. 1988. What an emotion is: A sketch. *Philosophical Review* 97:183–209.

Rorty, A. 1976a. Character, Persons, selves, individuals. In A. Rorty 1976b. (Reprinted in A. Rorty, *Mind in Action: Essays in the Philosophy of Mind*, Beacon Press, Boston, 1988.)

Rorty, A. ed. 1976b. *The Identities of Persons*. Los Angeles: University of California Press.

Rorty, A., ed. 1980a. *Explaining Emotions*. Berkeley: University of California Press.

Rorty, A., ed. 1980b. *Essays on Aristotle's Ethics*. Berkeley: University of California Press.

Rorty, A. 1990. Pride produces the idea of self: Hume on moral agency. *Australian Journal of Philosophy*.

Rorty, R. 1989. *Contingency, Irony, and Solidarity*. Cambridge: Cambridge University Press.

Ross, L., and Anderson, C. A. 1982. Shortcomings in the attribution process: On the origins and maintenance of erroneous social assessments. In Kahneman, Slovic, and Tversky 1982.

Ross, W. D. 1930. *The Right and the Good*. Oxford: Oxford University Press.

Ross, W. D. 1939. *The Foundations of Ethics*. Oxford: Oxford University Press.

Rotter, J. B. 1980. Interpersonal trust, trustworthiness, and gullibility. *American Psychologist* 35:1–7.

Rousseau, J.-J. 1961. *Émile*. Paris: Garnier-Flammarian. (First published 1762.)

Rousseau, J.-J. 1985. *A Discourse on Inequality*. Translated by M. Cranston. Harmondsworth: Penguin. (First published 1755.)

Ruddick, S. 1989. *Maternal Thinking*. Boston: Beacon Press.

Ryle, G. 1949. *The Concept of Mind*. London: Hutchinson's University Library.

Sandel, M. 1982. *Liberalism and the Limits of Justice*. New York: Cambridge University Press.

Sartre, J.-P. 1943. *L'Etre et le Néant*. Paris: Gallimard.

Sartre, J.-P. 1964. *L'Existentialisme est un Humanisme*. Paris: Nagel.

Scheffler, S. 1982. *The Rejection of Consequentialism*. Oxford: Oxford University Press.

Schiffer, S. 1976. A paradox of desire. *American Philosophical Quarterly* 13:195–203.

Schoeman, F. 1985. Aristotle on the good of friendship. *Australasian Journal of Philosophy* 63:269–282.

Schopenhauer, A. 1965. *On the Basis of Morality*. Translated by E. F. J. Payne. Indianapolis: Bobbs-Merrill. (First published 1841.)

Schuman, H., Steeh, C., and Bobo, L. 1985. *Racial Attitudes in America: Trends and Interpretations*. Cambridge: Harvard University Press.

Seabright, P. 1988. The pursuit of unhappiness: Paradoxical motivation on the subversion of character in Henry James's *Portrait of a Lady*. *Ethics* 98:313–331.

Selby-Bigge, L. A. 1964. *The British Moralists*. New York: Library of Liberal Arts.

Sherman, N. 1989. *The Fabric of Character*. Oxford: Oxford University Press.

Shoemaker, S. 1963. *Self-Knowledge and Self-Identity*. Ithaca: Cornell University Press.

Shoemaker, S. 1984. Personal identity: A materialist's account. In S. Shoemaker and R. Swinburne, *Personal Identity*. Oxford: Blackwell.

Shweder, R., and Bourne, E. 1984. Does the concept of the person vary cross-culturally? In R. Shweder and R. Levine (eds.), *Culture Theory: Essays in Mind, Self, and Emotion*. Cambridge: Cambridge University Press.

Sidgwick, H. 1893. Unreasonable action. *Mind* 2:174–187.

Sidgwick, H. 1981. *The Methods of Ethics* (7th ed.). Indianapolis: Hackett. (First published 1907.)

Slote, M. 1978. Time in counterfactuals. *Philosophical Review* 87:3–27.

Slote, M. 1983. *Goods and Virtues*. Oxford: Oxford University Press.

Slote, M. 1984. Morality and self-other asymmetry. *Journal of Philosophy* 81:179–192.

Slote, M. 1985. *Common-sense Morality and Consequentialism*. London: Routeledge and Kegan Paul.

Slote, M. 1988. Critical notice of C. Taylor, *Human Agency and Language: Philosophical Papers*, vol. 1. *Canadian Journal of Philosophy* 18:579–587.

Slote, M. 1989. *Beyond Optimizing*. Cambridge: Harvard University Press.

Smith, A. 1976. *The Theory of Moral Sentiments*. Indianapolis: Liberty Classics. (First published 1759.)

Smith, B. H. 1988. *Contingencies of Value*. Cambridge: Harvard University Press.

Stern, D. 1985. *The Interpersonal World of the Infant*. New York: Basic Books.

Stocker, M. 1966. Supererogation. Unpublished doctoral dissertation, Harvard University.

Stocker, M. 1976a. The schizophrenia of modern ethical theories. *Journal of Philosophy* 73:453–466.

Stocker, M. 1976b. Agent and other: Against ethical universalism. *Australasian Journal of Philosophy* 74:206–220.

Stocker, M. 1981. Values and purposes: The limits of teleology and the ends of friendship. *Journal of Philosophy* 78:747–765.

Stocker, M. 1986. Friendship and duty: Toward a synthesis of Gilligan's contrastive ethical concepts. In E. Kittay and D. Meyers (eds.), *Women and Moral Theory.* Totowa, N.J.: Rowman and Allanheld.

Stocker, M. 1989. *Plural and Conflicting Values.* Oxford: Oxford University Press.

Strawson, P. F. 1962. Freedom and resentment. *Proceedings of the British Academy* 48:1–25. (Reprinted in Watson 1982.)

Stroud, B. 1977. *Hume.* London: Routledge and Kegan Paul.

Sullivan, W. 1988. Calling or career: The tensions of modern professional life. In A. Flores (ed.), *Professional Ideals.* Belmont, Calif.: Wadsworth.

Taylor, C. 1971. What is involved in a genetic psychology? In C. Taylor 1985a.

Taylor, C. 1976. Responsibility for self. In A. O. Rorty 1976b. (Reprinted in Watson 1982.)

Taylor, C. 1977a. What is human agency? In T. Mischel (ed.), *The Self: Psychological and Philosophical Issues.* Oxford: Basil Blackwell. (Reprinted in C. Taylor 1985a.)

Taylor, C. 1977b. Self-interpreting animals. In C. Taylor 1985a.

Taylor, C. 1979. Atomism. In C. Taylor 1985b.

Taylor, C. 1981. The concept of a person. In C. Taylor 1985a.

Taylor, C. 1982. The diversity of good. In C. Taylor 1985b.

Taylor, C. 1985a. *Human Agency and Language: Philosophical Papers,* vol. 1. Cambridge: Cambridge University Press.

Taylor, C. 1985b. *Philosophy and the Human Sciences: Philosophical Papers,* vol. 2. Cambridge: Cambridge University Press.

Taylor, C. 1989. *Sources of the Self: The Making of Modern Identity.* Cambridge: Harvard University Press.

Taylor, G. 1985. *Pride, Shame, and Guilt.* Oxford: Oxford University Press.

Taylor, M. 1987. *The Possibility of Cooperation.* Cambridge: Cambridge University Press.

Taylor, R. 1985. *Ethics, Faith, and Reason.* Englewood Cliffs, N.J.: Prentice-Hall.

Telfer, 1970/1971. Friendship. *Proceedings of the Aristotelian Society* 71:223–241.

Theophrastus. 1967. *Characters.* Baltimore: Penguin.

Thomas, L. 1988. Rationality and affectivity: The metaphysics of the moral self. *Social Philosophy and Policy* 5:154–172.

Thomas, L. 1989a. Trust and survival: Securing a vision of the good society. *Journal of Social Philosophy* 20:34–41.

Thomas, L. 1989b. *Living Morally: A Psychology of Moral Character.* Philadelphia: Temple University Press.

Thompson, J. 1983. Parenthood and identity across time. *Journal of Philosophy* 80:201–220.

Trianosky, G. 1988. Rightly ordered appetites: How to live morally and live well. *American Philosophical Quarterly* 25:1–12.

Urmson, J. O. Aristotle's doctrine of the mean. In Rorty 1980b.

Van Gulick, R. 1988. A functionalist plea for self-consciousness. *Philosophical Review* 92:149–181.

Walker, M. U. 1987. Moral particularity. *Metaphilosophy* 18:171–185.

Wallace, J. 1978. *Virtues and Vices.* Ithaca: Cornell University Press.

Wallace, J. 1988. *Moral Relevance and Moral Conflict.* Ithaca: Cornell University Press.

Watson, G. 1975. Free agency. *Journal of Philosophy* 72:205–220. (Reprinted in Watson 1982.)

Watson, G. 1977. Skepticism about weakness of will. *Philosophical Review* 86:316–339.

Watson G., ed. 1982. *Free Will.* Oxford: Oxford University Press.

Watson, G. 1987a. Responsibility and the limits of evil: Variations on a Strawsonian theme. In F. Schoeman (ed.), *Responsibility, Character, and the Emotions*. Cambridge: Cambridge University Press.

Watson, G. 1987b. Free action and free will. *Mind* 96:145–172.

Wescott, M. 1986. *The Feminist Legacy of Karen Horney*. New Haven: Yale University Press.

White, S. L. 1988. Self-deception and responsibility for the self. In B. P. McLaughlin and A. O. Rorty (eds.), *Perspectives on Self-Deception*. Berkeley: University of California Press.

Whiting, J. 1986. Friends and future selves. *Philosophical Review* 94:547–580.

Wiggins, D. 1980. Weakness of will, commensurability, and the objects of deliberation and desire. In Rorty 1980b.

Williams, B. 1973. Ethical consistency. In *Problems of the Self*. Cambridge: Cambridge University Press. (Reprinted in Gowans 1987.)

Williams, B. 1976a. Morality and the emotions. In *Problems of the Self*. Cambridge: Cambridge University Press.

Williams, B. 1976b. Persons, character, and morality. In A. Rorty (ed.), *The Identities of Persons*. (Reprinted in Williams 1981a.)

Williams, B. 1981a. *Moral Luck*. Cambridge: Cambridge University Press.

Williams, B. 1981b. Moral luck. In Williams 1981a.

Williams B. 1981c. Internal and external reasons. In Williams 1981a.

Williams, B. 1985. *Ethics and the Limits of Philosophy*. Cambridge: Harvard University Press.

Williamson, J. 1974. *A New People*. New York: Free Press.

Winters, B. 1981. Hume's argument for the superiority of natural instinct. *Dialogue* 20:635–643.

Wolf, S. 1980. Asymmetrical freedom. *Journal of Philosophy* 77:151–166.

Wolf, S. 1982. Moral saints. *Journal of Philosophy* 79:410–439.

Wolf, S. 1986. Above and below the line of duty. *Philosophical Topics* 14:131–148.

Wolf, S. 1987. Sanity and the metaphysics of responsibility. In F. Schoeman (ed.), *Responsibility, Character, and the Emotions*. Cambridge: Cambridge University Press.

Wollstonecraft, M. 1982. *A Vindication of the Rights of Woman*. Harmondsworth: Penguin. (First published 1792.)

Wong, D. 1988. On flourishing and finding one's identity in community. In P. A. French, T. E. Uehling, and H. K. Wettstein (eds.), *Ethical Theory: Character and Virtue*, vol. 13 of Midwest Studies in Philosophy. Notre Dame: Notre Dame University Press.

Wootton, B. 1959. *Social Science and Social Pathology*. London: Allen and Unwin.

Wootton, B. 1963. *Crime and the Criminal Law*. London: Stevens and Sons.

Workman, P. L., Blumberg, B. S., and Cooper, A. J. 1963. Selection, gene migration, and polymorphic stability in a U.S. white and negro population. *American Journal of Human Genetics* 15, no. 4: 429–437.

Zipursky, B. 1987. Objectivity and linguistic practice. Unpublished doctoral dissertation, University of Pittsburgh.

Contributors

Annette C. Baier teaches philosophy at the University of Pittsburgh. She has written about Hume, Descartes, and various topics in moral philosophy. She is the author of *Postures of Mind: Essays on Mind and Morals* (University of Minnesota Press, 1985). Her current work is about trust in various spheres: what it enables us to do, what makes it sometimes appropriate, what risks it brings.

Lawrence A. Blum is Professor of Philosophy and Women's Studies at the University of Massachusetts in Boston. He is the author of *Friendship, Altruism, and Morality* (Routledge and Kegan Paul, 1980). His research interests are in the areas of moral theory, moral education, feminist ethics, racism and multiculturalism as moral issues, and the social philosophy of Simone Weil.

David O. Brink is Assistant Professor of Philosophy at the Massachusetts Institute of Technology. His primary interests are in ethical theory, the history of ethics, and legal theory. He is the author of *Moral Realism and the Foundations of Ethics* (Cambridge University Press, 1989).

Claudia Card is Professor of Philosophy at the University of Wisconsin and has teaching affiliations also in the Women's Studies Program and the Institute for Environmental Studies. Her research interests and principal publications are in ethics and social philosophy, feminist theory, and lesbian culture.

Owen Flanagan is Class of 1919 Professor of Philosophy at Wellesley College. His work is in the philosophy of mind and ethics. He is the author of *The Science of the Mind* (MIT Press, 1984) and *Varieties of Moral Personality: Ethics and Psychological Realism* (Harvard University Press, 1991). He is currently studying work in psychology and anthropology that has bearing on three related issues: the role of the emotions in morality, the connection between different conceptions of the self and different moral systems, and the way the moral-conventional distinction is drawn in different cultures.

Barbara Herman is Associate Professor of Philosophy and Law at the University of Southern California. Her main areas of interest are Kantian ethics; the idea and practice of casuistry; and the connections between morality, agency, and conceptions of the self.

Marcia Lind is Assistant Professor of Philosophy at Duke University. Her main areas of research are moral psychology, the history of ethics, and feminist theory. She is particularly interested in the role emotions have been given in traditional philosophical texts.

Alison McIntyre is Assistant Professor in the Department of Philosophy at Wellesley College. Her interests lie in the area where philosophy of mind, philosophy of action, and moral philosophy intersect. Her current research is concerned with practical reasoning and the nature of intention, Aristotle's ethics, and deontological constraints on agency.

Michele Moody-Adams is Assistant Professor in the Philosophy Department of the University of Rochester. Her publications and research interests are in moral and political philosophy, the philosophy of law, and the history of modern philosophy.

Adrian M. S. Piper is Professor of Philosophy at Wellesley College. Her research interests and principal publications are in metaethics and moral psychology. Her contribution to this volume is excerpted from "Rationality and the Structure of the Self," an examination of the metaethical and psychological foundations of moral theory.

Ruth Anna Putnam is Professor in Philosophy at Wellesley College. Her publications and current research interests lie in the areas of ethical theory, American philosophy (with special emphasis on James and Dewey), and applications to specific moral and poltical problems.

Amélie Oksenberg Rorty is the Matina Souretis Horner Distinguished Visiting Professor at Radcliffe College and Professor of Philosophy at Mount Holyoke College. Her *Mind in Action* includes papers on personal identity, the emotions, self-deception, akrasia, and ethics. Her history of philosophical conceptions of the emotions, *From Passions to Emotions and Sentiments*, will be published by Oxford University Press. She has begun a project on some political aspects of moral education.

Nancy Sherman is Associate Professor of Philosophy in the Department of Philosophy at Georgetown University. She has published *The Fabric of Character: Aristotle's Theory of Virtue* (Oxford University Press, 1989) and articles on Aristotle's ethical theory and is presently working on a comparative study of the theory of virtue in Aristotle and Kant.

Michael Slote is Professor of Philosophy at the University of Maryland, College Park. He has published books and articles in ethics. These include *Goods and Virtues* (Oxford University Press, 1983), *Common-sense Morality and Consequentialism* (Routledge and Kegan Paul 1985), and *Beyond Optimizing: A Study of Rational Choice* (Harvard University Press, 1989). He is currently engaged in a large-scale project on virtue ethics.

Michael Stocker is Professor of Philosophy at Syracuse University. He teaches and writes on ethics and moral psychology, most recently on affectivity, akrasia, friendship, and plural and conflicted values. He is the author of *Plural and Conflicting Values* (Oxford University Press, 1990).

Laurence Thomas is Professor of Philosophy at Syracuse University and an affiliate member of the Department of Political Science. He is the author of a number of articles in moral psychology and social philosophy and the book *Living Morality: A Psychology of Moral Character* (Temple University Press, 1989).

Gregory Trianosky is Assistant Professor of Philosophy in the Department of Philosophy at the University of Michigan, Flint. His publications and work in progress focus on the ethics of virtue, supererogation, and the eighteenth-century British moralists.

Gary Watson is Associate Professor and Chair of the Philosophy Department at the University of California at Irvine. He writes primarily on issues in the theory of agency and in moral psychology.

Stephen L. White is Assistant Professor of Philosophy at Tufts University. His publications are in the philosophy of language, the philosophy of mind, and moral psychology. His *Unity of the Self* (MIT Press) is forthcoming.

David Wong is Associate Professor in the Department of Philosophy at Brandeis University. He is the author of *Moral Relativity* (University of California Press, 1984). His research interests and publications are in the areas of ethical theory, comparative ethics, the history of philosophy, and Chinese philosophy.